Dostoevsky (1847)

Fyodor DOSTOEVSKY

Complete Letters

Volume One

1832-1859

Edited and Translated by
David Lowe and Ronald Meyer

Ardis, Ann Arbor

Copyright © 1988 by Ardis Publishers
All rights reserved under International and Pan-American Copyright Conventions.
Printed in the United States of America

Translated from the original Russian

Ardis Publishers
2901 Heatherway
Ann Arbor, Michigan 48104

Library of Congress Cataloging in Publication Data

Dostoyevsky, Fyodor, 1821-1881
Complete letters.

Includes index.
Contents: v. 1. 1832-1859.
1. Dostoyevsky, Fyodor, 1821-1881—Correspondence.
2. Dostoyevsky, Fyodor, 1821-1881—Translations,
English.   Authors, Russian—19th century—
Correspondence.   I. Lowe, David Allan, 1948-
II. Meyer, Ronald.   III. Title
PG3328.A3L68 1987   891'73'3 [B]   87-17510
ISBN 0-88233-898-6 (set)
ISBN 0-88233-897-8 (v. 1)

Contents

Illustrations

Introduction

The Ardis complete collection of Dostoevsky's letters in English translation will occupy five volumes. Volume I, covering the years 1832-1859, comprises 171 private letters and ten letters of an official nature. These 181 documents offer invaluable insights into Dostoevsky and his world. On the most obvious level, the letters report most of the crucial public and private events in the first four decades of Dostoevsky's life and thus acquire the retrospective function of a diary or epistolary autobiography.

The earliest letters, having Moscow and its environs as their place of origin and often bearing a collective sibling signature, reveal the Dostoevsky children's devotion to their chronically ill mother. The letters from 1837 to 1843 issue from St. Petersburg (now Leningrad) and tell the story of Dostoevsky's preparation for a military career through studies at the Main Academy of Engineering and of his service as a draftsman following graduation. A nearly total and therefore all the more eloquent silence surrounds the death of Dostoevsky's father in 1839, under still unexplained circumstances, but the letters also trumpet Dostoevsky's mounting dissatisfaction with military life and his nearly frantic desire to try to make his own way as a writer.

In 1844 Dostoevsky retired from the service and launched his literary career. The letters from that year to 1849 chronicle the successes and disappointments that kept the young Dostoevsky on an emotional roller coaster. As the letters from the period evidence, these peripeties in Dostoevsky's literary career led to at least one nervous breakdown.

The history behind the publication of *Poor Folk* (1846), Dostoevsky's first novel, represents one of the most famous episodes in the history of Russian literature. Dmitry Grigorovich, a friend of Dostoevsky's and fellow budding writer, took the manuscript of the sentimental novel to the publisher and poet Nikolay Nekrasov. At four in the morning Grigorovich and Nekrasov, after staying up all night to read the novel, rushed into Dostoevsky's rooms to congratulate him on a major achievement and to hail him as a new Gogol. Nekrasov then took the manuscript to the influential literary critic Vissarion Belinsky, who went into raptures over the work and soon greeted Dostoevsky with the rhetorical question: "Do you understand what you have written?" With each of Dostoevsky's subsequent works, however, Belinsky's enthusiasm waned, and his insistence on an overtly *engagé* literature led him utterly to dismiss *The Double,* a brilliant work much more interesting from the psychological point of view than from a socio-economic one. The development of frankly adversarial relations with such other early admirers as Nekrasov and Ivan Turgenev, both of whom made Dostoevsky's monumental ego and apparent lack of social graces the target of derision, no doubt aggravated Dostoevsky's sense that his literary career was foundering.

The letters from 1844 to 1849 give absolutely no hint of Dostoevsky's participation in the clandestine meetings of the somewhat radical Petrashevsky Circle and its very radical and perhaps even revolutionary subgroup, the Palm-Durov Circle, but they describe the consequences— his incarceration in St. Petersburg's Peter-Paul Fortress. There Dostoevsky penned a remarkable series of letters testifying to true nobility of spirit and grace under duress. It is almost impossible to believe that those letters were written by a man living under a sword of Damocles.

It seems likely that Dostoevsky smuggled letters out of prison, but there are none extant from the period of his *katorga* (penal servitude), which lasted from 1850 until 1854. The letters from 1854 to 1860 tell of Dostoevsky's exile and military service in Semipalatinsk, his falling in love with Marya Dmitrievna Isaeva and eventual marriage to her, and his constant efforts to have his exile lifted and to regain permission to publish. The exile was lifted in stages. In 1859 Dostoevsky was allowed to return to European Russia, first to reside in the city of Tver (now Kalinin), and finally, in his beloved Petersburg. He reentered the literary arena the same year with the publication of *Uncle's Dream* and *The Village of Stepanchikovo* ("A Little Hero" had appeared in 1857, anonymously).

In addition to providing information about Dostoevsky's public and private life, the letters also help scholars chart the evolution of the writer's plans and works. In this sense the letters describe Dostoevsky's creative laboratory. At another level, however, they take us directly *into* the laboratory, for Dostoevsky's personality as it is reflected in his letters, the role that he allots to literature in his letters, and the language in which he expresses himself in writing all have direct relevance for Dostoevsky's novelistic world.

To read Dostoevsky's letters is to encounter Dostoevsky's most Dostoevskian character—himself. The personality that emerges from the letters reveals all the passionate contradictions, the dialectical psychology, the struggle between the spirit and the flesh, and the sudden flights of morbid humor that mark Dostoevsky's most brilliant creations. To judge by the letters that have survived, much of what Dostoevsky learned or realized about the complexities of the human personality derived from his own pursuit of fame and fortune. The letters that he wrote to his brother Mikhail at the height of his early success and in the aftermath of successive failures reveal the vision associated with Dostoevsky's major novels, often calling to mind the character of Dmitry Karamazov in particular. In those letters written shortly after his literary debut Dostoevsky's moods, attitudes, and values shift and replace one another with a rapidity verging on the nihilistic. In the second paragraph of his letter to Mikhail of 16

November 1845 (No. 56), for instance, Dostoevsky writes: "Well, brother, I think that my fame will never reach such an apogee as now. There's unbelievable admiration everywhere, terrible curiosity about me." After running on in that vein for several pages, Dostoevsky abruptly adds: "I have read over my letter and found out that in the first place, I'm illiterate, and in the second, I'm a braggart." That apparently chastened confession does not prevent Dostoevsky, however, from concluding with a final paragraph complaining about how much money he is spending on prostitutes and describing to what an extent Belinsky and Turgenev love him and wish he were less dissolute.

The psychological ambiguities in the letter to Mikhail draw the reader into a maze of paradoxes. Does Dostoevsky's boasting about his fame spring from megalomania or an inferiority complex, or both? Does the confession of illiteracy and boastfulness represent true penitence or, instead, merely a cynical and calculated attempt to ingratiate himself with Mikhail? Or does it somehow embrace both attitudes? Does the conclusion of the letter invite Mikhail's compassion, envy, or disgust? The possibilities are nearly unlimited, and the paradoxical vision of the world and the human personality that the young Dostoevsky projects in his letters is merely sharpened, but not fundamentally altered, in his great novels from the last two decades of his life.

Dostoevsky's pursuit of fortune has even more twists and turns than his pursuit of fame and is of even greater relevance for his art. The single most common topic in his letters from the first four decades of his life is money—schemes for earning it, hopes for repaying it, but most often pleas for loans. One realizes early on that like his hero Dmitry Karamazov, Dostoevsky was in fact one of those people who are criminally irresponsible with money, so unrestrained in their spending habits, so generous when given the chance to be so, that if they are left in charge of their own finances no amount of money will ever be sufficient for them. Such indeed was Dostoevsky, who did not in fact know financial security until his second marriage, when his wife took over the family finances. Until then Dostoevsky was trapped in an endless cycle of borrowing and borrowing more.

In the process of wheedling, cajoling, begging, and extorting loans, all too often accompanied by the assurance that no further need for assistance would ever arise, Dostoevsky learned enough about the psychological subtleties of giving and receiving, generosity and gratitude, wealth and poverty, domination and subjugation, to fill several novels. All the major novels dramatize the distinction between true generosity and counterfeit charity, heartfelt thankfulness and camouflaged resentment. Dostoevsky demonstrates his awareness of the subtle psychological politics of charity most clearly in the letter to Alexander Vrangel of 14 August 1855, where he writes: "Believe me, Alexander Yegorovich, I know very well that you understand, perhaps better than another, how one should deal with a person to whom one has had occasion to lend money. I know that you will double, triple your courtesy with him; you need to be careful with a person who has borrowed; he is overly sensitive; *he thinks that through discourtesy towards him and lack of ceremony people want to make him pay for the loan* made to him." Clearly Dostoevsky's perspicacity with regards to the role that money can play in human relations was based on first-hand experience, an experience documented in exhausting detail in his letters and frequently reflected in his works.

Along with money, the topic that seems most to fire Dostoevsky's imagination is literature. Often enough the themes are linked, because beginning very early in life Dostoevsky dreamed of a literary career and pegged his hopes for financial success and security on publications of various sorts, whether translations or original works. In this regard, the letters in Volume I offer a catalogue of schemes proposed with passionate enthusiasm but doomed to remain unrealized, or worse, to bring disastrous consequences. They additionally survey Dostoevsky's literary tastes and distates, many of his letters to Mikhail revolving exclusively around his breathless reports on recent reading or around his own esthetic satisfactions and dissatisfactions with his works in progress. The letters show clearly that as for many of Dostoevsky's characters, literature provided the author himself with an all-embracing, all-consuming way of knowing the world and of responding to it.

The fact that so much of Dostoevsky's writing, if not in fact all of it, represents Dostoevsky's impassioned response to other authors, both living and dead, Russian and non-Russian, led the influential Soviet critic and theoretician Mikhail Bakhtin to speak of Dostoevsky's "dialogic imagination" and of the "polyphonic" interplay of voices in Dostoevsky's works. Not surprisingly, that peculiarity of Dostoevsky's manner also extends to his letters, whose manner paradoxically suggests a spontaneous, living human voice reflecting a personality conditioned by written literature. In his letters Dostoevsky genuinely seems to *speak* to his addressees, so that one hears Dostoevsky in his letters even as one is also aware of their dependence on written conventions and traditions. At moments of great haste and high emotion, Dostoevsky's epistolary voice is capable of imprecise and repetitive diction, non-neutral and inefficient word order, illogical appeals to logic, grammatical lapses, and all the other typical features of unedited, non-textbook speech. At the same time, many of Dostoevsky's turns of phrase, lexical choices, or even concepts derive from formal written literature, whether poems, novels, plays, or bureaucratic documents. The resulting blend of living and dead forms, of the carefully organized and naturally disorganized, of the imitation of other voices and Dostoevsky's own constantly changing tone and intonation, offers a potent but unstable linguistic brew that represents the essence of Dostoevsky's style.

To the greatest extent possible, the present translation attempts to reproduce in English the salient characteristics of Dostoevsky's epistolary style. The word order in the translations generally duplicates that of the original, which often means that subjects find themselves far removed from verbs, the placement of modifiers can lead readers into semantic labyrinths, and subordination reaches dizzying heights. In short, the sentence structures, both in the original Russian and in the English translation, violate canonical standards of taste, clarity, efficiency, and readability. The fact remains, however, that Dostoevsky generally strives for maximal expressiveness rather than for clarity or brevity, and the translations herein try to capture that unorthodox but distinguishing feature of Dostoevsky's style.

One of the most common examples of Dostoevsky's accent on expressivity is his use of diminutives, endearments, and exclamations in contexts and quantities that contemporary English usage generally associates with camp or kitsch. In spite of the risk of cultural misinterpretation, the translation retains Dostoevsky's gushiness. The letters thus bristle with turns such as "darling," "my dear," "for Heaven's sake," "for God's sake," and teems with exclamation marks. Contemporary readers may shudder at the emotional excesses in which Dostoevsky indulges, but at least they will be confronting the real Dostoevsky, not a sanitized version of him.

Another aspect of Dostoevsky's style that upsets literate English speakers' notions of correctness is his frequent reliance on what English stylists regard as run-on sentences or comma splices. Although such highly regarded writers as Isek Dinesen and Christopher Isherwood regularly indulge in the same practice in English, style manuals continue to insist on periods or semicolons where Russians view the comma as a free variant. In other words, so-called run-on sentences are stylistically neutral in Russian, and they allow such authors as Dostoevsky to construct extraordinarily long sentences. Since sentence length is among the most important features of an author's style, the present translation generally follows Dostoevsky's often long-breathed periods, even when that means subjecting readers to multiple comma splices.

For the texts and annotations in the Ardis edition of Dostoevsky's letters the editors have taken full and grateful advantage of the on-going *Polnoe sobranie sochinenii v 30-i tomakh* [complete collected works in 30 volumes], a monumental feat of scholarship being carried out by the Academy of Science Pushkin House in Leningrad. The numeration for the letters in the Ardis edition follows that of the *Polnoe sobranie sochinenii,* as does the convention of heading each letter with the date and place. The annotations for the Ardis Dostoevsky draw selectively on those in the *Polnoe sobranie sochinenii.* They have been modified when they seemed likely to overwhelm the English-speaking reader with excessive details. Conversely, the Academy commentary has been expanded in the case of Russian figures whom the Pushkin House editors deem too well-known to require identification. In general, the Ardis volume aims the annotations at cultured Western readers who know enough about world literature and civilization not to need to have Balzac or Goethe identified for them but who nonetheless may not be very familiar with the literature and history of Russia. Readers desiring more detailed information about Dostoevsky and his times than the commentary provides are urged to consult Joseph Frank's superb series of volumes devoted to Dostoevsky's life and writings.

The first occurrence of any given name in the letters is accompanied by a footnote supplying biographical information and any specific facts essential for understanding the context of the letter. Thus, if one wishes biographical information for anyone listed in the index, one need only turn to the footnotes for the letter in which the person's name first appears. The transliteration of Russian names and places generally follows the conventions of Shaw's Popular System I except when standard English spellings already exist, for instance, the first name Alexander or the last name Herzen.

David Lowe
Ronald Meyer

LETTERS
1832-1859

Dostoevsky's parents, Mikhail Andreevich and Marya Fyodorovna (1823).

The building in which Dostoevsky was born.

1832

1. To Mikhail Dostoevsky[1]
29 June 1832. Darovoe[2]

We all send you our most profound regards and kiss your hands, dearest Papa. Mikhayla,[3] Fyodor, Varvara,[4] and Andryusha[5]

Dostoevskys[6]
29 June 1832

---

1. Mikhail Andreevich Dostoevsky (178-1839), Dostoevsky's father.
2. The Dostoevsky family estate.
3. Mikhail Mikhaylovich Dostoevsky (1820-64), the eldest of the Dostoevsky children. Mikhail and Fyodor were close friends from childhood on and collaborated on publishing projects after Fyodor's return from Siberian exile.
4. Varvara Mikhaylovna Dostoevskaya (1822-93), the eldest of the Dostoevsky sisters. In 1840 she married P. A. Karepin.
5. Andrey Mikhaylovich Dostoevsky (1825-97), the elder of Dostoevsky's two younger brothers.
6. In the original letter the children all signed their own names.

1833

2. To Maria Dostoevskaya[1]
23 August 1833. Moscow

Dearest Mama,

We have already arrived at Papa's, dearest Mama, in good health. Papa and Nikolinka[2] are also in good health. God grant that you be well, too. Come to Moscow, nearest Mama, I don't think it will take long to harvest the rest of the wheat and I think that you're already harvesting the buckwheat a little at a time. Good-bye, dearest Mama, I kiss your hands with respect and will remain your obedient son

Fyodor Dostoevsky

1. Maria Fyodorovna Dostoevskaya (1800-37), Dostoevsky's adored mother. Her relatively early death was the consequence of tuberculosis.
2. Nikolay Mikhaylovich Dostoevsky (1831-83), the youngest brother in the Dostoevsky family. During most of his adult life he suffered from poor health and had to be supported by his brothers and sisters.

1834

3. To Maria Dostoevskaya
April-May 1834. Moscow

Dear Mama,

When you left, dear Mama, I started to miss you terribly, and when I think of you now, dear Mama, I am overcome by such sadness that it's impossible to drive it away, if you only knew how much I would like to see you and I can hardly wait for that joyous moment. Every time I think of you I pray to God for your health. Let us know, dear Mother, whether you arrived safely, kiss Andryushenka and Verochka[1] for me. I kiss your hands and will remain your obedient son

F. Dostoevsky

---

1. Vera Mikhaylovna Dostoevskaya (1829-96), Dostoevsky's middle sister. In 1846 she married A. P. Ivanov.

1835

4. To Maria Dostoevskaya
9 May 1835. Moscow

Dear Mama,

Here we are notifying you in writing for the third time that we are well and fine, thank God. Today, that is, Thursday, Papa has brought us home because of the holiday,[1] and we're all together but without you, dear Mama. It's a pity that we'll still have to be separated from you for so long; God grant that this time pass quickly. The weather here is very bad, I think that you're having the same, and I think that you aren't enjoying the spring; how boring it is to be in the country during bad weather. I think that Verochka and Nikolenka are even more bored, and that Nikolya isn't playing horsey, as he used to with me. I feel sorry for Alyona Frolovna, she is suffering so, poor thing, soon she'll disappear altogether because of the consumption that has attacked her.[2] Good-bye, Mama. In expectation of seeing you soon, I remain your obedient son

Fyodor Dostoevsky
and Andrey Dostoevsky

P.S. Don't forget to kiss Verochka and Nikolenka.

1. Mikhail, Fyodor, and Andrey Dostoevsky were studying at L. I. Chermak's boarding school, the best in Moscow, and usually came home only for holidays. The holiday in question, May 9, derived from Emperor Nikolay I's name day.
2. Alyona Frolovna (c. 1780-1850s) was the family nanny. The reference here is a jocular response to a letter from Dostoevsky's mother to his father. His mother had remarked that the extremely heavy Alyona Frolovna was suffering from a cough that she, Alyona Frolovna, claimed was tuberculosis.

5. To Maria Dostoevskaya
16 May 1835. Moscow

Dearest Mama,

We are sincerely glad that we can talk to you at least in a few lines. We spent today at Papa's; we went to see Mama's godmother,[1] where we had a fairly good time. Varenka asked us to kiss your hands for her in a letter.[2] We're going to have an examination soon, and we're studying for it, after which, perhaps, we'll soon see you, oh! how nice that moment will be when we press you to our hearts. Good-bye, dear Mama, wishing you all the best in the world, we have the honor to remain your obedient children

Mikhail, Fyodor, Andrey Dostoevsky

Kiss Verochka and Nikolenka for us.

6. To Maria Dostoevskaya
19 May 1835. Moscow

Dearest Mama,

We're sincerely glad that we can write at least a few lines to you; how delightful your letters are for us, how we look forward to receiving them from you in order to find out whether you're well, dear Mama, and how you're getting along apart from us. We just went to Maria's Grove[1] with Papa and had a good long walk. Mama's godmother[2] came to see us today with Varenka, who kisses your hands, and with her we all kiss your hands and have the honor to remain your obedient children

Mikhail, Fyodor, Andrey Dostoevsky

P.S. We kiss Verochka and Nikolenka and wish them good health.

1. Alexandra Fyodorovna Kumanina (1796-1871). She and her husband, Alexander Alexeevich Kumanin (1792-1863), raised the younger Dostoevsky children after the death of their father.
2. Varvara Dostoevskaya spent holidays with the Kumanins, not at home.
1. At that time Maria's Grove was a park district on the outskirts of Moscow.
2. See Letter 5, note 1.

7. To Maria Dostoevskaya
26 May 1835. Moscow

Dearest Mama,

I am very glad that thanks to the Creator's all-benevolent providence you are in good health. We're spending these two days, that is, Pentecost and Whitmonday, at Papa's. I think that the weather here is the same as you're having, it has been changeable all these days, but Saturday and today have been marvelous, although there was in fact a big rain, but that was during the night, and the weather after it cleared up and has become superb, but I don't think that you had this rain, because it wasn't a downpour.—Our examination will be at the end of June, as it was last year, and because of that we are deprived of the hope of seeing you soon. You write that the children are having a good time and that Nikolya has even put on weight: so now the weather is the very best, and, consequently, he can enjoy it out in the fresh air; kiss them for me, tell them to be good and that we'll soon come to see them. Good-bye, dear Mother, I have nothing more to write; I remain your obedient son

Fyodor Dostoevsky
and Andrey Dostoevsky

8. To Maria Dostoevskaya
2 June 1835. Moscow

Dear Mama,

We are sincerely glad to see from your letter that you are well, thank God. As for the examination, it will probably be on the 24th of June, and we're now studying for it. The weather has been marvelous yesterday and today; and now we're planning to take a walk with Papa. Good-bye, dearest Mama, wishing you good health and kissing your hands, we have the honor of remaining your children

Mikhail, Fyodor, Andrey Dostoevsky

Kiss Verochka and Nikolenka.

9. To Maria Dostoevskaya
23 June 1835. Moscow

Dearest Mama,

 We're very glad that we have the chance even if only in a few lines to wish you good health and every good fortune; as for us, we're all well, thank God. We've now been at Papa's since Friday waiting for the examination that is to take place on Monday. Kiss Nikolenka and Verochka for us. Good-bye, dearest Mama, kissing your hands, we have the honor to remain your obedient children

Mikhail, Andrey, Fyodor Dostoevsky

1837

10. To Mikhail Dostoevsky
3 July 1837. Petersburg

Petersburg. July 3

Dear Papa,

We received your letter.[1] How rare those letters are and by the same virtue how dear to us. We wait for them for weeks on end, and what a pleasure it is when we receive them! In addition to your letters I also hear rather often from Kudryavtsev.[2] You're well—thank God! If only He would grant that your affairs be put in order! Yes, He will, He will grant us His mercy, too. Up until now He seems to have protected us in all our undertakings. Let us rely on His providence, and everything will go as it should. Of ourselves we will say that, thank God, we are healthy—a most ordinary occurrence. Things are going well for us in their usual way. We go back and forth between studying geometry and algebra, drafting plans for field fortifications—redoubts, bastions, and so forth, and drawing mountains in ink. Koronad Filippovich[3] is very pleased with us and is especially nice to us. He bought us excellent instruments for 30 silver rubles, and in addition, paint for 12 rubles. It was absolutely impossible to do without them, because plans are always drawn up in paint, and our present comrades are too stingy to lend us any of theirs. We have no outside expenses except for paper for writing and for plans, because we are about to begin preparing them for the examination, and much attention is paid to that, and that will contribute to our being accepted more than anything else. We began artillery this week, too; it is also essential for the second class. From that you can now see, dear Papa, whether we could have entered the Academy without preparation!

We didn't receive the books from the post office until today, and for that reason aren't answering your letter right away. How very, very

---

1. Mikhail and Fyodor Dostoevsky were in Petersburg studying at K. F. Kostomarov's preparatory school for students planning to enroll in the Main Academy of Engineering.

2. Kondraty Kudryavtsev was a friend of Mikhail's from Chermak's boarding school in Moscow.

3. Koronad Filippovich Kostomarov (1803-73). See note 1.

grateful we are to you for them! We received them all in good condition. We kiss your hands for them many, many times!

Last week we saw our former comrade Garner and Vessel. They came to say good-bye to Koronad Fil[ippovich], because they were leaving for Peterhof for camp. Today is K[oronad] F[ilippovich]'s birthday. The weather now is excellent. We hope that it won't change tomorrow, either, and if it's good, Shidlovsky[4] will come to see us, and we'll go wander around Petersburg and examine its famous sights. Speaking of him, he asked me to write you to ask whether you received his letter and *The Agricultural Gazette.* He sends you his regards.

Now about ourselves. The rash seems to be going away, and by the time of the examination it will probably have gone away entirely. As for *the other thing,* no one notices it. Be quite reassured about that. There has not yet been a single example of one of K[oronad] F[ilippovich]'s pupils not being accepted at the Academy. Koronad Filippovich sends you his regards. It's already eleven o'clock! Time to sleep! Good night! Good-bye.

With sincere respect and filial devotion we have the honor of remaining your children

Mikhail and Fyodor Dostoevsky.

Kiss Andryusha, Nikolya, Verochka, and especially Sashurka[5] for us.

I spoke to Koronad Filippovich about the money. He said that it's all the same to him; he said all sorts of polite things, which usually happens in such cases. And what could he say? Could he really have any doubts? I don't know why he bothered you for that.

Please be so kind as to write, dear Papa, whether you'll be in Moscow for long. I think that you're probably upset now and troubling yourself, and all on account of us!! How will we repay you for that!

Together with your letter we're writing to Auntie,[6] too. It seems rather polite.

4. Ivan Nikolaevich Shidlovsky (1816-72), with whom Dostoevsky became acquainted in Petersburg, was the closest friend of his youth. They shared a passionate enthusiasm for literature.

5. Alexandra Mikhaylovna Dostoevskaya (1835-89), the youngest of the Dostoevsky children. In 1854 she married N. I. Golenovsky. Largely because of the difference in age, Dostoevsky hardly knew her.

6. See Letter 5, note 1.

11. To Mikhail Dostoevsky
23 July 1837. Petersburg

St. Petersburg, July 23

Dearest Papa,

Today is Saturday, and we, thank God, have time to write you at least a few lines; so busy are we all the time. It's already close to September, and with it to the examinations as well, and we can't lose even a minute a week. Only on Saturday and Sunday are we free; that is, Koronad Filippovich[1] doesn't show us anything on those days; and consequently, we haven't found the time to have a talk with you in writing until now.

Mathematics and science are now going along as they should for us, and also fortificat[ions] and artillery. On Sundays and Saturdays we draft plans and drawings. Koronad Filippovich works with everyone almost every day, and especially with the two of us, because of all those who are studying with him, we're the only ones who want to enroll in the second class, and all the others want to enter the lower one.[2] Koronad Filippovich places greater hopes on us than on all the eight pupils who are studying with him. We'll soon begin studying military formation with a noncommissioned officer whom Koronad Filippovich has invited, and we'll be studying that right up to matriculation, that is, until December. Extraordinary attention is paid to formation, and even if you know everything superbly, you can wind up in the lower classes because of formation. And moreover, only with that can we win gain the favor of His Royal Highness Mikhail Pavlovich.[3] He is an extraordinary admirer of order. And so you can judge how much we must study that in spite of the fact that after the September examination everyone is supposed to go to the Engineers' Castle to learn formation. What will happen? Our only hope now is in God. We will not fail to apply our best efforts.

Out in the country you're now harvesting the wheat, and as we know, that's your favorite activity; we don't know what the harvest is like at home or how the weather is. As for Petersburg's weather, it's marvelous, Italian. We haven't seen Shidlovsky yet and consequently have been unable to give him your regards.

What are our little brothers and sisters up to in the country? They all must have strolled, run, stuffed themselves with berries and sunbathed to

---

1. See Letter 10, note 3.

2. At the Main Academy of Engineering the fourth class was the lowest, the first the highest.

3. Mikhail Pavlovich (1798-1849), Emperor Nikolay I's brother, was the Inspector General for Engineering Affairs.

their heart's content. We guess that Sashenka has grown a great deal; the fresh air is good for her. Varenka is probably doing some needlework and surely won't forget to study her lessons and read Karamzin's *History of Russia*.[4] She promised us that.

As for Andryusha, in the midst of his country pleasures he surely won't forget history either, which he often used to be lazy about [?] knowing well. In the fall you'll most likely take him to Moscow, to a vacant place at Chermak's.[5]—So! You'll still have to take care of your children's education for a long time: you have many of us. Just judge how we should pray to God for the preservation of your precious health.

With the most profound respect and devotion we remain your sincerely loving

Mikhail and Fyodor Dostoevsky

Kiss all our brothers and sisters for us.

12. To Mikhail Dostoevsky
6 September 1837. Petersburg

St. Petersburg. September 6, 1837

Dearest Papa,

It has been a long time since we wrote you, and our long silence must have been causing you no little worry, especially in such circumstances. We have just now found the time to notify you, we are so busy: the examination is near at hand, constant preparations; we are quite overwhelmed by everything.

On September 1st, as was announced in the program for the Academy of Engineering, we were to be presented at the Castle. We all reported at the appointed time and were presented by Koronad Filippovich[1] to Inspector Lomnovsky[2] and General Sharngorst,[3] the director-in-chief of the

---

4. *The History of the Russian State* (1818), by N. M. Karamzin (1766-1826), was the first serious work of Russian historiography. In his youth, Dostoevsky read and reread it.

5. See Letter 4, note 1.

1. See Letter 10, note 3.

2. Pyotr Karlovich Lomnovsky (d. 1860) became the director of the Main Academy of Engineering in 1853.

3. Vasily Lvovich Sharngorst (1798-1873).

Academy of Engineering. The General treated everyone kindly, and everyone was ordered to be in readiness, as we will be summoned rather often to the Academy of Engineering. *Such boredom!* Just now a document has arrived from the General for Koronad Filippovich ordering us all to be presented at the Academy of Engineering. I don't know what for. I think it's for certificates, since the General has ordered us to bring certificates from the earlier institutions where each of us was. We could hardly wait for the main examination, which is slated for the 15th. There are 43 candidates in all. We're so happy that there are so few. Last year there were 120, and in former years 150 and more. And Kostomar[ov]'s pupils were always among the first. What will happen now, when there are so few? True, the total number to be admitted is 25, but they'll probably reject rather many, because apparently they're all empty people, and they're all trying for the fourth class. Apparently they are very much afraid of *Kostomarov's* pupils. They have such respect for all of us. What will happen after that?

It has been a long time since we've had any news from you either. But we don't even dare to trouble you in your work. This letter will arrive when our fate will be being decided, that is, when the real examination takes place. In our next letter we'll try to inform you of everything. Now our studies have tripled. Time itself can't keep us with us. We're always over a book. We can hardly wait for the examination. I'm writing you now from the post office. How many things there are to take care of after the letter. I've been writing it to you no more than 1/4 hour.— I'll tell you in addition that we were compelled to buy new hats for the examination; that cost us 14 rubles. It had been a long time since we'd seen Shidlovsky. Today, finally, we spent an hour with him at the Kazan Cathedral. We had wanted to do that for a long time; especially just before the examination. Shidlov[sky] and Koronad Fil[ippovich] send their respects. Good-bye until the next letter. We have the honor of remaining your always loving sons

Mikhail and Fyodor Dostoevsky

13. To Mikhail Dostoevsky
27 September 1837. Petersburg

27 September

Dear Papa,

It has been a long time since we wrote you, because we were awaiting the end of the examination that was to decide our fate.

Even before the examination, at the doctor's examination, they said that my health was poor; but that was just a lame excuse. They had no basis for it except perhaps for the fact that I'm not fat. And really, what could they have said, when they couldn't have noticed a single one of my defects, because my face had cleared up, and they didn't even take a look at the other thing. Besides, they're not even considering those defects, because this year they've accepted many candidates in whom one could notice many more. The main reason, in the first place, must be that both of us brothers are trying to enroll in the same year, and the second is that we are trying to enroll at public expense. I can't think of anything else. They expressed the opinion that I'm not up to bearing all the hardships of drill and military service, when my health allows me to be absolutely certain that I could bear even much more. That cost me a lot of tears, but what could I do? I hoped that it would still be possible to patch things over somehow. And besides, K[oronad] F[ilippovich][1] kept reassuring me and trying to convince me. The General,[2] on his part, was ready to accept me after he saw my certificate, if the doctor were willing to do that. But this can still be fixed up. There's still time. They accept students in January as well. The main thing right now consists in having a certificate from a good doctor who would vouch for my health. Who could do that better than M[ikhail] A[ntonovich] *Markus.*[3] He has great influence in Petersburg. Moreover, I've heard that he's supposed to be in Moscow this month. His word alone could change everything. They would accept me at the Academy even without that, but they're afraid to, because this year—something that has never happened before—five of their pupils died.

The General is a very kind person. K[oronad] F[ilippovich] recommends that you write him a letter in which you ask him to admit me to the examination and mention that we have petitioned the Emperor. My

1. See Letter 10, note 3.
2. See Letter 12, note 3.
3. Mikhail Antonovich Markus (1790-1895), appointed personal physician to Empress Alexandra Fyodorovna in 1837. His brother was a friend of the Dostoevsky family (see following note).

brother passed the examination with flying colors. We presumed that he surely would be among the first, since hardly anyone has more points than he does. For geometry, history, French, and theology he received the maximum number of points, that is, 10. For everything else he earned 9 each. Which hardly anyone had. In spite of all that he became the 12th, because now they were probably looking not at knowledge, but at age and the time when one started school. Therefore, almost all the firsts were young ones and those who gave money, that is, made gifts. This injustice annoys my brother no end. We have nothing to give; and even if we had something, we surely wouldn't give it, because it's unscrupulous and shameful to purchase first place with money instead of performance. We serve the Emperor, and not them. But this doesn't really matter, because personal merit will never be eclipsed by position, and if he turned out not to be first—which he didn't at all deserve—he can be first at the Academy. The main thing is that the General has announced that there is not a single subsidized vacancy; con[sequently], despite the Emperor's permission, they can't accept him at public expense. A disaster through and through! Where are we to find 950 rubles now? Does this really mean surrendering our last possessions? My God! My God! What will happen to us? But He won't abandon us. Our only hope is in Him.

It's also good that there is sufficient time to do all of this. Perhaps everything will work out for the best. We'll pray to God! He won't abandon poor orphans! He still has a great deal of mercy. Good-bye. Take care of yourself: be well. That's the wish of your eternally loving children.

Mikhail and Fyodor Dostoevsky

Give our regards to Fyodor Antonovich.[4] Tell him that we beg his pardon a thousand times for not having written him. Until now there has been absolutely no free time. We barely found the time to write you a few lines.

---

4. Fyodor Antonovoich Markus, brother of Mikhail Antonovich (see preceding note). Fyodor Antonovich had worked in the same Moscow hospital as Dostoevsky's father.

14. To Mikhail Dostoevsky
8 October 1837. Petersburg

Petersburg. October 8

Dearest Papa,

Today we suddenly received two letters: one from you, the other from Auntie.[1] My God, how bitter it was for us to learn that you have not yet received a single line from us. We don't understand what the cause of that could be; whether it's the post office's carelessness or inaccurate delivery to the post office; because our man is not too good at that. In addition, right after the 15th of September Koronad Filippovich wrote a letter to you at Darovaya. We had assumed that it arrived there while you were away in Moscow; meanwhile, as we now see from your letter, you haven't received it at all. We didn't write you in Moscow because we were waiting for the end of the examination, which went on for a little over two weeks and ended very happily for my brother. He has already been completely accepted and now attends lessons in military formation. Today all the new students were presented to Grand Duke Mikhail Pavlovich at the M[ain] A[cademy] of E[ngineering], and that review, which everyone very much feared, ended happily. After the end of the examination Koronad Filippovich and I immediately sent you and Auntie a letter[2] in which we described everything in detail; it probably didn't catch you in Moscow. We think, though, that it has already reached you. My God, if only we'd known that this would happen this way. Dear, dear Papa! How much grief we cause you! Will we ever be able to at least somehow thank you! When will the time come, the time when we will be able to make you happy? Every day I pray with tears to God for that. What can be done when nothing but misfortunes are fated for us![3] But there is still hope that all this will take a different, a better turn. You write that we are carrying on a correspondence with Kudryav[tsev] and Lamovsky.[4] We haven't written the latter even a single letter, because we don't know him at all well. And I haven't written to Kudryavtsev in over a month-and-a-half, although I've received several letters from him.

We received a letter from Auntie today—a reply to ours, which we sent along with a letter to you. They feel very sorry for us and definitely

---

1. See Letter 5, note 1.
2. Apparently a reference to Letter 13.
3. Mikhail probably has in mind the death of his mother, Maria Fyodorovna Dostoevskaya, along with his failure to gain admission to the Main Academy of Engineering.
4. Alexander Mikhaylovich Lamovsky (d. 1893) was a friend of Fyodor and Mikhail Dostoevsky from Chermak's boarding school in Moscow.

want to pay in 950 rubles for each of us, if only you will allow it. That surprised us very much, the more so as in our letter we didn't hint at that at all and didn't ask at all. Allow them to do that just for us. We are expecting a reply from you in your next letter. It won't cost them anything, and for us it will have a great influence on our fate. Moreover, until now they haven't done anything; so in this instance, which one may call critical, let them oblige just my brother and me. Without it it will be absolutely impossible for my brother to enter the school, because he has already signed for the payment of that money; otherwise he would have immediately lost his right to enroll, and his place would have been taken by someone else. Perhaps our sinful prayers have reached God, and our situation is taking a turn somewhat for the better. As for me, that's not difficult to fix up either. Koronad Fillippovich and all our people are advising me to enroll directly in the so-called Engineering Cadets, which will cost us hardly anything. And that's not a bit worse than the Academy of Engineering. In 2 years *at the very most* I can be an officer; *at the very most,* and perhaps even in 1 1/2 or a year, because that will depend on an examination. These cadets also live in the Engineers' Castle, and those who want to live by themselves usually live at home. The maintenance is all at public expense. Their job consists of drafting plans and being present at construction projects in the summer. They study on their own. But that's not a problem at all, because I could now take the officer's examination myself. On it they demand algebra up to indeterminate equations, geometry and trigonometry, which I've already had, fortifications and artillery, which I already know somewhat, but I have the means for studying on my own by borrowing notes from the petty officers (I have several close acquaintances among them). And they also demand architecture. I can also study for that by reading good books. And so, in a year or *at the most* in 2 I'll be exactly the same officer that I would have been had I graduated from the Academy of Engineering, with the only difference being that there (in the A[cademy] of E[ngineering]) I can receive the rank of ensign in only a year by taking an examination, as long as I study well, while here—only by serving the necessary time as an ensign. For examination preparation and for studies in general I'll have free time after dinner, since I'll only be on duty in the morning. Judge for yourself how good that is, and moreover, then it won't cost anything. Even the dress coat is the same as for petty officers. Here I can be an officer much sooner than in the Academy of Engineering. And that's all that I need. Actually, though, that could be done at any time, because there are a lot of vacancies there now. But perhaps I'll still be able to enroll in the Academy of Engineering. May everything work itself out as God sees fit. He does everything for the best and will arrange our affairs correctly too. There's only one thing we beg of you, dear Papa! Don't grieve over this; believe that God is arranging this, too, for our happiness. Perhaps I would have had to endure mnay misfortunes if I had enrolled in the Academy of Engineering. I will always pray to God, and He won't abandon us. Good-bye, kind, dearest Papa! Again, for Heaven's sake, don't grieve. Everything will work itself out for the best. With filial love and devotion, we have the honor of remaining your obedient sons

Mikhail and Fyodor Dostoevsky

For Heaven's sake, notify us immediately of the receipt of this letter. Then we'll write Auntie right away.

We kiss our sisters and Nikolochka.

K[oronad] F[ilippovich] and *Ivan Nikolaevich* Shidlovsky send you their regards.

15. To Mikhail Dostoevsky
3 December 1837. Petersburg

Petersburg. 3 December. Friday

Dearest Papa,

We received your letter today and along with it 70 rubles, money washed with the sweat of your labors and your own deprivations. Oh, how we appreciate that now! We thank you and thank you from the bottom of our heart, which fully feels everything that you are doing for us.

It may seem strange to you why we just now received your letter. The notification of the money had arrived already last Saturday; but K[oronad] F[ilippovich] didn't sign for it until Tuesday and didn't pick up the money at the post office until today. You write, dearest Papa, that you haven't received a reply to your last two letters, but for a month-and-a-half now we have been writing you punctually once a week. I don't know whether you received the letter in which in a postscript I informed you that I had asked at the office with regard to the letter to General Sharngorst.[1] The money that you sent is more than enough for us. I spoke to Koronad Filippov[ich] today; he assures me that there is no doubt about my being accepted. However, I have asked him to inform you of that himself; and he has promised to do that, saying that on Sunday he will find out in advance everything concerning me. About three days ago this week he called me in and told me to write you not to worry about money. That he won't trouble you about it any more if I, beyond his expectations, stay at his place the

---

1. A reference to the letter from Doctor Markus mentioned in Letter 13.

first few days of January. Con[sequently] he should now be trying for his own sake to send me on my way as soon as possible. But I wonder whether he isn't using this *noble* pretext to somehow deflect the 300 (hundred)-ruble claim on our part. The Lord only knows! But he vouches for my entrance and orders me to prepare more fortification and architectural plans. The petty officers live either in the Engineers' Castle or in the Peter-Paul Fortress, which is across the Neva. He wants somehow to place me in the Engineers' Castle, in the Drafting Department. That will be even better. He'll submit the request in December; the reasons for that I laid out in the last letter. If the Lord allowed me to enroll there, that would be very good for me. In a year I would be an officer, and from there the road is wide open.

K[oronad] F[ilippovich] asked the General to allow my brother to take the examination for the third class.[2] The General gave his permission. He is doing marvelously on the examination. With mathematics he couldn't have done better. Catechism too. Geography, history, and fortif[ications] are left, but we hope that they will go very well, too. Would you believe that they refuse even to examine people on fortifications and artillery, because they'll start them from the beginning in the 3rd class. Con[sequently], K[oronad] F[ilippovich] didn't need the 300 rubles at all. Until now, however, he hasn't been spending any of it, except for 10 rubles that he lent us.

You write, dearest Papa, that we correspond with the Kumanins. That is so. But if you only knew that I write them exactly the same things, about money, as to you. They write us all sorts of nonsense. Only about doings. Sometimes they reproach me for *lack of candor,* that I don't write them about the Engineering Cadets in sufficient detail. But honest to God, sometimes you forget, and sometimes you haven't yet found out everything properly for yourself. And besides, what sort of *lack of candor* can there be here? Funny people! The money for my brother has already been deposited and a receipt received. We recently received a letter from them in which among other *shortsighted* questions they write that they haven't had any news from you in a long time. In general, their letters are full of just questions, about things that we're doing, about the details on these petty officers. Their letters consist of a few lines. Rarely 2 pages long. A[lexander] Alexeev[ich][3] does the writing. He addresses us by first name and patronymic. Good-bye. Be well and as happy as possible! God hears prayers for that from your children.

M. and F. Dostoevsky

---

2. In the Academy of Engineering, the fourth class was the lowest, the first the highest.
3. See Letter 5, note 1.

The money is quite sufficient for us. Please don't worry.

We have the honor of congratulating you on two name day boys.[4]

[Ivan] Nikolaevich Shidlovsky sends you his regards. He visits us on Sundays or sends for us—and we spend the whole morning with him. Winter hasn't yet begun here. The snow falls, but then it goes away again. We think that my brother will definitely be accepted in the 3rd class. The General and Colonels Lomnovsky and Fere[5] are of an excellent opinion of him. They're being tormented a lot with formation drill. The Prince[6] is very strict. He's in Moscow.

16. To Varvara Dostoevskaya
3 December 1837. Petersburg

Dear sister Varenka,

Happy birthday and name day! May God grant you all the best. How are you going to spend the day? I guess that by now you play the piano very nicely. Kiss dear Sashurochka[1] for us. Does she talk? Does she walk? We don't know anything about that yet. Kiss the name day boy Kolechka[2] for us. Does he like *shepelenoski*[3] as much as he used to? Good-bye.

Your brothers M. and F. Dostoevsky

4. Andrey and Nikolay Dostoevsky.

5. A. Ch. Fere.

6. Grand Duke Mikhail Pavlovich.

1. Alexandra Mikhaylovna Dostoevskaya.

2. Nikolay Mikhaylovich Dostoevsky.

3. *Shepelenoski* does not turn up in any Russian dictionary, nor do any of the native Russians consulted know what the word means. Presumably it belonged to the Dostoevsky family's private language.

17. To Mikhail Dostoevsky
End of December 1837—Beginning of January 1838. Petersburg

[. . .]but I'll try to stand my ground. Oh, Papa, how bitter it sometimes is amid these people when you don't know to whom to turn with your request, when you see the absolute impossibility of enrolling, and God only knows how long you'll have to wait. But don't worry! I've already gotten to know these people's ways a bit and will be able to manage them. The main thing is not to be *tactful.* Good-bye, dear, kind Papa! Kissing your hands, we remain your loving children

M. and F. Dostoevsky

We kiss our dear sister Varenka, Sashechka, and our little brother Nikolya. Good-bye!

1838

18. To Mikhail Dostoevsky
4 February 1838. Petersburg

St. Petersburg.—1838.—February 4.

Dearest Papa,

I've finally enrolled in the M[ain] Academy of E[ngineering], I've finally donned a dress coat and fully entered the Tsar's service.[1] I've just barely managed to squeeze out a free moment from classes, studies, and service, a precious moment in which I can have a talk with you at least in writing, dearest Papa. It's been so long since I wrote to you, and after hearing at my last meeting with my brother that you reproached me for that, I very much wished to correct my fault, involuntary as it was. And just at that time I suddenly received a letter from you; I didn't know with what to compare your love for us. Without even knowing the address, dearest Papa, you sent me a letter, and in the meantime I hadn't written so much as a single line for over a month; but that was absolutely because I didn't have a single free moment. Just imagine that from early morning until late evening we can hardly keep up with the lectures in our classes. In the evening we not only have no free time, but not even a minute to look over properly, at our leisure, what we heard in classes during the day. We are sent to formation drill, we are given lessons in fencing, dancing, and singing, in which no one dares not participate. Finally, we are put on guard duty, and all the time passes at that; but after receiving the letter from you, I abandoned everything and now hasten to answer you, dearest Papa. Thank God, I'm gradually getting used to life here; I can't say anything good about my comrades. The administration is of a good opinion of me, I hope. We have a new Inspector of Classes. Lomnovsky (the former Inspector) ceded his position to Baron Dalvits; I don't know what's going to happen, but the former Inspector was pleased with me.—I received the 50 rubles. My brother has the money now. How much I must thank you, Papa. I really need it, Papa, and I'm hastening to acquire everything that I need. I don't go anywhere on Sunday or on other holidays, because the

1. Dostoevsky was officially enrolled at the Academy on 16 January 1838.

parents have to sign for each petty officer that they're taking him home.—
And so for the meantime I'm deprived of the chance to see my brother, and
consequently I couldn't read your last letters. Only once was I able to
petition to go see Kostomarov, and there I learned of the pleasant news
about my brother's enrolling in the Engineering Cadets. Thank God, our
longtime common wish has been realized, and my brother has at last found
the perfect path for himself. Now we hope that everything will go better. In
your letter to me you nevertheless express doubts about that. But it's all
quite finished, and surely in the best possible way. And besides, it would
always have been possible to hope for such a resolution, had it not been for
Kostomarov, who always wanted to drag out this matter, to keep my
brother beyond the specified time in order to be at least partially right
regarding our 300 rubles that he coerced from us so despicably.—You are
probably aware from my brother's recent letters that he was presented to
Gerua[2] and Truson,[3] his future generals. They received him most cordially,
as one who has already entered the service: con[sequently], the decision is
indubitable and there's no reason to doubt. Truson also promised to try to
do something for my brother when it's time to receive his officer's rank,
and we can hope that he'll keep his promise. I recently found out that after
the examination was already over the General arranged to have four new
people study at public expense in addition to the candidate who was at
Kostomarov's and who won my place. What baseness! That completely
stunned me. We, who struggle for every ruble, have to pay,[4] while others—
the children of wealthy fathers—are accepted without fees. To heck with
them!—You ask, Papa, whether I have need of anything. For the time
being nothing. My brother has my linen and clothes. I can hardly wait for
him to be completely enrolled. Then, at least, we'll be closer and closer to
each other. Good-bye, dearest Papa. With wishes for all God's blessings
for you.

I have the honor of remaining your humble and obedient son

F. Dostoevsky

I've heard that before moving into the Engineers' Castle my brother
will live for about two weeks at the Fortress.[5]

With regard to the new decree that you wrote me about, there's no
reason to be alarmed. We haven't heard anything about it. And besides, it
lacks a sufficient basis and is simply an empty rumor.

Kiss all my brothers and sisters for me. When will we see each other?

2. Adjutant-General Alexander Klavdievich Gerua (1784-1852).
3. Pyotr Khristianovich Truzon.
4. The Kumanins paid Dostoevsky's matriculation fee of 950 rubles.
5. The Peter-Paul Fortress.

Andryusha hasn't yet written us so much as half-a-line.

You write that I should send you Shidlovsky's address, but he's leaving Petersburg for Kursk[6] to visit relatives for a while. You'll surely meet him in Moscow, and he can find you through the Kumanins.

19. To Mikhail Dostoevsky
5 June 1838. Petersburg

St. Petersburg. June 5, 1838

Dearest Papa,

My God, how long it's been since I wrote to you, how long it's been since I tasted those moments of true heartfelt bliss, the true, pure, elevated . . . bliss experienced only by those who have someone with whom to share their hours of delight and their calamities, by those who have someone in whom to confide everything that transpires in their souls. Oh, how greedily I now revel in that bliss. I hasten to reveal to you the reasons for my long silence.

After my brother's letter, where I made a short postscript wishing you a Happy Easter, I was for a long time unable to take up anything extraneous. Our trimester examinations began immediately and lasted at least a month. We had to work day and night; especially the drafting did us in. We have four subjects for drawing: (1) fortificational, (2) situational, (3) architectural, (4) from nature. I don't draw well, as you are aware. Only in fortificational drafting am I fairly good, and what am I to do with that? And that hurt me a lot. In the first place, because I became one of the middle students in the class, when I could have been first. Just imagine, for all the intellectual subjects I have perfect scores, so that I have 5 points more than the first student for all subjects except drawing. But they pay more attention to drawing than to mathematics. That grieves me a great deal. The second reason for my long silence is formation drill service. Just imagine. Five reviews by the Grand Duke and the Tsar have worn us out. We were at the mounting of the guard, at the riding arenas we performed a ceremonial march together with the Guard, did maneuvers, and before every review we were tormented in the company with instruction at which we prepared ahead. All these reviews preceded a huge, resplendent,

6. Actually, Shidlovsky was on his way to Kharkov.

brilliant *May Parade* where the entire royal family was present and there were 140,000 troops. That day completely exhausted us. In the coming months we're going out to the camps. Because of my height I ended up in a company of skirmishers to whom now falls double instruction—in battalion training and skirmishing. What can we do, we don't have time to study for classes. Those are the reasons for my long silence.

Now let's talk about something else. Yes, who would have thought or supposed that my brother would be sent off?[1] But what can be done? That's what God sees fit to do.—And what is the result of His will cannot be changed by any force. Fate usually plays with the world as with a toy. It assigns roles to humanity . . . but it is blind. But God will show one a path along which one can make one's way out of any sort of misfortune. And my brother is not yet in misfortune.—Of course, it's bitter and painful for us to see the grief of a father like you. We mourn that with all our heart. But calm down, dearest Papa, my brother's position and service have their own advantages too. For engineering service the main thing is practical experience. He is having it now. And he can get schooling anytime and anywhere. Perhaps God is arranging everything for the best. I recently received a letter from my brother, and to judge by his description, I think his life enviable. But you must be aware of all that from his letter to you. Because I'm sure that you didn't have to wait to hear from him.

You must now be diverting your solitude with rural pursuits and work. Yes! What will the present year be like and what will God gladden us with? Oh, God grant us good fortune.

I still continue to visit the Merkurovs.[2] They are people worthy of friendship and respect. They receive me like a relative. God grant good fortune to all our well-wishers!

My present financial circumstances are somewhat bad. The trip to Revel cost my brother rather a lot! But besides that I spent a a fair amount of the money that you sent on school necessities. Because for the May Parade the dress coats and accoutrements needed many repairs and additions. Absolutely all my new comrades have acquired their own shakos; and the one that I had, from the Academy, could have caught the Tsar's attention. I was forced to buy a new one, and it cost me 25 rubles. With the rest of the money I repaired my instruments and bought brushes and paint. All necessities! By the time to set off for the camps the most horrific need will set in, because to be there without money is a catastrophe. If you can, Papa, send me at least something. Send your letter directly to the Main Academy of Engineering. Because I don't know how to tell you the apartment address for the Merkurovs. They've moved from

---

1. Mikhail Dostoevsky was transferred to the Revel Engineering Command on 22 April 1848.

2. The Dostoevsky brothers met the Merkurovs through Shidlovsky.

their old one, and I've forgotten the name of their present landlord. We're leaving for the camps around June 12.

Good-bye, dearest Papa. Kiss all my brothers and sisters. With sincere respect and filial devotion, I remain

F. Dostoevsky

20. To Mikhail Dostoevsky
9 August 1838. Petersburg

St. Petersburg. August 9, 1838

Dear brother,

How your letter surprised me, dear brother: can you really not have received even a half-line from me; since your departure I've sent you 3 letters: the 1st soon after your departure; I didn't reply to the 2nd, because I didn't have a single kopeck (I didn't borrow from the Merkurovs). That continued until the 20th of July, when I received 40 rubles from Papa; and finally, the 3rd just recently. Con[sequently], you can't boast that you didn't forget me and wrote more often. Con[sequently], I too was always true to my word. True, I'm lazy, very lazy. But what can I do when there's only one thing left for me in the world: continually relaxing! I don't know whether my melancholy ideas will ever subside. Only one condition has been given man's lot: his soul's atmosphere consists of a merging of heaven and earth; what an unlawful child is man; the law of spiritual nature has been broken... It seems to me that our world is a purgatory of heavenly spirits bedimmed by sinful thought. It seems to me that the world has taken on a negative meaning, and from elevated, refined spirituality there has emerged satire. If a person who shares neither an effect nor an idea with the whole, in a word, if a total outsider should wind up in this picture, what will happen? The picture is spoiled and cannot exist!

But to see only the cruel covering under which the universe languishes, to know that a single explosion of will is enough to smash it and merge with eternity, to know and to be like the last creature ... is awful! How cowardly man is! Hamlet! Hamlet! When I recall those stormy, wild speeches in which the moaning of a benumbed world can be heard, neither mournful grumbling nor reproach grips my breast ... My soul is so overwhelmed by grief that it fears to understand it so as not to tear itself to pieces. Pascal once said he who protests against philosophy is himself a philosopher. A pitiable philosophy! But I have gotten carried away with my chattering.—I received only two of your letters (besides the last one). Well, brother! You complain of your poverty. There's no need to tell you that I'm not rich either. Would you believe that on a march away from the camps I didn't have a single kopeck; on the road I fell sick from a cold (the rain poured all day, and we were out in the open) and from hunger and didn't even have half a kopeck so as to be able to moisten my throat with a swallow of tea. But I recovered, and in camp my lot was most distressing until the receipt of money from Papa. I immediately paid off my debts and spent the rest. But the description of your situation exceeds everything. Is it really possible not to have even 5 kopecks, *to feed oneself* on God knows what and with a fond gaze feel all the sweetness of the marvelous berries that you like so much! How sorry I am for you! You'll ask what happened to the Merkurovs and to your money. Here's what: I visited them a few times after your departure. But then I couldn't because I was on duty. In extremity I sent to them, but they sent me so little that I was embarrassed to ask them for any more. Just then I received your letter to them care of me. I didn't have anything and decided to ask them to include my letter in theirs. Apparently you didn't receive either one. They seem not to have written you. Just before the camps (not having any money to send Papa a letter long since ready), I appealed to them to send me at least something; they sent me all our things, but not a kopeck of money, and they didn't write a reply; I was on the rocks! From all of that I concluded that they wish to rid themselves of our annoying requests. I wanted to have things out with them in a letter, but I've been on duty since camp, and they've moved from their former apartment. I know the building where they live, but I don't know the address. I'll inform you of it later.—But it's long past time to change the subject of our conversation. Well, you boast that you've read a great deal, but please don't imagine that I envy you. At Peterhof I read at least as much as you. All of Hoffmann in Russian and German (i.e., his untranslated "Mur the Cat"[1]), almost all of Balzac (Balzac is great! His characters are the products of a mind of the universe! It's not the spirit of time, but whole millenia that prepared, with their struggling, such a culmination in the soul of man).[2] Goethe's *Faust* and his short poems, Polevoy's *History*,[3] *Ugolino*,[4] *Undina*,[5] (I'll write you a few things about *Ugolino* later). Also Victor Hugo except for *Cromwell* and *Hernani*. Now

1. E.T.A. Hoffmann's *Liebensansichter des Katers Murr* (1820-22).

2. On Dostoevsky and Balzac see Donald Fanger, *Dostoevsky and Romantic Realism* (1965).

3. Nikolay Alexeevich Polevoy (1796-1846), journalist, writer, early propagandist for romanticism, published his *History of the Russian People* in the years 1829-33.

4. *Ugolino* (1838), romantic drama by Polevoy.

5. *Undina* (1837), V. A. Zhukovsky's verse adapation of Fouqué's *Undine*.

good-bye. Write me, do me a favor, comfort me and write as often as possible. Reply to this letter right away. I count on receiving a reply in 12 days. At the latest! Write or you'll wear me out with worry.

Your brother F. Dostoevsky

I have a project: to become insane. Let people rave, let them be treated, let them be made intelligent. If you've read all of Hoffmann, then you surely remember the character Alban.[6] How do you like him? It's horrible to see a person who has the inscrutable in his power, a person who doesn't know what he should do, who plays with a toy that is—God!

Do you write to the Kumanins often? And write whether Kudryavtsev has told you anything about Chermak. For Heaven's sake, write about that too; I want to know about Andryusha.[7]

But listen, brother. If our correspondence continues in this manner, than it seems better not to write. Let's agree to write each other every other Saturday. That will be better. I received another letter from Shrenk[8] and haven't answered him for three months. That's what having no money means!

21. To Mikhail Dostoevsky
30 October 1838. Petersburg

St. Petersburg. 30 October 1838

Dearest Papa,

Please don't be angry at my silence after the receipt of your letter, dearest Papa. I have many reasons and justifications for the silence. I'll just say that your letter caught me at the beginning of an examination: it has now ended. I hasten to inform you about everything. Before our examination ended I had prepared a letter for you . . . I wanted to make you happy, dearest Papa, with my letter, I wanted to fill your heart with joy;

6. Alban is the hero of Hoffmann's story "Der Magnetiseur" (1813).
7. Andrey Mikhaylovich Dostoevsky.
8. L. I. Shrenk, an acquaintance of Dostoevsky's from Chermak's boarding school in Moscow.

that was all I saw and heard both awake and dreaming. Now what can I do? With what can I make you happy, my tender, dearest parent? But I'll speak more clearly.

Our examination was approaching the end; I was proud of my examination; I gave *outstanding* answers, and what happened? I was held back in the class for another year. My God! How have I angered Thee? Why dost Thou not send my Thy blessing from on high so that I might make my most loving parent happy? Oh, how many tears that cost me. I became physically ill when I heard about it. People who performed 100 times worse on the examination than I did were passed into the next class *(by reason of favoritism)*. What's to be done? Obviously you can't forge your own path. I'll tell you one thing: I was out of favor with some of the teachers and those with the loudest vote in the conference chamber. I have had personal trouble with two of them. A single word from them, and I was kept back. (I heard all of this later.) Judge for yourself how I did on the examination when I tell you my scores: I won't conceal anything—I'll be candid:

Out of possible perfect scores of 10 (15 for algebra and fortifications) I received:

For algebra—11 (the teacher definitely wanted me to be kept back; he's angrier at me than anyone else is)—

Fortifications—12	Russ[ian]—10
Artillery—8	French—10
Geometry—10	German—10
History—10	Catechism—10
Geography—10	

Now judge for yourself how I must have felt when I heard that I had been kept back in spite of such marks. Note that in algebra and fortifications I distinguished myself, and they gave me scores that don't correspond to that.[1]

What do I care that I'll be the 1st in our class. What do I care. In half-a-year I'll be in the second class. The examination is set for May. But I've lost a whole year! Don't be upset, Papa! What can be done! Spare yourself. Look at our poor family, at our poor little brothers and sisters who live only through your life, who seek support only in you. Why be upset and not take care of yourself, giving over to despair. You love us so much that you don't want to see a single failure in our fate. But who hasn't had them. And now you're tormenting yourself with the groundless idea that if I am kept behind, I'll be expelled from the Academy. But can I really lack all

---

1. Dostoevsky was also kept back because of his poor performance at military drill.

talent, so that I could be expelled? Or do I not know the Academy's regulations? I've been kept back for a 2nd year! O baseness! Tomorrow I'll ask the General[2] why I was kept back. I'll be told something or other. You write, dear Papa, that you're all alone now and that even our sister Varenka has left you. Oh, don't grumble at us, too, dearest Papa. Believe that my whole life will have the single goal of loving and pleasing you. What's to be done, such is God's pleasure. I remain your loving and respectful son

Fyodor Dostoevsky

P.S. I'll be more punctual in my letters now. Kiss Kolya and Sasha.[3] Oh, when will the time come when I'll embrace you with love and joy. Yet another year of wretched insignificant petty-officer duty!

You ordered me to be candid with you, dearest Papa, about my needs. Yes, I'm quite poor now. I have borrowed in order to send you this letter and have nothing with which to repay. Send me something right away. You'll extract me from hell. Oh, it's awful to be in extremity!

Iv[an]Nikolaevich[4] is in Petersburg, he sends you his greetings and tenders you his respects.

There will soon be a holiday in our family: your festive name day; I melt into tears brought about by memories. I wish you, our angel, every good fortune in the world! Oh, how glad I would be if my greeting found you in a merry and joyous mood.

22. To Mikhail Dostoevsky
31 October 1838. Petersburg

St. Petersburg. 31 October 1838

Oh, how long, how long it's been since I've written to you, my dear brother...The wretched examination! It prevented me from writing to you, to Papa, and from seeing Ivan Nikolaev[ich],[1] and what was the result? I didn't pass! O horror! Another year, an entire extra year! I

---

2. General Sharngorst.
3. Nikolay Mikhaylovich and Alexandra Mikhaylovna Dostoevsky.
4. Ivan Nikolaevich Shidlovsky.
1. Ivan Nikolaevich Shidlovsky.

wouldn't be so furious if I didn't know that baseness, baseness alone deposed me; I wouldn't regret it if our poor father's tears weren't scorching my soul. Until now I hadn't known what wounded pride meant. I would have blushed if that feeling had possessed me... but you know what? I'd like to crush the entire world at a single stroke... I lost, killed so many days before the examination, fell ill, lost weight, performed on the examination superbly, in the full force and scope of that word, and was kept back... That was the wish of one teacher (of algebra) to whom I was rude in the course of the year and who today had the audacity to remind me of that, giving that as the reason for my being kept back... On a 10-point system I had averages of 9 1/2, and was kept back... But to hell with all that. If I have to put up with it, then I will. I won't waste the paper, for some reason or other I rarely have a talk with you.

My friend! You philosophize like a poet. And just as the soul withstands a degree of inspiration in an unstable way, so is your philosophy unstable and inaccurate. In order *to know* more, one needs *to feel* less, and in reverse the rule is rash, ravings of the heart. What do you mean by the word *know?* To know nature, the soul, God, love... Those things are known by the heart, not the mind. If we were spirits, we would live and hover in the sphere of that thought over which our soul hovers when it wishes to decipher it. We ashes, however, people, have to try to decipher but they cannot suddenly embrace a thought. The conductor of thought through the perishable outer shell into the composition of the soul is the mind. The mind is a material capacity... but the soul, however, or spirit, lives on thought, which the heart whispers to it... A thought arises in the soul. The mind is an implement, a machine powered by the fire of the soul... Moreover (2nd point), the mind of man, when drawn into the field of knowledge, functions independently of *feeling,* con[sequently] *of the heart.* If, however, the goal of knowledge is love and nature, at that point a clear field opens up for *the heart.* I'm not going to argue with you, but I'll tell you that I disagree with your opinion about poetry and philosophy... You shouldn't assume philosophy to be a simple mathematical problem where the unknown is nature.... Note that the poet, in a transport of inspiration, makes out God, con[sequently], he fulfills the purpose of philosophy.[2] Con[sequently], poetic rapture is the rapture of philosophy... Con[sequently], philosophy is that same poetry, only in the highest degree!.. It's strange that you think in the spirit of today's philosophy. How many unintelligible systems of it have been born in intelligent fiery heads; in order to derive a correct result from this diverse heap you need to fit it into a mathematical formula. Those are the rules of

---

2. Dostoevsky's pronouncedly romantic notions about poetry and philosophy suggest the influence of such Russian Schellingians as the publisher and editor N. I. Nadezhdin and the young critic Vissarion Belinsky.

today's philosophy...[3] But I've gotten carried away in dreaming with you. Without recognizing your flaccid philosophy, I do, however, recognize the existence of the flaccid expression of it, with which I do not wish to weary you...

Dear brother, it's sad to live without hope...I look ahead, and the future horrifies me...I'm floating in some sort of cold, polar atmosphere into which no ray of sunshine has ever crept...It's been a long time since I've felt bursts of inspiration...but I'm often in the same sort of condition as, you remember, the prisoner of Chillon[4] after the death of his brothers in the prison...The heavenly bird of poetry doesn't visit me, doesn't warm my cold soul...You say that I'm secretive; but now even my former dreams have abandoned me, and my marvelous arabesques that I created once upon a time have shed their gilt. Those thoughts that used to scorch my soul and heart with their rays have now lost their flame and warmth; either my heart has become hardened or...I'm terrified to continue...It's awful to say, if all the past was only a golden dream, flowery daydreams...

I read your poem, dear brother...It wrung several tears from my soul and lulled my soul for a time with the salutatory whisper of memories. You say that you have an idea for a drama...I'm glad...Write it...Oh, if you were deprived of even the last crumbs from a paradisiacal feast, what would there be left for you to do...It's too bad that I couldn't see Iv[an] Nikolaev[ich][5] last week. I was sick!—Listen! It seems to me that fame also facilitates a poet's inspiration. Byron was an egoist: his idea about fame was insignificant, vain...But the single thought about the fact that sometime, following your former rapture, a pure, loftily beautiful soul will wrest itself from the ashes, the idea that inspiration, like a heavenly mystery, will illuminate pages over which you wept and posterity will weep, I don't think that that thought didn't steal into the poet's soul even at the very moments of creation. The crowd's empty cries are insignificant. Ah, I just recalled two lines by Pushkin, when he describes the crowd and the poet:

> And the crowd spits on the altar where your fire burns
> And in childish playfulness rocks your tripod![6]

Isn't that really wonderful! Good-bye. Your friend and brother F. Dostoevsky

---

3. Dostoevsky's criticism of mechanistic philosophy echoes various articles by Russian Schellingians in the Russian press in the 1830s.

4. *The Prisoner of Chillon* (1816), narrative poem by Byron.

5. Ivan Nikolaevich Shidlovsky.

6. A quotation from Pushkin's poem "To the Poet" (1830).

Yes! Write me about the main idea of Chateaubriand's work *Génie du Christianisme*.[7]—I recently read in *Son of the Fatherland* an article by the critic Nisard[8] about Victor Hugo. Oh, how low he stands in the opinion of the French. How insignificant Nisard makes his dramas and novels out to be. They're unjust toward him, and Nisard (although an intelligent person) talks nonsense.—In addition: write me about the main idea of your drama. I'm sure that it's excellent, although 10 years is too little for working out dramatic characters. At least that's what I think.—Oh, my brother, how sorry I am that you're short of money! I can't fight back the tears. When did this happen to us? But by the way. Best wishes, my dear, for your name day and your past birthday.

In your poem "Vision of the Mother" I don't understand the strange shape in which you clothed the deceased woman's soul. That character from beyond the grave is not complete. The verses are good, however, although in one place there's a blunder. Don't be angry with me for the analysis. Write more often. I'll be more punctual.

Ah, soon, soon I'll read through all of Ivan Nikolaevich's[9] new poems. How much poetry! How many brilliant ideas! But there's something else I forgot to tell you. I think you know that Smirdin[10] is preparing a pantheon of our literature in book form: portraits of 100 authors with one of their best compositions appended to each portrait.[11] And imagine Zotov (!?)[12] and Orlov (Alexande[r] Anfimov[ich])[13] among them. It's killingly funny! Listen, send me another poem. That would be marvelous!—The Merkurovs are soon going to Penza, or they've already left, I think.

I feel sorry for poor Papa! A strange character! Oh, how many misfortunes he has borne! It's bitter to the point of tears that there's nothing to console him with.—And you know what? Papa doesn't know the world at all: he has lived in it for 50 years and has kept the same opinion of people that he had 30 years ago. Happy ignorance. But he's very disappointed with it. That seems to be our common lot. Good-bye again.

Yours

7. Thanks to its psychologism and appeal to the irrational, *Le Génie du Christianisme* (1802), by François René Chateaubriand (1768-1848), gave a major impetus to the French romantic movement.

8. Désiré Nisard (1806-1888), French historian of literature and foe of romanticism. Dostoevsky has confused authors and articles, however. *The Son of the Fatherland* for March-April 1838 included both articles by Nisard about Lamartine and articles by Gustave Planche about Hugo.

9. Ivan Nikolaevich Shidlovsky.

10. Alexander Filippovich Smirdin (1795-1857), major Russian bookseller and publisher in the first half of the nineteenth century.

11. Smirdin published three volumes of 100 Russian Authors (1839-45).

12. Rafail Mikhaylovich Zotov (1795-1871), author of popular historical novels.

13. Alexander Anfimovich Orlov (d. 1840), author of popular novels in a pseudo-folk style.

1839

23. To Mikhail Dostoevsky
23 March 1839. Petersburg

St. Petersburg. March 23, 1839

My God! I just now learned that you didn't receive my last letter either, dearest Papa. The one I'm writing you now is the fifth. I,too, am finally running out of patience. My God! Can it really be that I must always be the reason for your despair. Everything that I was so afraid of has happened; I'm in despair, in absolute despair!

Listen now, dearest Papa, to everything that I'm about to explain to you briefly.

Immediately after the receipt of your letter with the 25 paper rubles enclosed I answered and thanked your for your help. I sent the letter a week later, and on that same day both your letter and my brother's got lost. Not having had any news in a long time, in despair about your fate, our dear Father, in despair about our family's fate, I wrote you another letter just before Christmas. That one had the same fate, too. I sent the third one the week before Lent. The fourth one at the beginning of Lent. The 5th one I'm writing now, at Ivan Nikolaevich's,[1] not having found him at home; I learned of the fate of my letters, and in sorrow, in despair, with tears in my eyes, I take pen in hand. Tomorrow, that is, Friday, this letter will start off on its way to you. Ivan Nikolaevich is a noble person and will carry out what I ask of him in a note I'm leaving for him now.

I now know the reason why my letters did not reach you. We had a horrible incident occur in the Academy that I can't explain to you on paper now,[2] because I'm certain that this letter will also be read by many third parties. Five petty officers were reduced to the ranks for this incident. I'm not at all involved. But I received the same punishment as everyone else. All of us innocent parties were confined to the Academy for about 2 months. During that time all our letters were unsealed and read in the

---

1. Ivan Nikolaevich Shidlovsky.
2. Dostoevsky may be referring to an incident wherein in the middle of the night students beat a fellow student whom they suspected of being an informer, threw potatoes at the officer who came to see what was going on, and on the following day refused to salute their commanding officer. As a consequence, all the students were confined to quarters.

Office, and they must have been held up at the post office. That's why you didn't receive any either.—I intended to send my 4th letter to you via Ivan Nikolaevich (in that letter I responded to your insured one, which had wounded me mortally), and the soldier whom I sent, as I have just now learned, deceived me and didn't fulfill my assignment. Con[sequently], I am completely in the right before you, dearest Papa. I swear that. My God! But you're in despair about the fate of your son! At your feet, I beg your pardon for all the unintentional annoyance that I've caused you.

Although I've been kept behind in the class, I haven't lost time. I've been studying military science and have accomplished a lot. I've followed the highest class's courses and intend to skip over a class and pass into the first through an examination.[3] But I've spent a lot of money (on the purchase of books, things, etc.) and had to keep borrowing. I'm in debt all the way around and very much. I owe at least 50 rubles. My God! Will I continue to take your last kopecks for a long time. But that help is essential, or I'm lost. The deadline for payment has long since passed. Save me. Send me 60 rubles (50 rubles for debts, 10 for my expenses before camp). We'll soon be heading for the camps, and there will be new needs again. My God! I know that we're poor. But God is my witness that I'm not asking for anything nonessential. And so I implore you to help me as soon as possible.—Time is passing, I'm all out of paper. Yours to the grave and to the end of time. Your son

F. Dostoevsky

P.S. I'm writing to you in terrible haste.

My brother writes that he'll soon be ready to take the entrance examination for the field engineers here. God grant him luck. By the way, best wishes for Easter, our dearest Papa. I wish you good fortune from the bottom of my heart.

I have just taken Communion. I borrowed money for the priest. It's been a long time since I had so much as a kopeck.

I recently received a letter from my brother. He writes that he hasn't received even a line from me.

My notion of taking the entrance examination for the highest class attracts me very much. I can pass it. But for that I need money. If you can send me 100 rubles, I'll take the examination. If not, then that will be another year. This is for you, dearest Papa; it's all the same to me.—Goodbye again.

Kiss our little ones and my sister. I received a letter from Khotyaintsev (Alexander).[4] I replied to him that I sent a letter via Ivan Nikolaevich. I'm

---

3. The first class was the highest in the Academy.

4. Alexander Fyodorovich Khotyaintsev was a neighbor who lived not far from the Dostoevsky family estate of Darovoe.

terribly irritated that Khotyaintsev didn't inquire much earlier.
Address your letter to me care of Ivan Nikolaevich.

24. To Alexander Khotyaintsev
23 March 1839. Petersburg

Dear Alexander Fyodorovich,[1]

I consider it my duty to express to you my sincere thankfulness for
your concerning yourself with my father's affairs! I can well imagine his
alarm; but at the same time I am amazed at how as many letters as I have
sent him have not reached him. I wrote to him quite recently; and today I
sent another letter through an acquaintance. The reasons why they did not
reach him are laid out in the last letter. I think that this last letter will reach
him.

It only remains for me to declare my gratitude for your indulgence.—
Allow me to assure you of the sincere respect with which I have the honor
of remaining your most obedient servant

Fyodor Dostoevsky.

25. To Mikhail Dostoevsky
5-10 May 1839. Petersburg

May 5, 1839

Dearest Papa,

I presume that even now you're worried about me, since you didn't
receive a reply from me right away. Dearest Papa! I hasten to reassure you
and I'll to justify my present silence as much as possible. Our examinations

1. See Letter 23, note 4.

have set in. We need to study, but meanwhile we use all our free time for formation drill, because the May parade is coming up soon. All we can do is look for free time late at night. I'm very glad that I've finally found a free moment to talk to you. Oh, how I reproach myself for having been the reason for your grief! I'll try to make up for it now as much as possible.—I received your letter and with all my heart thank you for the enclosure. You write, dearest Papa, that you yourself have no money and that you won't be able to send me anything for the camps. Children who understand their parents' situations must themselves share all joy and sorrow with them; children must fully bear their parents' need. I won't ask much of you.

After all, if you don't have tea to drink, you won't die of hunger. I'll get by somehow! But I beg you for at least something for boots for the camps, because I need to stock up on them for the road. But let's finish with this. I've already begun my examinations, and very well. I'll finish well, too. I'm certain of that.—Many of the teachers in whose disfavor I was last year are now as favorably inclined to me as they could possibly be. And in general, I can't complain about the people in charge. I remember my responsibilities, and they treat me justly. But when will I be finished with all this.

You write, dearest Papa, that I must not forget my responsibilities. I repeat: I remember them very well, and I'm already bound to service through the oath that I took upon enrolling at the Academy.—I haven't received any letters from my brother for a long time. He seems to have forgotten me. But recently I received from [him] a wad of paper all covered over with writing, where he attacks me violently for my imaginary silence toward you, and I confess that with that letter he wounded me to the depths of my soul, making me in his eyes a most vile creature. I let that pass, however, because his letter was not addressed to me. I consider myself much better than the person with whom he is conducting such a correspondence. But I am forgetting that and am preparing to reply to him this week. His situation is not at all bad now. He could take the entrance examination here at the Academy for the lower officer class. Advise him to do that. Many of the petty officers from the Fortress[1] do that. There are examples of that every year. He can be ready in a year. I'm ready to see that he gets all the notes and everything he needs. As it is, he already knows quite a bit of mathematics. But he needs to study fortifications better (which is our main subject in the petty officers classes) and artillery, because artillery, too, is treated in great detail, as a component of fortification.—Oh, how you gladdened me when you wrote that, thank the Lord, you are well. And I thought and assumed that your constant illnesses surely were made even worse by your distress (at not having received letters from me). I kiss my little brothers and sisters. What is Andryusha[2] doing;

1. The Peter-Paul Fortress.
2. Andrey Mikhaylovich Dostoevsky.

how is he getting along with his schooling? Don't you want to send him here to the Academy?[3] When I become an officer, I'll take it upon myself to prepare him for enrolling here, because enrolling here is rather easy. Kostomarov fooled us and simply took money from us when we could have enrolled in the Academy even without preparation. But good-bye, dearest Papa. I wish you happiness countless times.

Your obedient and loving son,

F. Dostoevsky

Belated best wishes for Easter Sunday. With what sadness do I recall spending the day in the family circle! And now? But the only important thing is to get myself out of the Academy.

Having passed into the highest class, I find it *absolutely essential* to subscribe to the French reading library here. How many great works by geniuses in mathematics and by military geniuses there are in French. I see the necessity of reading that, because I'm passionately fond of military science, although I can't stand mathematics. What a strange science! And what stupidity to study it. For me as much as is demanded of an engineer or a little bit more is sufficient.

But why should I become a Pascal or an Ostrogradsky.[4] Mathematics without application is a pure 0, and there's just as much usefulness in it as in a soap bubble. I'll tell you that I'm sorry that I gave up Latin. What a marvelous language. I'm reading Julius Caesar now, and after a 2-year separation from Latin I understand absolutely everything.

10 May

It's strange: these stupid circumstances of my present life deprive me of many things. I had to hold off sending you my letter for 5 days. The parade was postponed until the 10th of May. I wanted to write this postscript to you, and will you believe, dearest Papa, that because of drill exercise (which they're torturing us with) and examinations, I was unable to. I'm writing to you now at the post office.

My dear, kind parent! Can you really think that in asking financial assistance of you, your son is asking for anything nonessential. God is my witness if I want to cause you even the slightest deprivation, not only out of personal gain, but even out of necessity. I have a head, I have hands. If I were free, at liberty, my own master, I wouldn't even ask for a kopeck from

---

3. A. M. Dostoevsky attempted to enroll in the Main Aacademy of Engineering in 1842 but was not accepted. He enrolled in the Academy of Civil Engineering the same year.
4. Mikhail Vasilevich Ostrogradsky (1801-61), well-known mathematician in his day.

you; I would learn to feel comfortable with iron need. I would be ashamed then even to utter a peep about myself. I'm now expressing myself with nothing but promises in the future; but that future is not far off, and with time you'll see it.

Now, however, dear Papa, recall that I am *serving* in the full sense of the word. Will-nilly, I have to conform fully to the regulations of my present society. Why make of oneself an exception? Such exceptions sometimes are subjected to horrible unpleasantness. You understand that yourself, dear Papa. You have lived with people. Now: camp life for every student from institutions of military education demands at least 40 rubles. (I'm writing you this because I'm speaking to my father.) I'm not including in this sum such needs as, for instance, having tea, sugar, and so on. Those things are essential no matter what, and they're essential not just because of decency but also because of need. When you get soaked through in a canvas tent in raw, wet weather, or come home in such weather, tired, chilled, without tea you can fall ill, which happened to me last year on the march. Nevertheless, respecting your need, I won't drink tea. I'm asking only what is essential for 2 pairs of plain boots—16 rubles. Now my things—books, boots, pens, paper and so on and so on have to be stored somewhere. For that I must have a trunk, because there are no other structures in the camps besides tents. Our beds are heaps of straw covered with a sheet. The question arises of where I'm going to put all of this if I don't have a trunk. You should know that the treasury doesn't concern itself with whether I need a place; it doesn't concern itself with whether I have a trunk. Since the examinations are coming to an end, con[sequently], I don't need any books; the treasury outfits me, con[sequently], I don't need boots, and so on. But how will I spend the time without books? Three pairs of treasury-issue boots won't last half-a-year even in town! Con[sequently], there's no official place provided for me to place the trunk, which is essential for me.[5] In a common tent I'll crowd my neighbor, con[sequently], I'll cause others trouble, besides which, I simply won't be allowed to keep a trunk in the tent, because no one keeps them in a tent; con[sequently], I'll have to find a place for my baggage. I'll find a place by making arrangements (as everyone does) with one of our soldiers, our servants, to put my trunk somewhere. For that you have to pay. Con[sequently], at least a silver ruble for the purchase of a trunk.

> For transportation of it there and back....5 r.
> For a place....2 silver r.
> For having it cleaned....5 r.

5. After this line Dostoevsky erased the following phrase: "For a place in a tent one has to pay money to guard."

That's a conventional tariff charged by the servant. In town it's another matter, but in camp you have to pay them for their every step. And the authorities do not enter into this.

Now.... 16

16
3.75
5
7 (2 silver r.)
5
———
36 or 40.

(For sending letters, for pens, paper and so on.) I have saved 15 rubles from what you sent. You can see, dear Papa, that I absolutely need at least another 25 rubles. We'll be marching out to the camps in the first days of June. And so, send me the money by June 1st if you want to help your son in his horrible need. I don't dare to demand; I'm not demanding anything excessive; but my gratitude will be limitless.[6]—Send the letter care of Shidlovsky again. Good-bye, dear Papa.

Entirely yours,
F. Dostoevsky

26. To Mikhail Dostoevsky
16 August 1839. Petersburg

St. Petersburg. August 16, 1839

Yes, my dear brother, that's the way it always happens with us: we make promises without knowing ourselves whether we're capable of fulfilling them; it's good that I never promise rashly. For ex[ample]. What would you say about my silence? That I'm lazy . . . that I forget you and so on and so on. No! The whole problem is not a single kopeck of money; now

6. In a letter of reply dated 27 May 1839, Dostoevsky's father painted a very gloomy picture of the family finances, appealed to his son to cut down on his expenditures, and sent thirty-five paper rubles.

I have some, and I'm indescribably glad to see it, this long absent guest.

Well, here at last is a letter to you, too!

Let's have a talk, let's have a chat!

My dear brother! I spilled many tears over Father's death,[1] but now our situation is still worse; I'm speaking not of myself, but of our family. I'm sending my letter to Revel without knowing myself whether it will reach you there... I assume that it won't catch you here... God grant that you be in Moscow; then I would be more reassured about our family; but tell me, please, is there anyone in the world more unfortunate than our poor brothers and sisters? The idea that they will be raised at someone else's hands kills me. And that's why I think your idea of going to live in the country after you receive the rank of officer is excellent. There you would take up their education, my dear brother, and that upbringing would be good fortune for them. The harmonious organization of the soul amid one's own family, the development of all aspirations from a Christian foundation, the pride of family virtues, fear of vice and ignominy—those are the consequences of such an upbringing. Our parents' bones will sleep calmly in the damp earth then; but, dear brother, you'll have to put up with a great deal. You'll have either to break off with our relatives or to make peace with them. To break off with them is fatal; our sisters would perish. If you make peace with them you'll have to court them.[2] They'll call your disdain for government service indolence. But, dear brother, endure that. Spit on those miserable little souls and be a benefactor to our brothers. You alone will save them... I know that you've learned to be patient; fulfill your intention. It's excellent. God grant you the strength for that! I declare that I'll be in accord with you in everything from now on.[3]

What are you doing now?[4] You're more candid with [Ivan] Nikolaev[ich][5] than you are with me; [you told] him that you were swamped with work and didn't [have] time; yes, your job is hellish, but [what] can be done about it; relieve yourself of it as quickly as possible.

What should I tell you about myself... It's been a long time since I

---

1. M. A. Dostoevsky died 8 June 1839 under circumstances that still await satisfactory elucidation. Until quite recently it was generally believed that Dostoevsky's father was murdered by his peasants, and given Dostoevsky's curious reticence about his father's demise, it seems likely that he, too, thought that his father had come to a bad end. Modern scholarship has cast doubt on the notion that M. A. Dostoevsky met his death at the hands of his peasants, but no arguments in the matter can yet be called absolutely persuasive.

2. See the following letter, No. 27.

3. After M. A. Dostoevsky's death the Kumanins looked after the five youngest Dostoevsky children—Alexander, Nikolay, Vera, Andrey, and Varvara—but refused to be legal guardians. That position eventually fell to P. A. Karepin when he married Varvara Dostoevskaya.

4. The original of the present letter is torn in many places and indecipherable in others. Missing passages and conjectures are indicated by brackets.

5. Ivan Nikolaevich Shidlovsky.

talked to you candidly. I don't know whether even now I'm in the mood to talk to you about this. I don't know, but much more often now I look with complete callousness at the world around me. Moments of awakening occur more forcefully, too, however. My own goal is to be on my own. For it I'm sacrificing everything. But I often, often wonder what freedom will bring me... Will I be alone in a crowd of strangers? I'll be able to get free from all that; but I confess that I need a strong faith in the future, a solid sense of myself in order to live on my present hopes; but so what? It's all the same whether they come to pass or not; I'll accomplish my own purposes. I bless the moments when I am reconciled to the present (and those moments have begun visiting me more often now). At those moments I [recognize my] situation more clearly and I am certain [that these] sacred hopes will come to pass.

[spiri]t is not calm now; but in this [struggle] of the spirit strong characters usually mature; the clouded gaze becomes clear, and faith in life receives a purer and more elevated source. My soul is not open to the former stormy impulses. Everything in it is quiet, as in the heart of a person who has concealed a deep secret; I'm making fair progress at studying "what a man means and what life means"; I can study characters from writers, with whom the best part of my life flows freely and joyously; I won't say anything more about myself. I'm sure of myself. Man is a mystery. It needs to be unravelled, and if you spend your whole life unravelling it, don't say that you've wasted time; I'm studying that mystery because I want to be a human being. Good-bye. Your friend and brother

F. Dostoevsky.

[...] with my favorite ideas every moment [...] dreams and thoughts life is more unnoticeable. One more [...]: I can love and be a friend. I recently [...]. How many sacred and great, pure [...] in this word. Moses and Shakespeare all [...] on[ly] by half.

Love, love! You say that you are plucking its flowers. I think that there is no purer self-sacrificing person than a poet. How can you share your delight with paper. The soul always conceals more than it can express in words, colors or sounds. Because of that it's difficult to carry out the idea of creativity.

When love binds two hearts. From [...] and all the more doesn't show the tears [...] only in the breast. The on[ly] person who can weep [...] needs to have pride and Christ[ian] faith [...] you anything about M[...].

If I haven't received a letter from you by a week from today, I'll conclude that you're in Moscow and will write to you care of the Kumanins. Write me in detail, dear brother, about how you or how the others have managed all this. I'm anxiously awaiting a reply. Now, my dear friend, there won't be a cessation in our correspondence. I'll send you the list of books soon. *Write*. I don't have any time right now.

27. To Alexander and Alexandra Kumanin
25 December 1839. Petersburg

St. Petersburg. December 25, 1839

Dearest Uncle and Aunt,

My long, unjustifiable, and inexcusable silence may have seemed to you, dearest Uncle and Aunt, strange, incomprehensible, and unpardonable rudeness to you, and finally, black ingratitude. I am taking pen in hand, but not in order to justify myself. No! I know that my guilt, whatever circumstances might excuse it, is far beneath justifications. And besides, could I hope that my justifications would be accepted? I'll say just one thing: if my sincere, candid confession, my attempt to explain my misconduct with regard to you, is rewarded with even the slightest bit of your attention, I will consider myself fortunate, for I will have recovered what I had no hope of recovering—and least some slight attention from you and your favorable disposition toward me.

After entering the M[ain] Ac[ademy] of En[gineering], studies, the novelty and diversity of a new sort of life, all of that diverted me for some time—and that is the only period in which my conscience reproaches me grievously for forgetting my responsibilities, for my terrible misconduct toward you, for my silence; there is no explanation for it! There are no justifications for it, except perhaps in my strange absent-mindedness.

I know that this confession of absent-mindedness greatly lowers me in your eyes; but I must and will bear my shame, because I deserve it. My deceased parent's reminders and orders to break my strange silence with those of our relatives who so often showered us with their favors[1] forced me to examine thoroughly my conduct, and I have seen it in the most unfavorable light in regard to you, dearest Uncle and Aunt. Besides my

---

1. See Letters 18 and 26. There is no evidence that M. A. Dostoevsky encouraged his son to renew contact with the Kumanins. On the contrary, it would appear that the elder Dostoevsky disliked the Kumanins and resented his children having anything to do with them.

grievous fault—my absent-mindedness, I saw that my misconduct would acquire an even gloomier appearance, the appearance of rudeness and ingratitude...That made me confused and embarrassed...

It goes without saying that this embarrassment ought not to have continued for long; correcting my fault was my first matter of business, my first thought; but the mere thought that I had violated my primary responsibilities, that I had not fulfilled an obligation laid upon my by nature itself, that idea devastated me. I didn't rely on many people's rule that paper doesn't blush and that two or three banal excuses (lack of time and so forth) would be sufficient for the correction of the error, I blushed without your seeing me, grew irritated with myself, didn't know what, how, and with what a countenance I would write to you; I would take pen in hand and throw it down without finishing my letter. I beg and implore you, dearest Uncle and Aunt, to believe that; these are the pure outpourings of a repentant heart; this embarrassment and onerous situation with regard to you were the reason for my so lengthy silence.

My father's sad death and the charity that you have shown our family, the charity for which I do not even know how to learn to be grateful to you, evoked feelings in me which evoked to a larger extent all the former ones, both the feelings of shame and the torments of repentance. I feel my guilt; I don't dare hope for forgiveness; but it would be the greatest clemency for me if you would allow me to write to you or at least to my sister,[2] from whom I could learn about everything that is dear to my heart; the New Year, which I greet with the wish for your good fortune and happiness, dearest Uncle and Aunt, the New Year will be witness to my reform.

During it I'll try to deserve your attention by declaring my sincere attachment to you, my gratitude for your charity to our family, and the continual preservation of that sacred feeling of love, respect, and devotion with which I have the honor of remaining your obedient and devoted nephew

F. Dostoevsky

2. Varvara Mikhaylovna Dostoevskaya.

1840

28. To Mikhail Dostoevsky
1 January 1840. Petersburg

St. Petersburg. January 1, 1840

I thank you from the bottom of my heart, my kind brother, for your nice letter. No, I'm not like you; you won't believe what a delightful fluttering of the heart I feel when a letter from you is brought to me; and I've invented a new kind of pleasure—a very strange one—tormenting myself.

I'll take your letter, turn it over and over in my hands for a few minutes, feel it to see whether it weighs as much as it should, and having looked at it and admired the sealed envelope to my heart's content, I put it in my pocket... You won't believe what a delightful state of the soul, feelings, and heart that is! And I wait like that, sometimes for about 1/4 hour; finally, I greedily attack the package, rip open the seal and devour your lines, your dear lines. Oh, what does my heart not feel when reading them! How many sensations crowd the soul, both nice and unpleasant ones, sweet and bitter; yes, dear brother—both unpleasant and bitter; you won't believe how bitter it is when you're not comprehended, not understood, when everything is placed in a completely different light, not at all as you meant, but in a different, hideous form... After reading your last letter, I was *un enragé* [an enraged person] because I wasn't with you: the best of my heart's dreams, the most sacred of the rules given to me by bitter, difficult, arduous experience were distorted, mutilated, displayed in a very pathetic form. You yourself write to me: "Write, object, argue with me,"—and you find some sort of use in that! None at all, my dear brother, absolutely none; only the fact that your egoism (which all us sinners have) extracts a *very useful* conclusion about another person, about his opinions, rules, character, and poverty of intellect... After all, that's very offensive, dear brother. No! A polemic in friendly letters is sweetened poison.—What will happen when we see each other? That, it seems, will be the regular reason for discord between us... But I'm dropping that! We can talk about that some more on the last pages.

The Military Academy—*c'est du sublime* [that's sublime]![1] Do you know that that's a very brilliant idea (?!). I've been thinking a great deal

---

1. Mikhail apparently intended to enroll in the Academy of Engineering after graduating from the Petty Officer School in Revel.

about your fate in order to bring it into line with our circumstances, and the Military Academy occurred to me too; but you have anticipated me; con[sequently], you like the idea, too . . . But here's the problem: you need to serve at least a year before enrolling in the Military Acad[emy]; stay with the drafting office for this year.

But why are you going on about *notebooks,* when I don't know your program; what on earth shall I send you? I'll definitely send artillery, the petty officer course (which seems to be precisely what you need), the notes from the course taught by Major-General Dyadin,[2] who will conduct your examination in person. But I can't send you these notebooks for any longer than a month. They are not mine. I had trouble getting them. Not a day longer than one month. Copy them or give them to someone to have them copied (Dyadin is an eccentric person, for him you have to memorize by rote or speak in your own words as though from the book). Field fortifications is such nonsense that you can cram it in 3 days. But in May I'll send it to you, too. The other thing requires a lot of time; I'll try to take care of it. We have lithograph[ed] notebooks for differentials, too; but they're taken word-for-word from Brashman,[3] and, of course, abridged. And so we go through Brashman, and you should memorize him too. Buy a copy for yourself.

Do you know geodesy? We have it (Bolotov's[4] course). Physics (Ozemov's course). I'll try to get the lithograph[ed] notebooks for differentials. Our history course is very full and very huge (lithographed)— I can't get it. Philology and Russian literature are Plaksin's,[5] who teaches here.—I'll tell you that your examination to become a field engineer is very easy. They pretend not to see mistakes, and they all rely on the logic of not keeping down a fellow engineer. I see very frequent examples of that.

I sent a very decorous letter to the Kumanins.[6] Don't worry. I expect good results. I haven't yet written to our guardian[7]: honest to God, there isn't time!

Best wishes for the New Year, my dear brother. What will it bring us? Say what you wish, but the last 5 years have been horrible for our family.— I read your New Year's epistle from last year. The idea is good; the spirit and expression of the verses are under the strong influence of Barbier;[8] by

2. Alexey Vasilievich Dyadin (1791-1864) taught artillery theory at the Academy of Engineering.

3. Nikolay Dmitrievich Brashman (1796-1866), mathematicin, author of *Course in Analytical Geometry* (1836).

4. Alexey Pavlovich Bolotov (1803-53), geodesist and topographer, author of *Course in Higher and Lower Geodesy* (1837).

5. Vasily Timofeevich Plaksin (1796-1869), historian of Russian literature, taught at various military academies in Petersburg.

6. See Letter 27.

7. The reference is to N. P. Yelagin, who served as legal guardian for the Dostoevsky children until Varvara Dostoevskaya's marriage to P. A. Karepin.

8. Henri Barbier (1805-82), French satirical poet whose collections *Jambes* (1831; Iambs) and *Il pianto* (1833; The Lament) were popular in Russia in the 1830s.

the way, you had his words about Napoleon fresh in mind.[9]

Now about your poems. Listen, dear brother! I believe that in a person's life there are many, many sorrows, much woe, and many joys. In a poet's life these are thorns and roses. Lyricism is the poet's constant companion, because he's a verbal creature. Your lyric poems were marvelous: "The Walk," "Morning," "Vision of the Mother," "The Rose" (I think that's what it's called), "Phoebus's Steeds," and many others are marvelous. What a vivid tale about you, dear friend! And how closely it spoke to me. I could understand you then, because those months were so memorable for me, so memorable. Oh, how many strange and wonderful things happened in my life then. It's a very long story, and I won't tell it to anyone.

Shidlovsky showed me your poems then . . . Oh, how unfair you are towards Shidlovsky. I don't want to defend what anyone who doesn't know him and is not very changeable in his opinions won't see—his knowledge and rules. But if only you had seen him last year. He lived the entire year in Petersburg without anything to do and without a job. God knows why he lived here; he was not at all so rich as to be able to live in Petersburg for pleasure. But it's obvious that that was precisely why he came to Petersburg—to escape to somewhere.—All you had to do was take a look at him: he was a martyr! He shrivelled up; his cheeks became sunken; his damp eyes were dry and feverish; the spiritual beauty of his face rose with the decline of the physical beauty. He suffered! Suffered grievously! My God, how he loves a girl (Maria, I think her name is). She married someone. Without that love he would not be a pure, exalted, selfless priest of poetry . . . While making my way to see him at his poor apartment, sometimes on a winter evening (f[or] ex[ample], exactly a year ago), I couldn't help recalling Onegin's sad winter in Petersburg (the 8th chapter).[10] Only before me there was not a cold creature, an ardent dreamer against his own will, but a beautiful, elevated creature, a person the correct sketch of whom both Shakespeare and Schiller introduced us to; but he was ready even then to subside into the gloomy mania of Byron's characters.—We would often sit together whole evenings through, talking about God only knows what. Oh, what a frank, pure soul! My tears flow now as I recall the past. He concealed nothing from me, and what was I to him? He needed to talk to someone; oh, why weren't you there with us! How he wished to see you! Calling you a personal friend was a designation he took pride in. I remember how his tears poured when reading your poems; he knew them by heart! And you could say of him that he was

---

9. Barbier's satire "L'Idole" (The Idol), included in the 1831 collection of *Jambes*, takes the cult of Napoleon as its target.

10. A reference to Alexander Pushkin's novel-in-verse, *Evgeny Onegin*, where the heroine, Tatyana, while actually in love with the hero, Yevgeny, marries another man.

laughing at you! Oh, what a poor, pitiable creature he was! A pure, angelic soul! And during that difficult winter he didn't forget his love. It flared up more and more strongly.—Spring came; it enlivened him. His imagination began creating dramas, and what dramas, dear brother. You would change your opinion of them if you read his reworked *Maria Simonova.* He reworked it all winter long, he called its old form hideous.—And his lyric poems! Oh, if you knew the poems that he wrote last spring. For ins[tance], the poem where he speaks of fame. If you read it, dear brother!

After I came back from camp we spent little time together. At our last meeting we walked at Yekaterinhof. Oh, how we spent that evening! We re-called our winter life, when we would talk about Homer, Shakespeare, Schiller, Hoffmann, about whom we spoke just as much as we read him. He and I talked about ourselves, about our past life, about the future, about you, my dear brother.—Now he has long since left, and not so much as a peep about him. Is he alive? His health was suffering grievously; oh, write to him!

Last winter I was in a rapturous state. The friendship with Shidlovsky gave me so many hours of a better life; but that wasn't the reason for this then. You have perhaps reproached me and will reproach me because I didn't write. Stupid circumstances in the company were the reason.[11] But can I possibly tell you, dear brother; I was never indifferent to you; I loved you for your poems, for the poetry of your life, for your misfortunes—and just that; there was neither the love of a brother nor that of a friend . . . I had a friend, a certain being whom I so loved![12] You wrote me, brother, that I haven't read Schiller. You're mistaken, dear brother! I memorized Schiller, quoted him, raved about him; and I think that fate has never done anything more to the point in my whole life than to have allowed me to come to know the great poet at that period of my life; I could never have gotten to know him as I did then. Reading Schiller *with him,* I checked the noble, fiery Don Carlos as well as the Marquis of Posa and Mortimer[13] *against him.* That friendship brought me such a lot of both grief and enjoyment! Now I'll be silent forever about this; Schiller's name has become dear to me, a sort of magic sound that produces so many dreams; they are bitter, dear brother; that's why I've never talked to you about Schiller, about the impressions made by him: it's painful for me when I just hear the name Schiller.

I wanted to write you a lot in answer to your attacks on me, to your not having understood my words. Also to talk over several things; but the present letter to you has given me so many sweet moments, dreams, and

11. See Letter 23, note 2.

12. The reference is probably to Ivan Ignatievich Berezhetsky (b. 1820), one of Dostoevsky's fellow students at the Academy of Engineering.

13. Don Carlos and the Marquis of Posa are the heroes of Schiller's drama *Don Carlos* (1787); Mortimer is the youthful hero of the same author's *Maria Stuart* (1799-1800).

memories that I'm absolutely incapable of talking about other things. I will acquit myself on only one point: I never categorized great poets, and especially without knowing them. I never drew such parallels as, f[or example], Pushkin and Schiller. I don't know where you got that; please copy out my words for me; but I repudiate such a categorization; perhaps in speaking of something, I put Pushkin and Schiller next to each other, but I think that there's a comma between those two words. They don't resemble each other in the least. Pushkin and Byron, yes. As for Homer and Victor Hugo, you seem purposely to have refused to understand me. Here's what I say: Homer (a legendary person incarnated as God, perhaps like Christ, and sent to us) can be a parallel only to Christ, and not to Goethe. Get to know him deeply, brother, understand *The Iliad,* read it thoroughly (after all, you surely haven't read it? Confess). After all, in *The Iliad* Homer gave to the entire classical world an organization for both spiritual and earthly life, with absolutely as much force as Christ did for the new world. Do you understand me now? As a lyric poet Victor Hugo is of a purely angelic character, with a childlike, Christian direction to his poetry, and no one can compare with him in that, neither Schiller (no matter to what an extent Schiller is a Christ[ian] poet), nor the lyrical Shakespeare, I read his sonnets in French, nor Byron, nor Pushkin. Only Homer, with such unshakable certainty in his calling, with his childlike faith in the god of poetry whom he serves, resembles Victor Hugo in the direction of the source of his poetry, but only in the direction, and not in the idea, which was given to him by nature and which he expressed; I'm not even talking about that. I think that Derzhavin[14] can stand higher than both of them in lyric poetry. Good-bye, dear friend!

Your friend and brother F. Dostoevsky

Here's a scolding for you: in talking about form, you've nearly lost your mind; I've long since suspected that slight unease in your mind, and no joking. You recently said something like that about Pushkin! I let it pass, and not without reason. I'll talk about form in the follow[ing] letter. There's neither room nor time now. But tell me, please, in speaking of form, what made you say that neither Racine nor *Corneille* (?!?!) can please us, because their form is bad. You pathetic person! Why in addition the brilliant thought occurs to me: *Can you really think that they lack poetry?* Racine has no poetry? Racine, the ardent, passionate Racine enamoured of his ideals, Racine has no poetry? Can you even ask that? Why, have you read *Andromaque?* Huh? Brother! Have you read *Iphigénie?* Surely you won't say that it isn't marvelous. Isn't Racine's Achilles really Homeric?

14. Gavrila Romanovich Derzhavin (1747-1816), Russia's first indisputably great modern poet.

Racine in fact plundered Homer, but how he plundered him! What women he has! Understand him. Racine was not a genius; could he create a drama? He only had to imitate Corneille. And *Phèdre?* Dear brother! You will be God only knows what if you don't say that that's the most elevated, purest nature and poetry. After all, the outlines are Shakespearian, even though the statue is made of of plaster, not marble.

Now about Corneille? Listen, brother. I don't know how to talk to you; à la Ivan Nikiforovich, it seems, "after having eaten lots of peas."[15] No, I can't believe it, brother. You haven't read him and that's why you are so wide of the mark. Why, do you know that by virtue of his gigantic characters and the spirit of romanticism he is almost Shakespeare. Poor boy! You have the same rebuff to everything: "classical form." You poor fellow, why, do you know that Corneille didn't appear until 50 years after the pathetic, wretched, hapless Jodel,[16] with his lampoon, *Cleopatra,* after Trediakovsky-Ronsard[17] and after the cold poetaster Malherbe,[18] who was nearly his contemporary. How could he invent the form of a plan? It's a good thing that he at least borrowed it from Seneca.[19] But have you read his *Cinna.* Before that divine sketch of Octavius, before whom [. . .][20] Karl Moor, Fiesco, Tell, Don Carlos.[21] That would do honor to Shakespeare. Poor fellow. If you haven't read it, then do, especially August's conversation with Cinna, where he forgives him for his betrayal (but how he forgives [?]). You'll see that only wounded angels speak in that way. Especially where August says: "Soyons amis, Cinna" [Let us be friends, Cinna].[22] And have you read *Horace?* Perhaps only in Homer can one find such characters. The old Horace is Diomedes. The young Horace is Ajax Telamonides, but with the spirit of Achilles, and Curias is Patrocles and Achilles and everything that the sadness of love and duty can express. How great it all is. Have you read *Le Cid.* Read it, pitiable person, read it and fall in the dust before Corneille. You have offended him! Read him, read him. What does romanticism require if its highest ideas are not developed in *Le*

---

15. Ivan Nikiforovich is a comic character from Gogol's 1834 story "The Tale of How Ivan Ivanovich Quarrelled with Ivan Nikiforovich."

16. Etienne Jodelle (1532-73), French playwright and member of Ronsard's "Pleiade." His first tragedy, *Cléopâtre captive* (1552), was greeted by his contemporaries as evidence of the rebirth of ancient Greek and Roman theater.

17. Vasily Kirillovich Treidakovsky (1703-69), lackluster poet and major theoretician of eighteenth-century Russian classicism; Pierre Ronsard (1524-85), central poet of the French Renaissance. In linking the two names, Dostoevsky has in mind the epic poems that both wrote.

18. François de Malherbe (1555-1628), French classical poet best known for his odes.

19. The plan for Corneille's early one-act play *Medée* closely follows Seneca's play of the same name.

20. A corner of the original letter is torn off at this point, rendering the passage indecipherable.

21. All heroes of plays by Schiller.

22. A quotation from Act IV, Scene 3 of Corneille's *Cinna* (1639).

Cid. How splendid are the characters Don Rodrigue, his son, and his mistress! And what an ending!

But don't be angry, dear brother, at the offensive expressions, don't be an Ivan Ivanovich Perepenko.[23]

The present letter has made me spill several tears because of memories of the past.

The plot of your drama is lovely, you can see a correct idea, and what I especially like is that your hero, like Faust, while seeking the limitless and the boundless goes insane just when he finds the limitless and boundless— when he is loved. That is superb! I'm glad that Shakespeare has taught you something.

You're angry at me for not answering all your questions. I'd be glad to, but it's impossible! There's neither paper nor time. Besides, if one were to answer all your questions, including such ones as "Do you have a moustache?" one would find no room to write anything better. Good-bye, my dear, kind brother. Good-bye again. Write.

29. To Alexander and Alexandra Kumanin
28 January 1840. Petersburg

St. Petersburg. January 28, 1840

Dearest Uncle and Aunt,

Never has any joyous news made such a pleasant and delightful impression in my soul as what I experienced while reading my sister's letter.[1] Ought I to have expected, and judging by my guilt, could I have expected such good will and favor on your part, dearest Uncle and Aunt. I cannot comprehend those feelings that stirred in me upon the receipt of your letter. All the weight of my guilt, all your justified irritation, dearest Uncle and Aunt, vividly presented themselves before me! But what a change! You are returning me your favor readily, with love, to me, who has not in the least deserved it. But I did not know and I cannot tell you what was then transpiring in my heart. I ought to have rejoiced, but I didn't

---

23. Another character from Gogol's story "The Tale of How Ivan Ivanovich Quarreled with Ivan Nikiforovich."

1. Varvara Mikhaylovna Dostoevskaya.

know how to rejoice at that letter, because nothing in the world could have made me happier than your forgiveness; but vexation with myself, shame, your unparalleled indulgence toward me, who had for so long abused your good will, all of that weighed down my heart with a terrible burden.[2] The punishment of one's own conscience is the strongest, and I bear upon myself all the weight of that punishment ... I am indebted to you, dearest Uncle and Aunt, indebted beyond my means, and if the correction of my guilt, and my repentance and attachment to you have even the slightest value in your eyes, I'll consider myself still fortunate, because I will lighten my conscience considerably.

But what excited me more than anything else, what filled my soul with so many pleasant things in the past, what made my heart beat even more ardently for you, were the lines written in your own hand, dearest Aunt. I couldn't have expected such indulgence and good will ... Those lines were all the more pleasant for me in that it had been such a long time, exclusively because of my own guilt and mistake, since I had heard words so delightful for the heart, and your expressions of love for me, dearest Aunt, which reminded me of my departed mother ... With what ardor I kissed those lines; with what ardor I kiss your hands 1,000 times, dearest Aunt!

But there's no happiness without grief. The letter rubbed much salt on the scarcely mended wounds in my heart. Uncle's death[3] caused me to spill several sincere tears in his memory. Father, Mother, Uncle, and all of that in two years![4] Horrible years!

I would have hastened with my letter even earlier had it not been for examinations that held me up. They have ended now, and I'm not wasting a moment. But I sense that I'm already wearying you with my letter.—So allow a sincerely loving and respectful nephew to remain forever humble and obedient to you.

F. Dostoevsky

---

2. See Letter 27.

3. Mikhail Fyodorovich Nechaev, Dostoevsky's uncle on his mother's side.

4. Dostoevsky is mistaken in his dates. He really means three years, because his mother died 27 February 1837.

30. To Varvara Dostoevskaya
28 January 1840. Petersburg

My dearest Varenka,

Your letter made me indescribably happy: in it you announced to me Uncle and Aunt's forgiveness.[1] But how could you have thought, dear sister, that I had forgotten you; about whom am I more likely to remember if not my relatives—our benefactors, and you, my dear brothers and sisters. No! I never forgot that; always believe, Varenka, that you have brothers who love you more than their own lives. Your eldest brother,[2] dear sister, loves you just as ardently, indescribably; be able to revere him and if, possible, to love him as much. Remember how many misfortunes he bore, poor fellow, in order to calm Father while he was alive;[3] on that basis you can judge about his love for his relatives. The firmest friendship binds me to him.

Dear sister, you wrote me so many bits of pleasant news about our family...But not a word about our sister Verochka...She seems to be forgotten. Write me as much as you can about all of them. How are they doing? Have our little ones grown up, have they changed? I kiss them all from the bottom of my heart, just as I kiss you, my dear sister. Tell Andryusha that I would like to have received a few of his own lines in your letter. Teach him to be grateful to our benefactors. Tell him that for me.

Good-bye, my dear sister.

Your friend and brother F. Dostoevsky

1. See Letter 29.

2. Mikhail Mikhaylovich Dostoevsky.

3. The reference is probably to Mikhail's having to subjugate his romantic nature to the prosaic demands of officers' training.

31. To Olga Nechaeva
28 January 1840. Petersburg

Dear Grandmother,[1]

How delightfully my sister's words, mentioning the fact that you haven't forgotten me, echoed in my heart.[2] If in my last letter I had had the right to ask dear Uncle to give you my humblest regards, love, and respect, then, to my indescribable pleasure, I could have anticipated you. Now all I can do is thank you most humbly for that. Please believe that I'll never forget the respect and devotion with which I have the honor of remaining your loving and devoted

F. Dostoevsky.

I send my most humble regards to Aunt Katerina Fyodorovna.[3]

32. To Mikhail Dostoevsky
19 July 1840. Peterhof

Peterhof. 19 July 1840

I'm taking pen in hand again, my dear though implacable brother, and again I must begin a letter with a request for good will, a request that will be all the firmer the more you are stubborn and angry. No, my dear, kind brother! I won't leave you in peace until you extend your hand to me as before. And I don't know, dear brother, you were always fair to me (although there were exceptions), always forgave me in the case of a long silence, but now, when I offer a reason, an incontestable reason, you know yourself, you seem deaf to my words; forgive these reproaches, my kind friend; I won't conceal from you the fact that they came directly from the heart; I love you, my dear brother, and it's painful for me to see your indifference. In your place I would long since have forgotten everything so

---

1. Olga Yakovlevna Nechaeva (1794-1870), Dostoevsky's maternal grandmother. For much of her life she lived with the Kumanins.

2. See Letter 30.

3. Yekaterina Fyodorovna Nechaeva (1823-1855), Dostoevsky's mother's stepsister.

as to forgive my friend as quickly as possible rather than force him to beg even longer for forgiveness! I, at least, on my part, seeing myself now in decent circumstances, that is, with money (our guardian has already sent me some), although not a great deal of it, definitely promise to write absolutely every week. I'm writing in haste now because I don't dare go on and on in a long letter; at any moment we expect an alarm and maneuvers that will continue for about 3 days.

Oh, my dear brother, for Heaven's sake write me at least something. If you only knew how I worry about your fate, about your decisions, intentions, about your examination, my dear brother, because it's just around the corner. God only knows whether this letter will catch you still in Revel;[1] God grant that all go well for you, my dear brother; oh, if we continue this discord any longer, this disharmony in our *inseparable* friendship, I don't even know what torture I'll experience because of your silence.—After all, this stupid, yet at the same time decisive, turning point in your fate is coming up soon, the turning point that I have always awaited with a sort of trepidation. Really: what hinges on this? Remember, after all. Your life, your leisure, your happiness, my dear brother, yes, your happiness; because if you yourself really have not changed, or your fate has not changed since you wrote me with such delight about your hopes, about your Emilia,[2] then of course you can judge for yourself what a change in your fate a successful examination could produce. Well, take even just this circumstance in your fate, my dear brother! Do you really think that it wouldn't be too cruel to deprive your brother of your confidence, when perhaps through my friendship I could share either your happiness or your misery, my friend; oh, my kind friend! God is your judge for leaving me in such uncertainty, in such terrible uncertainty.

But what has happened to you, my dear brother! Has there come to fruition—I won't say your dreams, but has there come to fruition what fate flashed before your eyes after pointing to a bright corner in the dark perspective of your life, a corner where the heart has promised itself so many hopes and so much happiness; time, time shows a great deal; time alone can evaluate and clearly determine the whole meaning of these periods in our life. It can determine, forgive me for these words, my dear brother, it can determine whether that activity of the soul and heart was pure and correct, clear and bright, like our natural striving in the full life of a person, or incorrect, pointless, vain activity, a delusion forced from a lonely heart that often does not understand itself, is often still as senseless as a babe, but also pure and ardent, captive, seeking food for itself around

1. By an order dated 19 February 1840, Mikhail Dostoevsky was transferred from the Engineering Command in Revel to Petersburg, where he was to take the examination to become a field officer. To judge from the present letter, however, Mikhail was detained in Revel.

2. Emilia Fyodorovna von Ditmer (1822-79) married Mikhail Dostoevsky in 1842.

itself and wearing itself out in an unnatural striving for an "ignoble dream." Really, sad as your life sometimes is and burdensome as its other moments are, when a person, sensing his delusions, recognizing in himself boundless energy, sees that the energy is wasted in false activity, in unnatural things, in activity unworthy of your nature; then you sense that the spiritual flame has been crushed, extinguished by God knows what; when the heart has been torn to pieces, and by what? By a life worthy of a pigmy, and not a giant, of a child, and not a man.[3]

Here again friendship is essential; because the heart will fetter itself with unbreakable chains and a person will become depressed, droop before circumstance, before his heart's whims as before the commands of fate,[4] and will dismiss as an insignificant spider web those horrible nets from whose threads no one ever frees himself, before which everything wilts: it is then that fate is truly the command of Providence, that is, it acts on us with the irresistible force of our entire nature.

I interrupted my letter for a time; I was distracted by service; oh, dear brother, if you only had any idea of how we live! But come visit as soon as possible, my dear friend; for Heaven's sake, come. If you only knew how essential it is for us to be together, dear friend! Whole years have passed since we were separated. A scrap of paper sent by me from month to month was our entire link; meanwhile, time passed, time aimed both storm clouds and buckets at us, and all of that passed for us in terrible, sad soltitude; oh, if you only knew how savage I've grown here, my dear, kind friend! Loving you is an absolute necessity for me. I'm completely free, don't depend on anyone; but our bonds are so firm, my dear brother, that I seem to be knitted together with someone by life.

How many changes in our age, dreams, hopes, and thoughts have escaped us unnoticed, and which we have kept in our hearts. Oh, when I see you, I feel that my existence will be renewed; I feel somehow agitated now; the course of my time is so incorrect . . . I don't know myself what's wrong with me. Come visit, for Heaven's sake, come visit, my friend, my dear brother.

I don't know whether to be worried about your examination. How well prepared are you? As for your examiners, I'm certain of them. Here at the Academy they always test you so easily and simply that if you've studied anything, you'll pass; many people less talented than you have passed.[5] I've seen heaps of examples.—I think that you aren't angry with

---

3. This purple prose may be an echo of a passage in Mikhail Lermontov's novel *A Hero of Our Time*, first published in May 1840.

4. See previous note.

5. Mikhail passed the test and was promoted to Ensign-Engineer on 9 January 1841.

me about the notebooks; I repeat again that because of their insignificance you don't need them, they're all pathetic abridgements, it's a shame even to say; and besides, no one has them.

Our sister[6] wasn't in Petersburg. We'll soon be leaving Peterhof. Write to me in Petersburg. Good-bye, my kind, dear brother. Here are a few lines to you, written at odd moments. If you only knew how unbearable now it is for us to live.

Good-bye, my dear, my kind brother and friend. Be sure to write soon.

F. Dostoevsky

---

6. Varvara Mikhaylovna Dostoevskaya, who married P. A. Karepin on 21 April 1840.

1841

33. To Mikhail Dostoevsky
27 February 1841. Petersburg

St. Petersburg. 27 February.

So now we're back to letters again, my dear friend! Was it so long ago that we thought we'd almost never be parted and spent our time haphazardly, merrily, lightheartedly, and suddenly in a single instant you've been taken away from me for a long, long time.[1] I've grown very sad being all alone, my dear brother. There's no one to talk to, and besides, there's no time. So much cramming that Heaven help us, there's never been anything like it. They're squeezing the life out of us, my dear friend. I sit and study even on holidays, and now March is already approaching—spring, it's thawing, the sun is warmer, brighter, the air smells of the south—pure pleasure. Only what can I do? But there's not much left to cram!

You'll probably guess why this letter is written on 1/4 of a sheet. I'm writing it late at night, when I've grabbed some time.

Well, my dear brother, I'm very, very glad to gladden you with at least one thing—if you haven't yet been gladdened and if my letter catches you while you're still at Narva. On Monday (the day of your departure) Krivopishin[2] came to see me; we were having dinner then, and I didn't see him. He left a note—an invitation to to visit them. On Sunday evening I was at his place and he showed me [...]'s[3] report about the order given regarding your assignment to Revel. You are probably (why, and even without a doubt) in Revel already, kissing your Emilia[4] (don't forget to kiss her for me, too); otherwise there's no explanation for the slowness of the assignment. Only with regard to money, you probably have a bad case of consumption. I wrote to our guardian and sent the letter on Monday (the day of your departure). But his letter, if in fact there is anything from him, will come to Narva, cons[equently], you still won't receive it soon, and

---

1. Mikhail had been assigned to the Revel Engineering Command.
2. Lieutenant General Ivan Grigorievich Krivopishin (1796-1867), relative of P. A. Karepin and Vice-Director of the Inspection Department of the Ministry of War.
3. At this point in the original Russian text Dostoevsky uses initials and abbreviations whose meaning several generations of scholars have failed to decipher.
4. Mikhail's future wife. See Letter 32, note 2.

meanwhile you'll start piling up debts. There's a little still to be received from the castle.[5] All in all, the circumstances are not auspicious. There's hope neither for the present nor for the future. True, I'm mistaken! There's one chance in 1,000,000 that I'll win—a rather likely hope! 1 in 1,000,000!

Don't die of longing in Narva, my dear brother, before you receive a further assignment.

Thank Krivopishin. He's an invaluable person! Just try to find someone like him! I've been accepted by them God knows how. I alone am accepted, when they reject everyone, just as last time. Your case was decided in a moment, but otherwise

"you wouldn't have a chance in the world!"[6]

Thank him. They're worth it. What did we do to merit their attention? I don't understand! I haven't yet been to see any of my Petersburg acquaintances. Neither to Mme Zubatova nor to Grigorovich[7] nor to Rizenkampf[8] nor to the fortress.[9] I'm waiting for good weather.

I have a killing headache. Marino's and Zhillome's systems[10] lie before me and invite my attention. I can't stand it, my dear friend. Look for greater coherence in the next letter, but now, honest to God, I just can't. I hope to catch you at Narva, that's why I'm writing now.

Oh, brother! Dear brother! To the wharf quickly, to freedom quickly! Freedom and a calling are a great thing. I'm dreaming and fantasizing about them again as I can't remember when. The soul somehow expands in order to comprehend life's greatness. More about that in the next letter.

You, my dear brother—God grant you happiness in the peaceful, delightful family circle, in love, in enjoyment—and in freedom.—

Oh, you will be more free than I—if appearances work out!

Good-bye, my friend.

Yours,
Dostoevsky

5. The reference is to the Engineers' Castle in Petersburg.

6. A quotation from Act IV of the verse play *Woe from Wit* (1822-23) by Alexander Griboyedov (1795-1829).

7. Dmitry Vasilievich Grigorovich (1822-99), writer sometimes remembered for his philanthropic novels *The Village* (1846) and *Anton Goremyka* (1847). Grigorovich and Dostoevsky were both students at the Academy of Engineering and later roomed together, in 1844 and 1845.

8. Alexander Yegorovich Rizenkampf (1821-95), a doctor friend of both Dostoevsky and his brother Mikhail. Dostoevsky and Rizenkampf shared an apartment in 1843.

9. The Peter-Paul Fortress.

10. The reference is probably to textbooks on fortifications.

34. To Mikhail Dostoevsky
22 December 1841. Petersburg

22 December

You write, my priceless friend, about the woe that has crushed your heart, about your catastrophe, you write that you are in despair, my dear, dear brother![1] But judge for yourself about my misery, about *my* woe when I learned of all this. I became sad, very sad: it was unbearable. You are approaching that moment in life when all our hopes and our wishes blossom, when happiness grafts itself to the heart, and the heart is full of bliss; and then what? These moments are defiled and darkened by the woe of labor and cares.—My dear, dear brother! If you only knew how happy I am that I can at least help you in some way. With what pleasure I send you this trifle, which at least can restore your calm somewhat; it's not enough— I know that. But what can I do if I can't send any more—dear brother—I swear that I can't! If I were alone, I would go without bare essentials for you, my dear brother, but I have our brother[2] on my hands; and if I write to Moscow soon[3]—God knows what they'll think! And so, I'm sending you this little trifle. But my God. How unfair you are, my dear priceless friend, when you write such words as *a loan—I'll repay*. Aren't you ashamed, isn't it sinful, and between brothers! My friend, my friend, can it really be that you don't know me. That not all I could sacrifice for you!! No! You were in a bad mood, and I forgive you for that.

When is the wedding? I wish you happiness and expect long letters. I, however, can't write you a decent one even now. Would you believe that I'm writing you at 3 AM, and last night I didn't go to bed at all. The examinations and classes are terrible. They ask everything—and you don't feel like losing your reputation—and so you cram, "*with repugnance,*" but you cram.

I'm extraordinarily guilty before your dear fiancée[4]—my sister, dear and priceless, like you, but forgive me my incomprehensible character, my good friend. Can she really have so little of a relative's trust in me, or has a hideous notion of me already been created—of impoliteness, discourtesy, hostility, and lastly, of every vice, for her to be so predisposed against me, not to believe my avowals of an absolute lack of time, and to grow angry at

1. The letter from Mikhail seems not to be extant, but it is likely that his complaints had to do with financial difficulties arising from preparations for his marriage.

2. Andrey Mikhaylovich Dostoevsky.

3. Dostoevsky probably has in mind either the Kumanins or P. A. Karepin, who had married Varvara Dostoevskaya and was in the process of becoming the legal guardian for the Dostoevsky family.

4. See Letter 32, note 2.

my silence; but I don't deserve that—*on my honor I don't.* I beg her pardon most humbly; I ask her indulgence, and lastly, the complete forgiveness and absolution of my sins, cursed one that I am. I would be flattered to be called her good, sincerely loving brother, but what can I do? But I always flatter myself and will continue to do so with the hope that I'll at last achieve that.

I'm not writing anything about myself in this letter. I can't, there's no time—I'll leave it until the next time. Andryusha is sick; I'm very upset. What terrible fussing with him. And there's another problem. His studies and his living with me, a free, solitary, independent person, are unbearable for me. I can't get down to any business or amuse myself—you understand. Moreover, he has such a strange and shallow character that everyone is repelled by that; now that I've given him shelter, I greatly repent of my stupid plan.—Good-bye, my priceless one! May happiness be with you.

Yours,
Dostoevsky

I'm sending you 150 rubles. (This is for accuracy.)

150

1842

35. To Andrey Dostoevsky
December 1842. Petersburg

My dear brother! If you received the money,[1] for Heaven's sake please send me about 5 rubles or at least one silver one. I haven't had any firewood for three days now, and I'm sitting here without a kopeck. Next week I'll receive 200 rubles for certain (I'm borrowing), I'll pay you back then. If you still haven't received any, send me a note care of Krivopishin; Yegor[2] will deliver it. And I'll send it on to you right away.

Dostoevsky

1. The Kumanins had sent Andrey 100 rubles in celebration of his acceptance at the Academy of Civil Engineering.
2. Dostoevsky's orderly.

1843

36. To Andrey Dostoevsky
January 1843. Petersburg

Have you managed to get anything from Pritvits,[1] dear brother? If you have, send me some. I don't have any. And write me when you'll come, and if you don't send any now, be sure to bring it. Please, for Heaven's sake. Even if you have to go to Pritvits's apartment. Please.

Your brother F. Dostoevsky

37. To Andrey Dostoevsky.
January—Beginning of February 1843. Petersburg

You wrote me, dear brother, that you couldn't get money any earlier than Shrovetide. But here's what's occurred to me: together with this letter I'll send you another one, in which I ask you for a loan of 50 rubles. You show it to the General[1] right away and ask him to give you the money immediately so that it can be sent with Yegor.[2] Tell him, of course, that you gave me your word of honor and that it's your desire to help me. For Heaven's sake, please don't refuse, dear brother; and just as soon as I receive a loan from our brother[3] I'll repay you; you won't be without money. Take what you need for yourself out of the 50 rubles. And at Shrovetide, word of honor, I'll repay everything, you don't need the money now, and you can't imagine in what terrible, horrible need I am.

Help me, please.

Yours,
Dostoevsky

1. Fyodor Karlovich Pritvits (d. 1849), Director of the Academy of Civil Engineering, where Andrey Dostoevsky was enrolled. Krivopishin had passed on to Pritvits money that the Kumanins had sent for Andrey. See previous letter.

1. F. K. Pritvits. See preceding letter, note 1.

2. Dostoevsky's orderly.

3. Mikhail Dostoevsky.

P.S. If I don't have any money by Shrovetide, I'll get an advance on my salary and repay you.

38. To Pyotr Karepin
End of December 1843. Petersburg

Dear Pyotr Andreevich, kind sir and brother,[1]

First of all, allow me to wish you all the best for the New Year, and although the respected descendants have found our ancestors' custom of wishing new happiness along with old trite and outmoded, I nevertheless shall include in my greetings wishes from the bottom of my heart for the continuation of the old happiness, if it was according to your wishes, and for new happiness in accord with the wordly custom of wishing more and more. Your happiness, of course, is inseparable from that of my sister—your wife,[2] and of your dear little ones. May their happiness, too, be assured for their entire lives—may it bring your family the delightful, radiant harmony of bliss.

Thank you for what you sent, although it was very, very late. I was already so in debt that I immediately gave away everything you sent, down to the last kopeck. I myself was left with nothing. I trust completely in your calculation for the remaining allowance for this year; but nonetheless, if you sent me 150 rubles or so now, in a few days, my circumstances would be secured for a long while. My present request is explained by the needs stated in the last letter; moreover, I shall seek to beg your forgiveness for several careless words torn from my soul by need and necessity.

In expectation of your reply, dear brother, with the most profound respect and devotion, allow me to remain your loving relative,

F. Dostoevsky.

---

1. Really brother-in-law, but in informal relations Russians tend not to distinguish such gradations in kinship.

2. Varvara Mikhaylovna Karepina (née Dostoevskaya).

39. To Varvara Karepina
End of December 1843. Petersburg

My dear sister,

I haven't written you in a long, long time; I confess sincerely, but you see, I've been spoiled by your kindness and good will toward me and therefore always rely on your forgiveness. With me you need to be more severe and unforgiving—two qualities quite contrary to your kind, loving heart. I wish you greater and greater happiness, dear sister. I wish your little ones happiness and health too. May they grow up to bring you joy and comfort. Accept my sincere wishes, and don't be angry at my apparent coldness (silence).

I repent before you! But after all, you'll forgive me, I know that.

Good-bye, dear Varenka. Kiss the little ones—Sasha, Verochka, and Kolya.

Your loving brother F. Dostoevsky

40. To Mikhail Dostoevsky.
31 December 1843. Petersburg

31 December 1843

We haven't written each other in quite some time, dear brother, and believe me that that does honor to neither of us. You're slow to get moving, my dear friend . . . But since the deed is done, there's nothing else to do but to seize the future by the tail and wish you happiness for the New Year, and a little one as well. If you have a daughter, name her Maria.[1]

Give my most humble regards to Emilia Fyodorovna,[2] whom I wish all the best for the New Year. I wish her the best of health, and I kiss Fedya[3] and wish that he may learn to walk.

1. In memory of their mother, Maria Fyodorovna Dostoevskaya.
2. Mikhail's wife.
3. Fyodor Mikhaylovich Dostoevsky (1842-1906), Mikhail and Emilia Dostoevsky's son. In family circles he was known as Fyodor Mikhaylovich the Younger.

Now, my dearest brother, let's have a talk about business. Although Karepin did send me 500 rubles, by following the former system, which it is impossible not to follow if you have debts at home, I again have debts of 200 silver rubles. I need to work myself out of these debts somehow. I'm stuck until I do.—Fate has blessed me with an idea, an undertaking, call it what you wish. Since it's an incredibly profitable one, I hasten to propose that you participate in the labor, risk, and profits. Here's the point.

2 years ago there appeared in Russian a translation of 1/2 of the first part of *Mathilde* (Eug. Sue),[4] i.e., 1/16th of the novel. Since then nothing has appeared. Meanwhile, the public's attention has been roused; from a single province 500 demands for and inquiries about a speedy continuation of *Mathilde* were sent.

But there was no continuation. Serchevsky, the translator, a muddle-headed speculator, had neither the money nor the translation nor the time. Thus the matter stood for 1 1/2 years. Near Holy Week a certain Chernoglazov paid Serchevsky 2,000 silver rubles for the right to continue the translation of *Mathilde* and for the already translated 1st part. Having bought it, he hired a translator, who translated all of *Mathilde* for him for 1600 paper rubles. Chernoglazov received the translation and put it aside, because he didn't have a farthing to pay either to publish it at his own expense or even to pay for the translation. *Mathilde* sank into oblivion.

Patton,[5] you, if you want, and I are uniting our labor, money and efforts for carrying out this undertaking and are publishing the translation by Easter Week. We are keeping this undertaking a secret, examined from all sides and made by us *irrévocablement* [irrevocably].[6]

Here's how the business will go.

We divide the translation into 3 equal parts and work at it assiduously. We calculate that if each person can translate 20 pages of the small Brussels edition of *Mathilde,* he'll have his share finished by February 15. We need to do a fair, i.e., legible, copy directly. You have a fine hand, and you'll be able to do that. The translation will be censored as it comes out. Patton knows Nikitenko,[7] the main censor, and the matter will be taken care of more quickly than usual.—In order to publish it at our

4. A complete Russian translation of the novel *Mathilde* (1841) by Eugène Sue (1804-57) did not appear until 1846-47. Dostoevsky rated Sue highly, and the latter's highly-plotted novels of the city exerted a considerable influence on Dostoevsky's art. In particular, scholars have noted parallels between the heroines' childhoods in *Mathilde* and in Dostoevsky's unfinished *Netochka Nezvanova.*

5. Oskar Petrovich Patton (1822-?), one of Dostoevsky's friends from the Academy of Engineering.

6. The publishing venture never went beyond the planning stages.

7. Alexander Vasilievich Nikitenko (1805-77), a well-known critic of his time and a censor from 1833 on. Nikitenko merited his reputation as one of the most liberal censors of his time.

own expense we need 4500 paper rubles. We've found out the prices for paper and the printing.

They demand 1/3 down for the paper, and the rest they give on credit. The copies of the book serve as collateral.

A printer whom I know, a Frenchman, told me that if I give him 1000 rubles, he'll print all the copies (a total of 2500) rubles,[8] and he'll wait for the rest until the book is sold.

We need a minimum of 500 silver rubles. Patton has 700 ready. I'll be sent about 500 rubles in January (if not, I'll take an advance on my salary). On your part, take steps to have 500 rubles by February (by the 15th of the month), even if you have to take your salary. With that money we print, announce, and sell copies at 4 silver rubles each. (The price is cheap, French.)

The novel will sell out. Nikitenko predicts success. Moreover, curiosity has been aroused. 300 copies will cover all the printing expenses. If we sell the whole novel in 8 volumes at a silver ruble each, we have a profit of 7,000. The booksellers assure me that the book will be sold out in 6 months. The profits are split 3 ways. If we sell the novel at a paper ruble each, your 500 rubles will be returned to you and the edition will pay for itself.

There's our venture; do you want to enter the union or not. The advantages are obvious. If you want, start translating at "la cinquième partie" [the fifth part]. Translate as much as you can, I'll write you about the boundaries of your translation.

Write me immediately. Do you want to or not?

Dostoevsky

Write immediately. Good-bye.[9]

---

8. Dostoevsky has left out one or more words or numbers here.
9. Mikhail's reply is not extant.

1844

41. To Mikhail Dostoevsky
Last Half of January 1844. Petersburg

Dear brother,

I had the pleasure of receiving your reply and I myself hasten to write a few lines to you. You write that you didn't know my address. But my dear brother, you knew, after all, that I work in the Drafting Room of the Engineering Department. Could one make a mistake by using the place of work as an address? Your address is absolutely accurate. But I'm glad for your excuse and I accept it. At least you haven't completely forgotten me, dear brother. I'm very glad for your happiness, and I wish you a daughter and that Fedashka[1] grow handsome. If I'm fated to be a godfather for someone in your family, then may it be the Lord's will. Only God grant the godchildren good fortune. I kiss Emilia Fyodorovna's[2] hands and thank her for remembering me. With regard to Revel, *we'll think about it,* nous verrons cela [we'll see] (Papa Grandet's expression[3]).

Now to business; this is a business letter. Things are going well for us, to the point of nec plus ultra [could not be better]. The editing has been entrusted to me, and the translation will be good. Patton is a priceless person when profit is concerned. And after all, you know that in business such cohorts are better than the most selfless friends. Be sure to help us and try to do an elegant translation. I meant to send you the book with the same post, but Patton has it, and he has gone off somewhere. I'll send it with the next one. But for Heaven's sake, please don't let us down, dear brother. Give us a clean copy of the translation. It wouldn't be a bad idea if you could send us the translation no later than March 1st. We'll all finish our parts here, and the translation will go to the censorship. The censor Nikitenko knows Patton, and he has promised to pass it through the censorship in 2 weeks. On March 15 we'll print everything at once and put

---

1. Mikhail's son, Fyodor Mikhaylovich. See Letter 40, note 3.
2. Mikhail Dostoevsky's wife.
3. As Dostoevsky goes on to explain, he had recently finished a translation of Balzac's novel *Eugénie Grandet* (1833). The translation was published in 1844. The subject of Balzac's influence on Dostoevsky is explored by Vasily Grossman in two essays translated into English and included in the volume *Balzac and Dostoevsky* (1973).

in on sale by the middle of April at the very latest.—You'll ask where we will have gotten the money; I'll scrape together 500 and contribute it. Patton—700; he has it; and Patton's mother, 2000. She's lending the money to her son at 40 per cent. That much money is quite sufficient for the printing. The rest on credit.

We've run around to all the booksellers and publishers and here's what we've learned.

Chernoglazov, the translator of *Mathilde,* un homme qui ne pense à rien [a man who doesn't think about anything], has neither money nor sense. He does have the translation, however. We'll announce the translation when it's half printed, and that will be the end for Chernoglazov. He has himself to blame; why did three years pass between the 1st and 2nd parts. Anyone has the right to come out with 2 or 3 translations of one and the same work. The booksellers vouch for 1000 copies in the provinces; moreover, the money will be received immediately; only they take 40 kopecks per ruble. The booksellers said that it's senseless to charge less than 6 silver rubles for the book (the price of a French book in a Bruss[els] edit[ion]). Cons[equently], we'll get 3500 silver rubles all at once in May. According to the assurances of those same booksellers, 350 copies will definitely sell nowadays in Petersburg, 20 percent to go to the storekeepers; reckoning on 1500 copies, we can't receive less than 5000 silver rubles. We'll have a debt of 1000 rubles. 4,000 silver rubles profit. We have decided to share everything fraternally, three ways, and you'll definitely receive 4,000 paper rubles for your share. But finish the translation now.

In the copy leave proper names in pencil or let's write each other about that.

My dear little brother, I have a slight little request of you. I am without money now. You should know that over the holidays I translated Balzac's *Eugénie Grandet* (marvelous! marvelous!). The translation is superb.—At the very least I'll be given 350 paper rubles for it. I have the fervent desire to sell it, but the future man of wealth lacks the money to have it copied; the time, too. Please, for the sake of the angels in Heaven, send me 35 pap[er] rubles (the price of the copying). I swear by Olympus and by my *Jew Yankel* (a completed drama),[4] and what else? Perhaps by the moustache which I hope will grow out sometime, that half of what I receive for *Eugénie* will be yours.—Dixi [I have spoken].

Dostoevsky

You understand—with the first post.

---

4. Dostoevsky's play *The Jew Yankel* is not extant. The scholar M. Alexeev suggests that the play presented variations on characters and themes in Shakespeare's *Measure for Measure* and Gogol's novella *Taras Bulba.*

42. To Mikhail Dostoevsky.
14 February 1844. Petersburg

14 Feb 1844

Dear brother,

You ordered me to inform you regarding the circumstances of the translation. To my extreme regret, my priceless friend, I'll tell you that it seems the business won't work;—and therefore I am asking you to wait for a while and not translate further until you receive a more definite notification from me, my dear brother... You see: I really have no basis for suspecting failure. But caution is never superfluous in any event. As for me, I'm continuing to translate. I'm asking you to stop for a while so that just in case you won't have troubled yourself for nothing. I feel very bad even as it is, my dear friend, that perhaps even now you have wasted your time.—The failure that I suspect is located neither in the translation itself nor in its literary success (the venture would be brilliant), but in the strange circumstances that have arisen among the translators. The 3rd translator was Patton, who for an agreed upon sum hired Captain Gartong[1] to correct his translation. That's the same Gartong who translated *Plik and Plok,*[2] *The Lame Devil,*[3] and wrote the story "Requiem" for *The Reading Library.* All was going very well. We were going to be lent money by Patton's mother, who had given her word of honor about that. But Patton is going to the Caucasus in April, to serve under his father's command, together with his mother; he says that he'll definitely finish the translation and will entrust me with the printing and sale. But for some reason I don't believe that Jews like the Pattons would want to entrust me with up to 3000 rubles in a matter that, say what you may, is a risky one; for them it's a double risk. In spite of that Patton is translating. I know that and have seen it with my own eyes.

All these reasons have forced me to ask you, my dear friend, to abandon the translation for the time being. In a very short while I'll notify you of the final decision; but it probably won't be in favor of the translation: judge for yourself. And how sorry I feel, my friend, how sorry I feel for you. Please forgive me too, dear friend, poor thing that I am; after all, I'm unlucky Murad.[4]

1. Vasily Andreevich Gartong. See the rest of the present letter for further identification.

2. *Plik and Plok* (1831), seafaring novel by Eugène Sue. The Russian translation appeared in 1832.

3. *Le diable boiteux* (1707), novel by LeSage. The Russian translation appeared in 1832.

4. Murat is a mountain boy consumed by a passion for knowledge in P. P. Kamensky's 1830 novel *The Seeker after Strong Sensations.*

I wish Emilia Fyodorovna[5] a very beautiful daughter and much, much good health. I kiss her hands and Fedya's.

Yours always,
F. Dostoevsky

Write me what happened to Yegor Rizenkampf. The father wrote something to his son. And in my next letter I'll write you about my Alexander Rizenkampf.

43. To Mikhail Dostoevsky
March-April 1844. Petersburg

Dear brother,

I'm writing you in haste and just a few lines. I assume that after you received my letter, you immediately set to work. For Heaven's sake, please get going with the translation of *Don Carlos*.[1] It will be a glorious thing. Get going with it as soon as possible. A few days ago an idea flashed through my mind. It is to print *Don Carlos* at my own expense as soon as I receive it. I'll get the money, to wit, I'll take an advance on my salary (which I've already done several times). Here's the bill for what the printing will cost, which I've reckoned approximately:

The best vellum paper for 1000 copies—about 5000 sheets. 500 sheets of the best paper cost 10 rubles, a sum total of 100 rubles. Printing with small legible type (a little larger than the Belgian), 30 paper rubles a sheet, and there will be 5 sheets in all (at most)

con[sequently]. . . . . . in all 500
and *100* for the pap[er]
250

attractive salmon-colored
or light green wrapper. . . . . *30* paper rubles
in all 280 rubles

---

5. Mikhail's wife.
1. Schiller's drama. Nothing came of the scheme.

A copy costs 1 silver ruble. 100 copies will pay for the edition, with a high return.

The remainder, if sold at 10 silver kopecks a copy, in the event of a failure you'll clear 350 paper rubles—the price you'll be given at *The Repertory*[2]—that's the most.

Think about it, dear brother. A translation of *Don Carlos* will be a gratifying novelty in literature. It will be bought by admirers, it will sell at least 300 copies. Just think! You aren't risking anything. Don't worry about me; I understand these affairs and won't get in over my head, I'll always manage to pay for the edition.

You have a family. While sitting or sweating away at work, watching people lay bricks, not many happy thoughts enter one's head. The pay is little. You'll have bread; but you won't have the new frock coat when you absolutely have to have it. Woe in youth is dangerous! Cons[equently] you need to work. You have a marvelous command of verse. And from French a translator can have bread in Petersburg; and what bread; I'm testing it on myself (I'm translating George Sand[3] and charging 25 pap[er] rubles per signature sheet). Why is Strugovshchikov[4] already famous in our literature? Because of translations. And do you think you translate worse than he does? He has made a fortune. You could have done so long since, it's just that earlier we didn't know how to go about it. I'll write the introduction, and you do the verses for Schiller. We can start printing in June, and by July 1st I would send you a copy in gold wrapper. In literature the field is clear; it will be received with delight. I'm sure that you're translating. Write me soon, for Heaven's sake, and reassure me. I haven't sent the epaulets, because I forgot them. I'll definitely send them. I'm awaiting your reply, for Heaven's sake.

Yours,
Dostoevsky

I'm getting sick of the service.

I'm as sick of the service as I am of potatoes. Good-bye.

My regards to Emilia Fyodorovna.[5] Kiss my niece and nephew. I can't come visit you. They aren't giving leaves, my dear brother. But I'll come for two weeks in Semptember, when I retire. Then we'll have a talk.[6]

---

2. The journal *The Repertory of the Russian Theater and the Pantheon of All European Theaters*, published by I. P. Pesotsky and V. S. Mezhevich. The journal published Dostoevsky's translation of *Eugénie Grandet* in 1844.

3. Dostoevsky was translating Sand's Venetian novel *Le dernière Aldini* but did not manage to have the translation published. See the following letter.

4. Alexander Nikolaevich Strugovshchikov (1808-78), translator and poet.

5. Mikhail's wife.

6. Dostoevsky did not go to Revel.

44. To Mikhail Dostoevsky
July-August 1844. Petersburg

Dear brother,

The interval between your last letter and my reply was fraught with various occurrences. Not all of them were successful, but some are quite auspicious.

Upon receiving *The Robbers*[1] I immediately set to reading it; here is my opinion of the translation: the songs are translated brilliantly, the songs alone are worth the money. The prose is translated superbly—in regard to the force of expression and accuracy. You complain about Schiller for his language; but note, my friend, that that language could not have been any different. But I noticed that you got too carried away with the conversational language and often, quite often sacrificed the correctness of the Russian word for the sake of naturalness. Moreover, here and there non-Russian words pop up (but not *study*, not *little souvenirs*—the use of those words is the summit of art and resourcefulness). Finally, certain phrases are translated with great carelessness. But in general the translation is amazing in the full sense of the word. I cleaned up a few spots and and got down to business immediately. I went to see Pesotsky and Mezhevich.[2] The rogues are being stingy. They refuse even to think of printing all of Schiller in their journal; they don't understand a good idea, they speculate. They refuse to take *The Robbers* separately, they're afraid of the censorship. Nikitenko really can't and doesn't want to take responsibility without crossing out a whole third. I gave him the piece to censor, however, and later we can fix up the uneven places. What can we do! After I heard Pesots[ky's] and Mezh[evich's] decision I didn't even let them sniff *The Robbers*. But then here's what I decided: to publish *Don Carlos* in their journal. That will get the public interested; it will see that the translation is good. To announce in the same edition of the journal the edition of all of Schiller. They'll pay us for *Don Carlos,* and I'll insist that they pay well. So please finish it, for Heaven's sake, quickly. In the fall, all at one blow, we'll print *The Robbers, Fiesco, Don Carlos,* and *Maria Stuart* (for Heaven's sake, *Maria Stuart* too. You need to do it in verse, that's essential if you want a success).[3] There will be money for the printing. We need a little over a 1000 rubles. Cons[equently], we need 700 in cash, because they'll always give you a third on credit. That's what everyone

1. Mikhail's translation of Schiller's drama *Die Räuber.*
2. See Letter 43, note 2.
3. The scheme to publish a complete edition of Schiller came to naught. Mikhail eventually managed to get a few translations into print, including *Don Carlos* and *The Robbers,* which were published in 1848 and 1850, respectively.

does, and I'll always undertake to get 700 rubles. Having named a proper price for the edition, sales of 100 copies can not only cover all our expenses but even give a slight profit, and 100 is a trifle; the intention, cons[equently], is good, and the venture absolutely reliable. Write, my friend, translate. I'll vouch for success with my head, and I won't leave you without money. Just wait and see, they'll come flying at us in swarms when they see the translations in our hands. There will be plenty of offers from booksellers and publishers. They're dogs—I've come to know several of them.

And so hurry with *Don Carlos:* be sure to hurry; that will both give us money and set our edition in motion. We'll have the money right away. I imagine that you haven't been lazy and have been translating all this time. If you had wanted a lot of money at the outset, you ought to have begun the translation not in sequence, but right off with *Don Carlos.* But it's better to make a good job of it.

Mezhevich asks most humbly to send him as soon as possible all of Schiller's prose compositions about drama and the dramatic art, if they're ready in translation. Especially about *the naive and the sentimental.*[4] I advise you to translate them, there will be money, and translate quickly. (I won't let anything out of my hands without money, don't worry.) And so, do *Don Carlos* and the prose now. *Fiesco* and *Maria Suart* afterwards. I'm relying on you, dear brother; above all, don't get discouraged. Remember *Semela*[5] and *Hermann and Dorothea.*[6] *Semela* was rejected in one place, and you left off the translation: and recently *Semela* appeared in *Notes of the Father*[*land*]] in the vilest translation. *Hermann and Dorothea,* too, and they both had a success. And why; because you got discouraged too early, my dear brother; for Heaven's sake, please hurry and work. The profit will be marvelous. Afterwards you can do *Fiesco* and *Maria* at your leisure. And we'll print them just as soon as we have the money. And we'll have it. In this case we can put the squeeze on the Muscovites.[7]

Well, now may all the devils help you, but you won't be able to guess whom I discovered in Petersburg, dear brother.—*The Merkurovs!* I met them by accident, and of course, I renewed the acquaintance. I'll tell you everything. In the first place, dear brother, they're good people. Maria Kreskentievna is a remarkable woman. I respect her with all my heart. Merkurov is un peu picardo [a bit coarse], but a fine fellow. They have grown rich and have an annual income of about seven thousand. They live very well. Apparently the old man Merkurov died and they divided the estate. You were wrong in assuming that he is in the police. He only served

4. Schiller's essay "On Naive and Sentimental Poetry" (1795-96). Mikhail's translation of the piece was published in 1850.
5. *Semela* (1779-80), opera libretto by Schiller.
6. *Herman and Dorothea* (1797), verse epic by Goethe.
7. Dostoevsky means the Kumanins.

in the police for half a year; then he transferred to the Olviopol Hussar Regiment (in the south). Then he was assigned to Petersburg to *a model regiment.* That was when you were being made an officer (and we didn't know). Finally, he served again, and now as a staff officer, retired completely, and lives in Petersburg. They received me marvelously. They are exactly as they were before. But not a word about money at the 1st, 2nd, 3rd, or 4th meeting; nor did I say anything either, and besides, I would have been ashamed to. Finally, an unpleasant *incident happened* to me. I was without money. But my translation of George Sand's novel *(La dernière Albini)* was coming to an end. Just imagine my horror—the novel was translated in 1837.[8] But who the Devil knew that, I was in a frenzy. I wrote to Moscow, but meanwhile was perishing in Petersburg. Need forced me *to ask for a loan* from Merkurov. Instead of an answer I received an invitation to tea. I arrived: he said that my letter made him blush. That he didn't know why I had asked him for a loan when I had the right to demand what was owed. That he had been silent because he hadn't had any money (he really didn't have any, because before my very eyes he spent 2000 on purchases), that he had expected to get some very soon and then wanted to prove his firmness of character by giving us the money without our having asked. But now he was blushing because I had reminded him about it. Since he had no money, he asked me to accept 50 paper rubles. I took them (you don't know in what need I was, dear brother). They told me to send you their regards. Write to them, dear brother, they're very interested in you, they were surprised that you're married. What luck! Now the money is assured, he didn't want to repay it earlier, but now, after seeing me again, I'm sure that he has made up his mind to repay at the very first meeting, moreover, he has the means. Please write, best as cordially as possible, and don't ask for too much money. We'll have it in a short time just the same. But you can mention it casually and name *the entire debt,* he's forgotten *how much,* and I don't know myself. Good-bye, my friend, congratulations on the unexpected windfall. Give him your address *in Revel* and let me know when he sends it all to you. Because the money isn't mine, and I won't be the one receiving it. He lives near me: at the Vladimir Church, on Vladimir Street, in Nashchokin's building (His Exc[ellency]).

Good-bye. Give my regards to your dear wife, kiss the children, be diligent and happy.

Yours,
Dostoevsky

I'm notifying you that Obodovsky[9] has translated *Don Carlos.* Look sharp, dear brother, and hurry up: Obodovsky hasn't published it yet and

---

8. Dostoevsky was mistaken. A brief extract of the novel, more a retelling than a translation, under the title "Il primo tenore," appeared in *The Library for Reading* in 1838.
9. Platon Grigorievich Obodovsky (1805-64), writer and translator.

besides, he doesn't even intend to.

I can free up about 500 rubles for *Don Carlos.*

We can't issue the translation an installment at a time. The public remembers the Goethe installments. It's impossible.

45. To Pyotr Karepin
Circa 20 August 1844. Petersburg

Dear Pyotr Andreevich,

I hasten to inform you, Pyotr Andreevich, that as a consequence of the natural and quite unpleasant course of my affairs I have been forced to retire. The request was submitted about 10 days ago; the authorities have given their assent. The Imperial decree will be issued in two weeks at the latest.[1] Since I had no money for mail, I did not notify you immediately. The reason for this upheaval in my fate was the critical situation with regard to money. Seeing the natural impossibility of receiving aid from anywhere, I didn't know what better to devise. Life is bad just now. Neither from above, nor from below, nor from the sides is there anything good. A person can rot and perish like a lost dog, and even if nearby he had brothers from the same womb, they not only won't share with him (that would be a miracle, and therefore no one can hope for that, because he ought not to), but even what by right ought to belong to the person who is perishing they try to take away with all the force and all the capabilities given them by nature, and also even by what is holy.

Everyone for himself and God for all![2] That's an amazing proverb, invented by people who have managed to live a bit. On my part, I'm ready to admit all the perfections of such a wise rule. But the fact is that this proverb was altered at the very beginning of its existence. Everyone for himself, everyone against you, and God for everyone. After that it's natural that hope for a person remains quite bad.

I was assigned to the Fortress. I owed about 1200 rubles and was supposed to get ready a supply of clothes, was supposed to live on the road, perhaps on the way to Orenburg or Sevastopol or somewhere even farther, yes, finally, to have the means of acquiring a few things on the spot. Since I

---

1. Dostoevsky clearly exaggerated the brevity of the waiting period. The decree was issued 19 October 1844.

2. Dostoevsky is quoting the French saying "Chacun pour soi et Dieu pour tous."

was firmly persuaded (by experience) that if I'd been assigned even to Kamchatka, I could not have expected financial assistance from anywhere, I was forced to choose the lesser evil, that is, to postpone the catastrophe of my life at least for two months; and then they can go ahead and drag me off to prison; but then I would lawfully receive what I've been begging for for God knows how long.

I'm notifying you, Pyotr Andreevich, that I have the greatest need of clothing. The winters in Petersburg are cold, and the autumns are quite raw and dangerous for one's health. From which it obviously follows that one can't get along without clothing, lest one kick the bucket. Of course, in this regard there is a quite noble saying: *It serves you right!* But that saying is used only in extreme cases, and I haven't yet reached extremes. Since I won't have an apartment, because I definitely have to move out of the old one due to non-payment of rent, I will have to live on the street or sleep under the colonnade of the Kazan Cathedral. But since that's unhealthy, I need to have apartment. There exists a half-saying that in such cases one may find a *government* apartment, but that's only in extreme cases, and I haven't yet reached such an extreme. Finally, I need *to eat,* because *not eating* is unhealthy, but since on this point there's neither means nor a saying, all that's left is to die of hunger; but that's possible only in extreme cases, and, thank the Lord, I have not yet reached such an extreme. For three years I have demanded, asked, and implored that my part of the estate inherited from my father be allotted to me. There has been no reply, people refused to reply to me, I was tormented, humiliated, and mocked. I bore everything patiently, made debts, went through my money, endured shame and grief, endured illnesses, hunger and cold, now my patience has come to an end and all that's left for me is to use all the means given me by laws and nature to make people hear me and hear me with both ears.

In almost every letter of mine I proposed to you, as the manager of our family's affairs, a plan for the allotment, deal, contract, concession, or whatever you please, of the part of my estate for a certain sum of money. There has been absolutely no answer. The fact of the matter is that the sum that I requested in exchange was so insignificant that the family's interests demanded a detailed examination of the proposal. The matter was to be handled in accordance with the law, and cons[equently] there was no reason to fear (fear is allowed in deals). Since I have received no reply, I now want to use every means for receiving one.

Since I don't want anyone to dare to say that I am ruining our family, I am saying now, for the last time, of my own will, in accordance with my own wish to act in a way that will be best for all, *that I renounce my entire allotment (which brings an income of up to 1000 rubles) for 1000 silver rubles,* of which half is to be paid at once, and the remainder at fixed times. Otherwise I will be compelled to use all my efforts to get the allotment off my hands even if that means an outside party, which will be rather bad for everyone. At first glance this thing cannot be permitted by the law; but they recognize *the obligations of paying off debts with income, settlements for the receipt of income only rather than of the estate.* That's possible, but if it can't be done then we can work out something else, and so on. The smallness of the proposed sum will not stop me. What am I do to do? I need money. I do not want to be a hopeless case. I need to arrange my affairs. Now I'm free and nothing will stop me.

In addition, I will ask you, Pyotr Andreevich, to send me on the account of whatever you want, even for 10 years in advance or of the entire price of the settlement, to send me as much as possible in order to satisfy the requirement indicated on the fourth page. I am notifying you that I took an advance on my salary in May (I needed to eat). Cons[equently], I don't have even a kopeck right now, moreover, I have no clothes, and finally, I have to pay my debts. There is nothing I desire as much as to finish with the above-mentioned affairs. They are ruining my life.

F. Dostoevsky

46. To Pyotr Karepin
7 September 1844. Petersburg

Dear Pyotr Andreevich,

In my last letter to my brother Mikhaylo I wrote to ask him to vouch for me to all of our family that after the receipt of a certain sum now I will in no way violate the agreement which it will be your pleasure to offer me on the part of all our family, and that in response to my future requests, my brother Mikhaylo either will have to answer me himself or, finally, in the event that I do not keep my word, he will have to pay me himself out of his own part. Since I am firmly convinced that my brother Mikhaylo has carried out what I wrote him,[1] I find it essential to trouble you once more with a letter of mine.

My brother thinks, just as I used to a long time ago, that although it is indeed difficult to do a legal division, it's quite easy to perform a familial one, to observe it without violation on either part, and to finalize it later legally; of course, it was not for me to suggest such a solution to you; now my brother's notion naturally may somewhat facilitate the course of matters.—Guessing and always being certain that in response to the action

---

1. Mikhail vouched for his brother twice.

being taken by me now, i.e., retiring as a consequence of debts and disorder in my affairs, cries and accusations are being sent, among which a certain phrase will be pronounced—to wit, he wants to live off his brothers and sisters, I even consider myself obliged to receive my portion and separate, in spite of the fact that in and of itself this action is necessary in my circumstances. As a consequence of the above-mentioned reasons I am naming a price of 1000 silver rubles, which, with the payment of just my debts, both public and private, etc., etc., etc., turns out to be quite compliant and even lower and definitely lower than what it should be, taking into consideration your estimate at one time.

Of this sum of 1000 silver rubles I ask that 500 silver rubles be paid out at once, and the remaining 500 silver rubles be paid out at 10 silver rubles a month. In naming the 500 rubles at once, I am naming the most essential— 1500 for the repayment of debts and 250 for covering my present expenses, which in actuality require three times more than 250 rubles.—Of course, Pyotr Andreevich, I must admit that the agreement and resolution of the matter are now in your hands. You can reject all these proposals on a thousand pretexts. But a few very candid lines on my part, the essence of everything that has been written and said up to now on both our parts, are essential at the present moment. Never having doubted that intelligence, nobility, and sympathy always accompany your every action, I presume that you will forgive the unpleasantness of the meaning of the following lines; necessity dictates them.

Here they are.

Can it really be, Pyotr Andreevich, that after everything that has transpired between us on a certain point, i.e., the management of my inexperienced and misguided youth, after everything that has been written and said on my part, after (I'm not arguing—and I admit it) after several brazen escapades on my part in regard to advice, rules, constraints, deprivations, etc., you would still want to use that power, which has not been granted you, to act in accordance with those motives that can only guide the decision of parents, finally, to play a role vis-à-vis me which at the first moment of irritation I attributed to you as indecent. Can it really be that even after all this you will oppose my intentions, *for the sake of my own good and out of compassion for the pathetic daydreams and fantasies of errant youth.* If it is not these reasons moving your heart and prohibiting you from helping me in the most horrible circumstance of my life, then can it be only irritation over a few expressions that tore themselves from my pen. There can and should be irritation, that's natural, although I regret that, but there can be *no prolonged rage and desire to harm*—that, as I have always assumed, is against the rules of noble conduct in general and yours in particular; I am firmly convinced of that; although I still cannot comprehend the reason that has forced you, considering your interest in our family affairs, to keep aloof from me and to condemn me to the most unpleasant vileness and circumstances that have ever existed on earth.

And here are what my circumstances are. In the middle of August I resigned as a consequence of the fact that I have a mountain of debts, and an assignment doesn't tolerate the repayment of them, and that a defamed officer would begin his career quite badly. Finally, life was no paradise for me. A rich man is forgiven debts that exceed one's earnings. In certain cases this circumstance is viewed with respect. But the poor man gets a fillip. It would have been wonderful to continue the service, accompanied by the dissemination of complaints to all possible commands. Finally, my retirement was the result of hastiness. I was tormented by debts that I have not been able to pay for three years.[2] I was tormented by the lack of hope of paying them off in the future. And therefore I retired solely with the goal of paying off my debts in a well-known way—through the division of an estate (which as you justly remarked, is quite and even impossibly miniature, but suitable for certain purposes). As for respect for my parent's memory, it is precisely for the sake of that circumstance that I want to use my parent's property for what my father himself would not have begrudged it. That is, for his son's peace of mind, for the means for a new road and for delivery from the name of cad, i.e., although not of the name, of the opinion, which is one and the same thing. Petitions because of domestic circumstances will be submitted for Imperial decision beginning October 1st—the whole business takes about 10 days, a little less than two weeks. The middle of the month approaches. My retirement will be granted, creditors will attack me without mercy, the more so as I won't even have any clothes to wear, and I will be subjected to very unpleasant affairs. Although I foresaw this in part, and if my assumptions and premonitions turn out to be justified, and I was ready for this, still, you have to concede that I won't go off to prison singing songs out of stupid bravado. That's even funny. That's why, Pyotr Andreevich, I'm writing this letter for the last time, I'm depicting the extremity of my needs for the last time, for the last time I'm asking you to help me as soon as possible, on the proposed conditions, although not all at once but enough to stop up hungry mouths and dress myself.—Finally, I'm telling you for the last time that now, being absolutely ignorant of your decision, I will sooner rot in prison than enter into service before my affairs have finally been put in order.

F. Dostoevsky

---

2. Dostoevsky told Mikhail that he had debts of 800 rubles. See Letter 48.

47. To Pyotr Karepin
19 September 1844. Petersburg

19 September 1844

Dear Pyotr Andreevich,

I have received your letter of 5 September, filled with advice and ideas, and I hasten to reply to you.

It is natural that in any other instance I would begin with gratitude for your familial, friendly concern and for your advice. But the tone of your letter, a tone that would deceive an ignoramus so that he would take it for the genuine coin, that tone does not sit well with me. I understand it well and it has done me a service by delivering me from gratitude.

You, let's assume that as guardian you have the right to do so, reproach me for financial greed and for doing harm to my younger brothers, on whose account I have up to now made use of large sums of money. After everything that I have written over the course of the last two years I consider it unnecessary even to reply to you on that point. You could clearly see from my letters that it's not on the amount of money, up to a certain point, of course, that my salvation and putting my affairs in order depends, but on the timely sending of the money. I have explained the situation to you a thousand times—I'm not the one to blame.

But how can you possibly say the same things now and incite all our family against me with your words? You should have understood my requests. Can it really be that the request for 500 silver rubles at once and for the other 500 silver rubles to be paid, let's say, over a period of three years, can that really be such a huge request in exchange for the separation of my portion of the estate? As for all the difficulties with the Council of Guardians, the Trusteeship for the Nobility, the Civil Chamber and all those names that you threw at me hoping to stun me, I imagine that those difficulties do not exist. Aren't estates sold with the transferral of debt? Will anyone really lose out or lose a great deal if the estate remains the property of our family, as before; after all, it isn't passing into someone else's hands, it isn't becoming someone else's property. Finally, paying out 500 silver rubles in consideration of however many years of income—even ten—is a very private matter.

At least I'm retiring. I submitted my petition in the middle of August (as I recall). And it goes without saying that for the very same reasons by virtue of which I'm retiring, I cannot again enter the service. That is, I must first pay off my debts. One way or another, they must be paid.

You are up in arms over my egoism and are more apt to agree to accept the frivolousness of youth.

But none of that is your business. And I find it strange that you take upon yourself a labor no one asked you to and no one gave you the right to.

Be assured that I revere the memory of my parents no worse than you do yours. Allow me to remind you that this material is so thin that I would not care to have you occupy yourself with it. Moreover, bringing one's parents' peasants to ruin doesn't mean honoring their memory. And besides, finally, everything remains in the family.

You say that you were silent in response to many of my letters, ascribing them to superficiality and youthful fancy. In the first place, you couldn't have done that; I assume that you know why: the codex of courtesy should be open for everyone. If, however, you consider it banal and despicable to discuss anything with me, thinking, of course, that "he's a little boy and only recently donned epaulets," then nonetheless you ought not so naively to have expressed your superiority, through arrogant abasement of me, through advice and admonitions suitable only for a father, and with Shakespearian soap bubbles. I'm curious: for what reason did Shakespeare get such a going over from you. Poor Shakespeare!

If you choose to be angered by my words, allow me to remind you of a sentence of yours: "To exceed the size of the possibility of repayment is encroachment on another's property." Since you know very well yourself that a debt of only 1500 rubles in all is not the entire size of my repayment, how could you write that? I am not offering any other reasons to you for your not being able to write that. I am just giving you the fact, the sum, the number. You are even aware of the history of those debts; I am not the one who ran them up, and I am not to blame for the fact that the business protected by Bentham[1] prospers in Petersburg as nowhere else. In any event, I must and will put your naivete (out of respect for your years I cannot take it for intentional rudeness and the desire to wound) in the same category as the Shakespearian soap bubbles.

If this angers you, too, then please recall your letter to His Exc[ellency] Iv[an] Gr[igorievich] Krivopishin. For Heaven's sake, Pyotr Andreevich, how could you do that? You see, I can't accept that, because I refuse to accept it in the sense that you write a letter about me without consulting me, with the goal of harming my intentions and stopping my Shakespearian fantasy.

But listen to me—who on earth can stop the lawful will of a person who has the same rights as you ... But what's the point of talking about it! In order not to be an Ivan Ivanovich Perepenko[2] I am ready to take even that as naivete, for the above-mentioned reasons.

The fourth page of your letter seems to have avoided the overall tone of your letter, for which I am sincerely grateful. You are absolutely right:

1. Dostoevsky is referring to a treatise by Jeremy Bentham defending usury.
2. Character from Gogol's comic story "The Tale of How Ivan Ivanovich Quarreled with Ivan Nikiforovich."

real good is a great thing. A certain wise person, namely Goethe, said long ago that a *little* thing done well fully reveals a person's mind and is absolutely worth something great.[3] I took that citation in order that you could see how I understand you. That was precisely what you meant when you dug into me at first and quite awkwardly with the hook of your ridicule. Studying the life of people is both my primary goal and pastime, so I have now come to believe completely in the existence of Famusov, Chichikov, and Falstaff.[4]

In any event, the deed is done, I have resigned, and I haven't so much as a farthing for my debts and equipment. If you don't send me some right away, my last letter will quite justify itself.

Yours,
F. Dostoevsky

You know the reason for my retirement—the payment of debts. Although the two ideas don't square, that's the way it is. The retirement will be finalized by October 1.[5] Bear that in mind.

You were pleased to say a few sharp things in regard to the *miniature size* of my *inheritance*. But poverty is not a vice. It's what God sent. Let's presume that the Lord has blessed you. But not me. But even if only in a small way I still want to help myself as much as possible, while doing minimal harm to others. Can my requests really be so enormous? As for the word *inheritance*, why shouldn't we call a thing by its proper name?

48. To Mikhail Dostoevsky
30 September 1844. Petersburg

Dear brother,

I have received *Don Carlos* and hasten to reply as quickly as possible (there's no time). The translation is quite good, in places amazingly good, some lines are bad; but that's because you translated in haste. But there are perhaps only five or six poor lines in all. I took upon myself the boldness to correct a few things, also to make the verse more sonorous here and there.

---

3. This is perhaps a reference to an aphorism from *Wilhelm Meister* to a similar effect.
4. Windbags and liars from Griboedov's play *Woe from Wit* (1824), Gogol's novel *Dead Souls* (1841), and Shakespeare's *Henry IV,* Parts 1 and 2, respectively.
5. The formal order was signed 19 October 1844.

It's all the more vexing that in places you put in foreign words, for instance, *complot.*[1] That cannot be allowed. Also (however, I don't know how it is in the original) you use the word "sir." As far as I know, that word didn't exist in Spain, but was used only in Western Europe in countries of Norman origin. But that's all absolute trifles. It's amazing how good the translation is. Better than I expected.—I'll take it to the fools at *The Repertory.*[2] Let them have their mouths drop open. If, however (as I fear), they already have Obovodsky's translation, then I'll take it to *Notes of the F[atherland].*[3] I won't sell it for small change, be assured. As soon as I sell it, I'll send you the money. As for the edition of Schiller, I agree with you, of course, I was even about to suggest myself that it be divided into 3 installments. We'll publish first: *The Robb[ers], Fiesco, Don Carlos, Treachery,* Letters about Carlos and the Naive.[4] That will be very good. In regard to publishers we'll see. But the fact is that it would be much better to do it ourselves; otherwise there's no profit. You just translate and don't worry about the money: we'll find it somehow, one way or another—just the same. But here's the problem, brother, we need to finish this business in a month, that is, we need to decide, because *an announcement* cannot be put out later, and without *an announcement* we're done for. That's why I'll go ahead and order a few words printed about this in *The Repertory.*

The translation will produce a sensation. (With even a minimal success the profit will be amazing.)[5]

Well, brother, I myself know that I'm in hellish circumstances; I'll explain:

I retired because I retired, that is, I swear to you that I couldn't serve any longer. You hate life when the best time is taken away from you for naught. The fact is that in the final analysis, I had never wanted to serve a long time, cons[equently], why waste good years? And finally, the main thing: they wanted to send me off on assignment—well, tell me, please, what would I do without Petersburg? What would I be fit for? Do you understand me well?

Don't worry about my life. I'll soon find a piece of bread. I'll work like the devil. Now I'm free. But what I'm going to do now, at the present moment—that's the question. Just imagine, brother, I owe 800 rubles, of that, 525 paper rubles to my landlord (I wrote home that my debts were 1500 rubles, knowing their habit of sending 1/3 of what you ask).

No one knows that I'm retiring. Now, if I retire, what will I do then. I don't have even a kopeck for clothes. My retirement becomes official by

1. *Komplot* in the original Russian, from the French *complot,* "conspiracy."
2. See Letter 43, note 2.
3. The translation was published in the journal *Library for Reading* in 1848. See Letter 44, note 3.
4. See Letter 44, notes 3 and 4, for publishing information.
5. The projected edition of Schiller failed to come about.

the 14th of October.[6] If the Moscow swine delay, I'm lost. And very seriously, I'll be dragged off to prison (that's clear). A most comical situation. You say a family division.[7] But do you know what I'm requesting? For my removal from any participation in the estate now, and for the complete alienation when circumstances permit, i.e., for the concession of my estate to them from this moment on—I'm asking 500 silver rubles at once and another 500 at ten silver rubles a month (that's all that I'm asking). You must agree that that's not much and that I'm not hurting anyone. They refuse even to hear of it. And you have to agree as well that it's not for me to propose that to them now. They don't trust me. They think that I'll trick them. Please vouch for me, my friend. Tell them exactly the following: *that you're ready to vouch with everything that I will not extend my requests any further.* If they don't have that much money, then in my situation 700 or even 600 rubles could be gratifying; I can still turn things around, and vouch for that, *that it will be taken in payment of the entire sum of 500 silver rubles and 500 silver rubles at intervals.*

You say that my salvation is a drama. But after all, a production requires time. The same goes for payment. And I have retirement right around the corner (however, my dear brother, if I hadn't already submitted my resignation, I would do so now. I don't repent of it.).

I have a hope. I'm finishing a novel the length of *Eugénie Grandet.*[8] The novel is rather original. I'm already copying it over, by the 14th I'll surely receive a response to it as well. I'll give it to N[otes] *of the* F[atherland]. (I'm satisfied with my work.) I'll get perhaps 400 rubles or so, those are all my hopes. I would go on about my novel, but there's no time. (I'll definitely mount a drama. That's what I'm going to live on.)

The swine Karepin is as stupid as an ox. Those Muscovites are inexpressibly vain, stupid, and casuists. In his last letter Karepin, apropos of nothing, advised me not to amuse myself with Shakespeare. He says that Shakespeare and a soap bubble are the same thing. I wanted you to understand this comical trait, the irritation with Shakespeare. But what does Shakespeare have to do with anything? I wrote him such a letter![9] In a word, a model of polemics. How I dressed him down. My letters are a chef-d'oeuvre of *belles-lettres.*[10]

Brother, write home as quickly as possible, please, for the Lord's sake.[11] I'm in a terrible way; after all, the 14th is the absolute deadline; it's already been 1 1/2 months since I submitted my resignation. For Heaven's

---

6. See Letter 47, note 5.
7. Dostoevsky means dividing the family estates of Darovoye and Cheryomoshnya.
8. The reference is to the first version of *Poor Folk*.
9. Letter 47.
10. The Russian original is *letristika,'* a substandard form of *belletristika,* which Dostoevsky uses here with ironic intent.
11. Mikhail complied with his brother's request.

sake! Ask them to send me some money. The main thing is that I won't have any clothes. Khlestakov is willing to go to prison, but only *in a noble fashion.*[12] Well, and if I don't even have any *pants,* will that be in a noble fashion?

Karepin drinks, fucks, shits,[13] drinks vodka, has a rank, and believes in God. I thought it up myself.

My address: Near the Vladimir Church in Pryanishnikov's Building in Grafsky Lane. Ask for Dostoevsky.

I'm extraordinarily pleased with my novel. I can't get over it. I'll surely get money from it, and then—

Excuse me that the letter lacks any logical connection.

49. To Pyotr Karepin
Circa 20 October 1844. Petersburg

Dear Pyotr Andreevich,

In my last letter I declared to you that I was writing for the last time, until a turn for the better in my circumstances. I thought that way because I had nothing more to write, having exhausted all my means of persuasion and having presented to you all the horror of my situation.[1] Now the critical deadline for me has already passed, and I am alone, without hope, without help, handed over to all the calamities, all the trials and tribulations of my horrible situation—destitution, nakedness, humiliation, shame, and intentions on which I would not have resolved at another time. What else is left for me to do except to begin. Where to appeal to—judge for yourself.

You should know that at the moment you are reading this letter of mine I will already have received my retirement (check the newspapers). I have neither clothing nor money nor anything with which to pay my creditors, and I won't have an apartment, because I doubt that the landlord will keep me in the old one.—I started to write you in order to elucidate for you a few of the things that were incorrectly expressed in my last letter. I will try to speak as clearly as possible.

From your letters, Pyotr Andreevich, I see that a division, as you say,

12. A quotation from Gogol's play *The Inspector General* (1835).
13. The preceding three words have been crossed out in the original of the letter, but it is unclear by whom.
1. The letter to which Dostoevsky refers is not extant.

is impossible, in the first place, because the estate has public and private debts attached to it, and in the second place, since over the course of three years I took more money than was my proper share, in time, when the accounting is done, I will have to make up for it at a loss to myself by contributing an additional sum for the others.

All of this is so, but my brother Mikhaylo and I propose a *family division,* which will exist inviolably until the final one. But if there's even the slightest obstruction on anyone's part in this matter, then of course it can't be done. The matter is founded on the fullest mutual trust, and if a misunderstanding is encountered in this regard, then there can be no agreements whatsoever. I presume that you in your capacity as guardian may have doubts about fidelity and fairness on my part and finally, some incident—that is why I propose the following.

But before getting down to the matter at hand, you know what price I'm proposing—1000 silver rubles, of which 500 silver rubles at once and the remaining sum to be dispensed over the longest possible period. In its moderation, this price does not fear any demands by creditors, public or private, nor any difficulties during the division. Why am I fixing such a moderate sum, why do I want, in the words of certain people, *to throw away* my father's (miniature) property—those questions, in your own present opinion, Pyotr Andreevich, are superfluous. The fact is that I see in this my deliverance from troubles and the chance for arranging things for the better, and for me that's worth something. Finally, 1000 silver rubles with the proposed allotment of payment of it is a sum that may give birth to assumptions about youthful superficiality and wastefulness. But in the first place, I'm not dealing with profiteers, and in the second, I was far from thinking of being anyone's benefactor, I simply in my circumstances find it immoderate to ask for more, and for the elimination of suspicions I am resolved to do the following:

To give an acknowledgement of debt addressed to one of the members of our family, if it can't be addressed to everyone, or even to you, Pyotr Andreevich. This acknowledgement of debt will be for such a sum as will cover completely both the sum to be paid out to me now in a lump sum and my further requests for income until the final division. The acknowledgement of debt will be made out, for example, for January 1, 1845. I won't pay it, of course. Then you will have the full right to act in accordance with the laws, and my income will be applied formally in the family's favor right up until the final division itself. At the time of the division I will give you formal notice that I have received the money in full, the acknowledgement of debt will be torn up, and everything will take its proper course. If there should be any difficulty in the last instance, then I could give a promissory note of such a sum that all my claims at the time of the (real) division would be destroyed.—It seems to me that this is quite simple and possible, Pyotr Andreevich. I cannot express to you what a beneficent deed that will be for my fate. I will completely provide for myself now, extract myself from the vile situation in which I've been struggling along for more than two years, and will be able to continue service. There's no point in my writing you this, however. I understand that the enumeration of my hopes is out of place here. I could also depict for you a picture of my miserable situation. But it will be sufficiently comprehensible from this one-hundredth part that I have written.

Since I am without means, with debts, without clothing, and in addition, sick, which, however, is neither here nor there, then I am naturally coming to the decision to somehow, one way or another, correct my circumstances. You are a *practical* person, Pyotr Andreevich, with us, too, you behave as a *practical* person, and in no other way, and since you are a *practical* person, you will not have time to pay attention to my affairs, even though they are miniature, or perhaps precisely because they are miniature. But if these miniature affairs comprise a person's entire salvation, his well-being, all his hope, then you need to pardon his persistence and importunity. That's why I ask you most humbly to help me in the sense in which I have written you. My situation is now decided and definite—that is, all the horrors that are possible have fallen onto my head, so that now I have decided that what will be, will be. Since according to your reckoning I see that there is no money, borrow it. Because the matter is beneficial for the whole family, and you are sufficiently secure. Finally, Pyotr Andreevich, if you again leave me without any answer for even the shortest amount of time, I will perish.[2] And therefore I am forced to ask of you a certificate showing that you really are our guardian (drawn up according to the rules of proper form) and how much income (minimum) the estate gives me under any circumstances, even the most remote. I am asking you for this in order to be able to show my creditors the possibility of payment if worst comes to worst, and therefore I ask you to send me the certificate as soon as possible. I ask your forgiveness, Pyotr Andreevich, in the first place, for tearing you away from your business with my requests, and in the second, for requesting it immediately. I ask you once again most earnestly to examine my proposal and agree to it. The matter can be concluded just as I have described to you. There is no difficulty. I would have sent the acknowledgement of debt ahead myself, but I have no money. You, however, can entrust this matter to someone in Petersburg. Finally, in the most desperate case (and therefore I ask you to reply to me as soon as possible), in the most desperate case I will perhaps venture to earn myself even more creditors and concede everything to them as a consequence of acknowledgements of debts and certain obligations at a price ten times more than what I used. In Petersburg that can be done. But what the consequence will be, you can judge for yourself: trouble for everyone. And therefore I ask you once more, Pyotr Andreevich, for

2. Karepin acceded to Dostoevsky's demands in part and sent him 500 silver rubles.

Heaven's sake, to please answer me soon. In addition to all my other calamities, I don't have even a farthing for my daily needs. God forbid that you should have to endure what I am going through. Finally, don't leave off sending the certificate. You have to agree that in my situation it's absolutely essential.

I have the honor to remain

Yours,
Dostoevsky

I assume that in regard to sending the certificate I will not encounter any difficulties from your side. That seems clear to me.

50. To Mikhail Dostoevsky
November 1844. Petersburg

...I should point out to you, dear brother, that my last letter to Moscow was a little too bilious, even rude. But I had been thrown into every possible calamity, I was suffering in the full sense of the word, I had not the slightest hope—it is not surprising that physical and moral torments forced me to write the bilious, harsh truth...

And so, I have quarreled with everyone. Uncle[1] probably considers me an ignoble miscreant, and our sister and brother-in-law,[2] a monster. That torments me very much. But with time I hope to make up with everyone. Of our relatives you alone are left to me. All the others, even the children, have been set against me. They probably tell them that I am a spendthrift, debauchee, lazybones, don't follow his bad example, there's an example—and so on. That thought is horribly depressing for me. But God sees that I have such lambish good-heartedness that I think that neither from the side nor from the front do I resemble a miscreant or a monster of ingratitude. With time, brother, we'll wait. Now I have been cut off from all of you from the point of view of everything *common;* what are left are the fetters that are stronger than anything else on earth, either movable or immovable. And whose business is it what I do with my fate? I even consider this risk noble, this imprudent risk of changing my situation, risking my whole life for a shaky hope. Perhaps I am mistaken. But if I am not?...

1. A. A. Kumanin.
2. P. A. Karepin.

And so, to heck with them! Let them say what they want, let them wait. I'll take the hard road!...

51. To Andrey Dostoevsky
Fall 1844. Petersburg

It's a shame that you left, brother! I didn't have a single kopeck myself, and that's why I was in low spirits. I still haven't been able to make ends meet. I'm sending you such a tiny sum now that I'm embarrassed, but honest to God, there's no way I can manage any more. Come see me if you can.

F. Dostoevsky

Varvara Dostoevskaya (1840)

Vera Dostoevskaya (1860s)

Andrey Dostoevsky (1860s)

Alexandra Dostoevskaya (1860s)

1845

52. To Mikhail Dostoevsky
24 March 1845. Petersburg

24 March

Dear brother,

You're probably tired of waiting for my letter, d[ear] b[rother]. But I was held back by the instability of my situation. I cannot possibly do anything thoroughly when nothing but uncertainty and indecision are before my eyes. But since I still haven't done anything good in regard to my own circumstances, I'm writing all the same, because I should have written long since.

I received 500 sil[ver] rubles from the Muscovites.[1] But I had so many debts, both old and newly accumulated, that there was nothing left for the printing. That would have been quite all right. I could have borrowed from the printer or not paid off all the domestic debts, but the novel[2] was not yet ready. I had completely finished it almost in November, but in December I took it into my head to redo it all; I redid it and copied it, but in February I again began cleaning it up, ironing it out, making insertions and deletions. About the middle of March I was ready and satisfied. But then there was another story: the censor takes at least a month. It's impossible to get anything passed earlier. They claim that they're swamped with work. I took the manuscript back without knowing what to make up my mind to do. Because in addition to the three-week censoring, the printing will eat up about three weeks. It would come out around May. That will be too late! At that point people right and left began trying to persuade me to submit my work to *Notes of the Fatherland*. But that's nonsense. If you submit it, you'll be sorry. In the first place, they won't even read it, and if they do, then only six months later. They have enough manuscripts there without this one. If they print it they won't pay you any money. It's an oligarchy. And what do I care about fame when I'm writing because I need bread? I've decided on a desperate leap: to wait, perhaps enter into debts again, and around the 1st of September, when everyone will have moved to Petersburg

1. P.A. Karepin and his wife, Dostoevsky's sister Varvara.
2. *Poor Folk.*

and everyone, like hounds, will be sniffing out something new, to use my last crumbs, of which there may not perhaps even be any, to publish my novel. To give one's thing to a journal means not only to yoke oneself to the main maitre d'hotel, but even to all the sluts and kitchen boys who nestle in the nests from which enlightenment is disseminated. But there's not just one dictator: there are some twenty of them. To have something printed yourself means to make your own way, and if the thing is good, then not only will it not sink into oblivion, but it will buy me out of this cabala of debts and allow me to eat.

And now about food! You know, brother, that in this regard I am left to my own resources. But no matter what, I have sworn that even if things reach the point of desperation, I will stand firm and won't write to order. An order will crush and ruin everything. I want every work of mine to be distinctly good. Look at Pushkin and Gogol. They didn't write a lot, but both are awaiting monuments. And even now Gogol charges 1000 silver rubles per signature page, while Pushkin, as you know yourself, would sell at ten silver rubles per 1 line of verse. But to make up for that, their fame, especially Gogol's, was purchased with years of destitution and hunger. The old schools are disappearing. The new ones are daubing, but not writing. All the talent is being spent on broad scope alone, in which one sees a monstrous underdone idea, and the strength of the muscles of the scope, but only a crumb of anything worthwhile. Béranger[3] said of today's French practitioners of the feuilleton that they were a bottle of Chambertin[4] in a bucket of water. People imitate them here in Russia too. Raphael would paint for years, polishing, reworking, and the result was a miracle, gods were created under his hand. Vernet[5] paints a picture a month, and exhibition halls of special dimensions are ordered for it, the perspective is rich, sketches, on a grand scale, but there's not a farthing of anything worthwhile in it. They're decorators!

I'm seriously pleased with my novel.[6] It's an austere and elegant work. There are horrible deficiencies, however. Its publication will reward me. Now for the time being I'm empty. I'm thinking of writing something for an opening move or for money, but I don't feel like writing trifles, and for anything worthwhile you need a lot of time.

The time is approaching when I promised to visit you, dear friends. But I won't have the means, that is, money. I've decided to stay in my old apartment. Here at least I've made a contract and you don't know anything at all for about six months. The fact is that I hope to redeem all of this with

---

3. Pierre-Jean Béranger (1780-1857), whose humorous and satirical verse made him phenomenally popular in his lifetime.

4. A type of Burgundy.

5. Horace Vernet (1780-1863), French painter noted for his enormous canvases on historical themes.

6. *Poor Folk*.

my novel. If the business is not a success, I may hang myself.

I would like to save up at least 300 rubles by August. Even for three hundred I could print the novel. But the money crawls like crayfish, all in different directions. I had debts of about 400 silver rubles (with my expenses and the addition of clothing), at least I'm dressed decently for two years. I'll definitely come visit you, however. Write me as soon as you can what you think about my apartment. That's a decis[ive] step. But what can I do!

You write that you're horrified by a future without money. But Schiller will redeem everything, and in addition, who knows how many copies of my novel will be bought. Good-bye. Answer me soon. I'll announce to you all my decisions in the next mail.

Your brother Dostoevsky

Kiss the children for me and give my regards to Emilia Fyodorovna.[7] I think of you often. Perhaps you want to know what I do when I'm not writing—I read. I read a terrible lot, and reading acts on me strangely. I'll read something again that I've long since read and reread, and I seem to acquire new energy, to go deeply into everything, to understand distinctly, and I myself extract the ability to create.

Writing plays—well, brother. For that you need years of labor and calm, at least I do. It's good to be writing nowadays. The dramas now run to melodrama. Shakespeare pales in the dusk and through the fog of myopic dramatists, seems a god, like an apparition of a spirit on the Brocken or the Harz Mountains. But maybe I'll write in the summer. 2 or 3 years, and we'll see, but now let's wait!

Brother, in regard to literature I am *not the person* I was two years ago. That was childishness, nonsense back then. Two years of study have brought me a lot and taken away a lot.

In *The Invalid,* in a feuilleton, I just read about German poets who died of starvation, cold, and in a madhouse. There were about 20 of them, and what names! I'm somehow still terrified even now. You should be a charlatan...[8]

---

7. Mikhail Dostoevsky's wife.

8. The reference is to the article "Poets in Germany," by A. Veys, published in the March 22, 1845 issue of the journal *The Russian Invalid.*

53. To Mikhail Dostoevsky
4 May 1845. Petersburg

4 May. 1845

Dear brother,

Forgive me for not having written in a long while. I've been devilishly busy right up to this very moment. This novel of mine, from which I cannot at all disentangle myself, has set me such a task that had I known, I wouldn't have started it in the first place. I took it into my head to revise it once more, and honest to God, for the better; it has won nearly twice over in the process. But now it's finished and this revision was the last. I've given my word not to touch it. The fate of first works is always like that, you revise them to infinity. I don't know whether Chateaubrian's[1] *Atala* was his first work, but I recall that he revised it 17 times.[2] Pushkin made such revisions even with minor poems. Gogol polishes his marvelous creations for two years, and if you've read Stern's[3] *Voyage Sentimental*[4]—a tiny little book, then you remember what Valter Scott[5] says in his *Notice*[6] about Sterne, citing as his authority La Fleur, Sterne's servant. La Fleur said that his master covered nearly a hundred quires of paper about his journey to France. Well, one wonders, where did it go? It all made up a little book that a good scribbler like Plyushkin,[7] for example, would have fit on a half-quire. I don't understand how that same Walter Scott could write such a thoroughly finished piece as *Mannering*, for instance, in a few weeks![8] Perhaps because he was 40 years old.[9]

I don't know, brother, what's going to happen to me! You're unfair when you say that my situation doesn't torment me. It torments me to the point of sickness, nausea; I often stay awake the whole night through because of tormenting thoughts. Knowledgeable people tell me that I'll be lost if I publish my novel separately. They say, let's suppose that the book will be good, very good. But you're not a merchant. How will you publicize

---

1. Dostoevsky's spelling.
2. *Atala*, by Chateaubriand (1768-1848), was first published in 1801. It was not the author's first work.
3. Dostoevsky's spelling.
4. The reference is to the novel *A Sentimental Journey*, by Laurence Sterne (1713-68).
5. Dostoevsky's spelling.
6. A reference to Scott's "Life of Laurence Sterne," which Dostoevsky read in French translation.
7. The famous miser in Gogol's novel *Dead Souls*.
8. A reference to Scott's novel *Guy Mannering* (1815).
9. Scott was 44.

it? In the newspapers, do you think? You definitely need to have a bookseller on your side; but a bookseller is crafty; he's not about to compromise himself with announcements about an unknown writer. He'll lose credit with his pratiques [clients]. Each of the respectable booksellers is the owner of several journals and newspapers. The leading authors or those who lay claim to being leading authors participate in the journals and newspapers. If a new book is announced—it's in a journal certified by their signature, and that means a lot. Cons[equently], a bookseller will realize that he can squeeze you impossibly when you come to him with your unpublished ware. And that's the way things are! And a bookseller is a miserly soul, he'll definitely put the squeeze on me, and I'll definitely wind up holding an empty bag, definitely.

And so, I've decided to appeal to the journals and give my novel over for next to nothing—to N[otes of the] *Fatherland,* of course. The point is that N[otes of the] *Fatherland* sells 2500 copies, cons[equently], at least 100,000 people read it. If I publish there, my literary future, my life—all is assured. I will have made my way into the world. I always have entree at N[otes of the] *Fatherland,* I always have money, and in addition let my book come out, let's say in the August or September issue, and in October I'll reprint it at my own expense, by then firmly assured that the novel will be bought out by people who buy novels. Moreover, announcements won't cost me a farthing. So that's what I'm planning to do![10]

I can't come to Revel before taking care of the novel, because there's no time to be lost. I need to get busy. I have many new ideas which, if my first novel works out, will consolidate my literary renown. So there are all my hopes in the future.

As for money, alas, I don't have any. The Devil only knows where it disappeared to. But on the other hand, I have few debts. As for the apartment, in the first place, I still owe a bit; in the second, I'm in an uncertain situation—will I go to Revel or not? Will I place the novel or not? If I go, I'll have time then to move; because the expenses and fuss in moving will cost more than staying, no matter what apartment one rents. I've already counted it up. An apartment, the novel, Revel—3 fixed ideas—Ma femme et mon parapluie [my wife and my umbrella].[11]

Good-bye, in the next letter everything will be decided. But so long for now, and I wish you, along with your wife and little ones, every blessing.

Your Dostoevsky

---

10. *Poor Folk* was published in Nekrasov's *The Petersburg Miscellany* in 1846.

11. A reference to P. E. Chapelle's 1834 vaudeville *Ma femme et mon parapluie,* in which the hero regards a wife and umbrella as necessary attributes of bourgeois life. Dostoevsky's citation suggests that he viewed his concern over an apartment, his novel, and a trip to Revel as signs of his own aspirations for embourgeoisement.

If I place my novel, *Schiller* will find itself a place, or I'm not I. *The Eternal Jew*[12] is not bad. Sue is none too clever, however.

I just don't want to write, brother, but your situation and Schiller so disturb me that I forget about myself.[13] But things aren't easy for me either.

And if I can't place my novel, then perhaps I'll throw myself into the Neva. What can I do? I've already thought everything over. I won't survive the death of my idée fixe.

My most humble regards to Emilia Fyodorovna.[14] I want to see all of you.

We're having awful weather. It's raining torrents and Providence has sent the N[orthern] Palmira[15] several 1000 head colds, coughs, cases of consumption, fevers, temperatures, and similar gifts. Lord have mercy on us sinners! Did you read Veltman's *Emelya*[16] in the last issue of *L[ibrary] f[or] R[eading]*—what a marvel. *Tarantas*[17] is well written. What vile illustrations.

Answer soon, because I'm feeling depressed.

54. To Mikhail Dostoevsky
Beginning of September 1845. Petersburg

My priceless friend,

I'm writing to you immediately after my arrival, as we agreed. It is beyond my pen to tell you, my beloved friend, how much unpleasantness, depression, sadness, vileness, and vulgarity I endured on the road and on my first day in Petersburg. In the first place, after saying good-bye to you and dear Emilia Fyodorovna,[1] I boarded the ship in the most unbearable frame of mind. The crush was terrible, and my depression was unbearable. We set off a few minutes after twelve o'clock. The ship crawled rather than sailed. The wind was against us, the waves lashed across the whole deck; I

12. *Le juif errant* (1844-45), by Eugène Sue.

13. Dostoevsky is referring to the collapse of the plans for publishing an edition of Schiller.

14. Mikhail Dostoevsky's wife.

15. St. Petersburg.

16. *The New Emelya, or the Metamorphosis* (1845), by Alexander Fomich Veltman (1800-70), is a parody of Russian romantic clichés.

17. *Tarantas* (1845), by Vladimir Alexandrovich Sollogub (1813-82), a satirical account of a journey from Moscow to Kazan in a ramshackle cart.

1. Mikhail Dostoevsky's wife.

was chilled and frozen through and spent an unspeakable night, sitting up and nearly deprived of my senses and the ability to think. I only remember that I threw up about three times. On the next day at exactly four o'clock in the afternoon we arrived at Kronstadt, i.e., in 28 hours. After waiting about three hours, when it was already twilight, we set off on the vile, miserable little steamer *Olga,* which sailed for about three-and-a-half hours in the night and fog. How sad I felt as we sailed into Petersburg. In those deathly three hours of our arrival I dimly experienced all my future. Especially after having gotten used to being with you and getting so accustomed to it that it was as though I had lived my whole life in Revel, Petersburg and my future Petersburg life seemed to me so terrible, lonely, joyless, and necessity seemed so cruel that if my life had ended at that moment, I think I would have died with joy. I'm really not exaggerating. This whole show is absolutely not worth the candles. You, brother, want to visit Petersburg. But if you come, come by land route, because there's nothing sadder or drearier than an entrance into it from the Neva and especially at night. At least that's the way it seemed to me. You can probably notice that even now my thoughts are marked by the rocking of the boat.

When I arrived at my apartment at 12 midnight, my man turned out not to be at home; he was working for a time at another place, and the yardman, rejoicing at God knows what, handed over to me the orphaned key of my six-hundred rubles of apartment (in debts).[2] I couldn't even drink some tea and ended up just going to bed in an absolutely apathetic state. Today, after waking at eight o'clock, I saw my man before me. I questioned him a bit. Everything is just as it was, the same as before. My apartment has been slightly renovated. Grigorovich and Nekrasov[3] aren't yet in St. Petersburg, and it's only rumored that they'll perhaps turn up by September 15, and even then that's doubtful. After giving a very short but quite decisive audience to a few creditors, I set off on business and did absolutely nothing. I acquainted myself with the journals, ate something, bought some paper and pens—and that was all. I didn't go to see Belinsky.[4] I intend to go tomorrow, but today I'm terribly out of sorts. In the evening I sat down to write this letter, which is already almost finished, but the letter

2. The Russian original makes no more sense than the translation.

3. Nikolay Alexeevich Nekrasov (1821-77), poet, editor of *The Contemporary,* later *The Notes of the Fatherland.* A contradictory personality, he was always a thorn in the side of the Tsarist regime, but by the 1860s Dostoevsky's new-found conservatism and Nekrasov's unchanged radicalism strained their relations severely. See Sigmund Birkenmayer, *Nikolaj Nekrasov: His Life and Poetic Works* (The Hague, 1968).

4. Vissarion Grigorievich Belinsky (1811-48), the most influential Russian literary critic of the nineteenth century. A proto-radical, he is alternately praised and upbraided for having called for a socially-conscious literature, but his true and indisputable merit lies in his having acclaimed Pushkin, Lermontov, and Dostoevsky, among others. The best work on Belinsky in English is Victor Terras, *Belinsky and Russian Literary Criticism* (1974).

is dull, depressed, perfectly echoing my present distressing state: It's boring in this wide world, gentlemen!"[5]

I'm writing this letter to you, in the first place, as a result of the promise to write soon, and in the second, because of my depression, and the letter begged to be written. Oh, brother, what a sad business being single is, and I'm beginning to envy you now. You, brother, are lucky, really lucky, without even being aware of it. I'll write you more in the next mail. I'm a little bit bothered by the fact that I'm almost completely (until the 15th) without resources, but only a little, because at the present moment I can't even think about anything. That's all nonsense, however. I've grown terribly weak and I want to go to bed now, because it's already nighttime. The future will say something. How sad it is that you have to work in order to live. My work can't bear compulsion.

Oh, brother, you wouldn't believe how much I would like to spend another hour or two with you right now. What's going to happen, what's going to happen in the future? I'm really a Golydakin[6] now, on whom, by the way, I'll get down to work tomorrow. Good-bye for now! Until the next mail. Good-bye, my beloved friend; give my regards to Emilia Fyodorovna and kiss her for me. I send my regards to the children. Does little Fedya[7] still remember me or is he showing indifference? Well, good-bye, my dearest friend. Good-bye.

Yours,
Dostoevsky

Golyadkin has profited from my spleen. Two ideas have been born and one new situation. Well, good-bye, my dear. Listen, what will happen to us in twenty years? I don't know what will happen to me; I only know that now I'm painfully sensitive.

Give my most humble respects to M. I[vanovna] and A[lexander] Ada[movich] Bergman.[8] Petersburg is still empty. Everything is quite dull.

---

5. Dostoevsky slightly misquotes the last line from Gogol's story "How Ivan Ivanovich Quarreled with Ivan Nikiforovich."
6. The long-suffering, paranoid protagonist of Dostoevsky's *The Double* (1846).
7. Mikhail and Emilia's son Fyodor Mikhaylovich.
8. Mikhail's landlord in Revel.

55. To Mikhail Dostoevsky
8 October 1845. Petersburg

Dear brother,

Until now I've had neither the time nor the mood to let you know about anything concerning me. Everything was so vile and repellent that it was nauseating to look at God's world. In the first place, my dearest and only friend, all this time I was without a kopeck, and I was living on credit, which is quite bad. In the second place, it was altogether somehow sad, so that you involuntarily lose heart, don't take care of yourself, and become not brainlessly indifferent, but what's worse than that, you cross over the boundary and are angry and furious in the extreme. At the beginning of the month Nekrasov showed up, repaid me part of the debt, and I'll receive the other part in a few days. You should know that about two weeks ago Belinsky gave me complete instructions on how one can get along in our literary world, and in conclusion declared to me that I definitely, for the salvation of my own soul, must demand no less than 200 paper rubles per signature sheet. Thus, my Golyadkin[1] will go for at least 1500 paper rubles. Tormented by pangs of conscience, Nekrasov ran ahead like a hare and promised me 100 silver rubles by January 15 for the novel that he bought from me, *Poor Folk*.[2] Because he confessed frankly himself that 150 silver rubles is not Christian payment. And for that reason he's adding an extra 100 silver rubles out of repentance. All of this is good so far. But here's what's bad. That absolutely nothing has been heard about *Poor Folk* from the censorship yet. They're dragging such an innocent novel round and round, and I don't know what they'll end with. Well, what if they forbid it? Cross it out from top to bottom? A catastrophe, pure and simple, and Nekrasov says that he won't have time to manage to publish the almanac, and he's already spent 4000 paper rubles on it.

Yakov Petrovich Golyadkin is standing quite firm in character. A horrible scoundrel, he's unapproachable; refuses to move ahead at all, claiming that after all, he's not yet ready, and that he's fine for the meanwhile just as things are, that he's all right, not at all drunk, and that perhaps, if it came to that, then he could do that too, why not, why shouldn't he? After all, he's just like everyone else, he's just so-so, but otherwise just like everyone. What does he care! A scoundrel, a horrible scoundrel! He absolutely refuses to finish his career earlier than mid-November. He's already had his explanation with His Excellency now, and

---

1. The central character in Dostoevsky's *The Double*.

2. *Poor Folk* was first published in 1846 in *The Petersburg Miscelllany*, a volume edited by Nekrasov.

perhaps (why not) he's ready to to tender his resignation. And he's putting me, his creator, in an extremely bad situation.

I visit Belinsky quite often. He's impossibly well-disposed toward me and seriously sees in me *proof to the public* and the validation of his opinions. A few days ago I met Kronenberg, the translator of Shakespeare (the son of the eld[er] Kronenberg, the Khark[kov] prof[essor]).[3] Generally speaking, the future (and none-too-distant) may be good and may be awfully bad. Belinsky is urging me to finish writing Golyadkin. After all, he has trumpeted it to the whole literary world and practically sold it to Kraevsky,[4] and half of Petersburg is already talking about *Poor Folk*. What is even Grigorovich worth! He tells me himself: "Je suis votre claquer-chauffeur" [I am your publicity agent].

Nekrasov is a shady dealer by nature, otherwise he couldn't even exist, he was just born that way—and therefore on the day of his arrival, at my place in the evening, he suggested a plan for a *breezy little almanac,* to be created to the best of our abilities by all our literary people, but the main editors will be Grigorovich, Nekrasov, and I. Nekrasov will bear the expenses. The almanac will take up 2 signature pages and will come out once every two weeks, on the 7th and 21st of each month. Its title is *The Scoffer;*[5] the point is to make jokes and laugh at everything, have mercy on no one, tackle the theater, the journals, society, literature, occurrences on the street, an exhibition, newspaper reports, foreign news, in a word, everything, all of this in the same spirit and same direction. It will begin November 7th. It has turned out wonderfully. In the first place, it will have illustrations. For the epigraph we'll take Bulgarin's[6] famous words from a feuilleton in *The Northern Bee* that "we are prepared to die for the truth, we cannot survive without the truth," and so on, and it will be signed "Faddey Bulgarin." The announcement that will come out November 1st will say the same thing.[7] The articles for the first issue will be Nekrasov's *"about certain instances of baseness in Petersburg"* (which happened a few days earlier, of

---

3. Andrey Ivanovich Kronenberg (b. 1885), well-known translator of Shakespeare in his time; Ivan Yakovlevich Kronenberg (1788-1838), philologist and historian of literature at Kharkov University.

4. Andrey Alexandrovich Kraevsky (1810-89) published and edited *Notes of the Fatherland,* where Belinsky's major articles appeared as well as all of Dostoevsky's pre-exile works except *Poor Folk.*

5. The censorship prohibited the publication of the proposed journal.

6. Faddey Benediktovich Bulgarin (1789-1859), publisher of the de facto government newspaper *The Northern Bee* and agent for the Third Section (secret police). One of the most distasteful figures in nineteenth-century Russian literature, Bulgarin generally characterized himself in print as a defender of the truth, but he was widely viewed as the embodiment of malevolence, deceit, and bad taste.

7. The announcement, written by Dostoevsky, was published in the November 1845 issue of the journal *Notes of the Fatherland.* At least one of the prospective editors, Grigorovich, believed that the wording and tone of Dostoevsky's announcement led the censorship to prohibit the planned journal.

course), (2) a future novel by Eug. Sue, *The Seven Mortal Sins* (the whole novel will take up 3 little pages). A survey of all the journals. A lecture by *Shevyryov*[8] about the fact that Pushkin's verse is so harmonious that when he was at the *Colosseum* and read a few stanzas from *Pushkin* to two ladies who were there with him, *all the frogs and lizards that were at the Colosseum came crawling around to hear him.* (Shevyryov read that at Moscow University.) Then the latest meeting of the *Slavophiles,*[9] where it will be solemnly proclaimed that Adam was a Slav and lived in Russia, and that on this occasion all the extraordinary importance and utility of the resolution of such an important social question for the prosperity and good of the whole Russian nation will be shown. Then in the section on art and the arts *The Scoffer* will give Kukolnik's *The Illustration*[10] its due, and in that connection it will even cite the following point in *The Illustration,* where it says that "iisktgezl-dtoom-dudurn" and so on, several lines in that form. (It's well known that *The Illustration* is quite careless in its proofreading; the transposition of words, words backwords mean nothing at all to it.) Grigorov[ich] will write *The History of a Week* and put several of his observations there. I'll write *A Servant's Notes about His Master* and so on.[11] You can see that the journal will be quite merry, rather like Karr's *Guêpes.*[12] It's a good business, because the minimum income for me alone may be 100-150 rubles a month. The booklet will sell. Nekrasov will publish

8. Stepan Petrovich Shevyryov (1806-64), a professor at Moscow University and leading man of letters in the 1840s and '50s. An adherent of German idealism, Shevyryov found all Russian poetry after Pushkin unacceptable. In particular, he denigrated the note of socio-political protest associated, rightly or wrongly, with Belinsky, Gogol, and the young Dostoevsky. In later life Dostoevsky would have found Shevyryov's views close to his own, but at this point in his development Dostoevsky was much under Belinsky's influence.

9. The Slavophiles and Westernizers, rival intellectual camps, had their roots in the 1830s and '40s and shared certain traits and convictions. Almost all of these thinkers came from the gentry, relied on philosophy and art for interpreting the world around them, and abhorred serfdom as well as the absence of the most elementary civil rights in Russia. In their views on Russia's past and future, however, the two groups differed fundamentally. The Slavophiles, passionately religious and anti-urban, saw Peter the Great as the arch-villain of Russian history. With his importation of Western European culture and technology, the Slavophiles averred, Peter did violence to Old Russia, destroying its patriarchal, communal, and allegedly idyllic way of life. To the Westernizers, however, with Belinsky at their head, pre-Petrine Russia seemed a barbaric wasteland. Russia's sole hope for the future, the Westernizers proclaimed, lay in the cultivation of Western European political institutions and cultural norms. In its most extreme varieties, Westernizing thought flirted with socialism and revolution, while Slavophilism became identified with crude reaction. Dostoevsky began his career as a Westernizer but ended as a staunch Slavophile.

10. Nestor Vasilievich Kukolnik (1809-68) wrote once enormously popular but now quite forgotten romantic dramas and published several journals, among them *The Illustration* (1845-47).

11. As far as is known, Dostoevsky did not write the sketch mentioned here.

12. Alphonse Karr (1808-90), a celebrated French wit of his day, founded the satirical newspaper *Les Guêpes.* To Karr belongs the aphorism "Plus ça change."

poems there too.

Well, good-bye. I'll write more the next time. I'm terribly busy now, but you see, by the way, that I've penned you a whole letter, but you won't even write me half-a-line without a letter from me. You reckon in visits. You're such a lazybones, Fetyuk, simply a Fetyuk.[13]

Read *Teverino*[14] (George Sand in *Notes of the Fatherland,* October). There's been nothing like it in our century. There are people for you, prototypes.[15]

Good-bye, my friend. I send my regards to Emilia Fyodorovna[16] and kiss her hands. Are the children well? Write me in detail.

Translate Schiller little by little, although it's absolutely impossible to say when the edition will come to fruition. I'm trying to sniff out a translation for you now. But alas, at *Notes of the Fatherland* there are three offic[ial] translators. Perhaps you and I can work out something together. Everything is in the future, however. If I make it, so will *Schiller's Theatrical Works*—that's all I know.

Yours,
F. Dostoevsky

56. To Mikhail Dostoevsky
16 November 1845. Petersburg

16 November 45.

Dear brother,

I'm writing you in haste, the more so as I'm short of time. Golyadkin[1] is still not finished; but I definitely need to finish by the 25th. You took quite a long while to answer me, and I was beginning to be very worried. Write more often; and your pleading lack of time is nonsense. You don't

---

13. In Gogol's novel *Dead Souls* the character Nozdryov applies the name "Fetyuk" to people whom he dislikes.

14. *Teverino* (1845-46), novel by George Sand.

15. Dostoevsky's evaluation of *Teverino* perhaps reveals the influence of Belinsky, who also rated the novel very highly.

16. Mikhail's wife.

1. The protagonist of the story *The Double.*

need much time for that. Provincial laziness is destroying you in the flower of your years, dear brother, and that's all there is to it.

Well, brother, I think my fame will never reach such an apogee as now. There's unbelievable admiration everywhere, terrible curiosity about me. I've met a heap of the most respectable people. Prince Odoevsky[2] is asking me to pay him the honor of a visit, and Count Sollogub is tearing his hair out from despair. Panaev[3] announced to him that there is a talent that will trample them all into the dirt. Sollogub ran around to see everyone, and stopping in at Kraevsky's, suddenly asked him: "Who is this Dostoevsky? Where can I *get Dostoevsky?*" Kraevsky, who doesn't care a whit about anyone and cuts everyone left and right, answered him that "Dostoevsky will not wish to do you the honor of bestowing a visit upon you."[4] And that's really so: the trashy little aristocrat is now getting on stilts and thinks he'll destroy me with the grandeur of his cordial attention. Everyone is receiving me like a miracle. I can't even open my mouth without having it repeated in all corners that Dostoev[sky] said such-and-such, Dostoev[sky] wants to do such-and-such. It would be impossible to like me more than Belinsky does. A few days ago the poet Turgenev[5] returned from Paris (you probably have heard) and from the very first time attached himself to me with such an attachment, such a friendship, that Belinsky explains it as Turgenev's having fallen in love with me. But, brother, what sort of person is he? I also have nearly fallen in love with him. A poet, a talent, an aristocrat, a handsome fellow, wealthy, bright, educated, 25 years old[6] — I don't know what nature has denied him. Finally: an inexhaustibly direct, excellent personality, formed in the best school. Read his story "Andrey Kolosov"[7] in *Notes of the Fatherland.* It's he himself, although he didn't plan on exhibiting himself there.

I'm still not rich in money, but I'm not in need. A few days ago I didn't

2. Prince Vladimir Fyodorovich Odoevsky (1803-69), influential man of letters, especially in the 1830s and 1840s. An adherent of Schelling's philosophy, Odoevsky made his mark on Russian literature with *Russian Nights* (1844), a collection of philosophical tales. His talent also embraced society tales and science fiction, along with music criticism.

3. Ivan Ivanovich Panaev (1812-62), minor writer of the 1830s. Together with Nekrasov he edited *The Contemporary* from 1847 until its demise in 1866.

4. Sollogub soon visited Dostoevsky— apparently toward the end of 1845— and expressed to him his admiration for *Poor Folk.*

5. Ivan Sergeevich Turgenev (1818-83) and Dostoevsky were ill-suited to one another in almost every way imaginable. Soon after meeting Dostoevsky, Turgenev began making fun of the swaggering young author. Their relations remained outwardly correct until Dostoevsky's parody of Turgenev in his novel *The Possessed* (1871-72) occasioned a permanent rift between the two. Dostoevsky always admired Turgenev's literary style but often polemicized with the ideological content of Turgenev's works, especially in the novels *Fathers and Sons* (1862) and *Smoke* (1867). *The Possessed* arose in part as a reaction to both of those novels.

6. Turgenev was 27 at the time.

7. Turgenev's story "Andrey Kolosov" was first published in *Notes of the Fatherland,* No. 11, 1844.

even have a farthing. Nekrasov, meanwhile, started up *The Scoffer*[8]—a delightful humorous almanac for which I wrote the first announcement. The announcement made a splash, because it's the first announcement of such lightness and such humor in things of that sort.[9] It reminded me of Lucien de Rupembré's[10] first feuilleton. My announcement has already been published in *Notes of the Fatherland* in the Miscellaneous News.[11] I took 20 silv[er] rubles for it. And so, a fews days back, not having any money, I dropped in on Nekrasov. While I was at his place, the idea for a novel in 9 letters occurred to me.[12] After coming home, I wrote the novel in a single night; its size is half a signature. The next morning I took it to Nekrasov and received 125 paper rubles for it, i.e., my page in *The Scoffer* is valued at 250 paper rubles. In the evening my novel was read to our whole circle at Turgenev's, that is, among 20 people at least, and it produced a furor. It will be published in the first issue of *The Scoffer*. I'll send you the book by December 1 and you'll see for yourself whether it's worse, for instance, than Gogol's *Lawsuit*.[13] Belinsky said that he's now absolutely certain of me, because I can tackle absolutely different elements. A few days ago Kraevsky, on hearing that I had no money, beseeched me most humbly to take a loan of 500 rubles from him. I think that I'll sell him my signature sheet for 200 paper rubles.

I have a mountain of ideas; and I can't tell any of them even to Turgenev, for instance, without people knowing the next day in almost all corners of Petersburg that Dostoev[sky] is writing such-and-such and such-and-such. Well, brother, if I were to begin enumerating to you all my successes, there wouldn't be enough paper for them. I think that I'll have money. Golyadkin is turning out superbly; that will be my chef d'oeuvre. Yesterday I was at Panaev's for the first time, and I seem to have fallen in love with his wife.[14] She's intelligent and attractive, in addition kind and wonderfully direct. I'm spending the time merrily. Our circle is very large. But I keep writing about myself; forgive me, my dear brother; I'll tell you quite frankly that I'm now nearly intoxicated with my own fame. I'll send *The Scoffer* with the next letter. Belinsky says that I'm profaning myself by publishing my pieces in *The Scoffer*.

Good-bye, my friend. I wish you happiness. I congratulate you on

8. See preceding letter for details.

9. Grigorovich felt that the wording of Dostoevsky's announcement probably led to the censorship's decision to prohibit the planned journal.

10. The hero of Balzac's novel *Illusions perdues*.

11. See preceding letter, note 7.

12. *A Novel in Nine Letters* was published in the first issue of *Notes of the Fatherland* for 1847.

13. Gogol's short play *The Lawsuit* was published in 1842.

14. Avdotya Yakovlevna Panaeva (1819-93), Panaev's wife and eventually Nekrasov's mistress. She wrote under the psuedonym "N. Stanitsky" and left interesting if not always reliable memoirs.

your new rank. I kiss Emilia Fyodorovna's[15] hands and your children. How are they?

Yours,
Dostoevsky

Belinsky is protecting me from entrepreneurs. I have read over my letter and found that in the first place, I'm illiterate, and in the second, I'm a braggart.

Good-bye. For Heaven's sake, write.

Our Schiller will definitely work out. Belinsky praises the idea of *a complete edition*.[16] I think that with time we'll be able to sell it profitably, at least to Nekrasov, for instance. Good-bye.

The Minushkas, Klarushkas, Mariannas, and so on have grown impossibly attractive but cost a terrible lot of money. A few days ago Turgenev and Belinsky gave me a good scolding for my disorderly life. Those gentlemen cannot even fathom how to love me, they're all in love with me, every last one. My debts are at their former point.

15. Mikhail Dostoevsky's wife.
16. See Letter 48 for details of the planned edition of Schiller in Russian translation.

БѢДНЫЕ ЛЮДИ.

РОМАНЪ

Ѳедора Достоевскаго.

С. ПЕТЕРБУРГЪ.

ВЪ ТИПОГРАФІИ ЭДУАРДА ПРАЦА.

1847.

Title page of the first book edition of *Poor Folk* (1847)

1846

57. To Mikhail Dostoevsky
1 February 1846. Petersburg

1 February

Dear brother,

First of all, don't be angry with me for not having written for such a long time. Honest to God, there was no time, and I'll prove that right now. The main thing that held me up was that fact that up until very recently, that is, until the 28th, *I was finishing my scoundrel Golyadkin.*[1] Terrible! So much for human calculations: I wanted to finish before August and dragged it out until February! I'm sending you the almanac[2] now. *Poor Folk* came out the 15th. Well, brother! What fierce abuse it met everywhere! In *The Illustration* I read swearing, not criticism.[3] There was the Devil only knows what in *The Northern Bee.*[4] But I remember how Gogol was received, and we all know how Pushkin was received. Even the public is in a frenzy: 3/4 of the readers rail at it, but 1/4 (not even that much, actually) praise it extravagantly. Terrible debates have started up. They rail at it, rail, and rail at it, but nevertheless read it. (The almanac is being bought up unnaturally, terribly. There's the hope that in 2 weeks not a single copy will be left.) That's how it was with Gogol, too. They railed at him, railed at him, railed at him, but nonetheless read him and now they've made their peace with him and have begun praising him. I've thrown them all a dog bone! Let them gnaw away—the fools are building my fame. To disgrace yourself the way *The Northern Bee* does with its criticism is the height of disgrace. How frantically stupid! But on the other hand, what praises I hear, brother! Just imagine, all our people and even Belinsky have

1. Dostoevsky is probably referring to the final proofing of the story *The Double,* which was published in *Notes of the Fatherland,* No. 2, 1846.

2. *The Petersburg Miscellany,* where Dostoevsky's *Poor Folk* was published. See Letter 55, note 2.

3. The anonymous reviewer in the 26 January 1846 issue of *The Illustration* complained about a lack of form in *Poor Folk.*

4. Writing in the 30 January 1846 issue of *The Northern Bee,* L. B. Brant called *Poor Folk* a failure.

found that I've even gone far away from Gogol. In *The Library for Reading*, where Nikitenko writes the criticism, there will be an enormous analysis of *Poor Folk*, in my favor.[5] Belinsky is setting the bells ringing in March.[6] Odoevsky is writing a separate article about *Poor Folk*.[7] Sollogub, my friend, is too.[8] I've entered high society, brother, and in about three months I'll tell you all my adventures in person.[9]

Our public has an instinct, as does any crowd, but it lacks education. They don't understand how one can write in such a style. They've gotten used to seeing the author's mug in everything; I didn't show mine, however. But they can't even imagine that it's Devushkin[10] speaking, and not I, and that Devushkin can't speak in any other way. They find the novel drawn out, but there's not an extra word in it. They (Belinsky and the like) find in me a new, original current consisting of the fact that I operate by Analysis, not Synthesis, that is, I go into the depths, but by taking things apart atom by atom I seek out the whole, while Gogol takes the whole directly and for that reason is not as profound as I am.[11] You'll read and see for yourself. And I have a brilliant future, brother!

Golyadkin[12] is coming out today. *4 days ago* I was still writing him. He'll take up 11 signature pages in *Notes of the Fatherland*. Golyadkin is 10 times higher than *Poor Folk*. Our people say that not since *Dead Souls*[13] has there been anything like it in Russia, that it's a work of genius, and what don't they say about it! With what hopes they all view me! I really was incredibly successful with Golyadkin. You'll like it like I don't know what! You'll like it even better than *Dead Souls*, I know that. Does anyone where you are get *Notes of the Fatherland?* I don't know whether Kraevsky will give me a copy.

Well, brother, it's been such a long time since I wrote you that I don't remember at what point I stopped back then. So much water has flown under the bridge! We'll see each other soon. In the summer I'll definitely come to see you, my friends, and I'll be terribly busy writing all summer: I

5. Nikitenko praised the novel's social-analytical basis, as he called it, but found fault with its language and composition.

6. Belinsky's critique was published in *Notes of the Fatherland*, No. 3, 1846. He was not entirely enthusiastic, admiring Dostoevsky's humanism and artistic independence but also criticising the novel for its longueurs.

7. Odoevsky failed to publish anything about *Poor Folk*.

8. Sollogub did not publish any remarks about *Poor Folk*.

9. Although little is known about Dostoevsky's "adventures" in high society, it is clear that he cut a poor figure there, striking people as either swaggering or morbid or both.

10. The main male protagonist in *Poor Folk*.

11. The notion of analysis as the basis of Dostoevsky's art belongs to the critic V. N. Maykov, not to Belinsky. Maykov first voiced the idea in print in the article "Something about Russian Literature in 1846," *Notes of the Fatherland*, No. 1, 1847.

12. The main protagonist in the story *The Double*.

13. Novel by Gogol (1842).

have ideas. I'm writing now, too. I charged exactly 600 silver rubles for Golyadkin. In addition to that I've also been receiving a mountain of money, so that I've spent 3000 since saying good-bye to you. I'm living in a very disorderly fashion—that's the whole problem! I've moved from my apartment and I'm now renting two marvelously furnished rooms from tenants. I'm enjoying life very much.

My address: by the Vladimir Church, at the corner of Grebetsky Street and Kuznechny Lane, the merchant *Kuchin's* building, No. 9. Please write, for Heaven's sake. Write whether you like *Poor Folk*. Give my regards to Emilia Fyodorovna[14] and kiss the children. I was really in love with Panaeva, but that's passing now, but I don't yet know. My health is terribly unstrung; my nerves are sick and I'm afraid of a nervous fever or an inflammation. I can't live in an orderly way, I'm so dissolute. If I don't get to bathe in the sea this summer, it will simply be a disaster. Good-bye, for Heaven's sake, write. Forgive me for having written the letter badly. I'm in a hurry. I kiss you. Good-bye.

Y[ours,]
Dostoevsky

Well, brother, for the Lord's sake, please forgive me for not yet having sent anything. I'll bring everything in the summer. Well, good-bye, for the third time.

I'll bring you all gifts.

In the summer, my friend, you and I will spend the time more merrily than right now. I won't be rich, but I hope for 800 or 1000 rubles. That's enough for the summer.

Verochka[15] is getting married. Do you know that?

14. Mikhail's wife.

15. Vera Mikhaylovna Dostoevskaya, who married the doctor and teacher Alexander Pavlovich Ivanov (1813-68) on 7 January 1846.

58. To Mikhail Dostoevsky
1 April 1846. Petersburg

1 April 1846

Dear brother,

I'm sending you a helmet with accessories and a pair of epaulets. The covering on the helmet is not affixed, because, as I was told, the shako would get a little damaged in the transporting. I don't know whether I've served you well. If not, I'm not to blame, because I understand absolutely nothing in these things. I'm behind the times, my friend.

Now the 2nd question. You'll ask why I'm so late. But I, my dear friend, have been at such hard labor that strange as it may seem to you, I couldn't find time for your request. True, I missed two mailings out of sheer negligence. I'm at fault. Don't be angry.

Now on to other things. My friend. You're probably reproaching me for not having written in such a long time. But I'm in complete agreement with Gogol's *Poprishchin: "A letter is nonsense, letters are written by pharmacists."*[1] What could I write you? I would have to fill entire volumes if I were to begin to speak as I would like. Every day in my life there are so many new things, so many changes, so many impressions, so many good things and things that are advantageous for me, so many unpleasant and disadvantageous things, that even I have no time for pondering them. In the first place, I'm busy all the time. I have tons of ideas and I'm writing constantly. Don't imagine that I'm completely on a bed of roses. Nonsense. In the first place, I've gone through a lot of money, i.e., exactly 4500 rubles since saying good-bye to you and 1000 paper rubles as an advance on my future work. Thus, with the tidiness of mine with which you are familiar, I've completely robbed myself and am again beginning to live, as before, without a kopeck.

But that's all right.—My fame has reached its apogee. In 2 months, according to my calculations, I've been spoken of about 35 times in various publications. In some of them praise to the skies, in others, praise with exceptions, and in still others out-and-out cursing. What could be better and higher? But here's what's vile and painful: our own people, our kind, Belinsky, and everyone are displeased with me for Golyadkin.[2] The first

1. A quotation from Gogol's "Diary of a Madman."
2. In *Notes of the Fatherland*, No. 3, 1846, Belinsky praised the originality of Dostoevsky's talent as revealed in *The Double* but criticized the story for its excessively drawn-out quality. In the major article "A View of Russian Literature of 1846," however, published in *Notes of the Fatherland*, No. 1, 1847, Belinsky thoroughly revised his opinion of *The Double,* calling the work a failure and cavilling at its fantastic coloration.

impression was uncontrollable delight, clamor, noise, talk. The second, criticism. Specifically: everyone, everyone in the general clamor, i.e., *our people* and the entire public have found Golyadkin so boring and flaccid, so drawn out that it's impossible to read it. But what's most comical of all is that everyone is angry at me for long-windedness and every last person is reading me in a frenzy and rereading me in a frenzy. And all one of our people does is spend his time reading a chapter a day, so as not to exhaust himself, and all he does is smack his lips from pleasure. Some of the readers yell that this is quite impossible, that it's stupid both to write and to print such things; others, on the other hand, yell that it's modelled directly on them, and I've heard such madrigals from some people that it's embarrassing even to speak of them.

As for me, I was even depressed for a certain time. I have a terrible vice: boundless vanity and ambition. The idea that I had failed to meet expectations and had ruined a thing that could have been a great work was killing me. Golyadkin became repulsive to me. Much in him was written in haste and exhaustion. The first 1/2 is better than the last. Along with brilliant pages there is foul stuff, trash, it's nauseating, one doesn't want to read it. That is exactly what created hell for me for a time, and I fell ill from misery. Brother, I'll send you Golyadkin in about two weeks, you'll read it. Write me your full opinion.

I'm passing over my life and my *apprenticeship* and will say a bit about our news. The 1st (enormous piece of news). *Belinsky* is leaving *Notes of the Fatherland*.[3] He has ruined his health terribly and is heading off for the waters, perhaps for abroad. He won't take up any criticism for a couple of years. But in order to support his finances he's publishing an almanac of *gigantic* size (60 signatures).[4] I'm writing two stories for him: the 1st, "Shaved Sideburns," the 2nd, "A Tale about Destroyed Offices," both with stunning tragic interest and— I'm already answering— condensed as much as possible.[5] The public is anxious for my works. Both stories are short. In addition, something for Kraevsky and a novel for Nekrasov. All this will take a year from me. I'm finishing "Shaved Sideburns."

The 2nd piece of news. A whole horde of new writers has appeared. Some are my rivals. Of them Herzen (Iskander)[6] and

---

3. Belinsky had been thinking seriously of leaving Kraevsky's journal since the middle of 1845.

4. Belinsky's plans for an almanac came to naught.

5. Dostoevsky did not finish either story. He reworked some of "A Tale about Destroyed Offices" for the story "Mr. Prokharchin," and echoes of "Shaved Sideburns" can be heard in *The Village of Stepanchikovo*.

6. Alexander Ivanovich Herzen (1812-70), Russian radical who spent the last half of his life in exile in London, from where he published *The Bell* (1857-67) and *Polar Star* (1855-62), "underground" periodicals that wielded enormous influence in Russia in the 1850s and 1860s. His best-known writings are the novel *Who Is To Blame?* (1845-47) and his memoirs, *My Thoughts and Past* (1852-68). For a detailed English-language study of Herzen's life and

Goncharov[7] are especially remarkable. The former has already published, the latter is only beginning and hasn't yet published anywhere. People praise them terribly. I'm in first place for the time being and I hope forever. All in all, literature has never been in such full swing as now. That's for the best.

The third. I'll come to see you either very early, or very late, or I won't come at all. I'm in debt, I won't have any money (and without money I won't come for anything, and in the third place, I'm swamped with work. The future will tell all.).

The 4th. Shidlovsky has given notice of himself. His brother visited me. I'm beginning a correspondence with him.

The 5th. If you want, my beloved friend, to earn something in the literary field, there's a chance to show off and produce an effect with a single translation. Translate Goethe's *Reineke Fuchs*.[8] I was even asked to entrust the translation to you, because Nekrasov needs the piece for his almanacs. If you want, translate it. Don't rush. And even if I don't arrive by May 15 or June 1, send what you have ready. Everyone is heading off for the summer; but if it's possible, I'll perhaps place it somewhere even in the spring and bring you the money. If not in the spring, then in the fall, *but definitely*. There will definitely be money. Nekrasov is a publisher, he'll buy it, Belinsky will buy it, Ratkov[9] will buy it, and Kraevsky is completely at my disposal. It's a profitable matter. People here have talked about this translation. And so start, if you want, and I vouch for success with my head. If you translate about three chapters, send them to me, I'll *show* them to the gentlemen, and it may happen that they'll give you an advance.

I've never been as rich in activity as now. Everything is moving along, in full swing... But what will happen? Good-bye, my beloved.

Good-bye, my dear. I kiss you all and wish you all the best. I kiss both Emilia Fyodorovna's[10] hands. The children, too. How are you? Write about yourself. Oh, my friend. I want to see you. But what can I do.

Entirely yours,
Dostoevsky

work, see Martin Malia, *Alexander Herzen and the Birth of Russian Socialism* (Cambridge, 1961).

7. Ivan Alexandrovich Goncharov (1812-91), the author of the novels *A Common Story* (1847) and *Oblomov* (1859). The best study of Goncharov in English is Vsevolod Setschkareff, *Ivan Goncharov* (1974).

8. *Reineke Fuchs* (1794), poem in twelve cantos by Goethe. Mikhail Dostoevsky's translation was published in *Notes of the Fatherland* in 1848 and remains one of the classic Russian renderings of the work.

9. Pyotr Alexeevich Ratkov, St. Petersburg publisher.

10. Mikhail Dostoevsky's wife.

Verochka[11] has been married 3 months already. They say happily so. Uncle[12] gave just as much as he did to Varya.[13] She married *Ivanov* (His Excellency). He's 30. He's a professor of chemistry somewhere.[14] Verochka wrote to me and told me that she wrote to you, too.

59. To Mikhail Dostoevsky
26 April 1846. Petersburg

26 April

Dear brother,

I haven't written to you because up until today I haven't been able to take pen in hand. The reason for that was that I was sick and near death in the full sense of the word. I was ill to the greatest degree with an irritation of the entire nervous system, and the illness headed for my heart, produced a rush of blood and an inflammation in the heart, which was barely restrained by leeches and two blood lettings. In addition, I ruined myself with various decoctions, drops, powders, mixtures and similar such abominations. Now I'm out of danger. But only because I still have the illness, and according to my doctor's statement, since it was prepared over the course of three of four years, curing it will not take a short time. My treatment has to be both physical and psychic—in the 1st place, with a diet and continual physical deprivations that are prescribed for me. In the 2nd, a change of place, abstention from all strong sensations and shocks, a balanced and tranquil life, and, finally, order in everything. In this instance a trip to Revel (but not for sea bathing, since bathing has been deemed harmful for me) for a change of place and style of life has been prescribed for me as a drastic remedy. But since I don't have a single kopeck, and I need enormous amounts of money for this trip, not so much for Revel as for the expenses and the payment of debts in Petersburg, because of this circumstance everything, practically my life and my health, depend on Kraevsky. If he gives me an advance, I'll come; if not, I won't come at all. And because of this circumstance, after this letter I won't write you for about three weeks, at the conclusion of which time either I'll present myself

11. Vera Mikhaylovna Dostoevskaya. See preceding letter, note 15.
12. A. A. Kumanin.
13. Varvara Mikhaylovna Dostoevskaya.
14. A. P. Ivanov was a doctor and a professor of physics. See preceding letter, note 15.

to you in person or I won't turn up the whole summer long.[1]

I'm writing you in haste and with a business matter. I have a request to make of you that you should fulfill and take care of to the utmost of your energies. Here's what it is. Belinsky is going for the summer (he left yesterday) to Moscow, and then together with his actor friend Shchepkin[2] and a few other people he's undertaking a trip to the south of Russia, to the Ukraine, and to the Crimea. He's returning in September[3] and will try to take care of his almanac.[4] His wife,[5] however, and her sister and a year-old baby are setting out for Gapsal. Maybe I'll arrive with them and maybe not. The ship stops at Revel for a few hours.[6] Now, the problem is that their household people refuse to go with them to a foreign place, even for the summer. They are left without a nanny. It's impossible to hire one here, either, because they won't agree to leave the country except for an enormous sum, which they are unable to pay. And therefore they ask me most humbly to write you their following request. Beginning on the day you receive this letter, try with all your might (which I also ask) to find in Revel a nanny, *a German and not a Finn* (that's essential), if possible an older one who would agree to go with them to Gapsal until September. Their price will be 15 paper rubles a month; if, however, she agrees to go with them later to Petersburg, then 25 paper rubles, they can't give any more than that. It goes without saying that it is quite desirable to find a woman with a good reputation, in a word, a respectable nanny. When you have found her, keep her in readiness from the 5th of May on, i.e., ready for departure in a moment, because of the circumstance that since the ship stops in Revel for four hours, Mme. Belinskaya in those four hours will come to see you, you'll send for the nanny, and the whole business will be taken care of. That's their plan. Everything depends on whether you agree, and I fall before you at your feet for this. I implore you for myself. I like and respect these people. I ask you most humbly, you and Emilia Fyodorovna,[7] try your best. Mme. Belinskaya, a quite weak, aging and ailing woman, is forced to travel all alone, moreover, with a baby. One could do no better than to work for them. They are good people, they live in contentment and treat people superbly well. A nanny for them is only a nanny and doesn't do anything else. For Heaven's sake, brother, please try your best. In addition, answer me as soon as possible. The Belinskys may be in Revel by the 10th. Write me soon and also explain whether

1. Dostoevsky arrived in Revel on 25 May 1846.
2. Mikhail Semyonovich Shchepkin (1788-1863), the most famous Russian actor of the nineteenth century.
3. Belinsky left Moscow on May 16 and returned there in the last half of October 1846.
4. See preceding letter, note 4.
5. Maria Vasilievna Belinskaya (1812-90).
6. Mrs. Belinskaya, her daughter, and her sister spent the summer in Revel.
7. Mikhail Dostoevsky's wife.

passengers are accepted on the ship that goes from Petersburg to Gapsal via Revel. Otherwise they won't take the nanny on the ship.

Before my departure I have to finish a short story,[8] for money that I borrowed from Kraevsky, and then take an advance.

The enormous activity in our literature is in full swing. You won't write anything new. I have great hopes. When we see each other I'll tell you all about them, but for now good-bye.

Entirely yours,
F. Dostoevsky

I'm anxious to receive your letter. I send my love and admiration to Emilia Fyodorovna, my most humble respects to Fedya,[9] and my most humble admiration, mixed with respect, to Masha.[10]

60. To Mikhail Dostoevsky
16 May 1846. Petersburg

1846. 16 May

Dear brother,

Before you are the ladies who have delivered this message to you. Please receive them well and if possible, it would not even be a bad idea to invite them to dinner, both Mme Belinskaya and her interesting sister. They ask to be introduced to Emilia Fyodorovna[1] too. Nourish their feminine egoism with your attention as much as possible, and of course, talk about literature as little as possible. You understand these matters better yourself than I do, however. Instruct them where to stay and what to do. I don't know what's better for them—to stay in Revel or go on to Gapsal.[2]

About myself I'll say that I absolutely don't know what's going to happen to me. I don't have even a kopeck, and moreover, I don't know where I can get any money. I can't get myself out of here unless I have 500

8. The reference is to the story "Mr. Prokharchin," first published in *Notes of the Fatherland*, No. 10, 1846.

9. Mikhail and Emilia's son, Fyodor Mikhaylovich Dostoevsky.

10. Mikhail and Emilia's daughter Maria Mikhaylovna Dostoevskaya.

1. Mikhail Dostoevsky's wife.

2. Mrs. Belinskaya, her sister, and the Belinskys' daughter spent the summer in Revel.

rubles specifically for paying off Petersburg debts. Cons[equently], judge for yourself. It's likely, and even more than likely, that we simply won't see each other, brother, and that I won't come.[3] I'm depressed and feeling bad here. I'm writing and don't see an end to the work. I send my regards to Emilia Fyodorovna. I petition her on behalf of the Belinsky ladies and rely on all her indulgence and kindness. It won't be bad if on their part Fedya and Masha[4] also show cordiality and express their opinion frankly, to the extent of their well-known reliability. Well, good-bye, brother, there's no time. I've absolutely never had such a difficult time. Depression, misery, apathy, and the feverish, convulsive expectation of something better torment me. And then my illness to boot. The Devil only knows what this is. If only all of this would somehow blow over.

Yours,
F. Dostoevsky

61. To Andrey Dostoevsky
24 May 1846. Petersburg

Brother. I'm leaving for Revel right now. I'm sorry that I didn't drop by to see you. Recently I've kept having different apartments, and in general, disorder has prevailed around me because of uncertainty whether I would remain in Petersburg or not. You probably looked for me but didn't find me. My health isn't bad, although I haven't yet recovered entirely.[1] I'm leaving in order to take a cure, I'll give your regards to our brother. And now good-bye.

I'll return in October[2] and after I get myself fixed up I'll come to see you myself.

Yours,
F. Dostoevsky

---

3. Dostoevsky arrived in Revel 25 May 1846.
4. Son and daughter of Mikhail and Emilia Dostoevsky.
1. See Letters 59 and 60 for information about Dostoevsky's health.
2. Dostoevsky returned to Petersburg September 1.

62. To Mikhaïl Dostoevsky
5 September 1846. Petersburg

I hasten to inform you, dear brother, that I made it to Petersburg with difficulty and am staying with Trutovsky,[1] as I wished. I didn't experience any seasickness, but on the way and here in Petersburg I got soaked to the skin and caught cold. I have a cough, head cold, and all of that to the highest degree. At the beginning I was terribly depressed. I went to rent an apartment and for 14 silver rubles have already rented from tenants two little rooms with good furniture and a servant, but I haven't moved yet. The address is: *opposite the Kazan Cathedral, in Kokhendorf's building, number 25*. Write me at this address soon, because I very much wish to have a letter from you. A terrible melancholy has settled over me.

The Belinskys arrived without any problems, and since docking I haven't yet seen them. I dropped by to see Nekrasov the next day. He and the Panaevs live in the same apartment, and for that reason I saw everyone. The almanac[2] is moving along; it's necessary to hurry. I didn't want to ask about the shop and I don't know, but it's probably coming along too.[3] But here's some news: in order to find out Nekrasov's address, I dropped by to see Prokopovich.[4] He explained to me the reason for Nekrasov's arrival in Revel—a reason that he kept secret for various political aspects and didn't even tell Prokopovich; but the latter figured it out from various data. He came to see Masalsky[5] in order to buy *The Son of the Fatherland* from him. The business seems to have worked out, and by the New Year we may have a new journal.[6]

I haven't been telling you anything about Gogol, but here's a fact for you. In next month's issue of *The Contemporary* a piece by Gogol will be published—his will, in which he disavows all his works and considers them useless and even more than that. He says that he will not take up the pen for the rest of his life because his business is praying. He agrees with all the opinions of his opponents. He orders his portrait to be printed in a huge number of copies and the profits to be assigned for financial assistance to travelers to Jerusalem and so on. There it is. Draw your own conclusions.[7]

1. Konstantin Alexandrovich Trutovsky (1826-93), painter who studied with Dostoevsky at the Academy of Engineering.

2. See Letter 58, note 4.

3. It is unclear to what Dostoevsky is referring here.

4. Nikolay Yakovlevich Prokopovich (181-57), poet and friend of Gogol's.

5. Konstantin Petrovich Masalsky (1802-61), popular novelist and editor of the journal *The Son of the Fatherland*.

6. In fact, Nekrasov and Panaev acquired the journal *The Contemporary*.

7. Dostoevsky perhaps heard of Gogol's "Will" from Prokopovich. The piece did not appear in print until 1847, and then as part of *Selected Passages from a Correspondence with Friends*.

I visited Kraevsky too. He has begun setting Prokharchin;[8] it will appear in October. I haven't yet spoken about money; he is fawning and flirtatious, however. I haven't yet visited anyone else. Yazykov has opened an office and put out a sign.[9] It's raining terribly outside and therefore it's difficult to go out. I'm still living at Trutovsky's, but I'm moving to the apartment tomorrow. It's also been absolutely impossible to see about an overcoat because of all the errands and the rain. I want to live in the most modest fashion. I wish the same thing for you. One needs to accomplish things little by little. We'll live a bit and see. And now good-bye. I'm in a hurry. I would like to write a lot, but sometimes it's better not to speak. Write. I'm expecting a reply from you in the shortest possible time. Kiss the children. Give my respect to Emilia Fyodorovna.[10] Also give my regards to whomever appropriate. I'll write much more in the next mail. This is just a note. Good-bye. I wish you all the best, my priceless friends—and most importantly for the time being, patience and health.

Your brother F. Dostoevsky

63. To Mikhail Dostoevsky
17 September 1846. Petersburg

17 September

Dear brother,

I'm sending you the overcoat. Forgive me for being so late. The delay wasn't on my part, I was looking for my servant and finally found him. I couldn't buy it without him. The overcoat has its virtues and its inconveniences. The virtue is that it is unusually full, in fact double, and the color is good, just what you need for a uniform, gray; the shortcoming is that the material sells only at 8 paper rubles. There was nothing better. But on the other hand, it only cost 82 paper rubles. The remaining money has been used for the mailing. There wasn't anything I could do: there was

8. Dostoevsky's "Mr. Prokharchin" was published in *Notes of the Fatherland,* No. 10, 1846.
9. Mikhail Alexandrovich Yazykov (1811-85), a friend of many leading men of letters of the 1840s and 1850s, especially Belinsky. In 1846 Yazykov and M. M. Tyutchev opened an agency for providing people in the provinces with books and household goods.
10. Mikhail Dostoevsky's wife.

material at 12 paper rubles, but the color was bright steel-blue, excellent, but you disdain it. But I don't think you'll dislike it. It's still a bit long.

And I haven't written you until now because of the overcoat. I already announced to you that I've rented an apartment. Things aren't bad; it's just that in the future I have almost no money. Kraevsky gave me 50 silver rubles, and to judge by his look, he won't give any more; I'm going to have to endure a great deal.

"Prokharchin" has been terribly disfigured at a certain place.[1] The gentlemen of the certain place forbade even the word *bureaucrat,* and God only knows why; even as it was, everything was too innocent, and they crossed things out all over the place. All the life has disappeared. Only the skeleton of what I read to you is left. I'm renouncing my story.

I haven't heard anything by way of news. Everything is as before; people are waiting for Belinsky. Mme Belinskaya sends you her regards. All the ventures that there were seem to have gotten mired in place; or perhaps they're being kept secret—the Devil only knows.[2]

We're pooling our resources for dinners. Six friends have gathered at the Beketovs,[3] including Grigorovich and me. Each one contributes 15 silver kopecks a day, and we have two good simple dishes for dinner and are satisfied. Cons[equently], dinner costs me no more than 16 rubles.

I'm writing to you in haste. Because I'm running late, and the servant is waiting with the package to take it to the post office. I have even more nonsense than when your teeth were aching. I'm very much afraid that the overcoat will be too late for you. What can I do? I tried my hardest.

I keep on writing "Shaved Sideburns."[4] The thing is going so slowly. I'm afraid of being late with it. I have heard from two gentlemen, namely, from the second Beketov and Grigorovich, that *The Petersburg Miscellany* is known in the provinces exclusively as *Poor Folk.* No one cares about the other things in it, although they snatch it up out there like crazy, outbidding each other and paying a huge price to buy it from people lucky enough to have gotten it. And in the bookstores, for instance, in Penza and Kiev, it officially costs 25 and 30 paper rubles. What a strange fact: here it's not selling at all, and there you can't get it.

Grigorovich has written an amazingly good story,[5] through my efforts and those of Maykov,[6] who, by the way, wants to write a long article about

1. Dostoevsky is referring to cuts in "Mr. Prokharchin" required by the censorship.

2. See Letter 58, note 4, for the details on Belinsky's plans for an almanac.

3. Nikolay Nikolaevich Beketov (b. 1827) and Andrey Nikolaevich Beketov (1825-1902) both became professors at Petersburg University. Their elder brother, Alexey Nikolaevich (b. 1823), studied at the Academy of Engineering with Grigorovich and Dostoevsky. Dostoevsky shared an apartment with the Beketov brothers from October 1846 until the spring of 1847.

4. Dostoevsky did not complete the work. See Letter 58, note 5.

5. The reference is to Grigorovich's novella *The Village,* first published in *Notes of the Fatherland,* No. 12, 1846.

6. Valerian Nikolaevich Maykov (1823-47), one of the few nineteenth-century Russian

me by January 1st,[7] the story will be published in *Notes of the Fatherland*, which, by the way, has become completely impoverished. They don't have a single story in reserve.

I'm in a horrible depression. And you work worse. I lived with you as though in paradise, and the Devil knows, give me something good, and with my character I'll definitely make it as bad as possible. I wish Emilia Fyodorovna[8] pleasures, and more importantly, health, I sincerely desire that; I think about all of you a lot.—Yes, brother: money and security are a good thing. I kiss my niece and nephew. Well, good-bye. I'll write more in the next letter. And now, for Heaven's sake, don't be angry with me. And be healthy and don't eat so much beef.

My address:

Near the Kazan Cathedral, at the corner of Bolshaya Meshchanskaya and Cathedral Square, in Kokhendorf's building, No. 25.

Good-bye.

Your brother F. Dostoevsky

Try to eat as healthily as possible, and please, without mushrooms, mustard, and similar such junk. For Heaven's sake.

Y[ours,]
D

64. To Mikhail Dostoevsky
7 October 1846. Petersburg

7 October 1846

Dear brother,

I hasten to answer your letter and together with that to write you about what I wanted to notify you of even without your letter.

I wrote you the last time that I'm planning to go abroad.[1] The

---

literary critics who valued aesthetics more highly than ideology. His early death robbed Russian literary criticism of what no doubt would have been a major figure.

7. Reference to Maykov's "Something about Russian Literature in 1846," where several pages are devoted to Dostoevsky. See Letter 57, note 11.

8. Mikhail Dostoevsky's wife.

1. Dostoevsky did not realize his plans for a trip to France and Italy in 1846.

booksellers are giving me four thousand paper rubles for everything. Nekrasov was going to give me 1500 silver rubles. But it seems that he won't have any money for that and will renege. If my price seems low (judging by my expenses), I won't take it and I'll publish my volume myself, perhaps even by November 15.[2] That's even better, because the business will be right before my eyes, they won't mess up the volume, for instance, and in a word, there will be distinct advantages. Then by January 1st I'll sell all the copies to the booksellers wholesale. Perhaps I'll earn 4,000, and although that's the same that the booksellers are giving, I won't publish everything in my volume. Cons[equently], if I add a little bit, a second volume will come out after my return from Italy, and I'll arrive to money straightaway.

I'm not going for a good time but to take a cure. Petersburg is hell for me. It's depressing, so depressing to live here! And my health is noticeably worse. Moreover, I'm terribly afraid. What will October say, for instance, so far the days are clear.—I'm very much looking forward to your letter, because I want to know your opinion. But for the time being here's the following for you: help me, brother, until December 1 at the most. Because until December 1st I absolutely don't know where to get any money. That is, there will be money, Kraevsky, for instance, is thrusting some at me, but I've already borrowed 100 silver rubles from him and now I flee him. Because 50 rubles is the same as a signature sheet. And in Italy, at my leisure, at freedom, I want to write a novel for myself and be able finally to raise my price. But the system of continual indebtedness that Kraevsky practices is the system of my slavery and literary dependence. And so, give me some money, if you can. In leaving for abroad, I wrote you that I would repay the 100 silver rubles; but if you can send me 50 silver rubles now, I'll give that money back, too; everything will be arranged by January 1st. Figure out if you can lend me money until January 1st, then give it to me. With regard to repayment, rely on me as on a stone mountain. I'm writing the last actually so that it will be clearer for you to calculate.

I need this money for an overcoat. I no longer have clothing sewn for me; I'm entirely taken up with the system of literary emancipation, and it, that is, my clothing, is already indecent. I really need an overcoat. I'll use 120 for one with a collar, and the rest I want to use to get by somehow until publication. Kraevsky has offered to help me himself. Ratkov and Kuvshinnikov publish things upon his recommendation. I've already spoken with them. They offered 4,000 for a manuscript.

I intend by January 1st to write some other trifle for Kraevsky and then to get away from everyone. In order to betake myself to Italy I need to pay various debts (including to you) in the sum of 1600 paper rubles. Cons[equently], at the very, very most, 2,400 paper rubles will be left. I've

---

2. Of Dostoevsky's various publishing plans, the only one on which he was able to follow through in the 1840s was a separate book edition of *Poor Folk* in 1847.

asked about everything: the trip costs 500 (at the most). And in Vienna I'll have clothes and linen made for 300 rubles, things are cheap there, for a total of just 800; that means that 1,600 will be left. I'll get by for eight months. I'll send *The Contemporary* the first part of a novel,[3] get 1200 and from Rome go to Paris for 2 months and then back. When I arrive, I'll publish the 2nd part right away, and I'll bȩ writing the novel until the fall of 1848 and then immediately publish its 3rd and 4th parts. The first part, the prologue, will be published in *The Contemporary* in the form of a prologue. I have both the plot and the idea in my head. I'm now almost in panicky terror over my health. My palpitations are terrible, as during the 1st period of my illness.

The Contemporary is being published by Nekrasov and Panaev January 1st. The critic is Belinsky. Various journals and the Devil only knows what else are arising. But I flee from everything because I want to be healthy in order to write something healthy. Nekrasov's shop is on the wane.[4] But Yazykov and Co. are flourishing.[5] He also has commissions and books. I've already spoken with him about depositing copies with him for the management and distribution of them.

Give my regards to everyone. Especially to Emilia Fyodorovna.[6] The children too, and for Heaven's sake, answer me with the first mail. I'm waiting for your letter. Write as soon as possible; because if you won't send any money, then at least say so (for which, honest to God, I won't hold anything against you), so that I can look elsewhere.

Entirely yours,
F. Dostoevsky

I'll be writing you letters very often now.

It will be a long time before we see each other, brother. But when I return from abroad I'll come directly to see you, no matter where you may be.

By October 20, the time of finishing the raw material, i.e., "Shaved Sideburns," my situation will become apparent in the clearest way, since the printing of *Poor Folk* will begin on October 15th.

3. Dostoevsky may be referring to *Netochka Nezvanova*.

4. Dostoevsky may be referring to the commission sales of *The Petersburg Miscellany*, edited by Nekrasov.

5. See Letter 62, note 9.

6. Mikhail Dostoevsky's wife.

65. To Mikhail Dostoevsky
17 October 1846. Petersburg

17 Octob[er] 46

I hasten to inform you, d[ear] b[rother], that I received your money, for which I am inexpressibly grateful, since I no longer feel the cold and other unpleasant things. I hasten to tell you also that all my hopes and calculations seem to be postponed until a more convenient time. At least right now I still don't know much myself. Conditions keep being offered the likes of which one cannot accept; either the money is too little, or the money is decent, but you don't get it all at once and have to wait. It goes without saying that if I'm to sell, I can do that only for cash. Finally, I'm being advised to wait. That's both bad and good. Bad for my health. What's good is that if I wait, I can get a more significant sum. In the latter case, there's no prospect of publishing by Christmas. Since I need to live on something; cons[equently], I need to sell stories to journals; and then I'll have to wait; and therefore the earliest that the publication can occur is perhaps by May 1st. Moreover, I'll have to exert myself in order to arrange everything; and publish two thick volumes and not for 2 [rubles] 50 kopecks, as I had presumed; but for 3 and perhaps more. And so, perhaps we'll see each other again this summer, and the trip will not take place until perhaps the fall, if I have a lot of money.

All of this so upsets me, brother, that I'm like a crazy person. Oh, how much labor and how many difficulties of various kinds one has to go through at first in order to establish oneself. I have to leave my health, for instance, to luck, and the Devil only knows when I'll ever have any security. I'm writing you a short letter, because I don't yet know anything for certain myself. I'm not entirely in the dumps, however. How are you? You write that you're expecting a new guest in the family. God grant that all go well.[1] And may your circumstances, too, right themselves. I haven't stopped thinking about our goals, brother. Our association can be realized. I keep on dreaming. I absolutely have to have a complete success, without that there won't be anything, and I'll just barely get by. All of this depends not on me but on my energies.

"Shaved Sideburns" is not yet quite finished.[2] "Prokharchin"[3] is being praised highly. I've been told a lot of judgments.[4] Belinsky hasn't arrived yet. The gentlemen at *The Contemporary* keep on hiding. So I'm still

1. Mikhail Mikhaylovich Dostoevsky was born 5 November 1846.
2. Dostoevsky did not finish the piece. See Letter 58, note 5.
3. Reference to the story "Mr. Prokharchin."
4. The published reviews of "Mr. Prokharchin" were generally critical of the story.

hanging on to "Shaved Sideburns" and haven't yet promised it to anyone. Perhaps Kraevsky will publish it. I don't yet know how I'll manage things with that, however. I'll take advantage of circumstances and enter the story into the fray, and whoever fights harder will get it. Then I'll surely pull down some decent money. But if it happens that I publish it separately, so that I'm given a certain sum in advance, I won't give it to the journals.

Our brother Andrey sends his regards. The Belinskys too, both to you and to Emilia Fyodorovna.[5] I visit them from time to time. How they play games of chance![6] I kiss the children, I often think of them. If I do a good job of selling the story, I'll send them some candy and various sweets for Christmas. Emilia Fyodorovna has all my devotion. Let's be patient, brother, perhaps we'll get rich. We need to work. But for Heaven's sake look after your health. And I would advise you and ask you not to work a lot. Let the Devil have it! Please take care of yourself. And most importantly, eat more healthily. Less coffee and meat. They're poison. Good-bye, brother. I'll write again soon. It's so dark.

F. Dostoevsky

October here is dry, clear, and cold, There have been few illnesses. Don't forget me and write. Give my regards to the Forshtadtskys, Reyngardt, and the others.[7]

66. To Andrey Dostoevsky
18 October 1846. Petersburg

Dear brother Andrey,

I've long since arrived from Revel,[1] and every Saturday circumstances of one sort or another have kept me from notifying you. Forgive me. Come to see me tomorrow about 10 AM. I live opposite the Kazan Cathedral, on the corner of Cathedral Square and Bolshaya Meshchanskaya, in Kokhendorf's building, No. 25, Mme Capdeville's apartment.

And now good-bye.

Your brother F. Dostoevsky

5. Mikhail Dostoevsky's wife.
6. Apparently a reference to the game preference, which somewhat resembles whist.
7. Friends of Mikhail and Emilia Dostoevsky in Revel.
1. Dostoevsky had returned to Petersburg on 1 September 1846.

67. To Mikhail Dostoevsky
Last part of October 1846. Petersburg

Dear brother,

I want to write you a couple of words, but no more, because I'm running around and beating my head against the wall. The problem is that all my plans have collapsed and been destroyed all by themselves. The edition won't come off.[1] Because not a single one of the stories that I have told you about has come off. I'm not writing "Shaved Sideburns," either. I've given up everything: because it's all nothing but a repetition of old things that I've long since said. Now more original, lively, and radiant ideas are begging to be put down on paper. When I finished "Shaved Sideburns," all of this presented itself to me on its own. In my position monotony is ruination.

I'm writing another story,[2] and the work is going as it once did with *Poor Folk,* crisply, easily, and successfully. I intend it for Kraevsky. Let the gentlemen from *The Contemporary* be angry; that doesn't matter.[3] Meanwhile, after finishing the story by January I'll cease publishing entirely until next year and write a novel that even now is giving me no peace.[4]

But in order to live, I've made up my mind to publish *Poor Folk*[5] and a revised *The Double*[6] as separate books. I won't put Part 1 and Part 2 on them, for instance, it will simply be *Poor Folk* separately and *The Double* too—all my work for the year. I hope to do exactly the same thing with my future novel.

And finally, perhaps in 2 years or so I'll tackle a complete edition, and in that way I'll gain extraordinarily, because I'll get money twice and create renown for myself.

I'm starting to print *Poor Folk* tomorrow or the day after. I'll do that through *Ratkov,* he promises. And now I only curse fate that I don't have 700 paper rubles in order to publish it at my own expense. Publishing at your own expense is everything. At someone else's means taking a risk; you can perish. The booksellers are scoundrels. They have scads of tricks that I don't know and with which they can swindle you. But their most barbarous thing is the following: he publishes an edition at his expense, and for that he receives from me 350 or 400 copies (the price covering his expenses), he

---

1. The reference is to a planned volume of stories by Dostoevsky.
2. The reference is probably to the story "The Landlady," first published in *Notes of the Fatherland* in 1847.
3. Reference to Nekrasov and Panaev.
4. Probably a reference to *Netochka Nezvanova*.
5. Dostoevsky was unable to publish *Poor Folk* in a separate book edition until 1847.
6. Dostoevsky did not publish a revised version of *The Double* until 1866.

takes 40 per cent, i.e., 40 silver kopecks per copy (I'm selling them at a ruble each). That's for *the turnover of his capital* and for *the risk*. He has in his hands, let's say, 300 copies. He's the one who sells them. I, however, do not have the right to sell a single copy until all of his are sold, because I would be undercutting him. He'll sell them all and tell me that the public doesn't want any more and that the books won't sell. It's impossible to check him. That means quarreling with him. That is done only in extreme cases. I have copies. I need money. Finally, after having made me starve, he buys a couple hundred copies from me at half price. Finally, there are rascals of the sort who hold back requests from other cities and don't release copies even to the Petersburg public that is asking for them. Now, if I publish myself, I suddenly sell to all the booksellers in Petersburg, for hard cash. They take a certain percentage. Each one gives more than the other, trying to undercut each other if the book sells well, and finally, the main stockpile is set up at Yazykov's office.

Listen, brother: I request an immediate reply from you, and here's what I propose. If only you have money, *200 silver rubles* (I need more, but I can go slightly into debt), don't you want to do some speculation? If you're saving up, then the money is just lying there and going to waste. I propose that you give me some money for the edition. I can have it printed by November 15. The edition will pay for itself by January 1st. I'll send you your 200 silver rubles right away. Later, 1/4 of the profits. The edition will pay for itself with 350 copies. There will be 850 left at 75 silver kopecks each = 635 paper rubles. I'll give that profit to a bookseller. But I'd prefer to share it with you. My money wouldn't be lost. Then, if it smelled of success, we would publish *The Double*. Finally, in any event, your money will be returned to you by January. I give my word of honor that I won't drag you into a false position. Finally, I expect success. Even if a slow one. It will take at least a year for the *whole* edition to sell out. Here's an example: Osnovyanenko's *Mr. Kholyavsky*[7] was published in *Notes of the Fatherland* 3 years ago. Then it was published separately and now they already want to do a 3rd printing.

If you want, brother, answer me right away and with money. In the meanwhile I'll correct a few things, go to the censorship, and make arrangements with the printer. If you send some and you don't have that much, then for a starter send at least 120 silver rubles, no less, for a deposit, and then the remaining 80 silver rubles absolutely by November 15.

Finally, if you can't do all this, you won't put me in straitened circumstances, at least as far as time. I'll go to the booksellers, and we'll publish *The Double* later.

---

7. Grigory Fyodorovich Kvitka (pseud. of Grigory Fyodorovich Osnovyanenko, 1778-1843), wrote most of his works in Ukrainian. *Mr. Khalyavsky* (1839) is a humorous portrait of life among the Ukrainian gentry.

Cast aside in this matter all fraternal love, tactfulness, and similar things. Regard this matter as speculation. Don't rob yourself out of the desire to do me a good turn, even if only for a short time. You have a new child on the way. Good-bye, kiss everyone. Give my regards to everyone you should. I'm still sick all the time. But after all, you know me.

Yours,
Dostoevsky

Good-bye, dear brother. I await your immediate reply. For Heaven's sake, don't put yourself in a false position, that is, if you were giving me the last of your money. Then it's better not to. After all, I'm only making a proposal. But if you're rich and willing, send the money with the first mail, for instance, by the 2nd or 3rd of the month.

Well, listen to me. I've written you everything and I'm saying for the last time: if you have money, don't be afraid and agree. If you don't have any or very little, for Heaven's sake, don't enter into this venture. Answer right away.

Give my regards to Emilia Fyodorovna.[8] I wish you all happiness, my friends. Gogol died in Florence 2 months ago.

68. To Mikhail Dostoevsky
26 November 1846. Petersburg

26 November 1846

Well how could you, my priceless friend, write that I was allegedly angry with you for not having sent money and therefore was silent. How could such an idea occur to you? And how, finally, could I have given you a pretext to think that about me? If you love me, then do me the favor of renouncing such ideas from now on and forever. Let's try to have everything between us direct and simple. I'll tell you aloud and straightforwardly that I am obliged to you for so much that it would be ridiculous and base swinishness on my part not to admit that. Now enough about this. I will do better to write about my circumstances, and I'll try to make everything as clear as possible.

In the first place, all my editions have burst and come to nothing. It

8. Mikhail Dostoevsky's wife.

wasn't worth it, it took too much time, and it was too early. The public might not have gone for it. I'll do the edition sometime toward next fall. The public will become better acquainted with me by then and my position will be clearer. Besides, I'm expecting several advances. *The Double* is already being illustrated by a Moscow artist. *Poor Folk* is being illustrated in two places here—whoever does the better job.[1] Bernardsky[2] says that he's not opposed to the idea of starting negotiations with me in February and of giving me a certain sum for the right to publish an illustrated version. Until then he's busy with *Dead Souls*. In a word, for the time being I've grown indifferent to the edition. Besides, there's no time to bother with it. I have scads of work and orders.—I'll tell you that I had the unpleasant experience of quarreling decisively with *The Contemporary* in the person of Nekrasov. Complaining about the fact that I'm still giving my stories to Kraevsky, to whom I'm in debt, and that I refused to declare publicly that I do not belong to *Notes of the Father*[*land*], and despairing of receiving a story from me in the near future, he made a number of rude remarks to me and imprudently demanded money. I took him at his word and with an acknowledgement of debt promised to pay him a sum by December 15. I want them to come to me themselves. They're all scoundrels and enviers. After I had given Nekrasov a royal dressing down, he could only mince and try to get away, like a Jew who's having his money stolen. In a word, a dirty story. Now they're claiming that infected by vanity, I conceived a high opinion of myself and am going over to Kraevsky because Maykov praises me. Nekrasov is planning to criticize me. As for Belinsky, he's such a weak person that even in literary opinions he keeps changing his mind. Only with him have I retained my former good relations. He is a noble person. Meanwhile Kraevsky, rejoicing at the chance, gave me some money and promised in addition to pay off all my debts for me by December 15. In return I'm working for him until the spring.—You see what, brother: out of all this I have extracted a very wise rule. The 1st disadvantageous thing for a beginning talent is friendship with proprietors of publications, from which as an unavoidable consequence favoritism and then various obscenities proceed. Then independence of position, and finally, work for Holy Art, work that is sacred and pure in the simplicity of a heart that has never before so trembled and moved in me as now before all the new images that are being created in my soul.[3] Brother, I am being reborn, not just morally, but physically as well. Never before has there been in me such an abundance of clarity, such equilibrium in my character, such physical health. I'm much obliged in this matter to my good friends the Beketovs,[4] Zalyubetsky, and the others with whom I'm living; they're sensible, bright

---

1. Dostoevsky's revised version of *The Double* was not published until 1866; the book edition of *Poor Folk* that came out in November 1847 lacked illustrations.

2. Yefstafy Yefimovich Bernardsky (1819-c.90), wood engraver, began publishing illustrations for Gogol's novel *Dead Souls* in 1846.

3. Dostoevsky was working on "The Landlady."

4. See Letter 63, note 3.

people, with an excellent heart, with nobility, with character. They have cured me with their company. Finally, I proposed that we all live together. A large apartment was found, and all the expenses, for all the parts of the household, don't exceed 1200 paper rubles per person per year. How great are the boons of an association![5] I have my own room and I work days on end. My new address, to which I request that you address letters: Vasilevsky Island, 1st Line at Bolshoy Prospect, in Soloshich's building. No.26, opposite the Lutheran church.

I congratulate you, my dearest friend, on the arrival of my third nephew.[6] I wish every blessing for both him and Emilia Fyodorovna.[7] I love you all now three times as much. But don't be angry at me, my priceless friend, for writing a scribbled over wad of paper instead of a letter; there's no time, people are waiting for me. But I'll write again on Friday. Consider this letter unfinished.

Your friend,
F. Dostoevsky

69. To Mikhail Dostoevsky
17 December 1846. Petersburg

St. Petersburg, 17 December 46

What has happened to you, dear brother, that you have fallen completely silent? With every mail I've been expecting something from you, and not a word. I'm worried, I often think of you, about the fact that you sometimes fall sick, and I'm afraid to draw conclusions. For Heaven's sake, write me at least a couple of lines. Please write and reassure me. Perhaps you've been waiting the whole time for the continuation of my recent letter.[1] But don't be angry with me for keeping my word so inaccurately. I'm swamped with work now and have pledged by the 5th of January to give Kraevsky the 1st part of the novel *Netochka Nezvanova,* about the publication of which you've probably read in *Notes of the Fatherland.*[2] I'm writing you this letter in fits and starts, because I'm

5. "Association" was a code word for "socialism."
6. Mikhail Mikhaylovich Dostoevsky (1846-96).
7. Mikhail Dostoevsky's wife.
1. See the conclusion of the preceding letter.
2. Although *Netochka Nezvanova* was announced in *Notes of the Fatherland,* No. 12, 1846, the novel did not begin to appear in print until issues No. 1, 2, 5 of *Notes of the Fatherland* for 1849.

writing day and night except from 7 o'clock in the evening on, when I go to the gallery of the Italian Opera to listen to our incomparable singers. My health is good, so there's nothing more to write about it. I'm writing with fervor. I keep feeling that I have started up a lawsuit against all our literature, journals, and critics, and with the three parts of my novel in *Notes of the Fatherland* I'm establishing my primacy for this year to spite my ill-wishers. Kraevsky is discouraged.[3] He's nearly perishing. *The Contemporary,* however, is performing brilliantly. They've already started up a crossfire.[4]

And so, brother, I won't go abroad either this winter or summer, but will come to see you again in Revel.[5] I can hardly wait for the summer. In the summer I'll redo my old things and prepare an edition for the fall, and then we'll see what happens. Is your family well, brother? Is Emilia Fyodorovna[6] by any chance ill? I request an immediate response to this letter, brother. I'm living, as I've already written you, brother, with the Beketovs on Vasiliev Island; it's not boring; it's good and economical.[7] I sometimes visit Belinsky. He's ill all the time, but he has hope. Mme Belinskaya has given birth.

I'm paying off all my debts, thanks to Kraevsky. My task for myself is to work and repay him everything over the winter and not owe a kopeck for the summer. When will I get out of debt? It's a bad thing to work as a day laborer. You'll destroy everything, including talent and youth and hope, grow disgusted with your work, and in the end become a pen pusher, not a writer.

Good-bye, brother. You've torn me away from the most interesting page in my novel, and there's still a mountain of things ahead. Oh, my dear, if only you're successful. I'd love to see you soon, and before seeing you, to settle and resolve my situation. I've bound myself hand and foot with entrepreneurs. And meanwhile, from the side I'm receiving brilliant offers. *The Contemporary,* which in the person of Nekrasov wishes to criticize me, will give me 60 silver rubles per signature page, which equals the 300 rubles at N[otes of the] *Fatherland, The Library for Reading*—250 paper rubles per its signature page and so on, and I can't give them anything: Kraevsky has taken everything for his 50 silver rubles given as an advance. By the way, Grigorovich has written a physiology,[8] *The Village,*[9] in *Notes*

3. Dostoevsky did not fulfill his contractual obligations to Kraevsky, a situation that led Belinsky, for one, to conclude that Dostoevsky had taken advantage of the publisher.

4. Valerian Maykov, writing in *Notes of the Fatherland,* and Belinsky, in *The Contemporary,* polemicized with each other in 1846 and 1847.

5. Dostoevsky did not go to Revel in 1847.

6. Mikhail Dostoevsky's wife.

7. See Letter 63 for details of Dostoevsky's communal arrangement with the Beketovs.

8. This is Dostoevsky's shorthand for "physiological sketch," a plotless genre that attempted to portray the daily lives of typical representatives of the urban lower classes.

9. See Letter 63, note 5.

of the Fatherland, which is creating a furor here. Well, good-bye, dear brother. Give my regards to Emilia Fyodorovna, Fedenka, Mashenka, and Misha.[10] Have the children forgotten me or not? Give my regards to Reyngart and the others. Does Anna Ivanovna[11] visit you? Regards to all the old friends too.

Yours always,
F. Dostoevsky

My address:
On Vasiliev Island on the 1st line along the Bolshoy Prospect, in Soloshich's Building, No. 26, in Beketov's apartment.

Now, brother, here's what: come to Petersburg this year for Shrovetide. Even if only for two weeks. But definitely come. Room and board won't cost you anything. Nor will tea, sugar, and all your keep. You'll hardly spend any pocket money at all. The whole trip will cost only a trifle. Well? What do you think? Think about it. Why not? I would be so glad to see you. And it would be pleasant for you to live awhile in Petersburg too. You don't even need to take any money with you to come here. I owe you and will pay for everything. We'll get some money. For Heaven's sake, come, brother. You're a stay-at-home. Can you really want to reach the point where you'll have to be extracted from Revel with tongs? Joking aside, come visit at Shrovetide.

Yours,

10. Mikhail Dostoevsky's wife and children.
11. Perhaps a reference to Anna Ivanovna Shtremmer (1830-1911), A. N. Maykov's future wife.

I. I. Panaev

N. A. Nekrasov

Valerian Maykov

D. V. Grigorovich
(Self-portrait)

1847

70. To Alexander Poretsky
January 1847. Petersburg

Dear Alexander Yustinovich,[1]

We have a box, reserved, in the fifth tier on the left side, let[ter] M.
When Shtrandman's[2] note arrived, I was at the Maykovs'; there I was notified of the second one. They jotted down the box and promised to inform you; that is why on my part I didn't let your messenger know.
And will there be bouquets?

Entirely yours,
F. Dostoevsky

NB. Borsi[3] is very ill, in a fever, at the Palace they're having unction or something like that. Therefore the royal family may not be at the theater. And if they aren't, it seems that the administration has taken measures to postpone the performance. Read the theater bill tomorrow.
Good-bye.

D.

1. Alexander Yustinovich Poretsky (1818-79), minor writer who in later life collaborated with Dostoevsky on the journals *Time* and *Epoch*.
2. Roman Romanovich Shtrandman (1822-69), friend of Valerian Maykov's and member of the Petrashevsky Circle.
3. Giulia Borsi (1817-77), Italian soprano.

71. To Mikhail Dostoevsky
January-February 1847. Petersburg

Dear brother,

Again I beg your absolution for my not keeping my word and not writing you with the next mail. But such a depression settled on me this whole time that it was impossible to write. I thought of you a great deal and agonizingly. Your fate is a hard one, dear brother! With your health, with your thoughts, without people around, with depression, instead of a holiday mood, and with a family about which, although it's a sacred and sweet worry, the burden is still heavy—life is unbearable. But don't lose heart, brother. The time will brighten up. You see, the more spirit and inner content we have in ourselves, the better is our corner in life. Of course, the dissonance and disequilibrium that society present to us are terrible. *The external* must be balanced with *the internal.*[1] Otherwise, with the absence of external phenomena, the internal will gain too dangerous an influence. Nerves and fantasy will occupy too much space in a being. Any external phenomenon, for want of habit, seems colossal and frightens one somehow. You begin to be afraid of life. You're fortunate that nature has provided you abundantly with love and a strong character. In addition, you have. strong common sense and flashes of brilliant humor and merriness. All of that saves you too. I think about you a lot. But Lord, how many disgusting, vilely-limited, gray-bearded wisemen, authorities, Pharisees of life there are who *pride themselves* on their experience, that is, their lack of individuality (because they're all cut from the same cloth), useless people who eternally preach contentment with fate, belief in something, limitation in life and satisfaction with one's place, without penetrating the essence of those words—a contentment resembling monastic torture and limitation, and with the inexhaustibly petty malice of those who condemn the strong, ardent soul of one who cannot bear their banal daily schedule and calendar of life. They're scoundrels with their earthly vaudeville happiness. They're scoundrels! I come across them sometimes and they drive me into a rage.[2]

For instance, just now the unbearable windbag Sviridov[3] interrupted me with his wittily-social visit. He, brother, seems a most importunate fool. He brought me a question from analytical geometry and brought some wretched old odd sheets of paper with which it seems to be impossible

1. The notion of man's need for harmony between the inner and outer links this letter to ideas that inform Dostoevsky's story "The Landlady" (1847).

2. Dostoevsky develops notions similar to these in the story "The Little Hero" (1849).

3. Nikolay Sviridov, acquaintance of Dostoevsky and his brother Mikhail.

to do anything. He wants me to ask Beketov to correct these sheets. A funny person. He doesn't understand anything in them and wants others to do something. I'll do something about your reply. I'll go see everyone who has notes.[4]

But the time is getting away. I wanted to write you a great many things. How irritating that everything has been interrupted. For that reason I'll limit myself to the latest things and write a bit about myself. I'm working, brother: I don't want to publish anything before finishing it. In the meantime I have no money, and were it not for the existence of kind people, I would perish. The degeneration of my renown in the journals is bringing me more profit than loss.[5] All the more quickly will new things be snatched up by my admirers, who seem to be many and who will defend me. I'm living very poorly and since leaving you I have spent only 250 silver rubles, I used up to 300 silver rubles on debts. I was clipped most badly by Nekrasov, to whom I returned his 150 silver rubles because I didn't want to get involved with him. Toward spring I'll get a large loan from Kraevsky and will definitely send you 400 rubles. That's a sacred vow, because the thought of you tortures me more than anything else. I doubt that I'll come to Helsingfors[6] early. Because perhaps I'll try to cure myself completely with Priesznitz's[7] cold water method. And therefore I won't arrive any earlier than July. However, I don't know anything yet, my dear. My future lies ahead. But even if thunder were to crack over me I won't move now, I know everything that I can do, I won't spoil my work, and I'll correct my financial circumstances with the successful sale of a book that I'll publish in the fall.[8] The damned Spiridov. It's already nearly two o'clock. Imagine: I tried with all my might to give him to understand that I have no time. He kept on sitting and chattering about how he composed your question, letting me understand how important help was for you in this matter, how he would travel to the Caucasus and write a work about the flora there such as has never been written. The Devil take him, the fool! Honestly, you talk to some people and it's just as though you had come out of some office. He tore me away from you, my dear. Take care of yourself, brother. Especially your health. Amuse yourself and wish me well in finishing my work quickly. Following that I'll have money right away and will visit you. I have treatment by Priesznitz on the brain. Perhaps the doctors will talk me

4. A reference to Mikhail's preparations for an examination that would lead to a promotion. In the belief that they would be of help to Mikhail, Sviridov had brought the mathematics notes Dostoevsky mentions.

5. In 1846 several journals printed highly unflattering articles about Dostoevsky's early works.

6. The Swedish name for Helsinki. Mikhail Dostoevsky was transferred there in 1847, but Dostoevsky did not go visit his brother there.

7. Vincent Priessnitz (1799-1851), German doctor, one of the founders of hydrotherapy, which became very popular in the late 1830s.

8. Reference to a book edition of *Poor Folk*.

out of it. How I would love to see you. Sometimes I'm tormented by such depression. Sometimes I recall how awkward and difficult I was with you in Revel. I was ill, brother. I remember you once telling me that my treatment of you excluded mutual equality. My dear. That was absolutely unfair. But I have such a vile, repulsive character. I have always valued you higher and better than myself. I'm ready to surrender my life for you and your family, but sometimes when my heart is swimming in love you can't get a tender word from me. My nerves don't obey me at such moments. I'm funny and disgusting, and because of that I constantly suffer from an unfair conclusion about me. People say that I am callous and lack a heart. How many times have I been rude to Emilia Fyodorovna,[9] the most noble of women, 1,000 times better than I. I remember how I sometimes was purposely spiteful to Fedya,[10] whom I loved at the same time even more than you. I can only show that I'm a person with a heart and love when the very exterior of a circumstance, an incident extracts me violently from my usual banality. Until that point I'm disgusting. I attribute that inequality to illness. Have you read *Lucrezia Floriani,* take a look at *Carl.*[11] But soon you'll read *Netochka Nezvanova.* That will be a confession, like *Golyadkin,*[12] although in a different tone and form. I hear on the sly (and from many people) such rumors about Golyadkin that it's simply horrible. Some say right out that the work is a *wonder* and hasn't been understood. What difference if he has a terrible role in the future, what if I had written only Golyadkin, that would be enough from me, and for some it's more interesting than Dumas's sort of interest. Well, now my vanity has come gushing forth. But brother! How nice it is to be understood. Brother, why do you love me so!—I'll try to embrace you soon. We'll love each other passionately. Wish me success. I'm writing my "Landlady." It's already turning out better than *Poor Folk.* It's in the same manner. My pen is being guided by a well of inspiration springing directly from my soul. Not as with "Prokharchin," with which I suffered all summer long. How much I would like to be able to help you soon, brother. But rely, brother, on the money that I've promised you as on a wall, as on a mountain. Kiss your family for me. And for the meanwhile, I am

Yours,
Dostoevsky

Will we sometime get together in Petersburg, brother? What would

---

9. Mikhail Dostoevsky's wife.

10. Fyodor Mikhaylovich Dostoevsky, Mikhail and Emilia Dostoevsky's son.

11. Carl von Roswald is the hero of George Sand's novel *Lucrezia Floriani* (1846). Oblique reflections of him may be seen in the character Ordynov in Dostoevsky's "The Landlady."

12. A reference to *The Double.*

you say about a civilian job with a decent salary?

I don't know whether Mme Belinskaya gave birth to a son or a daughter.[13] I've heard a baby crying two rooms away, but it seems a bit embarrassing and strange to ask.

72. To Mikhail Dostoevsky
April 1847. Petersburg

Dear brother,

I'll write you two lines, because I'm busy. I don't know where my letter will find you. I'll try with all my might to finish up my affairs so that I can visit you for a week even if not until September.[1] As for money, I was a little mistaken in my calculations. I'll have to write perhaps even two feuilletons a week,[2] that is, no more than 250-300 paper rubles. And since I need to pay back the Maykovs,[3] from whom I have borrowed a lot (although they aren't even asking), and for the apartment, I don't even know how much I'll be sending you; but I'll be sending something. I'm in such a state, brother, that if by October 1st I repay you only 100 silver rubles, I'll consider myself a most fortunate person. But from the 1st of October on or September[4] things will change. I'll take an advance of 1000 silver rubles from Kraevsky after finishing my novel and on no condition other than for *an indefinite period.* Since *The Contemporary* is making a go of it and fiercely luring contributors away from *Notes of the Father[land]*, he, *Andr[ey] Alexan[drovich] Kraev[sky]*, is very frightened. He'll agree to anything. Moreover, it's his good fortune and *mine* that my novel is being published at the end of the year.[5] It will crown the year, appear during the subscription period, and most importantly, it will be, if I'm not mistaken now, the capital thing of the year and will get the better of my friends "the Contemporaries," who are absolutely trying to bury me. But to hell with them. Then after receiving 1000 silver rubles, I'll

---

13. Mme Belinsky had given birth to a son, Vladimir, who lived only a very short time.

1. Dostoevsky did not go to visit his brother Mikhail in the summer of 1847. Instead, Mikhail went to Petersburg.

2. Dostoevsky surely means two feuilletons a month, not a week.

3. Apollon Nikolaevich Maykov (1821-97), minor poet whom Dostoevsky admired throughout his life, and his brother Valerian. The reference may also be to the Maykov brothers' parents, Nikolay Apollonovich Maykov (1794-1873) and his wife Evgenia Petrovna (1803-80).

4. I'll come to visit you then, on the last ships. *Dostoevsky's own note.*

5. The reference is probably to *Netochka Nezvanova.*

come to see you with the money and with the final decision regarding you. You can come to Petersburg even alone, taking a leave of 28 days, find a position and—or continue service in the engineers, or leave it forever.

My address:

On the corner of Malaya Morskaya Street and Voznesensky Prospect, in Shil's building, in Bremmer's apartment, ask for F. Dostoevsky.

I don't know about a translation, I'll work all summer and try to find one. We had in Petersburg (he's abroad now), a fool, Furmann,[6] he receives up to 20,000 a year just on translations! If you had even only so much as a year of financial security, you could definitely make a go of it. You're young; you could even make a lit[erary] career. Nowadays everyone is making one. In ten years or so you could even forget about translations.

I'm writing very zealously, perhaps I'll finish. Then we'll see each other earlier. What does Emilia Fyodorovna[7] have to say? I send her my most humble regards, the children as well. Good-bye, brother. I have a slight fever. I caught cold yesterday by going out at night without a frock coat in just an overcoat, and it was sleeting along the Neva. It's as cold here as in November. But I've already caught cold up to six times—it's nothing! All in all, my health has much improved.

Good-bye, brother. Wish me success. After the novel I'll get down to printing my 3 novels (*Poor Folk, The Double,* redone and the last one) at my own expense,[8] and then perhaps my fate will clear up.

God grant you happiness, my dear.

Yours,
F. Dostoevsky

You won't believe it. For the third year of my literary activity it's as though I'm in a daze. I don't see any life, there's no time to come to my senses; study disappears for lack of time. I want to establish myself. They've created a dubious renown for me, and I don't know how long this hell will continue. Poverty, rush work—if only there were some peace!

My most humble regards to Nikolay Ivanovich Reyngardt, to the Bergmans.

6. Pyotr Romanovoch Furman (1809-56), translator.
7. Mikhail Dostoevsky's wife.
8. See Letter 67, notes 5 and 6.

73. To Albert Starchevsky[1]
April-May 1847. Petersburg

I sat for five hours without a break over the form that is being sent to you. The article about the Jesuits[2] ought to be entirely rewritten. The difficulty and slowness lie in the fact that one has *to repair* things and not completely redo them; and for that you need to observe the printer's interests and not rub everything out. To do corrections, and not even elegant corrections, you sit a quarter of an hour over two little lines. The little tickets you can strike out as you please.

I'll bring you the other 2 forms myself, I'm working on them now without a break, I have only 10 forms left. To do 3 forms I have to sit over them 12 hours a day.

F. Dostoevsky

74. To Albert Starchevsky
April-June 1847. Petersburg

Dear Albert Vikentievich,

Not even once was I told about your messenger, and I was anxiously waiting for him myself. I'm sending you your sheets; they haven't been looked through. I'm unwell, with rushes of blood to the head, and on doctor's orders absolutely cannot work. When I'm capable of working, I'll start. If there won't be any work for me, I'll return the advance as soon as the *Dictionary*[1] comes out. With that I remain

Yours,
F. Dostoevsky

1. Albert Vikentievich Starchevsky (1818-1901), journalist, critic, and publisher.

2. Apparently Dostoevsky was editing the proofs of an article on Jesuits for the fifth volume of the *Reference Encyclopedia Dictionary* (1847), published by Kray and edited by Starchevsky.

1. See Letter 73, note 2.

75. To Nikolay Nekrasov
End of August-Beginning of September 1847. Petersburg

Dear Nikolay Alexeevich:

Of course the conditions that you were pleased to offer me at our last meeting at Maykov's are quite advantageous. But at the present moment I am in such a difficult position that the money promised by you will not bring me any benefit at all, and will only extend my desperation for no good purpose. You may be partly aware of my circumstances.

I need 150 silver rubles in order to get on my feet at least a bit. And therefore, Nikolay Alexeevich, if you do not wish to give me that money in a lump sum, then to my greatest regret, it will be impossible for me to deliver my story to you. Because I will not have the material means for writing it.[1]

If, however, you agree to give me such a sum in advance,[2] then—

in the 1st place, the date by which you will receive the story will be January 1, 1848, no earlier. You probably would prefer for me to say *for certain,* not about. Therefore, *for certain, by January 1, 1848.*

and in the 2nd place, I will ask you to pay out the money to me in the following manner: 100 silver rubles on October 2, 1847, and 50 silver rubles right now, that is, with *my* messenger.

Pardon me, Nikolay Alexeevich, for negotiating with you via a letter instead of personally, as would be more convenient for us. I kept planning to come to see you after I had completed my current work.[3] But now, at the present moment, I am in such a disgusting position that I decided to begin the business now, about which I am writing you frankly.

I cannot leave the house, because I caught a cold this morning and now it seems that I'll have to stay home for about four days.

Y[ours,]
D

P.S. *In any event,* I ask you most humbly to send an answer with my messenger, because afterwards I won't need him.

---

1. Dostoevsky is referring to a story promised for Nekrasov's planned *Illustrated Almanac,* but it is unclear precisely what story Dostoevsky has in mind.

2. Since at the time of his arrest Dostoevsky owed Nekrasov 165 silver rubles, it seems likely that Nekrasov agreed to the request for 150 silver rubles contained in the present letter.

3. Dostoevsky is probably referring to "The Landlady."

76. To Mikhail Dostoevsky
9 September 1847. Petersburg

9 September 1847

I hasten to reply to your letter, brother. Well, do as you wish with your family, as you yourself consider best, but you, in regard to yourself, don't change your disposition for anything.[1] You're afraid that they won't grant you an extension; but can't you take a leave for 2 or 3 months? And if you can't, then consult the district commander and simply ask him to see that there be no delay with the extension. After all, that's if they want to squeeze you; but I don't think they'll squeeze someone who's retiring. But come anyway. You write that you'll arrive by October 1st; but in that case you won't apply for leave until September 2nd, cons[equently], its final date will be in 1/2 of November, but your retirement may be issued in the middle of November.

You say that people are shaking their heads; and I say to you— don't be upset by that. You write that I've made a slow start too. But after all, that's only right now; wait a bit, brother, things will improve. And we have an association.[2] It's impossible that we should both fail to make our way out onto the road; nonsense! Just remember what sort of people are shaking their heads! What you're getting now you'll always get in Petersburg, but not at the cost of such hard work. I'll stay in my apartment and wait for you. I'm not well now and am finishing a story so that it can be printed in October.[3] And therefore I'm hurrying.

You don't say on what date you're leaving for Revel. But it doesn't make any difference; my letter may reach you on the eve of your departure. How will you arrange things for your family there? 125 silver rubles is not much money. I'll write to the Muscovites,[4] but you write, too, from Helsingfors,[5] and tell them to send the money to my address. It's clear that Karepin is a son of a bitch and a scoundrel of the first degree.

Come soon, brother. In a fit of terrible need I can get some money. But do you know how much I need myself? At least 300 silver rubles by October 1. Out of that sum 200 rubles will be used for debts and 100 will be spent on me personally, and all of that is only if there is any money. Just in case, I'll write down for you everything that I can realize by the first days of October

1. Mikhail Dostoevsky planned to retire from government service and move to St. Petersburg. His retirement became official in May 1847.

2. A reference to Dostoevsky's communal living and eating arrangements. At the time, the word "association" generally served as a code word for "socialism."

3. Dostoevsky is referring to "The Landlady."

4. The reference is to P. A. Karepin.

5. Swedish name for Helsinki.

if some extreme need should present itself.

From Kraevsky 50 silver rubles		50 silver rubles
From Nekrasov 100 silver rubles		100 silver rubles
At a certain place 50 silver rubles		50 silver rubles
And selling the right to a		
printing of *Poor Folk* 200 silver rubles		200 silver rubles
		400 silver rubles

That sum is good, but it will ruin me, taking into consideration the sale of *Poor Folk*. I have no time to publish *Poor Folk*. But through a certain printer I hope to print it without money. If you turned up here, you would take care of this and then all winter we would keep getting money.— You won't be making a mistake if you come as soon as possible. I'll tell you that perhaps there's hope that if you're in town you'll have the work that I wrote you about the last time. In addition, there's a certain publication towards the New Year, a colossal one, started with huge capital, in which you'll be able to furnish a lot of translation-compilation work. In addition, you can get translations from Kraevsky or from Nekrasov, with whom I'll enter into a definite arrangement, which he wants awfully much. In addition, there is yet another publication toward the New Year, and still *another one*. And all of them will be brought to fruition.[6]

It's too bad that you didn't finish translating Schiller's plays. If you had them all, they could be sold.[7] Gather together everything that you have. A few days ago, when I told Kraevsky that you could translate a book for the Geographic Society (in the last letter), and that you knew German and had translated all of Schiller, Kraevsky suddenly asked rashly: "And where is his translation?" And then he suddenly fell silent, thinking the better of it. Even if not in *Notes of the Fatherland,* Kraevsky could facilitate its acquisition.

Well, good-bye, my dear. I didn't write much of what I wanted to, honest to God, there's no time.

Your F. Dostoevsky

Regards to Emilia Fyodorovna.[8] Kiss the children.

---

6. In 1848 three large new journals were launched: *The Geographic News of the Russian Geographic Society, The Northern Survey,* and *The Naval Miscellany*. Kraevsky was an influential member of the Geographic Society, and Dostoevsky obviously counted on his connections and help.

7. See Letter 48.

8. Mikhail Dostoevsky's wife.

Do you see what an association means? If we work apart we'll fall down, become timid, and lose heart. But two people together for a single goal— that's another matter. There you have a hearty person, boldness, love, and twice as much energy.

Write me about everything in as much detail as possible. Write me about figures (money, time, and so on) carefully and precisely.

1848

77. To Yevgenia Maykova[1]
14 May 1848. Petersburg

Dear Yevgenia Petrovna,

I hasten to apologize to you; I sense that I left you yesterday in such a rush that it turned out indecent, without even paying my respects to you and not remembering that until after you called to me. I'm afraid that you may think me gruff and (I agree) rude, with some sort of strange intention. But I ran away on instinct, having a premonition of the weakness of my nature, which can't help bursting forth in extreme cases and bursting forth precisely in excesses, *hyperbolically*. You'll understand me: because of my weak-nerved nature it's difficult for me to endure and answer ambiguous questions that are posed to me, not to become enraged precisely because those questions are ambiguous, to become enraged most of all at myself for not having known how to do things to make those questions direct and not so intolerant; and finally, at the same time, it's difficult for me (I admit this) to maintain my composure when I see before myself a majority which, as I recall, acted against me with precisely the same intolerance with which I acted against it. It goes without saying that the result was a row—hyperbole, conscious and unconscious, flew from both sides, and I instinctively took to my feet, for fear that these hyperboles might acquire even greater dimensions . . .[2] But judge about all the weakness of the nature of a person such as I!— I took pen in hand in order to apologize simply and with all humility, and meanwhile I've begun writing my justification in all due form! . . But really sensing that I was gruff, difficult, and irritating to you, I fall back on your tolerance and beg your pardon. I am certain that you will understand all my importuneness with my apologies: I value your good opinion too much, therefore I am afraid of losing it. Perhaps this letter is superfluous, perhaps I'm exaggerating, as is my habit, perhaps you forgave me from the very first moment and did not blame me; but this unwarranted fear, this timidty about myself before you will show you, if

---

1. Yevgenia Petrovna Maykova (1803-80), mother of A. N. and V. N. Maykov. A writer herself, Yevgenia Petrovna and Dostoevsky got along particularly well in the late 1840s.
2. Presumably Dostoevsky is referring to a scene with someone representing the journal *The Contemporary*, perhaps Nekrasov.

you will allow me to say it, all the extent of that filial respect that I have always felt for you—

Your entirely devoted
F. Dostoevsky

78. To an Unknown Addressee
3 June 1848. Pargolovo

Dear Sir,

Not until *today* did I receive your letter in which you express the desire to have *my autograph*. This happened in the following way.

When it arrived in Pargolovo, I was in Petersburg. My servant received the letter, put it on my table and forgot about it, but forgot about it so well that I found it only by accident today under some books.

I hasten to fulfill your wish and am sending you immediately a page from a story of mine that has not yet been published anywhere.

With absolute respect I have the honor of remaining your humble servant

F. Dostoevsky

48. June 3

The first page of Dostoevsky's letter, written in the Peter-and-Paul Fortress on 22 December 1849, to his brother Mikhail.

1849

79. To Andrey Kraevsky
1 February 1849. Petersburg

Dear Andrey Alexandrovich,

A misunderstanding has arisen between us, and besides that, I am
perplexed myself from another, private vantage point that more concerns
me. Both these misunderstandings need to be cleared up quickly and soon,
otherwise it's impossible to get anything done. Judge for yourself.

In the first place: Two years ago I had the misfortune of borrowing a
large sum of money from you. That sum, instead of diminishing, has grown
to impossible proportions. Since before anything else I want to square
accounts and pay you, I've found it essential to propose decisive measures.
But first of all it is necessary to seek out the reason why this sum has not
diminished, but increased. I have long since figured it out and it turns out
that it is for the following reasons:

(1) Because I had to write and not receive anything *regularly*. That is,
although I did receive money *from time to time,* it was from time to time;
but since you have to pay for your life monthly, I should have been
receiving money not from time to time, but regularly, for instance, at least
a half for the value of things already written, and a half would have gone on
account. That happened, of course, but again *not regularly*.

(2) Because in order to keep my word and deliver on time, I pushed
myself, wrote, by the way, such bad things or (in the singular)—such a bad
thing as "The Landlady," as a result of which I gave way to bewilderment
and self-deprecation and for a long time afterward could not get down to
writing anything serious and decent.[1] Every failure of mine has produced
an illness in me.

(3) The illness which formally hindered me, which continued for a year
and which ended, as you know, with an inflammation of the brain.

(4) A purely psychological reason, which made me hate urgent work
that did not even bring me my daily bread, and finally, the slavery in which
I found myself, of course, of my own free will. That is an important reason.
Whether out of self-deprecation or I don't know from what sort of false

---

1. Dostoevsky enjoyed writing "The Landlady" and counted on the work's success, but
he changed his attitude toward the piece as a result of published negative criticism.

delicacy I considered that in lending me money, you were doing me a favor, when in fact it was purely a matter of *one good turn for another.* The first money I received from you couldn't be considered a loan to me. We were very little acquainted with each other. I think I couldn't have done anything to acquire your good favor, so that you could, as you told me last time yourself, *take a risk* and give me, as I recall, 400 silver rubles. Finally, one more consideration: I wouldn't even have taken it gratis. Cons[equently], this was not a loan; and if you do say that it's a *loan* (since you told me that the last time)— then allow me, too, to say that money is not given gratis, that you gave it to me in the hope of a service, that is, my work, which was also worth something.

I know, Andrey Alexandrovich, that I, meanwhile, in several times sending you notes with a request for money called each fulfillment of my request a *loan.* But I was in frenzies of unwarranted self-deprecation and humility as a result of false delicacy. I, for instance, understand Butkov,[2] who is ready, after receiving 10 silver rubles, to consider himself the most fortunate person in the world. That is a momentary, morbid state, and I have come out of it.

Proof that I was in frenzies of unwarranted delicacy is the following:

(1) In order to repay you for the loan I, in spite of my illness, wrote a bad story and risked my signature, which for me is my only capital.[3]

That I did not polish my works sufficiently and wrote for a deadline, that is, I sinned against art.

That I did not spare my health and made attempts worthy of a martyr to square accounts.

That I rejected an offer by Nekrasov, who was willing to give me 75 silver rubles for your signature sheet, with the offer to repay you immediately the entire debt in cash.

And so on, and so on, in a word, there were a great many feats, that is, I acted very honestly.

But in spite of all this, since the 1st of January of last year my works have been receiving steadily greater and greater praise from the public. That is so and I know it. That is, what was going on here and why have they, in spite of my fall in 47, in spite of Belinsky's *authoritative attacks,*[4] and so on, begun to be read and find an audience? The answer: that this means there is sufficient talent in me that I have been able to overcome indigence, slavery, illness, the heat of criticism that was solemnly burying me, and the public's prejudice. Cons[equently], if I really do have talent, I need to tackle it seriously, not risk it, polish my works, and not enrage my

2. Yakov Petrovich Butkov (1820?-57), minor writer occasionally remembered for his *Attics of Petersburg* (1844-45), a sentimental depiction of the lives of poor government clerks.

3. Dostoevsky is referring to his story "A Weak Heart" (1848).

4. In speaking of his "fall," Dostoevsky is referring to negative reviews of "The Landlady," including one by Belinsky.

own conscience against me and torment myself with repentance, and finally, spare my name, that is, the only capital that I have.

Finally:

I know very well, Andrey Alexandrovich, that the first part of *Netochka Nezvanova,* which I published in January, is a good work, so good that *Notes of the Fatherland,* of course, *can find a place for it in its pages without shame.* I know that it is a serious work. Finally, it is not me saying that, but everyone.

I don't want to spoil it:

And therefore, taking into consideration our recent argument, I have made up my mind to propose to you the following, if you want to follow my suggestion, everything will be very good. If not, then as you please. But I am acting as will be most advantageous for me. I am acting, finally, as a consequence of need and fully realizing that my proposal is moderate and modest in the highest degree.

Here's the point:

We have an agreement according to which I receive 50 silver rubles every month—a good agreement, since the debt has suddenly begun to diminish very quickly since the contract came into existence. It was established on the basis that I firmly and absolutely wanted to repay you the debt quickly.

I took the *minimum* for existence, that is, 50 silver rubles. On that money you can live with want—but you cannot at all deal with creditors and needs, you cannot at all insure yourself against *unforeseen surprises.* In a word, it is only a *minimum.*

On the other hand:

Since I'm now writing (and take this into consideration) not simply in order to drag out my existence, that is, not just for money.

(2) Not so that *Notes of the Fatherland* will have large type in its literature section every month.[5]

(3) In a word, not just to write something for the repayment of a debt.

But because:

(1) I like my novel, (2) because I know that I'm writing a good thing, so good that it will not bring any *risk* but, rather, the goodwill of the readers (I never boast, allow me now to tell the truth, I have been provoked to do that), (3) because, finally, it's sinful for me to spoil my work and because it's dearer to me than even *Notes of the Fatherland.*

I, finding myself in the following circumstances:

(1) Being pressed by an unforeseen expense.

(2) Placed in a difficult position by our last calculation.

(3) In order to have a certain sum of money right now, having to begin writing a story precisely two signature sheets in length for *The St.*

---

5. The literature section of *Notes of the Fatherland* was printed in larger type than was the rest of the journal.

Petersburg News, The Library for Reading, or *The Contemporary.*

(4) Since in connection with this, forced to distract myself from my novel with work on the side, I cannot polish it properly (but I am polishing it; proof is the fact that I have thrown out of the 2nd part an entire 1 1/2 signature sheet of things that were not at all bad, for the shape of the thing, that is, I am scratching out and cutting rather than writing all over the place, which is what a person who did not value his work would do).

(5) Since I cannot have fewer than 5 signature sheets in the 3rd part (that is, I can't have *2* or *3*, but an entire *5* for the full effect).— And taking into consideration that I now need to set to work on an extraneous piece and write 2 signature sheets in order to get money— and that I can't write 7 signature sheets by the 15th, I have made up my mind, that is, *I have been forced by necessity,* to make you the following proposal.

(1) Considering that for me not to violate our contract (about the 50 rubles) precisely because that is irregular, and to exert myself in labor that would kill an elephant is impermissible and even indecent,

(2) that if I'm to write a good thing, then I need to write it,

(3) that if I'm to pay back money, I need to pay it,

(4) that not for anything will I agree to spoil my novel and won't take 1000 silver rubles per signature for it,

(5) not for anything will I agree to break it up and not print it on 5 signature sheets (which is necessary for the full effect),

(6) that there's no way that I can publish other than every month, at least the first six parts.

I propose to dissolve the contract for our common good in the following way:

I have written a novel worth 315 silver rubles, I have received 100 silver rubles on account,

I have paid you

215 silver rubles on the debt.

But since I need 100 silver rubles (minimum) *immediately,* I request that you pay that to me. In exchange for that

by the 15th of the month you will receive 5 signature sheets,

that is, the equivalent of 250 silver rubles,

that is, subtracting the 100 taken now, 150 silver rubles will be paid off on the debt, and therefore, by the 20th of February (after clearing the censorship), 365 rubles will be paid off.

I, on my part:

feeling that for me to borrow money from you (1) is disadvantageous, (2) after our last conversation is indecent, (3) that the bad and disadvantageous relations between us can end only when the debt is repaid,

(4) that the debt will not be repaid if sensible measures are not taken on both sides,

(5) that more than anything else I desire the repayment, and not the borrowing of money, and in taking 100 rubles now, that is, seemingly diminishing your benefit, by the 15th will increase it practically threefold,

that is, by at least 250 silver rubles, and that that is a sensible measure,

(6) that only such a calculation moves me to make you such a proposal now, after our recent conversations,—

I pledge *seriously*

not to take any money for the 3rd and 4th parts, that is, in February and March.

The guarantee for this promise:

(1) my word of honor,

(2) the desire to finish the novel, which is dearer to me than anything else, and to deliver myself from literary slavery, which is worse than anything else for me,

(3) that having an entire month before me, I can find the time for an outside story and earn 50 rubles for March without appealing to you.

In conclusion, I ask you:

to note that (1) I am speaking and acting seriously, (2) that most of all I desire to remain on good terms with *The Notes of the Fatherland*, (3) that I understand my position, (4) that I like my novel and will not spoil it, (5) that I can earn not 50, but 100 rubles a month, and in addition have *Netochka* ready by the fall, publish it, and return your money to you, (6) that, finally, I am so poor that I am forced by necessity to do what is most advantageous for me. With that I have the honor of remaining your

F. Dostoevsky

1st of February

P.S. I will have the honor of coming to see you for your reply tomorrow.

80. To Andrey Dostoevsky
20 February 1849. Petersburg

Dear Andrey Mikhaylovich,

Your note found me with 2 silver kopecks to my name and in the same situation as you. But meanwhile I would terribly like to help you, the more so as I am tormented to death by pangs of conscience in regard to my debt. Well, what am I to do? I'll try to drop by to see you at the beginning of the week. Whatever I get, I'll share with you. And now, my dear, good-bye.

And don't drink coffee, and don't eat meat either or anything at all that arouses and works on the blood strongly. Please!

Entirely yours,
F. Dostoevsky

81. To Andrey Kraevsky
25-26 March 1849. Petersburg

Dear Andrey Alexandrovich,

I'm sending you the end of the 1st chapter.[1] In all there will be, as in the 2nd part as well, two large ones. I'll deliver the 1st half of the second chapter (which is now being copied here at my place) to the print shop today at 8 PM. And I'll try to get the other half in order overnight. In that way the matter will be done.

Andrey Alexandrovich, I, in trying to make ends meet for the 2 1/2 months since the last receipt of money from you, have been exhausting myself completely. Exclusively for the support of my momentary need, sweeping aside any notion of asking anything more of you before the established date, I am appealing to you with the most humble request not to deny me 10 silver rubles, which I needed in fact yesterday for payment to my landlady. Because the date of my moving to the apartment was yesterday, and I hadn't paid for two months. The ten rubles will satisfy her at least for the moment, and in so doing will provide me with the necessary peace, light, and provisions without which it is impossible to write anything in the world.

For Heaven's sake, please do not deny this request, Andrey Alexandrovich. Your humble servant

F. Dostoevsky

1. The reference is to *Netochka Nezvanova*.

82. To Andrey Kraevsky
31 March 1849. Petersburg

Dear Andrey Alexandrovich,

In your last letter you mentioned that you were sending me money for the last time and that I needed to work everything off in order to have the right to receive anything.

That's precisely the sort of arrangement I wanted to make. That is, first to deliver the 3rd part,[1] which I presumed I would finish by Monday. After that to set immediately to work on the 4th and fifth parts, which I scheduled for May. But above and beyond all my calculations, I finished the 3rd part by Wednesday (it turned out to be 3 signature sheets and a bit), in the 4th there will be about 4, $3 + 4 = 7$, that is, 350 silver rubles, and 100 have already been worked off, cons[equently] from 450 to 500 silver rubles. With the 4th part I am counting on the rapid working off of the debt (because you surely will admit, Andrey Alexandrovich, that to repay 500 rubles on a debt of 800 in a few months, and in addition to that to live, is a decent accomplishment), I planned to report to you with the third part in hand at the end of this week and ask you for assistance before the holiday,[2] by the 10th I wanted to deliver the 5th part.

I'm now working without pause on the 4th part, in spite of the fact that I just finished the 3rd, I'm not allowing myself a scrap of rest; because I definitely want (basing myself on your promise in Shidlovsky's presence[3]) to publish the 2 parts in May (that is, the 4th and 5th ones). Even now I'm tearing my hair out over the fact that the episode hasn't been presented in its entirety, but split up into 3 parts. Nothing has been finished, only curiosity has been aroused. But curiosity aroused at the beginning of the month, in my opinion, is not the same thing as at the end of the month; it cools down, and even the best works lose. It's the same thing as though I had divided the scene with Pokrovsky, the best one in *Poor Folk*, into 2 parts and had tormented the public for a month. Where is the impression? It will disappear. And so here is in regard to the two parts. I'm working on the 4th part. And I'll deliver the 4th and 5th on time, no later than by the 15th; because in addition, we need to deliver a response to *The Contemporary*.[4] But in connection with the work consider the following:

1. Reference to the novel *Netochka Nezvvanova*.
2. Easter.
3. Probably a reference to Yury Shidlovsky, the censor responsible for *Notes of the Fatherland*.
4. Dostoevsky is probably referring to an article in the first issue of *The Contemporary* for 1849, Pavel Annenkov's "Notes on Russian Literature Last Year," which criticized the young writers associated with *Notes of the Fatherland*, of whom Dostoevsky was the most notable.

(1) that if I didn't take any money now, by May I would have worked off 650 silver rubles. And if in this interval I received 100 rubles from you, then it would be only 550—the balance for the whole winter of what I had worked off and the remaining debt would be 250 rubles,

(2) that I would long since have worked everything off, not just that sum, if I hadn't worked on the side.

Andrey Alexandrovich, tell me, please, can it really be that in the 4 years of my work for you you haven't noticed that I will never be able to repay you my debt if we keep on with this system of taking money in advance and working it off in which we have been up until now? Why, judge for yourself: just take the present winter! I have worked like a horse and the harder the better, so that the public likes what I'm doing, and in spite of all my calculations last fall, I cannot work off more than 650 silver rubles by May. I'll still be in debt. How has this happened? Isn't it really quite clear how, Andrey Alexandrovich! And meanwhile I borrowed money from you. I borrowed a lot. But here's a fact for you: after borrowing from you 100 the last time (2 months ago), I spent an entire month thinking up a story that would earn me another 50 silver rubles, because I was short your 100, in order to be at ease. And since while thinking up the story I kept in mind the tendency and character of the publication where I wanted to get it printed, I thought for an entire month and didn't come up with anything other than a migraine and unstrung nerves, plus 3 marvelous subjects for three large novels. If I had had the 50 silver rubles, you would have received 150 silver rubles extra in repayment.

In borrowing 100 rubles from you the last time, I swore that I would never again take an advance from you. But I was reckoning without the manager from Moscow.[5] They'll send some money after the holiday. But meanwhile there is *the Holiday*—what a word! I don't care in the least, but the creditors can hardly wait to besiege people in hordes, because those unfortunates only have 2 dates in the year on which almost everyone pays up.

Listen, Andrey Alexandrovich. Can it really be that it has never occurred to you that I lived, lived, and died. What will happen to my debt then? I have so many debts that not even the Moscow money would be sufficient for paying off yours. Let's finish with this system of indebtedness quickly and enter into peaceable payment for work completed by inviolable deadlines at the first of each month. To my greatest regret, if I worked until I had calluses on my hands, it is physically impossible for me to bring you the 4th part by Saturday, but I'll bring it by the 7th. But in the meantime it will be impossible for me to write. I've been tortured to death, because 7 years of dealing with creditors have made me irritable, and I'll leap at outside work, that is, I will be forced to write a fairy tale of some

---

5. Reference to P. A. Karepin, the executor of Dostoevsky's estate.

sort on the side. The most lamentable thing here is that the energy for our novel[6] and the desire to continue it will be interrupted by work on the side again for half a month, and perhaps even for a month.

Andrey Alexandrovich, I will report to you Saturday morning. For Heaven's sake, please see me out with the hundred rubles borrowed from you. I will return it to you, I won't say a hundred times over, but 5 times over, by the 15th of April. And I'll never borrow from you again, and the witness to that is my brother.[7] Ask him: the Moscow money will definitely arrive in April, and then I *naturally* will not ask you for any, but I won't forget your helping me for this last time. *Remind me of that some time.* You'll see for yourself. Judge for yourself: during all of Lent I have been awaiting Easter Sunday with fear and trepidation because of creditors. Remember *Good Friday* of last year. I remember it even now. My brother's family came from Revel then, too. Now I'll just have a hellish time and nothing else. Where's the poetry in all this?

Your F. Dostoe

31 March

83. To Andrey Kraevsky
First Half of April 1849. Petersburg

Dear Andrey Alexandrovich,

We have an agreement according to which I receive 50 silver rubles for each month that I publish, or rather, for each part. Last time the agreement was altered somewhat: I took an advance of 100 silver rubles for 2 parts, namely, for the 3rd and 4th ones.[1] The 3rd has been delivered, the 4th not yet. If I had been delivering the parts uninterruptedly, that is, if they had been in March and April, then at the end of April, that is, after the May issue had passed the censorship, I would have received the 50 silves rubles. That is, that would be for the 5th part.

In the present month, that is, for the May issue, according to the agreement, to your promise, 2 parts are included: the 3rd and 4th (which I will deliver by the 15th). Cons[equently], at the end of May I'll receive 50

---

6. A reference to *Netochka Nezvanova*.
7. Mikhail Dostoevsky.
1. Reference to the novel *Netochka Nezvanova*.

silver rubles for the June issue.

But here's what: you will have the 4th part by the 15th. Andrey Alexandrovich, judge for yourself: the 100 rubles taken as an advance have been earned, we're on our former basis. I'm not asking you for an advance now, but here's what I'm asking for: give me 15 silver rubles for the 5th part; it will now go without interruption. I borrowed 10 before the holiday, and so it will turn out that together with this 15 I'll take 25 silver ruble for the 5th part and in May I'll receive, cons[equently], not 50, but 25. I ask you most earnestly to do this for me. The present time is urgent. I'm fighting with my petty creditors like Laocoön with the snakes; I need 15 now, just 15. That 15 will pacify me. I'll have more readiness and desire to write, you may be certain. What's 15 rubles to you? But for me that will be a lot. Have mercy on me, I've been without a cent the whole week long, if only I had something! If you only knew to what I have been reduced! Only it's embarrassing to write about it, and besides, it's unnecessary. After all, it's simply shameful, Andrey Alexandrovich, that *Notes of the Father[land]* has such poor contributors. Well, I've borrowed a lot, too: of course, that's bad! But after all, there is repayment, and there is work! After all, there seems to be, Andrey Alexandrovich.

For Heaven's sake, Andrey Alexandrovich, send me the galley sheets for the 3rd part. I need them terribly badly!

Entirely yours,
F. Dostoevsky

84. To Andrey Dostoevsky
20 June 1849. Petersburg, Peter-Paul Fortress[1]

20 June 49

My dear brother Andrey Mikhaylovich,

I have been allowed, in accordance with my request, to write you a few lines, and I hasten to inform you that I, thank God, am healthy and

1. Early on the morning of April 23, 1849, Dostoevsky was arrested for his participation in the Petrashevsky Circle and a satellite group, the Palm-Durov Circle. The groups, composed of officers and literati, met to discuss radical politics and social philosophy. Several members were revolutionaries, and there is evidence that Dostoevsky himself was flirting with the idea of revolutionary terrorism during the last few months before his arrest. At the time of the present letter Dostoevsky was incarcerated in the Peter-Paul Fortress awaiting trial and sentencing. For more about Dostoevsky and the Petrashevsky and Palm-

although I'm sad, I'm far from despondency. Every condition has its consolations. And therefore don't worry about me. Please let me know about our brother's family—how are Emilia Fyodorovna and the children?[2] Kiss them for me.

I have a request to make of you: all this time I've been suffering an extreme need of money and great deprivations. You probably didn't know that you could give me any help and therefore have been silent until now. Don't forget me now. I ask you, if our Moscow financial business has not been settled,[3] to write to Moscow and ask Karepin to send me immediately, out of the sum that is rightfully mine, *twenty-five silver rubles.* I don't need any more that that for the time being.

If the business has been settled, however, then have him send everything that I have coming to me. But I assume that I have already received something, and according to my calculations, the matter should be drawing to a close. Don't forget our brother's family either and write to Moscow for him.

But in expectation of the Moscow money, if you can, send me 10 silver rubles. I've borrowed that amount here; I need to repay it. I'll be greatly obliged to you for that. Do it. Write our sisters and give them my regards, tell them that I'm all right, fine, and don't frighten them. Give my regards to Uncle and especially to Auntie.[4] Take care not to forget about her.

One more request. I don't know whether it's possible, that is, whether they'll allow one to do it, but as far as I can guess, it's possible. Namely: our brother Mikhail has a ticket entitling him to *Notes of the Fatherland.* The May issue for this year must not have been picked up yet. Ask Emilia Fyodorovna for the ticket, pick the issue up for me, and send it to me. The third part of my novel[5] was printed there, but without me, without my supervision, so that I didn't even see the proofs. I'm worried about what they printed there and whether they didn't mutilate my novel.[6] So send the volume to me.[7] Address it to: the Office of His Excellency the Commandant of the St. Petersburg Peter-Paul Fortress or, better, come in person.

Durov Circles, see Joseph Frank, *Dostoevsky: The Seeds of Revolt, 1821-1849* (1976), pp. 239-91, and Liza Knapp, *Dostoevsky as a Reformer: The Petrashevsky Case* (1987).

2. Mikhail Dostoevsky's family. Mikhail, too, had been arrested in connection with the activities of the Petrashevsky Circle and was incarcerated at the Peter-Paul Fortress.

3. Reference to the proposed sale of the family estate (the hamlet Darovoye and the village Cheryomoshnya) to either the Karepins or the Ivanovs, i.e., to Dostoevsky's married sisters. The estate in fact passed to the Karepins, but not until 1852.

4. The Kumanins.

5. *Netochka Nezvanova.*

6. The Third Department (secret police) allowed the publication of the third part of *Netochka Nezvanova* after Dostoevsky's arrest, but on the condition that it be published without any indication of the author's identity.

7. Upon his release from the Peter-Paul Fortress, Mikhail Dostoevsky carried out the requests contained in the present letter.

I'm sure you were glad when they released you after the erroneous arrest.[8] Good-bye, I wish you all the best. Wish me the same.

Your brother Fyodor Dostoevsky

85. To Mikhail Dostoevsky
18 July 1849. Petersburg. Peter-Paul Fortress

I was gladdened beyond words, dear brother, by your letter. I received it July 11. You're finally free,[1] and I can imagine what happiness it was for you to see your family. How they must have been waiting for you! I see that you're beginning to get yourself fixed up along new lines. What are you doing now, and most importantly, what are you living on? Do you have work, and what precisely are you doing? Summer in the city is depressing! And in addition, you say that you've taken another apartment and you're probably more crowded. It's a pity that you can't finish the summertime out of town.

Thank you for the packages; they've given me great relief and amusement. You write, dear brother, that I should not be despondent. But I'm not despondent; of course, I'm bored and miserable, but what can be done? But I'm not even always bored. All in all, my time goes along extremely unevenly—sometimes too quickly, and then it drags. At other times you even feel that you seem to have gotten used to such a life and that it doesn't make any difference. I of course chase temptations from my imagination, but sometimes you can't cope with them, and one's former life simply forces its way into the soul, and the past is relived again. But that's in the nature of things. The days are clear now, at least for the most part, and it's grown a bit more cheerful. But inclement days are unbearable, the casemate looks more grim. I have some pursuits, too. I haven't lost any time, I've thought up three stories and two novels; one of them I'm writing now,[2] but I'm afraid to work a lot.

This work, especially if it is done with enthusiasm (and I have never worked so con amore [with love] as now), always exhausted me, irritating my nerves. When I worked at freedom, I constantly needed to interrupt myself with diversions, but here the agitation after writing has to pass on its

8. In connection with the arrest of his brothers, Andrey Dostoevsky was arrested by mistake and spent the time from 23 April to 5 May 1849 in the Peter-Paul Fortress.

1. Mikhail had been released from the Peter-Paul Fortress 24 June 1849.

2. "The Little Hero."

own. My health is good, except for my hemorrhoids and the derangement of my nerves, which is proceeding at a crescendo. I've begun having throat spasms, as before, my appetite is very slight, and I get little sleep, and even at that with painful dreams. I sleep about five hours in twenty-four and wake up about four times a night. That's the only thing that's depressing. The hardest thing is the time when night falls, and at 9 o'clock it's already dark here. I sometimes can't get to sleep until one or two AM, so that enduring five hours or so of darkness is depressing. That undoes my health more than anything else.

I can't tell you anything about the time of the conclusion of our case, because I've already lost all reckoning, and I just keep a calendar in which I passively note each passing day—phew! I've read a little bit here: two journeys to holy places and the works of St. Dmitry of Rostov. The last interested me very much; but that reading is a drop in the ocean, and I think I would be unbelievably happy to receive a book. The more so as it will even be curative, because you refashion your own thoughts using other people's or rethink your own along new lines.

That's all the details about my life; there's nothing else. I'm very glad that you found your family well. Have you written to Moscow about your release? It's a great pity that the business there is not being resolved.[3] How I would love to spend even a single day with you! It will soon be three months that we have been incarcerated; what will happen after this? Perhaps you won't even see the green leaves this summer. Do you remember how they sometimes took us out to walk in the little garden in May? The greenery was just beginning then, and I was reminded of Revel, where I used to visit you at about that time, and the garden in the Engineering Building. I kept thinking that you would make that comparison too—it was so sad. I'd like to see a few other people too. Whom are you seeing now; everyone must be out in the country. Our brother Andrey certainly must be in town; have you seen Nikolya?[4] Give my regards to them. Kiss all the children for me, give my regards to your wife, tell her that I'm very touched that she remembers me, and don't worry about me much. I only desire to be healthy, and boredom is a passing matter, and besides, good spirits depend on me alone. There is a huge amount of malleability and vitality in man, and I really didn't think that there was so much, but now I've learned from experience. Well, good-bye! Here are a couple of words from me, and I hope that they give you pleasure. Give my regards to everyone you see and whom I knew, don't neglect anyone. I have been recollecting everyone. What do the children think about me and I'm curious what assumptions they're making about me: where, for instance, has he disappeared to! Well, good-bye. If you can,

3. See the preceding letter, note 3, for details of the family inheritance.
4. Nikolay Mikhaylovich Dostoevsky.

send me *Notes of the Fatherland.* You'll read anything. Write a couple of words, too. That will make me extraordinarily happy.

Good-bye.

Your brother F. Dostoevsky

18 July

86. To Mikhail Dostoevsky
27 August 1849. Peter-Paul Fortress

27 August 49

I'm very glad that I can reply to you, dear brother, and thank you for the parcel of books. I'm especially grateful for *Notes of the Fatherland.* I'm also glad that you're well and that incarceration didn't leave any bad traces on your health. But you write very little, so that my letters are much more detailed than yours. But that's a minor matter; you'll get better later.

I can't say anything definite about myself. There's the same obscurity about the conclusion of our case. My *private* life is monotonous, as before; but I've again been allowed to walk in the garden, in which there are almost seventeen trees. And that's a great happiness for me. In addition, I can now have a candle in the evenings— and that's another happiness. There will be a third if you answer me soon and send *Notes of the Fatherland;* because I, like an out-of-town subscriber, wait for it as for an epoch, like a bored landowner in the provinces. Do you want to send me some historical works. That will be marvelous. But best of all if you would send me a Bible (both Testaments). I need it. But if it's possible to send it, send it in a French translation. And if you'll add a Slavonic one, that will be the height of perfection.

I cannot say anything good about my health. For an entire month now I've been eating nothing but castor oil and only in that way managing to remain on this earth. My hemorrhoids have grown fierce to the highest degree, and I feel a chest pain that I never had before. And in addition, especially towards night, my impressionability becomes greater, at night I have long, hideous dreams and in addition, beginning quite recently, the floor keeps seeming to sway beneath me, and I sit in my room as though in a ship cabin. From all this I conclude that my nerves are in disarray. When such a nervous time would come upon me in the past, I would take advantage of it to write—in such a state you'll always write better and more, but now I refrain from it so as not to do myself in completely. I had an interval of about three weeks in which I didn't write anything; now I've begun again.[1] But none of this really matters; I can still live. Perhaps I'll manage to recover.

You simply amazed me when you wrote that you thought that our Moscow people[2] didn't know anything about our adventure. I thought about it, reasoned, and concluded that that's absolutely impossible. They surely know, and in their silence I see a completely different reason.[3] That's exactly what one should have expected, however. The matter is perfectly clear.

How is Emilia Fyodorovna's[4] health? What a misfortune for her! For the second summer now she's having to suffer unbearable boredom! Last year cholera and other reasons, and this year God only knows what! Really, brother, it's a sin to give in to apathy. Intensified work con amore [with love]—that's real happiness. Work, write—what's better than that!

You write that literature is sick. But nonetheless the issues of *Notes of the Fatherland* are very rich, just as before, but not in regards to belles lettres, of course. There's isn't a single piece that can't be read with pleasure. The science and scholarship section is magnificent. *The Conquest of Peru* alone is an entire *Iliad,* and really, is in no way inferior to last year's *The Conquest of Mexico.*[5] What difference does it make that the piece is translated!

I read the second analysis of *The Odyssey* with great pleasure, but the second article is much worse than the first one, by Davydov.[6] That was a brilliant article; especially where he refutes Wolf,[7] it's written with such profound understanding of the matter, with such passion, that it was difficult even to expect that from such an ancient professor. Even in that article he managed to avoid the pedantry typical of all scholars in general and of Moscow ones in particular.

From all this you can conclude, brother, that your books gave me extraordinary pleasure and that I'm impossibly grateful to you for them. Well, good-bye; I wish you every success. Write soon. It wouldn't be at all bad if you wrote to the Muscovites about our affairs and asked them

1. Probably a reference to the story "The Little Hero."

2. The Karepins, Ivanovs, and Kumanins.

3. The Karepins, Ivanovs, and Kumanins did not in fact learn of Dostoevsky's arrest until very late in 1849.

4. Mikhail Dostoevsky's wife.

5. Reference to works by William Prescott (1796-1859), American historian.

6. The first article was written by P. A. Lavrovsky and edited by I. I. Davydov; the second article belonged to B. I. Ordynsky.

7. Friedrich August Wolf (1757-1824), philologist who suggested in his *Prolegomena in Homerum* that *The Iliad* and *The Odyssey* were the works of numerous anonymous authors, not of Homer.

formally what state the matter of the village is in.[8]

Kiss all the children. I imagine that they're being taken to the Summer Garden. Give my regards to Emilia Fyodorovna and to everyone you see from among our acquaintances. You write that you would like to see me . . . When will that be! Well, good-bye.

Your Fyodor Dostoevsky

Write me who the gentleman (Vl. Ch.) is who publishes his articles in *Notes of the Fatherland*.[9] Also, who is the author of the analysis of Shakhova's[10] poems in the June issue of *Notes of the Fatherland*.[11] Find out if you can.

My money will become available between the 10th and the 15th of September, brother. If you can, help me again. I need a little. I have an account with Sorokin[12] for *Poor Folk*, but I've forgotten how much; in any event, it's an extremely small one. He's paid almost all of it.

F. Dostoevsky

87. To Mikhail Dostoevsky
14 September 1849. Petersburg. Peter-Paul Fortress

I received your letter, dear brother, the books (Shakespeare, the Bible, *Notes of the Fatherland),* and the money (10 silver rubles), and I thank you for all of that. I'm glad that you're well. I'm still the same as before. The same upset stomach and hemorrhoids. I really don't know when this will pass. The difficult autumn months are approaching, and with them my acute depression. Now the sky is already glowering, but the bright bit of sky visible from my casemate is a guarantee of my health and of good spirits. But still and all, for the meanwhile I'm still alive and well. And for me that's quite a fact. And therefore please don't think anything especially bad about me. For the time being everything is fine in regard to my health. I expected much worse and now I see that there is so much vitality stored

8. See Letter 84, note 3, about the Dostoevsky inheritance.
9. Vladimir Chachkov.
10. Elizaveta Nikitichna Shakhova (1821-99), poet, contributor to *The Contemporary.* Shakhova later became a nun and turned to religious poetry.
11. The review, unsigned, was by Apollon Maykov.
12. Petersburg bookseller.

up in me that you can't exhaust it.

I thank you again for the books. They're at least a diversion. It's been nearly five months now that I've been living on my own means, that is, on my head alone and nothing else. For the time being the machine has not yet come unstrung and is still functioning. Constant thinking, however, and just thinking, without any outside impressions to revive and support thought is hard going! It's as though I were under an air pump from which the air is being pumped out. Everything in me has gone to my head, and from my head to thought, everything, absolutely everything, and in spite of that this work increases with every day. Books, even though only a drop in the ocean, still help. But work itself seems only to drain my last juices from me. I'm glad for it, however.

I've read through the books that you sent. I thank you especially for Shakespeare. How did you guess! The English novel[1] in *Notes of the Fatherland* is extraordinarily good. But Turgenev's comedy[2] is unpardonably bad. How did this misfortune come about? Can it really be that he is definitely fated after all to spoil every one of his works that exceeds a signature sheet in size? I didn't recognize him in that comedy. No originality: an old, beaten track. All of this has been said before him and much better than by him. The last scene reeks of infantile weakness. There are flashes of something here and there, but that something is good only by virtue of the lack of anything better. What an excellent piece about banks! And how accessible to everyone!

I thank everyone who remembers about me. Give my regards to Emilia Fyodorovna,[3] our brother Andrey, and kiss the children, whom I especially wish good health. I really don't know, brother, how and when we'll see each other. Good-bye and please don't forget me. Write me in at least two weeks.

Good-bye.

Your F. Dostoevsky

14 Sept. 49

Please don't be so worried about me. If you find anything to read, send it.

---

1. Emily Brontë's *Jane Eyre.*

2. *The Bachelor* (1849). It is worth noting that Turgenev's comedy shows the influence of Dostoevsky's *Poor Folk,* especially in the two central protagonists.

3. Mikhail Dostoevsky's wife.

88. To Mikhail Dostoevsky
22 December 1849. Petersburg. Peter-Paul Fortress

Peter-Paul Fortress
22 December

Brother, my dear brother! Everything has been decided! I have been sentenced to four years of labor in a fortress (Orenburg, I think) and then to the ranks.[1] Today, December 22, we were taken to Semyonov Square. There we were all read the death sentence, allowed to kiss the cross, had sabers broken over our heads and our pre-death attire put on (white shirts). Then three people were stood against the stakes for the carrying out of the execution. I was the sixth in line, people were summoned by threes, cons[equently], I was in the second row and had no more than a minute left to live. I remembered you, brother, and all of your family; at the last moment you, only you were in my mind, only then did I realize how much I love you, my dear brother! I had time also to embrace Pleshcheev,[2] Durov,[3] who were nearby, and to say farewell to them. Finally a retreat was sounded, the ones tied to the stake were led back, and it was announced that His Imperial Majesty was granting us our lives.[4] Then the real sentences followed. Palm[5] alone was pardoned. He'll go back into the army at the same rank.

I've just been told, dear brother, that we're to set off today or tomorrow. I asked to see you. But I was told that was impossible; I can only write you this letter, which you should hurry to give me a reply to.[6] I'm afraid that you might somehow have known of our sentence (to death). From the windows of the wagon, when we were being taken to Semyonov Square, I saw a throng of people; perhaps the news had already reached you too and you were suffering for me. Now you'll be able to feel better for me. Brother! I'm not despondent and I haven't lost heart. Life is everywhere, life is in us ourselves, and not outside. There will be people by

---

1. Dostoevsky served his term of labor at the Omsk Fortress, not Orenburg.

2. Alexey Nikolaevich Pleshcheev (1826-93), poet, one of the earliest members of the Petrashevsky Circle. He and Dostoevsky remained on good terms for the rest of their lives but were especially close in the 1850s and early 1860s.

3. Sergey Fyodorovich Durov (1816-69), writer, translator, and one of the two organizers of the Palm-Durov subset of the Petrashevsky Circle. Dostoevsky used Durov as one of the prototypes for Stepan Verkhovensky in the novel *The Devils*.

4. The melodramatic eleventh-hour pardon was choreographed by Nicholas I personally.

5. Alexander Ivanovich Palm (1823-85), one of the two organizers of the Palm-Durov subset of the Petrashevsky Circle. His novel *Alexey Slobodin* (1872-73) recreates the atmosphere of the circles of the 1840s.

6. Dostoevsky was allowed to see his brother Mikhail on December 24, the day of his departure for Siberia.

my side, and to be a *human being* among people and to remain one forever, no matter in what circumstances, not to grow despondent and not to lose heart—that's what life is all about, that's its task. I have come to recognize that. That idea has entered my flesh and blood. But it's the truth! The head that created, lived the higher life of art, that recognized and grew accustomed to the higher demands of the spirit, that head has already been cut from my shoulders. What remains is memory and images created and not yet embodied by me. They will ulcerate me, really! But there remain in me a heart and the same flesh and blood that can also love, and suffer, and pity, and remember, and that's life, too! On voit le soleil! [One can see the sun!][7]

Well, good-bye, brother! Don't grieve about me! Now about the disposition of my things: the books (the Bible has remained with me) and several sheets of my manuscript (the rough plan for a drama and a novel and the finished story "A Children's Tale"[8]) have been taken from me and in all likelihood will wind up with you. I'm also leaving my coat and old clothes, if you'll come to pick them up. Now, brother, I'm faced with what may be a long journey to prison. I need money. Dear brother, as soon as you receive this letter, and if you can get any money, send it to me immediately. I need money now more than I do air (because of a special circumstance). Send me a few lines from you too. Then, if the Moscow money[9] comes through, look after my interests and don't abandon me . . . Well, that's all. There are debts, but what can be done about them?!

Kiss your wife and children. Remind them about me; see to it that they don't forget me. Perhaps we'll see each other sometime? Brother, take care of yourself and your family, live quietly and with foresight. Think about your children's future . . . Live positively.

Never before have such abundant and healthy reserves of spiritual life teemed in me as now. But I don't know whether my body will endure it. I'm setting out unwell, I have scrofula. But perhaps somehow! Brother! I have already experienced so much in life that there's very little that will frighten me. Let come what may! I'll let you hear from me at the first possible opportunity.

Give the Maykovs farewell and final greetings from me. Tell them that I thank them all for their constant concern for my fate. Say a few words for me, as warm as possible, whatever your heart dictates, to Yevgenia Petrovna.[10] I wish her much happiness and will always remember her with

7. A partially distorted quotation from Victor Hugo's "Le dernier jour d'un condamné" ["The Last Day of a Condemned Man"], a work several echoes of which may be found in the present letter.

8. Reference to the story "A Little Hero."

9. A reference to money from the sale of the Dostoevsky family estate. See Letter 84, note 3, for details.

10. Yevgenia Petrovna Maykova.

grateful respect. Shake Nikolay Apollonovich's and Apollon Maykov's hands for me, and then everyone's.

Find Yanovsky.[11] Shake his hand and thank him. Finally, shake the hand of everyone who hasn't forgotten me. And remind those who have. Kiss our brother *Kolya*. Write a letter to our brother *Andrey* and tell him about me. Write our uncle and aunt.[12] Write to our sisters: I wish them happiness!

But perhaps we'll even see each other, brother. Take care of yourself, live, for Heaven's sake, until we can meet each other. Perhaps we'll embrace each other sometime and recall our young, our past golden time, our youth and our hopes, which at this moment I am tearing out of my heart with blood and am burying.

Can it be that I'll never take pen in hand? I think that in 4 years it will be possible. I'll send you everything I write if I write anything. My God! How many images, cast out, created by me anew will perish, will expire in my head or contaminate my blood like a poison! Yes, if I won't be able to write, I'll perish. Better fifteen years of imprisonment and a pen in hand!

Write me often, in great detail, a lot, and fully. Go on at length in every letter about your family details, about trivialities, don't forget that. That will give me hope and life. If you only knew how your letters enlivened me here in the casemate. These two-and-a-half months (last), when correspondence was forbidden, were very difficult for me. I was unwell. The fact that you didn't send any money from time to time worried me to death about you: evidently you were in great need yourself! Kiss the children one more time, I can't get their dear little faces out of my mind. Oh, may they be happy! May you be happy, too, brother, be happy!

But don't grieve, for Heaven's sake, don't grieve about me! Know that I haven't lost heart, remember that hope has not abandoned me. In four years there will be an easing of my lot. I'll be a common soldier— no longer a prisoner, and keep in mind that someday I'll embrace you. After all I was at death's door today, I lived with that thought for three-quarters of an hour, I faced the last moment, and now I'm alive again![13]

If anyone remembers me with malice, and if I quarrelled with anyone, if I made a bad impression on anyone—tell them to forget about that if you manage to see them. There is no bile or spite in my soul, I would like to so love and embrace at least someone out of the past at this moment. It's a comfort, I experienced it today while saying farewell to my dear ones before death. At that moment I thought that the news of the execution

---

11. Stepan Dmitrievich Yanovsky (1815-97), a doctor and close friend of Dostoevsky's. Their relations became somewhat strained in the 1860s but the two continued to see each other.

12. The Kumanins.

13. Dostoevsky used his recollections of those three-quarters of an hour at death's door in Prince Myshkin's protest against the death penalty in the novel *The Idiot*.

would kill you. But now be calm, I'm still alive and will live in the future with the thought that someday I'll embrace you. That's the only thing I have in my thoughts now.

What are you doing? What did you think today? Do you know about us? How cold it was today!

Oh, if only my letter would reach you soon. Otherwise I'll be without news of you for about four months. I saw the packages in which you sent money the last two months; the address was written in your hand, and I was glad that you were well.

When I look back at the past and think how much time was spent in vain, how much of it was lost in delusions, in errors, in idleness, in the inability to live; how I failed to value it, how many times I sinned against my heart and spirit— then my heart contracts in pain. Life is a gift, life is happiness, each moment could have been an eternity of happiness. Si jeunesse savait! [If youth knew!] Now, changing my life, I'm being regenerated into a new form. Brother! I swear to you that I won't lose hope and will preserve my heart and spirit in purity. I'll be reborn for the better. That's my entire hope, my entire consolation.

Life in the casemate has already sufficiently killed off in me the needs of the flesh that were not completely pure; before that I took little care of myself. Now deprivations no longer bother me in the slightest, and therefore don't be afraid that material hardship will kill me. That can't be. Oh, if only my health holds out!

Good-bye, good-bye, brother! When will I write to you again! You'll receive from me as detailed a report as possible about my journey. If only I can preserve my health, everything else will be all right!

Well, good-bye, good-bye, brother! I embrace you firmly, kiss you soundly. Remember me without pain in your heart. Don't be sad, please don't be sad about me! In my very next letter I'll write you about how things are. Remember what I've told you: calculate your life, don't waste it, put your fate in order, think about the children.— Oh, to see you someday! Good-bye! Now I'm tearing myself away from everything that was dear to me; it's painful to leave it! It's painful to break yourself in two, to tear your heart in half. Good-bye! Good-bye! But I'll see you, I'm certain, I hope, don't change, love me, don't let your memory grow cold, and the thought of your love will me the best part of life for me. Good-bye, once more good-bye! Good-bye to everyone!

Your brother Fyodor Dostoevsky
22 December 49

At the time of my arrest several books were taken away from me. Of them only two were forbidden. Won't you get the rest of them for yourself? But here's a request: of those books one was *The Works of Valerian*

Maykov, his criticism—Yevgenia Petrovna's copy. She had given it to me as her priceless treasure. During my arrest I asked an officer of the gendarmes to give the book back to her and gave him the address. I don't know whether he returned it to her. Check on that! I don't want to take that memory away from her. Good-bye, once again good-bye.

Your F. Dostoevsky

I don't know whether I'll be walking or riding to prison. Riding I think. I hope!

Once more: shake Emilia Fyodorovna's hand and kiss the children.— Give my regards to Kraevsky, perhaps...

Write me in detail about your arrest, imprisonment, and release.

1854

89. To Mikhail Dostoevsky
30 January-22 February 1854. Omsk

It seems that finally I can talk to you at greater length and with greater assurance.[1] But before writing a line I'll ask you: tell me please, for the love of God, why have you not yet written a single line to me?[2] And could I have expected that? Would you believe that in my remote, isolated state I fell into real despair several times, thinking that you were no longer alive, and then for nights on end I would meditate on what would happen to your children, and I would curse my fate that I couldn't be of use to them. At other times, when I would learn for certain that you were alive, I would be seized by irritation (but that happened during morbid periods, of which I had many) and would reproach you bitterly. But then that too would pass; I would pardon you, try to find all the justifications, would take comfort in the best ones and not once did I lose faith in you: I know that you love me and remember me fondly. I wrote you a letter via our headquarters. It must surely have reached you, and I was expecting a reply from you and didn't get one. But can it really be that you were forbidden to write? After all, that's allowed, and all the political prisoners here receive several letters a year.[3] Durov received them many times, and many times in reponse to inquiries to the authorities about letters, permission to write them was confirmed. I think that I've guessed the real reason for your silence. Because of your lethargy you didn't go to ask the police, and even if you did, you contented yourself with the first negative answer, perhaps from a person who didn't know his business very well. In so doing you caused me a great deal of selfish grief as well: "So," I thought, "if he can't even trouble himself about a letter, will he trouble himself about anything more important for me!" Write and reply soon, and first of all write officially, without waiting for an occasion,[4] and write in detail and at length. I'm like

1. This is Dostoevsky's first extant letter written after his release from prison (15 February 1854), although there is evidence that he sent a number of unauthorized letters to his brother Mikhail while still in prison.
2. Mikhail replied that he had not written because of the official prohibition against writing as long as Dostoevsky was in prison.
3. Mikhail replied that his several attempts to receive official permission to write Dostoevsky in Siberia all ended in his being informed that such correspondence was forbidden.
4. Dostoevsky means a chance to send a letter with someone personally rather than through the open mail.

a branch cut off from all of you, and I would like to grow back, but I can't. Les absents ont toujours tort. [Those absent are always wrong.] Can it really be that that must happen between us too? But don't worry, I believe in you.

It's already been a week since I was released from prison.[5] This letter is being sent to you in the deepest secrecy, and not even half a word about it to anyone. But I'll send you an official letter, too, via the headquarters of the Siberian Corps. Answer the official one immediately, and this one at the first convenient opportunity. But in the official one, too, you must give a very detailed account of all the important things about you for all these 4 years. As for me, I would be happy to send you entire volumes. But since I scarcely have time even for this letter, I'll write you the most important things.

What are the most important things? And what precisely has been the main thing for me recently? When you think about it, it turns out that I won't be able to describe anything fully to you in this letter. Well how can I convey to you my head, an idea, everything that I've experienced, of which I've become convinced and which I've dwelled on in all this time. I'm not going to undertake that. Such a labor is absolutely impossible. I don't like to do anything by halves, and to say anything would mean precisely nothing. The main report is before you, however. Read and extract what you will. I'm obliged to do this and therefore I'm tackling my recollections.

Do you remember how we parted, my dear, my beloved brother? As soon as you left me, the three of us, Durov, Yastrzhembsky,[6] and I were led off to be put in leg irons. At precisely 12 o'clock, that is, precisely on Christmas Day, I put on irons for the first time. They weighed about 10 pounds and it was extraordinarily awkward walking. Then we were put in an open sleigh, each of us separately, with a gendarme, and in 4 sleighs, a courier out ahead, we set out from Petersburg. I had a feeling of heaviness in my heart and a sort of vagueness and indefiniteness because of many diverse sensations. My heart was caught up in a bustling of some kind, and therefore it ached and grieved dully. But the fresh air invigorated me, and since you usually feel a sort of vitality and energy before every new step in life, in essence I was very calm and gazed intently at Petersburg as we rode past the gaily illuminated houses, and as I bade farewell to each separate one. We were driven past your apartment, and Kraevsky's was all lit up. You had told me that he was having a Christmas party, that Emilia Fyodorovna[7] and the children had gone to his place, and right at that building I began to feel fiercely sad. I seemed to be saying good-bye to the

---

5. Dostoevsky's prison term expired 23 January 1854.

6. Ivan-Ferdinand Lvovich Yastrzhembsky (1814-80), one of the most active members of the Petrashevsky Circle. He served a prison term of six years in Siberia, and in 1857, a year after his release, was allowed to return to Petersburg.

7. Mikhail Dostoevsky's wife.

children. I felt sorry for them, and later, years afterwards, how many times I recalled them, nearly with tears in my eyes. We were being driven toward Yaroslavl, and therefore towards morning, after three or 4 stations, we stopped at the crack of dawn at an inn in Shlisselberg. We attacked the tea as if we hadn't eaten for a whole week. After 8 months of incarceration we had gotten so hungry after 60 versts[8] of winter travel that it's pleasant to recall it. I was in a cheerful mood, Durov was gabbing non-stop, but Yastrzhembsky had visions of some sort of unusual terrors in the future. We were all getting accustomed to our courier and testing him out. It turned out that he was a marvelous old fellow, as good and kindly toward us as one can possibly imagine, a worldly-wise man who had travelled through all of Europe with dispatches. On the road he did many a kindness for us. His name is Kuzma Prokofievich Prokofiev. By the way, he transferred us to covered sleighs, which was very beneficial for us because the cold was terrible. The next day was a holiday, the drivers got in dressed in coats of gray German cloth with scarlet sashes, on the streets in the villages there wasn't a soul. It was a marvelous winter day. We were driven through empty land, along the Petersburg, Novgorod, Yaroslavl roads, etc. Sparse, indifferent little towns. But we had left during the holiday season and therefore we found something to eat and drink everywhere. We got horribly cold. We were dressed warmly, but sitting, for instance, for some 10 hours without leaving the sleigh and making 5 or 6 relay stops was almost unbearable. I would get chilled to the bone and could hardly warm up later in warm rooms. But strange to say: the journey cured me completely. In Perm province we endured a night of forty degrees.[9] I don't recommend that to you. It's rather unpleasant. The moment of crossing the Urals was a sad one. The horses and sleighs got stuck in the drifts. There was a snowstorm. We got out of the carriages, this was at night, and stood waiting for them to pull the carriages out. There was snow and a snowstorm all around; the border of Europe, Siberia ahead and an enigmatic fate in it, all the past behind—it was sad, and I was moved to tears. All along the way whole villages would run out to look at us, and in spite of our leg irons, they soaked us for all we were worth at the stations. Kuzma Prokofich alone took nearly half our expenses on his own account, took them forcibly, and in that way we only paid 15 silver rubles each for our expenses on the road. On January 11 we arrived at Tobolsk,[10] and after being presented to the authorities and searched, where all our money was taken from us, we were led, Durov, Yastrzhembsky, and I, to a special cubicle; the others, however, Speshnyov[11] and the others, who had arrived

8. One verst = 3500 feet.

9. Presumably Dostoevsky means -40 Reamur, which equals approximately -55 Fahrenheit.

10. According to official documents, Dostoevsky arrived at Tobolsk 9 January 1850.

11. Nikolay Alexandrovich Speshnyov (1821-82), perhaps the most vivid character in the

before us, were confined in another section, and the whole time we hardly saw each other. I'd like to talk in great detail about our six-day stay in Tobolsk and the impression that it made on me. But this isn't the place.[12] I'll simply say that we were rewarded with compassion, the keenest sympathy, almost with happiness. The old-time exiles (that is, not they, but their wives[13]) looked after us as though we were family members. What marvelous souls, tried and tested by 25 years of woe and selflessness. We saw them only at a glance, because we were held under strict detention. But they sent us food, clothing, comforted us and cheered us up. I, who had set out lightly, without taking even my own clothes, repented of that [*indecipherable*]. They even sent me clothing. Finally we started out and three days later arrived in Omsk.[14] While still in Tobolsk I had found out about our future immediate authorities. The commandant was a very decent person, but Deputy Commandant Krivtsov[15] was a scoundrel the likes of which are few, a petty barbarian, quarrelsome, a drunkard, everything repellent that one can possible imagine. It began with his calling us both, Durov and me, fools because of our case, and he promised to have us flogged at the first opportunity. He had already been deputy commandant for two years and was responsible for the most horrible injustices. Two years later he was tried. God delivered me from him. He always came riding in drunk (I never saw him sober), would pick on a sober prisoner and flog him on the pretext that the latter was as drunk as a cobbler. At other times while visiting at night, he'd do the same thing for someone's not sleeping on his right side, for someone's crying out in his sleep or hallucinating at night, for whatever idea came into his drunken head. It was with that sort of person that I had to live without harm to myself, and that same person wrote reports and submitted recommendations about us to Petersburg every month. While still in Tobolsk I had gotten acquainted with convicts, and there in Omsk I settled down to live with them for four years. They are coarse people, irritable and spiteful. Their hatred of the nobility exceeds all bounds, and therefore they greeted us nobles with hostility and with malicious joy over our woe.[16] They would

Petrashevsky Circle. An atheist and communist with strong revolutionary leanings, Speshnyov was freed from prison in 1856. In 1860 he returned to European Russia, where he occupied a minor government post in Pskov Province. Commentators consider Speshnyov one of the prototypes for Stavrogin in Dostoevsky's novel *The Devils*.

12. Tobolsk was a central clearing station for convicts serving terms in Siberia, so Dostoevsky probably had his first exposure to violent criminals there.

13. Dostoevsky is referring to the Decembrists and their wives. Many of the former were exiled to Siberia after an abortive uprising in Petersburg in 1825, and in several famous instances their wives followed them to Siberia, acquiring in the process nearly legendary status as ideals of selfless Russian womanhood.

14. Dostoevsky arrived in Omsk on 23 January 1850.

15. Krivtsov is described vividly in Dostoevsky's *Notes from the House of the Dead*.

16. Dostoevsky expands on the conflict between the common folk and the nobility in *Notes from the House of the Dead*.

have eaten us up if they had been allowed to. However, judge for yourself how much of a defense there could be when we had to live, eat and drink, and sleep with those people for several years, and when there wasn't even time to complain because of the infinite number of outrages of all kinds. "You nobles, iron noses, pecked us to death. You used to be a gentleman and torment the common folk, and now you're worse than the worst, you've become just like us"—there is a theme that was played upon for 4 years. 150 enemies couldn't tire of persecuting one, that was a pleasure for them, an amusement, a pastime, and if we could in any way save ourselves from grief, then it was through indifference, moral superiority, which they couldn't help but understand and respect, and through resistance to their will. They always realized that we were higher than they were. They had no notion of our crime. We kept silent about that ourselves, and therefore didn't understand each other, so that we had to endure all the vengeance and persecution, which they live and breathe, of the class of the nobility. Our life was very hard. Military penal servitude is more severe than civilian. I spent the entire four years in prison without going out, behind walls, and went out only for work. The work that fell to us was difficult, of course not always, and on occasion I exhausted myself in bad weather, in the wet, in the slush, or in the wintertime in unbearable cold. Once I spent about four hours at special work when the mercury had frozen, and it was perhaps 40 degrees below freezing.[17] My foot got frostbitten. We lived in a heap, all together, in one barracks. Imagine for yourself an old, dilapidated, wooden building that should have been torn down long since and that could no longer serve. In the summer the stuffiness is unbearable, in the winter the cold beyond enduring. All the floors have rotted through. The floor is an inch thick with mud, you can slip and fall. The little windows are covered with hoarfrost, so that for the whole day it's almost impossible to read. There's an inch of ice on the windowpanes. There is a drip from the ceiling—it's all full of holes. We're like herring in a barrel. If they stoke the stove with six logs there's no warmth (the ice barely melted in the room), but the fumes are unbearable—and that's our whole winter. The prisoners do their laundry right there in the barracks and splash water all over the whole little barracks. There's no room to turn around. It's impossible to go outside to answer the call of nature between sunset and sunrise, because the barracks is locked and a tub is placed in the hall, and therefore the stuffiness is unbearable. All the prisoners stink like pigs and say they can't help doing swinish things because, they say, "a man's a living thing." We slept on bare plank beds, one pillow was allowed. We covered ourselves up with short half-length fur coats, and your feet are always bare all night. You shiver the whole night. Mountains of fleas, lice, and cockroaches. In the winter we wear half-length fur coats, often very bad

17. A reading of -40 Reamur is approximately -55 on the Fahrenheit scale.

ones that hardly keep one warm, and boots with short tops—try walking around in the freezing weather like that. For food we were given bread and cabbage soup in which there was supposed to be 1/4 pound of beef per person; but the beef that they put in is chopped, and I never saw it. On holidays gruel with hardly any butter. During fasts cabbage with water and hardly anything else. I ruined my digestion unbearably and was sick several times. Judge for yourself whether one could live without money, and if I hadn't had money, I definitely would have died, and no one, no prisoner, could endure such a life. But everyone does some sort of work, sells something, and has a kopeck. I drank tea and sometimes ate my piece of beef and that saved me. It was also impossible not to smoke, because one could have suffocated in such stuffiness. All of that was done on the sly. I was often in the hospital. Because of unstrung nerves I came down with epilepsy, but attacks occur rarely, however. I also have rheumatism in my legs. Except for that I feel quite well. Add to all these delights the near impossibility of having a book, if you get one, you have to read it furtively, constant hostility and squabbling all around you, cursing, yelling, noise, clamor, always under guard, never alone, and four years of that without a change—one really can be forgiven for saying that it was miserable. In addition to that the ever-present responsibility, leg irons and complete constraint of the spirit, and that's my way of life. What happened to my soul, my beliefs, my mind and heart in those four years—I can't tell you. It would take too long to tell. But constant concentration within myself, where I escaped from bitter reality, brought its fruits. I now have many needs and hopes such as I had never even thought about. But this is all riddles, and therefore I'll pass over it. One thing: don't forget me and help me. I need books and money. Please send them, for the love of Christ.

Omsk is a vile little town. There are hardly any trees. In the summer there's heat and wind with sand, in the winter, snowstorms. I haven't seen any nature. It's a filthy army town and depraved to the highest degree. I'm speaking of the people. If I hadn't found people here I would have perished completely. K. I. I[vano]v[18] has been like a brother to me. He's done everything for me that he could have. I owe him money. If he visits Petersburg, thank him. I owe him about 25 silver rubles. But how can I repay him for that cordiality, that constant readiness to fulfill every request, attention and care as though for one's own brother. And he's not the only one! Brother, there are many noble people in this world.

I've already written that your silence sometimes tormented me. Thanks for sending money. In your very first letter (even if it's an official one, because I don't know whether I can give you news now), in your very first letter write me in detail about all your affairs, about Emilia

---

18. Konstantin Ivanovich Ivanov (d. 1887), general and military engineer whose position and connections enabled him to help Dostoevsky in a number of ways, eventually by arranging for permission for Dostoevsky to return to Petersburg.

Fyodorovna, the children, about all the relatives and friends, about the Muscovites,[19] who's alive, who has died, about your business[20]; write me about what capital you used to start your trade, whether it's profitable, whether you have anything, and finally, whether you can help me with money and how much you can send me annually. But don't send any money in an official letter, unless I can't find another address for you. For the time being use the name *Mikhail Petrovich* (you understand)[21] when you send it. But I still have money; I don't have books, however. If you can, send me the journals for this year, at least *Notes of the Fatherland.* But here's what's essential: I need (desperately) historians, ancient (in French translation) and modern,[22] economists, and the Church fathers. Choose the cheapest and most compact editions. Send them right away.[23] I've been assigned to Semipalatinsk, nearly in the Kirghiz steppe. I'll send you the address. Here it is in any event: *Semipalatinsk, 7th Siberian Line Battalion.* That's the official address. Use it for sending letters. But for books I'll send another. But for the time being use the name Mikhail Petrovich for the sender. Just bear in mind that the very first book I need is a German dictionary.[24]

I don't know what awaits me in Semipalatinsk. I'm rather indifferent to that fate. But here's what I'm not indifferent to: take up my case, petition someone. Couldn't I be sent to the Caucasus in a year or 2—still and all, it's Russia! That's my ardent desire, please ask for me, for Christ's sake! Brother, don't forget me! Here I am writing to you and giving instructions about everything, even your money. But my faith in you hasn't extinguished. You're my brother and you loved me. I need money. *I need to live, brother. These years won't pass fruitlessly.* I need money and books. What you spend on me won't be lost. You won't be robbing your children if you give me money. If only I'm alive, I'll return it to them with interest. After all, I'll be allowed to publish in six years or so, and perhaps even earlier. After all, a lot can change, and I won't write any nonsense now. You'll hear about me.

We'll see each other, brother, very soon. I believe in that as in two times two. There is clarity in my soul. It's as though I have my whole future and everything that I'll do right before my eyes. I'm satisfied with my life. There's only one thing to fear: people and tyranny. You can wind up with a commander who takes a dislike for you (there are such people), who'll pick on you and wear you down or kill you with duties, and I'm so weak that of course I'm incapable of bearing the whole burden of soldiering. "All the

---

19. The Karepins, Kumanins and Ivanovs.
20. Mikhail had opened a cigarette factory.
21. Dostoevsky is recommending the use of a fictitious name.
22. Vico, Guizot, Thierry, Thiers, Ranke, etc.—*Dostoevsky's note.*
23. Mikhail complied with Dostoevsky's request, but the latter did not receive the books.
24. Dostoevsky was planning to undertake translations from the German.

people there are simple folk," I'm told encouragingly. But I fear a simple person more than a complicated one. People are people everywhere, however. Even in prison among brigands, I, in four years, finally distinguished people. Believe it or not, there are profound, strong, marvelous personalities there, and how delightful it was to find gold under a coarse crust. And not one, not two, but several. You couldn't help respecting some of them, and others were absolutely marvelous. I taught one young Circassian (sent to prison for robbery) Russian and reading and writing.[25] Another prisoner burst into tears when saying good-bye to me.[26] I had lent him some money—but could it have been much? But his gratitude for that was limitless. And meanwhile my character turned rotten; I was capricious and intolerant with him. They respected the state of my spirits and bore everything without a murmur. A propos. How many types and characters from among the common people I brought out from prison! I got accustomed to them, and therefore I think I have a decent knowledge of them. How many stories of vagrants and robbers and in general of the whole dark and wretched side of life! It will be enough for entire volumes. What a wonderful people. All in all, the time hasn't been lost for me. If I have come to know not Russia, then the Russian people well, and as well as perhaps few people know them. But that's my petty vanity! I hope it's forgivable.

Brother! Be sure to write me about all the main details of your life. Address your letters to *Semipalatinsk officially,* and *not* officially, as you already know. Write about all our Petersburg acquaintances, write about literature (with as many specifics as possible), and finally, about the Muscovites. How is our brother Kolya? How (and this is the main thing) how is our sister Sashenka? Is Uncle alive?[27] How is our brother Andrey? I'll write to Auntie[28] through our sister Verochka when there's an opportunity. This letter is in secret. For Heaven's sake, keep this letter of mine in secret and even burn it: don't compromise people. Don't forget books for me, dear friend. The main things: historians, economists, *Notes of the Fatherland,* the Church fathers, and the history of the Church. Send them at different times, but send them right away. I'm managing your pocket as though it were mine, but that's because I don't know your financial circumstances. Write me something precise about those circumstances so that I have some notion of them. But know, brother, that books are life, my food, my future! Don't abandon me, for Heaven's sake. Please! Ask for permission to send me books officially. Be careful, however. If it can be done officially, then send them. If not, then through K[onstantin] I[vanovich]'s brother, addressed to him; they'll be passed on

---

25. Dostoevsky mentions this episode in *Notes from the House of the Dead.*
26. This episode, too, is cited in *Notes from the House of the Dead.*
27. Dostoevsky is referring to A. A. Kumanin.
28. A. F. Kumanina.

to me. K[onstantin] I[vanovich] will be in Petersburg himself this year, however; he'll tell you everything. What a family he has! What a wife! She's a young lady, the daughter of the Decembrist Annenkov,[29] what a heart, what a soul, and how much they have endured!

I'll try to find you another address from Semipalatinsk, where I'm headed in a week. I'm still a bit unwell and therefore have been delayed for a time. Send me the Carus, Kant's *Critique de raison pure* [*Critique of Pure Reason*], and if you can send it to me unofficially, be sure to send me *Hegel,* especially Hegel's *History of Philosophy.* My entire future is connected to that! But for Heaven's sake try and ask for my transfer to the Caucasus, and find out from knowledgeable people whether I'll be able to publish and how to petition for that. I'll ask in about two or three years. But until then please feed me. Without money I'll be crushed by soldiery. Take care! Won't some other relatives help me with at least something, if only at the outset? In that case, have them give the money to you, and you forward it to me. In my letters to Verochka and Auntie, however, I'm not asking them for anything. It will occur to them on its own if the heart so wills.

When leaving for Sevastopol, Filippov[30] gave me 25 silver rubles. He left them with the commandant, Nabokov,[31] so that I didn't even know. He thought I wouldn't have any money. A kind soul. All our exiles are getting along so-so. Tol[l][32] has finished his term at labor, he is in Tomsk and living decently. Yastrzhembsky is finishing his at Tara. Speshnyov, in Irkutsk Province, has acquired universal love and respect. That fellow's fate is marvelous. Wherever and however he shows up, the most ingenuous, most impenetrable people surround him with reverence and respect. Petrashevsky,[33] as before, is mentally unbalanced. Mombelli[34] and Lvov[35] are well, but Grigoriev,[36] the poor man, is quite mad and is in the

29. The reference is to Olga Ivanovna Ivanova, née Annenkova (1830-91), daughter of I. A. and P. Ye. Annenkov.

30. Pavel Nikolaevich Filippov (1825-55), a member of the Petrashevsky Circle.

31. General Ivan Alexandrovich Nabokov (1787-1852), in his old age Commandant of the Peter-Paul Fortress. I. A. Nabokov was the great-great-uncle of the novelist Vladimir Nabokov.

32. Felix Gustavovich Toll (1823-67), writer and member of the Petrashevsky Circle. In the late 1850s he regained the right to live in Moscow and St. Petersburg and gained a certain renown as a teacher and critic of children's literature.

33. Mikhail Vasilievich Butashevich-Petrashevsky (1821-66), admirer of French utopian socialism, founder of the Petrashevsky Circle. The most comprehensive work on him in English is John L. Evans, *The Petrashevsky Circle 1845-1849* (1973).

34. Nikolay Alexandrovich Mombelli (1823-91), officer and member of the Petrashevsky Circle. After being amnestied in 1856 he served out the remainder of his military career in the Caucasus.

35. Fyodor Nikolaevich Lvov (1823-85), officer and member of the Petrashevsky Circle. Amnestied in 1856, Lvov returned to Petersburg in 1863, where he had a successful career in various trade organizations.

36. Nikolay Petrovich Grigoriev (1822-86), member of the Petrashevsky Circle. In 1857 he was entrusted to the care of his family by reasons of his mental illness.

hospital. And how are things with you? Do you see Mme Pleshcheeva,[37] how is her son? From prisoners passing through I heard that it's the Orsk Fortress he's living in,[38] and Golovinsky[39] has long since been in the Caucasus. How are you doing with literature and in literature? Are you writing anything? How is Kraevsky and what are your relations with him? I don't like Ostrovsky,[40] I haven't read Pisemsky[41] at all, Druzhinin[42] nauseates me, Yevgenia Tur[43] drove me to ecstacy. I also like Krestovsky.[44]

I'd like to write you a lot; but so much time has passed that I'm even at a loss with this letter. But after all, it can't be that we have both changed a lot toward each other. Kiss the children for me. Do they remember Uncle Fedya? Regards to all our acquaintances; but this letter is a deep secret. Good-bye, good-bye, my dear! You'll hear about me and perhaps you'll see me. But we'll definitely see each other! Good-bye. Read over carefully everything that I write to you. Write to me often (even officially). I embrace you and all your family a countless number of times.

Yours.

P.S. Did you receive my "A Children's Tale"[45] that I wrote in the Ravelin?[46] If you have it, keep it and don't show it to anyone. Who is the Chernov who wrote "The Double" in 1850?[47] Yes, please send me some cigars, not exceptionally good ones, but American, and some cigarettes, but be sure they have a surprise.[48]

22 February

37. Mother of A. N. Pleshcheev, member of the Petrashevsky Circle.

38. A. N. Pleshcheev was serving in the Orenburg Batallion.

39. Vasily Andreevich Golovinsky (1829-70), member of the Palm-Durov subgroup of the Petrashevsky Circle.

40. Alexey Nikolaevich Ostrovsky (1823-86), prolific Russian playwright. Though hardly known in the West, his plays retain a central position in the Soviet repertory.

41. Alexey Feofilaktovich Pisemsky (1821-81), author of the novel *A Thousand Souls*. The best English-language study of Pisemsky is Charles Moser, *Pisemsky: A Provincial Realist* (1969).

42. Alexander Nikolaevich Druzhinin (1824-64), minor writer who served as the main critic for *The Contemporary* in 1855.

43. Yevgenia Tur, pseudonym of Elizaveta Vasilievna Salhias de Turnemir (1815-92), who specialized in historical tales and novels.

44. Krestovsky, pseudonym of Nadezhda Dmitrievna Khvoshchinskaya (1826-89).

45. Reference to "A Little Hero."

46. The Ravelin is the prison within the Peter-Paul Fortress.

47. The story "The Double," by A. Chernov (pseudonym of N. D. Akhsharumov), published in *Notes of the Fatherland,* No. 3, 1850, is an imitation of Dostoevsky's *The Double*.

48. It is unclear what Dostoevsky means by "surprise."

'It seems that I'll definitely be going to Semipalatinsk tomorrow. K[onstantin] I[vanovich] will be here until May. I think that if you want to send me something—books, for instance, send them to the name we used before—Mikhail Petrovich.

I may give you another address (not official) for Semipalatinsk. Be sure to write me officially, as soon and as often as possible. For the Lord's sake, take up my case. Couldn't I be transferred to the Caucasus or somewhere out of Siberia? Now I'm going to write novels and plays, but I still need to read a lot, lots and lots. Don't forget me, and once more good-bye. Kiss the children. Yours. Good-bye.

90. To Natalya Fonvizina[1]
End of January—Third Week of February 1854. Omsk

Finally, dear N[atalya] D[mitrievna], I'm writing to you after having left the former place. The last time I wrote you I was sick in soul and body. Melancholy was eating me up, and I think I wrote you a very muddle-headed letter. That long, colorless life that was difficult physically and psychologically had broken me. I always feel sad writing letters at such moments; and to impose one's melancholy on others at such a time, even if they're well-disposed towards us, is, I think, faint-heartedness. I'm sending this letter with someone and I'm very, very glad that I can talk with you this time; the more so as I have been assigned to the 7th Battalion at Semipalatinsk, and therefore I don't know whether I'll be able to write you and receive letters from you. You wrote me about my brother[2] a long time ago. At that time I had already prepared both a letter to you and one to my brother, but I became wary and decided not to send it, and it seems that I was right to do so. I read all your addresses in the letter to S[ergey] D[urov] and I'll take them just in case. They may indeed be reliable, but your last letter arrived opened, and therefore we need to be very careful. It would be better, if you want to grant me the happiness of writing to me, to address the letter to my brother in Petersburg, or perhaps (but not for certain) he'll

1. Natalya Dmitrievna Fonvizina, née Apukhtina (1805-69), wife of the Decembrist Ivan Alexandrovich Fonvizin. She followed her husband into Siberian exile and thus became one of the legendary "Decembrist wives." In 1850 Fonvizina managed to visit Dostoevsky and other members of the Petrashevsky Circle in the transit prison at Tobolsk, an incident that Dostoevsky remembered for years afterwards.
2. Presumably a reference to Mikhail Dostoevsky.

see you in person, or, finally, send you a trustworthy person. My brother is now in business, and therefore, I think, it is not difficult to find his address, for instance, in publications. I don't know his address myself. However, I don't advise you to rely on the postal service either. But since, I assume, acquaintances of yours travel between Moscow and Petersburg, it would be best of all to use such an opportunity to deliver a letter for me to him. That way I will have dealings only with my brother, and it's best of all in such instances to have one set of relations rather than two. It's less dangerous. However, if you find a perfectly harmless opportunity for writing to me by another channel, then of course that will be wonderful, even better, because I still don't know how I'm going to write to my brother. I keep counting on him only because he's the person with whom I'll definitely start up a correspondence. Moreover, you live in Marino, and that's the usual route between Moscow and our little village in Tula Province.[3] I've been down that road back and forth 20 times, and therefore I can clearly imagine for myself the place of your refuge, or rather, of your new incarceration.[4] With what pleasure I read your letters, dear N[atalya] D[mitrievna]! You write them marvelously, or, better to say, your letters come directly from your kind, loving heart easily and without strain. There are reserved and bilious natures that rarely find in themselves a kind moment of expansiveness. I know such people. And meanwhile they are not at all bad people, even quite to the contrary.

I don't know, but on the basis of your letter I surmise that it's with sadness that you have come again to your native region. I understand that; I've thought several times that if I ever return to my native region, I'll find more suffering than joy in my impressions. I haven't lived your life, and I don't know much about it, just as no one knows much about another's life, but we have human feelings in common, and I think that upon returning home, every exile has occasion to experience anew, in his consciousness and recollection, all his past woe. It resembles scales on which you weigh and find out exactly the real weight of what you have suffered through, endured, lost, and what good people have deprived you of. But God grant you many more long years! I've heard from many people that you are very religious, N[atalya] D[mitrievna]. Not because you're religious, but because I have experienced and felt this myself, I'll tell you that at such moments you thirst for faith like "a withered blade of grass," and find it, precisely because the truth shines through clearly in the midst of misfortune. I'll tell you of myself that I have been a child of the age, a child of disbelief and doubt up until now and will be even (I know this) to the grave. What horrible torments this thirst to believe has cost me and

---

3. A reference to Darovoye.
4. In 1853, after having spent twenty-five years in Siberian exile, the Fonvizins were allowed to return to European Russia, but on the traditional Russian condition that they live in the country, far from any large cities.

continues to cost me, a thirst that is all the stronger in my soul the more negative arguments there are in me. And yet God sometimes sends me moments at which I'm absolutely at peace; at those moments I love and find that I am loved by others, and at such moments I composed for myself a credo in which everything is clear and holy for me. That credo is very simple, here it is: to believe that there is nothing more beautiful, more profound, more attractive, more wise, more courageous and more perfect than Christ, and what's more, I tell myself with jealous love, there cannot be.[5] Moreover, if someone proved to me that Christ were outside the truth, and it *really* were that the truth lay outside Christ, I would prefer to remain with Christ rather than with the truth.

But it's better to stop talking about this. I don't know why, however, certain subjects of conversation have been completely excluded from use in society, and if people do sometime start talking about them, others seem to be shocked. But let's pass over this. I've heard that you want to travel somewhere to the south?[6] God grant that you be given permission. But whenever, please tell me, whenever will we be completely free, or at least, like other people? Perhaps only when we won't need any freedom at all? As for me, I desire the best of all or nothing. In a soldier's coat I'm just as much a prisoner as before. And how glad I am that I find in my soul patience that will last a long time, that I don't desire earthly blessings, and that I need only books, the chance to write, and to be alone several hours every day. I'm very worried about the last point. It will soon be five years that I've been under guard or in a crowd of people, and I haven't been alone for a single hour. To be alone is a normal need, like drinking and eating, otherwise in this forced communism you'll become a misanthrope. Human company will become a poison and an infection, and it's from that unbearable torment that I suffered most of all these four years. I have had moments when I hated every single person around me, the just and the guilty, and I saw them as thieves who were stealing my life from me with impunity. The most unbearable misfortune is when you become unfair, spiteful, vile yourself; you recognize all that, even reproach yourself—and can't overcome it. I've experienced that. I'm certain that God has spared you that. I think that in you, as a woman, there was much more strength for enduring and forgiving.

Write me something, N[atalya] D[mitrievna]. I'm going into the wilds, to Asia, and it's there, in Semipalatinsk, that I think all my past, my impressions, and my recollections will abandon me, because the last people whom I loved and who were before me, like the shadow of my past, will have to part with me. It's terribly easy for me to get accustomed to a place, I immediately graft myself onto whatever surrounds me, and then with pain

5. Dostoevsky's credo is repeated by the character Stavrogin in the novel *The Devils*.
6. Fonvizina wished to visit Odessa, where her sons were buried.

later tear myself away from it. Live, N[atalya] D[mitrievna]. Live happily and long! When we see each other we'll get acquainted anew, and perhaps each of us will still have many happy days allotted to him. I'm in some sort of expectation of something; I seem to be still sick now, and it seems to me that in a very, very short time something very decisive has to happen to me, that I'm approaching the crisis of my whole life, that I seem to be ripe for something, and that there will be something, perhaps calm and clear, perhaps more threatening, but in any event something inescapable. Otherwise my life will be a nonexistent life. But perhaps this is all my sick ravings! Good-bye, good-bye, N[atalya] D[mitrievna], or better to say until we meet again, let's believe that it's until we meet again.

Your D

For Heaven's sake, please forgive me for writing you such untidy and blotchy letters. But honest to God, I can't help crossing things out. Please don't be angry with me.

91. To Mikhail Dostoevsky
27 March 1854. Semipalatinsk

27 March 54.

I hasten to inform you, my dear friend, that I received your letter with the 50 silver rubles, for which I sincerely thank you. I wanted to reply to you right away, but I missed a mailing. I'm to blame, please don't be angry. I hope, my priceless friend, that now you'll write more often. Bear in mind that your letters are a real holiday for me, and therefore don't be lazy. We haven't written anything to each other in such a long time! But could you really not write to me? That's very strange and painful for me. Perhaps you didn't ask for permission yourself; but letters are permitted. I know that for certain. But now you're not going to forget about me, isn't that so?

You write about your family; thank you for that. A week doesn't pass without my dreaming of all of you. How glad I am that all my former ones, Fedya, Masha and Misha[1] are alive and well. I'm very happy for our brother Kolya.[2] Kiss him for me. I love him very much. I was thinking all

1. Dostoevsky's niece and nephews.
2. In 1854 Nikolay Dostoevsky graduated from the Directorate of Communication's

along that our brother Andrey should be getting married.[3] I guessed that on my own a long time ago. If you write him, give him my regards. I wrote you, about three weeks ago, a letter that you may not have received yet. There's a letter in it for our sister Varenka. Be sure to forward it to her and soon. I'm very curious to know about them, and especially about Sasha.[4] Finally, I definitely want to know something about Auntie.[5] Write me about them. I'll be greatly obliged. I addressed your letter to Neslind's building, to the old apartment. It will reach you, of course, but nevertheless I don't know whether you live there, and therefore I'm addressing this letter to Loginov's building, where your business is, about which I learned from advertisements.[6]

I'm extraordinarily glad that you've taken up a business. You have a family; money is essential for you; make it. Increase your activity if you can. In a word, don't abandon what you've begun.

You congratulate me on my release from prison and lament the fact that because of my poor health I can't petition to be transferred to the active army. But I wouldn't worry about my health. That's not the point. But do I have the right to petition? A transfer to the active army is a royal favor and depends on the will of the Emperor Himself. Therefore I cannot petition myself. If only it depended on me!

For the time being I'm serving, going to instruction, and remembering old times. My health is rather good, and has gotten much better in these two months; that's what it means to leave closeness, stuffiness, and painful imprisonment. The climate here is rather healthy. The Kirghiz steppe begins here. The town is rather large and populous. There are many Asiatics. The steppe is wide open. The summer is long and hotter, the winter shorter than in Tobolsk and Omsk, but severe. There is absolutely no vegetation, not a single tree—bare steppe. At a distance of several versts from town is a pine forest that stretches for many tens and perhaps hundreds of versts. Here it's all fir, pine, and white willows, there aren't any other trees. Hordes of foul. There is decent trade, but European items are so expensive that they're inaccessible. Sometime I'll write you about Semipalatinsk in greater detail. It's worth it.

And now I'll ask you for some books. Send them to me, brother. I don't need any journals; but send me European historians, economists, the Church fathers, as far as possible all the ancients (Herodotus, Thucidides, Tacitus, Pliny, Flavius, Plutarch and Diodorus and so on. They've all been

Institute of Civil Engineering in Petersburg and, according to his brother Mikhail, showed promise as an architect.

3. Andrey Dostoevsky married Dominika Ivanovna Fyodorchenko in 1850.

4. In 1854 Alexandra Dostoevskaya married N. I. Golenovsky (d. 1872), an officer serving in Petersburg.

5. The reference is to A. F. Kumanina.

6. See Letter 89, note 20, for details about Mikhail's business.

translated into French). Finally, the Carus and a German dictionary. Of course, not everything at once, but whatever you can. Also send me Pisarev's physics[7] and a work on physiology (even in French if one in Russian is expensive). Choose the cheapest and most compact editions. Not everything at once, a bit at a time. I'll be grateful to you even for a little. You can imagine how much I need this food for the soul! But there's no need for me to tell you that. Good-bye, my dear. Write often. For Heaven's sake, please don't forget your

F. Dostoevsky.

92. To Mikhail Dostoevsky
30 July 1854. Semipalatinsk

Semipalatinsk. July 30/54

It's been two months now since I wrote you you, my dear friend and brother. I couldn't, it was nearly impossible. But tell me why you are being silent.[1] How many letters I've already sent you! You, on the other hand, besides your January letter, have answered only one of mine, the first. That answer, that is, your second letter, written in April, I received at the beginning of June and had not answered until now. I assure you, my dear brother, that up to this very moment there was hardly any time. Finally, if there were actually even a few free moments, I purposely put off writing until a more convenient time,[2] all the while expecting that it would come soon. I wouldn't want to write to you in fits and starts and in haste. You know, of course, or, finally, can guess what I'm busy with now. Exercises, reviews by the brigade and division commanders and preparations for them. I arrived here in March. I hardly knew drill formation at all and nonetheless in July I stood at review along with the others and knew my stuff no worse than the others. How tired I got and what that cost me is

---

7. Probably a reference to N. Pisarevsky's *Course of General Physics* (1852; second edition, 1854).

1. In a letter written in 1856 Mikhail justified his silence by saying that since he was unable to say what he wanted to in letters going through official channels, he found it preferable not to write at all.

2. Dostoevsky probably means until a reliable person can be found to deliver a letter in person.

another question; but they're satisfied with me, and thank God! Of course, none of this is very interesting for you; but at least you know what I was exclusively occupied with. No matter what you write, you end up not telling anything in writing. No matter how alien all this is to you, I think you'll realize that soldiering is no joke, that a soldier's life, with all the obligations of a soldier, is not an entirely easy business for a person with such health and such a lack of habit, or better to say, with such complete ignorance in such matters. In order to acquire those skills, you have to do a lot of work. I'm not grumbling; it's my cross, and I deserve it. I'm writing this only so as to force a few lines from you, without which it really is hard for me to live on this earth. Understand, finally, that if we wait for a reply to each other's letters and don't write otherwise, the intervals will perhaps last three months or so. Just imagine enduring all that! You know what a letter from you means for me. Surely we're not going to reckon in letters as though they were visits. Even as it is it's been so long since we saw each other, and even as it is it's been so long since we wrote anything to each other!

I finally received letters from our sisters Varenka and Verochka. What angels! I'm sure they love me just as much as they say they do. How sweetly Varenka wrote. Her whole soul is in that wonderful letter. I planned to answer them with the very first post, but I've already put it off for the third time. I was very busy, and I don't want to write them a short letter. I don't know how to show them my love and attention. May God bless them! Now you know my main activities. To tell the truth, other than ones connected with service there haven't been any. Nor have there been any external events, upheavals in life, or extraordinary incidents. And as for my soul, heart, and mind—what has grown up, what has matured, what has withered, what has been cast out along with the weeds—you can't convey that or tell about it on a scrap of paper. I live here in solitude; as is my custom, I hide from people. Moreover, I was under guard for five years, and therefore it's the greatest pleasure for me to find myself alone sometimes. All in all, prison took a lot out of me and implanted a lot in me. I've already written you about my illness, for instance, strange attacks that resemble epilepsy and yet aren't, however. I'll write about it in greater detail sometime.

Please do me the favor, however, of not suspecting that I am the same melancholic and just as overly anxious about my health as I was in Petersburg in the last years. Everything has absolutely gone away, vanished, as though by magic. Everything comes from God and is in His hands, however. I thank our brother Kolya for his postscript. I intended to write to him myself, but let him wait for the right time and forgive me, wretched thing that I am. May he be assured of one thing—that he is very dear and near to my heart, and that I remember him with a warm feeling. Kiss him for me and wish him all the best. Give my regards to Emilia

Fyodorovna.[3] I sometimes recall with horror the year 1849 and those two months that she spent alone when your were arrested. Is she well and happy now? In prison I dreamed and thought so much about the past and the future, and mainly, about all of you. Certain recollections are painful and bitter, but I don't drive them off. Even the bitter is sweet to me.

Give my regards to our sister Sashenka; kiss her and give her my congratulations.[4] Is she well now? Kiss her for me and tell her something good about me. In general, recommend me to her. Wish her every sort of good fortune for me.

My dear, you write about money and ask whether I need any. But you know my situation yourself. If you can send some, do. After all, you're my main hope. I don't rely on anyone the way I do on you.

Good-bye, my dear! Write more about yourself. Be sure to write me about your health and more details about how your children are being brought up. Good-bye, my friend, now the letter is finished, and what have I written? It's sad to live in letters without having seen each other in 5 years. I'll write more, and more often now. But you answer me as soon as possible. Good-bye, until we see each other.

Your brother Fyodor Dostoevsky

93. To Andrey Dostoevsky
6 November 1854. Semipalatinsk

Semipalatinsk. November 6, 1854

Dear brother Andrey Mikhaylovich,

I did not receive your letter of 14 September, my beloved, until the end of October, missed one mailing, and am now hurrying to answer you. In the first place, thank you for your greeting and for not forgetting me, wretched thing that I am. You won't believe how happy your letter made me! No one in our entire family has forgotten about me! Every last one has written to me, every last one takes the most sincere, fraternal interest in me, and for me, who has grown unaccustomed to anything kind, friendly, and familial, this has all been a great happiness. It will soon be 10 months since

---

3. Mikhail Dostoevsky's wife.
4. A reference to Alexandra Dostoevskaya's getting married. See Letter 91, note 4.

I left prison and began my new life. And those 4 years I consider a time during which I was buried alive and locked up in a coffin. I can't even tell you, my friend, what a horrible time that was. It was inexpressible, unending suffering, because every hour, every minute weighed on my soul like a stone. In all those 4 years there was not a moment when I didn't feel that I was in prison. But what's the point of telling about it! Even if I wrote you 100 pages, even then you would have no notion of my life at that time. You need at least to see it for yourself, but I don't claim that you have to experience it. But that time has passed and now it's behind me, like a depressing dream, just as I imagined release from prison as a bright awakening and resurrection into a new life.[1] During all that time I had absolutely no news about all of you. I was like a severed branch. After coming out from prison I soon received a letter from Mikhail Mikhaylovich, my faithful brother, friend, and benefactor. After that our sisters soon gladdened me. From those letters I learned all about each member of your family, including you, my friend. Finally, you're writing to me, too, and at the same time my dear sister Domnika Ivanovna[2] has been so good as to send me her kind greeting. For Heaven's sake, please don't be angry with me, dear brother, for not writing to you first. I would definitely have written, however. But in my new life I've come across so many new cares and things to attend to that until now I've hardly had time to settle in! In accordance with the Imperial Decree of Clemency, I joined the 7th Line Battalion. At that point a new concern began for me: service. My health and strength were little help to me. I had left prison a very ill person. And meanwhile I had to take up drill, instruction, and inspections. I was so busy the whole summer that I hardly found time to sleep. But now I've gotten a little used to it. My health has also gotten a bit better. And without losing hope, I look ahead rather cheerfully. But enough about me; let's talk about something else, something more interesting.

In the first place, I'm indescribably glad that, to judge by all appearances, you are happy. I congratulate you on your marriage, even though the 4th anniversary of it has already passed.[3] Even before, I always thought that there is nothing in the world more lofty than family happiness. I sincerely wish it for you without end. Your lot in life is quiet, modest, but correct, and that's wonderful. It's hard to make your own way, at random, without discernment, to the right and to the left, as was the case with me my whole life long. They write a lot of good things about our brother Nikola, and he always adds a note to me in each letter himself. Our brother Mikhail Mikhaylovich and I write to each other as often as we can, but my letters take a long time to get to Russia, exactly two months, and

---

1. This passage, as well as others in the present letter, foreshadows themes and images in *Notes from the House of the Dead*.
2. Andrey Dostoevsky's wife. See Letter 91, note 3.
3. Andrey Dostoevsky had married in July 1850.

therefore you probably won't receive the present one, my dear, until Christmas. The only person to whom I haven't written is our sister Sashenka, although I send my regards to her in letters to Mikhail Mikhaylovich. She hasn't written to me, and it's a ticklish situation for me. I don't want them to think that I'm hoping to take advantage of them, since I'm in a condition that is in any case impoverished. I'm not talking about her, but about her husband, whom I don't yet know. But I'll write nontheless, and let this last business remain just between the two of us. Good-bye, my dear, write often; I thank you, don't forget me. I'll never forget about all of you.

Your loving brother F. Dostoevsky.

I urgently request that you kiss all my dear ones for me right away, and of course, my dear little nieces Evochka and Mashenka, too.[4]

94. To Domnika Dostoevskaya[1]
6 November 1854. Semipalatinsk

Dear sister Domnika Ivanovna,[2]

Your kind, friendly letter, in which you come right out and call me your brother, gave me inexpressible pleasure. Through it I learned that I have another sister, that there is yet another loving and compassionate heart that has not denied me greeting and sympathy. That was doubly pleasant for me. It was pleasant to get to know such a sister and to see her as my dear brother's wife. But there's something strange in this exchange of feelings and thoughts between us. To know that we'll never get together, never see each other—unless a miracle intervenes in my fate and God finally performs it for me—to know this, and how, please tell me, can one not feel a longing, at least for one's native region and for all that is dear in it, a longing that darkens the bright feeling that visits me when I reread your letter? May God grant you every happiness and joy. I wish you that as a brother; for you are already near and dear to me as a sister. I thank you

---

4. A reference to Andrey and Domnika Dostoevsky's children.

1. Domnika Ivanovna Dostoevskaya, Andrey Dostoevsky's wife.

2. The addressee is actually Dostoevsky's sister-in-law, but in common Russian parlance the terms "brother" and "sister" extend to in-laws and cousins.

again for your letter. Love me as I love you, and don't forget

a brother who is devoted to you with all his heart,

F. Dostoevsky

Marya Dostoevskaya (1850s)

Pavel Isaev, Dostoevsky's stepson (1870s)

1855

95. To Yevgeny Yakushkin[1]
15 April 1855. Semipalatinsk

April 15

I thank you, dear Yevgeny Ivanovich, for remembering me and for your attention to me. I unexpectedly, to my good fortune, seem to have found in you a good friend. I thank you once again. Of myself I'll say that I'm living for the most part on hopes alone, and my present is not very pretty. Moreover, ill health has been added in here too. My comrade D[urov] has left military service and, as I have heard, has found employment with civilian duties in Omsk. (That's all because of his illness.)

I received the Pushkin.[2] I thank you very much for it. My brother wrote me that as long ago as last spring via you he sent me certain books, for instance, the Church fathers, ancient historians, and things—a box of cigars. But I didn't receive anything from you. Please let me know now whether you sent anything to me. If you did, then it got lost on the way. If you didn't send anything, then of course you didn't receive it yourself. Please do me a favor and let my brother know about this.

My endeavors here are very vague. I'd like to do something systematically. But I read and write a bit in fits and starts. There's no time, especially now; absolutely none. You write about collecting songs.[3] I'll be very happy to try, if I find anything. I doubt that, however. But I'll try. I have never collected anything like that myself up until now. I was always stopped by the thought that if you're going to do something, you should do it well. But if you collect casually, even folk songs, you won't really end up collecting anything. Nothing is granted to one without effort. Moreover, my activities now are of another sort. How much I need to read, and how far behind I've fallen! In general, there is disorder in my life.

Please let me know who *Olga N.*[4] and *L. T.*[5] are (the latter published

---

1. Yevgeny Ivanovich Yakushkin (1826-1905), jurist ethnographer, and literary historian. Yakushkin became acquainted with Dostoevsky in Omsk in 1853.

2. The first volume of Pavel Annenkov's edition of Pushkin's works had just come out in 1855.

3. Apparently Yakushkin was interested in collecting Siberian folk songs.

4. Pseudonym of Sofia Vladimirovna Engelgardt (née Novosiltseva, 1828-94).

5. Lev Nikolaevich Tolstoy (1828-1910).

"Adolescence" in *The Contemporary*).

Good-bye, dear Yevgeny Ivanovich. Don't forget me, and I'll never forget you.

Your D

I'm enclosing a letter to K. I. Ivanov. Please forward it to Petersburg, to Lisitsyn's Building, near the Church of the Transfiguration. But you probably know the address yourself.

96. To Mikhail Dostoevsky
14 May 1855. Semipalatinsk

Semipalatinsk. 14 May 1855

My dear brother and good friend,

I finally received your letter of 26 January and 21 March and I thank you for it and for the parcel from the bottom of my heart. It came at a very opportune time, but I have to confess—and for Heaven's sake don't be angry with me for this confesion—that I had almost ceased hoping ever to receive a letter from you. It's no laughing matter! Since the 3rd of October, the date on which you wrote me the next-to-last time, nothing, not a single line until now! What things didn't occur to me! In the first place, your health: I thought, I was absolutely certain that you were either seriously ill or dead. You know how over-anxious I am about health. How I was tormented!

But, fortunately, just before spring I came across newspapers with your advertisements.[1] Then other thoughts began to torture me. Namely: how are your business affairs going? They must be bad, I thought to myself, when he either can't tear himself away from them or doesn't want to write about them. Please note, my dear, that not once did I think that you weren't writing because you were fed up with me and that you wrote letters to me out of a sense of decency. Not once did I doubt your wonderful heart. I wrote to our sister Varenka, who also hasn't written to me for a long time (and the others have stopped writing completely), that

1. Mikhail had a tobacco and cigarette factory.

you had surely forgotten me and that that was very depressing for me. But those words were wrung from my heart by misery, and don't be angry for them; I was very depressed. I'm very glad that your business is getting along. Don't abandon it, my friend. It's the only hope for you and your family. I always read your stories about your family with pleasure. How happy I am for your children! I love them so much, just as though I had never left them. I don't want to believe that Mashenka isn't attractive. That is impossible. In your other letters write me more about Moscow. How glad I am that you have become friendly with them and were well received by Uncle and Auntie.[2] You know what, write me in detail all about their life (that is, about Uncle), what they're doing and how they are. Also acquaint me with our new relatives, Golenovsky,[3] Ivanov, in detail. I've heard very little by way of particulars and details about them from you.

What can I tell you about my life? I live a day at a time and nothing more. My health is not entirely good and therefore my life is not entirely wonderful. I'm still subject to various fits, and although they happen at long intervals, they're still very unpleasant. Now I'm busy with service. Don't be angry with me, for Heaven's sake, for writing so little about myself!

How is Emilia Fyodorovna's[4] health? God grant her all the best. Tell me, brother, all my life I've been supported by you, have been in debt to you. What a fate! Thank you, thank you for not abandoning me; and without you what would I be!

Good-bye, my dear. Love me as I love you.

Your F. Dostoevsky

2. A. F. and A. A. Kumanin.
3. N. I. Golenovsky, Alexandra Dostoevskaya's husband.
4. Mikhail Dostoevsky's wife.

97. To Marya Isaeva[1]
4 June 1855. Semipalatinsk

Semipalatinsk. 4 June 55

I thank you boundlessly for your kind letter from the road, my dear and never-to-be-forgotten friend, Marya Dmitrievna. I hope that you and Alexander Ivanovich[2] will permit me to call you both friends. After all, we were friends here, I hope that we will remain so. Can it really be that separation will change us?[3] No, judging by how difficult it is for me without you, my dear friends, I also judge by the strength of my attachment . . . Just imagine: this is already the second letter I've written to you. I had a reply ready for the last mail to your kind, sincere letter, dear Marya Dmitrievna. But it wasn't sent. Alexander Yegorych,[4] with whom I intended to send it to be posted, suddenly left for Zmiev, last Saturday, so that I didn't even know about his departure and didn't find out about it until Sunday. His servant also disappeared for two days and the letter remained in my pocket. Such grief! I'm writing now, and I still don't know whether this letter will be sent. A[lexander] Ye[gorovich] still isn't here. But a courier has been sent to fetch him. At any moment we're expecting the Governor-General, who at this minute may already have arrived. They say he'll spend about five days here. But enough about that. How was the trip to Kuznetsk, and, God forbid, did anything happen on the way? You write that you were upset and even ill. Even now I'm terribly alarmed for you. So many cares, so much unavoidable trouble, if only from the move, and now add illness to that, why how can one endure it! I think only of you. Besides, you know that I'm overly anxious about health; you can judge about my agitation. My God! But is this fate, are these cares, these petty troubles worthy of you, you who could serve as a decoration for any society! Cursed fate! I'm anxiously awaiting a letter from you. Oh, if only it

1. Marya Dmitrievna Isaeva (née Konstant, 1825-64), married Dostoevsky in 1857. Her first husband, Alexander Ivanovich Isaev, died in 1855, only a few months after his transfer to Kuznetsk, leaving his widow and son practically helpless.

The marriage between Dostoevsky and Marya Dmitrievna was not a happy one, and from 1859 on she was very much on the periphery of Dostoevsky's life. His early passionate feelings for her, as well as his fears that she might marry a rival, the teacher Vergunov, found reflection in the novel *The Insulted and the Injured*.

2. See note 1.

3. Isaev had recently been reassigned from Semipalatinsk to Kuznetsk, over 400 miles away.

4. Alexander Yegorovich Vrangel (1833-after 1912), diplomat, jurist, and archeologist. He and Dostoevsky became close in Semipalatinsk, where Vrangel served as the public procurator. Vrangel did much to improve Dostoevsky's lot while in exile. The close relations between the two men gradually came to an end after Dostoevsky's return to European Russia.

were with this mail; I went to check, but A[lexander] Ye[gorovich] still isn't here. You ask how I spend my time and write that you don't know how my schedule looks without you. It's two weeks now that I haven't known what to do with myself out of misery. If you only knew to what an extent I've been orphaned here alone! Really, this time reminds me of when I was first arrested in forty-nine and buried in prison, torn away from everything near and dear. I have become so accustomed to you. I never viewed our acquaintance as an ordinary one, and now, having been deprived of you, I've guessed about a lot of things on the basis of experience. I lived for five years without people, alone, without having, in the full sense of the word, anyone to whom I could pour out my heart. You accepted me like a member of the family. Alexander Ivanovich wouldn't have looked after his own brother the way he did me. How much trouble I caused you with my difficult personality, and you both loved me. After all, I realize that and sense it, after all, I'm not lacking a heart. You, you amazing woman, a heart of amazing, childlike kindness, you were a sister to me. The mere fact that a woman extended her hand to me made for an entire epoch in my life. A man, the very best, at certain moments, if you'll allow me to say so, is no better or worse than a blockhead. A woman's heart, a woman's compassion, a woman's sympathy, infinite kindness, of which we have no notion and which because of our stupidity we often fail to notice, is irreplaceable. I found all of that in you; a sister would not have been kinder and more gentle toward me and my flaws. Because if there were in fact flare-ups between us, then, in the first place, I was an ungrateful swine, and in the second, you (yourself) were ill, irritated, insulted, insulted by the fact that foul society had failed to appreciate you, did not understand you, and with your energy it's impossible not to be indignant about injustice; that is noble and honest. That is the basis of your character; but grief and life, of course, exaggerated a lot, irritated a great deal in you, but my God, all of that has been redeemed with interest, a hundred times over. And since I'm not always stupid, I saw that and appreciated it. In a word, I could not help becoming attached to your home with all my heart as though to a native spot. I'll never forget the both of you, and I'll be eternally grateful. Because I'm certain that you both fail to understand what you did for me and to what an extent I needed people such as you. That has to be experienced and only then will you understand. If you hadn't been here, I might have become completely apathetic, but now I'm a human being again. But enough; you can't tell about all of that, especially in a letter. A letter is cursed immediately because it reminds me of the separation, and everything reminds me of it. In the evenings, at twilight, at the time when I used to set out to see you, I'm overcome by such melancholy that if I were given to tears, I would cry, and you surely wouldn't laugh at me for that. My heart has always been of such a character that it grows attached to what is dear to it, so that later it has to be torn away and bloodied. I now live completely alone, I've absolutely nowhere to go; I'm fed up with everything here. Such emptiness! There's only A[lexander] Ycgorych, but it's difficult for me to be with him, simply because I cannot help comparing you with him, and of course, the result is well known. And besides which, he isn't even at home. I went twice without him to the Kazakov Gardens,[5] where he has moved to, and it was so sad. When I recall last summer, when I recall that you, poor thing, all summer long wished to go somewhere out in the country, at least to breathe some fresh air, and couldn't, then I feel so sorry for you, so sad for you. But remember how once we did manage to visit the Kazakov Gardens, you, Alexander Ivanovich, Elena, and I. How clearly I recalled everything when I arrived at the Gardens this time. Nothing has changed there and the bench on which we sat is the same... And I felt so sad. You write that I should live with Vrangel, but I don't want to, for many important reasons. (1) Money. If I live with him, I obviously will have to spend more: apartment, servants, food, and I would find it hard to live at his expense. (2) My personality. (3) His personality. (4) When I took a look, I saw that people often hang around his place, and even a lot of them. To excuse oneself from company is sometimes impossible, and I can't bear strangers. Finally, I like to be alone, I'm used to it, and habit is second nature. But enough. I still have told you hardly anything. After seeing you to the forest and parting with you at that pine tree (which I noticed), Vrangel and and I returned arm in arm (he led his horse) to the Peshekhonovs'[6] hospitable farm. Right then and there I felt that I had been completely orphaned. At first we could still see your carriage, then hear it, but, finally, everything disappeared. After we got into the sleigh, we talked about you, about how your trip would be, about you in particular, and then, by the way, Vrangel told me something that made me very happy. Precisely on the day of your departure, in the morning, when Pyotr Mikhaylovich[7] invited Vrangel somewhere for the whole evening, he excused himself and to the question "why" answered: "I'm seeing the Isaevs off." There were some people there. P[yotr] M[ikhaylovich] immediately asked: "You mean, you know them well?" Vrangel responded sharply that although it was a recent acquaintance, nonetheless it was one of the most pleasant homes for him, and that the mistress of the house, that is, you, was such a woman as he had not yet met since Petersburg and didn't ever hope to meet again, and such a woman "as you," he added, he "perhaps had never even seen, and the acquaintance with whom I consider the highest honor." I liked that story a lot. A person who inarguably has seen women of the very best society (for he was born into it), has the right to authority, I think, in such a judgment. With those

5. Reference to an attractive country home and estate in Semipalatinsk where Vrangel lived at the time of the writing of the present letter and to where Dostoevsky later moved.

6. Pyotr Mikhaylovich Peshekhonov, a judge in Semipalatinsk. Dostoevsky was a frequent guest at his farm.

7. P. M. Peshekhonov.

conversations and railing at the Peshekhonovs, we arrived in town almost at dawn, and the driver, to whom we had not given any preliminary instructions, drove us right to my apartment. In that way the proposed tea fell through, for which I was very glad, because I very much wanted to be left alone. At home it was a long time yet before I went to bed, I paced around the room, looked at the dawn that was breaking and recalled this whole year, which had passed for me so quickly, recalled everything, everything, and I began to feel melancholy when I pondered my fate. Since then I've been wandering around without a destination, a real Eternal Jew. I hardly visit anyone. I'm fed up. I visited Grinenko, who has been assigned to Kopal and is leaving in a few days (he'll be in Verny, too), Meder, who finds that I have lost weight, Zhunechka (I wished him a happy nameday), where I met the Peshekhonovs and talked with them, I visit Belikhov,[8] and finally, I go to camp for instruction. Sometimes I'm sick. With what impatience I waited for the Tatar drivers. I kept going to see Ordynsky,[9] and Sivochka ran off every evening to check. I dropped by your apartment, took the ivy (it's with me now), saw the orphaned Surka, who rushed to meet me but doesn't go far from the house. Finally, the drivers returned. Your letter, for which I thank you endlessly, was a joy for me. I asked the Tatars about you, too. They told me a lot. How they praise you (everyone praises you, Marya Dmitrievna!). I gave them some money. On the following day I saw Koptev[10] at Vrangel's. He also told me a few things, but I couldn't ask him about the most interesting thing, about your money for the trip: it's a ticklish question. I still can't imagine how you managed the trip! How nicely you wrote the letter, Marya Dmitrievna! That's exactly the sort of letter I wanted; as many details as possible, and in the future do the same. I can almost see your grandmother. The good-for-nothing old woman! And she'll hound you to death. Let her stay with her pug dogs "to the end of her days." I hope that Alexander Ivanovich will extract a will, as he should, but not take her. She needs to be persuaded that things will be better that way: otherwise she should give you a signed statement that she'll die in three months (1,000 rubles a month), don't take her in otherwise. Can it really be that you, you, Marya Dmitrievna, will have to look after her pug dogs, and with your health! My, but these old woman are unbearable! I read your letter to Vrangel (parts of it, of course). I couldn't restrain myself and ran to see Elena: she's all alone, poor thing. How sorry I was that you were ill on the trip. I can hardly wait for your letter! I'm so worried. How did the trip go? I press Alexander Ivanovich's hand firmly and kiss him. I hope that he'll write me soon. I embrace him with all my

8. Lieutenant-Colonel Belikhov, Commander of the 7th Siberian Line Battalion, in which Dostoevsky served.

9. Karl Ordynsky, the treasurer of the 7th Siberian Line Battalion.

10. Ivan Kharitonovich Koptev, a captain who served in the office of the Governor-General for Western Siberia.

heart, and both as a friend and as a brother I wish him the best company. Surely he won't be as lacking in discrimination in Kuznetsk as he was in Semipalatinsk? And are such people worth it, spending time with them, eating and drinking with them and putting up with their vileness! Why, that means consciously doing harm to oneself. And how repellent they are, and mainly, how filthy it is. Sometimes after their company it's just as filthy in your soul as though you had gone to a tavern. I hope Alexander Ivanovich won't get angry with me for my wishes. Good-bye, never-to-be-forgotten Marya Dmitrievna! Good-bye! After all, we will see each other, won't we? Write me often and a lot, write about Kuznetsk, about the new people, about yourself as much as possible. Kiss Pasha[11]; I'm sure he acted up on the trip! Good-bye, good-bye! Surely we'll see each other.

Your Dostoevsky

98. To Alexander Vrangel
14 August 1855. Semipalatinsk

Semipalatinsk, 14 August / 55

Beginning with the very first word I beg your pardon, my dear Alex[ander] Yegorovich, for the future disorder of my letter. I'm already certain that it will be full of disorder. It's two o'clock in the morning now, I've written two letters. My head aches, I'm sleepy, and in addition I'm all upset. This morning I received a letter from Kuznetsk. Poor unfortunate Alexander Ivanovich Isaev is dead.[1] You wouldn't believe how sorry I am for him, how torn to pieces I am. I may be the only person here who was able to appreciate him. If he had flaws, his black fate is half to blame for them. I'd like to see anyone who would have sufficient tolerance in view of all those failures. But on the other hand, how much kindness, how much sincere nobility! You didn't know him well. I'm afraid that I may be guilty before him for having at times, at bilious moments, conveyed to you, and perhaps with excessive enthusiasm, only his bad sides. He died in unbearable torments, but beautifully, as God grant you and I may die. And death makes a person beautiful. He died steadfastly, blessing his wife and

11. Pavel Alexandrovich Isaev (1848-1900), Dostoevsky's stepson-to-be. For most of his life he lived on handouts from Dostoevsky or on the charity of Mikhail Dostoevsky's family.
1. A. I. Isaev died 4 August 1855.

children,[2] and only worrying about their fate. Poor Marya Dmitrievna[3] informs me about his death in the most minute details. She writes that recalling those details is her only comfort. In the greatest agony (he suffered terribly for two days) he kept calling her, embracing her, and repeating endlessly: "What's going to happen to you, what's going to happen to you?" In his torments about her he would forget his own pain. Poor man! She is in despair. In every line of her letter there is such melancholy apparent that I couldn't read it without tears, and even you, an outsider, but a person with a heart, would cry. Do you remember their boy, Pasha? He has gone out of his mind from tears and despair. In the middle of the night he leaps from his bed, runs to the icon with which his father blessed him two hours before his death, falls to his knees and prays, in her words, for the repose of his father's soul. The funeral was poor, on other people's money (kind people were found), she was as though unconscious. She writes that she feels herself in bad health. She spent several sleepless days and nights at his bedside. Now she writes that she is sick, has lost sleep, and can't eat a bite. The district police officer's wife and another woman have been helping her. She has nothing except debts at the store. Someone sent her three silver rubles. "Need forced my hand to accept them," she writes, "and I accepted ... the alms!"

If you, Alexander Yegorovich, have the same idea as a few days ago, in Semipalatinsk (and I'm certain that you have a noble heart and that you don't renounce good ideas *because of some empty reason that has nothing to do with the matter),* then send now, with the letter than I'm enclosing from myself to her, the sum of which we spoke. But I repeat, dear Alexander Yegorovich, even more than then I am planning to consider the whole 75 rubles (formerly 25) my debt to you. I'll definitely pay it back to you, but not soon. I know very well that your kind heart thirsts to do a good deed itself ... But consider: you are a recent acquaintance of theirs, you hardly know them, so little that although the deceased Al[exander] Iv[anovich] did borrow money from you for the trip, your offering her any, in your own name—is difficult!

On my part, in my letter to her I'm writing her all about your readiness to help and that without you I wouldn't be able to do anything. I'm not writing that so that the honor of a good deed belongs to you or so that they'll be grateful to you. I know that as a Christian, you don't need that. But I don't want them to be grateful to me when I don't deserve it; because I took from someone else's pocket, and although I'll try to repay it soon—I borrowed it practically for an indefinite period.

If you intend to send the money, put it in with my letter to her, which I'm enclosing (unsealed). It would be very good of you if you were to write

2. The Isaevs had only one child, their son Pavel Alexandrovich.
3. M. D. Isaeva.

her at least a few lines. Let's grant that you were not very well acquainted. But he remained in debt to you; now she knows that you gave me the money—and therefore there's a chance for you to write, you even ought to—what do you think? Not a lot, just a few lines . . . But my God! I seem to be teaching you how to write! Believe me, Alex[ander] Yegorovich, I know very well that you understand, perhaps better than another, how one should deal with a person to whom one has had occasion to lend money. I know that you will double, triple your courtesy with him; you need to be careful with a person who has borrowed; he is overly sensitive; *he thinks that through discourtesy towards him and lack of ceremony people want to make him pay for the loan* made to him. You know all of that as well as I do; if God gave us sense and nobility, we can't be any other way. Noblesse oblige, and you are noble, I know.

But I also know, from your own words, that your pocketbook is not absolutely in good repair right now. And therefore, if you can't send the money, don't send her my letter, but return it to me afterwards. Please do me the favor of letting me know, with the first post, *WHETHER YOU SENT THE LETTER OR NOT.*

He recalled you as he was dying. I think that it was this way, that he (his words) said he "*didn't dare even to think of offering it to you in place of the debt,*" but he asked to forward the book to you, *as a reminder of himself (Alexander's Associates,*[4] remember that beautiful edition; he received it from Petropavlovsk, where he had left it). The book will be sent to you.

I'm writing to you in Barnaul, to the address that you gave me, but I still don't know whether you're in Barnaul. I think you wrote then that I should address letters to Barnaul after the 23rd. I'm sending it on the off chance, via Krutov. Is it all right via Krutov? Write me. What are you doing, are you having a good time? By the way, is it true, as I heard (and several times, already), that Mlle A[ba]za[5] is getting married?

If you're going to send money, don't delay. Of course there can never be a more difficult position than right now.

Since I don't know whether this letter will catch you in Barnaul and whether it might not sit there until your arrival, with this post I'm writing Marya Dmitrievna another letter, which I'm sending tomorrow, *hoping for the best!* I'm also sending you your Saturday correspondence. I opened the letter, as you told me to do. If Krutov has time to bring me *MONDAY'S* letters tomorrow, too, I'll enclose them as well.

Good-bye. I have a terrible headache. I'm so upset. The pen won't stay in my hand. I embrace you from the bottom of my heart.

Your. F. D.

---

4. *Alexander I and His Associates in 1812, 1813, and 1814,* by A. I. Mikhaylovsky-Danilevsky (1845-50).

5. Olga Abaza. She lived in Zmeinogorsk and knew both Dostoevsky and Vrangel. The latter refers to her in his memoirs as "the beauteous Olga Abaza."

99. To Mikhail Dostoevsky
21 August 1855. Semipalatinsk

Semipalatinsk, 21 August 1855

My good friend, my dear brother Misha! It's been a very long time since I had so much as a line from you, and as usual, I'm beginning to be alarmed and to complain. Apparently things will be the way they were last summer. My friend, if only you knew what bitter isolation I am in here, you really wouldn't torment me so long and wouldn't feel it a burden to write me at least a few lines. You know what? A depressing thought sometimes occurs to me. I think that time is gradually having its way; the old attachment is weakening and former impressions are growing dim and being erased. I think that you're beginning to forget me. How else can I explain such long intervals between letters? Don't reproach me if I sometimes go for a long time myself without writing you. But in the 1st place, I always write more often, and in the 2nd, I swear to you that I sometimes have very difficult duties, I get tired and—I miss a mailing, which in our case goes out only once a week. Yours is a different case. Even if in fact, for instance, there's nothing to write, then at least something, at least two lines. The thought wouldn't occur to me that you're abandoning me. My dear friend, last year, in October, in response to similar reproaches, you wrote me that it was very sad and depressing for you to read them. My dear Misha! Don't be angry with me, for Heaven's sake, remember that I'm lonely, like a cast off stone; that in character I have always been melancholy, ill, and overly anxious. Take all of that into consideration and forgive me if my reproaches are wrong and my assumptions stupid; I'm even convinced myself that I'm wrong. But you know that a doubt even the size of a poppy seed is depressing. But after all, there's no one who can dissuade me other than you yourself.

Are you alive, are you well? Those are the questions that so often torment me. I read the 4th page of the newspapers, hoping at least to see your advertisements. Is all your family well? God grant it! I love you all just as much as before, and I remember you as though I had never been separated from you. How are your business affairs? Are they going well? That is so important! You know, I think so much about your business enterprises. Surely they will reward you for everything that you have given up for them (literature, government service, activities more in line with your character). You've had the factory for several years now, and what do you think, are there at least positive hopes for the future?[1] And

1. Mikhail had a tobacco and cigarette factory.

meanwhile time is passing, the children are growing, expenses are increasing. Oh, if only I could know all of these things in greater detail.

What can I tell you about my life? Everything is as before, and since my last letter hardly anything has changed. I live quietly. In the summer the service is more difficult, there are inspections. I can't boast of my health, my good friend. It's not entirely good. The older you get, the worse. If you think that there's still anything left in me of that irritable over-anxiousness and suspicion of every disease in me, as was the case in Petersburg, please be disabused of that, there's not a bit of that left, just as together with that a lot of other things are gone too.

Write me, for Heaven's sake, about our sisters. How is dear Varenka doing? Is everyone well? I can hardly wait for a letter from her. You must see Sasha often.[2] Write me about what she is like, whether she is kind, and what sort of character she has. And by the way, give her my regards and kiss her for me.

In your last letter you wrote about the children, that Fedya is a good boy but of limited talents and that Mashechka is not as attractive as she was when I knew her as a baby. But at such an age, it seems to me, it is difficult to notice either of those things.

Write me something about Kolya,[3] and especially whether you've heard anything from our brother Andrey, and where should I write him now. He wrote me once and then fell silent. I wouldn't want to break off correspondence with him.

Write me, for Heaven's sake, my dear, my kind brother, and don't abandon me! It's difficult for me here, and most importantly, it's sad. A desperate and constant longing. Good-bye, I embrace you! Give my regards to Emilia Fyodorovna.[4] Wish her all the best. I wish her that with all my heart. I remember her and remember her well. My God! Where is everything that used to be and where has life gone! Good-bye, my friend. Yours always,

Fyodor Dostoevsky

---

2. Alexandra Mikhaylovna lived in Petersburg after her marriage.
3. Nikolay Mikhaylovich Dostoevsky.
4. Mikhail Dostoevsky's wife.

100. To Alexander Vrangel
23 August 1855. Semipalatinsk

My dear and kind Alexander Yegorovich,

This is the second letter that I'm writing you. I would very much like to receive at least two lines from you, which you surely will do, that is, you'll send. I'd also like to press your hand. I miss you! And everything all around is so bad and there aren't any people. I hardly go anywhere. I can't stand meeting new people. You really have to look at every new person, I think, as at an enemy with whom you'll have to enter into battle. And then you can get the true measure of him. What are you doing and are you having a good time? Are you in Barnaul? I took a chance and put Barnaul on the last letter, although I recall that you said you wouldn't be in Barnaul until after the 23rd. But God knows whether you're in Barnaul even now. Now allow me to beg your pardon: I have sent my own letters on to you and am still doing so, but I entrusted your letters to Demchinsky.[1] For me to send them on myself is difficult, and for a quite simple reason: a thick package insured at the post office will cost a great deal, and I, if you will allow me to say so, haven't a penny. And therefore let Demchinsky do the forwarding.

In case you don't receive the letter that I sent you a week ago, to Barnaul, to the address you indicated (although it would be difficult not to receive it)[2]—I'm informing you that Al[exander] Iv[anovich] Isaev died (August 4th), that his wife is left alone, with questionable help, in despair, not knowing what to do, and—of course, without money.

Today I received from her the 2nd letter since her husband's death. She writes that she's very melancholy, that God has sent people all around who are sympathetic, that they help her at least a little, that she's very melancholy, and she asks what she should do. She writes that the attorney and the district police officer offer her hope by saying that Bekman[3] may give her a government subsidy (of 250 sil[ver] rubles). If anything can be done, then God grant it! For the time being she wants to sell her things. If you haven't changed your mind—(as we spoke back then) about sending 50 rubles, then send it now. It was never more needed. But I think this way: send 25 instead of 50, since with the former 25 and with the sale of things and perhaps with outside help, she'll have something to live on for a while. Some can be sent later. I'm writing this, in the 1st place, so as not to burden

---

1. Vasily Petrovich Demchinsky, Adjutant Major-General at the Main Headquarters for Western Siberia and friend of Dostoevsky in Semipalatinsk.

2. Vrangel did in fact receive Dostoevsky's letter of August 14.

3. Valerian Alexandrovich Bekman, the civilian governor of Tomsk in the 1850s.

you, since 25 is less than 50, and you surely need the money. 2) As it is, I caught hell from her for the first 25 rubles. She reproached me highly, saying that I didn't have anything myself and that I was not sparing myself. I answered that the money was yours, not mine, that without you I wouldn't have done anything, that she shouldn't worry about me, that friendship has its rights, and so on and so forth, and that—finally, without that money she would have had to endure terrible misery—she'll surely agree with that. I'll show you the letter when you arrive. My God! What a woman! It's a shame that you don't know her well.

One additional circumstance. She knows that money has been sent to her, and suspects that it's from me, but the letter is still at the Kuznetsk post office. Although she knows him, the postmaster can't make up his mind to hand it over, so as not to wind up in a mess. The address is to blame. You're right. It should have been addressed to her. It's addressed to her husband. He is dead. And therefore the postmaster (who is certain that you're the one writing) asks that you be told: *to send to the Kuznetsk post office an official or private authorization to deliver the letter to the widow Isaeva.* For Christ's sake, dear Alexander Yegorovich, do that and, most importantly, without delay. For Heaven's sake. Do you know the proper form for these authorizations? I don't. There are probably forms at the Barnaul post office. It's most unfortunate that the Kuznetsk postmaster is a stickler for form!

What can I tell you about myself? The time is dragging by listlessly. I'm not entirely well; I feel sad. I don't know any news except that (and it seems to be true) the Chinese burned down one of our trade offices in Chuguchak and the consul saved himself by fleeing. I would wish with all my heart that you be 10,000 times happier than I am. If you come across a good book during your wanderings, hang on to it. Good-bye, Alexander Yegorovich. I wish you all the best, and from the bottom of my heart. I remind you about the post office. For Heaven's sake don't delay. I press your hand firmly.

Your F. Dostoevsky

Semipalatinsk. Sunday, 23 August 55.

I've informed her, too, that 25 is being sent instead of 50. She wants to thank you. Will you write her something?

101. To Praskovya Annenkova[1]
18 October 1855. Semipalatinsk

Dear Praskovya Yegorovna,

I've wanted to write you for so long and have been waiting for a convenient opportunity for so long that I cannot pass up the present one. The bearer of my letter, Alexey Ivanovich Bakhirev,[2] is a very modest and very kind young man, a simple and honest soul. I've known him a year-and-a-half already and I'm certain that I'm not mistaken about his qualities.

I will always remember that from the very moment of my arrival in Siberia, you and all your wonderful family took a great and sincere interest in my comrades in misfortune and in me. I can't recall that without a special, consoling feeling, and I think I'll never forget it. Whoever has experienced a hard lot in life and has known its bitterness, especially at certain moments, understands how sweet it is at such a time to meet with fraternal sympathy, completely unexpectedly. You were that way with me, and I remember the meeting with you when you came to Omsk and when I was still in prison.

Since my arrival in Semipalatinsk I've received hardly any news about Konstantin Ivanovich[3] and Olga Ivanovna,[4] the acquaintance with whom will always be one of the best memories of my life. A year-and-a-half ago, when Durov and I left prison, we spent almost an entire month in their home. You'll understand what an impression such an acquaintance must have made on a person who for four years, to use the expression of my former prison comrades, was like a severed branch, like someone buried in the ground. Olga Ivanovna extended her hand to me like a sister, and the impression of that beautiful, pure soul, elevated and noble, will remain bright and clear for my whole life. God grant her much, much happiness—happiness for herself and for those dear to her. I would very much like to learn something about her. It seems to me that such wonderful souls as hers ought to be happy; only evil ones are unhappy. It seems to me that

---

1. Praskovya (Polina) Yegorovna Annenkova (née Gebl, 1800-76), wife of the Decembrist Ivan Alexandrovich Annenkov. When her husband was exiled to Chita in 1826, she followed him. The two of them lived in Nizhny-Novgorod upon Annenkov's return from exile in 1856. Praskovya Yegorovna made Dostoevsky's acquaintance in Tobolsk at the transfer prison, where she and other Decembrist wives greeted the members of the Petrashevsky Circle. She also visited Dostoevsky in Omsk in 1853.

2. Alexey Ivanovich Bakhirev and Dostoevsky shared an apartment for a time in Semipalatinsk.

3. Konstantin Ivanovich Ivanov.

4. Olga Ivanovna Annenkova, the Annenkovs' daughter.

happiness is in a radiant view of life and in an unblemished heart, not in external things. Is that so? I am sure that you understand this profoundly, and that's precisely why I'm writing it to you.

My life is dragging on so-so, but I'm informing you that I have great hopes... My hopes are based on certain facts; people are exerting themselves very hard for me in Petersburg, and perhaps I'll learn something in a few months.[5] You probably already know that by reason of poor health Durov has been released from military service and has entered the civil service, in Omsk.[6] Perhaps you have news of him. He and I don't write each other, although of course we remember each other very well.

Baron Vrangel, your acquaintance, sends you his regards. I'm very friendly with him. He is a marvelous young soul; God grant that he always remain such.

My deepest respects, full and sincere, to your spouse. I wish you complete happiness.

Have you by any chance heard anything about a certain session of fortunetelling, in Omsk, while I was there? I remember that it impressed Olga Ivanovna.[7]

Good-bye, dear Praskovya Yegorovna. I'm sure that God will allow us to see each other, and perhaps soon. I very much desire that. I remember you and all your family with reverence.

Allow me to remain, with the most profound respect, your completely devoted

F. Dostoevsky.

18 October 55.

I received a few lines from Konstantin Ivanovich this summer.

I very much respect A. I. Bakhirev, but I'm not completely candid with him about everything.

---

5. Dostoevsky tied his hopes to a poem that he wrote in the summer of 1855 on the occasion of the Empress's birthday and which the Empress received thanks to Baron Vrangel's efforts. In a petition attached to a copy of the poem and submitted to G. Kh. Gasfort, the Governor-General of Western Siberia, Dostoevsky asked to be promoted to the rank of noncomissioned officer.

6. See Letter 88, note 3, and Letter 95 for the details of Durov's biography.

7. Olga Ivanovna Ivanova had told Dostoevsky about a séance at which her receiving a large inheritance was predicted.

102. To Mikhail Dostoevsky
17 December 1855. Semipalatinsk

Semipalatinsk, December 17/55

My dear and never-to-be-forgotten friend, my brother Misha. I'm taking advantage of an opportunity to write you this letter.[1] Soon I'll have the chance to send you the fullest, most detailed account of my life here for all this time.[2] And therefore forgive me for just sending you a few lines now, from which, except for my request, you will hardly learn anything more. I could have put off the request as well until the long letter that I promise you, my friend, this winter. But my circumstances are such that I'm forced to write to you now. My friend! I'm sure that you love me and therefore will be indulgent toward me. If you only knew how hard it is for me to beg, even from you. I need money, my friend, because I've long since been reduced to extremity. It's been two years now since I've asked you for so much as a kopeck. You were so kind that you didn't forget me. Our sisters also sometimes sent something. And in spite of that, in these two years I've amassed rather a lot of debts—a lot for me at least! One thing I beg you to believe, my dear brother (I'm afraid that you may think that I understand my situation poorly, allowing myself to spend so much and even to create debts)—one thing I beg you to believe is that I'm very little to blame for my debts. There were circumstances and there were irrefutable needs. I'm not giving you any explanations now—I can't. Nor am I writing how much I owe. I'll only say that I absolutely must repay 50 silver rubles. In addition, I've rather worn out my clothes in these two years, I need to get new linen, clothes (my own); I need to replace everything. And therefore, if you send me 100 rubles, for which I ask you most earnestly, after paying my debts and buying new clothing I'll have hardly anything left. But I'm asking for only 100 rubles, dear brother. Don't send any more for the time being. I know that you won't be stingy if you have it. But I wouldn't want you to think badly of me.

Yes, brother, it is hard to beg, I repeat, even from you, especially sensing in myself everything—both the strength and the capability of getting essential things for myself. But what can I do—I can't now, and therefore I'm saying to you as to a brother—help. I won't conceal from you that I have great hopes that perhaps this unbearable situation of mine will end and will take a turn for the better. You may have heard partly about this.[3] Then my life will take a different course. But I won't conceal from

---

1. The present letter was delivered to Mikhail by Baron Vrangel.
2. Dostoevsky is referring to Letter 103, which Vrangel also delivered for him.
3. Dostoevsky has in mind his poem on the occasion of the Empress's birthday and his petition to be promoted to the rank of noncommissioned officer.

you, my friend, that I may soon need rather a large amount of money considering me and my situation. All of that will be linked in part to a change in my fate, if only my hopes are realized.[4] Now, however, I'm writing you only about my daily bread; because I'm in great need and that 100 silver rubles will only just help me.

I want to appeal to Uncle,[5] my friend. I need to have someone to help me. I so don't want to ask him! But what can I do, if any change in my fate occurs, money will be essential. You last wrote me on September 15. Your letter reached me around November 15. You see how long! During that time I had to live on something. With the money that you sent I could hardly do anything.

Don't be angry with me for frankly telling you the naked truth. Just remember one thing: I'm not demanding anything at all from you, because I know that I have no right to do that. It's one of two things: either you love me very much and want to help—or you don't. If you love me, then I ask you without ceremony, because I know that I would help not only a brother myself, but even a stranger, denying myelf. That's why I'm telling you this straight out. There were people here who helped me in extremity. Of course, I won't take money from just anyone. But there are people who have done so much selfless good for me, so much good, that *no one* as yet has done so much. I borrowed money from such a person. I need to repay him. Out of the 100 silver rubles, however, I won't be able to repay him anything. That person is Baron Vrangel.

My dear friend, I hope that you'll help me willingly and with a brotherly feeling. I believe in you, and I have never offended you with doubt. You should believe, too, that I don't want to live my whole life at your expense, and I hope that I'll finally be allowed to earn my own bread. I ask you: please send it very soon, if you can, immediately, to "His Excellency Stanislav Avgustovich Lamot,[6] Semipalatinsk." (Tout court [quite simply].)

In your letter to Mr. Lamot, write the following, word for word: "Dear Sir: You were so good as to declare your willingness to pass on to Baron Vrangel money if I sent it care of you. I am enclosing ___ rubles. Please pass them on. Allow me once more to thank you and to be allowed to remain etc." Do not put your signature on it. Don't deliver the letter to the post office yourself.

Good-bye, my priceless one. You'll soon receive a long letter from me. A lot has happened to me, I've been through a lot! Good-bye, don't forget me. Give my regards to Emilia Fyodorovna,[7] kiss all the children.

Your Dostoevsky

4. Dostoevsky is referring here to his plans to marry M. D. Isaeva.
5. A. A. Kumanin.
6. Stanislav Avgustovich Lamott was the doctor for the 7th Siberian Line Battalion.
7. Mikhail Dostoevsky's wife.

1856

103. To Mikhail Dostoevsky
13-18 January 1856. Semipalatinsk

Semipalatinsk. 13 January/56

I am taking advantage of the opportunity to write you, my friend. Since last year, when I wrote you via M. M. Kh[omentovsky],[1] I haven't been able to find, until now, a single other opportunity. Now it has presented itself. I have to confess that last year you repaid my poorly for my long letter: you hardly answered anything, didn't even answer certain of my questions to which I expected a detailed answer from you. I don't know what stopped you: laziness?—but that was completely inappropriate; business?—but I've already written that I'll never believe in the existence of business affairs that don't give even a single free moment. Carefulness? But if I write you, surely there's no reason to fear. I hope that this time you'll write me at greater length, although I'll still have to wait a long time to receive your reply—about seven months. This time I also wanted to write you a great deal and in detail, about all my life since I left Omsk and arrived in Semipalatinsk.

But I'm limiting myself to this one signature sheet, actually, because Alexander Yegorovich Wrangel, the bearer of this letter, can inform you in greater detail and very intimately about me, if not in all, then in many regards. Receive him as well as possible and try with all your might to make friends with him. This young man is worth it: a good, pure soul, and I won't even mention the fact that he has done so much for me, has shown me such devotion, such attachment, as not even my own brother would do. (That does not refer to you.) Please do me the favor of trying to like him and become good friends with him. I've already given him the best possible recommendation of you. And besides, remembering your easygoing, kind and tactful nature, which pleased everyone and everyone likes, that won't be difficult for you. Just in case, in a couple of words I'll depict Al[exander] Ye[gorovich's] personality for you, to make things easier for you, and so that you won't have any further difficulty. He is a very young, very gentle person, but with a strongly developed point d'honneur [point of

---

1. Mikhail Mikhaylovich Khomentovsky, brigadier general, acquaintance of Dostoevsky's in Semipalatinsk.

honor], incredibly kind, a bit proud (but that's from the outside, I like that), has a few youthful flaws, is educated, but not brilliantly and not deeply, likes to study, has a very weak character that is impressionable in a feminine way, he's a bit prone to depression and rather over-anxious; what infuriates and enrages someone else saddens him—the sign of a superior heart. Très comme il faut [very correct]. In the most selfless way he has undertaken to look after my concerns and help me with all his might. We're good friends, however, and he loves me. Later on I'll tell you a little more about him, but now, for the time being, I'll move on to myself.

You probably already know, my dear friend, that people are working hard to intercede for me in Petersburg and that I have great hopes.[2] If I don't manage to get everything, that is, if not complete freedom, then at least some. Al[exander] Ye[gorovich's] brother[3] (who serves in the Horse Guard) has been to see you; I know that from his letter to his brother, and he has probably informed you of the efforts being made on my behalf. Alex[ander] Yegor[ovich], I'm certain, remuera ciel et terre [will move heaven and earth] on his part, after his arrival in Petersburg, on my behalf. He'll tell you more about all this and in greater detail that I can write in this letter. On my part, I'll just tell you that I'm now in an absolutely passive state and have made up my mind to wait (I'll announce to you in passing that I've been promoted to the rank of noncommissioned officer, which is rather important, since the next act of clemency, if there should be one, will have to be, naturally, more significant than noncommissioned officer). People here assure me that in about two years or even one I may be officially admitted to the rank of officer. I'll confess that I would like to transfer to civilian service and even now wish for that, and I may even try for that. But for now at least I've made up my mind to wait passively for a response to all these current efforts that are now being made on my behalf in Petersburg. I repeat, Al[exander] Yegor[ovich] will tell you much more about this and in greater detail. I'll add this, however: my friend, don't think that any sort of social advantages or anything like that forced me to such an extent to work so zealously on my own behalf. Believe that after you've been in such scrapes as I have, you extract at least a bit of philosophy—a word that you may interpret as you wish. But there are two circumstances that force me to get out of my straits as quickly as possible and are plunging me into feverish concern for myself. It is precisely of those circumstances that I ought to inform you. (1st) It is that I want to write and publish. More than ever before I know that it was not in vain that I took this road and that I will not burden the earth with myself for naught. I'm convinced that I have talent and that I can write something good. For Heaven's sake, don't take my words to be foppery. But to whom

2. See Letter 101, note 5 for details on Dostoevsky's reasons for hoping for an imminent improvement in his lot.

3. Mikhail Yegorovich Vrangel.

am I to confide my dreams and hopes if not to you? In addition, I definitely wanted you to know for what reasons I need freedom and a certain social position.

I'm now coming to the second point, a very important one for me, but about which you have never heard anything from me. You should know, my friend, that when I left my melancholy prison, I arrived here with happiness and hope. I resembled a sick person who is beginning to recover after a long illness, and having been at death's door, even more strongly feels the pleasure of living during the first days of his recovery. I had a lot of hope. I wanted to live. What can I tell you? I didn't notice how the first year of my life here passed. I was very happy. God sent me the acquaintance with a family that I'll never forget. That's the Isaev family, about which I think I wrote you a bit, even asked you to take care of a matter for them. He had a position here, not at all a bad one, but couldn't make a go of it, and because of trouble retired. When I met him he had already been in retirement for several months and he kept trying to find another position. He had lived on his salary, had no fortune, and therefore, when he lost his position, they gradually fell into terrible poverty. When I met them they were still just managing to support themselves. He had made a lot of debts. He lived in a rather disorderly way, and besides which, his nature was rather disorderly. Passionate, stubborn, somewhat callous. He had fallen very low in the common opinion and had a lot of trouble; but he endured a great deal of undeserved persecution from the local society. He was as carefree as a gypsy, vain, proud, but didn't know how to control himself, and, as I already said, had degenerated terribly. But, by the way, his was a strongly developed and very kind nature. He was educated and understood everything that people might start in talking about with him. He was, in spite of a lot of filth, extraordinarily noble. But it wasn't he who attracted me, but his wife, Marya Dmitrievna. She is still a young woman, 28 years old, attractive, very well educated, very intelligent, kind, nice, graceful, with an excellent, wonderful heart. She bore that fate proudly, without a murmur, performed the duties of a maid herself, looking after her carefree husband, to whom I, by right of friendship, read many lectures, and after their little son. It's just that she became ill, overly impressionable, and irritable. Her character, however, was cheerful and frisky. I hardly left their house. What happy evenings I spent in her company! I have rarely met such a woman. Almost everyone broke off with them, in part because of the husband. And really, they couldn't have maintained the acquaintances. Finally a position came for him, in Kuznetsk, in Tomsk Province, as an assessor, but he had formerly been a clerk for special commissions at the customs office; the move from a rich and prominent position to an assessor was very humiliating. But what could he do! There was hardly a slice of bread, and I was just barely able to manage, after a lengthy, sincere friendship, to get them to allow me to share with them. In May 1855 I saw them off to Kuznetsk, two months later he died from kidney stones. She was left in alien surroundings, alone, exhausted and racked by long-term sorrow, with a seven-year-old child, and without a piece of bread. She didn't even have the means to bury her husband. I didn't have any money. I immediately borrowed first 25 and later 40 silver rubles from Alex[ander] Yegor[ovich][4] and sent it to her. Thank God she is now being helped by her relatives, with whom she had been somewhat at odds, because of her husband. Her relatives are in Astrakhan. Her father, the son of a French émigré, is M. de Constant; he is an old man and occupies the important position of director of quarantine in Astrakhan. He is not independently wealthy, but lives on his very large salary. Now, however, he'll soon retire and therefore his income will be diminished. Besides that, he has two other daughters on his hands. Finally, there are her husband's relatives, distant ones; one of her husband's brothers is a captain in the Finn[ish] Inf[antry] Guard Battalion. I know that her husband's family was very respectable too. Now here's what, my friend: I have loved this woman for a long time and I know that she can love me, too. I can't live without her, and therefore, if only my circumstances change at least somewhat for the better and the positive, I'll marry her. I know that she won't refuse. But the problem is that I have neither money nor social position, and meanwhile her relatives are inviting her to come live with them in Astrakhan. If my fate does not change by the spring, she will have to leave for Russia. But that will only put the matter off, not change it. My decision has been made, and even if the earth collapses beneath me, I'll carry it out. But I cannot now, not having anything, take advantage of this noble creature's attachment to me and incline her toward marriage. Since May, when I parted from her, my life has been hell. We write to each other every week. Al[exander] Ye[gorovich] knew the Isaevs, but only during the last part of their life in Semipalatinsk. He saw Marya Dmitrievna, but only knows her slightly. I have been somewhat frank with him on this point, but not completely. He doesn't know the content of this letter, but I think that he'll talk to you about all of this. Until now I've been constantly thinking of transferring to civilian service. The head of the Altay factories, Colonel Gerngross,[5] a friend of Al[exander] Yegor[ovich's], very much wants me to transfer to his service and is ready to give me a position, with a small salary, in Bárnaul. I'm thinking about that, but again I'm waiting to see whether there will be any news from Petersburg before spring. If I won't be able to leave Siberia, I'm determined to settle in Barnaul, where Al[exander] Yegor[ovich] will be coming to work as well.[6] In a little while, I know for sure, I'll be returning to Russia. But in any event I don't know when I'll be

4. A. Ye. Vrangel.

5. Andrey Rodionovich Gerngross (b. 1814).

6. Dostoevsky's hopes for transferring to civilian service and moving to Barnaul proved groundless.

able to count on a salary alone. It can't be much. Of course, I'll investigate all means and will earn money. For that purpose it would be marvelous if I were allowed to publish. In addition to that, here in Siberia, with very small capital (insignificant) one can undertake good and reliable speculation. If I only had 300 extra silver rubles here in Semipalatinsk, I would definitely earn an additional 300 in a year; it's a new and curious region. In any case, I'll be ashamed, my never-to-be-forgotten friend, to ask you to support me. But I'm sure that you'll help me a little for at least another year. Most importantly, help me now. If any sort of clemency is granted me, I'll ask Uncle[7] for help; let him at least give me something with which to start a new life. It goes without saying that before the event I won't write anyone in the world that I'm planning to marry. I'm telling you this now in great secrecy. And I confess that I didn't even want to tell you. This is a matter of the heart, which fears public discussion, fears an outsider's gaze and touch. At least that's the way my character is. And therefore, for Christ's sake, don't tell anyone about this, absolutely no one. And about my letter in general don't say anything to anyone and don't show it to anyone. For Heaven's sake, not a word about this to our sisters; they will immediately start worrying about me, and the advice to be prudent will start. But for me, without what has now become the main thing in my life, I won't even need life itself. You're the only person I believe in, my good, my best friend. You're the only one I have. Now I'll say a few words about my circumstances here in general, but only a few words, because the Baron will tell you everything better than I can. My health is very decent; I haven't had any attacks for a long time. I've established myself here on a firm footing. In spite of the fact that I'm a common soldier, everyone here who has a higher rank knows me and even considers it an honor to do so. The authorities like me and respect me. The commander of the corps (the Governor-General)[8] knows me and does his best for me. In Barnaul the head of mining, a general, is ready to do everything on his part that he can, and in his position he can do a lot.[9] But I would consider the very best thing for me is to get to Russia, at the beginning just to serve anywhere. Later, if I got permission to publish, I would be financially secure. All of that will happen, too; I'm certain of that, but perhaps I'll still have to wait awhile. Until then I may have to live in Siberia. What can I do, I'll wait. The main thing is if even the slightest clemency were visited upon me—to transfer to the civilian service and for the time being to get any old little position with a salary. I don't know whether my dreams will work out, whether they will be realized. Perhaps the possibility of this marriage will even fall through. Then, I know myself, I'll be murdered and miserable again. I need money—that's what!

7. A. A. Kumanin.
8. A. R. Gerngross.
9. See Letter 102 for details.

I tell you that I will feel guilty asking anything of you then, but at least a little, at least in the beginning, help me. Now I'll say a few words about my present financial circumstances. In a letter via Al[exander] Yegor[ovich's] brother I asked you to send me 100 silver rubles. My friend, that 100 rubles will hardly help me, because I've borrowed a great deal. In all, I have debts of 50 silver rubles, and if your money arrives soon, I'll still have 50 silver rubles left with which I can wait for a change in my circumstances, for instance, in the event of clemency. Then I'll need a significant amount of money; I'll need to dress myself, I'll need to acquire essential things, but there's no point even in listing what I'll need. I'll also have to use up very soon the 50 silver rubles that will be left; I've worn out everything I have, I'll have to get linen and repair my dress coat, have a new overcoat made. I'll have little left; it's impossible to live on less than 15 silver rubles a month, excluding unforeseen expenses, check about that with Wrangel. Everything is expensive here. I'm not even asking for any more, however. I'll get by somehow on that 100 silver rubles. Perhaps Varenka[10] will send me something—angelic soul. (How sweetly she writes letters, where did she learn that, what a delight her letters are! Not like yours, my dear sir, but better.) In the event of a change in my fate, when I'll need a significant amount of money, as I've already written to you, I'll ask Uncle. Surely he won't refuse. But my friend! If only you knew how difficult it is for me to confess one additional circumstance to you! I have one other debt, besides this one. I owe Al[exander] Yegor[ovich], having borrowed from him at various times, 125 silver rubles. Don't ask where they went! I don't even know myself! I only know that I live in great poverty, deny myself everything, and in the meantime I've made debts! I'm not requesting, my friend, that you repay Alex[ander] Yegorovich for me. That would be too much! But I only know that I must repay him, and even though he blushes when I start up about my debt and is even annoyed if I remind him of it. (He is a most tactful person!) But enough about money! I know that you won't forget me! My only thought is of somehow providing for myself as soon as possible and not being a burden to all of you. I'll add a few more words about Alexander Yegorovich. Listen! If you manage to become friendly with him, look after him, don't leave him on his own. I'll tell you a big secret, and perhaps it's bad of me to tell you this about him, but it's for his own good. Il est amoureux fou d'une dame ici, d'une dame parfaitement comme il faut, très riche et d'une famille considérée. [He is madly in love with a woman from here, a perfectly respectable woman, very rich and from a respected family.] She'll arrive in Petersburg at almost the same time.[11]

Don't let on to Vrangel that you know about this, but be like a brother

---

10. Dostoevsky's sister Varvara Mikhaylovna (Karepina).
11. The reference is to Yekaterina Iosifovna Gerngross (b. 1818).

to him, as I have been to him, take my place, look after him, because he's capable of the most horrible, that is, tragic foolishness dans cette affaire[in this affair], and I wouldn't like that to happen. There is a certain Marquis de Traverse (the son of the one in Revel), and although they grew up together and are friends, my Baron has reason to consider him his rival, and therefore the two of them together could do a lot of stupid things. I won't write anything more. If you make friends with Alex[ander] Yegorov[ich] and earn his confidence, he'll tell you all about it himself. If not, there's no reason for you to know any more. But in any event, using this little information that I've written you, look after him. He has a weak, gentle, even over-sensitive character; stop him. But in any event, for Heaven's sake, *not a single word to anyone* about this. And don't tell Vrangel that I wrote you about this, even in a moment of candor if the two of you become close. I did this for him because I like him very much. This secret is known by *him, me,* and now *you;* but by no one else. Give me your word of honor that you'll keep your silence. He's not at all candid with his brother, but I take such an interest in everything that concerns Alex[ander] Yegor[ovich] that I'm thinking of writing his brother a few words. In addition to this secret, I'll tell you that he doesn't quite get along with his father, who is a person of a stubborn, strange, overly-anxious, and suspicious character. His father loves him terribly much, but demands, for instance, that he not dare take a step without his permission, up to the most minor matters (all from love), is himself rich and even very much so, but is miserly with his children; and my Baron doesn't even want to take from him, because his father has the habit of reproaching his children for money given them. But I foresee and know that he may have great difficulties with his father. If he's candid with you—comfort him in his troubles, impress him with the fact that a father is nonetheless a father, and that he needs to get along with him somehow. He has a sister who seems to be the guardian angel for the whole family. I have read her letters and know of her from the Baron's stories.

18 January—I've written letters to our sisters, to Uncle (from whom I'm not asking anything), Ivanov, Maykov, and Prince Odoevsky. I'm asking the Prince to help when I seek permission to publish. Perhaps I'll soon have time to write a patriotic article about Russia.[12]

If I'm allowed to publish, I'll petition for that, and there will be money. Do you happen to know Yevg[eny] Nik[olaevich] Yaku[shkin]?[13] If not, make his acquaintance. He takes great interest in me. Please get to know Ivanov better.

---

12. The general drift of Dostoevsky's planned patriotic article can be gleaned from Letter 104. Dostoevsky dropped his plans for the article after the humiliating Treaty of Paris (1856), whose conditions placed Russia in a situation quite at odds with the optimistic picture that Dostoevsky no doubt would have painted.

13. Dostoevsky has the patronymic wrong. It should be Ivanovich.

Please don't get yourself into a stew and get all alarmed about what I've told you about my attachment. Perhaps it will come to be, perhaps not. I'm an honest person and don't wish to use my influence to force that noble creature to sacrifice herself to me. But when the chance comes, even if 5 years from now, I'll carry out my intention.

Please don't be angry with me for my request for money. Just help me now. Soon, very soon perhaps, my fate will change.

Good-bye, my friend, live happily, don't forget me. Now that Vrangel has left, I'm completely orphaned. It's very sad.

Kiss the children, give my regards to Emilia Fyodorovna.[14] Is she well? May God grant you all happiness. Love me and remember me. I love you very much, too.

Your D

104. To Apollon Maykov
18 January 1856. Semipalatinsk

Semipalatinsk. 18 January 56.

I've wanted to reply to your dear letter for a long time, my dear Ap[ollon] Nik[olaevi]ch. I was somehow reminded of old, former times as I read it. I thank you countless times for the fact that you haven't forgotten me. I don't know why I always thought that you wouldn't forget me, probably for the simple reason that I couldn't forget you. You write that a lot of time has passed, many things have changed, much has been experienced. Yes! That must be so. But at least the fact that we as people haven't changed is good. I am answering for myself. I could write you a lot of interesting things about myself. Just don't reproach me for writing you now in haste, in fits and snatches, and perhaps things that are unclear. But at this moment I'm feeling what you also probably did when writing to me: the impossibility of revealing oneself after so many years not just in one, but even in 50 sheets. For that one needs to talk eye to eye, so that the soul can be read on the face, so that the heart can be felt in the sounds of a word. A single word, spoken with conviction, with complete sincerity and without hesitation, eye to eye, face to face, means much more than dozens of sheets of paper covered over with writing.

14. Mikhail's wife.

I thank you especially for the news about yourself. I knew ahead of time that that was how things would work out and that you would get married. You ask whether I remember Anna Ivanovna.[1] But how could I forget? I'm glad for your happiness, it was no stranger to me even before; remember 1847, when all of that began.[2] Mention me to her and assure her of my boundless respect and devotion. Tell your parents that I remember and continue to remember their friendship and kindness with pleasure. Did Yevgenia Petrovna[3] get the book—analyses and criticism in *Notes of the Father[land]*, written by the never-to-be-forgotten Valerian Nikolaevich?[4] When I was arrested the book was taken away from me, then returned, but under arrest there was no way I could deliver it to Yevgenia Petrovna, and I knew that it was very dear to her. All of that saddened me greatly. 2 hours before setting off for Siberia I asked the Commandant, Nabokov, to return the book to its owner. Did they give it back? Give my regards to your parents. With all my heart I wish them happiness and a long, long life. Perhaps you know some details about me through my brother. In the hours when I have nothing to do, I've been jotting down some things from my recollections of the time spent in prison, the things that were most interesting. There's very little there that is strictly personal, however. If I finish it and there is ever a very covenient opportunity, I'll send you a copy, written in my own hand, as a remembrance. (By the way, I forgot, and am now forced to make a digression.) This letter will be delivered to you by Baron Alexander Yegorovich Vrangel, a very young peron with excellent qualities of soul and heart, who arrived in Siberia directly out of the lyceum, with the *generous* dream of getting to know the region, being useful, and so on. He served in Semipalatinsk; we became close, and I have come to like him very much. Since I will ask you very earnestly to take note of him and get to know him, if possible, very well, I'll give you a couple of words about his character: an extraordinary amount of kindness, no special convictions, a noble heart, he has intelligence—but his heart is weak, tender, although at first glance his appearance has a certain aspect of inaccessibility. I would very much like for you to get to know him altogether for his own good. The half-aristocratic, or 3/4 aristocratic, baronial circle in which he grew up is not entirely to my liking, nor to his, since he has superior qualities, but a lot is noticeable from the old influence. Have your influence on him, if you have time. He is worth it. He has done me a multitude of kindnesses. But I like him and not only for the kindnesses done me. In conclusion: he is a bit

1. Anna Ivanovna Maykova (née Gusyatnikova, 1830-1911).

2. Dostoevsky is referring to the period when he first made the acquaintance of Maykov's future wife.

3. Ye. P. Maykova.

4. Reference to V. N. Maykov. For more details on the fate of the missing book, see Letter 88.

oversensitive, very impressionable, sometimes reserved and somewhat uneven in his moods. If you make friends with him, talk to him simply, as sincerely as possible, and don't begin from afar. Forgive me for pleading for the Baron. But I repeat, I like him very much. (Keep my remarks about him, and this letter in general, secret; there's no need for me to instruct you, however.)

You say that you used to reminisce about me warmly and say "Why? Why?" I reminisced about you warmly, too, and in answer to your word *"Why?"* I won't say anything—it would be superfluous. You say that you have been through a lot, changed your mind about a lot of things, and have experienced many new things. It couldn't have been otherwise, and I'm certain that even now you and I would agree with each other about our ideas. I have also thought and agonized, and there were such circumstances, such influences, that I had to live through, think over, and chew over too much, even beyond my endurance. Knowing me well, you surely will do me the justice of realizing that I always followed what seemed best and most direct to me and didn't dissemble, and whatever I gave myself up to, I gave myself up to passionately. Don't imagine that with these words I'm making some sort of hints about why I wound up here. I'm speaking now of what followed that, it would be inappropriate to speak of the past, and in any event that was no more than an incident. Ideas change, the heart remains the same. I read your letter and didn't understand the main point. I'm speaking of patriotism, of the Russian idea, of the feeling of national duty and honor, of everything of which you speak with such enthusiasm. But my friend! Were you ever any different? I always shared precisely those feelings and convictions. Russia, duty, honor?   Yes, I have always been truly Russian—I'm telling you that frankly. What is there new in that movement that has taken shape around you and of which you write as though about some sort of new direction?[5] I confess to you that I didn't understand you. I read your poem and found it excellent; I share with you completely the patriotic feeling of the *moral* liberation of the Slavs. That is the role of Russia, noble, great Russia, our holy mother. How beautiful the ending is, the last lines in your "Clairemont Cathedral."[6] Where did you

---

5. Dostoevsky is referring to Slavophile notions, or perhaps more accurately, Pan-Slavic ideas.

6. Rendered in a prose translation, the conclusion of Maykov's "Clairemont Cathedral" (1854) runs:
> And, perhaps, enemies foresee,
> That from icy Russia
> An unprecedented tribe of giants
> Will emerge a threat to them,
> Giants with an unquenchable thirst
> For immortality, glory and goodness,
> Giants such as their world once saw
> In the threatening image of Peter.

find the language for expressing such an enormous thought so superbly? Yes, I share with you the idea that Europe and its mission *will be completed by Russia.* For me that has long since been clear. You write that society[7] seems to have awakened from apathy. But you know that in our society no demonstrations ever occur. But who ever concluded from that that it lacks energy? Explain an idea well and appeal to society, and society will understand you. That's just the way it is now: an idea was illuminated superbly, in a thoroughly popular and knightly way[8] (that's true, you have to give justice its due)—and our political idea, bequeathed to us already by Peter, has been justified by everyone. Perhaps you were disturbed, and disturbed quite recently, by the influx of French ideas into that part of society that thinks, feels, and studies?[9] That really was an exceptionality, too. But every exceptionality by its nature creates an antipode. But you have to agree that all sober-minded people, that is, those who set the tone for everything, viewed French ideas from a learned angle—and no more, and they themselves, perhaps, even though devoted to exceptionality, were always Russian. Where do you see the novelty? I assure you that, I, for instance, have everything Russian so much in my blood that not even convicts frightened me—they were the Russian people, my brothers in misfortune, and I had the good fortune on more than one occasion to find generosity even in the soul of a bandit, especially because I could understand him, because I was a Russian myself. My misfortune allowed me to learn a great deal in practice, perhaps that practice had a great deal of influence on me, but I found out in practice as well that I had always been a Russian in my heart.[10] You can be mistaken about any idea, but you can't make a mistake with your heart and through a mistake become unscrupulous, that is, act against your own convictions. But why, why am I writing you all of this! After all, I know that I'll never manage to say anything in lines on a page, why write this then! I'll tell you a few more things about myself. In prison I read very little, there were absolutely no books. Occasionally some turned up. After coming out here, to Semipalatinsk, I've begun to read more. But I still don't have books, and even necessary books, and time is passing. I can't tell you how much torment I endured in prison because of not being able to write. But all the same, inner work was in full swing. Some things came out well; I sensed that. I created there in my head my long, definitive novel. I was afraid that

7. The Russian word "obshchestvo" suggests educated society.

8. "Popular" in the sense of expressing the essence of the people, the broad masses. The conclusion of Maykov's poem predicts that Russian enemies may yet be surprised by the giants who will emerge from the country.

9. This may be a reference to the attraction that French socialism held for the members of the Petrashevsky Circle.

10. The allegedly special nature of the Russian people became one of Dostoevsky's favorite themes from the 1860s on but is first broached in the present letter.

my 1st love for my creation would turn cold when the years passed and the time came for its fulfillment—that love without which it's impossible even to write. But I was mistaken; the character that I created and who is the basis of the whole novel required several years for development and I am certain that I would have spoiled everything if I had set to work on it hastily, unprepared. But after leaving prison, although everything was ready, I didn't write. I couldn't write. A certain circumstance, a certain opportunity that had been slow to appear in my life and finally visited me carried me away and swallowed me up completely.[11] I was happy. I couldn't work. Then grief and sadness visited me. I lost what had been everything for me. Hundreds of versts separated us. I won't explain the matter to you, perhaps I'll explain it sometime; I can't now. I wasn't completely idle, however. I worked; but I put my main work aside.[12] I need greater tranquillity of spirit. As a joke I started a comedy and as a joke I created such a comical situation, so many comical characters, and I so liked my hero that I have abandoned the form of the comedy, in spite of the fact that I was having a success with it, purely for the pleasure of following my new hero's adventures for as long as possible and to laugh at him myself. That hero is somewhat related to me. In short, I'm writing a comic novel,[13] but until now I've kept writing separate adventures, I've written enough, and now I'm sewing everything into a whole. Well, that's the report to you on my doings: I couldn't help telling; that's because I started speaking with you and recalled our past, my unforgettable friend. Yes! I was happy with you many times: how on earth could I forget you! You write me a few things about literature. I've hardly read anything this year. I'll tell you my observations, too: I like Turgenev best of all—only it's too bad that for all his enormous talent, there is a great deal of inconsistency in him. I like L. T.[14] very much, but in my opinion he won't write much (perhaps I'm mistaken, however). I don't know Ostrovsky at all, I haven't read anything in its entirety, but I've read a lot of excerpts in articles about him. He may know a certain class of Russia well,[15] but I don't think he's an artist. Moreover, I think he's a *poet without an ideal.* Disabuse me of this, please, send me some of his better things so that I can get to know him not just through the critics. Of Pisemsky's works I've read "The Braggart"and "The Wealthy Fiancé"—nothing else. I like him very much. He's intelligent, good-natured, and even naive; he's a good storyteller. But

---

11. Dostoevsky surely is referring to falling in love with M. D. Isaeva.

12. During the last half of the 1850s Dostoevsky frequently made reference to a major work that he had conceived in prison.

13. The comic novel mentioned here is not extant, but Dostoevsky later used episodes from the work for the stories *Uncle's Dream* and *The Village of Stepanchikovo and Its Inhabitants*.

14. Lev Nikolaevich Tolstoy.

15. Ostrovsky's plays often deal with the Moscow merchant milieu.

there's one thing about him that's sad: he writes in haste. He writes too quickly and too much. He needs to have more self-esteem, more respect for his talent and for art, more love of art. When you're young ideas just pour out, you shouldn't seize every one of them on the run and immediately express it, rush to have your say. It's better to wait awhile for more synthesis; to think more, wait for a lot of minor things expressing the same idea to gather into a large whole, into a single large-scale image, and then express it. Colossal characters created by colossal writers were often the result of a long, intense process of creating and refining. You shouldn't express all the intervening experiments and sketches. I don't know whether you understand me. As for Pisemsky, I think he doesn't much restrain his pen. Our lady writers[16] write like lady writers, that is, intelligently, nicely, and hasten extraordinarily to express themselves. Tell me, please, why is a lady writer almost never an exacting artist? Even the indubitable, colossal artist George Sand has often done harm to herself with her womanly traits. I've read many of your short poems in the journals *during this whole time.* I have liked them very much. Take courage and work. I'll tell you as a secret, as a large secret: Tyutchev[17] is quite remarkable, but...etc. What Tyutchev is that, not ours by any chance?[18] Many of his poems are marvelous, however.

Good-bye, my dear friend. Excuse me for the incoherence of this letter. You can never write anything in a letter. That's why I can't stand Mme de Sévigné.[19] She wrote letters entirely too well. Who knows? Perhaps I'll embrace you sometime. God grant that! For Heaven's sake, don't tell *anyone* (absolutely *no one)* about my letter. I embrace you.

Your D

16. Dostoevsky has in mind such authors as N. D. Khvoshchinskaya and Y. V. Salhias de Turnemir.

17. Fyodor Ivanovich Tyutchev (1803-76), one of the three or four greatest Russian poets of the nineteenth century.

18. "Our Tyutchev" would be Nikolay Nikolaevich Tyutchev (1815-78), a translator and member of Belinsky's circle. Dostoevsky's confusion about identity occurred because from 1840 until 1854 F. I. Tyutchev published hardly any of his poetry and had been forgotten by the reading public at large.

19. The Marquise de Sévigné (1626-96), famous for her letters to her daughter, *Lettres de Mme de Sévigné à mme la comtesse de Orignan sa fille* (1726), a chronicle of French life and thought of her time.

Alexander Vrangel (1858)

105. To Alexander Vrangel
23 March 1856. Semipalatinsk

Semipalatinsk, 23 March / 56. Friday.

Kindest, irreplaceable friend of mine, Alexander Yegorovich! Where are you, what's happened to you? You haven't forgotten me, have you? Starting next Monday I will wait for the promised letter from you with such impatience as though it were good fortune and the fulfillment of all my hopes.[1] In this envelope you will find three unsealed letters: one for my brother, another for Adjutant General Eduard Ivanovich Totleben.[2] Don't be surprised! I'll tell you everything. But now I'll proceed in order and begin with myself. If you only knew my melancholy and despondency, almost despair, now at this moment, then you would truly understand why I am awaiting your letter as though it were salvation. It should settle much, much in my fate. You promised to write me as soon as possible upon your arrival in Petersburg and inform me of everything for which I have hoped and about which you have, like a brother, troubled yourself for an entire year—frankly, without hiding anything, not coloring the truth and in no way reassuring me with false hopes. I've been waiting for such news from you as though it were my life. Don't show my letter to anyone, for God's sake. I'm informing you that my affairs are in an extreme state. *La dame (la mienne)*[3] [the good lady (mine)] is grieving, despairs, is sick every moment, loses faith in my hopes, in the settlement of our destiny, and what is worst of all, she is surrounded in her little town (she hasn't moved to Barnaul yet) by people who will contrive something very bad: there are suitors there. The obliging gossips are tearing themselves to bits trying to persuade her to marry, to give her word to somebody whose name I don't know yet. In anticipation they spy on her, trying to find out from whom she receives letters. She is still waiting for news from her relatives, who, over there on the other side of the world, are to decide her fate here, i.e., whether to return to Russia or move to Barnaul. Her last letters to me recently have become more and more sad and melancholy. She was writing in a morbid mood: I knew that she was ill. I guessed that she was hiding something from me. (Alas! I never told you this: but already during your stay here, par ma jalousie incomparable [through my incomparable jealousy] I drove her to despair and that's why she hides things from me now.) And what do you think? Suddenly I hear here that she has given her word to marry another,

---

1. Vrangel, who left Semipalatinsk for Petersburg in January 1856, intended to continue his brother's efforts to help Dostoevsky.

2. See Letters 106 and 107.

3. *La dame (la mienne)*. Marya Dmitrievna Isaeva.

in Kuznetsk. I was thunderstruck. In despair I didn't know what to do, I began to write her, but on Sunday I received a letter from her, a very nice one, as nice as ever, but even more reticent than usual. Fewer sincere words than before, as if she were avoiding writing them. Not a word about our future hopes, as if the thought of them had been completely put aside. A sort of total disbelief in the possibility of a change in my fate in the near future and finally the crushing news: she has decided to break with her secretiveness and meekly asks me: "If an elderly gentleman with good qualities were found, a civil servant and well-to-do and if this man proposed to her—what should she answer?" She is asking for my advice. She writes that her head is spinning from the thought that she is alone at the edge of the earth, with a child, that her father is old, may die—then what will become of her? She asks that I judge the situation coolly as a *friend* should and answer straight away. There were still, however, protestations d'amour [protestations of love] in her previous letters. [...] she adds that she loves me, that this is still only supposition and calculation. I was thunderstruck, I became unsteady, fainted, and cried the night through. Now I'm lying down in my room [...]. I have an idée fixe in my head! I can barely understand how I live, what people say to me. Oh, God save everyone from this terrible, threatening feeling. The joy of love is great, but the sufferings are so horrible that it would be better never to love. I swear to you that I fell into despair. I realized the possibility of something extraordinary, something which another time I would never have decided upon... I wrote her a letter that evening, a terrible, despairing one. My poor little one! My angel! She was already ill as it was, but I tormented her! I may have killed her with my letter. I said that I would die if I should lose her. There were threats and carresses and humble requests and I don't know what all. You will understand me, you, my angel, my hope! But just consider: what was she to do, the poor thing, abandoned, morbidly sensitive and, finally, having lost all hope in the settlement of our destiny! After all she's not one to marry a soldier. But I reread all her recent letters this week. God knows, maybe she still hasn't given her word and that seems to be the case; she has only wavered. Mais—elle m'aime, elle m'aime [But —she loves me, she loves me], I know it, I see it—in her grief, melancholy, in the repeated floods of emotion in her letters and in many other things about which I can't write you. My friend! I was never completely honest with you on this score. Now what should I do! I have never experienced such despair in my life... Deathly melancholy is consuming my heart, at night dreams, shouting, spasms in the throat suffocate me, tears are stubbornly dammed up and then gush out in a stream. Consider my situation, too. I'm an honest person. I know that she loves me. But what if I stand in the way of her happiness? On the other hand, I don't believe in her suitor from Kuznetsk! It's not for her, ill, short-tempered, spiritually refined, educated, intelligent, to give herself to God knows whom, who perhaps considers beatings a legitimate thing in marriage. She is kind and trusting. I know her well. She can be persuaded of anything at all. In addition those gossipy women (cursed things) and the hopelessness of the situation are confusing her. A definite answer, that is, I'll learn all the facts by the 2nd of April, but, dear friend, advise me, what should I do? Although, why do I ask your advice? There's no way I can possibly relinquish her. Love at my age is not a whim, it's been continuing for two years, do you hear, two years, and in the 10 months of separation it has not only not weakened, but has reached the point of absurdity. I will perish if I lose my angel: I'll either go mad or jump into the Irtysh. *It goes without saying that if my affairs were straightened out (by the manifesto[4]), then I would be preferred above everyone and everything;* because she loves me, I am certain of that. I'll tell you what we in our language (mine and hers) call the settlement of my fate: a transfer from military to civil service, a position with some sort of salary, a rank (at least the 14th) or hope for that soon and some kind of possibility of getting money to live on at least until the final settlement of my affairs. It goes without saying that leaving the military and entering the civil service—even if without rank and a lot of money—would be considered on her part as an extraordinary hope and revitalize her. I, for my part, will declare to you what my hopes are; what I need *for certain* to free her from the suitors and remain before her an honest person, and then I will ask you, since you are in Petersburg and know much that I don't know: what should I expect of that which I need, what may come to pass, what may not?

My hopes, my dear, priceless, and perhaps only friend, you, pure honest heart—my hopes—listen to them. However much I think about it they seem to me to be rather clear. In the first place, can it really be that there won't be some sort of amnesty this summer, either upon the conclusion of peace[5] or at the time of the coronation? (That bit of news is exactly what I'm waiting to hear from you now with feverish impatience.) Let's assume the second is still in the region of hopes for the time being; but is it really impossible for me to transfer from the military to the civil service and move to Barnaul, if there won't be *anything* else from the manifesto.[6] After all, Durov transferred to the civil service. I'm telling you that this change alone will revitalize her and she will drive all the suitors away; for in the last letter and the one before that she writes that she loves me deeply, that a suitor is only a *calculation,* that she implores me to not doubt her love and to believe that this is only a supposition, the latter I believe; maybe they have suggested it to her and are trying to persuade her, *but she has still not given her word;* I've inquired about the rumors, searched for their source and it turns out to be a lot of gossip. In addition, if she had given her

4. Dostoevsky hoped an amnesty would be announced in the manifesto to be issued in connection with the coronation of Alexander II. The manifesto was issued on 26 August 1856 and in fact pardoned the Petrashevsky Circle.

5. The Treaty of Paris was signed on 18 March 1856. It is likely that Dostoevsky was unaware of the treaty when he wrote Vrangel.

6. Dostoevsky was not allowed to transfer to the civil service until 1859.

word she would have written me. Consequently, it is far from being decided. I'm expecting a letter from her by April 2nd. I demanded complete openness and then I'll know all the facts. Oh, my friend! Am I to keep her or give her up to another? After all, I have *rights* to her, do you hear, *rights!* And so: my transfer to civil service will be considered a great hope and encouragement. 3) Will I be without rank for a long time? What do you think? Is it possible my career will be closed off? Have criminals such as I received everything? I don't believe that! I believe that in two years, even if nothing happens now, I will return to Russia. Now the most important thing is money. Two things, one an essay,[7] the other a novel[8] will be ready by September. I want to formally request to be published. If that is permitted, then I will have an income for the rest of my life. Now it's not like it was before, so many things have been worked over, so many things are planned, and such energy for writing! I hope to write a novel (by September) better than *Poor Folk*. After all, if they allow me to publish (and I don't believe, hear me: I don't believe that that is impossible to obtain), there will be a furor, the book will sell out, it will bring me some money, significance, draw the government's attention to me, and my return will come shortly. And what I need is: 2-3 thousand a year in paper currency. And so, will I be able to act honestly with her or not? Is this too little, after all, for our support? In two years or so we will return to Russia, she will live well and, perhaps, we'll even acquire something. Well, is it possible that after having such courage and energy in the course of 6 years for struggles with unheard of sufferings that I will not be capable of obtaining enough money to feed myself and my wife. Nonsense! After all, the main thing is that nobody knows either my strength or the degree of my talent, and that's mainly on what I'm relying. Finally, the last case: well, let's suppose they don't allow me to publish for yet another year. But, upon the first change of my fate I will write to my uncle, ask him for 1,000 silver rubles for beginning a new career, without saying anything about my marriage; I'm sure that he will give it to me. Well, is it possible that we couldn't live for a year on that? And then things will work themselves out. Finally, I can publish incognito and still take the money. You must understand that all these hopes are only in case nothing happens this summer (the manifesto). And what if it does happen? No, I am not being a scoundrel to her! And as she herself mentions that she would be glad to throw over all the suitors for me if only our affairs were settled, that means I can still deliver her from misfortune. But what am I saying! It's been decided that I will not leave her! She will perish without me! Alexander Yegorovich, my friend! If you only knew how I'm waiting for your letter! Perhaps there's positive news in it, then I'll send her the original, and if

7. See Letter 103 for details about the essay.
8. *Uncle's Dream* and *The Village of Stepanchikovo* are probably reworked episodes from this novel.

that's not possible, I'll tear out the lines about my hopes for the settlement of my destiny and send that to her.

But you understand how busy I am with troubles and worries! I have a lot of requests for you: for Christ's sake, please fulfill them all. *1st request.* You will find in here a letter to Ed[uard] Iv[anovich] Totleben. Here is my idea: at one time I was well acquainted with this person; I've been a friend of his brother's since childhood.[9] A few days before my arrest I ran into him by chance and we very cordially shook hands. Well, perhaps he has not forgotten me. He's a kind, simple person with a generous heart (he has proven this), a true hero of Sevastopol, worthy of the names of Nakhimov and Kornilov.[10] Take my letter to him. First read it through carefully. You probably will notice from the tone of my letter to him that I wavered and didn't know *how* to write him. He now has such a high position, and who am I? Will he want to remember me? In any case that's the way I wrote it. Now: go to him in person (I hope that he's in Petersburg) and give him my letter in private. You will immediately see from his face how he receives it. If badly, then there's nothing to be done; after explaining to him in a few words the situation and putting in a few good words, take your leave and go, asking him ahead of time to keep all of this a secret. He's a very polite person (his personality is a bit chivalrous), he will receive and see you out very politely, even if he doesn't say anything *satisfactory.* If you see by his face that he will take up my cause and show much sympathy and kindness, oh, then be completely frank with him; go into the affair, straight from the heart, tell him about me and tell him that *his word* means a lot now, that he could petition the Monarch on my behalf, vouching (as one who knows me) for the fact that I will henceforth be a good citizen and he surely will not be refused. The Sovereign has pardoned Polish criminals several times at Paskevich's request. Totleben is now in such grace, in such favor that, really, his request will be worth Paskevich's. In general I'm relying on you very much. You will say some heartfelt words, I'm sure. For God's sake, be so kind as to do this. Stress in particular my leaving military service (but the main thing if something more is possible, i.e., even a full pardon, don't lose sight of that). Couldn't I, for example, be discharged with the right to enter the civil service at the 14th rank and with the possibility of returning to Russia, and, mainly, of publishing? In general read my letter to Totleben carefully. Couldn't I try a poem?[11] I read in the newspapers that at dinner Maykov recited verses to him. Does he by chance know him? If so, tell Maykov everything, in confidence, and ask him to petition Totleben on my behalf and go together with you to see Totleben. Can you somehow meet Totleben's younger brother Adolf? He's a friend of mine. Tell him about me and he will throw himself on his brother's shoulder and beg him

9. Adolf Ivanovich Totleben.
10. Pavel Nakhimov and Vladimir Kornilov were both killed in the defense of Sevastopol.
11. Dostoevsky's poem "On the Coronation and Conclusion of Peace."

to intercede for me. It goes without saying that you should seal my letter to Totleben in an envelope and give it to him that way. And for me, as soon as you can, send me word about all of this, whether it be good or bad. But here's the problem: what if Lamotte goes on his rounds at that time. He'll be gone for a month! I think he won't go! Surely not, I think. Hurry to answer me. I'm worried about one more thing: whether Pr[ince] Odoev[sky] received my letter favorably. You may be discouraged and perhaps go to *Totleben unwillingly.* My angel! Don't abandon me, don't drive me to despair.

 2nd request. Write me in detail and soon: How did you find my brother? What are his thoughts about me? He used to be a person who loved me passionately! He cried when bidding me farewell. Has he cooled towards me! Has his character changed! How sad I would be! Has he immersed himself wholly in the pursuit of money and forgotten all the past? I somehow don't believe that. But again: what is the explanation for his sometimes not writing me for 7 or 8 months at a time, writing God knows what, even in an uncensored letter via Khomentovsky he didn't answer any of my questions and I see little of the former warm person. I shall never forget that he told Khomentovsky, who delivered him my request that he intercede for me: *that it's better that I remain in Siberia.* In December we wrote (through your brother, remember), I asked for money, asking that it be sent to Lamotte's address. You know what need I was in! And what happened—not a word! I understand that he may not have any, because he's in business, but in extreme cases you save a person. And what's more, I'll be on their hands for only a short time and will repay everything. And what's more I'm asking him for money, because I remember his own words at our parting. In my letter to him, enclosed here, I ask him to send me, besides the 100, as much more as he can. I need this just in case (if I were to receive my freedom, then I'd immediately go to Kuznetsk, but that's impossible without money). Besides, if she goes to Barnaul, I'll persuade her to take it from me; I can't write you everything, but I need, desperately need money; it's only once in a lifetime that one needs money so badly. 300 silver rubles would save me. But even 200 would be good, including the 100 I asked for in December. It goes without saying that I'm writing you this as a friend, but don't even think of helping me yourself in any way! I'm already a *scoundrel* before you, I owe you tons! In any case, read over my letter to my brother. Don't show him what I'm writing to you now. But I am sending him to you for explanations: tell him everything. But what if he, like all the uncles and relatives in novels, *gets angry at my love for her* and tries to dissuade you from helping me? But I'm 35 years old. What does he think? That I love him for the money that he sends me. Nonsense! I have my pride. I will eat bread alone and *she* and *I* will perish, but I don't need money from him sent with that sort of feeling. I don't want charity! I need a brother and not money! He and I used to quarrel, but we loved each other passionately, and I swear to you that I would give my life for him. I have an awful personality, but when it comes down to deeds, then I stand up for my friends. When they arrested us, at that point during the first moment of terror one would think that it would be permissible to think about oneself first of all. But guess what? I thought only about him, about how the arrest would shock his family, how it would shock his poor wife; I begged my third brother, whom they arrested by mistake, to put off as long as possible explaining the mistake to those who arrested him and to send money to my brother, because I assumed that he didn't have any.[12] Is it possible that he's forgotten all of the past and is angry at me for asking for a lot of money, and when? At the most critical moment of my life. Write me now he received you, how you found him (frankly), write me his views *regarding this whole matter,* and listen only to your golden heart, my kind friend; and be quite candid with Maykov about me. He's a marvelous person and likes me. It goes without saying that you should ask him to keep everything secret. *3rd request.* For God's sake, understand me, help me, without thinking that I may in some way harm my career through my love for her and 2nd) don't think that I have acted dishonorably with her, diverting her from an *advantageous marriage* to another, having in mind only my egoistic benefit. There is neither advantage for her in a marriage to another, nor *craven* egoism in me, and therefore one must not think that. Otherwise, I swear that I am ready to give my life for her and would relinquish my hopes in her favor. You judge: in every letter of hers and even in the last one she writes that she loves me more than anything on earth, she writes that the man seeking her hand in marriage is *only a calculation* on her part, and particularly begs me to believe that it is still only a proposition. Understand her position, too. She has been eagerly awaiting a change in my fate and there's nothing and nothing again! She is falling into despair and realizing that she is a mother, that she has a child, has wavered at the chance, if my affairs are not be set aright, to marry. Just two posts ago she wrote me, trying to calm my jealousy, that not a single person in Kuznetsk is worth so much as my finger, that she would like to tell me something, but is afraid of me, that all kinds of vipers are intriguing all around her, that this is all done so coarsely, without the slightest notion of decency, she assures me in the same letter that she feels more than ever that she needs me and I her, and writes: "Come soon, we'll have a laugh together." Of course, we'll have a laugh at the caprices of the old ladies who have sworn to marry her off. But, after all, the poor, weak thing is afraid of everything. In the end they'll confuse her, but mainly they'll tear her to pieces if they see that she isn't giving in to their caprices and she will live alone among enemies. Understand that it is death and ruin for her to get married there! I know that if there were the slightest hope for my fate she would revive, would

---

12. Andrey Dostoevsky was arrested instead of his brother Mikhail on 23 April and was not released until 6 May 1849.

become stronger in spirit and, after receiving her father's letter (with his permission), would go to Barnaul or Astrakhan. As for me, she and I, of course, would be happy. In a marriage to me she would be surrounded by good people all her life and by good, greater respect than with this person. I will be an official myself, after all, and perhaps soon. I'm sure that I can provide for a family. I will work, write. Even if there are not any pardons now, it will still be possible to transfer to the civil service, get the 14th rank soon, receive a salary, and, mainly, I can publish, I can even publish incognito. I'll have money. Finally, this is not right away, but by that time my situation will be settled. Do you know what I answered and what I'm asking of her? Here's what: that since she cannot marry before the end of her mourning, before September that is,[13] that she wait and not give *that person* a definite answer. If my affairs aren't settled by September, then, *perhaps,* she should announce her consent. You have to agree that if I had treated her dishonestly and selfishly, then I couldn't have harmed her with my request to wait until September. Besides, she loves me! The poor thing! She is being tormented to death! How could she, with her heart and with her mind, spend her whole life in Kuznetsk, God knows with whom. She's in the same position as my heroine in *Poor Folk,* who marries Bykov[14] (a self-fulfilling prophecy!). My friend! I'm writing you all this so that you will act with your whole heart and soul in my favor. I rely on you as on a brother! Otherwise I will be driven to despair! What purpose would life have then! I swear to you that I will do something drastic! I beg you, my angel! And if you ever need a person to send through fire and water in your stead, then that person is ready, *I am he,* and I don't desert people I love, either in happiness or in misfortune, and I have proven that! And therefore, my angel, *the 4th request.* For God's sake, without losing any time, write a letter to her in Kuznetsk and write her clearly and concisely all about my hopes. Especially if there is something *positive* in the change of my fate, then write her all the particulars and she will quickly go from despair to assuredness and will be revived by hope, write her *the whole truth* and *only the truth.* Most importantly, in great detail. It's very easy. Here's how: "F. M. sent me your regards (she sends you her regards and wishes you happiness)—as I know that you are greatly concerned about F. M.'s fate, I hasten to make you happy, there is such and such news and hopes for him. . ." and so forth. Finally: "I have thought about you a great deal. Go to Barnaul, they will receive you well there" and so forth. Write it like that, and also: she wrote me that you wrote her when you were leaving. She is happy and grateful that you haven't forgotten her, but writes that there is nothing in your letter that shows that she would be well off in Barnaul, that you didn't even write whether Barnaul would agree to receive me, and she doesn't know therefore whether they won't receive her with

---

13. Marya Dmitrievna's husband died on 4 August 1855.
14. In *Poor Folk* Varvara, seeing no other way out of her position, marries Bykov.

vexation, as if she were a beggar, when she turns up there. You were probably busy and upset yourself when you wrote her so incompletely and casually. I understand that and am not grumbling at you. But for God's sake set the thing right now. For me, do this for me, my angel, my brother, my friend! Save me from despair! After all, you more than anyone else *could understand me!*

Finally: for Christ's sake, inform me about the progress of my affairs, in as much detail and as quickly as possible; in this I rely upon you completely. Try to persuade my brother to help me, be my defender with him. Impress upon him that I will only make myself happy with my marriage to her, that we don't need much to live on, and that I will find the energy and strength to feed my family. That if I am allowed to write and publish, then I am saved, that I will not be a *burden to any of them,* will not ask them to help me, and *most importantly,* I'm not getting married *right away,* but will wait for something secure. She will gladly wait a bit, if she only had hope for a definite settlement of my fate. Say also that I'm 35 years old, and that I have enough sense in me for 10 people. Good-bye, my dear, my friend! Yes, I forgot! For Christ's sake speak to my brother about my financial matters. Persuade him to help me for the last time. *Understand* what sort of situation I'm in. Don't desert me! After all, such circumstances as mine only happen once in a lifetime. When should one help one's friends if not at such a time as this. I embrace and kiss you. How are things with *you?* I can hardly wait for a letter from you. I end this letter with regret; now I will be alone again with my tears, doubts and despair.

Write me for God's sake: is Katerina Osipovna[15] in Petersburg or not? Intercede about her and my affairs with the Gerngrosses. Good-bye; I embrace you and kiss you again! You are my hope, you are my savior!

Your D

106. To Mikhail Dostoevsky
24 March 1856. Semipalatinsk

Semipalatinsk, 24 March/56.

My brother and friend, my kind and dear Misha, Al[exander] Yegor[ovich] Vrang[el] will pass on this letter to you. I am writing to you, but for details send you to Al[exander] Yeg[orovich] with whom, I assume,

15. Katerina Osipovna is Yekaterina Iosifovna Gerngross, who earlier had helped Dostoevsky a great deal.

you have become well acquainted. One can't write much in a few lines of a letter, my good friend! I would like to see you, talk with you and, heart to heart, tell you everything that is worrying and torturing me now. I will say one thing: never in my life were there such grief, melancholy and despair as now! I ask you to help: you, if no one else, don't abandon me now. Al[exander] Yeg[orovich] will tell you a lot. In a letter I sent with him I already wrote you about a certain lady with whom I was acquainted in Semipalatinsk, who moved with her husband to Kuznetsk, where her husband died. I also wrote you about my hopes, about our love. My dear friend! This attachment, this feeling for her is now everything in the world for me! I live, I breathe only her and for her. In parting we exchanged vows, promises. She promised to be my wife. She loves me and has proven that. But now she is alone and helpless. Her parents are far away (they help her, send money). Seeing that my fate is taking such a long time to be resolved, there is nothing of what she and I expected, that the improvement of my fate is still doubtful (although I am convinced of it), she has fallen into despair, is melancholy, grieves, is ill. They are plotting in that little town. They are besieging her with marriage proposals, everyone has suddenly become a Kochkaryov.[1] If she doesn't consent, they will all become her enemies. They are wearing her down, pointing out the helplessness of her situation, and now, finally, after hiding it from me for a long time, she has written me about this. She writes that she loves me more than anything in the world, that the possibility of marrying another is still only a supposition, but she asks: "what is she to do?"—and implores me not to deprive her of my counsel in this critical moment. I was thunderstruck by this news. I'm worn out by torments. What if they confuse her, what if she destroys herself, she with her feeling, with her heart, by marrying some peasant, dolt, official, for a piece of bread for herself and her son, she could just do that! But how can she sell herself, when she has another love in her heart? And how about me? Perhaps, on the eve of a change in my fate and of her getting settled anew. Because I am too hopeful to lose hope. If not now, then sometime I will achieve a full settlement of my affairs, and now if not everything, then a little would save us both! And this little is so possible and soon! I've even found people here who are ready to give me a position[2] and it's always possible to get a transfer from the military service to the civil service. They may even transfer me with the 14th rank (they have, for example, assured me that next year they can recommend me for the rank of officer). I will receive a position, a salary. Even if there were no pardon[3] this summer and all the efforts on my behalf were in vain, then even this transfer to civil service would settle my affairs once and for all. And this is already possible! Finally, of course, the salary would be small, but I can get

---

1. Kochkaryov is a character from Nikolai Gogol's comedy, *Marriage*.
2. Dostoevsky refers to A. R. Gerngross' offer to give him a position in Barnaul.
3. The pardon expected to be forthcoming on Alexander II's coronation.

money on my own, I would secure the right to publish. Polezhaev, Marlinsky have been published, after all.[4] Then I will be provided for and by the standards here even rich (I expect a lot from literature. Imagine a wonderful composition like *Poor Folk;* and then I will have the attention of even those from above). Finally, if this winter, when I plan to ask permission to publish a novel and an article that I'm working on now, if in spite of my belief that I will secure this permission,—even if I were refused, for the first year of my marriage I would be able to provide for myself and live without coming running, for example, to you with a request for help; because if there is a change in my fate, even a slight one, then I intend to appeal to uncle and ask him (saying nothing about marriage) to help me for the beginning of a new life. He will give me money! I'm sure of that. Now, judge my situation yourself. She needs to be reassured, persuaded, saved; I'm far away from her; it's hard to take care of the matter through letters. Understand my despair! And understand as well, brother (for Christ's sake be a brother to me and understand that this is not the passion of a 20-year-old, that I'll soon be 35, that I will die from melancholy if I lose her!), that I wanted to devote my whole life to making her happy. I can't write you either about my hopes or despair. We haven't seen each other for over 6 years. Will we understand each other as we should, as a brother understands a brother? Do you love me as you used to, have you not, perhaps, changed—I don't know anything! My friend, my angel! I have hope and confidence that you are still a brother to me! Save me! Help me! I have 2 requests of you, one insignificant, the other important, but both, if they are fulfilled, would help me and you would have done *me a good deed,* do you hear brother, *a good deed!* Here are the requests (I beg you not to put them off, but fulfill them as soon as possible. Remember that, perhaps, I will be useful to you, too, that I didn't forget you either in a critical situation. You know that I love you. Brother, my angel, help me! Can it be that everyone, everyone will abandon me!): *the first thing I'm asking you for.* She has a son, a boy who is barely 8 years old. When her husband died, she, as a mother, as one cast to the end of the world and, finally, as a weak woman, was driven to horrible despair over the fate of her child. I gave her hope. Her father wrote her that he would not abandon his grandson, would send him to school and then to the university. But what will happen, she wonders, if the old man dies, then who will provide for her son? And therefore she thinks that it would be better to send him to *a military academy,* where the education is now wonderful and where the *government* doesn't abandon its pupils ever their whole lives, even during service, once they have been taken under its care. In line with her husband's rank it isn't possible to send him anywhere but to the Pavlovsky Military

---

4. Alexander Polezhaev (1805-38) was forced to serve as a soldier for his bawdy poem *Sashka.* The Decembrist Alexander Bestuzhev-Marlinsky (1797-1837) was exiled to the Caucasus in 1829, but began to publish under the pseudonym Marlinsky in 1830.

Academy. I agreed with her entirely, and told her that Golenovsky,[5] my relative, holds a significant post in this academy, that he would take special care of the child and his morals and that, finally, you as my own brother would not refuse to fulfill my earnest request to at least *sometimes* take him to your home on Sundays. In this way he wouldn't remain a complete orphan, he would visit a good home, where he would see excellent examples and in this way she could be easy in her mind regarding both the development of his character and his morals. When she gave me her consent to be my wife, I reaffirmed that I would plead to my relatives on behalf of her son, and that in the event she is successful in placing him in the Pavlovsky Military Academy (which she will do herself, without troubling anybody with requests), then my family, in some respects already family to her son, will take a warmer, more familial concern in him. She was very pleased by this. She, the poor thing, was so depressed. I will tell you, my dear, that I really was firmly relying on you. What effort would it cost you after all to take him in sometimes on Sundays. The poor orphan wouldn't eat you out of house and home. And God will give you even more for the orphan. Besides, once upon a time when your brother, who was in exile, in misfortune, thrown to the edge of the world, abandoned by everyone, was taken in by the father and mother of this child like their own brother; they fed him, provided him drink, soothed him and made his lot happier. Besides, the actual enrollment of the boy won't be soon, he's only 8 years old. Now understand me: I want to ask you to write her about this. Just like this: Dear Marya Dmitrievna! My brother, F. M. D., has written me many times how cordially, with what familial concern, he was received by you and your late husband in Semipalatinsk. There are not words to express the gratitude for what you did for a poor exile. I am his brother and therefore can feel this. I have wanted to thank you for some time. My brother has informed me that you intend to enroll your son, when he is of age, in the Pavlovsky Academy. If he is ever there, and if I can in some way ease the child's loneliness, in the event that he has neither relatives nor acquaintances in Petersburg, then, rest assured, I will consider myself a most fortunate person, all the more so if in this way I can show my earnest gratitude for my brother's cordial reception in your home. And rest assured as well that all that my brother has written me about you and his acquaintance with your home has been exceedingly pleasing for me and has filled my heart with happiness for my poor brother. There are no words to express to you all my respect. Allow me to remain, etc."[6]

Please write on this theme a bit more briefly and a bit better. Realize what you can do for me, all the more so that it doesn't cost you anything. You will infuse her with hope. She will see that she has not been

---

5. N. I. Golenovsky, the husband of Dostoevsky's sister Alexandra, was an inspector in the Pavlovsk Military Academy.

6. There are no opening quotation marks in the original.

abandoned, and mainly, you will help me terribly in my affairs. Because my family's good will towards her is exceedingly important to her now; because I informed her that I wrote you about the possibility of our marriage. It goes without saying that there should not be a word about this marriage. Address the letter: M[arya] D[mitrievna] Isaeva, city of Kuznetsk, Tomsk Province.[7]

For Christ's sake do this for me, brother. You will be doing me, I repeat, a good deed. I beg you this on my knees. Don't kill me with a refusal! The 2nd request is *important.* I've already written you, my friend, that I'm in terrible need and asked you for 100 silver rubles. Not a word from you. My God! What if you've had your fill of me, that you're glad to get rid of me *completely,* and I'm writing you *such letters!* But I have resolved to write you once more and ask you for enormous assistance. My friend! I need so much money that it's frightening to say how much. But I'm asking for the *last time,* I'll never again for the rest of my life trouble you and will repay you everything at the 1st change of my fortune.

Besides the 100 rubles that I already asked you for, I need another 200. Brother, listen to me! Remember the time when you were getting married? Didn't I share with you down to the last bit then? I know, don't reproach me for ingratitude! You've given me so much money during my life that my claim is nothing compared to *yours.* But everything will be all right *in its time.* Besides, can it really be that you are capable of refusing assistance to a brother in such misfortune. Realize that in my life there has never been such a horrible moment! This money could help me in the most critical situation. If 300 is impossible, then send 200. But, for God's sake, send it! I won't trouble you anymore.

I hope for a change in my fate and am convinced that I will soon be able to earn my own bread. Brother! I wanted to say a few other things, but I feel so sad, so sad! My brother, can it be that you have changed towards me! How cold you are, you don't want to write, once in 7 months you send some money and a letter of 3 lines. Just like charity. I don't want charity without a brother! Don't insult me! My friend! I'm so unhappy! So unhappy! I'm crushed now, tormented! My soul aches mortally. I've suffered for a long time, 7 years in all, everything bitter that one could imagine, but really there is a limit to suffering! I'm not a stone after all. Now all of this is overflowing. My angel! If I'm insulting you with my reproaches and if I'm being unjust to you, then I beg you on my knees for forgiveness. Don't be angry with me, I'm so miserable! Don't be so negligent towards me! Help me, hear me!

My cordial brotherly regards to Emilia Fyodorovna and the entire

---

7. In his reply to this letter, Mikhail reproaches his brother for the manner of Fyodor's request: "Again you have offended me to the bottom of my heart. To ask for two pages for something that one doesn't have to ask a brother. Of course, the child will be received like a son. There was no need to even worry about that."

family. For Christ's sake, not a word to anybody about my intentions regarding marriage. Write the letter to M[arya] D[mitrievna] as soon as possible, without delaying, and as respectfully as possible. This woman is worth it!

107. To Eduard Totleben
24 March 1856. Semipalatinsk

Your Excellency, Eduard Ivanovich,

Forgive me for being so bold as to trouble your attention with my letter. I fear that, having glanced at its signature, at a name probably forgotten by you—although I at one time (a very long time ago) had the honor of your knowing me[1]—I fear that you will become angry with me and my impudence and will throw it away without reading it. I beseech you, be indulgent. Do not accuse me of not realizing the entire, immeasurable difference between my position and yours. In my lifetime there has been all too much sad experience for me not to realize this difference. I also fully realize that I have no right whatsoever to recall now the fact that you once knew me, to recall that in order to consider that at least a shadow of the right to your attention. But I am so miserable that almost against my will I have come to believe in the hope that you will not close your heart to an unfortunate exile, that you will grant him at least a moment of your time, and will perhaps hear him out favorably.

I have asked Baron Alexander Yegorovich Vrangel to deliver this letter to you. When he was here in Semipalatinsk he did more for me than one's own brother could do. I was so happy for his friendship. He knows all my circumstances. I have asked him to deliver this letter to you personally, he will do this, in spite of the fact he does not have the pleasure of knowing you and that I cannot assure him that this letter will be received with indulgence. Doubt is understandable in the heart of a person who is a former convict. I have an enormous request of you, only the faint hope that it will be heard by you.

Perhaps you have heard about my arrest, trial and Imperial sentence resulting from the affair in which I was involved in 1849. Perhaps you have given my fate some attention. I base this supposition on the fact that I was friends with your younger brother, Adolf Ivanovich, loved him passionately almost from childhood. And although I have not seen him

---

1. Dostoevsky had shared an apartment with Totleben's brother, Adolf, a fellow engineer.

recently, I am certain that he pitied me and perhaps told you my sad story. I will not be so bold as to trouble your attention with the story of this affair. I was guilty, I admit that completely. I was convicted for the intention (but nothing more) of acting against the government. I was sentenced lawfully and justly; long experience, hard and painful, has sobered me and has changed my views on many things. But then—then I was blind, I believed in theories and utopias. When I set out for Siberia I had, at least, one consolation, that I had conducted myself before the court honestly, I did not shift my blame onto others and even sacrificed my own interests if I saw the chance of shielding others from misfortune with my confession. But I harmed myself, I did not confess everything and was punished more harshly for this. Before this I had been ill for two years in a row with a strange, psychological illness. I fell into hypochondria. There was even a time when I would lose my reason. I was too irritable with the susceptibility developed by the illness, with the capability of distorting the most ordinary facts and giving them another form and dimension. But I felt that, although this illness had a strong inimical influence on my fate, it would be a poor justification and even a debasing one. But I did not fully realize that back then. Forgive me for such details. But be magnanimous and hear me out to the end.

Imprisonment began for me—4 years of a grievous, horrible time. I lived with thieves, with people lacking human feelings, with perverted principles; I did not see and could not see for all of these 4 years anything cheerful, besides the blackest, most hideous reality. I had not a single being at my side with whom I could exchange even a single sincere word; I experienced hunger, cold, illnesses, work that was beyond my strength, and the hate of my thieving comrades, who took vengeance because I was from the nobility and an officer. But I swear to you there was no suffering for me greater than when I realized my errors, realized at the same time that I was cut off from society, an exile, and could not be useful to the extent of my energy, desire and capabilities. I know that I was condemned justly, but I was condemned for dreams, for theories. Ideas and even convictions change, a whole person changes too, and how painful it is to suffer now for what no longer exists, for what has been changed in me into the opposite, to suffer for former errors whose groundlessness I already see myself, to feel the energy and capabilities for doing at least something for the redemption of the past uselessness and—to languish in inactivity.

I am now a soldier, I am serving in Semipalatinsk and this summer was promoted to the rank of non-commissioned officer.[2] I know that many people have taken and continue to take a sincere interest in me, that they have interceded and petitioned for me. They have given and continue to give me hope. The Monarch is kind, merciful. I know, finally, that it is hard for a person who has resolved to prove that he is an honest person and

2. Dostoevsky was promoted on 20 November 1855.

wishes to do something good, not to achieve his goal sometime. I can do something too! I am not devoid of capabilities after all, or feelings, or principles. I have a great, immense request of you, Eduard Ivanovich! Only one thing hampers me: I have no right whatsoever to trouble you with my person. But you have a noble, exalted heart! One may mention that; not long ago you so gloriously proved it for all the world to see.[3] Long since, before others, I had the pleasure of forming this opinion about you and long, long since I had learned to respect you. Your word could mean a great deal now to our merciful Monarch, who is grateful to you and who loves you. Remember a poor exile and help him! I wish to be useful. It is difficult, having energy in my soul and a head on my shoulders, not to suffer from idleness. But military service is not my field. I am prepared to strive with all my might; but I am not well and, besides that, I feel that I am more inclined to another field, one more fitting to my abilities. My one dream is to be released from military service and enter the civil service somewhere in Russia, or even here; to have at least some freedom in choosing my place of residence. But I do not consider the service to be the main goal of my life. At one time I was given hope by the public's favorable reception on a literary path. I would like to have permission to publish. There have already been precedents for this: political criminals, through the favorable attention and mercy shown to them, have received permission to write and publish even before me. I have always considered the calling of the writer to be a most noble, useful calling. I am convinced that only on that path could I truly be useful, perhaps, I would attract at least some attention too, I would acquire a good name for myself again, and at least somewhat provide for my existence, because I have nothing, except for certain, and perhaps very minor, literary abilities. I will not conceal from you that in addition to a sincere desire to exchange my lot for another, one more suitable to my energies, a certain circumstance, upon which, perhaps, depends the entire happiness of my life (a purely personal circumstance), has induced me to be so bold as to remind you of myself. I am not asking for everything all at once, but only for the possibility of leaving military service and the right to enter the civil service.

After reading these requests of mine, do not accuse me of faintheartedness! I have borne such suffering that, truly, just by the chance to endure it I have proven both my patience and even a certain amount of courage. But now I have lost heart and I sense that myself. I have always considered it faintheartedness to trouble others about myself, no matter who it may be. Even more so to trouble you about myself. But have pity on me, I implore you! I have courageously borne my calamity until now. Now, however, circumstances have broken me and I resolved to make an attempt, only an attempt. The idea of writing you and asking you on my

---

3. Dostoevsky is referring to Totleben's exploits in Sevastopol, which had made him a national hero.

behalf did not occur to me earlier, I swear to you. I would have been somehow ashamed and it would have been difficult for me to remind you of myself. I have recently followed your triumph with the utmost disinterestedness and enthusiastic feeling. If you knew with what pleasure I spoke of you to others, you would believe me. If you knew with what pride I have recalled that I had the honor to know you personally! When they learned of that here, they showered me with questions, and it was so pleasurable for me to talk about you! I am not afraid to write you this. Your triumph is so glorious that even such words cannot appear to be flattery. The bearer of this letter can testify to you about the sincerity and disinterestedness of my feelings for you. A Russian's gratitude to the person who in an era of misfortune has covered the terrifying defense of Sevastopol with eternal, unfading glory is understandable. But, I repeat, I had no intention of troubling you with myself. But now, in a moment of despondency and not knowing to whom to turn, I recalled how you had always been cordial, unpretentious and kind to me. I recalled you always with bold, pure and exalted stirrings of the heart and took faith in my hope. I thought: surely you will not spurn me now, when you have risen to such a glorious and high position, and I have fallen so low, low. Pardon my boldness, in particular pardon me for this long (*too long,* I realize this) letter, and if you can do something for me, I implore you, do it.

I have one more extraordinary request of you, which, I implore you, do not refuse me. Remember me some time to your brother Adolf Ivanovich and tell him that I love him as before, that during my 4-year penal servitude, while sorting over in my head my entire life, day by day, hour by hour, I more than once came upon him in my recollections. But he knows that I love him! I remember that he was recently very ill. Is he well now? Is he alive? Pardon me for this request as well. But I do not know through whom I could have fulfilled this request of mine and have appealed to you.

I know that by writing this letter I have committed a new crime against the service. A simple soldier writing to an adjutant-general! But you are magnanimous and I entrust myself to your magnanimity.[4]

With the most profound respect and the sincere, grateful feeling of a Russian, I make so bold as to remain Your Excellency's humble servant
Fyodor Dostoevsky.

Semipalatinsk
24 March 1856

4. Dostoevsky's letter was given to Totleben by Vrangel (see Letter 105). Totleben was indeed magnanimous and took an active part in Dostoevsky's affairs. Dostoevsky was pardoned largely due to Totleben's influence at court.

108. To. Alexander Vrangel
13 April 1856. Semipalatinsk

Semipalatinsk, 13 April 1856

I hasten to answer your nice, most kind letter, my kind friend, which you wrote me on March 12th and which made me happy the day before yesterday. I waited for news from you so eagerly. But recently I'd quit even hoping for a speedy receipt; because Demchinsky, who arrived from Russia about 2 weeks ago, said that you were lingering in Kazan, and then they wrote here from Moscow (to Spirodonov) that you were in Moscow for only a day or two and had already set off on March 9th for Petersburg. From all these rumors I figured that I would receive something, at the earliest, at Easter; and here I've received it earlier! You will not believe how happy you have made me and how I *needed* your letter. And that I would receive it from *you,* the certainty that you would not forget me and would *do your utmost* for me—of none of that did it even occur to me to have any doubt, to think that you would forget me. I know you, your most kind, most generous heart, and I have not loved you without reason. You will not believe what a state I've been in recently. . . But about that later, and for the sake of order I'll begin first with your letter, my most kind Alexander Yegorovich. You begin with the fact that despite many distractions, you haven't been able to forget your *heart's* grief. I believe that, my friend; that isn't forgotten so easily; I know that very well *now,* and in general I've learned a lot that earlier I hadn't supposed would be that way. But, I confess to you, I would very much like to know what there is now exactly *between you;* because since your letter from Yalutorovsk, I have had no notion of these matters. Now you, of course, already have a definite opinion on this score, because, as far as I understand you, that person perhaps has already arrived in Petersburg.[1] But at least you're now among family; how happy I am that you and your father have come to terms. For Christ's sake, don't break this concord. Plan for the future and *keep it in mind.* It's already time for you, in my opinion, to begin to plan and assess your future. I don't at all mean that you should act contrary to your true feelings and thoughts. You write, for example, that they want to marry you off. It's profitable, but after all there's more to life than money. All of this has been well known long since and there's no need to talk about it. Each person acts according to his conscience, but a decent person plans according to his conscience, too. You write, my most kind and never-to-be-forgotten friend, that you are planning to be in Siberia in June and to pass through Semipalatinsk. You won't believe how happy I am that you

---

1. Dostoevsky is referring Yekaterina Gerngross.

haven't changed your plans and want to return to Siberia and that by winter you even intend to settle in Barnaul. I will wait for you like the sun. But, my friend, are the rumors that have been circulated here about you true: namely, that supposedly a corps commander has assigned you to himself in Omsk as an official for special commissions (they say that he was very surprised that you didn't go through Omsk), precisely what you didn't want to be. Then, perhaps, to avoid this and if there is no longer any chance of altering it, you will stay in Petersburg, and not come here! However, you already know about this. They've probably written you from here. For God's sake, my friend, for God's sake inform me *for certain* if you can. Whether you will come or not, when, where, how you're coming here and how you hope to arrange your business in Petersburg. Besides the fact that I'm dying to see you, you are indispensable to me now, like air, but you were always indispensable and I remember that.—You won't believe how happy I was that you liked my brother and that it seems the two of you will become close. Do this, for God's sake; you won't regret it.[2] How happy I am that he's still the same and loves me. I wrote you at length about my doubts even on his account in my last letter. But if you only knew what a sad, what a terrible state I was in and how I regret my suppositions in regard to my brother. Tell him that I kiss him; I'm not writing him because I hardly have time to answer even you. I'll write him an official letter soon that will say *"I'm alive and well"* and that's all. What can you write in an official letter besides that? But in the next letter to you I'll write him as well. In my last letter I asked him for another 100 rubles. Not for me, my friend, but for everything that now is the most dear in my life, and, mainly, *just in case.* If only he can fulfill my request, let him fulfill it and the Lord will reward him for it, and he, perhaps, in doing so can make me happy and deliver me from despair. How can one know what will happen? Besides, if I'm allowed to publish, I'll have my own money and will begin a new life and won't trouble him, which has always weighed on my heart, because my brother works for his piece of bread. I wrote you, my friend, to go to Totleben and deliver my letter. You may have already done that. You won't believe with what anxiety I'll wait for your answer on this score. I thank you beforehand for everything you are doing for me. Only, for Christ's sake, don't fill me with vain hopes out of a desire to calm me. Write me facts, only facts.

I also asked both you and my brother to write Marya Dmitrievna, and, if possible, soon. I repeat my request; for God's sake, do it. You write that something in the way of amnesty is being prepared for us, but what exactly—is being kept secret. Do me a favor, my priceless friend, couldn't you find out in advance at least something regarding me. I need that, need

2. Vrangel writes in his memoirs that he met Mikhail, who upon learning that Vrangel was going to Semipalatinsk, gave him some clothes, books, 50 rubles and a letter for Dostoevsky.

that, very much. If you find out something, let me know right away. I'm not even thinking about the Caucasus.[3] Or the Barnaul battalion. That's all nonsense *now*. You write that everyone loves the Tsar. I adore him myself. I confess that my promotion is personally very important to me. But to wait for an officer's rank is to wait a long time yet, and I'd like at least something now, in connection with the coronation. The best and most sensible, of course, is to petition for permission to publish. I'm thinking of sending you in the near future via a private route a poem written for the coronation.[4] But I'll send it the official route as well. You'll probably see Gasfort. He's going to the coronation, after all. Won't you have a talk with him and get him to present my poem himself? Couldn't you do that? Let me know as well until what date I can write you, because if you're leaving Petersburg, then it will be bad if the letters go astray. I told you about the article on Russia.[5] But it was turning out to be a purely political pamphlet. I wouldn't want to cut a word from my article. But I doubt that I'd be allowed to begin publishing with a pamphlet, despite the most patriotic ideas. But it was turning out well and I was satisfied. I was very interested in that article! But I gave it up. Well, how can they refuse to let me publish! Why should my labors be lost? But time is too dear to me now to spend it in vain, writing for my own pleasure. And besides, the political circumstances have changed. And so I have set to work on another piece: "Letters about Art." Her Highness Maria Nikolaevna[6] is the president of the Academy. I want to request permission to dedicate my article to her and publish it anonymously. My article is the fruit of a decade's deliberations. I'd thought the whole thing through down to the last word already in Omsk. There will be much that is original, passionate. I vouch for the exposition. Perhaps many people will disagree with me on many points. But I believe in my ideas and that is enough. I want to ask Ap[ollon] Maykov to read the piece beforehand. In several chapters there will be whole pages from the pamphlet. It is actually about the mission of Christianity in art. Only the problem is where to place it. Publish it separately—100 people will buy it, because it's not a novel. The journals will pay money. But *The Contemporary* was always hostile towards me,[7] *The Muscovite*, too.[8] *The Russian Messenger* published Katkov's introduction to a critique of Pushkin where the ideas are completely opposite to mine.[9] That leaves only

3. A year earlier Dostoevsky had wanted to serve in the Caucasus.
4. Dostoevsky's poem "On the Coronation and Conclusion of Peace" (see Letter 105).
5. See Letter 103, note 12.
6. Maria Nikolaevna—daughter of Nicholas I.
7. Dostoevsky's problems with *The Contemporary* began in 1846, when Belinsky left *Notes of the Fatherland* for the journal founded by Pushkin. Dostoevsky, however, refused to align himself exclusively with *The Contemporary*. Nevertheless, *The Contemporary* published *Novel in Nine Letters* in 1847.
8. *The Muscovite* printed harsh reviews of both *Poor Folk* and *The Double*.
9. Mikhail Katkov (1818-87), journalist and editor of *The Russian Messenger*.

Notes of the Fatherland, but I don't know what's going on with *Notes of the Fatherland* now. Therefore, talk to Maykov and my brother, but only as if it were just a plan, about whether it will be possible to publish it somewhere for money, and inform me. But the main thing is that I'm working on a novel, and that's my joy. Only that way can I make a name for myself and attract attention. But of course it's better to begin first with a serious piece (about art) and ask for permission to publish it, because they still view a novel as a trifle. That's how it seems to me.—If you have the chance to speak and petition for my transfer to civil service, *namely in Barnaul,* then for God's sake don't overlook that. If you can speak to Gasfort about this, then, for God's sake, speak to him; and if you can not only talk, but act, then don't let this chance slip by and petition for my transfer to Barnaul in the civil service. This is the *closest* and *most reliable* step for me. Nevertheless, I agree with you completely that I need to wait for the coronation. The Lord knows, maybe there will be even *more* than even we expect. The time is near, but God knows how much water can flow under the bridge by that time. I'm speaking about my situation, which you know.

My angel, I was distressed, I was delirious, in a fever when I wrote you and my brother the last time. That's really how it was: because now the matter has been cleared up *in many respects.* It seems to me that I ought to write you all of this after what I wrote you in my last letter. During Shrovetide I was at several places for bliny, I even danced at parties. Slutsky was here and I saw him often (we are acquaintances). I wrote Marya Dmitrievna about all of this, about even venturing to dance and about certain local *ladies.* She up and imagined that I was beginning to *forget* her and was taking a fancy to others. Then, when the explanation came, she wrote me that she was tortured by the thought that I, her last and true friend, was already forgetting her. She wrote that she suffered and was tormented, but that under no circumstances would she have betrayed to me her melancholy, doubts, "she would die, but not say a word." I understand that; she has a proud and noble heart. And, therefore, she wrote: "I involuntarily became cold to you in my letters, nearly convinced that I was not writing to the same person who had just a short time ago loved only me." I noticed this coldness in her letters and it killed me. Suddenly I was told that she was getting married. If you only knew what happened to me then! I wore myself out with torments, I reread her last letters, and because of their coldness I, against my will, fell into doubt and then despair. I hadn't yet had time to write her anything about this, when I received the letter from her about which I wrote you last time, when, speaking about her helpless, indefinite position, she asks for advice: "what should she answer if a man with some good qualities proposes to her?" After this direct confirmation of all my doubts, I could doubt no longer. Everything was clear and the rumors of her marriage were true, and she had been hiding them from me so as not to upset me. I spent two weeks in such torture, such hell, such agitation of thoughts and blood that even now I can't even recall it because of the horror. Honest to God, I wanted to hurry there to be with her if only for an hour, and then to hell with my fate! But the shadow of a hope stopped me. I waited for her answer and this hope saved me. Now here's what happened: in torments of jealousy and sadness about the friend lost to her, alone, surrounded by vipers and rubbish, sick and nervous, far from her family and from any kind of help, she decided *to find out for certain* what our relationship was, whether I was forgetting her, whether I was the same as before or not? Basing herself on certain things that had really happened, she wrote me: "what should she answer if someone proposed to her?" If I had answered indifferently, that would have proved to her that I had really forgotten her. After receiving that letter I wrote a despairing, terrible letter with which I tore her to pieces, and another one by the next post.[10] She had been ill all the time lately and my letter tormented her. But she seems to have been consoled by my melancholy even though she suffered on my account. The main thing was that she was reassured by my letter that as before I loved her boundlessly. After this she at last decided to explain everything to me: her doubts and jealousy and agitation and, finally, she explained that the idea of the marriage was invented by her as a means to know and test my heart. Nevertheless this marriage had a basis. Someone in Tomsk needs a wife, and having learned that there's a widow in Kuznetsk, moreover, quite a young one and, according to reports, interesting, proposed to her through the Kuznetsk gossips (the vile creatures who are continually insulting her). She burst out laughing and answered the Kuznetsk lady matchmaker that she would not marry anybody here and that they shouldn't bother her anymore. They didn't stop; gossip started, hints, interrogations: with whom does she correspond so often? She has a simple, but good, family of officials there whom she loves. In fact she told the wife of this official that if she were to marry, there was already a man whom she respected and who had almost proposed to her. (She was hinting at me, but didn't say who.) She announced this, knowing that even though they are good people, they wouldn't be able to resist spreading the news everywhere, and in this way, if people knew that she had a fiancé, they'd stop the matchmaking and leave her in peace. I don't know if her calculation was accurate, but Peshekhonov's son, who is in service there, wrote his father that Marya Dmitrievna was getting married and his father spread the rumor in Semipalatinsk; it was because of this I was certain for a short time that everything had ended for me. But my dear friend! If you knew what a sad state I'm in now. First, she's sick: the Kuznetsk vileness will do her in, she's afraid of everything, hypersensitive, I'm jealous of every name she mentions in a letter. She's afraid to go to Barnaul: what if they receive her

---

10. Dostoevsky's correspondence from 1856 with Marya Dmitrievna has not survived.

as a suppliant, unwillingly and proudly? I'm dissuading her of the opposite. She says that the trip is expensive, that in Barnaul she'll need new things. That's true. I wrote her that I'll use all my means *to split* the cost with her, she pleads with me in the name of everything sacred not *to do this*. She's waiting for an answer from Astrakhan, where her father will decide what she should do: stay in Barnaul or go to Astrakhan. She says that if her father demands that she go to him, then she has to go and at the same time she writes: shouldn't she write her father that I'm proposing to her and just hide my true circumstances from him? All this is depressing, hell for me. If only the coronation were sooner and if there were something *certain* and *soon* about my fate, if there were, then she would calm down. Do you understand my situation now, my good friend. If only Gerngross would take some interest. Truly I sometimes think I'll go mad!

109. To Alexander Vrangel
23 May 1856. Semipalatinsk

Semipalatinsk, 23 May 1856 (Wednesday)

My dear, most kind Alexander Yegorovich, I hasten (in the full sense of the word *hasten*) to answer you. And, therefore, do not censure me if this letter is written in a slapdash manner and carelessly. I'll explain everything later.

First, I thank you beyond words for everything that you have done, for all of your efforts on my behalf. You are my second brother, dear and beloved! Totleben is a most noble soul, I was always convinced of that. He is a knightly soul, exalted and magnanimous. His brother has the same character. For Christ's sake tell Ernst[1] that I couldn't read your letter without tears and that I don't know if there are words to express my feelings for him. Kiss Adolf for me. Something is going to happen! I myself realize that the business is on the right path. God grant good fortune to our magnanimous Monarch! And so, it is right that people continually spoke of everyone's ardent love for him. How happy this makes me! More faith, more unity, and if, in addition, there's love—then everything is taken care of.—How could anyone remain behind? Not join the general movement, not do his bit!? Oh, God grant that my fate will be settled soon. You write me to send something. I'm sending a poem for the *coronation* and the

---

1. The editors of the Academy edition suggest that the name Ernst is written mistakenly for Eduard (Totleben).

conclusion of peace. I don't know whether it's good or bad, but I sent it around to the authorities here with a request for permission *to publish* it (i.e., Pyotr Mikhaylov[ich][2] only informed Gasfort about this request). To officially ask (by petition) for permission to publish, without having presented a work at the same time, is, in my opinion, a blunder. Therefore, I started with a poem. Read it, copy it and try to get it to the Monarch. But here's the problem: I shouldn't bypass Gasfort. After all, I may have to serve here. Gasfort is going to Petersburg on the 10th of June. He will of course report to the Tsar. He'll take my poem, but it's imperative that he be forewarned and, the main thing, be inclined as much as is possible in my favor. Will you be in Petersburg when Gasfort arrives? Will you meet him? If you should meet, I ask you not to tell him about Totleben. He'll take up the task more ardently if the success of the affair will be attributed to him personally. But it would be marvelous if Totleben, after meeting him somewhere, or even (but I don't even dare to hope for such an act of kindness from Totleben) *after making a visit himself* to Gasfort (which would flatter Gasfort terribly), would ask him to present my poem to the Tsar with the request to publish it and say a kind word on my behalf if they ask him about me, i.e., that I'm worthy of a promotion. Don't you think the matter would be well handled then! And so, my friend, whether you will have a chance to see Gasfort in Petersburg or not, convey this idea to Totleben, carefully (for I'm asking a lot) and if you see that he approves of it, explain everything to him.—You can't believe how you have inspired me with this news. I can't wait to see you! Oh! The sooner the better! How much there is to talk over!

X. left Barnaul at the beginning of May and by now you've surely long since seen each other and—are happy.[3] God grant you good fortune, and not those horrors that can sometimes occur—I'm speaking from experience! But don't sit too long in Petersburg. Come here, for God's sake, come.—Tell my brother that I embrace him and ask his pardon for all the grief that I have caused him; on my knees before him.—*My* affairs are terribly bad and I'm almost in despair. It's hard to endure as much as I've suffered! But I won't weary you, all the more so as *I can't* convey everything, and thus, I am completely alone with my hopeless melancholy. Oh! If only you were here, without you around none of this would be! The thing is that she[4] has now formally refused to go to Barnaul; but that wouldn't matter! But in all of her recent letters, where there are nevertheless flashes of tenderness, affection and even more, she's been hinting to me that she can't make me happy, that we are both too unhappy and that it's better for us...[5] She asks me to petition for Pasha to be

2. Pyotr Mikhailovich Spiridonov, District Military Governor of Semipalatinsk.

3. X.: Yekaterina Gerngross.

4. She: Marya Dmitrievna.

5. The sentence is not complete. At this point the text that continued on the next sheet was torn off, most likely by Dostoevsky's second wife, Anna.

enrolled in the Siberian Academy, and asks you also to petition Gasfort to have him admitted this year to the juvenile division (Pasha's 9). I promised to petition unselfishly and therefore—I implore you—do what you can. But I also implore you, for God's sake, persuade my brother to ask in detail and assiduously whether it isn't possible to place Pasha in the Pavlovsk Academy, if not now, then next year. If it's possible, my brother should write Marya Dmitrievna all the particulars as soon as possible, reassure her completely and you, Al[exander] Yegor[ovich], for Christ's sake and for mine, reassure her that there may be a good chance of getting Pasha to Petersburg, that she needn't move an inch to send her son off to Petersburg, that others will take him and that Pasha will find friends in Petersburg. Assure her, calm her! I particularly implore my brother to do this... I haven't told Belekhov that I'm going to Kuznetsk, but I'll get there, if for only a few hours. I haven't told him because for some reason Belekhov has begun scratching his head at the last moment. However, he's letting me go. I'm going, almost for certain, if Bel[ekhov] doesn't change his mind tomorrow. Everything at my own expense. Don't accuse me of wasting money for no good purpose; but I'm prepared to be prosecuted, if only I can see her. My situation is critical. We need to talk things over and decide everything in one fell swoop! Don't worry; nothing will happen to me on the road; I'm careful. I'll return in 10 days, but I'll see her. I'm keeping it secret that I'm going to Kuznetsk. For Christ's sake don't you tell anyone either except my brother. My friend! I'm horribly agitated. You write that you are petitioning for my transfer to the Barnaul battalion. For the sake of everything you hold sacred *don't transfer* me before I get my officer's rank (if God sends it). That will be my death. First, elle ne sera pas là [she won't be be there]. Second, it's so difficult to get used to new people, to new superiors. Here I'm spared the watch, there I won't be. The battalion command is a bad one. And why? For what reason? In order to live together? But she may be in Omsk. For God's sake abandon this idea. It leads me to despair.

Demchinsky isn't completely well-disposed to you either. (My relations with him are friendly.—Lamotte is a superb person.) Everybody here is surprised that, according to your letters, you are being offered so much, but are coming *here,* where you were bored, why, for what reason? I told Lamotte in confidence that it's a consequence of your family relations and made up a story, very cleverly, let L[amotte] tell it. [I'll also visit] Poletika—if I catch her at home. I'm going for about ten days.

Good-bye, my friend, God preserve you, I'm waiting for you as an angel of God. You are more to me than a friend and brother. You were sent to me by God.

110. To Alexander Vrangel
14 July 1856. Semipalatinsk

Semipalatinsk, 14 July 1856.

I hasten to answer you by the first post, my most kind, priceless Alexander Yegorovich. And I've waited for at least a line from you for a long time! I'm not reproaching you; you have always been like a brother to me; I sense that and know it. But if you knew how much I needed your friendly concern, your remembrance of me all this time. I was planning to write you a thousand times, but I was always afraid that you were leaving for here at the same time and that my letter wouldn't find you. Besides, what would I have written you? You can't write anything *you need to* in a letter. And now also.— I thank you for the 100th time for all of your efforts on my behalf. Thank both of the Tot[lebens]. You can't imagine with what ecstasy I look upon the conduct of such souls as you and both of them in regard to me! What did I do for you to make you love me so much? What did I do for them, the noble souls! God bless you all! And so, now I can firmly hope but. . . it's already too late! I have been *there,* my dear friend, I saw her! I still can't understand how it happened. I had a letter of conduct as far as Barnaul, and I risked Kuznetsk, but I was there! But what can I write you? Again, I repeat, can one write everything on a scrap of paper! I saw her! What a noble, what an angelic soul! She cried, she kissed my hands, but she loves another. I spent two days there. In those two days she *remembered the past* and her heart was again turned towards me. Whether I'm right or not, speaking this way, I don't know! But she said to me: "Don't cry, don't be sad, not everything is decided yet; you and I and nobody else!" Those were absolutely her words. I spent I don't know what sort of two days, it was unbearable bliss and torment! Towards the end of the second day I left with *complete hope.* But it's a quite accurate thing that those who are absent are always guilty. And that's exactly what happened! Letter after letter, and again I see that she is depressed, cries and again loves him more than me! I won't say forget about her! I don't even know what will become of me without her. I am done for, but she is too. Can you imagine, my priceless and last friend, what she is doing and what she is deciding, with her extraordinary, limitless common sense! She is 29 years old; she is educated, a bright girl who has seen the world, knows people, has suffered, has been tormented, ill from the last years of her life in Siberia, who is searching for happiness, is self-willed, strong, she is *now* ready to marry a 24-year-old youth, a Siberian who hasn't seen anything, doesn't know anything, who is barely educated, who is beginning the 1st idea of his life, while she, perhaps, is living out her *last idea,* without significance, without a place in the world, with nothing, a teacher in a provincial school, who (very soon) has the prospect of a salary of 900 paper rubles.[1] Tell me, Alex[ander] Yegorov[ich], isn't she destroying herself a 2nd time after this? How can such different personalities with different views on life, with different needs make a life together? And won't he abandon her later on, after several years, when she moreover[...], won't he cause her death! What will become of her in poverty, with a heap of children and sentenced to Kuznetsk? Who knows how far the discord, which I unavoidably foresee in the future, will go; for even if he were an ideal youth, he's nevertheless not a strong person. And he's not only not ideal, but... Anything might happen later on. What if he should insult her with some base reproach, when he comes to believe [?] that she was counting on his youth, that she voluptuously desired to take away the taste of age and she! she! a pure, beautiful angel, may be forced to hear this! What then? Can that really not happen? Something like this will inevitably happen; and Kuznetsk? Baseness! My God—my heart is breaking. I love her happiness more than my own. I spoke with her about all of this, that is, one can't say everything, but only about a tenth of it. She listened and was astounded. But in women feeling wins out even over the obviousness of common sense. My reasons fell before the idea that I was attacking him, looking for something suitable (forget her); and when I was defending him (saying that he couldn't be such a person) I didn't persuade her of anything, but cast a doubt: she cried and suffered. I started to feel bad for her, and then she turned completely to me—she pities me! If you knew what an angel she is, my friend! You never knew her; every minute something original, sensible, witty, but paradoxical too, infinitely good, truly noble— she has a chivalrous heart: she will do herself in. She doesn't know herself, but I know her! At her invitation I decided to write *him* everything, the whole view of things; for, when we were parting, she turned her heart to me again completely. I became close with him: he cried, but that's all he knows how to do. I realized my false position; because if I started to advise them against it, to show them the future, they'd both say: he's doing this for himself, he's inventing these horrors in the future on purpose. Moreover, he's with her, and I'm far away. And that's just what happened. I wrote both of them a long letter. I presented everything that can result from an unequal marriage. The same thing happened to me that happened to Gil-Blas and Archeveque de Grenade, when he told him the truth.[2] She heatedly answered, defending him, as if I had attacked him. And he, in true Kuznetsk fashion *stupidly* took it as a reproach and as an insult—when I

1. Nikolay Vergunov.

2. Dostoevsky is referring to a scene from LeSage's novel *Gil Blas of Santillane* (1715-35). The archbishop of Grenada demands Gil Blas' honest opinion of his sermons. Gil Blas praises them, but remarks that the last sermon is inferior to the earlier ones. Gil Blas is thrown out of the archbishop's house for his honesty. Dostoevsky considered the scene a masterpiece and mentions it in "The Gentle Creature."

requested in a friendly, brotherly way (because he himself asked me to be a friend and brother) that he think about what he is striving for, whether he won't ruin a woman for his own happiness; for he's 24 years old, and she's 29, he doesn't have any money, anything definite for the future, and Kuznetsk forever. Imagine, he was offended by all of that; on top of that he set her against me by reading one of my thoughts inside out and convincing her that it was insulting to her. He wrote me an abusive reply. I think he has a nasty soul! After the first outbursts she already wants to make peace, she's writing me, again tenderly... again gently, when I still haven't had a chance to justify myself before her. I don't know how this will all end, but she will ruin herself and my heart is sinking. Believe me or not, Alex[exander] Yegor[ovich], I'm talking to you as one does to God, but her happiness is dearer to me than my own. I've been like a madman, in the full sense of the word, all this time. We've been having reviews, and I, tormented both spiritually and bodily, wander about like a shadow. My soul isn't healing and won't ever heal. I thought I'd receive at least a line from you (I have nobody with me), and you're silent; and now God knows if we'll see each other or not! For God's sake, don't abandon me! What effort does it cost you to dash off two or three words? Write me every other post, I beg you. After all, you're my friend, brother, aren't you? I don't know how this will all end. If only I could tear out my heart and bury it, and everything with it! For God's sake write as soon as possible about your fate: are you coming or not? I wouldn't dare to advise you of anything; you know yourself. But, for God's sake, let me know as soon as possible. You write about the Marquis[3] and ask for advice. I don't know what to say! You write that she[4] hates him, a bad sign! It would be better if she were indifferent! I heard from Demchinsky that Andr[ey] Rodion[ovich] told him that she supposedly wants to go abroad this winter. Is that so? What will you do then?

Write Marya Dmitrievna what you want. If you knew with what feeling and respect she speaks of you. But you never knew her! I asked Slutsky and some others to intercede in Omsk for Pasha, and also about an allowance (her father also doesn't forget her and helps). The allowance has moved forward. Slutsky is so responsible, he answered unbelievably politely. He did everything he could. But concerning Pasha he writes that there aren't any vacancies and that only the Sovereign can approve a supernumerary, but he will be registered in the list of candidates. Plead with Gasfort, for God's sake, maybe there's still hope that he'll be accepted for this year.[5] There's still one other, last request of you. *She* must not suffer. If she marries him, then let there be at least some money. And for that he

---

3. Marquis N. de Traverse.

4. Yekaterina Gerngross.

5. Pavel Isaev was appointed a pupil at the Siberian Academy, to be educated at the state's expense.

needs a position, to be transferred somewhere. He now receives 400 paper rubles and is petitioning to take the examination to raise his rank as a teacher, in Kuznetsk. Then he'll make 900 rubles. I still don't know what can be done for him; I'll write about this. But for now talk to Gasfort about him (as a worthy young man, excellent, capable; praise him for all the world, say that you knew him, that it wouldn't be wrong to give him a higher position. I think he has an official rank. If you're in Gasfort's good graces, for God's sake tell him; what will it cost you? Also write Gerngross something about him. I'll write you again and tell you what exactly: but for now just throw out a word to Gasfort when the occasion arises. His name is: Nikolay Borisovich Vergunov. He's from Tomsk. This is all for *her, for her alone.* If only so that she wouldn't be impoverished, that's all.)[6] Really and truly I don't know who was intriguing against you in Omsk. Everybody here talked about it; but nobody knows anything. However, a month ago there was a rumor that you had been appointed as an councilor in Barnaul and *just* from appearances it looked very probable. Is that so? For God's sake write me as soon as you can. You often write to others here that you are being offered positions, that you're making acquaintances, etc. Here this is viewed ironically, it seems, by everyone and therefore I'm warning you not to write them in this manner. Everybody is surprised that you are going to Siberia just when so much is being promised to you in Petersburg, and, not understanding *your* reasons, they think you are boasting. Even Lamotte smiles with high irony when speaking about you, and Demch[insky] says that in order to read your letters one has to put on a full-dress coat. Ignore all of this. Write them, but without injuring their petty vanity. Among the mining people I've only met Pishko and Samoylov; they're good people; I didn't catch the others. Gerngross and I missed each other. If I'm promoted, then I wish to go to Barnaul. And if some other way to Russia, too, all the better. For Christ's sake, don't forget me.

I have still one very special request. If you can—do it, and if not—that's all right! My friend, if I'm promoted and, in general, in August I'll need money, very much, terribly, desperately. You won't believe how much my expeditions cost me, but I will risk another.[7] I'm 100 silver rubles in debt. I live cheaply, but my expenses are special. I sense that I will need (just in case) will badly need money. I need money right now desperately. Implore my brother (whom I ask you to kiss without end) to send me some if he can soon. Of you I ask this: if you really have hope and assurance that I'll be allowed to publish (but only in that case), then for God's sake borrow (because you probably don't have it yourself) 300 silver rubles until January. If I'm allowed to publish, then I can more than pay back the

6. Scholars have noted the similarity between this episode from Dostoevsky's biography and the relations between Ivan Petrovich and Natasha in *The Insulted and the Injured.*

7. Dostoevsky's "expeditions" are his visits to Kuznetsk to see Marya Dmitrievna.

money in January. I won't compromise you. Only *if* you have somebody to borrow from. But if that is very difficult for you—don't bother, because it's excruciating to borrow. Don't borrow from X., for God's sake, because that would be too great a sacrifice for me on your part. If you do borrow the money, then send it right away care of Lamotte. For God's sake, forgive me for such requests. In the first place, I don't know your circumstances, and second, I'm like a madman. For God's sake don't think anything bad of me. Good-bye, I'll write you something soon. For God's sake write soon about everything. Don't forget me.

Your F. Dostoevsky

I embrace you together with my brother countless times. My regards to the others. Don't hide anything from me.

111. To Alexander Vrangel
21 July 1856. Semipalatinsk

Semipalatinsk 21 July 1856

Here's another letter for you, most kind, priceless Al[exander] Yeg[orovich]. Only I don't know how it will reach you—will it find you in Petersburg? This is a letter-request. My friend, my good friend, I am literally sprinkling you with requests. I know that what I'm doing is bad—but you are my only hope! Besides, I believe in you so, when I remember your pure, beautiful heart! Don't feel burdened by my requests. And I'd go through fire and water for you. Here's what it's about. I wrote you that I asked Slutsky to petition for Pasha and I asked Zhdan-Pushkin too, and that I had received replies from both of them. The prospects for this year are bad. I asked you to tell Gasfort about this. But now I've received another letter from Slutsky, whom I also asked to advance Marya Dmitrievna's application for an award of a one-time allowance, since she has the right by law to 285 silver rubles on the death of her husband. Slutsky really did advance the case, which had been completely stagnant. Unfortunately, Gasfort had left. The Central Administration, owing to his absence, forwarded the case to the Minister of Internal Affairs (7 July 1856, No. 972). Now: the application for the award of a one-time allowance to her can get *stuck* in Petersburg, particularly in the present circumstances, and God knows how much time may pass before it's acted upon. And besides this, will it in fact be decided in her favor? Well, how can they refuse? My friend, my good angel! If you still continue to love me, one who continuously besieges you with sundry requests, then help, if you can, in this matter as well. For God's sake, inquire about the fate of this *application;* you most likely will find you have acquaintances who will help you with this and people with influence, with weight. Couldn't you nudge the matter a little, so that it doesn't stagnate and so that it's decided in Marya Dmitrievna's favor? My angel! Don't be lazy, do this, for Christ's sake. Just think: in her situation this sum is a whole fortune, and in her *present* situation—salvation, the only way out. I tremble at the thought that she may give up waiting for the money and marry. Then, very likely (I think), they will even refuse her this. He doesn't have anything, nor does she. A marriage will entail expenses that it will take the two of them a couple of years to recover from. And again she will have poverty, again suffering. And then she won't be able to turn to her father for help, because she will be married. Why should she, the poor thing, suffer and eternally suffer? And therefore, for God's sake, fulfill my request; also fulfill (as much as is possible) those requests about which I wrote in my last letter. You don't know how happy you will make me!

I'm writing you but I don't know where and when you'll get this letter. If you are coming here, then it won't find you. If you remain there, then where will you be exactly? For God's sake let me know whether you received this letter. And don't be too lazy to write me, good friend! If only a few, just a few lines! If you only knew how I now need your heart! Maybe if I embraced you I would feel better. I'm so unbearably sad. Although I know that if you don't come to Siberia, then, of course, it's because it's much more advantageous for you to remain in Russia, but forgive my selfishness: I dream only of seeing you here as soon as possible. I need you, need you so much! Forgive me for writing on such a scrap of paper. In the first place, I'm hurrying, and second, at the present I'm capable of almost nothing and I look at everything with pain! If only I could see her again, even for just an hour! And although nothing would come of it, at least I would have seen her.

Embrace my priceless brother and tell him to forgive me for my silence. I'll write later, but now, really, I'm desperate! It's enough to start me drinking! Embrace him for me and tell him that I love him immensely.

Have you seen X? And what's the situation? I'm afraid that you'll be silent even longer now. Write me everything, for Our Creator's sake. If there's really hope that I'll be promoted to the rank of officer, then can't it be arranged that it be to Barnaul? Don't forget about Vergunov, for God's sake, speak to Gasfort and Gerngross. Convey my eternal gratitude to the Totlebens, my boundless love for them! May God grant you, my good, priceless friend, every happiness and may God preserve you from going through what I am experiencing. I will wait for your reply and write you (I promise) a more diverting and detailed letter. My regards to everyone, particularly Yakushkin if you see him. You asked if Gavrilov got married:[1]

1. Gavrilov was evidently one of Dostoevsky's fellow soldiers.

No, and, it seems he's not even thinking of it now. It was a very comic story. We became close not long ago. Demchinsky is the same as always, he's very good to me and does me a number of good turns. Zhoravovich (the artillery man) married Gavrilova and the wedding took place a few days ago. Good-bye, my priceless friend! Are you really not going to attend the coronation? Don't forget about my request for money. All my plans will be dashed without it! I repeat—it's desperate! Besides that I'm suffering need myself. Good-bye, good-bye! I kiss you countless times.

Your D.

112. To Alexander Vrangel
9 November 1856. Semipalatinsk

Semipalatinsk, 9 November 56

I'd already received your letter, my priceless friend, Alexander Yegorovich, on the 30th of October and didn't answer by the first post due to special circumstances. I was thinking about a trip to B[arnaul] and wanted to write you from there, after seeing X., and, of course, making my letter more diverting for you. But my trip still hasn't taken place, but I'm almost certain that it will take place next week, if, as promised, they send me some money. Then I'll write you from B[arnaul], and you should expect that letter in the very near future. But you shouldn't consider this letter that I'm writing now a real letter; it's just a few lines to answer you at least something more quickly. If you were here I couldn't tell you even in a week's time, my never-to-be-forgotten friend, everything that I would like to talk about with you.

You write that besides our infinitely merciful Monarch I should thank Totleben and His Highness Prince Oldenburgsky.[1] I thank them with an ardent heart and if you see Totleben, tell him that I don't have words to express my gratitude to him. I will remember his noble deed on my behalf my whole life. But my heart is fair: if it had not been for you, my dear friend, if you had not exerted yourself on my behalf, I'm certain, my case would not have advanced so quickly. God sent you to me. I thank you and embrace you very tightly. You know that I love you.

Now I'll tell you in a few short words (although there's a lot I would

---

1. Vrangel had informed Dostoevsky that he had been promoted to the rank of officer. Prince Pyotr Georgievich Oldenburgsky (1812-81), famous for his philanthropy, was the founder of the Institute of Jurisprudence, the Technical Institute and several hospitals.

like to say about this, but you can't get everything in)—you will never realize, my priceless one, into what sadness, what grief I was plunged by your long silence! My friend, I understand the psychic state in which one doesn't want to take pen in hand even to write that person who is capable of understanding us, to me, in a word, from whom you almost kept no secrets. The arrival of X. in Barnaul, at the time when there were rumors that she would be in Petersburg all winter, disturbed me. I knew very well that her arrival and departure would not go by without some influence on you. I had almost guessed everything about which wrote me. But such strange thoughts, such suspicions and conjectures occurred to me about you in regard to X. that I was in the deepest despair and fear for you. It was known here that you had been appointed to the expedition.[2] But that you were still in Petersburg, I was certain of that. Then why doesn't he write, that's the question I asked myself every day. But I swear to you that despite everything, I didn't once doubt your friendship, I didn't think that you'd forgotten me. You proved that by sending your portrait (which I haven't received yet). But, my friend, I understand that psychic alarm when one doesn't want to open an old wound in the heart by talking about it with another. But really, couldn't you have written me a couple of lines? Another reason that you advance to explain your silence to me (namely: that *you had not fulfilled any of my requests)*—is quite incomprehensible to me. I asked you for money, as from a friend, as from a brother, at a time and under circumstances when there remained either the noose or a decisive act. You were precisely the person I ventured to ask because I knew that I could burden you with my request, but that if you were in circumstances similar to mine and I were asked to risk something extreme for you I would do it. Feeling this way, I, without pangs of conscience, decided to trouble you (if I hadn't borrowed here and accumulated the debts, I would have perished—I needed the money so badly, not for my very existence, but for my *intentions.* You know from my previous letters what sort psychic state I was in. I don't know why I haven't gone mad yet!). But if, most good Alexander Yegorovich, if you didn't have the money yourself to help me (which is undoubtedly so, because you have never failed me before)—tell me, for God's sake, why couldn't you simply write: *no* or *I can't (if the impossibility of complying with my request was one of the reasons for your silence)?* Did you really think I was incapable of understanding that, of course, *impossibility* forced you to refuse me and not the lack of friendship? And what right would I have had to be vexed with you for not sending the money (even without that I'm entirely in your debt—to you, who have been and are for me like a beloved, dear brother. Because after all that you've done for me, you will allow me to address you

2. Vrangel was appointed secretary to the leader of a naval expedition that was to travel to China, Japan and to the mouth of the Amur River, which for more than 1,000 miles forms the border between the USSR and China. The expedition was postponed until the fall of 1857.

that way). Finally, my despair about you lately grew to impossible proportions (on top of everything I've been frequently ill lately). I even imagined that something tragic, of the sort we'd talked about at one time, had happened to you. And there was nobody who could give even the slightest piece of news about you. Finally, your letter arrived and it resolved many of the misunderstandings, many, but not all. My friend, I'm even glad, although it's hard for me to touch such a sore spot in your heart—I'm glad that God led you to finally break with X. Relations with her finally were taking on a most unsettling prospect for you. You would have ruined yourself, perhaps. My God! How curious I am to at least see X. (that soon will happen and you should be certain that I will relate to the last nuance, my priceless one, all of my impressions upon meeting with her). What can I say to you? Can you really be consoled by words? Oh, my friend, nobody understands your grief more than I, who have *suffered like you*. And whom should be consoled? Do you have a heart that can be healed by consolations? Time, time is what will right everything (I say that and don't believe it, judging by my own example). You will remain in Russia all winter. Throw yourself into something, into some kind of excitement, but for Christ's sake, for God's sake, write me more and more often, even if only a few lines, but write. How I would like to see you, but when? when?

You ask about my relations with M[arya] D[mitrievna]. If you wanted to find out something about me, then by asking just that question, because she is as before *everything* in my life. I've thrown over everything, I don't think about anything except her. If the promotion to an officer's rank gladdened me, it was precisely because I'll perhaps get to see her soon. There wasn't any money, and I still haven't gone. My brother gives me hope. I'm expecting some money next week and will set off immediately. *Father*[3] promised to give me leave for about 15 days. I love her madly, more than before. My longing for her would have driven me to my grave and *literally* reduced me to suicide, if I hadn't seen her [...]. Don't shake your head, don't condemn me; I know that I'm acting imprudently in many ways in my relations with her, since I have almost no hope—but whether there's hope or not—it's all the same to me. I don't think about anything else. If only I could see her, hear her! I'm an unfortunate madman! Love in such a guise is an illness. I sense that. I owe from the trip (I tried to go a second time, but got only as far as Zmiev; it didn't work out). Now I'm going again, I'll ruin myself, but what do I care? For Christ's sake, don't show this letter to my brother. I'm endlessly guilty before him. He, the poor thing, has been helping me with all his might and what am I wasting the money on! And I asked you too—either to drown myself or satisfy myself. My relationship with her is the same. Every week there are letters, long

3. Dostoevsky nicknamed Belikhov, the battalion commander, "father."

ones, full of the most sincere, most extreme attachment. But in her letters she often calls me her brother. But she loves me. My appearance alone in Kuznetsk almost caused her *to return* to me again. Oh, don't wish that I would abandon this woman and this love. She was the light of my life. She appeared to me at the saddest time of my life and resurrected my soul. She resurrected in me my entire being, because I had met her. But if you knew what an angel she is, what a soul! What a heart! The poor thing, she is suffering a cruel lot! It's horrible to live in Kuznetsk. She is trying to to get her son into the academy (I asked Slutsky, in writing, to do something for him, and he promised to do everything that he can), and she's petitioning for a pension and is living on the crumbs her father sends her, quietly, modestly, meekly, compelling the entire little town to respect her. She is a firm, strong personality. Her marriage to him (the other one) evidently is quite impossible, materially impossible (he has a 300-ruble salary), and she won't wish to burden him.[4] I'll write you about everything from Barnaul.

My friend, you ask me what I wish, what should be requested. And you also say that I can be transferred to Russia. But my friend: the mercy of our Angel-Tsar is boundless, and I know that I, even without serving, will be returned for good in a year or two. Transfer to the army is also bad because I'm in any case a poor officer, if for no other reason than my health. But I'll have to serve. If I wish to return to Russia, it's solely because I want to embrace my dear ones and consult with knowledgeable doctors and find out what sort of illness I have (epilepsy), what sort of attacks, which still repeat themselves and which each time dull my memory and all of my faculties and from which I fear, as a result, I'll go mad. What kind of officer am I? If they would retire me—even if they left me here *for a time*—that is all that I wish. I would secure myself some money to live on. I wouldn't perish here. And what's more there is *her (she* is the main thing) and therefore write me definitely (as much as possible): 1st) *can I* in the near future, owing to the weakness of my health, tender my resignation (requesting just in case my return to Russia, *for consultation with doctors?)* and 2nd) can I *publish*—this question for me is *the main one,* about which you write *nothing* in your letter. But, after all, that's the means for my existence *and a career,* because I *have faith* in myself and hope to be famous and make for myself a name, fate, and finally attract attention. And therefore I'm asking you to write me in the affirmative: if I should send something in the near future under my own name (or a pseudonym)— *will it be published?* For God's sake, my friend, my priceless brother, don't abandon me, don't forget me, and write me about this if you can, soon and affirmatively. I'll write more definitely about what I plan to achieve after the trip; *because* much will be decided by this trip. But now, in the meantime, answer me these two questions.

4. Nikolay Vergunov.

So, have you become acquainted with Goncharov?[5] How did you like him? A gentleman from the United Society,[6] of which he's a member, with the soul of a petty clerk, no ideas and with the eyes of a boiled fish, whom God, as though for a joke, has blessed with a brilliant talent.

How sorry I am that you and my brother haven't become close. He's a splendid person and, truly, you wouldn't have anyone beside you who would love you as passionately as he. I'm enclosing a letter to him. For God's sake, give it to him right away, don't hold on to it. I'm writing you in haste, because there are a lot of things that I can't write about definitely; I repeat; the *next letter* will be more even and substantive.

I can't tell you anything about your things and books. Stepanov doesn't have *anything*, he told me so himself. (Neither the samovar, nor the pans.) Last summer I saw 4 boxes that Demchinsky sent to Ostermeier. Stepanov says that you didn't leave anything for him. Demchinsky says that he doesn't know what's in the boxes. I'll find out everything in Barnaul, including the books, and will try to carry out everything you ask. If they give me your suitcase (which you are making a present of to me), then I'll take it, I thank you, my friend, you never cease to think about me.

I thank you immensely for your promise to outfit me. But I outfitted myself here, as much as was possible (by borrowing and one way or another). I'm very sorry that I couldn't let you know earlier; because you may have already sent everything! But I feel bad that you have spent so much on me. But I won't decline a helmet, half sabre and scarf—I'll even ask for them; because you can't get any of those things here (especially the helmet).

I'm not writing about the local news. Everything and everybody are the same here (I'll write you later). I'm fairly intimate with Demchinsky (he helps me a lot with the *trips,* because he accompanies me himself, since he has some affairs of the heart in Zmiev). For God's sake, don't think that he has replaced you, you know what he's like as a person. But he's terribly devoted to me (I don't know why) and I can't help being grateful. Why doesn't he especially like you? However, he does all these things by some sort of *inspiration.* Obukh [7] is in Verny.

Good-bye, my priceless friend, write me as soon as you can and expect something from me soon. I embrace you tightly.

Your D.

M[arya] D[mitrievna] has asked about you 1000 times. She is very

5. The novelist Ivan Goncharov served as a secretary under Admiral Putyatin on a naval voyage to the Far East (1852-54), the basis for his travel notes *The Frigate Pallada* (published 1855-57).

6. The United Society (formerly the American Society) was one of the Petersburg society circles.

7. Obukh has not been identified.

worried about you because of letters. She loves you extraordinarily and speaks about you almost with reverence. She respects you boundlessly.

113. To Mikhail Dostoevsky
9 November 1856. Semipalatinsk

Semipalatinsk. 9 November 1856.

My dear brother, my irreplaceable and faithful friend, Al[exander] Yegor[ovich], to whom I am so much obliged, will deliver this letter to you. I received your letter with the last post. I'm surprised that you learned of my promotion so late. I already knew about it on October 30th. (Thank K. I. Ivanova and Olga Ivanovna. They sent me the order; and in addition, a document from headquarters about my promotion arrived at the military governor's on October 30th.) Together with you I repeat: may our Angel-Monarch reign long and happily! There aren't words to express my gratitude to him. I embrace you with all my heart and thank you for your good wishes. I waited an eternity for your letter. My friend, get rid of your system: let me know about yourself more often, even if only a bit at a time. Sometimes you have nothing to send me, I know that, but who cares, write me anyway! You promise, my friend, to send me some money by a future post and assure me of help on the part of my dear sisters and aunt. My kind friend, if only you knew what need I am in. This help will arrive at a most opportune time, for I wouldn't know how to outfit myself. A uniform here costs a lot more (1 1/2 times more) than in Petersburg. I bought what was indispensable in the shops on credit. But a lot still remains to be acquired. By the way, I don't have any underclothes. Now I'm receiving a salary. But the salary, at first, with the deductions, etc., isn't much. In addition I've borrowed (of course, from such people who'll wait for me, but nevertheless I'm in debt). I'm writing you this, my friend, not because I haven't found anything more important than to immediately start talking about money and ask you about sending some. No! And you yourself don't consider me such a person, I'm sure of that, but here's why: in order to justify myself before you, if only a little bit, for I'm very guilty before you, *counting* on your money and *having spent more* than I can spend. But, my dear brother! If there were extreme expenses they were beyond my control. The woman whom I loved, I still adore. I don't know how this will end. I would go mad, or worse, if I didn't see her. All of this unsettled my affairs (don't think that I'm sharing with her, that I'm giving it over to her; she's not that kind of woman, she could be penniless, but she wouldn't accept it).

She is an angel from God, who turned up on my path, and suffering has bound us together. I would long ago have lost heart without her. What will be, will be! You were very worried by the possibility of my marriage to her. My dear friend, it seems tht this will never be, even though she loves me. I know that. But what will be, will be! She begs you to forgive her for not answering you. She was in horribly wretched circumstances at the time. But after long procrastination she was ashamed to answer. Your letter delighted her. But enough of that.

A new life is beginning for me now! Al[exander] Yeg[orovich] asks what else I ask for and what do I wish? (He's devoted to me like a brother). I don't even know myself now what to wish for, since I will soon achieve my return to Russia even without a transfer to the army. If I wished to return to Russia more quickly, it would be so that I could embrace you and consult with knowledgable doctors about my illness (the attacks). More than anything else I would like my retirement and therefore I'm asking Al[exander] Yegor[ovich] to write me soon and affirmatively whether I can hope to request my retirement owing to the weakness of my health? Retirement would be useful to me: 1) for the improvement of my health, 2) freedom; the opportunity to devote myself to literature (more conveniently) and, finally, it would give me more money. For even here they have 2 times offered me (counting on my being given complete freedom by the manifesto) work that would perhaps have totally provided for me. But I'm planning, waiting and hoping for permission to publish; having hoped for that ahead of time and too soon, I in fact borrowed senselessly (I was counting on "A Children's Tale," which you were thinking of publishing. Why wasn't it published, was there an attempt, and if so, then what was said?—For Christ's sake write me about all of this).[1] My friend, I have been so upset this past year, in such melancholy and suffering, that I was absolutely unable to work decently. I gave up everything that I'd begun writing, but was writing in fits and starts. But even that was not without results, for a good piece has matured, been thought out and is half written. Yes, my friend, I know that I will make myself a career and win a good place in literature. What's more, I think that through literature, *once having attracted attention to myself,* I'll extricate myself from these last difficulties that remain in my bitter lot. I'm greatly tormented by the sheer abundance of material for writing. And I'm tormented as well by things in a vein other than novels. I think I would say something even remarkable about art; a whole essay is in my head and on paper in the form of notes, but my novel has diverted all my attention. It's a big work. The novel is a comic one; it began with a humorous element and I am pleased with what has turned out. There will be very, very good things

---

1. "A Children's Tale," written in 1849 in the Peter-and-Paul Fortress, was published in 1857 with the title "A Little Hero" (under the pseudonym M-y).

in it. For God's sake, don't think me a braggart. There's not a man more just and strict than I am in regard to myself in this respect, and if only my former critics had known that! I would like to publish *now* excerpts, completely finished episodes, from this big novel.[2] It would give me both fame and money. For Christ's sake, find out as far as possible whether that is possible, and write me.

My angel, I feared for you horribly. Your cigars frightened me when I read about them in your letter, and later in the newspapers. I was horrified by your risking everything you have on such a risky undertaking. This is tempting fate. Once you had success with the cigarettes; but to venture a second success and to tempt fate—it's too risky.[3] I feared for you all summer. God grant that you were lucky! But I'm talking without knowing much about the business.

My dear friend, you write about our sisters: they're angels! What a wonderful family we have! What people there are in it! Where is brother Andrey and what's happening with him? I haven't heard a word for a long time; I'll definitely write him. I'm writing this letter in haste, only so as to reply to yours. But I'll write again soon to Al[exander] Yegor[ovich]. Then I'll write you again at greater length and in more detail, for I'll know more about myself as well then. I ought to write my sisters and uncle now, but I'll wait one more post for letters from our sisters. Varenka wanted to send me some underclothes (and I had worn everything out, and, the high cost of living notwithstanding, I was forced to borrow in order to have some underclothes made), she asks what address should she send the underclothes to. I still don't understand her question, but to the same address to which she sends her letters. If you see her, kiss her for me, and if you don't see her, write that I kiss them all. The good Varenka sent me 25 rubles (which I didn't receive until August, by special delivery) and God knows how much that helped me!

I've rented an apartment with a maid, heating and board for 8 silver rubles a month.[4] In a word, I'm living like a Jew. For God's sake, my brother, can it be that you still can't address your letters to me directly and not through headquarters? I'm sure that even by the proclamation you're free from this last surveillance. For God's sake, write to me directly. (The Monarch is angelic goodness itself!) I'm hurrying to finish this letter to you. My health is the same as before. But in the fall I was nevertheless somewhat ill. The attacks haven't stopped. They come on every once in a while. I lose heart after them each time and sense that I am losing my memory and faculties.[5] Despondency and a state of psychic abasement are

2. Dostoevsky wrote Maykov about his plans for a long, comic novel in Letter 104.

3. On 18 April 1856 Mikhail wrote Dostoevsky that besides cigarettes *(papirosy)*, he had begun to manufacture cigars and that he had spent "heaps of money" on this venture.

4. Dostoevsky rented his apartment from the Palshins in Semipalatinsk.

5. For a comprehensive study of Dostoevsky's epilepsy see James L. Rice, *Dostoevsky and the Healing Art* (Ann Arbor, 1985).

the consequence of my attacks. Are you well? Is everybody at home well? How is Emilia Fyodorovna, give her my regards and kiss the children for me. Write soon and without fail. If there's nothing to send, then send an empty letter. My angel, a letter is dearer to me than money! I'm alone, completely alone, and you don't know anything about my situation. And what can I tell on 4 pages of paper, when we need years to tell everything to each other! Oh, if only we could see each other. Good-bye, my angel, but not for long. I'll write again soon, only you write too, write as often as you can. I embrace you. All yours, F. Dost[oevsky]

Be sure to write!

114. To Chokan Valikhanov[1]
14 December 1856. Semipalatinsk

Semipalatinsk, 14 December 1856

Alexander Nikolaevich[2] passed on your letter, my dearest friend. You write so affably and tenderly that I seemed to see you before me again. You write me that you love me. And I declare to you without any ceremony that I've fallen in love with you. I've never felt for anybody, not even excepting my own brother, the attraction I feel for you, and God knows how this came about. A lot could be said here in explanation, but what's the use of praising you! You most likely believe my sincerity even without proofs, my dear Vali-khan, and if one were to write 10 books on this theme, you wouldn't write anything: feeling and attraction are an inexplicable thing. After we said good-bye from inside the sleigh we were all sad afterwards for the whole day. We reminisced about you the whole way and tried to top each other in praising you. How marvelous it would have been if you'd been able to travel with us! You would have made a great impression in Barnaul. In Kuznetsk (where I was alone) (NB This is a secret)—I talked a lot about you to a certain lady, a woman who is intelligent, kind, with a soul and heart, who is my best friend. I talked to her so much about you that she fell in love with you, without even seeing you, from my words, explaining to me that I painted you in the brightest colors. Perhaps you will see this superb woman sometime and will also be numbered among her

---

1. Chokan Chingisovich Valikhanov (1835-66), a Kirghiz by nationality, was an ethnographer and explorer. Valikhanov was a student in the Cadet Academy in Omsk, where he became acquainted with Dostoevsky.

2. Alexander Nikolaevich Tsurikov delivered Valikhanov's letter to Dostoevsky.

Chokan Valikhanov and Dostoevsky (1858)

friends, which I would wish for you. That's why I'm writing about this.[3] I spent hardly any time in Barnaul. However, I was at the ball and had time to get acquainted with almost everyone. I was in Kuznetsk longer (5 days). Then in Zmiev and in Lokt. Demchinsky was in his usual good humor the whole time. Semyonov[4] is a wonderful person. I took an even closer look at him. There's a lot I could tell you that can't be fitted into a letter. But sometime you'll find out a few things, but now, when so much grief, so many troubles and so much fear have accumulated in my soul suddenly, unexpectedly (I both expected it and didn't expect it) for what is *dearer to me than anything else on earth,* now, when I am completely alone (and it's necessary to act)—now I repent that I didn't reveal to you my major concerns and my aspirations and everything that has been tormenting my heart to death for more than two years! I would have been fortunate. My good friend, dear Chekan Chingisovich, I'm writing you riddles. Don't try to solve them, but wish me success. Perhaps, you'll soon hear about everything from me in person. Come visit us soon, if possible, but in April without fail. Don't change your intentions. How I would like to see you, and you certainly won't be bored. You write that you're bored in Omsk—I should think so! You ask for advice: what to do about your service and, in general, about your circumstances. In my opinion, here's what you should do: don't give up your studies. You have a lot of material. Write an article about the steppe. They'll publish it (remember, we talked about this). It would be best of all if you could write something like your *Notes* about life in the steppe, your school days there, etc.[5] That would be something new that would interest everybody. So it would be new and you, of course, would know what to write (for example, something like *John Tanner* in Pushkin's translation, if you remember).[6] You would receive attention both in Omsk and Petersburg. With the material you have you would interest the Geographical Society in yourself. In a word, people would look at you differently even in Omsk. Then you would be able to interest even your family *with the possibility of a new path for you.* If you want to spend a future summer in the steppe, you may have to wait a long time yet. But beginning the 1st of September of next year you apply for a *year's leave* to Russia. After living there a year, you would know what to do. You would have the means for a year; trust me that you don't need that much.

---

3. The woman is Marya Dmitrievna Isaeva.

4. Dostoevsky became acquainted with Pyotr Semyonov in the Petrashevsky Circle. Semyonov at this time was the head of an expedition sponsored by the Geographical Society.

5. Valikhanov's *The Kirghiz* was published in 1858.

6. The nine-year-old John Tanner (ca. 1780-1847), son of an American farmer, was kidnapped by Indians and did not return to "white man's civilization" until 1820. He later became a translator for the U.S. Government. Tanner's *A Narrative of the Captivity and Adventures of John Tanner* was published in 1830 and caused a sensation. Pushkin's essay "John Tanner," which includes numerous quotations (translated from the French), was published in *The Contemporary* in 1836.

The main thing is what budget to live on and what outlook to have on the matter. Everything is relative. By the end of that year you would be able to decide on the next step in your life. You would *find out* for yourself the result, that is, you would decide what to do next. After returning to Siberia you would be able to present such advantages or such considerations (there's a lot one can depict or present!) to your family that they would very likely allow you to go even abroad, that is, a couple of years' travel in Europe. In 7 or 8 years you would be able to arrange your fate so that you would be unusually useful to your homeland. For example: isn't it a great goal, isn't it a sacred mission to be practically the first of one's people who would explain in Russia what the steppe is, its significance and your people in regard to Russia, and at the same time to serve your homeland by means of *enlightened* intercession for her among the Russians. Remember that you are the first Kirghiz educated entirely on the European model. Fate herself has in addition made you a most excellent person, having given you both a soul and a heart. You absolutely must not lag behind; insist, endeavor, and even be cunning if possible. And after all, everything is possible, believe that. Don't laugh at my utopian calculations and conjurings about your fate, my dear Vali-khan. I love you so that I have dreamed about you and your fate for days on end. Of course, in my dreams I arranged and fostered your future. But among the dreams there was one reality: it is that you are the *first* of your tribe to have acquired a European education. That circumstance alone is astonishing and awareness of it involuntarily imposes duties upon you. It's difficult to decide what your first step should be. But here's one more piece of advice (in general)— ponder and dream less and do more: at least begin with something, at least do something for the furthering of your career. Something is better than nothing, after all. May God grant you good fortune.

Good-bye, my dear one, and allow me to embrace and kiss you 10 times. Remember me and write more often. I like Tsurikov, he's direct, but I don't know him well yet. Will you meet up with Semyonov and will you be together in Semipalatinsk? Then we'll have a big group. Then, perhaps, a lot will change in my fate, too. God grant that it be so! Demchinsky sends his regards. I'm writing you from his apartment, at the same table at which we usually had breakfast or drank tea at night, waiting for the offended orphans.[7]

Tsurikov is sitting across from me and is also writing you. Demchinsky, however, is sleeping and snoring. It's now 10 o'clock in the evening. I don't understand why I'm so tired. I'd like to write you a few things about Semipalatinsk; there are some very funny things. But one

---

7. It is unclear who the orphans are. Valikhanov wrote Dostoevsky: "By the way, about the orphans. Last night I was engaged in love on your suggestion with S. Question her, it seems we spent the evening pleasantly."

can't write even a tenth part of them, if one writes as one should. Good-bye again, my good friend. Write we more often. And I will always answer you. Perhaps another time I'll risk writing about my affairs too. Regards from me to D[urov], and wish him all the best from me. Assure him that I love him and am sincerely devoted to him.

Adio! [*sic*]

NB. S. sends her regards, she told me how you tried to entice her to Omsk. She remembers you and is very *interested in you.*

115. To Alexander Vrangel
21 December 1856. Semipalatinsk

Semipalatinsk. 21 December 1856.

My most kind, priceless, Alexander Yegorovich. I have been waiting with impatience so long for your letter and haven't received anything. Did you receive mine in which I informed you that I want to leave Semipalatinsk for a couple of weeks? But if you did receive it, then your reply to it couldn't have come yet; I'm speaking about the letter that you promised to write me without even expecting a reply. You wanted to send me some officer's things. I already informed you, my most kind friend, not to ruin yourself for me in vain, that I don't need all the clothing (for in any case it will arrive late) and that if I really needed some of those things, for instance, a shako, uniform epaulettes, military buttons, etc., it's only because there aren't any of those things here—one must order them. And that's why I informed you that I was prepared to accept these trifles from you gratefully. But if the preparation of these things and shopping for them have delayed you, so that you, waiting for the completion of these preparations, haven't even written me—then that's wrong, of course, it's wrong! My good and never-to-be-forgotten friend, you to whom I am so indebted even as it is—can it be that such trifles as these could prevent you from writing me? But perhaps I'm mistaken, perhaps time has succeeded in blotting out the memory of me in your soul, and you no longer love me as before! Who knows! But, no! I'm ashamed to say it. You've done so much for me that the doubt that could creep into my heart would be ingratitude toward you! I don't want these doubts, I shoo them away, and having embraced you with all my heart, I want to talk to you as before, as we used to in Semipalatinsk, when you were everything for me: both a friend and a brother and when we both shared with each other our cares. . . *of the heart.*

First, has it been a long time since you saw Totleben? Is he in Petersburg? And if he is, did you convey my gratitude to him? Tell him, my friend, that I don't have words to express it to him and that I shall eternally hold him in reverence, my whole life, and shall never forget what he did for me.[1] For God's sake, my good friend, write me about all of this as soon as possible. I promised you a long letter and here I am writing on half a sheet. The reason for this is that I don't know if my letter will catch you in Petersburg. You wrote me that you wanted to go to Irbit and God knows, perhaps you will take it into your head to go even as far as Barnaul. In that case I don't know if my letter will lie around until your return or if it will be forwarded from Petersburg to where you will be staying. That's why I'm writing you briefly about what I could write about at greater length. And there's another reason, which you will understand from the following words "God alone knows how I would like to talk over everything with you verbally, and not in writing!" If I could see you I would get a few things across to you, but that's not possible now. I'll say only one thing: I went to Barnaul and Kuznetsk with Demchinsky and Semyonov (a member of the Geographical Society). We arrived in Barnaul on December 24th[2] (X.'s name-day) and Gerngross, without having yet seen us, straightaway invited us to the ball through Semyonov. I liked him a great deal. I don't know *why he now, suddenly, has become somewhat prejudiced against you.* He told me that right out. I liked her a great deal, *everything about her,* but she was wrong in obviously distancing herself from me. She was courteous with me, sweet, everything was apparently fine, but she obviously didn't trust me. But even if she suspected that I know about your romance, could she really think me an ignoble person? It should be noted that she obviously tried to talk about you as drily as possible, even with a slight sneer. I don't know why I liked that so much, that is, not the sneer, but *the tactic.* She's very intelligent. I'm certain that when she wants to be, she is seductive. I wished with all my soul's might that in its qualities her heart corresponded to the rest of her. But she hid it far away from the curious. We met at the ball four times or so and talked. I purposely didn't dance in order to talk with her.

I'm not going to write you about the Barnaul people. I've become acquainted with a lot of them; it's a bustling city and how much gossip and how many homegrown Talleyrands there are! I spent a day in Barnaul and set off for Kuznetsk alone. I spent 5 days there and on returning spent another day in Barnaul. I dined at Gerngross' and stayed at his place until evening. He treated me superbly. I made a small gaffe at dinner: I very much liked their son, a boy of about 8 years; he looks awfully like his mother. I said that. She objected that there wasn't any likeness. I began to

1. Dostoevsky received his pardon due to Totleben's influence and intercession.
2. Obviously a slip of the pen—the month should read *November.*

analyze the likeness in detail. Just imagine—this boy, I later found out, is considered practically a freak by the family! What a great compliment I made!

My friend, you, it seems, were very frank with X. in Petersburg and showed her my letters? Is that so? At least when I went to Kuznetsk she told Semyonov (whom I got to know very well) that I went to Kuznetsk to get married, that there is a woman there whom I love, and she knows that from you?

I received your portrait. Thank you, my friend, thank you!—I haven't received the suitcase you gave me. Gerngross didn't say a word to me about it. And I was ashamed to ask. Of course, he forgot, but it doesn't make any difference, for, perhaps Ostermeier has the suitcase. I'll get it later, if he has it. Your books and minerals in all probability are in Zmiev at Ostermeier's, in those 4 boxes that were sent to him last summer. We arrived in Zmiev at night on our return journey. I wasn't able to go to Ostermeier's. But *rest assured* that everything will be saved and delivered to you. I still hope to go to Zmiev.

Now, my friend, I want to make known to you a matter very important to me. This should be revealed to you, since you're my friend. Short and sweet: *if a certain circumstance doesn't interfere*, then I am getting married by Shrovetide—you know to whom.[3] Nobody but this woman will be able to make me happy. She still loves me and I've carried out her wishes. She herself told me: "*Yes.*" What I wrote you about her last summer had too little influence on her attachment to me. She loves me. That I know for certain. I knew it then, too, when I wrote my letter to you last summer. She soon lost faith in her new attachment. I knew that already last summer from her letters. Everything was plain to me. She has never had secrets from me. Oh, if only you knew what this woman is!

I'm writing that I will *probably* be married, incidentally, there may be a certain circumstance about which it would take too long to tell, but which may postpone our marriage for an indeterminate period. This is a completely incidental circumstance. But, judging by all appearances, it seems to me that it *won't take place*. And if it doesn't, you will receive the next letter from me when *everything is over*.

I don't have even a kopeck. By the most modest and stingy calculations I need *600* silver rubles *for everything*. I'm planning *to borrow* it from Kovrigin (he's in Omsk, but will arrive soon). We've lately become very close. I hope that he'll give it to me. And if he doesn't, then everything will fall through, at least for an indeterminate period. I'll borrow from Kovrigin for a long term, that is, for at least a year. But with the next post I'm writing my uncle in Moscow, a wealthy person who more than once has

---

3. Dostoevsky was married to Marya Dmitrievna Isaeva on 6 February 1857.

helped our family, and I'm asking him for 600 silver rubles.[4] If he gives it to me then I'll pay back Kovrigin right away. If, however, he doesn't, then I'll need to get the money *myself,* for that debt is a *sacred* debt and I'll need to pay it back as soon as I can.

I can't count on my brother. If he had the money, he would give it to me. But he writes that his circumstances are poor, at least for now. And therefore, the only hope for both paying back my debt and for the funds for my future life is if I'm allowed to publish. Don't be astonished, my friend, that I, having nothing, am borrowing such large sums as 600 silver rubles. But I have material ready for publication worth 1000-odd silver rubles. Consequently, there will be something to pay it back with if I am allowed to publish and if my uncle doesn't send anything. But if I am not allowed to publish for yet another year—then I'm ruined. Then it would be better not to live! Never in my life has there been such a critical moment for me as now. And therefore, understand, my priceless friend, how important it is for me to have at least some *news about permission to publish.* And therefore, I implore you as one does God, if you have been able to find out something about this (I asked you about this in my last letter), then let me know *immediately.* I implore you, and if you still have the former feeling for me you will take on my request and fulfill it. Am I right, my friend, am I deceiving myself or not? (Why hasn't my "Children's Tale,"[5] which you wrote me about, been published? *Was it by chance rejected?* That is very important for me to know. It goes without saying that I'm ready to publish, *forever even, anonymously* or using a pseudonym.) If Kovrigin gives me the money, I'll try to leave between the 20th and 25th of Janury and in about 20 days will return to Semipalatinsk with a wife. *They're hoping* in Barnaul, I don't know why, that you will be there. Will we meet there?

Have you been seeing my brother? For God's sake see him, speak in my favor to him. I'm not asking him for money: he doesn't have any. But I'm asking him, if he can, to send me some things! I'd like to have them very much. And tell my brother that he should write me everything he knows about all the *behind-the-scene secrets* of current literature. This is very important to me.

But before I say good-bye to you in this letter—there's another request: I am asking you on my knees. Remember, I wrote you last summer about Vergunov. I asked you to intercede for him with Gasfort. He's dearer to me than a brother now. It would take too long to describe my relationship with him. But here's the point. His last hope to arrange his fate is to take the examination in Tomsk in order to receive the right to a rank and a position with a salary of 1000 paper rubles. He'll be given everything if he passes the examination. But nothing will come of it with-

<hr>

4. Dostoevsky's letter to his rich uncle, Alexander Kumanin, has not survived. Kumanin did send the money.

5. "A Children's Tale" was not published until 1858—under the title "The Little Hero."

out influence. Everything depends on the director of the Tomsk school, Councillor of State Fyodor Semyonovich *Meshcherin.*—If somebody *influential* were to write Meshcherin about Vergunov, telling him *to pay attention to him* when he takes the examination, then, of course, Meshcherin will do everything possible. It's not wrong to ask this for Vergunov: *he is worth it.* And therefore, I'm asking you, if you have somebody among your family or acquaintances in the Ministry of Education who holds an important post, would it be possible for him to write Meshcherin a letter about Vergunov? Do you see Apollon Maykov? He's acquainted with Vyazemsky. If only Vyazemsky would write! For God's sake do at least something, think about it and be like a brother to me.

Good-bye, my dear friend, I embrace you. Write, for Christ's sake, as soon as possible and let me know about everything. Good-bye.

Yours, Dostoevsky

NB. Don't write X. what I wrote you about her. Don't betray me. Who knows, perhaps, she won't like it...

116. To Mikhail Dostoevsky
22 December 1856. Semipalatinsk

Semipalatinsk 22 December, 56

Greetings, my good friend. How long I've been waiting for the promised letter from you—the letter which you promised to write me with the first post right after your letter dated 15 October. I don't know what has delayed you. I swear to you, my dear brother, that I can't reconcile myself to your reasons with which you have tried to explain the length of the intervals between your letters to me. No matter how busy a person is—he can always find 5 minutes to write a few lines to his own brother. But I understand: they probably informed you from Moscow that they had sent me money from there. In you letter dated October 14th[1] you promised to send me at least some money with the next post. "So, he received the money," you thought. "Consequently, he isn't in need and, therefore, I don't need to write him a letter too." Fine, my friend! But haven't I told you, haven't I written that I don't need money from you, but a brother's remembrance and attention. You wrote that that your affairs are in a bad way, that you don't have money. Do you really think that I can't

---

1. In the second sentence of this letter Dostoevsky writes *15th* October.

understand that you, a family man, obligated by many worries, may not have money for me! And what right would I have to hold a grudge against you for not sending me money, when you alone have helped and supported me till now! Do you think that I don't know and don't understand all the weight of your worries from your letters! And therefore, understand that I'm grumbling at you not because you promised me money and didn't send it (I know that if you didn't send any, then there probably wasn't any; I don't doubt your goodness or your heart). But realize, my friend, that what pains me is that, besides sending money, you, it seems, don't consider it necessary to have any dealings with me. Perhaps you will say that you don't have *anything* to write me. But judge objectively. In your last letter you write me that *your* affairs are in a bad way, you promise to write me another letter in the near future—and suddenly silence, not a line. What am I supposed to conclude? That your affairs are even worse, that they've affected our correspondence, that perhaps you're ill or find yourself in an extremely difficult situation. And if this is so, can it be that you think that I'm completely indifferent to all of this? No, I've worn myself out with worry for you, I've racked my brains over your situation, it was depressing for me to hear that you aren't being succeessful and I ardently wished to receive some news from you. You offend me by supposing me to be indifferent. Break your silence at last, my friend, answer me at least something, write and in particular answer this letter quickly. You will see for yourself that this letter is rather important, at least for me.

Perhaps you've been able to see from my previous letters over the last 2 years and my repeated hints that I love a certain woman. Her name is Marya Dmitrievna Isaeva. She was the wife of my best friend, whom I loved like a brother. Of course, my love for her was concealed and hopeless. Her husband was without a position; finally, after long waiting, he received a position in the city of Kuznetsk in Tomsk Province. He died 2 months after arriving there. I was in despair, being separated from her. You can imagine how my despair increased when I learned of her husband's death. Alone with a young son in a remote God-forsaken place in Siberia, with nobody to look after her, with no help! I lost my head. I borrowed money and sent it to her. I was so happy that she accepted it from me. I didn't discuss with her the fact that I had gone into debt. She finally exchanged letters with her family, with her father in Astrakhan.[2] Since then he has helped her and she's managed to get by. Her father invited her to come to live with him. She would have gone, but she first wanted to place her son in the Siberian Cadet Academy. She wouldn't have any means to educate him in Astrakhan; she would have to pay money. She was afraid of burdening her father and was afraid of her sisters' rebukes,

2. Marya Dmitrievna's father, Dmitry Konstant, was the director of a quarantine house for travelers in Astrakhan.

for whom she would be a hanger-on. They provide an excellent education in the Siberian Cadet Academy and the graduates are obligated to serve only 3 years in Siberia.[3] Our correspondence continued. I was certain that she at least realized that I loved her. But I, being a soldier, couldn't ask her to be my wife. For what would we have lived on? What fate would she have shared with me? But now, immediately following my promotion, I asked her whether she would be my wife and honestly, frankly explained all my circumstances to her. She consented and answered: *"Yes."* And therefore our wedding will *definitely* take place. There is only one circumstance that might thwart or at least postpone our wedding for an indeterminate period. But there are *90* chances out of 100 that this circumstance won't come up, although one has to foresee everything. (I'm not writing about this circumstance: it would take too long to tell, you'll find out everything later.) I can only say that I am almost certainly marrying her. If I marry, the wedding will be performed before the middle of February, that is, before Shrovetide.[4] That's what we've decided if everything is settled and ends satisfactorily. And, therefore, my priceless friend, my dear friend, I ask and entreat you not to grieve for me, not to be in doubt, and mainly, not to try to dissuade me. All that will be too late already. My decision is *unalterable,* and your answer, perhaps, will arrive when everything is already over. I realize the sense of all of your objections, notions and advice, they are all excellent, I am certain of your good, loving heart; but for all the common sense of your advice—it will be useless. I am certain you will say that at age 36 the body is asking to be left in peace, and it's dangerous to impose on oneself such a burden. But I will not answer this. You'll say: "What will I live on?" A reasonable question; for, of course, I'm ashamed, and a married man can't count on you, for instance, to support me and my wife. But realize, my priceless friend, that I need only a little, very little, in order to live together with my wife. I'm not writing you anything about Marya Dmitrievna. She is the sort of woman the likes of whom you won't find in 1000 to match her character, mind and heart. She knows that I can't offer her much, but she also knows that we will never be in *great* need; she knows that I'm an *honest* person and will make her happy. I need only 600 rubles a year. To get that amount of money yearly I'm counting on one thing, namely, the Tsar's mercy, on the mercy of that adored being who rules us. I'm hoping for permission to publish. I dare to nourish in myself confidence that my hope is not a chimera. I hope that our wise Monarch, that angelic heart, will turn his gaze towards me and permit even me, as much as it is in my power, to be useful. And I'm certain of my energies, if only I receive permission. Don't take this, for Christ's sake, as boasting on

3. See Letter 110 for Dostoevsky's efforts to get his stepson Pasha into the Siberian Cadet Academy.

4. The wedding took place on 6 February 1857.

my part, my priceless brother, but realize, be confidently assured that my literary name is not a name that is done for. I've accumulated a lot of material in 7 years, my ideas have grown clear and have taken shape; and now, when everyone is doing his bit for the common cause—they will not deny me the chance to be useful. I believe, I have hope and I revere the Monarch's decision. And if I'm allowed to publish—I am certain of 600 rubles a year. As for the possibility of having children—that's too far away to worry about yet. But if there are children, then they'll be educated, rest assured. You will say, perhaps, that petty worries will wear me out. But what kind of scoundrel would I be, imagine, if just so as to live the easy life, indolently and without worries, I were to reject the happiness of having as my wife a being who is dearer to me than anything in the world, to reject the hope of making her happy and to pass by her misfortunes, sufferings, agitations, helplessness, to forget her, to abandon her—only because, perhaps, a few worries may sometime trouble my most precious existence. But enough justifications! Make peace with the fact, my friend. It's irrefutable, if God arranges everything, and all possible reasons, the most prudent ones, will be like that famous exclamation:

Mais qu'allait-il faire dans cette galère [But what was he going to do in that galley, i.e., why did he have to get involved in that business?].

I agree that it was foolish for Oront's son to land in the galleys, a prisoner of the Turks, I agree entirely, entirely, with all the arguments, but no matter how you exclaim, pity, he's nevertheless dans cette galère, he's wound up there and the fact is irrefutable.[5] My priceless friend, my dear brother, don't rise up against me, but help me and then you will be more of a friend and brother than ever. For this reason I consider it necessary to inform you of the dispositions that I intend to make in order to achieve my goal and about some of the circumstances of the matter. I don't have a kopeck, and money is the 1st thing and therefore I am venturing to borrow. I know a certain person here who is disposed to me and who is wealthy and good. I will ask him. I need not a little. I have to make at least some preparations, rent an apartment with at least 3 rooms, have at least the most essential furniture. I have to dress and I have to help her too. I need 100 of the most essential things, but which cost money. I have to send a covered carriage for her which will be pulled by three horses 1500 versts there and back—you calculate the travelling expenses. I have to pay for the wedding. I myself have still not been able to finish with my officer's outfitting. My salary is sufficient to live on. But starting up everything at once is difficult. They sent me 200 rubles; out of that part went to pay a debt, another went for indispensable linen (for sister sent only shirts), and

---

5. An inexact quotation from Molière's *Les Fourberies de Scapin*. The phrase, repeated several times in the play by Geronte (not Oront as Dostoevsky writes) is taken from Cyrano de Bergerac's *Le pédant joué.*

for a multitude of the most indispensable things, the most crude and simple, but which cost money. And finally, since I'm a drill officer, I need at the very least 2 military coats immediately: one for service, instruction, watch, and another for review. I need an overcoat, I need officer's accoutrements—helmet, sword, scarf, sword-knot, etc., etc. Finally, I need boots—all this costs money and therefore 200 rubles, with the indispensable, extraneous expenses—was far from enough.

Finally, after the wedding we have to live until that time when the final circumstances of my fate become clear, namely: the possibility of publishing and therefore I intend to borrow *600* silver rubles. That will be just barely enough. I can borrow this amount for I already have in hand material for publication worth some 1000-odd silver rubles. I'm not deceiving by borrowing, the more so as I will borrow for a long period and will explain my circumstances straightforwardly to this person, without hiding anything. With this post I'm writing our sister Varenka and am informing her of everything as much as is possible.[6] I am warning her in my letter that with the next post I am writing uncle. I'm asking uncle for 600 silver rubles. The letter to uncle will be written very sensibly, rest assured. I'm asking Varenka not to be surprised, not to oh and ah, not to try to dissuade, but to persuade aunt to give my letter to uncle at a good moment, when he has one. I'm not hiding anything from uncle. If he gives me money, then I'll immediately pay back my debt *here,* and if he doesn't —my only hope is on me, on God, and His angel—our Monarch! I beg you, my good Misha, as soon as you've read this letter, to write our sister in Moscow and advise her definitely to have the letter passed on to uncle. For, fearing him, they might not give him my letter.[7] I'm writing uncle by post, the next post. For God's sake, brother, do this for me.—Now, I'll lay out yet another request of you, of you *directly.* My brother, my angel, help me for the last time. I know that you don't have money, but I need certain things, specifically for *her.* I want to give them to her as a present; I can't buy them here, because they cost twice as much. If I had money, I would send it to you; but I don't have any and therefore beg you not to refuse me in this *last* allowance. But I implore you as well: if it's the slightest bit *hard* for you (that is, if you don't have any money, for I'm certain of your desire to lend it to me)—then for Christ's sake don't torment yourself and don't send anything. I'll understand, I'm your brother, and I've had too much proof from you of your attachment to doubt you.

Here are the things that I would like to have; they are almost indispensable.

1) *For Easter*—a hat (there aren't any here), of course, a spring one.

2) *(Now, however)*—silk dress material (any kind except *glacé*)—in a

6. See Letter 117.

7. Dostoevsky's letter to his uncle, Alexander Kumanin, is not extant. We know from Letter 121 that Kumanin sent the money and a letter.

color they're wearing now (*she's* blonde, taller than average height, with a beautiful waist, her figure resembles Emilia Fyodorovna's as I remember her).

A mantilla (velvet or something)—to your taste.

A half-dozen fine Dutch handkerchiefs—women's.

2 caps (with blue ribbons if possible) not expensive, but attractive ones.

A scarf made of woolen lace (if it's not expensive).

NB. If these *requests* seem to you to be *demands,* if it makes you *laugh* when you read this list because I'm asking for things that cost almost 100 silver rubles—then laugh and refuse. If you understand my desire to make *her* this present and that I *did not hold back* from writing to you about it, then *you won't laugh at me,* but will forgive me.—But, good-bye! I kiss you with all my heart. Wish me happiness, my dear friend. I embrace you. My regards to Emilia Fyodorovna, kiss the children and, for Christ's sake, answer this letter immediately.

Your brother F. Dostoevsky

I wish you a Happy New Year. God grant you more success.

117. To Varvara Karepina
22 December 1856. Semipalatinsk

Semipalatinsk, 22 December 56

My dear, sweet friend, my most kind sister Varenka!

Perhaps you are surprised that you haven't received a letter from me for such a long time or an acknowledgment of receiving the money from you. My friend, there were certain circumstances that detained me. I wanted to wait until their conclusion, for I had a feeling that I needed to explain the matter to you as well; in such a way as to write everything all together, at once. I thank you and all of yours, particularly uncle and auntie, for the money (200 silver rubles). Also, kiss Verinka for me. I'm extremely guilty before her. I still haven't written her! But you will see for yourself that I've been somewhat busy. I will write everybody, but now, for the time being, hear me out about something I've wanted to write you for a long time. Here it is: the story is a bit long and therefore it's necessary to begin *from the beginning* two years ago. After arriving in Semipalatinsk from Omsk in '54, I became acquainted with a certain local functionary,

Isaev, and his wife. He was from Russia, an intelligent, educated and good man. I came to love him like a brother. He was without a position, but expected a swift placement in the service again. He had a wife and son. His wife Marya Dmitrievna Isaeva, a woman still young, and he accepted me in their home as if I were family. At last, after long efforts, he received a position in the city of Kuznetsk, in Tomsk Province, 700 versts from Semipalatinsk. I bade them farewell and parting with them was harder for me than parting with life. This was in May of '55. I'm not exaggerating. After arriving in Kuznetsk, he, Isaev, suddenly took ill and died, leaving behind his wife and son without a kopeck, alone in a strange place, helpless, in a horrible position. When I learned of this (for we corresponded), I borrowed and sent her money at the first opportunity. I was so happy that she accepted it from me! Finally, she succeeded in exchanging letters with her family, with her father. Her father lives in Astrakhan, occupies an important post there (the director of quarantine), with a significant rank and receives a large salary. But he still has three daughters on his hands, young girls, and his sons, in the Guards.[1] The father's surname is *Konstan*. He's the grandson of a French emigrant from the 1st revolution, a nobleman, who came to Russia and stayed to live here. But his children, through their mother, are Russian. Marya Dmitrievna is the eldest daughter and her father loves her more than the others. But, apart from his salary he has nothing, and he couldn't send her more than 300 silver rubles. At least she hasn't needed anything since she wrote her family that she lost her husband. Her father invited her to Russia. But she doesn't want to go there before placing her 8-year-old son in the Sib[erian] Cadet Academy. She wouldn't be able to educate her son if she went to Astrakhan with him. You have to pay there, and she didn't have any money. Her father wouldn't abandon her, but he's very old and doesn't have anything besides his salary. If he died, she would be left a hanger-on for her sisters. They provide an excellent education in the Siberian Cadet Academy, graduating the best students to the artillery with the obligation to serve only three years in Siberia. In short, she decided to remain. I have a lot of acquaintances here. There were people in Omsk who held fairly important posts, who knew me and were ready with all their hearts to do for me what they could. I petitioned for Marya Dmitrievna's son; they promised me, and it seems most likely that he will be admitted to the academy next year. My dear friend, I've been writing you the details, but haven't written the main thing. I've loved this woman for a long time, insanely, more than my own life. If you knew her, this angel, then you wouldn't be surprised. She has so many wonderful, excellent qualities. She is intelligent, sweet, educated, as women rarely are, with a meek character,

1. Besides his eldest daughter, Marya, Konstant (not *Konstan* as Dostoevsky writes) had 3 daughters: Varvara, Sofia, Lidia. Nothing is known of the sons.

who understands her obligations, is religious. I saw her in misfortune when her husband was without a position. I don't want to describe to you their former need. But if you had seen with what selflessness, with what strength she bore this misfortune that one could truly call misfortune. Her lot is terrible now: alone, in Kuznetsk, where her husband died, surrounded by God knows whom, a widow and orphan in the full sense of the word. Of course, my love for her was hidden and unspoken. I loved Alexander Ivanovich, her husband, like a brother. But she, with her mind and heart, couldn't fail to realize my love for her, to guess about it. Now, when she is free (1 1/2 years have passed since her husband's death) and when I have been promoted to an officer, my first act was to propose to her. She knows me, loves me and respects me. Since the time we parted, we have corresponded with every post. She consented and answered me *yes*. And, if a certain circumstance² doesn't come to pass (about which I'm not writing, too long to tell) that can, if not unsettle everything, then postpone the matter for a long time—then our wedding will be performed before the 15th of February, that is, before Shrovetide. My friend, dear sister! Don't object, don't be sad, don't worry about me. I couldn't have done anything better. We make a good couple. We are of the same upbringing at least, we understand each other, we are of the same inclinations, rules. We have been friends for a very long time. We respect each other, I love her. I'm 35 years old, and she's in her twenty-ninth year, from an excellent family, though not a wealthy one (she has almost nothing. However, she has property from her mother, a house in Taganrog, but it's pending the coming of age of her youngest sister, who has just graduated from an institute, is still not sold and divided up). I wrote our brother about this a long time ago, asking him not to say anything to any of you. But then I didn't have even the slightest hope. Now, when I've been promoted, it's permissible for me to have hopes for the future arrangement of my fate; the Monarch's mercy is boundless. I know, Varenka, that your first question, as a good sister who loves and worries about her brother's fate, will be "What will you live on?"—for, of course, my salary is insufficient for two. But, in the first place, my wife will not demand a lot; she has a sensible view of life; she was in misfortune, she bore it proudly and patiently; at least she isn't an extravagant woman, rest assured, but, on the contrary, she's an excellent housekeeper, and 2nd) if we don't live in Petersburg or Moscow, then 600 silver rubles a year is completely adequate for me. Where will I get it? But you know, Varenka, all of my goals. I rely on God and the Tsar. I firmly hope that I'll be allowed (and soon) to be understood—to write and publish. Wait a little, my friend, you will yet hear of me and you will hear a lot of me. I already have some things written and if I'm allowed to publish, then I'll get at least 1000 silver rubles. And that's my career. Nowadays

2. Dostoevsky writes Vrangel about this "certain circumstance" in Letter 115.

labor has long since begun to be compensated. I won't force myself as before, I won't bring shame upon myself and write abominations, force myself to get pieces in on time, according to contracts. (That work always killed all the energy in me, and I could never write anything businesslike.) But now the situation is different. I have no end of material. My thoughts have cleared up and taken shape. The journals won't refuse to print what I will write, but, on the contrary, they'll gladly accept it. I know that for certain. Of course, I can earn without a lot of effort much more than six hundred rubles a year. But I'm assigning only 600 for my needs and I'll have it. If this doesn't work out either, then there is such a need in Siberia for honest people who know something that they are given positions (private ones, for example, in the gold industry) with huge salaries. And I *know, for certain* that I won't be refused, but, on the contrary, will be gladly received. In a word, I will not perish. But for now, as long as I'm in service at least for this year, I need something to live on. After calculating everything (for I have to acquire both an apartment and some furniture, and clothe myself and her, and send her some money for the journey and pay for the wedding), for all of this I need 600 silver rubles. There is one of my acquaintances here, a person with whom I've become friendly, who is wealthy and kind.[3] I'm planning to ask him for a loan, without hiding from him my circumstances, hopes, and tell him straightforwardly that I can't pay him back for a year or 2. Otherwise, I won't borrow. I'm almost certain that he'll give it to me. But this debt will have to be paid back. It's a sacred debt. And therefore I'm planning to appeal to uncle, to write him a letter, to outline everything frankly and ask him for 600 silver rubles. Perhaps he'll give it—and then I'll be saved. If there weren't so little time remaining until the wedding (I don't want to postpone it until after Easter and can't), then I would appeal to uncle directly. If uncle will give it, then God bless him! He will save me from misfortune, for it's painful to shoulder a debt of 600 silver rubles. If he won't give it—it's as he pleases! He has done so much for us, dear sister, he's so taken the place of our father by his good works that I would be ashamed to grumble about him. Tell that angel, our auntie, about all of this and tell her that she should give me her blessing. I'm not sending the letter to uncle with this post and am doing that on purpose in order to forewarn you and auntie, who surely will help me. I'm sending the letter to uncle by the post. It will be written in my hand. For God's sake, give him this letter yourselves *at a good moment* and explain it. Rest assured that the letter will be superbly written. It won't be so difficult for you, my angel Varenka, to show uncle that my marriage is not completely a ridiculous thing, for the facts speak for themselves. Understand, my friend! I am still, and forever shall be, under surveillance, mistrusted by the government. I earned this through my errors. And believe me that a man

---

3. Nikolay Kovrigin (see Letter 115).

who has settled down, married, consequently changed his direction in life, will be believed more than one who is as free as the wind. It will be taken into consideration that a married man won't want to risk the fate of his family and won't be attracted by pernicious ideas as easily as a young person (as I was) who has only himself to account to. And I am seeking to gain the government's trust; I need that. My whole fate depends on that and I, of course, will soon achieve my goal, even if permission to write and publish doesn't come.

Good-bye, my angel, don't worry about me and take my side. Realize that I had decided long ago on this marriage, that it's been thought over and rethought for 1 1/2 years, although I didn't have any positive hopes until my promotion, and that now *I won't give up* my intentions *for anything.* I kiss you 1000 times, shower the children, Verinka, with kisses and tell auntie that I consider her my guardian angel.

Be sure to show uncle my letter. Don't unseal it beforehand. Good-bye, my dear. The letter to uncle will probably arrive with the next post.

Best wishes to all of you for the coming holidays.

Your brother Dostoevsky

Give my regards to Alexander Pavlovich. So much good is said and written about him that I have come to love him without seeing him.

118. To Susanna
22 December 1856. Semipalatinsk

Semipalatinsk, 22 December 56

Dear Miss Susanna,[1]

I hasten to thank you for your good, kind letter to me. You have proven by it that you don't forget old friends, and remembering one's friends is without question a sign of a wonderful heart. You write me about your loss. Of course, it's hard to lose those who are so close to us. I understand this very well and therefore sympathize with you completely. You write that you are depressed; but may you be consoled by those to whom you are dedicating all your concern. May God grant you to see

1. The identity of Susanna has not been established.

happiness in your family! We here are also living neither in depression, nor in gaiety. It's true that much has changed here in Semipalatinsk. But our domestic life has remained almost unchanged. We have no homes with families, or very few. A lot of single people have come here. Everyone, starting with the governor, is a bachelor. And only familial society gives a city a face. Here the only thing that can be is a diversity in life. The bachelor circle eternally and everywhere lives the same way. However, we do have both balls and holidays. You described in detail your impressions of the procession into the capital of our priceless Monarch for the coronation.[2] All of this, rest assured, echoed throughout all of Russia, from Petersburg to Kamchatka; and it didn't bypass Semipalatinsk, either! Our entire social world organized a ball, by subscription, and the day of the celebration of the coronation was spent with great pomp and gaiety. God grant the Tsar a long life.

Yes, of course, if you some day came to Semipalatinsk, you, of course, would not recognize it. It's even built better. But you are right: the past is always nicer than the present. You yourself with sadness admit it by saying that I reminded you of the past with my letter. You ask about Peshekhonov. They are alive and well. He, of course, is no longer in service, lives on the farm (remember, next to the pine forest). There were outstanding debts on it, and in order to pay them he sold his own house and built another one, which he rents out. My regards to Sofia.[3] I will write Marya Ivanovna separately. Good-bye, may God grant you every happiness, and I remain respectfully devoted to you.

119. To Marya Ivanovna
22 December 1856. Semipalatinsk

Dear Marya Ivanovna,[1]

Allow me to add a few lines to you as well. From Susanna's letter I see that you are alive, well and even remember old friends, such as I, for example, whom I hope you will allow to be called your friend. May God bless you for that and may He reward you with every happiness. With what

---

2. The procession into Moscow for the coronation took place on 17 August 1856. The coronation itself took place on 26 August in the Kremlin's Uspensky Cathedral, but the celebrations continued until 8 September.

3. Sofia is probably a former Semipalatinsk acquaintance.

1. Dostoevsky's correspondent has not been identified.

pleasure I read Susanna's letter. If she writes that I reminded her of the past with my letter, then, of course, her letter too resurrected in me what I had experienced long ago. Somehow it was better in the past! I wonder how you've been spending your time. Are you happy? Well, of course, if I'm ever in Moscow I won't pass up friends, and will consider it a particular pleasure to visit you. And God grant that I soon visit Russia. There, in Russia, one feels at home. Everything there is established, settled. While the character of our little Siberian towns is a sudden influx of society, the arrival of petty officials and later, at the 1st change of power in Siberia, all of this disappears as quickly as it appeared, making room for others. But it's not really very boring here. It's only that you aren't with us. I would be glad to go back about five years. Don't laugh at my wish. After all it's so natural to wish that! Good-bye. God preserve you and may He send you all the best. Perhaps, until we meet. Who knows! Perhaps, we will even see each other some day. In the meantime, accept the assurances of the feelings of respect and devotion with which I have the honor to remain

Your obedient servant.

22 December 1856
Semipalatinsk.

1857

120. To Alexander Vrangel
25 January 1857. Semipalatinsk

Semipalatinsk 25 February[1] 1857

I'm answering your letter, priceless friend, my priceless brother, with this short little letter. I ask you not to consider my letter an answer to yours, but only a preamble to an answer. I'll write you very soon, namely on the 10th of February, and if it turns out well, then even earlier, on the 3rd of February. Yes, my never-to-be-forgotten friend, my fate is coming to an end. I wrote you the last time that Mar[ya] Dm[itrievna] had consented to be my wife. All this time I've been involved in awful worries; I'm amazed that I didn't lose my head. The means for the wedding had to be arranged. Money had to be borrowed. I firmly hope that this year I will be allowed to publish something and then I'll give it back. Pending that it was necessary to borrow no matter what. I had only one person whom I could ask—Kovrigin. But he was in Omsk the whole time, finally returned and at my first word he gave me 600 silver rubles, he helped my like a brother. I took it on the condition that I would not have to return it earlier than in a year. He asked me not to trouble myself. He's a most noble person! It's only been 3 days since I received the money and on Sunday the 27th I go to Kuznetsk for 15 days. I don't know if I'll be able to get there and be married in such a short time. *She* may be ill, she may not be ready or for instance they may not marry us in such a short time (for a lot of rites are required)—in a word I'm taking an impossible risk, but there's no way I can help taking a risk, that is, postpone it until *after Easter. There's no possibility* of postponing it *due to several circumstances,* and therefore a decisive measure must be taken. I hope that it works out somehow. In all my decisive acts I've gotten away with things and things have worked out. But there are thousands of worries in view. Only one of them is the fact that out of the *600* rubles I'll have almost nothing when I return to Semipalatinsk: everything costs so much and is so expensive! And meanwhile I was barely able to buy a few chairs for furniture—so everything is meager. Outfitting, debts, payment and the indispensable

---

1. A slip of the pen—the month should read *January,* judging by the rest of the letter.

rites and the 1500 verst journey, finally everything that *her* moving from that place might cost—that's where all the money went. After all, the two of us had to start practically with shirts—we didn't have anything, we had to acquire everything. I've written to a relative in Moscow and asked for 600 rubles. If he doesn't send it—I'm doomed, I'll live like a pauper for at least 8 months, i.e., until that time when, by my calculations, I can publish something. Now I'm bustling about like a madman, there's no end of errands and I'm writing you this letter, my dear friend, at three o'clock in the morning, and tomorrow I have to be up at 7. In no later than 2 weeks I'll answer you about everything *in detail, not concealing* anything. But now just a few words and I'll answer only the most important things.

First about X.[2] I won't say a word about her now at all. I will soon have the opportunity to see her another time. I would have so much to tell you even now! But I don't want to tell you guesses, I want to tell you what I see for myself! I will say only that you are right. Gerngross has been incited against you, but by whom? That's another question. In addition I will say: console yourself, dear priceless friend, my never-to-be-forgotten angel! Afterwards you yourself will say: *"It's good luck that I have parted with her!"* But enough! Until the next letter about X.

You write (and ask for advice) about marrying mlle K. But my friend, it's impossible to give advice behind somebody's back. I'll say only this: if you yourself call her an angel, then don't miss the opportunity to be happy for the rest of your life. There's no chance of not coming to love a pure, pious creature, whom you will call your wife and will love, if not passionately, then more sacredly and loftily and *more steadfastly* than *anyone*—rest assured. That's how it seems to me! In addition: your position in your family demands a *real independence,* otherwise you will be unhappy, you *won't* be able to bear it and, at the least, you will be incapable of beginning anything at all in life. If your father is prepared to support you and give you 5000 rubles a year, then don't overlook that, but make sure that this 5000 is certain and wouldn't depend on how the wind blows, on your father's disposition. That is imperative. There are two words for you about that. In my next letter I'll write about this and will tell you everything as I see it.

I thank you without end for your letter, but for God's sake write more often, answer *this* letter immediately, without waiting for a second one. My address—others write directly to me by name. But I'll ask you to write care of Lamotte for F. M., that is, *for me.*—You write about my brother: I'm sorry that you don't see each other. I haven't heard a thing about him for God knows how long. He gives me 2 lines in 8 months, like alms, and he never writes about what he should, but God knows what. What's he afraid of? There's so much that one should write about and that it is *possible* to

2. Yekaterina Gerngross.

write. And I need news. He doesn't write me a word about literature, and after all, that's my bread, my hope. If only he would answer just my questions. For example, I badly need to know who the literary entrepreneurs are nowadays. That's critical for me. Can he be afraid? I don't understand, I don't understand him, despite all of his explanations. I know one thing: he's an excellent person! But what's happening to him? you write that I'm *lazy* about writing; no, my friend, but my relationship with M[arya] D[mitrievna] has completely occupied me for the last *2 years*. At least I *lived*, though I suffered, I lived!

I want to solemnly ask for permission to publish. Help, help me, when the time comes! Solicit permission, at least don't hold back news. Understand my position and be my guardian as you have been until now!

Until now I didn't know for certain where your things and books were. You wrote so definitely that Gerngross had them that I thought so too myself. Now it turns out that Ostermeier has them. I'm travelling through Zmiev, I'll ask about them! But I don't know how I will send them to you, because everybody has already left for Irbit.[3] It's late now.

P.S. I'm enclosing my head size for a shako. Priceless Al[exander] Yegor[ovich]! I *badly need* these things. They're not available here for any kind of money, and not even we really know what a real uniform is. Needed: *a shako, scarf, epaulettes, buttons,* —and that's all! But where can you get them if there aren't any. Send them for God's sake, as quickly as possible.

Forgive me, my most priceless friend, for writing so hastily. I'll write *about everything* soon, but, for now, so long. I embrace you. For God's sake write in more detail about everything, particularly about yourself.

121. To Varvara Karepina
23 February 1857. Semipalatinsk

My dear, Varechka, forgive me, for God's sake, for writing you hastily. But here's the reason: I went to Kuznetsk for 15 days, got married (January 6th), brought my wife back, was very sick on the road (I fell sick in Barnaul, the same attacks that I have constantly and about which I wrote you),[1] despite my sickness I continued the journey and arrived home

---

3. Irbit held an annual fair during February, where goods being sent east from Russia and goods being sent west to Russia were sold.

1. Dostoevsky describes this attack more fully in his letter to his brother (Letter 123).

in Semipalatinsk on February 20th, sick and worn out from all this worry, from the sickness and from the bad roads. My wife is sick from extreme exhaustion, though it's not dangerous. You judge whether there is even a minute to describe to you everything in detail. My wife, despite her desire to do so, is also unable to write you, the more so, despite her illness, she's busy with getting herself at least somewhat settled in a new place. And therefore I'm writing you only a few lines; but in the near future I'll write you another letter, together with my wife, a detailed and long one. For now, however, my wife embraces you, kisses you and asks that you love her. And she's loved you for a long time. She's known all of you from me since 1854. I read her all of your letters and she, a woman with a soul and heart, was always enraptured by them. I'm letting you know, my angel, that I'm writing uncle and auntie by this same post. May God bless them! I sincerely confess to you, Varenka, that I, despite their goodness and all that they have done for us, didn't expect my request to be fulfilled and am all the more touched by it. You write that auntie at first became a little angry with me. I attribute this to her familial and Christian love for me; how could she not be worried, how could she not shake her head, how could she not say what she said: "He's only just got himself out of unparalleled misfortune, isn't provided for and is pulling another being down into his misery, and in addition he's tying himself doubly, triply." You said the same thing, my angel, in your letter to me. I realize that you couldn't have answered differently and attribute all of this to your sincere feelings for me. The thing is out of your sight, remote; how can you judge! But I'll answer you that everything is in God's hands, and I, relying on God, will not doze off myself. It's true that there are more worries in life. There are stern responsiblities and, perhaps, difficult ones. But there are also immeasurable advantages for me. I'm not writing about them in detail, but they are obvious to me. What's more, I'm not afraid of *debt* and *responsibilities* in a certain respect. Sometimes debt and responsibilities are useful in another life, and it's even good *to bind* yourself with them. If a person is honest, then the energy will turn up too for the fulfillment of the debt. And not to lose energy, not to lose spirit   that's my chief need. But enough; the future is in God's hands. I thank you and Verochka for your efforts on my behalf and for your love. I'll soon write you all and brother Misha, who, it seems gave his word of honor to write me one letter a year, not more, not less. If you knew how bitter this is for me. A most noble person helped me here, a very good person, with whom I've always had a good relationship. He lent me money, with almost no time limit. Nevertheless, I must repay him as soon as possible. Good-bye, my dear, I kiss you and your children and all of you. Verochka too. Until my next letter. Then I'll write a few things in more detail. If not for this slight ailment that is still with me, I would be completely at peace and happy. Good-bye, until we meet.

Your brother F. Dostoevsky

23 February 1857

122. To Alexander Vrangel
9 March 1857. Semipalatinsk

Semipalatinsk, 9 March 1857

It's already been some two weeks that I've been home, my dear friend and brother, Alexander Yegorovich, and only now have I finally summoned the energy to write you. If you knew how many cares, troubles and duties, the most unforeseen, befell me with the new order of things, then you would surely forgive me for not writing you immediately upon my arrival. 1st, my wedding, which took place in Kuznetsk (February 6) and the return journey to Semipalatinsk took much more time than I had figured. I had an attack in Barnaul and I spent an extra 4 days there. (My attack shattered me both physically and psychically: the doctor told me that I have genuine epilepsy and predicted that if I didn't take immediate measures, that is, proper treatment, which is possible only in complete freedom, then the attacks can take on a most dreadful nature and I will suffocate during one of them from the throat spasms that almost always occur during the attack.) After arriving in Semipalatinsk, I was met by the worries of setting up the apartment; then my wife fell sick, then the brigade commander arrived and conducted an inspection, so that I was forced to postpone writing both you and my brother until today. And how I wanted to reply soon, my never-to-be-forgotten friend, to your good, kind, wonderful letter! Don't grieve, don't grieve, my friend, though I clearly see that you have woes on all sides. What worries me more than anything else for you, my friend, are your relations with your father. I know, I know extremely well (from experience) that such trouble is unbearable, and all the more unbearable because you both, I know this, love each other. It's a kind of never-ending misunderstanding on both sides, which the further it goes the more confused it becomes. There's absolutely no way to avoid it. No explanations can restore harmony, and if it is restored, then only for a moment. The only aid, the only medicine is separation. In the 1st days of separation you will again find a place in his heart and he will be the first to blame himself for everything. Personalities such as your father's are a strange mixture of the blackest suspicion, painful sensitivity and generosity. I'm concluding that about him without knowing him personally, for I've twice known in life precisely such relationships as yours with him.[1] He also needs to be spared, and you know that better than I. You know what, my dear friend: it seems to me that you have the same disposition, you are also ailing in heart and soul, and if nervousness and suspicion haven't yet developed in you, there wasn't an occasion, or it's still

---

1. Dostoevsky's own father by all accounts was not an easy man to deal with.

too early, that is, it will develop later. In return, you have a painfully developed sensitivity. Guard and save yourself from this; strong upheavals in life always help; I was a hypochondriac of the highest order, but I was completely cured by a sharp upheaval that took place in my fate. Travelling is superb; but since you, my dearest friend, were very open with me in your letter, I too consider it my duty to be completely open with you, though my conscience for a long time rebelled against me and my heart forbade me to express my opinion. In passing, I will say as well: you write about the possibility of marrying. To that I'll say to you that it is, in my opinion, the very best thing in your fate, for it will at once settle a great deal and will change the direction of your life. But here's the problem: I don't now all of the circumstances, I read only a hint about it in your letter. I'm therefore completely unable to judge, and therefore will give my opinion (and you ask for it) in general. But before that I'll speak of one other matter, namely about what I didn't want to speak openly with you until now, that is, you realize, about X. I didn't want to give my opinion first, because, knowing only a few of the facts, I didn't want to consider it certain and definite; 2nd, I didn't want to upset and poison your heart, 3rd) I didn't want to be a traitor and gossip; but now here's what forces me to be open. 1st) that in any case I am not giving out my opinion as definite and infallible, but only as an opinion and so why not say it; 2nd) I now presume that time has already blotted out and cured much in your heart, and you now see more clearly and healthily and 3rd (the main thing), that this woman, I am sincerely convinced, *is not worthy of you* and your love, is beneath you and you are only tormenting yourself with regret in vain. Finally, 4) I want to express one last opinion: weren't you completely wrong about her? Perhaps you assured youself that she could give what she is quite incapable of giving to anyone. Namely: you thought to seek in her constancy, faithfulness and all that there is in a *true* and complete love. But it seems to me that she's incapable of that. She's only capable of making a present of one moment of pleasure and complete happiness, but only a moment; she can't even promise more than that, and if she promised, then she herself was mistaken and you shouldn't blame her for this; and therefore accept this moment, be forever grateful for it and—that's all. You will make her happy if you leave her in peace. I am certain that she thinks so herself. She loves pleasure more than anything else, she herself loves the *moment,* and who knows, perhaps, she herself plans beforehand when that moment will end. The only bad thing is that she plays with the hearts of others; but do you realize how far the *naivete* of these creatures extends? I think that she is certain that she is not guilty of anything! It seems to me that she thinks: "I gave him happiness; be happy with what you got; after all, you don't always find that, and is it really so bad that *it* is *over;* what's he unhappy about." If a person resigns himself and is satisfied, then these creatures are capable of nursing forever for him (through memories) a never-ending, sincere friendship, even of repeating love on meeting. But to the point: I was struck on my very first arrival in Barnaul, in November, by the fact that she looked at me both suspiciously and at the same time with a certain curiosity. However, during the short period of my stay there she was both kind and polite to me. He, moreover, received me with unusual cordiality and I liked him extraordinarily.[2] The only thing that struck me then was that he was obviously strongly against you, and she, in the presence of him and many others spoke about you with disdain and even mockery, laughing at your portrait, which she gave me, and saying that your pretensions and coquetry were given expression in it, and, to my question whether she really considered you to be such a person?—she answered affirmatively: yes. I noticed and heard then a few more things. One can't tell everything; but during my last trip through here's what conduct regarding you I found out about for certain.[3] Le mari [the husband] said to me privately about you, extremely seriously, that he liked you very much before, but that you turned out to be a most wicked person and that he regretted that he knew you. It seemed to me (and perhaps I was mistaken) that he purposely, with intent, said this to me, wishing to suggest to me that I shouldn't believe a word of what you would say and write me about X., knowing that you and I have a friendly correspondence. From his seriousness I conclude that X. probably *took measures* and succeeded in inciting him against you by telling him, perhaps, that you boast of your relationship with her. Of course, all of this was done out of *caution* and you know what: either she really for some reason suspects you of indiscretion in regard to your relationship with her, or this is her usual tactic, that is, to blacken in her husband's eyes both the next lover and the lover who preceeded him. Let's suppose she was taking precautions with her husband; but you judge: can a loving heart blacken and make a laughing-stock of the person it loved, without having any reasons for this; and even if there were reasons, would this be noble? In Semipalatinsk I had already heard that general rumor throughout Altai ascribes to her a new lover. Since I had a friendly relationship with this new person (I won't name him to you; I'll only say that he's not a mountaineer, but a person who arrived for a time from Petersburg (and not the Marquis[4])—an excellent person, intelligent, gentle and sensitive, but with a few humorous oddities[5])—it was easier for me than others to find out whether this was true. I really saw something new, there *certainly* was something, but *to what degree*—was unclear. In any case, he spent time there without going out and was privy to a lot of secrets, he spoke a lot about you, of course not in the sense of a *liaison*. He evidently didn't believe it. He was instilled with most respectful thoughts about the Marquis (he knows the Marquis personally). He was

2. A. R. Gerngross.
3. Eleven lines are crossed out.
4. Marquis N. de Traverse.
5. Pyotr Semyonov, who lived in Barnaul 1856-57.

cunning with me and there was a lot he kept back. I even noticed that he acquired a slightly hostile disposition towards me (from the most friendly one earlier); at least he became secretive and careful. I'll see him again soon. However, I don't think he succeeded in getting everything from X. During my 1st stay (in November) Bob was at X's constantly; he's not in Barnaul now. The Marquis isn't there either. And so, my friend, I'm not claiming that my opinion is definitive; keep in mind that I was there in passing. But it seems to me that she is not worthy of your love; forget her and don't blame her a great deal. For you to meet with her again is very difficult, because le mari is angry with you. Forget her and if the idea of a marriage to K. has not yet vanished, then get married.[6] I'm speaking *in general* and am speaking as your friend, without knowing, however, many of the circumstances.

NB. on the other sheet.

NB. It seems to me, my friend, that K. must be wonderfully brought up, must be a superior tender heart. She will love you, and this is more lasting than anything else, because it cannot be that you won't come to love her. It seems to me that your heart will find rest in a quiet and calm life, and in addition, your character will change for the better. Let your father support you (don't take a wife wealthier than you are), select work at an embassy and go abroad (at least at first). That's my advice, friendly advice. Don't avoid me, don't deprive me of your trust and, for God's sake, write me more often.

Now in short about myself. Kovrigin and Khomentovsky helped me here with the wedding. When I returned to Semipalatinsk I received a letter and some money from my uncle in Moscow, whom I had asked for assistance. The whole business cost me 700 silver rubles; uncle sent me 600; I only repaid part of my debts; with the remainder I have provided for myself for only a few months. Illness and the chance to publish worry me. My brother encourages me and therefore I beg you, write me definitely and clearly whether attempts have been made to publish "A Children's Tale," if they've been made, then why hasn't it been published?[7] It's very important for me to know this. Don't accuse me of laziness. I'm writing a long piece and haven't yet finished. But perhaps I'll send it to Petersburg to find out more quickly whether it will be published—something very short and soon. All of my hopes are on this. My wife sends her regards; she loves you especially; she can't forget you and remembers with pleasure your short, but for her memorable, acquaintance. Everything that concerns you interests her to the utmost. Your portrait is in her room, she begged me for it. Will we meet some day, my friend? Both my wife and I would be good for you. You would find in us a brother and sister who love and understand you. Don't forget us, and we shall never forget you.

6. Vrangel did not marry until 1860. It is not clear whom Vrangel has in mind here.
7. The work in question is "The Little Hero."

I don't know what news to write you. They say a certain Colonel Panov of the General Staff has been appointed governor here—is that true?

Demchinsky is on leave. I don't know whether he's succeeding with his courting, but he's hoping to marry; I won't write whom he's courting: *it's a secret.*

What a pity that you're not closely acquainted with my brother. Visit him, I'm writing him with this post. Good-bye, my never-to-be-forgotten friend, my brother. Rest assured that I love you without end. Don't forget me.

Entirely yours, Dos.

NB. For God's sake not a word about what I wrote concerning X., and especially don't write X. herself. She's certain that I came to spy. Don't compromise me, for God's sake.

123. To Mikhail Dostoevsky
9 March 1857. Semipalatinsk

Semipalatinsk 9 March 1857

It's already been two weeks my priceless, dear brother, since I've returned to Kuznetsk with my wife, but I've only now found a moment to write you. My dear, my sweet, for God's sake, don't be angry with me for not writing you with the first post after my arrival. You are always in my thoughts and heart. I love you as much as it is possible to love anyone. But of course you, since you know life, will believe me that with the new order of things I have had so many worries, cares, and errands that I don't know why my head doesn't crack. However, I nevertheless managed to write uncle and sister (at her request at once). Uncle has helped me and for a time I'm provided for, and then I will rely on God's grace. I won't fail, I'll work even more zealously. But you probably will require a detailed description of how my affairs have been settled. Without going into great detail, I'll say in general that everything ended well. My good acquaintance, on whom I was relying while waiting for uncle's help, helped me and gave me 600 silver rubles for a year's term (or even longer). In general I'll say, my friend, that not just this person, but many others besides him took a sincere interest in me. Two others, for example, absolutely wanted me to borrow money from them (without any kind of due date)—they were going to quarrel with me if I wouldn't accept their friendly services. I was forced to borrow besides the 600 rubles another 200 silver rubles, 800 in all, of which after returning to Semipalatinsk I had spent almost everything, that is, I had spent exactly 700 silver rubles all in all. Perhaps you will wonder, my brother, how I could go through such a sum. I wouldn't have supposed myself that I'd spend so much; but there was absolutely no chance of spending less. Preparations for the road, my outfitting and hers (for she didn't have much of what's necessary)—but the most necessary outfitting, one could say a poor one, a journey of 1500 versts, in a closed carriage (her health is poor—the cold and bad roads—there was no other way)—for which I payed in round figures for four horses, the wedding in Kuznetsk, even though it was the most modest sort, renting an apartment, the acquisition of at least some furniture, dishes for the house and kitchen—all of this took so much money that it's beyond comprehension. I knew almost nobody in Kuznetsk. But there she acquainted me with those who are of the better sort and who all respected her. My sponsor at the wedding was the local district police officer and his wife, the best men were also rather decent people, simple and good, and if you count the priest and two other families of her acquaintance, then that's all of the guests at her wedding. On the journey back (through Barnaul), I stopped over at Barnaul at the home of a certain good acquaintance of mine.[1] There a misfortune befell me: completely unexpectedly I had an epileptic attack that scared my wife to death and filled me with grief and despondency. The doctor (learned and sensible) told me, contrary to all the doctors' previous opinions, that I have *genuine falling sickness* and that I should expect that during one of these attacks I will suffocate from a throat spasm and will die precisely from that. I myself asked for the doctor's complete candor, appealing to him with the name of an honest man. In general he advised me to be careful of new moons.[2] (A new moon is now approaching and I'm expecting an attack.) Now realize, my friend, what desperate thoughts drift through my head. But what's the point of talking about it! Still, perhaps, it's not even true that I have genuine falling sickness. When I married I completely believed the doctors who had assured me that they're simply nervous attacks that might pass with a change in my way of life. If I had known for certain that I had genuine falling sickness, I would not have married. For my peace of mind and so that I can consult with *genuine* doctors and *take measures* it's *essential* that I resign as soon as possible and move to Russia, but how am I to do this? There's one hope! I'm allowed to publish, I get some money and then move. Finally, besides that I'm scared that an attack

---

1. Dostoevsky and his bride stayed in Barnaul with Pyotr Semyonov.

2. James Rice writes that Dostoevsky sometimes noted the phases of the moon, weather conditions and coincidental happenings in his notebooks. Rice has collected Dostoevsky's seizure records for the years 1861-81 in his *Dostoevsky and the Healing Art* (pp. 287-98).

might occur during the exercise of duty. On watch, for example, trapped in a tight uniform—I'll choke for sure, judging from the accounts of witnesses who saw the attack and what happens to my chest and my breathing. But God is merciful, I'll just repeat to you for the 10th time: realize how important the possibility to publish is for me. I brought an ailing wife to Semipalatinsk. Although I, on leaving, prepared everything as far as possible, due to my inexperience not even half of what needed to be done was, and therefore, we had two weeks of constant bother. In this case, the brigadier commander arrived. Inspection, duty—in a word, I was completely fagged out—and therefore forgive me for not writing you immediately upon my arrival. My wife is better now. She asks you to forgive her for not writing you anything now. She'll write soon. She assures me that she *hasn't prepared herself.* She loves you all very much. She loved you all before as well, when I (in '54) read her each of your letters and she knew all the details about you. From my stories she respects you exceedingly and holds you as an example for me all the time. She's a good and gentle creature, a bit frisky, quick, intensely impressionable; her past life has left painful traces on her soul. Changes in her feelings are impossibly quick, but she never ceases to be good and noble. I love her very much, and she me, and for the time being everything is going along rather well. After receiving the money from uncle (whom I thank with all my heart) I paid off part of my debt; now I have 250 silver rubles in the chest of drawers; but we have to live at least until I receive permission to publish and therefore I'm glad that I'm provided for for at least this period. I somehow blindly believe in the future. If only God would grant me health. An astonishing thing: out of painful misfortune and experience I've taken away some sort of extraordinary cheerfulness and self-assuredness. Perhaps that is actually bad. God grant that I've acquired enough common sense so as not to be too self-assured. But don't worry and be sad about me. Everything will turn out fine. But I very much miss you, my priceless, dear friend, my good, noble brother! I received your letter, I thank you for your packages, which haven't arrived yet, but my friend, I was so pained when I read about the weight of your circumstances, that you spent so much on us![3] I thank you 1000 times, and my wife doesn't even know how to thank you. But, my angel, your business still isn't improving! It absolutely frightens me. You're putting your hopes on the cigars; what if they don't sell! And you know that can easily happen. It seems to me that the primary drawback is the high price of your cigars. But I don't know much about this. God grant that things work out! Weather this crisis—and for Christ's sake don't risk any more; don't reach for a lot; little by little is more sure. But how do you like our sister Sasha? Why is she making us all blush!

---

3. Mikhail had sent the presents for Marya Dmitrievna that Fyodor requested in Letter 116.

Literally blush! For everyone in our family is noble and generous. Whom does she take after to be so vulgar? I wondered long ago why she, the youngest sister, never wanted to write me so much as a line. Is it because she's a *lieutenant-colonel's wife?* But that's ridiculous and stupid. Write me more and in greater detail about her for God's sake. It's a pity that I'm hurrying or I'd write you more and in greater detail myself. Now I'll ask you a question: I, my dear, asked you about the fate of "A Children's Tale." Tell me *definitely* (and I beg you about this) whether they seriously wanted to publish it. If they did, did they try or not, and if they didn't try, then why exactly? For God's sake, write me everything about this. This request of mine will be the answer to your supposition that I'm not forbidden to publish. Admit that the fate of this little thing, "A Children's Tale," is of interest to me in many respects.

My friend, how sorry I feel for poor Butkov![4] And to die like that! And how could you watch them let him die in the hospital! How sad that is!

Good-bye, my angel. My regards to everyone who remembers me, I remember everyone and those whom I loved—I love as before. I'm guilty before Verochka and her husband—I haven't written them in a long time, soon I'll write everyone. Kiss the children for me and remember me to Emilia Fyodorovna in particular. May God grant her good fortune.

My wife isn't even adding anything to this letter to you. To my invitation she answered that she'll write you herself, a special letter, just as she'll do for Varenka too. But she asked that I convey her sincere regards and wishes all the best to you and Emilia Fyodorovna. Good-bye.

Your brother F. Dost.

124. Varvara Karepina
15 March 1857. Semipalatinsk

Semipalatinsk, 15 March 857

Here's yet another letter for you, dear Varenka. I'm informing you that my wife and I (she is writing you together with me), although we are somehow settling down and beginning a new life, are nevertheless inundated with such various bothers that against our will we missed the

---

4. Yakov Petrovich Butkov (1815-56) died in a charity hospital. He was praised by Chernyshevsky as one of Nikolay Gogol's most talented followers, but Butkov vanished from literature and died in poverty.

last post and didn't write you, even though I had promised to. In addition, my wife for some reason is often ill, and this week I fasted, today made my confession, am horribly tired, and can't boast of health myself. And therefore you will surely forgive me. My wife is asking you in her letter to love her. Please take her words—not for words, but for the real thing. She is truthful and doesn't like to speak contrary to her heart. Love her and I will be extremely grateful to you for this, forever. We're getting along so-so, not making numerous acquaintances, saving our money (though it goes frightfully), and hope for the future, which, if it pleases God and the Monarch, will come right. I don't think that I am mistaken in being persuaded that my hopes will be fulfilled. But I don't know how to live until I'll earn my own living. Then and only then will I have the right to call myself a man. But until then my gratitude to all of you for loving me and not forgetting me in my misfortune is boundless. I'm troubled somewhat by my attacks, it looks as if they've faded away again; God grant that they cease altogether. Because of them I view my service and activities now with a sense of a certain despondency. In addition, the conviction that I can be useful to myself and others, will restore my name and atone for the past *on another path, by other activities* is taking root in me more and more. Would that God grant that I be able to prove to all of you the truth of my words. It goes without saying that I will not change my present situation, my service, for something unknown. I will change all of this when I have the facts that I can exist otherwise and be employed in something else, something more profitable in all respects than now.

I received not long ago from brother Misha an exceedingly good and kind letter. There's truly a friend and brother (just like you—an exceedingly good sister to me!). But you won't believe, my dear, how worried I am by the state of our brother Misha's business affairs! He ventured too rashly with his cigars. God grant that his hopes be justified; but here (how many letters already) he writes me that he's buried in endless calculations, the most dreary tasks, and is living on hope.[1] I pity him to an unbelievable degree or to put it better, I worry about him as about myself. Without knowing lately if his affairs have improved, because he seldom writes me and not knowing whether uncle and auntie would help me, I asked Misha to help me, namely to send a few things, some of which were absolutely essential in order to get settled and make a present to my future wife. He writes me now that he will fulfill my request immediately. He still

---

1. In his letter dated 18 April 1856 Mikhail writes his brother: "I've now begun to manufacture, besides cigarettes, cigars and used a heap of money for this at the end of last year. I've taken a risk, and if they don't sell, then I don't know what I'll do. The money is spent, a mass of promissory notes have been signed, the terms of which are already coming to an end, and I still haven't started to sell the cigars. You know yourself that they have to mature well. But, on the other hand, if they sell, then everything will be fine. In general this is a critical year for me."

hasn't sent anything, but my conscience reproaches me for troubling him with expenses for me in his present circumstances. If it were possible to stop him, then I would happily take back my requests. But now, it seems, it's too late and most likely he will without fail send everything.

I very much wanted to write to Verochka but I don't know where she is (in Petersburg?) and will write without fail, but now for the meantime let her forgive me. Kiss her for me, my darling Varenka. Write me everything, about all of you; write about uncle and auntie (are they well, do they support me, are they satisfied with me). Write about Misha, what you think about his business. But now good-bye, my priceless sister. Be as happy as possible. You deserve that. I kiss your children, your hands and beg you to love me as before.

Good-bye, once and for all

Your loving brother F. Dostoevsky

For God's sake, forgive me for such a messy letter. Forgive me, as a favor, my darling.

125. To Dmitry Konstant
20 April 1857. Semipalatinsk

Semipalatinsk, 20 April 1857

Most respected Dmitry Stepanovich,

With a feeling of the most profound respect and sincere, genuine devotion to you and all your family, I make so bold as to present myself to you as a relative. God finally fulfilled my most ardent desire and I, two months ago, became your daughter's husband. Long ago, when Alexander Ivanovich was still alive, she spoke so much and so often of you, with such feeling, and often with tears, remembered her former life in Astrakhan, that I already then had learned to love and respect you. She always mentioned you with sincere love and I cannot but sympathize with her.

I became acquainted with Marya Dmitrievna in '54, when, after my arrival here in Semipalatinsk I was still a stranger to everyone. The late Alexander Ivanovich, about whom to this day I cannot recollect without special feeling, received me into his home like his own brother. His was a beautiful, noble soul. Misfortunes in his service had somewhat shaken his personality and health. After receiving a position in Kuznestk, he fell ill and passed away so unexpectedly for all those who loved him that no one could think of his fate without emotion. I couldn't imagine what would become of poor Marya Dmitrievna, alone, in a remote place, without support, with a young son. But God arranged everything. I don't know whether I will be able to fulfill what He put in my heart; but I assure you that there is in me a firm, unwavering desire to make my wife happy and to arrange poor Pasha's fate. I love him like my own; I loved his father so that I cannot but be a friend to the son too.

I will ask you, most respected Dmitry Stepanovich, to present me to your family and to express my regards and my sincere respect to Marya Dmitrievna's sisters. Perhaps you will some day come to know me personally. In any event, believe me, I hope to earn your good opinion and to prove worthy of having the honor of being close to your family. And now accept once more the assurance of my feelings of the most profound respect and allow me to remain your sincerely loving and most devoted servant.

F. Dostoevsky

126. To Yevgeny Yakushkin
1 June 1857. Semipalatinsk

Semipalatinsk, 1 June 857.

Dear Yevgeny Ivanovich,

Alexander Pavlovich[1] told me everything that you had instructed him to tell me. I do not know by what means and how I have earned your attachment and how I can ever return your kindness! I would like to see you and have the honor of getting to know you better. For the sake of brevity, I'm not writing you anything about myself and my circumstances or hopes. Alexander Pavlovich will be so good as to tell you everything that I hope to achieve shortly, as well as my hope to be in Moscow. But for the present let's turn straight to the matter that interests me almost more than anything else, in which all of my future hopes in life are contained, that is, my entry again into literature.

---

1. Alexander Pavlovich Ivanov, Dostoevsky's brother-in-law, a teacher in the Konstantin Land Survey Institute, was connected with Yakushkin, who worked in the Department of Land Survey.

Alexander Pavlovich sent me from you 100 silver rubles.

Dearest Yevgeny Ivanovich, tell me as soon as you are able what money this is, from where and whose? Probably yours, that is, you, moved by brotherly concern, are sending it to me in the hope of setting me to literary activity and in so doing wish to help me doubly. Alexander Pavlovich writes that you are taking on yourself the trouble to petition for the publication of my works and that you hope to secure a significant sum for me by selling them somewhere. Of course, I will not remain deaf to your call, only I don't know how to thank you for your attentions to me.—Until now, even though I wished to, I have refrained from publishing. It always seemed to me that I didn't have the right. But it seems that my fears were groundless. Many people already have pressed me to publish. I had long ago decided to begin, but I didn't know how to arrange the matter. 1st) I didn't know where to send things. For the most part I don't know the journals' editorial boards now. I definitely did not want (and so I wish even now) to publish under a name other than my own. Lately I've thought about *The Russian Messenger*.[2] My friend Pleshcheev (now in Orenburg) informed me that he wrote to Katkov about me.[3] And so I would like to begin with *The Russian Messenger*. But here's the problem: what to offer to the *Messenger*. I'll tell you straight out that it's already been determined by me long since what to begin with, and I won't begin with anything else. Although there are some other things, I won't begin with anything else except a novel and story.

Lately, that is the last 1 1/2 years now, I have been thinking over and working on a novel that, unfortunately, is too bulky. I say unfortunately, because will the *Messenger* want to publish a novel the length of Dickens' novels? Here's the main thing. 2nd) that I would like to know: do you already have in mind publishers or a journal with whom you would like to place something of mine? And 3rd) where would it be better and more profitable to place something, that is, which journal at present is preferable in this regard? I'll explain to you what exactly I'm writing, though, of course, I won't tell the contents. It's a long novel, the adventures of one person, which have an integral, general connection, but are nevertheless made up of completely separate and self-contained episodes. Each episode comprises a part. Therefore I, for example, can easily place them by episode and this will comprise a separate adventure or story. It goes without saying that I would like to place them all in order. I will tell you in addition that the novel consists of 3 books, each about 20 signatures, and of several parts. Only the 1st book made up of 5 parts has been written.

---

2. *The Russian Messenger* (1856-1906), founded by Mikhail Katkov (1818-87), became the leading "thick" journal of the period. Apart from Dostoevsky, its contributors would include Tolstoy, Turgenev, Goncharov, Aksakov, Fet, Tyutchev and many others.

3. Pleshcheev wrote Dostoevsky (20 January 1857) about *The Russian Messenger:* "Send me, my friend, everything you write. Rest assured that they'll gladly publish it."

The remaining two books will be written, not now, but some day, because, 1st) though they constitute the continuation of the adventures of the same person, it is in a different guise and character and several years later. The 1st book is complete by itself and is an absolutely separate novel in 5 parts.[4] It's all written, but not yet revised and therefore I'll start revising it in parts now and I'll deliver it to you in parts. After I receive your answer, I'll immediately send you the 1st part of the 1st book. That part constitutes an absolutely separate and finished story. I most earnestly ask you to answer my questions set forth above. Speak with the editors if you have any you know and offer it to them. What they will say and what they will give per signature. I'm not working on anything else (literary) now except this novel, because it is very close to my heart.

Excuse me, Yevgeny Ivanovich, for such details, but I want to take full advantage of your obliging proposal. I thank you once again. I press your hand firmly. You are setting me on the track and are helping me in the thing most important to me. Until we meet! I hope that it is until we meet. Yours forever,

F. Dostoevsky

127. To Ivan Zhdan-Pushkin
29 July 1857. Semipalatinsk

Dear Ivan Vikentievich,

You once took notice of the wretched fate of two unfortunates— myself and Durov—and received us in your home. I had always heard about you things that taught me to sincerely respect you; your kindness to us, however, taught me to love you as well. I'm appealing to you now without fear and trustingly with a most earnest request; because I know whom I am asking. But first of all I will inform you that I have been forgiven by the Monarch's mercy, I was promoted to the rank of officer almost a year ago now and not long ago received my former hereditary nobility—which is the equivalent of an almost full pardon.[1] After receiving

---

4. The first book of Dostoevsky's projected novel is probably the future *The Village of Stepanchikovo and Its Inhabitants.*

1. Dostoevsky was made an ensign on 1 October 1856 and was granted his former status by decree on 17 April 1857.

my rank, I was married to the widow of my late friend, whom I loved and respected, Alexander Ivanovich Isaev. I met him in '54 in Semipalatinsk; he was without a position then. But in a year's time he received a position in Tomsk Province, set off for work in the city of Kuznetsk and 2 months later died, leaving behind his wife and young son. The late Alexander Ivanovich Isaev spoke of you often with the greatest respect. He knew you personally; I don't know whether you remember him. I remember that I wrote to you about his orphaned son, when I was trying to think of a way to place him in the Siberian Academy, which was greatly desired by the poor widow, his mother, who had almost given into despair after her husband's death. She submitted requests, wrote letters—and now the decision has been issued (thanks to the thoughtfulness of good and noble Yakov Alexandrovich Slutsky) when she has already been my wife for six months. And though it's sad and difficult for me to let go of such a little boy, about whom I gave my word to look after out of respect for his father's memory, it is impossible to refuse such an opportunity, all the more so as the Academy's commandant has made an exception for him, by ordering that he be admitted at such a young age. The Siberian Academy is so well established that it is hard to wish anything better. There is one difficulty: the boy is too young, is still a child, and has never been parted from his family. For God's sake, be his protector! Give him your attention. I know and believe that you even without being asked will devoutly fulfill your duty as the superintendent; but sometimes a word of tenderness, of approval or indulgence will take the place of a lot for a poor orphan. Be generous! I remember your kindness, your nobleness, and therefore am boldly asking, in the hope that you will forgive me for this request.

I am now ill with a rather dangerous disease—falling sickness. I intend to undergo treatment and to go for this to Moscow. I hope that I will not be refused permission to go to the capital. In that case at the end of winter or next spring, I will travel through Omsk and then, in person, together with my wife, I will petition you about the poor orphan. Until the last minuté I had hoped that I would take him to the academy personally. But, they didn't let me go, since I've already taken leave twice this year;[2] and therefore I am sending him with a hired agent—a decent person, the postman Lyapukhin, who has my complete confidence.[3]

Forgive me for having been so bold as to enclose 10 silver rubles with this letter. He's still just a boy, some treat can console him a great deal. I don't dare to think (and consequently ask you either) that you would be so disposed to my request and take it upon yourself to treat him out of this money, though in doing so you would oblige me unspeakably. But you have things to attend to, important responsibilities—and therefore I don't dare even think about such indulgence. So, if it's not possible for you to keep the money, then entrust it to somebody you know among your subordinates; any decision of yours will be good.

If little Isaev has need of any expenses beyond the necessary keeping, then I am gladly ready to satisfy any request.

I taught my stepson to love and respect you as his future superintendent. Love him, if possible, most noble Ivan Vikentievich! He will soon be 10 years old. He is good, with wonderful inclinations, sharp abilities, ambition (I've noticed this), but hotheaded, frisky and, it seems, he will have a passionate and fiery temperament. I vouch for the accuracy of the portrait. But you must agree that if it's accurate, how easy it would be for this boy to be led astray and to acquire bad inclinations! At the same time, how easy, with supervision, to make a wonderful person out of him!

And that is precisely what I am asking of you, most noble Ivan Vikentievich, be his benefactor, sometimes look at him *a bit more intently,* and—that's all! I don't dare trouble you more with my requests. Anything further will come from your noble heart. Good works are free. I'm completely relying on you in everything.

Forgive me for this hope, so expressed, and allow me the honor to remain, with the feeling of the most profound respect, dear Sir, your most humble servant.

F. Dostoevsky

Semipalatinsk.
29 July 1857.

P.S. Forgive me for my miserable handwriting and don't mistake this for carelessness. I can't write better.

128. To Varvara Konstant
31 August 1857. Semipalatinsk

Dear Madam and most kind sister, Varvara Dmitrievna,

I thank you with all my heart for your letter to me. I sense the honor you have done me and see your favorable attitude toward me. Allow me to call you by the name of sister. One of my sincere wishes is to deserve your favor, together with that of your entire family, whom I respect. From my wife's letter to you you will learn the reason for our long silence: we wanted to write without fail the most certain and conclusive news about Pasha. I know how you love Pasha and, therefore, consider myself obliged to inform you about him in greater detail. I confess to you that placing him in the Academy was not to my liking at first. I reckoned differently and tried to persuade Marya Dmitrievna to wait a bit. I'm certain of my return to Russia (very soon). Both my health and my circumstances require it. There, in Russia, I have many means and very many devoted and powerful friends, who would help me to set up Pasha in the best manner, right before our eyes. In addition the commandant of the battalion of the Pavlovsk Cadet Academy is a relative of mine, my younger sister's husband. I thought that in that academy he would be as if in a relative's home. Having all of this in mind, I hoped that Marya Dmitrievna's previous request (before our marriage) about placing Pasha in the academy would not be followed by a swift response, owing to Pasha's young age. But the people whom I myself had asked earlier are so devoted to us that they successfully petitioned, despite Pasha's young age, as an exception to the general rule, for his acceptance into the academy. There was nothing to be done, we parted with him. Marya Dmitrievna reasoned as a mother and was happy with *the definite* and *the certain*. On reflection I, too, made peace with the idea of parting with Pasha and here's why: the Siberian Academy, 1st) is a most excellent institution, its privileges are great, the administration is extraordinary and inestimable. The director is the well-known, learned General Pavlovsky; his name is spoken with veneration in Omsk. The inspector is Zhdan-Pushkin, whom I know personally, a most cultured person, with most noble ideas about education. (He was well acquainted with the late Alexander Ivanovich, who, I remember, spoke to me of him with enthusiasm.) Finally, my illness and our not yet completely assured position—all this inclined us to prefer *the certain* to all our dreams about the best. In addition the latest decrees of our Sovereign-Emperor, concerning military education give the right to all provincial cadets to transfer, conditional on good progress, to the last special class in Petersburg, in the Constantine Corps, and from there to end up even in the Guard, depending on one's progress. I wrote about Pasha to Zhdan-Pushkin (from whom I received a warm, good-natured reply and who greeted him like a son and put him up at his home), then to Colonel Slutsky, a family man and an important person in Omsk, and Major General de Grave's wife, my kind acquaintance, a noble and intelligent woman. I asked them all to take an interest in Pasha: all gave their promise. Letters were also sent to the cadets in the senior classes so that they would receive Pasha better. We sent him off with a good and honest man, the landlord of the house in which we rent our apartment, and whom Pasha loved very much. He looked after Pasha like a nanny and did an excellent job of delivering him. Pasha was very happy that he was already a cadet, although he cried when we parted. I'm writing you all this, knowing the interest you take in him. He's a good, very sharp boy, with great abilities, noble and honest, with the capability of becoming strongly attached and of loving, but with the embryo of powerful passions. He's an exact portrait of the never-to-be-forgotten Alexander Ivanovich, both physically and psychically.

My wife has told me too much about you, and the late Alexander Ivanovich, who especially spoke of you with deep respect, for me, without even knowing you partially, not to treasure your favorable attitude towards me. I so wish to deserve your flattering attention.

Allow me to assure you of the feelings of my most profound respect for you and to remain, dear Madam, your humble and respectful servant

F. Dostoevsky.

31 August 1857.

P.S. Remember me to your most respected family and convey my most humble respect to your sisters. This is my most humble request.

129. To Dmitry Konstant
31 August 1857. Semipalatinsk

Dear Dmitry Stepanovich,

I must begin my letter with an apology. It has taken me too long to answer you. But this fault was involuntary. Marya Dmitrievna definitely wanted to write you the conclusive and definite news about our Pashechka. Marya Dmitrievna's long-standing request to have Pasha enrolled in the Siberian Cadet Academy was decided completely unexpectedly, and it was decided due to the governor-general's special attention and concern.[1] Pasha was admitted, and although it was hard to part with him, the thought that the Siberian Cadet Academy is one of the first-class institutions in Russia set us at ease somewhat. The administration is excellent there—friends both of mine and of the late Alexander Ivanovich. We have been busy all this time with sending Pasha off to Omsk. I, to my misfortune, was not able to accompany him personally; for I have already taken leave three times this year.[2] They didn't let me go this time. Instead we found a most devoted person, who has admirably fulfillled our

1. G. Gaslort was the Governor-General of Western Siberia.
2. In Letter 127 Dostoevsky writes that he has taken leave only *twice*.

assignment. He's already returned now and has brought us most welcome news; Pasha has been accepted; all of my letters about him to Omsk have been effective, but it could not be otherwise: I wrote to the most noble people. One can definitely say that the matter has ended very successfully. Pasha has been introduced excellently, he will constantly receive the attention of many important people in Omsk. That is the news we were waiting to inform you of, as a matter conclusively decided, and thus to set you at ease.

You wrote me so many flattering words, most noble and respected Dmitry Ivanovich, that I truly don't know how I deserved them; I swear to you that I will try to deserve your trust in me. I thank you with all my heart for your most kind wishes.

We are getting along all right and so far do not have any reason to complain of our fate. In May I received another monarchal favor: the return of my former hereditary nobility. This signifies a full pardon of my guilt. But my health is poor. I am thinking of going in about eight months (by my calculations) to Moscow. There it will be both better and easier to live, and my income will be more certain, and, finally, it will be more convenient to receive treatment from the best doctors.

Allow me, for my part, to wish you in all sincerity all the best. I place myself at your service. Allow me to be called your most respectful relative and accept the assurance of the profound respect with which I have the honor of remaining, dear Sir, your most humble and constant servant

F. Dostoevsky

Semipalatinsk
August 31, 1857.

130. To Varvara Karepina
7 Semptember 1857. Semipalatinsk

Semipalatinsk, 7 September 1857.

Kind friend, my dear sister, Varenka, I decided to write you again, without waiting for your reply. I want to remind you about me; this is so natural among people who love each other. A long time ago now, in early spring, my wife and I each sent letters to all of you: to you and sister

Verochka in Moscow and to our brother in Petersburg. We received a reply from our brother. But nothing yet from either you or Verochka. Tell me, Varenka, whether you are angry with me for something. If so, it's for no good reason! There are few who love and respect you as I do. I don't even think that, I can't imagine how that could have happened! I know that you are as kind as an angel and aren't capable of getting angry for no reason. I don't understand why Verinka hasn't answered anything either. Are you both well? Brother wrote that he was at your home in Moscow and found everything all right. Are uncle and auntie well? I've thought of them several times: If auntie were seriously ailing, I know you would not leave her side, and in that case you wouldn't have time for me. May God grant them good health, together with all of you! Write at least something, Varenka, and dispel this bewilderment.

About myself I'll only say that we are getting along so-so, so far we are fine. In the future there are only hopes, that is, hopes on myself, on my powers with God's help, and that's best of all. Perhaps God will arrange my fate. If certain things (literary) turn out well, then I'll resign. I can't be in the service any longer, in the 1st place it's expensive, and my time is taken up with the service. But there, free, I will of course gain more. But, it goes without saying that for this I have to move to Moscow. Perhaps this will come about. My illness isn't going away at all. On the contrary, the attacks occur more frequently. Since April I've had three when I was on guard duty, and besides these, three or four times in my sleep. After them there always lingers a weight, debility. It's difficult for me to bear this, Varenka. I hope that the Emperor will allow me to move to Moscow to be treated.[1] But here, with our doctors, there's no way to be treated. In Moscow, despite my illness, I hope to support myself. And renew my soul. Siberia is crushing me. But there's no sense in guessing about the future. Everything will still work out somehow.

I suppose that Verochka is now in the country. I also wrote (at the same time) to Alexander Pavlovich and another acquaintance of mine, Yakushkin, I wrote about things that are important to me and asked for as quick a reply as possible. But I haven't received anything yet.

I sometimes think, Varenka, that my letters have gotten lost. But again, let's suppose one letter was lost, but then another one arrived; otherwise it would be too strange.

Good-bye, Varenka, my dear friend. I just wanted to write you a few lines to remind you of me. Embrace Verochka for me, and convey my profound respect to uncle and auntie. Tell them that thanks to them I still have a piece of bread; I haven't yet spent her money. My gratitude to uncle and auntie is boundless. May God grant them both health and happiness.

Good-bye, my angel, be healthy and prosperous, I am your forever loving brother, F. Dostoevsky.

---

1. Dostoevsky submitted his resignation, citing illness, in January 1858.

NB. Where is brother Andryusha? If he was in Petersburg, was he successful there and where is he now? Where can one write to him?[2]

Good-bye.

131. To Mikhail Dostoevsky
3 November 1857. Semipalatinsk

Semipalatinsk, November 3, 1857.

Kind friend and brother, after receiving your short little letter in which you informed me of your trip abroad, or, to put it better, your attack on Europe, I didn't answer right away but waited for the promised shipment of cigars (since you promised to send them with the next post) to answer you then all at once. But there weren't any cigars or a letter, and therefore I'm writing without waiting any longer, in the first place, in order to chat with you sooner, and in the second to lay out before you some of my present circumstances. 1st, about my private life. We are getting along so-so, neither badly nor well. I serve, although I intend to request my retirement in the near future, because I consider it a sin to let my illness go on without treatment. And my conscience itself asks me whether this is how one serves, when I myself know and feel that on account of my illness I can barely fulfill the slightest duties. It's better to give up my position to another and step aside. I, both retired and ill, will find an opportunity to be useful with my literary activities. Every abnormality, every unnaturalness, will, in the end, avenge itself. To live continually in Semipalatinsk, intensifying my illness and neglecting it, in my opinion, I repeat, is a sin.

I rely on the imperial mercy of our excellent Monarch, who has already granted me so much. He will show me, an unfortunate sick person, charity and, perhaps, allow me to return to Moscow to take advantage of doctors' advice and for the treatment of my illness. Besides that, where will I earn my living if not in Moscow, where there are so many journals now and where they will probably accept me as a regular contributor. You can't understand, brother, what it means to negotiate, at least about literary things, face to face, to write—and not have even the most essential books and journals at hand. I was about to begin a series of writings about

---

2. Andrey Dostoevsky went to Petersburg at the end of 1856 to petition for a transfer. His transfer to Simferopol did not take place until 1858. The summer of 1857 Andrey lived 70 versts from Elizavetgrad (presentday Kirovgorod), where he supervised the construction of a church.

contemporary literature under the rubric "letters from the provinces."[1] I have a lot of ripe material in that regard, a lot jotted down, and I know that I would bring attention to myself. And what happened: owing to the insufficiency of materials, that is, the journals for the last decade—I stopped. And that's how everything of mine gets killed, both literary ideas and my literary career.

You write me, my dear, about my novel and ask me to send it directly to you; but here's what I'll say to you about that: I long ago received a proposal from *The Russian Messenger,* indisputably the premier Russian journal at present, and I've already started up a correspondence in Moscow through excellent acquaintances of mine, and through Pleshcheev, who is now in Orenburg and who has been working for *The Messenger* for a year now.[2]

As far as my novel is concerned, an unpleasant thing happened both to it and to me, and here's why: I resolved and vowed that now I will not publish just because of money anything hasty, anything immature, anything for a deadline (as before), that one must not trifle with an artistic work, that one must work honestly, and that if I write something bad, which will probably happen many times, then it will be because I have no talent, and not because of carelessness and frivolousness. That's why, seeing that my novel was assuming enormous proportions, that it had shaped up marvelously, but that I needed, unquestionably needed (for money) to finish it soon—I became pensive. There is nothing sadder than this meditation during work. Desire, will, energy—everything is extinguished. I saw myself needing to ruin the idea that I had thought out for three years, for which I had collected a mass of material (with which I won't even be able to cope—there is so much), and which I had already partially executed, having written a mass of individual scenes and chapters. More than half of the work was ready in rough draft. But I saw that I wouldn't be able to finish even half by the time I will need money deperately. I thought (and convinced myself) that I could write and publish it in parts, for each part had the appearance of a separate entity, but I was more and more tormented by doubt. I long ago took as a rule that if doubt creeps in, then you must give the work up, because work in the presence of doubt isn't any good at all. But I was sorry to give it up. Your letter in which you say that nobody will take it in parts forced me to give up the work for good. Two considerations were the reason for this: "What will happen?" I thought, "Either I will write well, but then will not receive any money even in a year because my work is useless, or somehow finish it and ruin everything, that is, act dishonestly; but I couldn't do do that." And,

1. Dostoevsky's planned "Letters from the Provinces" were never realized.

2. Pleshcheev published two works in *The Russian Messenger* in 1857: "The Inheritance" ("Nasledstvo") and "Everyday Scenes: Father and Daughter" ("Zhiteiskie stseny: Otets i doch'").

therefore, the entire novel with all the materials has been rolled up and put in the drawer. I have started to write a story, a short one (about 6 printed signatures nevertheless).[3] When I've finished that I'll write a novel based on Petersburg realia, like *Poor Folk* (but the idea is even better than *Poor Folk*[4]), both of these things were begun a long time ago and are partly written, they don't present any difficulties, the work is going along beautifully and on December 15th I will send my 1st story to *The Messenger*.[5] They will give me an advance, and a good-sized one. I'll have money. But here's the misfortune: I won't have any money at all by January 1st, and since, when I was beginning this letter, I decided to explain to you all of my circumstances and ask you about a few things, I'll proceed to that matter.

In February, when I married, I borrowed 650 silver rubles here. I borrowed them from a certain gentleman, a very proper, but strange person. We were on intimate terms. He is about 50, and when giving me the money (he's a rich man), he said to me: "Not for just a year, but even for two, don't deprive yourself, I have it and I am glad to help you," and he didn't even want to take a promissory note.[6] Later, after arriving from Kuznetsk, I received from Moscow, from uncle, 600 silver rubles and even later another 100. The only wordly possesions I had, besides my uniform dress coat, were a pillow and a straw mattress. Everything, down to the last trifle, had to be acquired anew, besides: in a year's time I had traveled to Kuznetsk and back four times, spent a lot of money on the affairs of my wife, then still my fiancée, paid off debts acquired over three years to Khomentovsky and some others for up to 300 silver rubles (for I *needed* money when her husband died) etc., etc. Semipalatinsk is the most expensive city on earth. It's like the uninhabited island here where Robinson found gold nuggets and couldn't buy anything he needed for any money whatsoever.[7] With the opening up of the province everything has become more expensive. I pay, for instance, 8 silver rubles a month for an apartment—without firewood or water. I would like to find a smaller and cheaper apartment but there aren't any, because everything is occupied, 3 years ago up to 100 officials came and not one of them as yet has built a house. According to provincial custom, no matter who comes, he must get a bite to eat; realize that a pound of the most awful Russian cheese costs up to a silver ruble. There are 150 merchants here, but the

3. *The Village of Stepanchikovo.*

4. The work that was to be even better than *Poor Folk* is probably *The Insulted and the Injured.*

5. *The Village of Stepanchikovo* was not finished until 1859.

6. Dostoevsky is referring to N. Kovrigin (see Letter 115).

7. Daniel Defoe, *Robinson Crusoe:* "...as for the money, I had no manner of occasion for it. It was to me as the dirt under my feet, and I would have given it all for three or four pairs of English shoes and stockings and a good coat."

trade is Asiatic. Three or four merchants deal in European (i.e., upper-class) goods. They bring defective goods from Moscow factories and sell them for an unbelievable price, for a price that only a delirious and insane person would ask. Try to order a uniform dress coat or pants; for a cloth that costs 2 silver rubles in Moscow, they charge up to 5. In a word, this is the most expensive, vile little town in the world. And, therefore, it's not surprising that travel, journeys, the wedding, payment of debts, purchasing all of the essential things for our initial settling down and living have eaten up all of our money. By December 1st not a ruble will be left. And meanwhile, only three months after my wedding, the gentlman who had given me money began to remind me of it. This surprised me; I had told him specifically: "If you can wait a year for me, then give it, if not, don't." In answer he said precisely: "Even for two years." I hastened to give him a promissory note with the date of January 1st of the coming year. I had hoped to receive money for my novel. Now all of my hopes are dashed; at least they're dashed as far as January 1st is concerned. By the way, this gentleman has married, is angry at me for an unknown reason and—now the situation is such that I regret that I got involved. He's all tact, but I know that he plans to protest by January 1st   I'm not writing you everything, but the situation is too depressing. In a word, on January 1st I must pay come what may. Incidentally, unexpected help arrived, which will influence my future too. This help is Pleshcheev. I've been corresponding with him for a long time now. He's the same likable, noble, gentle soul that he was before. He's in the civil service in Orenburg, he doesn't travel to Russia, because he fell in love and will marry a 16-year-old poor, but educated, girl (he may be married even at this moment; I'm waiting for a letter from him, we correspond often). About 2 months ago he informed me that he was receiving an inheritance. A relative about whom he hadn't given a thought died in Moscow. There are a lot of heirs, but his portion according to the will comes to exactly 50,000 silver rubles. Pleshcheev wrote me right away that if I needed money, he would give me *as much as I wanted,* even as much as five thousand silver rubles.[8] But he won't receive his inheritance earlier than April of next year ('58). He writes that if we manage to get together in Moscow, we'll never part, and says that he's ready to use his capital on any certain literary venture, and writes that, of course, the central figure will be me (that is, I). I answered that I would borrow 1,000 silver rubles. This thousand together with the money I'll receive for my 2 stories will help me pay my debts, retire, and in June of '58 come to Russia. For the 1st story, which (if you figure 75 rubles per signature) will be worth 500 silver rubles, I'll receive the money around February. But I will ask for 300 rubles in advance and therefore will get up

8. Pleshcheev was married in the fall of 1857. He later loaned Dostoevsky 1000 rubles, a loan which Dostoevsky paid back in installments until 1880.

to 800 silver rubles. Both of my novels will be worth up to 1000. And so: in February I'll receive money *for certain,* in April from Pleshcheev is also for certain—but what am I to do by January 1st '58? More importantly, what am I to do in December of this year? By December 1st the last remaining ruble I have will be spent; what am I to live on? There's nobody to borrow from now! There isn't anyone from whom I would venture to borrow! There's nothing to sell. I can't get an advance on my salary (we have a new commandant, and besides, getting an advance is always a bother). Finally, this debt that tortures, torments me. This is why, my kind friend, I'm appealing to you for the last time: help me this last time. Send me 650 silver rubles, if only you can, for only some three months. You have two guarantees that I will without fail pay you back for certain: if you don't believe that in February I'll receive *for certain* the money for my work, then in April I'll receive it from Pleshcheev for sure. I'll send it to you immediately in February, you'll receive it in March. I swear! And therefore if you can sacrifice 650 rubles for three months, then save me for the last time, as you've saved me 1000 times. Once more be my benefactor, believe me, my friend, that I wouldn't venture to ill-use your trust for anything in the world, in March you'll get it—I swear to you by all that is holy! Help me, my friend and brother. This debt tortures me so morally that I have never in all my life been in such an ambiguous, *vile* situation. I'm not writing you everything, but this incident from my life will make a splendid episode for a novel. Good-bye, my dear brother. Know that all my hopes are on you. I would ask Pleshcheev, but he has *nothing* now, in addition he's getting married. I beg of you one thing: don't delay your answer and answer immediately after you receive my letter, because I'll be waiting for it with extreme impatience and longing.

My wife sends her regards. She wrote Varenka and Verochka, but neither has answered. This is very distressing for her. She says that you, then, are all angry with her and don't want her in your family. I try to dissuade her, but it's useless. She doesn't know you personally. She's very sad.

My stepson Pashechka was accepted into the Omsk Cadet Academy, on his mother's request, which had been submitted a year-and-a-half ago. We sent him off. The academy is excellent, the inspector a man with a lofty heart. I know him personally. But I'm sorry for the little boy, he's only 10, and I have come to love him so. But they accepted him, it was impossible to refuse, and ridiculous besides.

For God's sake, brother, answer at once, don't delay your answer. Realize how much this means to me!

132. To Yevgeny Yakushkin
23 November 1857. Semipalatinsk

Semipalatinsk, 23 November 57.

Dear Yevgeny Ivanovich,

I don't know what you can have thought of me, after not receiving an answer from me to your letter. It's so depressing for me to imagine that I involuntarily blush for my position. But hear me out and you will see that I'm not as guilty as it must seem to you. I sent an answer to your letter on June 1st; I would have sent it even earlier, but the arrival of Fyodor Krestyanovich compelled me to rewrite the letter I'd already written to you. Finally, on September 3rd, I received a letter from Fyodor Krestyanovich Meyn, from Zmeinogorsk. My letter to Alexander Pavlovich Ivanov was enclosed in his letter, in the same package in which I had sent it to Moscow. In this same package there was also the letter to you which I had sent on June 1st, asking Alexander Pavlovich to pass it on to you. I addressed it to the Land Survey Institute. They didn't accept it at the Land Survey Institute. It was returned to Semipalatinsk. Since Fyodor Krestyanovich addressed all of his letters to Moscow to the Land Survey Institute too, the Semipalatinsk post office guessed that it was probably his letter and sent it to him in Zmeinogorsk, from Zmeinogorsk it finally came to me, with an explanatory letter from Fyodor Krestyanovich in which he wrote, by the way, that he was soon going to Moscow by way of Semipalatinsk. It then occurred to me to write to Moscow with him; I was afraid to trust the post a second time, even though he did give me Alexander Pavlovich's new address. But I didn't wait for him. Lately, I haven't been entirely free: I've been distracted by both service (we have a change in administration) and other circumstances; that's why I've missed several more posts. And now at last I'm writing to you, again through Alexander Pavlovich. I'm putting all of the previous letters and even a letter from Fyodor Krestyanovich in my letter to him. And therefore, you'll receive 2 letters: one from June 1st, the second—this one.

My work lately has come to a halt, owing to both ill health and official distractions. A new commandant, new procedures. But since I still haven't managed to send anything to Moscow, you will see that I erred a bit in my calculations. I'm crossing out and revising a lot. I want to send something very good. And there were other cirucmstances too, rather sad ones. I could write a lot now about my affairs, but I'll wait a bit. I hope, however, to send something soon to *The Russian Messenger.*[1] If I receive an answer

---

1. Dostoevsky planned to send *The Village of Stepanchikovo* to *The Russian Messenger.*

from Alexander Pavlovich before that, I'll send it first to you, for I'll be sure of the address. I've resumed correspondence with Pleshcheev, who's in Orenburg. Perhaps you know him or have heard of him. He published in *The Messenger* last year, is acquainted with the editors and offers his mediation.

Good-bye, most kind Yevgeny Ivanovich; if you write me something, I'll write you something more detailed. I'd like to tell you a lot. I have a strong belief that I will be in Moscow this year. This has turned into an idée fixe in me. Entirely yours

Fyodor Dostoevsky.

133. To Varvara Konstant
Semipalatinsk, about 30 November 1857

Most kind sister Varvara Dmitrievna,

My wife just told me that she's writing to you. There remains only a little time until the last call for letters, and, therefore, I, against my will, must hurry and limit myself to just a few lines in order to thank you for your sweet, friendly letter, full of pure, familial interest. If you write that you had heard about me long ago, much earlier than my marriage to your sister, from the deceased and never-to-be-forgotten Alexander Ivanovich, then I'll say to you that I had heard about you many, many times from the departed, who spoke of you even with a sort of veneration. Believe that I very much wish to see you and your entire family some day. I don't know whether these dreams of mine can ever come true. I firmly hope to return to Moscow next year, and I long ago promised myself not to sit at home, but as much as possible get to know our priceless motherland—spend some time in Little Russia, in the South and in the East. Won't it happen then? But, of course, I'll go to Astrakhan with my wife. But God, and He alone, disposes. Do you know that I have a prejudice, a premonition that I am to die soon? Such premonitions almost always occur from being overanxious about one's health; but I assure you that in this instance I'm not being overanxious and my belief in an imminent death is completely dispassionate. It seems to me that I've already experienced everything on earth and that there will not be anything more to strive for. I thank you with all my heart for the medicine for my disease that you enclosed. Believe me, I'm not at all against sympathetic and magnetic medicines. Folk medicine, for example, sometimes has remedies wonderful in their effects.

I'll try to use your medicine in due course. I'll say as well that it's already been more than three months since I've had an attack and I'm very glad of this. Don't blame poor Pashechka. He didn't forget you at all and often mentioned Auntie Varya. Now he's getting used to the academy, and I keep thinking that he's too young for it. I received a letter from Zhdan-Pushkin, the academy's inspector, filled with news about Pasha. He writes that he misbehaves a lot and is doing poorly at his studies. It seems to me that's all in the nature of things. How can he get used, so suddenly, to a completely new order of things, which until now he had never even dreamed of? I wrote to Pushkin, too, about this, begging him to keep Pasha under unremitting supervision. Pushkin is an excellent person, understands his job and we rely firmly on him.

Convey my profound respect to your papa and sisters. Assure them of my deep, heartfelt liking for them. I've heard so much about Dmitry Stepanovich from my wife, who adores him, that I have automatically learned to love and respect him.

With the most profound respect and devotion I remain your sincere brother

F. Dostoevsky.

NB. For God's sake, forgive the untidiness of my letter. Don't take it for disrespect. I always mess up paper this way.

Dostoevsky in dress uniform (1858)

1858

134. To Mikhail Katkov
11 January 1858. Semipalatinsk

Dear Sir,

As far back as August I received from your contributor, A. N. Pleshcheev, notification that you would not refuse to publish something of mine in *The Russian Messenger*.[1] I long ago wished to make you a proposal—to publish the novel that I am now working on. But since it was not finished there was no point in proposing anything. I specifically wanted you to first read my novel and then later time would be found to enter into negotiations. I happened to publish so much bad stuff nine years ago or so that now I can't help not wanting to take any action without seeing people in person. But my circumstances have changed and I am forced to proceed not as I had at first supposed. Permit me to explain.

I conceived my novel at leisure, during my residence in the city of Omsk. After leaving Omsk three years ago I was able to have paper and pen and immediately set to work. But I didn't hurry my work; it was more pleasant for me to think everything over, down to the last detail, to compose and harmonize the parts, to write down individual scenes in their entirety and most importantly—to collect material. In three years of such work I haven't cooled to it, but, on the contrary, have developed a passion for it. The circumstances, moreover, were such that I absolutely could not work systematically, assiduously. But in May of last year I sat down to work on a final draft. Almost all of the 1st book and part of the 2nd were already in rough draft. This notwithstanding, I have not yet managed to finish even the 1st book; but, nevertheless, the work goes on without interruption. My novel is divided into three books; but each book (although it could be divided into parts too, I am noting only the chapters)—but each book is by itself a completely independent thing. And therefore I wanted at first to offer you only one book. I cannot and do not wish to publish the 2nd book in the same year; the same with the 3rd. But all three books can be published in three years. After reading the 1st book, you will see for yourself that such a division is quite possible. My

---

1. Mikhail Nikiforovich Katkov (1818-87) founded the journal *The Russian Messenger* in 1856. Pleshcheev was a contributor to Katkov's journal.

circumstances this year were such that I, upon the change of my way of life, have come to need money badly. After presenting you my novel (the 1st book) in manuscript, I had intended to ask you for some money in advance of publication, and perhaps you would have honored my request. For that reason I hurried to finish it. But working for money and working for art are two incompatible things for me.[2] All three years of my distant literary career in Petersburg I suffered because of that. I did not want to profane my best ideas and the best plans for stories and novels by working in haste and for a deadline. I loved them so much, so wished to create them not hastily, but with love, that it seems to me, I would rather have died than venture to deal dishonestly with my best ideas. But, being constantly in debt to A. A. Kraevsky (who, nevertheless, never extorted work from me and always gave me time)—I was bound hand and foot.[3] Knowing, for instance, that he did not have anything for the publication of an issue, I sometimes on the 26th, that is 4 days before publication, forced myself to think up some story and frequently would think up and write it in 4 days. Sometimes it turned out badly, other times rather well, at least judging from the reviews in other journals. Of course, I often had several months at a time to prepare something better. But the fact was that I myself never knew that I had so many months ahead; because I always set a deadline for myself of not more than a month, because I knew I would have to help out Mr. Kraevsky by the following month. But a month would pass, five months would pass, but I was only tormenting myself trying to think up a better story, because I didn't want to publish anything bad either, and besides, it would have been dishonest to Mr. Kraevsky. At the same time I, in addition to all of this, was morbidly depressed, frequently to a very high degree. Only youth kept me from wearing myself out, from losing my passion and love for literature, and in addition to my youth, love for the sincere ideas of the novels I had planned and for which I was waiting for the time to begin and finish. Those years left a heavy imprint on me, so heavy that now the thought of hurrying to finish the 1st book of my novel in order to get money soon was almost unbearable for me. That's why I haven't hurried. In addition, various concerns and illness have held me up somewhat. Despite that I wanted to send you in January (that is, now) half of the 1st book, and the 2nd half not more than a month later, so that in March the whole novel (that is, the 1st book) would be in your hands. But a certain unforeseen circumstance has stopped me here too. (Incidentally, you probably are surprised and, perhaps, wondering as you read my letter "Why has he gone into such detail?" But do me the favor of reading me to the end. The fact is that I have an enormous request to make of you and all of these details are relevant.) The circumstance that has halted my novel at

2. Dostoevsky is quoting from Pushkin's *Mozart and Salieri.*
3. Dostoevsky writes of his relationship with Kraevsky in Letter 64.

present is the following: last year I badly needed money and therefore entered into debts. To pay them back and for my further maintenance I badly needed to have 1000 silver rubles by January 1st. I wrote my brother in Petersburg about this money. Two weeks ago I received a letter from him. He writes that he obtained for me only 500 silver rubles by entering into certain literary obligations in my name; a certain Count Kushelev plans to publish beginning with next year a journal, *The Russian Word*.[4] His factotum, a certain Mr. Moller, came to see my brother and through him asked for my collaboration. Knowing that I needed money, my brother, not knowing my intentions, but knowing that I was writing a novel, took it into his head to sell it to the future *The Russian Word*.[5] They gave 500 rubles in advance and both parties wrote and signed an agreement. What am I to do now? I'm receiving the money with the next post and I see the necessity of coming to the aid of my brother who has signed the agreement. I had a novel planned a very long time ago which I liked very much and had even begun to write at one time. Now I've taken it out of the drawer and I've decided to continue and finish it so that I can send it to my brother right away. The novel is very short; in two, at the most in two-and-a-half months I hope to both finish and send it off and then immediately take up my old work. But since I received 500 rubles and not the 1000 that I absolutely needed, since I not only cannot pay back my debt for good, but cannot provide for myself with this 500, I have decided on an extreme measure: namely, to appeal to you with a most humble request and offer to you, if you would like to have it, for publication this year, my novel, then couldn't you send me now, as an advance on the novel, the 500 silver rubles that I'm short and badly need. I know that my proposal is fairly eccentric; but it's all a matter of how you take it. There's only one thing I wouldn't want: for you to somehow think that I value my talents so highly that I think nothing of such proposals. Believe me that only extremity has forced me to this. In exchange for the 500 rubles (if you send it), I pledge to send you *all* of the 1st book of my novel during the course of the summer, so that if you want, you can begin publishing it in September.[6] It will be fourteen or fifteen printed signatures, so that it will in any case be worth more than 500 silver rubles and you, when you receive the manuscript, will deduct at once that part of the payment that you send now. I *without fail* pledge to send the novel at the promised time (I purposely have taken a bit more time). Moreover, since you will pay out money to me (if that is the case) in

4. *The Russian Word (Russkoe slovo)*, a St. Petersburg monthly, was published 1859-66. Yakov Polonsky and Apollon Grigoriev initially served as editors, but left in mid-1859. Pisarev joined the journal's staff in 1860 and became its leading critic.

5. The work intended for *The Russian Word* is *Uncle's Dream*, which was published in that journal in 1859.

6. Dostoevsky missed this deadline too. *The Village of Stepanchikovo* was not finished until 1859.

advance, without even glancing at the manuscript, then I on my part pledge that in the event that you don't like my work, to take it back and write another one for you as quickly as possible.[7] After all I used to write some decent things in between the bad ones. Perhaps I'll succeed now, too. We will arrange the price per page when you have read the manuscript. However, you set the price yourself and I completely defer to your decision. Apart from these attestations, that is apart from *my word of honor*, I am unable to give you any more guarantees, at least now. However, if you should require some other guarantee—I will comply. Finally, as the greatest guarantee I will tell you that the novel that I am promising you is my most heartfelt work and has been for a long time. I, however, understand that this is also a small guarantee and it does happen that a writer's favorite work is sometimes exceedingly bad as a result of various factors. In any case I pledge to make it as good as possible.

I hope that you will be so good as to honor me in any event with at least some kind of acknowledgment. I am now applying for retirement and hope that by the end of the summer, after petitioning for permission, to arrive in Moscow to live.[8] Then I will have the pleasure of reporting to you in person. My address now is: *Semipalatinsk, Western Siberia, Fyodor Mikhailovich Dostoevsky.*

Forgive the surface sloppiness of my letter, the ink blots and so forth, and don't take this as a sign of disrespect. I, really and truly, don't know how to write any better. As a precaution I'm addressing this to two addresses: to the editorial office of *The Russian Messenger* and to your printing house.

Accept, dear Sir, the assurance of the feelings of deepest respect with which I remain

Your most humble servant
F. Dostoevsky

Semipalatinsk
11 January 1858

P.S. You may ask why I don't give the novel that I'm writing for *The Russian Messenger* to *The Russian Word*. But 1st, I don't know what *The Russian Word* will be, either the editorial board, or the orientation—nothing. 2) I must send a piece as soon as possible for the money they've sent (500 rubles) and the short novel that I've designated for them, of

---

7. Katkov did send the 500-ruble advance Dostoevsky requested, but categorically rejected *The Village of Stepanchikovo* when it was offered for publication. The work was eventually published in *Notes of the Fatherland* in 1859.

8. Dostoevsky was not permitted to live in either Moscow or St. Petersburg when the order concerning his resignation was issued (dated 18 March 1859).

course, I will finish sooner than the long one that I'm writing for *The Russian Messenger*. My fate, probably, is to work *for money,* in the most constraining sense of the word.

D.

135. To Mikhail Dostoevsky
18 January 1858. Semipalatinsk

Semipalatinsk. 18 January 1858.

I received three letters from you, my dear friend; one dated November 25th, the other two December 17 and 19. I wanted to answer the first one immediately, but it was impossible. You wrote about the fact that you would be sending me money and about the dealings with *The Russian Word.* Since I didn't know whether you would send the money, I absolutely couldn't write you anything. That's why I waited to receive the money. Now I'll reply to everything. But first of all, let me thank you with all my heart for sending the money. You have saved me and I'm now provided for for at least a while. And without it I would have perished; there wasn't a single way of somehow pulling through.

I hasten to answer your letters in order—in the same order as you wrote them.

I received the cigars (I don't know whether I wrote you about that). But, the gentleman for whom I ordered them turned them down, and for a most respectable reason: they were too mild for him. He used to give me some of his. Ten-Cate swindles him, but they send him very strong ones; and that's just what he needs. I smoked your cigars myself. I remain in debt to you for them. We'll settle up. I'll say as well that your cigars are excellent, but shredded awfully en route. In any case, I'm surprised that they didn't *go* for you. Next: you write about *The Russian Word.* Let's suppose that the lordly idea is a good one; that capital for assistance appears. But can an editorial board really be created with money? And without an editorial board and without originality a journal is nonsense! I don't know whom he'll hire to be the editors.[1] But I have little faith for some reason in the success of *The Russian Word.* As an almanac, the journal might be good for a short time.

---

1. Count Grigory Alexandrovich Kushelev-Bezborodko (1832-76), the publisher of *The Russian Word* chose Apollon Grigoriev and Yakov Polonsky to be co-editors.

However, what business is it of mine so far? May God grant it success. I thank you, my friend Misha, my devoted friend, for striking up dealings with *The Russian Word* and doing the thing so masterfully. Now listen to me about my circumstances. I'm giving up my novel (the long one) for the time being. I can't finish it in time! It would only wear me out. It's already worn me out so. I'm giving it up until there are tranquility and stability in my life. This novel is so dear to me, has become so much a part of me, that I won't give it up completely for anything. On the contrary, I plan to make it my chef-d'oeuvre. The idea is too good and it's cost me too much to give it up completely. Now here's what I'm up to: I conceived the idea eight years ago now for a short novel the length of *Poor Folk*. Lately I somehow knew, recalled and created the plan anew. Now this has all come in handy. I'm getting down to work on this novel and writing. I hope to finish it in about two months. Besides this: there's an episode in my big novel that's completely finished and good on its own, but detrimental to the whole. I want to cut it out of the novel. It's also the length of *Poor Folk,* only with a comic content.[2] There are fresh characters in it. They give a deadline of a year at *The Russian Word.* And so here is what I'm asking you: write me immediately, if I, for example, send you the novel in April for *The Russian Word* and the number of signatures (in comparison to the signature sheet size of other journals) is more than 5 (and it will be), whether *The Russian Word* will send me immediately, in April, money for the remaining signatures or will they wait until next year, that is until publication? If they will send it, then I'll immediately upon your notification send the novel to you for *The Russian Word.* If they won't send it, then I figure: let *The Russian Word* wait until autumn; in the autumn I'll send them a finished piece (namely the episode from the long novel redone absolutely separately)—and I'll send the other novel, which will be ready at the end of March, to Katkov at *The Russian Messenger.* The plan is clear: I won't be late for *The Russian Word;* there will be a piece by the journal's appearance, even if I deliver it in the autumn. But now I must save myself. Katkov has made me a proposal through Pleshcheev. Having received 500 rubles from you, and not 1000, I still don't know what to do, because I've given almost all the money, of the 500 you sent, to creditors. I'm left with almost nothing and I still remain in debt for exactly 350 silver rubles. That's exactly why I've done the following: I wrote to Katkov with the last post, in detail and thoroughly, that I wish to participate in his journal; I'm offering him my long novel (which I now, for the time being, have definitely decided to give up), informing him that I will deliver it to him in August (not earlier) and am asking him, owing to my difficult circumstances, for an advance of 500 silver rubles, which I am asking him

2. The episode from the big novel is probably *Uncle's Dream,* which was published in 1859 in *The Russian Word.*

to send immediately upon receiving my letter. Having written this, I figured this way: "After all, they're giving an advance at *The Russian Word* without seeing anything, why shouldn't *The Russian Messenger* give one too?" This way they might send me in March (in the middle) another 500 silver rubles (in general I think that I have nothing to lose; I haven't published anything for 8 years and therefore, perhaps as a novelty, I will be interesting for the public! The editors most likely know this and perhaps just because of it they'll give an advance, and what do I have to lose, especially and being in a difficult situation?). If Katkov will send the money, then I would immediately send him, *not the long* novel (which I've given up), but another one, a *short* one, which I am writing now, even though I did write him about the long novel (I didn't know then that I would give it up). But after all, it's all the same to Katkov as long as the thing is good. If I send it to Katkov, then I can probably take another 500 rubles from him immediately, since the novel will turn out to be about eight printed signatures in length; consequently, having taken another 500 I'll remain a bit in debt. Katkov, seeing my punctuality and a good novel (assuming that it will be good) will probably send another 500. And that couldn't be better. It goes without saying that *The Russian Word* will receive something from me then by September (namely, the superfluous episode from the long novel). I'll deal honorably with *The Russian Word:* deliver by the deadline and, moreover, will try to make it as good as possible; because I like this episode for the idea alone; and besides, it will be a complete, finished thing. And so, there are all my instructions. Write what you think of all this.

And now something else: you write me in the first letter that you will need my story by next year. Then in the other letters you mention that you have some business concerning me (probably the same thing). I strongly reproach you for not writing in detail, that is, what do you want to publish, with whom and how? As far as the story is concerned, rest assured: I give my word, you'll have it. Having disentangled myself from the long novel, I seem to have become inspired again: I will finish the piece for *The Russian Messenger,* then the one for *The Word* and there will still be a lot of time. Only write me about everything in more detail.

You should also know, brother, that I submitted my application for retirement (a few days ago), citing illness. You know my plans. If I'm not permitted to live in Moscow (which I request in the application for retirement), I will write a letter to the Monarch; He is merciful and will perhaps allow an ill person that; because I will request "to make use of the advice of the capitals' doctors."[3] If I'm not allowed even in that case (but how are Tol[l] and Palm in Petersburg, if they don't allow others? Perhaps

---

3. Dostoevsky wrote his letter to Alexander II at the beginning of March (see Letter 5 of Business and Official Letters).

they really have found it necessary to forbid entry to some, but probably not to all), then I will go to Odessa, where one can live both well and cheaply and probably not forever. The Monarch is merciful and with time will allow entry into the capitals. That's my plan. Consequently, I will leave, if everything works out, in the summer and only then. I'm definitely considering borrowing 1000 rubles from Pleshcheev. He and I will settle up and I know how to settle up. I can't move from this place without his money. That's why another enormous and vital request to make of you has has been conceived in me; I appeal yet again to your kindness, which[. . .][4]

A frank explanation. Even though I wrote about the clothes, I've now suddenly begun to feel ashamed. No, brother! I'm worrying you too shamelessly, and therefore I'll say: write frankly, that is, if you have to pay cash, then don't send them, I'll manage. If you, as a merchant, can buy ready-made clothes on credit, then buy them, but only if it's possible on credit; also write me how much they cost. There are, it seems, cheaper ones too, otherwise my conscience will torment me. But if it's on credit, then I'll be able to send you money too. The money will be good in the summer.

Pleshcheev got married. He often reminisces about you and sends his regards.

NB. Don't worry about a bad fit. Buy your own size. I can wear your clothes. Perhaps tell them to make it a *hair looser* and *longer* than for you.

NB. If you have to spend even a kopeck *cash* for the clothes, don't send them.

You write about portraits of the whole family. I'm terribly glad for that and my wife talks of nothing else. Send them quickly, for God's sake. My wife sends both you and Emilia Fyodorovna her regards. I also kiss Emilia Fyodorovna's hand, and heartily, heartily embrace you. My regards to everyone to whom it occurs to you. Kiss brother Kolya if he's in Petersburg.

Entirely yours, F. Dostoevs

Kiss especially your children, down to the last one. Do they remember me? When you send the portraits, enclose a *description,* so I can recognize each of them.

---

4. The continuation at this point has not survived.

136. To Yevgeny Yakushkin
8 February 1858. Semipalatinsk

Semipalatinsk 8 Feb. 1858

I thank you for all the information that you have reported and for your efforts on my behalf. As far as my novel is concerned, here's what I must write you finally: I have given it up (for the time being). A significant part of it was already quite ready. But just the idea that I would have to finish it for money, on posthorses, as had happened with me earlier, was killing me so that I had become sick in both mind and body. I remember how I used to destroy decent things because I had to meet the conditions of the journals that had given money in advance. I have fallen in love with my novel and expect something from it.

Instead of it I've begun a long story of about 8 signatures, which is easier and so far is going along well. Work usually agitates me very much, I can't write dispassionately and, consequently, quickly. In any case by the end of March, I hope to finish, send it to you and even find you in Moscow with my letter. But first of all, I'll tell you that I wrote Katkov myself—a strange, but necessary letter. I have debts here of 600 silver rubles (made at the time of the wedding). The term for them was January 1st of '58. My brother Mikhaylo (in Petersburg) wrote me that a journal, *The Russian Word*, is being planned for next year. A certain Count Kushelev gave money for it, I don't know the editors. Kushelev's business factotum is a certain Moller. The latter presented himself to my brother and asked for my novel, story and so on. My brother, knowing that I need money and not having the means to help me himself, entered into a contract with Moller on the following terms: 1) I deliver the story by the end of 1858. 2) The pay is 100 silver rubles per signature 3) 500 rubles is paid in advance, immediately. And that's exactly how things worked out, and I've already received the money (500 rubles). I already have a story about 5 signatures long for Moller. But, consequently, I'm at ease as far as meeting the terms with the proposed *The Russian Word*. But 500 rubles wasn't enough for me. I needed 1000; for after having paid everybody back I needed something to live on. I wrote Katkov a frank letter (I don't think that Katkov could be offended by it) in which I offered him my novel (for this year) and asked him to send me 500 rubles immediately. After having sent my letter, I decided not to work on the novel (I put it aside for the time being), but to work on the short novel (about 8 signatures) that I mentioned above.[1] If Katkov sends the money, I hope that he won't repent it greatly.

---

1. The short novel is *The Village of Stepanchikovo.*

I'm not saying, however, that I'll write something very good. But perhaps it will be decent. If he doesn't send the money—it's his choice. But if he sends it, I'm in a bind again. 50 rubles per signature isn't enough for me. And so I decided this: you, most kind Yevg[eny] Ivanov[vich], after you have received my novel, will take it to Katkov and if he likes it then he'll add some more for me, if he doesn't, then I'll get the money to pay him back. The whole problem is due to the fact that Pleshcheev assured me that the pay was more than 50 rubles. But this is all nothing; it will work out somehow. As far as the novel is concerned (the long one), I'll get down to work on it in earnest at the end of the year. I hope to receive money this summer and leave this place. I have submitted my resignation and am asking to be allowed to go to Moscow: perhaps I'll be allowed. Good-bye, most noble Yevgeny Ivanovich, don't censure me if there's great disorder in my letter, I had an attack of falling sickness the day before yesterday and am now literally not in my right mind. My head is not clear and all my limbs hurt. Good-bye. I hope to see you this year.

Your Dostoevsky.

NB. However there's no sense in guessing ahead of time. I'll deal with Katkov in such a way that he won't repent. At least as well as I am able.

137. To Mikhail Dostoevsky
1 March 1858. Semipalatinsk

Semipalatinsk, 1 March 1858

I hasten to answer you, my most kind friend, Misha. Pardon me for writing you so briefly. This time there is little time, and besides the letter to you, I must send off 2 long letters. Listen.

The news about the publication of "A Children's Tale" was not completely pleasant. I long ago had thought of reworking it and reworking it well, and in the 1st place, of throwing out the good-for-nothing beginning. But what can I do? It's been published, so you can't take it back. In addition I still haven't been able to get the August issue of *Notes of the Fatherland.* They get it here. They have promised to give it to me. But so far I don't have it. And therefore I still haven't read what was published.[1]

---

1. Mikhail's attempts to publish "A Children's Tale" were made on Dostoevsky's instructions (see Letters 113, 115, 123), but Dostoevsky was not aware of the story's actual appearance. Dostoevsky made some changes in later editions of the story, retitled "The Little Hero" (1860, 1866): among other things he cut the sentimental dedication to Mashenka.

The second circumstance. It makes me very sad, my dear friend Misha, that you don't treat me in a brotherly fashion, namely: in the event that I don't consider myself in debt to Kr[aevsky], you want to send me *immediately* 200 rubles, and you even add: *"even if it comes to borrowing."* Aren't you ashamed to act like that with me! With what shameless eyes would I demand these 200 rubles from you, when I'm in debt to you all around, moreover, when you have done me so much good, because without you I wouldn't have known what to do in many instances during my life here. And so, get this nonsense out of your head and if "A Children's Tale" can be of use to you for settling your accounts with K[raevsky], then use it for that, as you please. I find Mr. Kr[aevsky] and his magnanimity funny. Here's what I've decided:

Tell him the following word for word:

In the 1st place I didn't owe him 800-odd silver rubles, but exactly 650. To add on 150 rubles is completely unacceptable. I remember the amount of the debt very well. However, I'm sure that he's not deliberately mistaken and I know the reason for his mistake. Namely: when he paid out the money to me in installments, he always took a receipt (on scraps of paper) from me. When I would bring him something for publication (in repayment of the debt) I never took back the receipts and didn't cross out what went to repayment. The remaining receipts he has are probably confusing him.

2) If I do recognize that I owe him 650 rubles and if *I wish* to pay him back (I wish to with all my heart), then at the same time *I do not recognize that he has the right* to demand from me the immediate payment of these 650 rubles or to arrange for the repayment of my debt to him by publishing a piece that belongs to me. This decision of mine has the following grounds:

a) that according to the law I don't owe him anything and if I recognize the debt and wish to repay it, then only out of of a feeling of honor and my own desire.

b) if I took money from Kr[aevsky], I *never* pledged to pay him back with money, but on the contrary, with works. That's why he gave me money, so that I would bring him works. He would not ever have given me anything under any other circumstances. And since the ten-year circumstances which were beyond my control, may be such that I cannot repay my debt even with works, then what grounds has he *to demand* the debt from me?

c) If he brags that *until now* he has not demanded my debt from me, then I can in no way recognize this as generosity, on the basis that he, even if he had wanted to demand, *could not* have done so.

d) if he appeals to me as one man to another, and apart from all considerations based *on the law,* demands the debt *in the name of my honor,* then I answer him this: in the 1st place, I didn't pay him back for ten years *due to circumstances beyond my control. These same circumstances* make it physically impossible for me to pay him back now or in the near future, although I would wish that. In the 3rd place, I ask him again to recall that I pledged to repay him not in money, but with works.[2]

e) if he says that in that case I must indeed pay him back with works and that he had a right to publish my "Children's Tale," then I answer that due to the same *circumstances beyond my control* I consider that I now have the right to dispose of my property according to my will, not someone else's. 2) that he can only make repayment to himself, by force, after having received such power from the law, as is done with insolvent debtors.

f) Finally (and *mainly):* recognizing myself to be your debtor for a sum four times more than what "A Children's Tale" is worth, and besides which, recognizing myself to be in debt to you through eternal gratitude for your generous and selfless help, which has saved me in the most difficult circumstances, *I wish first of all to pay you back.* While recognizing "A Children's Tale" to be my property (for it ended up at Kraevsky's after circumstances beyond my control, and mainly, since I in *the very beginning* left it to you, ceding to you the right of full ownership) (if the opportunity presented itself to make use of it), then on the basis of the abovementioned, I recognize *you alone* to be the sole owner of "A Children's Tale" with the right to do with it what you will, but any arbitrary appropriation of this story by another party (even though he may be my creditor) I consider an unlawful act of violence, as I look at this affair now from the sidelines. And therefore, the last thing: don't send me money for the story; use it for your own benefit; and since you write that you were in debt to him, then, now having in hand my certification that the story belongs to you and not to me, you have the full and lawful right to consider yourself not at all in debt to Kraevsky. If my receipt for the 200 rubles received from you in November is needed in connection with this, I enclose it for you in any case (date it yourself). Don't send me money under any circumstances, for in so doing you will seriously offend me, my friend Misha.

If, for example, Mr. Kr[aevsky] says that the previous fee was 50, and is now 100, and that a fee of 100 per signature is high, then explain to him that a person who has bought a sack of flour at the market for such-and-such doesn't have the slightest right to protest if in a week the price at the market has risen. He can only regret that. If he says that the agreement was formerly for 50 per signature, then tell him that that was before, only because I was in debt and out of *delicacy* could not raise the price; and finally, *then* nobody would have given any more. Now I'm being offered *100;* and since I recognize "A Children's Tale" not to be the property of Mr. Kraev[sk]y, I am selling it for what I please, taking into consideration the market prices. Mr. Kr[aevsky], who willfully published the piece, must naturally pay what others have offered for it.

---

2. There is no "2nd place" in Dostoevsky's letter.

Good-bye, my priceless friend Misha, I embrace you with all my heart,

Your F. Dostoevsky.

My wife and I send regards to you all, Emilia Fyodorovna in particular. What's happened, brother: you boasted that you would send portraits and still nothing! And we can hardly wait, especially my wife. Kiss the children.

Again: don't send me those 200 silver rubles under any pretense. My regards to Shrenk. That's really a case of when will we have a chance to meet.

I'll inform you how my business with *The Russian Messenger* ends. But I'm writing. I don't know now when I'll finish. My situation is critical. I rely on God. If Pleshcheev gives me 1000, I'll go to Russia immediately, and if he doesn't—I don't know how I'll even exist. He promised. I know how to settle up with him. Good-bye. Write, for God's sake.

I remember *The Russian Word*. There will be a piece. *However, I'll write you about this in the near future* and announce my plans.

I remain 350 silver rubles in debt (here). I must without fail repay it, but I have only 20 silver rubles on hand. I asked Katkov (*Russ[ian] Mess[enger]*) for 500 silver rubles in advance, promising him a piece. (I don't have anything finished yet.) I expect his reply two posts from now. If I'm refused, not only will it be impossible to repay the debt, but also I will have nothing to live on. Pleshcheev promises the 1000 silver rubles not earlier than June.

I wrote you about clothes. For God's sake, do it if on credit and it doesn't exceed 100 rubles! My retirement is soon. We'll settle up without fail. There's not a cent now.

Received by me, in November 1857, from Mikhail Mikhaylovich Dostoevsky, two hundred silver rubles.

Fyodor Dostoevsky.

138. To Dmitry Konstant
15 March 1858. Semipalatinsk

Dear Dmitry Stepanovich,

It has been a long time since I had the pleasure of writing you. I am doubly glad to fulfill my duty now, hastening to greet you on the coming holiday of Easter Sunday. May God grant that you celebrate it many times more in your family circle, gaily and happily. Trust that this is my most sincere wish, as Masha is my witness. She will tell you how much I respect you, knowing you only from her stories. She doesn't tire of talking about you. Her most sincere and most impatient desire is to see all of you soon, her sisters, whom she loves so. She and I often talk about that and, who knows, perhaps our dream will come true some day. I am informing you, most respected Dmitry Stepanovich, that I have submitted my resignation, owing to my impaired health and I hope that I will be allowed to live in Moscow. I am doing this, first, because I really am ill; second, because I have nothing to gain from a career in the service here, and, third, my means of support will double with my move to Moscow. Everything here is expensive and rotten. We spend an awful lot. Remaining in Siberia offers nothing but disadvantages. Masha and I are planning, if we are fortunate enough to move to Moscow, to take Pashechka with us. It's bad for him to remain alone in Siberia without us. And it's an unenviable future to enter the officers' ranks of the Siberian Academy. If you knew everything that goes on in Siberia, that is, if you were an eyewitness, then I'm certain you would approve of our intention. As long as we are in Siberia, he nevertheless is getting an education at the Siberian Academy. But when we go, to leave him alone would be a sin, all the more so since in Russia, I'm certain, there will be a chance to give him an education in a better institution. Trust as well that if we did not have this certainty, we would not want to act rashly.

Pasha writes us fairly often. He is received in good homes in Omsk. He sends his regards to you and his aunts and asks that he be remembered to you.

I also commend myself to your good graces, most respected Dmitry Stepanovich. How I wish, together with Masha, to see you and become acquainted with you in person. Perhaps God will soon fulfill our wish.

With feelings of the most profound respect and devotion, allow me to remain, dear Sir, your most respectful relative.

Fyodor Dostoevsky

139. To Mikhail Katkov
8 May 1858. Semipalatinsk

Dear Mikhail Nikiforovich,

I have long since received your pleasant letter and if I didn't answer it immediately, it was only because I was waiting for the promised money, supposing that it would arrive right after the letter.

I wanted to inform you all at once of the receipt of it too. And therefore don't be angry with me for my long silence. Allow me, 1st, to thank you for sending the 500 rubles and 2nd, for your letter full of concern and support. It gave me enormous pleasure. I'm very, very grateful to you, most respected Mikhail Nikiforovich.

I will try to follow your advice in all respects, but I will nevertheless try to deliver the piece earlier. I submitted my application for retirement long ago. I'm expecting it any moment. Since in the Omsk jail I developed falling sickness, which continues to this day vehemently and which causes me great suffering, I requested permission to live in Moscow in order to take advantage of the advice of Moscow doctors. I don't think that our merciful and noble Emperor would refuse a poor, sick person, the more so as everything has been returned to me long since. And therefore I firmly hope to settle in Moscow. You won't believe how necessary it is for me to return to Russia for the success of my literary endeavors. Would you believe that I have a novel, begun a long time ago, which I abandoned long ago, only because I lacked certain material and impressions that I need to gather myself, in person, from nature. But I worked on that novel with love, and it was difficult to abandon it. And if that were all! To say nothing of the fact that books alone are not life, that provincial life, to which one involuntarily becomes accustomed, is at odds with all my needs and you don't notice how monotony of thought and exceptionality rise up in everything. But this is difficult to describe. You can imagine how pleasant I found your words and the promise that I will be welcome among you and your staff.

I'm not writing you anything about my novel now, although I feel the need to speak about it. But there's too much that needs to be said and therefore I will say nothing for the present. I'll say only this: I'll try to comply with your wish that the novel not be dragged out over several years. I hope to give you more news about myself before I arrive in Moscow. I also hope that you won't leave me without your advice, which perhaps I will need.

Accept the sincere assurance of my respect and devotion.

Fyodor Dostoevsky

8 May 1858. Semipalatinsk.

I enclose a receipt for the money, which the editorial board of *The Russian Messenger* requested.

140. To Ivan Zhdan-Pushkin
17 May 1858. Semipalatinsk

Semipalatinsk 17 May 1858

Dear Ivan Vikentievich,

I thank you for your letter and for your favorable reply to my request. Everything you write about the public education of society and *certain* of its disadvantages, in *some* instances is so true that I'm surprised that only now has it begun to be noticed! Honor and glory to the public education of society—that's indisputable. It has done it's job and done it well. Incidentally, there was one extraordinarily important feat that it accomplished. It began when our public-minded society was still forming and was just beginning its new direction. There were neither *common* laws, nor a *common* truth, nor a *common* clear consciousness, nor a *common* feeling of honor. At that time it sometimes happened that two noblemen, fathers of families, differed in their notions of everything, like Europe and China, and the government, which has always taken the lead with us and has been the head of thinking society—which Peter himself bequeathed to his successors when he was dying—the government realized that in Russian education the intelligentsia must, for the time being, be the first priority.[1] But now it is no longer the same with educated society. We have gone far, have worn down the sharp corners and have in part come to agree on those concepts. That's what it is inclining to. Consequently, the public education of society (which was so convenient for some parents, because it gave them the chance to be relieved of their fledglings, particularly at public expense) was already beginning to be harmful for youth, the more so as exclusiveness has been raised to such a high degree by both the former routine and the comforts of the parents themselves. Our good Tsar, the golden, Russian soul, now thinks otherwise—and glory to Him![2] I'm

1. Dostoevsky wrote further on Peter I's education reforms in the essay "Pedantry and Literacy" (1861).
2. A concerted effort to reform Russia's educational system at all levels was begun when Alexander I assumed the throne in 1855.

writing you all this now because your letter awakened in me all the painful memories of my own education. But I was in my father's house until I was 15 and didn't stagnate in an academy. But what I saw around me, what examples! I saw boys of thirteen who had already planned their whole lives: where to get which rank, what's more advantageous, how to rake in the money (I was in the engineers) and how to reach a secure, independent command as quickly as possible! I saw and heard this with my own eyes and not one, or two such people.[3] That's why it always seemed to me that Pasha entered the academy too early. But what could be done? My wife was left a widow and without great hopes for the future. It was better to get him a place quickly than to lead a wretched life with him and leave him without an education. They began to petition long ago. Good people nobly helped her. Pasha was fixed up, but she had already married and Pasha could have stayed at home. Could we really ignore the opportunity and say that now we don't want to send our son to the academy?

Next Saturday I will send an authorized person with a letter to the academy's director.[4] I think I can manage to have the same person who brought him to the academy. This person can be trusted; I know him well. I'll furnish him with a letter for you too, most respected Ivan Vikentievich, and I have several things to ask you for. You write that it's enough to just send a letter to the director and ask him to let him go. That's what I'll do and I will confidently believe your words that there won't be any delay. Allow me to offer you my most sincere gratitude for everything. I know that you are taking a sincere interest in our orphan. May God reward you for this! My wife presents you her most profound respect and gratitude.

Accept the assurances of my feelings of the utmost respect and devotion, with which I have the honor to remain

Your most humble servant

F. Dostoevsky

---

3. This sentiment is echoed in Dostoevsky's *Notes from Underground.*
4. Dostoevsky plans to send Lyapukhin (see Letters 123, 127).

141. To Mikhail Dostoevsky
31 May 1858. Semipalatinsk

Semipalatinsk. 31 May 1858.

I hasten to answer you, kind friend, with the first post. I'm surprised that my letters take so long to reach you. Meanwhile, I'm not lazy about writing. If you were worried about me, I was also about you. Particularly recently. I had decided in fact that something had happened to you, and mainly—that you were ill. The news about your loss (3,000 rubles) saddened me greatly. You say that it's not the loss of money that saddened you, but the critical situation and so forth. No, brother, one can regret money as well. Your children are growing, and you won't get 3,000 soon. Can it really be there's no hope of retrieving it? I'm vexed, my friend, that I, as if on purpose, turned up with my commissions and requests. But what's to be done? You write that you'll send the things soon. Thank you, brother. I hope that I'm troubling you for the last time. I meant to wait for the things and answer then. But the things can still be long in coming. You write that you'll send tails and just pants. In my opinion, a frock coat would be better. That's always more useful. I'll scrape together some money and have one made here, though I'm in desperate financial straits. You write, my friend, that I should send you what I've written. I don't remember (in general, my memory has become very poor)—I don't remember whether I wrote you that I've opened up dealings with Katkov (*The Russian Messenger)* and sent him a letter in which I offered to contribute to his journal, and promised a story this year if he would send me 500 silver rubles right away. I received the 500 rubles from him about a month or five weeks ago, with a very intelligent and kind letter. He writes that he's very glad of my participation, is fulfilling my request (500 rubles) immediately and asks that I stint myself as little as possible, work unhurriedly, that is, not for a deadline. This is wonderful. I'm engaged now on my work for *The Russian Messenger* (a long story[1]); but it's a shame that I didn't come to an agreement with Katkov about the payment per signature, writing that I rely in this instance on his fairness. I'll also send something to *The Russian Word* this year; I hope so. Not my novel, but a story.[2] I've put aside writing the novel until my return to Russia. I've done that out of necessity. It has a rather fortunate idea, a new character that hasn't yet appeared anywhere. But since this character is probably now in wide circulation in Russia, in real life, particularly now, judging from the movement and ideas that everyone is so full of, I'm certain that I will enrich my novel with new observations

---

1. *The Village of Stepanchikovo.*
2. *Uncle's Dream.*

by returning to Russia. One shouldn't hurry, my dear friend, but one should try to do something well. You write, my dear, that I'm probably proud and wish now to make my appearance with something very good and therefore am sitting and hatching this very good think like one hatches eggs. Let's suppose that's so; but since I've ceased worrying about making my appearance with a novel, and am writing two stories that will be only passable (and that by the grace of God), there's no hatching in me now. But what sort of theory, my friend, do you have that the picture must be painted at once and so on and so on? When did you become convinced of that? Believe me—work is necessary in everything, and an enormous amount of it. Believe me—a light, exquisite poem of a few lines by Pushkin seems to have been written all at once because it took a long period of time for it to be glued together and was corrected over and over by Pushkin.[3] These are facts. Gogol spent eight years writing *Dead Souls.*[4] Everything that was written all at once was immature. It is said that Shakespeare didn't have any corrections in his manuscripts. That's why he has so many monstrosities and lapses of taste, but if he had worked—it would have been better. You clearly are confusing inspiration, that is, the first momentary creation of a picture or stirring in the soul (which always takes place), with work. I, for example, jot down a scene immediately, just as it first appeared to me, and I'm happy with it, but then I revise it for entire months, a year, I'm inspired by it *several times,* not just once (because I love this scene) and several times will add or take out something, as has already happened with me, and believe me that it's turned out much better. If only it were inspiration. Of course, there would be nothing without inspiration.

True, they're paying larger fees in Petersburg now. So, Pisemsky got 200 or 250 rubles per signature for *1000 Souls.*[5] One can live and work without hurrying that way. But can you really think Pisemsky's novel wonderful? It's only a mediocrity and, although a golden one, nevertheless only a mediocrity. Is there even one new character, *created,* which had never appeared before? All of this is old stuff and appeared long ago in our writer-innovators, especially in Gogol. These are all old themes in a new key. A superb pasting together using other people's models, a work by Sazikov based on Benvenuto Cellini's designs.[6] True, I've only read two

3. Yevgeny Yakushkin (see Letter 95) sent Dostoevsky Pavel Annenkov's *Materials for a Biography of A. S. Pushkin (Materialy dlia biografiia A. S. Pushkina,* 1855), in which Annenkov describes Pushkin's manuscripts.

4. Gogol began work on *Dead Souls* in 1835. The first part was published in 1842.

5. Alexey Pisemsky's *A Thousand Souls* (1858) was enormously popular as soon as it was published. The novel traces the rise and fall of Kalinovich, who marries an heiress, uses his wife's money and connections to promote himself in the world, throws her over when he has achieved his goal, but loses all when he prosecutes the evil and powerful Prince Ivan (his wife's lover), because he resorts to illegal measures.

6. I. P. Sazikov was a Petersburg silversmith whose commissions primarily consisted of

parts; the journals reach us late. The ending of the 2nd part is absolutely improbable and completely ruined. A Kalinovich who consciously deceives is impossible. Kalinovich, from what the author showed us earlier, ought to have made a sacrifice, proposed marriage, shown off, in his heart of hearts delighted in his nobility, and been convinced that he would not deceive. Kalinovich is so vain that he can't consider himself, even to himself, a scoundrel. Of course, he will delight in all that, sleep with Nastenka, and later, of course, dupe her, but this is *later,* when reality demands it and, of course, he will comfort himself and say that even in this instance he acted nobly. But a Kalinovich who consciously dupes and *sleeps* with Nastenka is repulsive and *impossible,* that is, possible, only not Kalinovich. But enough about these trifles.

My friend, I can hardly wait for my retirement. I didn't come out directly and request to live in Moscow, but it's written about directly in my request for retirement, since the form demands it: *I will have residence in the city of Moscow.* If they don't object, I'll go. I'll go, but on what? I won't have any money until the story is finished. What will I live on in two months?—I don't know. Because I won't have any money in two months either. Out of the 500 Katkov sent, a debt of 400 silver rubles was paid immediately. I spend 40 silver rubles a month, but I can't get away from *emergency expenses.* For 1 1/2 years it's been this and that and everything unexpected. My only hope is Pleshcheev. He promised me 1000 rubles, but he may not get it himself or not for two years. What will become of me before the end of the year, when I'll get something for my work? (I won't get anything for my work earlier.) I don't know; I have a splitting headache. There's nobody even to borrow from now. But don't worry about me a lot; everything will work out somehow.

Pleshcheev will come to Moscow and Petersburg. He's going in May. Receive him kindly and get acquainted with his wife. I just received Milyukov's package (his book).[7] Some officer dropped it off; but I didn't see the officer. Perhaps he'll drop by. My regards to Milyukov and everybody.

What's with our family? Varenka, Verochka? Not a word, not a word yet. Where's brother Andrey, where's Kolya?

Good-bye! I embrace you. Regards to Emilia Fyodorovna, kiss the children! My wife sends her regards to you all. Good-bye.

Yours, F. Dostoevsky

---

designs based on other artists' models. Dostoevsky is comparing Sazikov, a talented copyist with the work of Benvenuto Cellini (1500-71), the Italian sculptor and metalsmith, who is generally considered to be the greatest of his time.

7. Probably Alexander Milyukov's *Essay on the History of Russian Poetry (Ocherk istorii russkoi poezii,* 2d ed., 1858).

I'll write again when I receive the things and the *retirement*. I'll apprise you of my situation. But, for God's sake, don't delay and write yourself.

142. To Mikhail Dostoevsky
19 July 1858. Semipalatinsk

19 July 1858.

My priceless friend and brother Misha, I answered your letter (dated May 5th) immediately after I received it. In that letter, by the way, you wrote me: "*I'm sending you the clothes, etc. this week or the next.*" This means that the latest date of dispatch would be May 15th, no later. That at least is how it turns out based on the sense of your letter. Now figure it out for yourself, my priceless one: the mail usually takes 22 or 25 days (between these figures) to get from Petersburg to Semipalatinsk. What am I supposed to think about you now, your situation, and your circumstances?

And above all realize, my priceless one, that it's not the sending of the clothes that worries me (although God knows how valuable these clothes are to me now; for I don't have a kopeck to buy clothes with). But forget about it and the clothes!

Above all realize that it is *you* who are worrying me, *you* alone, and that I absolutely don't know now what to think about you. In your last letter you wrote me of difficult business trouble. Is it the cause even now of your silence? Realize, my friend, that I'm worried sick over you: are you well? Are you alive? I don't know anything. Nobody writes, nobody lets me know! Not a line from Moscow in more than a year now. I dream of you every night, I am terribly alarmed. I don't want you to die; I want to see you once more in my lifetime and embrace you, my priceless one. Reassure me, for God's sake, and if you are well, then, for Christ's sake, throw aside all your business and concerns and write me immediately, this very minute, otherwise I'll go mad. Understand, my friend, my position. If you can't send the clothes, then don't send them (if that's all that's delaying you). But I don't think that this alone has been delaying you. Reassure me, my dear, I swear my missing you has become unbearable.

I can't say anything comforting about myself. My resignation still hasn't been approved (it's already been 6 months since I applied; I can't imagine what the reason is for the delay). My health isn't getting better. The attacks come now and then and leave behind distressing after-effects. There's no money; I have literally *a few rubles* left. There's nobody to borrow from now; for the people who would always loan me money before aren't here now. Pleshcheev promised me last year 1000 silver rubles as soon as he receives his inheritance. But he still hasn't sent any money, nor is he able to say anything definite. I definitely can't get out of Siberia to go to Russia without 100 rubles (everything's figured down to the last kopeck; because when I arrive in Russia I need to have something in reserve for the first months). Now Pleshcheev has gone to Moscow and Petersburg for a 6-month leave (with his wife). He will be in Petersburg too; he will call on you too. Ask him frankly and in detail about 1) whether he can send me 1000 rubles, 2) when can he send it. Get *firm* answers from him and write me immediately with complete frankness. I don't doubt Pleshcheev's friendship. But I realize what it means to receive an inheritance: you hope to receive it in 6 months, but receive it in 6 years. I absolutely don't know where to get money for living expenses. You write to send you a story and say that you will sell it immediately and send the money. But, my friend, I will never write to order; I swore an oath. I'll go mad from that kind of work. I'm writing 2 stories now. One, a long one (the length of *The Double)* for *The Russian Messenger,* the other, 5 printed signatures, for *The Russian Word,* which is expecting a novel from me; I'll deliver it at the very end of the year. I quit work on the novel, because it by all indications will be *my* chef-d'oeuvre, and I don't want to spoil it by hurrying, and besides, information on certain points of the novel needs to be gathered in person in Russia. The story for *The Russian Messenger* will be good in the details, but as a whole will be flawed (it's long-winded and I'm crazy about brevity, which I can't manage). Perhaps it won't be bad for *The Russian Word.* I've already taken 500 rubles in advance from Katkov. There are 13 chapters (one chapter per printed signature in all) in my story (for Katkov). I'll send him on August 10th 7 chapters, completely finished and revised and will ask him for another 600 silver rubles.[1] *I know for certain that he won't give it.* But this is my last desperate attempt. Everything now depends on the Emperor's mercy: if he wishes to make me a happy man—he will allow me to come to Moscow. I'm not treating my illness with anything now. There's nothing easier to ruin completely. I want to consult with the best Moscow doctors; then I'll decide what to do.

If it's difficult to send the clothes—the hell with them, don't bother. Good-bye, my dear.

My wife sends her regards. She tries to reassure me, but is just as worried about you as I am. I embrace all of your family. I particularly send my regards to Emilia Fyodorovna. Good-bye, my priceless one, my one and only. Reassure me, calm me with even just a single line. I implore you.

Write, for God's sake, about what publication you are organizing for

---

1. Dostoevsky did not send the first chapters of *The Village of Stepanchikovo* until April 1859. The finished version has 18 chapters, not the 13 he mentions here.

next year.[2] Write in more detail.

Now I'll count on my fingers the days and hours until I receive an answer from you to this letter.

143. To Mikhail Dostoevsky
13 September 1858. Semipalatinsk

Semipalatinsk. 13 September 58.

My priceless friend Misha, so, nothing happened to you, you simply didn't write me. But you can't imagine how worried I was about you! What didn't cross my mind. For God's sake, write more often in the future. Just a few lines and 10 minutes of your time, after all. Do me this favor, don't torment me. What is always happening with your business, my priceless friend Misha! You're always *all caught up in a setback*. But, my friend, I, of course, don't know your business, but judge for yourself: isn't it time to bring something *to fruition*? You must agree, what have you labored for like an ox for so many years? People make huge millions in this line. If only you'd succeed in getting a hundred thousand. May God grant it, my priceless one; you have a family. At least you have lived on this money and raised your children. And that's already good. But I, let's assume, will never make anything all my life! I don't have children. But it's still devilishly hard to live. All of my hopes are on moving to Moscow as quickly as possible. I realize full well that everything is expensive in Moscow and Petersburg—and more expensive than it was before. But, besides the fact that it's not so cheap in Semipalatinsk either, I'm certain that I'll get double in Moscow what I get here. I'm working in the dark, I don't know anything, I could find myself a good spot as a contributor to a journal, I could get into the middle—in a word, I know what I could do. Besides that, I could meet many good people who would be able to help me. I can hardly wait for my retirement, but even if the retirement comes—there won't be any money. Pleshcheev wrote me, reassures me that he will help, but he writes that perhaps he will not send all that I had asked (1000 rubles), but half (500 rubles), and the other half later. If it's not all of it—then I'm stuck here again until spring and I'll be spending money all for nothing and will still not be treated. However, in any case I would not leave

---

2. Mikhail submitted a request on 19 June 1858 for permission to publish the political and literary journal *Time (Vremia)*.

earlier than January, because I haven't yet finished my literary obligations for *The Russian Messenger* and Kushelev, and am still far from finished! All of this worries me unbearably. Oh, my dear, if I could tell you everything in person and in detail, you can't say anything in a letter. You write about the Contemporaries' proposal.[1] But I can't decide about their proposal. Probably only as a last resort. I swear to you that I don't bear them any malice, although those people behaved maliciously and ignobly towards me. Now they feel sorry for me; I thank them for this with all my heart. But I don't want them too to think badly about me now: they just promise some money and I come running. Perhaps this is ugly pride—but it exists. And therefore it's better that I wait a bit and only in an extreme— in an extreme case will I enter into financial dealings with them. It goes without saying that you should not pass on to them these thoughts of mine. It's not good, after all, to repay their kind feelings with ones that are if not malicious, then at least somewhat offensive to them. I'm saying this only to you. I'll borrow from Pleshcheev without shame. I know that if I had it and he didn't, I would give him everything. Moreover: I'll earn it back for him. And even if I had no hope of earning it— I'd take it anyway. He's a person à parti, and besides, we're comrades in the same misfortune. I also borrow from you, but my heart aches when I borrow from you. And I'm continually borrowing from you. I realize that you need every kopeck. But I on my part firmly intend to pay you back. Your newspaper, about which you wrote me, is a very nice thing. I had in mind long ago the idea of a similar publication, but only a purely literary newspaper. Mainly: a literary feuilleton, analyses of the journals, analyses of what's good and what's mistaken, an enmity towards *nepotism*, which is so widespread now, more energy, passion, wit, staunchness—that's what is needed now! I'm saying this so passionately now because I have several literary pieces in this manner jotted down and outlined: e.g., *about contemporary poets, about the statistical movement in literature*, about the futility of *directions* in art—essays that are written provocatively and even sharply, but mainly, with a light touch. But a question: are you really going to publish a newspaper? Isn't it a difficult thing to do with the factory? Watch out, brother. A second thing: I will never live in Petersburg, and therefore it will be hard for me to help you! But it goes without saying that I will help you— but only if you wish it.

My illness isn't abating, but is intensifying. Last month there were four attacks, which has never happened before—and I did almost no work. After the attacks I am for a while in despair and depression and completely undone. I can't finish soon either for Kushelev or for Katkov. I very much

1. *The Contemporary* had offered to send Dostoevsky money in advance for anything he might want to contribute. The journal was a "last resort" because it had published Belinsky's unflattering review of Dostoevsky's work since *Poor Folk* as well as the poem, "Belinsky's Message to Dostoevsky," penned by Nekrasov and Turgenev.

dislike the long story I'm writing for Katkov, it's become loathsome! But a lot is already written, I shouldn't quit so as to start another one, and the debt must be paid. And I'm going to be writing for money my whole life long! Even if I had a great talent, even it would perish in this depression. My friend, I kiss you 1000 times and your children too, and I kiss Emilia Fyodorovna's hand.

I'm enclosing a letter for Pleshcheev. He wrote me himelf that it's better through you and therefore give it to him or forward it immediately.

NB. My friend, I'm enclosing another letter for Count Kushelev. He wrote me a polite letter himself a month ago, and though he claimed that he didn't wish to hurry me, it's understandable that he needs the piece. And therefore give him the enclosed letter. I'm answering him in his manner. Write his name next to the word *Count*, for I don't know what his name is. No matter that it will be in your hand, no matter! You can give him the letter even through Moller. Seal it. Tell Moller that I will try with all my might to finish the piece soon. Be so kind as to do everything just as I am asking.

The story for Kushelev will be full of certain comic and even considerable details, but almost implausible ones.[2] What can I do, I would be glad if it were better, but all the *ideas* I have for novels are larger in scope and for this length there's no other story but this one. And I won't have time to write a large-scale one. Good-bye, my dear. If you write Varenka, send her my regards.

Kiss Kolya for me. I want to write Varenka, Verochka, and without fail, Andryusha. My wife sends you all her regards. I'm very glad that Pleshcheev's wife is pretty, very glad. Beauty doesn't hurt at all.

144. To Yevgeny Yakushkin
12 December 1858. Semipalatinsk

Semipalatinsk, 12 December 58.

It's been a long time since I've written you anything, most kind and noble Yevgeny Ivanovich, and I consider that unpardonable on my part. You have continually expressed your concern to me so nobly and simply that I can never forget you and very much fear that you will call me a person without a heart and memory. But I assure you that this will be

2. *Uncle's Dream.*

unjust. If it's been such a long time since I wrote you, that isn't due to inattentiveness or forgetfulness. I've been planning to write you for three months now and haven't for various reasons, among them the fact that I would like to write you something definite about myself. I'm expecting the resolution of my fate any day and hour and can hardly wait for it. You won't believe how sickening this is, Yevgeny Ivanovich.

Now in a few days it will soon be a year since I submitted my resignation, mentioning in my request (as directed by the form) that I will have my residence in Moscow. My resignation was sent, and there has still not been a word about it. I don't know what's holding it up. I requested my retirement due to illness (falling sickness). The retirement will be announced some day, but will there be obstacles to going to Moscow: that is the question. My brother and others who are taking an active interest in me assure me that there can't be any doubt. I don't know, but my situation is most unpleasant. I can't even undertake anything definite in many things which are of particular interest to me, because I don't know what's ahead and how to reckon. I'm living in Semipalatinsk, with which I'm sick to death; life in it torments me painfully. I can't explain everything to you for lack of space. Can you imagine that even the very pursuit of literature has become not a respite, not a relief for me, but a torment. That is the worst thing of all. My surroundings and painful situation are to blame for everything. I don't read the journals, and it's now half a year since I've touched even newspapers. Assuming that I would soon leave for Russia, I didn't subscribe, and there's nobody to borrow from, because I don't want to owe certain people anything. And I assure you, this is not pride or bitterness on my part. And so—one can't tell everything.

Katkov wrote me a letter and in accordance with my request sent me an advance of 500 silver rubles. I promised him a novel, set to work on it with enthusiasm, but quit, for I want to write it well, but I'm lacking certain information which I need to find out for myself, in person, in Russia. I don't want to write haphazardly. And therefore, having put aside my long novel, I started another. I forced myself to start working on it, but then I soon got carried away and was writing with pleasure. But it's turning out too long—12 signatures. Having finished 2/3, I gave it up for the following reason. Since I constantly need money and a lot of it (particularly in connection with my marriage), since I had gone completely into debt (not so now), my brother entered in Petersburg into agreements with the future editorial board of the future journal *The Russian Word*—it will come out in 1859, concluded a contract in my name, took an advance of 500 rubles (100 rubles per signature) and sent me the money. I couldn't refuse the money and approved all the terms, thinking I would finish everything by New Year's. But after not finishing a piece by September for *Katkov*, I came to my senses and set to work on the story for *The Russian Word*, and am now writing it very quickly, I'm almost completely finished. I'm sending it off in a few days.[1] I'll start the one for Katkov immediately upon sending off the one for *The Russian Word*, and in a short time will send half—so that he can see that I'm working. But don't think that Katkov is hurrying me. On the contrary, he wrote me a most decent letter in which he asked me not to feel burdened by the debt and not to force myself. That's why I just want to finish soon. I'm very guilty before him, having taken on the committment for *The Russian Word*, when I was obliged to finish the piece for him first. I'm not even going to mention how much time my sickness (falling) has taken from me, but mainly, my spirits. In addition, there have been other circumstances as well. There you are, most kind Yevgeny Ivanovich, a short story about me. I repeat, you have become so close to me through your deeds on my behalf that I can no longer be silent with you and not tell you *all my things* frankly. However, there's *much* that I still haven't written you.

Good-bye, most kind Yevgeny Ivanovich, don't forget me, and I will always remember you. Perhaps we shall soon see each other.

Yours truly, Fyodor Dostoevsky.

I'm writing to the former address and don't know whether it will reach you.

145. To Mikhail Dostoevsky
13 December 1858. Semipalatinsk

Semipalatinsk. 13 December 58.

I want to write something to you, too, my dear brother. Why do you keep on being silent? I wait impatiently for a letter from you. And what are your letters like? A few lines. And in my backwoods receiving a letter, for the lack of anything else, is complete happiness for me. Now Pleshcheev always answers my letters immediately. You say, my dear friend, that you have business and worries. That's very true. But after all, a letter takes all of five minutes, no more. How can you not find five minutes a month? I don't understand. However, this point has been an issue between us for a long

---

1. *Uncle's Dream* was received by the editorial board of *The Russian Word* not later than January 1859 (Pleshcheev gives Dostoevsky his opinion of the work in his letter of 10 February) and was published in the March issue.

time now. I know, my dear, that you love me very much, more, perhaps, than I deserve. But nevertheless you're stingy with letters, very stingy. But forget it.

I informed you in October that I would definitely send you a story on November 8th. But now it's already December, and my story isn't finished. Many reasons interfered. My ill health and bad mood and the provincial torpor, but mainly, my disgust with the story. I don't like it and I'm sad that I'm forced to make such a poor appearance in public again. The saddest of all is that I'm *forced* again to appear before the public in such a poor light. I have in mind (and partly on paper) things that I value very much and which really would immediately make a name for me. But what can be done. It's my long novel which I, for various reasons, can't write here, and besides which, I don't want to write to order. I want to leave after me at least one irreproachable work. But what can be done? You can't write what you want to, but you have to write about what, if you didn't need money, you wouldn't want even to think about. I am obliged to *purposely invent* stories to get money. And that's so hard! The vile trade of the poor writer. My story has stretched out to six signatures and, it seems, I'll send it to you soon.[1]

My friend, I asked you about money from the editorial board of *The Russian Word* (1000 rubles); you could at least inform me whether this is possible.[2] You won't believe how I tremble at the thought that this hope will burst. Then I will definitely have nothing to get out of here with. And 1000 rubles will just barely be enough for the move; I'll arrive in Moscow without a cent. (But it's better to be without a cent in Moscow than to waste energy and use up all my money to get by in Semipalatinsk.) Upon receiving my story, no matter what, see what you can do about this loan. Say that I will be their permanent contributor and they can depend on me, since I fulfilled the first contract. Without this money I'm done for. But, the main thing is that it must be sent to me as soon as possible upon receipt of my story. By that time my retirement will come through and I don't want to spend one extra day in Semipalatinsk. Realize, brother, how I need all this and, for God's sake, act accordingly. For God's sake, show yourself to be a brother, kind, as you were and are in fact. My request for retirement was sent in a year ago now and still—no decision. But now I think they will soon be done; if you, brother, could ask and inform me about this! How grateful I would be to you! But I don't dare to even ask.

I have another request of you, one that is very important to me, but may seem funny to you. I asked you for clothes and linen a long time ago. The time is approaching, but I don't have them. Of course I'm embarrassed

1. *Uncle's Dream.*

2. Dostoevsky had asked Mikhail to appeal to *The Russian Word* for an advance of 1000 rubles for a future, unspecified work, because the advance for *Uncle's Dream*, received in 1857, had long been spent.

to ask you to buy everything on credit, when I am receiving money (but all of my money went on debts, housekeeping expenses and flows out like water); I've decided now that I'll somehow have the frock coat and trousers made myself—as far as the linen goes I don't know anything either, and I don't have any civilian linen. One can't go around in Moscow like a ragamuffin, although I don't at all want to be a dandy. But here's what I earnestly ask of you: send me two waistcoats, which you can even buy ready-made. I'll wear out a frock coat, for example, even before I arrive in Moscow, I'll still have to get a new one made in Moscow. But one can wear waistcoats for three years, it's expensive to get them made here and they'll do a dreadful job of sewing, consequently I'd have to throw them away in Moscow, and I want to economize and not throw them away. And therefore send me two waistcoats, rather good ones, and send them, if you can, immediately upon receiving this letter. Deduct the money for them for yourself when you receive the 1000 rubles from Kushelev. In any case there will be money, because my story is 6 signatures long, consequently, in any event I'll pay you.

I don't dare ask for shirts; but if you sent me 3 shirts (no more) and, moreover, decent ones—what a favor you would do me! Deduct the money.

Good-bye, my friend, I heartily embrace you. My life is difficult and bitter. I'm not writing you a word about it. Perhaps we shall soon see each other.

Good-bye! Kiss the children and Emilia Fyodorovna's hand. I love you all boundlessly.

Your F. Dostoev

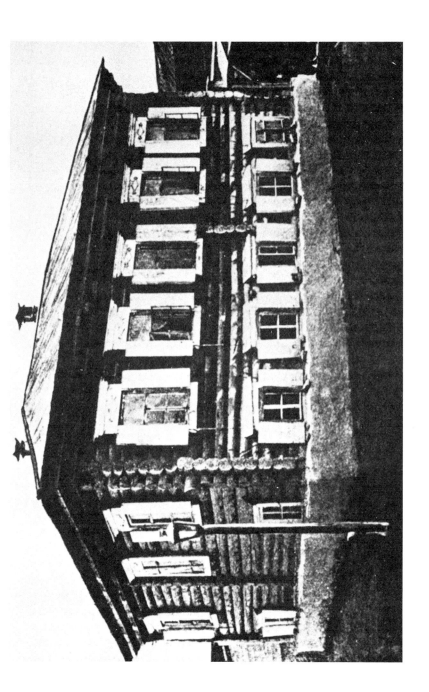

The house in Semipalatinsk in which Dostoevsky and his wife rented rooms in the first years of their marriage.

1859

146. To Mikhail Dostoevsky
14 March 1859. Semipalatinsk

Semipalatinsk. 14 March 59.

My dear friend Misha, I hasten to answer you; I have only an hour's time, and I need to write you and reply to Pleshcheev, or else I'll be late for the post. First, I thank you, my dear friend, for all the trouble you have taken about my business with Kushelev.[1] That is all very good. But I fear that you didn't insist, didn't say that I need the money right now and not later. Otherwise, very likely, he'll drag it out God knows how long. The mail from Russia comes on Monday (it's Saturday today) and if I don't receive it on Monday, then things will be unbelievably bad. My situation, with regard to money, is now horribly strained. Oh, my friend, perhaps my retirement is near, but I have big worries. Now, of course, I'm not worried about the money. They'll send it: but will 1000 be enough for the move, for the journey and for everything? I've calculated it and it won't be enough. Out of this thousand I must pay 350 silver rubles as soon as I get it, within two hours, the remaining 650 is for everything, and mainly, for life here, which owing to the delay in the retirement, will take a lot of money, because we now will have to leave, perhaps, in August, and before I had figured on leaving in April. The main thing is that you don't know all my expenses! But what of it! Just so they send the money! I thank you again.

You write that Kushelev wants to publish *Uncle's Dream* in March.[2] That's very good. The sooner, the better. But, for God's sake, find out precisely and in detail, if you can, whether Kushelev and the entire editorial board liked it. This is extremely important for me, my friend. 2) Can it really be that I won't be sent *The Russian Word*? I was published and can't read my own piece in print! I already wrote you to ask them to send it to me. You may have forgotten. Ask now. There will still be time to send it. I suggest that they charge it to my account and add it to the 1000. I'll pay. Otherwise, just imagine, I won't know anything about the journal that is publishing my story. That's impossible. Send it, for God's sake, and

---

1. Thanks to Mikhail's efforts, Kushelev, the publisher of *The Russian Word*, had promised to send Dostoevsky an advance.

2. *Uncle's Dream* was published in the March 1859 issue of *The Russian Word*.

quickly. I'm curious to know if the censor threw anything out.[3] You write about *Poor Folk,* my dear. Could you really not have written that a copy of it now costs 15 rubles. This flatters my vanity and might have comforted me a great deal earlier. It's excusable, brother! If it's so expensive now, then, of course, it wouldn't be bad to sell it now, when it's so expensive. How well Kushelev would do to publish it with illustrations! That would be very good.

Pleshcheev is half dissatisfied with my story. Perhaps he's right.

I now have big worries and cares. Here's what the problem is: you write that it will be bad if Katkov reads *Uncle's Dream* before receiving my story for *The Russian Messenger.* But that's precisely what will happen, my friend! My story can't be published by them before autumn.[4] It's too long (about 12 signatures and even more). I'm polishing it and don't want to hurry. There will be a lot of shortcomings in it, I know that myself, and I don't like it too much, but some things in it will really be good. And therefore I don't want to hurry. After I sent the story to Kushelev I immediately informed Katkov myself, with complete frankness, telling him that, owing to my poverty I couldn't refuse the 500 rubles sent in advance and set to work on the piece for Kushelev, having too much confidence in my energy, i.e., thinking I could finish both things by the deadline. But that my illness and my wish to do a good job forced me to tarry. Let Katkov be angry (he seems to be angry, because he hasn't answered). On the other hand, I'm working conscientiously for him, and perhaps I'll give him a good piece. That's better than hurrying and making a fool of oneself. I cranked out *Uncle's Dream* in a hurry. But good-bye, my dear friend, there's still a lot that I need to write you, but for the next post, after receiving Kushelev's money. Good-bye. I embrace you and all your family. My wife sends her regards.

Your F. Dostoevsky.

I myself dream, my dear friend, about our seeing each other and I dream of this often. Then we'll really have a talk, and there's a lot that needs to be said. It thrills my soul. NB. I'm writing for Katkov day and night. Good-bye.

If Pleshcheev is in Moscow, send him my letter at once.

3. There is no information available about censorship problems with *Uncle's Dream.*

4. Dostoevsky was writing *The Village of Stepanchikovo* for *The Russian Messenger.*

147. To Mikhail Dostoevsky
11 April 1859. Semipalatinsk

Semipalatinsk, 11 April 1859.

My dear brother Misha, I'm writing you just a couple words. There's no time. I'm sending *Katkov three fourths* of my novel with this post.[1] I still haven't managed to finish it all. I worked almost all night; got up late, there's no time at all, the post is leaving. It's already two weeks since I received the 1000 rubles from Kushelev together with a letter of praise. I haven't informed you until now, because I was expecting a letter from you the whole time and wanted to answer everything all together at once. Your beautiful soul can be seen in your happiness that many people like my story. But you write on *March 6th* and don't mention that my story has already been published. Isn't *The Russian Word* published on the first of the month?[2] For God's sake, send me *The Russian Word,* or at least the issue in which my story is printed. Ask Kushelev, tell him that it should be charged to my account. Arrange it somehow, for God's sake.

Thank you for the promise to send me the linen and waistcoats. I had hoped that you would send them out of Kushelev's thousand. Now we won't be able to will square up until after my arrival in Tver.[3]

My friend, only 600 rubles are left out of that thousand. With this I have to leave and live until the departure; but that's impossible and it won't be enough. I'm writing Katkov to send me another 200 rubles and that I'll wait for a reply from him until June 15th. But after that I won't be able to wait any longer, I'll leave. I also wrote him about the 100 rubles per signature. What will his answer be? He's angry with me and didn't answer my last letter. How difficult these dealings are, brother, by correspondence and not in person!

I consider the novel that I'm sending to Katkov to be incomparably superior to *Uncle's Dream.* There are two serious characters there and they are even new, without precedent anywhere.[4] But how will I still finish the novel? I'm terribly fed up with it, it's even exhausted me (literally). It will appear, I hope, in *The Russian Messenger* in August or September.[5]

---

1. The novel is *The Village of Stepanchikovo and Its Inhabitants.*

2. The third issue of *The Russian Word,* in which *Uncle's Dream* was published, passed the censor on 13 March 1859.

3. Dostoevsky was informed in December 1858 that he would not be permitted to live in either Petersburg or Moscow.

4. The characters Foma Opiskin and Rostanev in *The Village of Stepanchikovo and Its Inhabitants.*

5. Relations between Dostoevsky and Katkov were broken off when Katkov did not reply to Dostoevsky's request for an increased royalty. *The Village of Stepanchikovo* was finally published in *Notes of the Fatherland* (1859).

I'm expecting a letter from you soon. I'm certain that you will write me about everything, that is, about the literary opinions that greet *Uncle's Dream*. Please, write me in great detail! I beg you.

You don't write anything about Pleshcheev. Has he left for Moscow? Zavyalov visited us often. He's a good and gentle fellow. I like him very much.

You write about Tver and say that I have to live there for 2 years. But, my friend, that's horrible. I am hoping, on the contrary, to immediately obtain permission to live in Moscow. I'll begin requesting it on my arrival in Tver, of course. I was refused, after all, not by Imperial decree, but simply the Inspector's Department *precisely* and *clearly* wrote to them here that it (the Inspector's Department) *is not taking upon itself* to decide this question *without knowing* whether I am permitted to live in Moscow and advises that I apply for permission to the Sovereign Emperor through the Third Section. There's yet another hope: on September 8th the Heir to the Throne comes of age.[6] On the coming of age of the now-reigning Emperor enormous favors were shown to political prisoners.[7] I am certain that our Sovereign, on this present celebration as well, will remember us unfortunate ones and will pardon everything else. I reckon that it's imperative to request permission to live in Moscow by that time (September 8), if only I am in Tver by then.

Good-bye, my good Misha. I heartily, heartily embrace you and all of yours. My wife sends her regards to you. Tomorrow is Easter: Christ is risen! My health is the same as before.

Your F. Dostoevsky.

See what you can do for my Pasha.

148. To Mikhail Dostoevsky
9 May 1859. Semipalatinsk

Semipalatinsk. 9 May 1859.

My dear friend Misha, I finally received your letter of April 8th with the last post and was extremely saddened and frightened by your illness.

---

6. The coming of age of Alexander II's son, Nikolay, was celebrated on 8 September 1859.

7. Some of the Decembrists received commutations of their sentences in 1834 when Alexander II came of age.

My fear has still not passed. I understand very well that such attacks can have a most dangerous outcome and if I don't receive new letters from you about your complete recovery, I'll be beside myself the whole time. I'm leaving, God willing, on June 15th, but not earlier, and maybe much later.[1] I already wrote you that my retirement was approved in Petersburg, by Imperial decree, March 18th, but it's only just been received here and I must wait at least until the beginning of June before all the formalities in the corps are over and I am completely discharged. But if I leave June 15th, then I will probably not receive a reply from you to *this* letter of mine, all the more so as the post is now much slower because of the rivers' spring flooding. But nevertheless, if you really love me, answer this letter immediately (and in more detail about your health) and address it directly to Semipalatinsk. I have to stay in Omsk two or three weeks in connection with taking Pasha out of the academy, and they'll forward your letter to me from Semipalatinsk. (NB. Don't address it to Omsk, but address it to Semipalatinsk.)

My friend Misha, I so strongly imagined that you would die suddenly and that I would never see you, that fear still lies heavy on my heart. Oh, to receive a letter from you soon—even if only 4 lines!

I thank you, my friend, very much for sending the waistcoats, shirts, etc. But I haven't received anything yet. I see by your letter that you sent all this in the middle of March. Your letter, dated April 9, arrived a week ago already, but the package from the middle of March is still somewhere en route. I don't understand any of this.

I informed you that I received the money from Kushelev. But I haven't received the journal from him. Perhaps I'll still receive it: he informed me that he'd send me a bill. Perhaps together with the journal.

My friend Misha, I ask you to fulfill my request, write me frankly everything you hear about my novel, that is, how it is spoken of, if anyone has in fact spoken of it. Realize that this is of extreme interest to me.

I wrote Kushelev with the last post. I had to inform him about receiving the money. I asked him myself for the journal. As far as taking part in his journal (he wrote me in his letter that he would be waiting impatiently for my next story)—I wrote him that I wished first of all to see him and talk things over with him in person. I explained to him that I have in mind a long novel, of about 25 signatures, that I would very much like to begin writing it immediately (and only it), but that owing to certain circumstances I am completely unable to begin this work and *that I would like to talk with him in person about these very circumstances.* I concluded my letter to Kushelev with this, without any explanations, but I'll explain to you what these circumstances are. 1st) I need 1 1/2 years in order for me to sit down and write this novel. 2) In order to spend 1 1/2 years writing it, I

---

1. Dostoevsky did not leave Semipalatinsk until 2 June 1859 (see Letter 150).

need to be provided for during that time, but I have absolutely nothing. 3rd) You continually write me news such as that Goncharov, for example, got 7000 for his novel (in my opinion an abomination), and that Katkov (whom I'm asking for 100 rubles a signature) gave Turgenev 4000 rubles, that is 400 rubles a signature, for his *Nest of Gentlefolk* (I finally read it. Extremely good).[2] My friend! I know very well that I write worse than Turgenev, but not all that much worse and, finally, I hope to write something no worse at all. Why do I, with my needs, charge only 100 rubles, when Turgenev, who has 2000 souls,[3] gets 400? *I am forced* because of poverty to hurry and write for money, consequently *definitely to spoil things.* And therefore, when I see Kushelev, I plan to ask him plainly to give me a period of a year-and-a-half, 300 rubles a signature, and, in addition, in order to live while working—3000 silver rubles in advance. If he agrees, then I additionally will pledge to give him for next year (toward the beginning) a short story of 1 1/2 printed signatures. I have a lot of plots for long stories, but not for short ones. But I hope that I can somehow stumble upon inspiration by the new year and cook up a short story for Kushelev. It will perhaps seem to you that my conditions have suddenly gone from humble to arrogant; but, my friend, all of this is connected with a certain circumstance that you do not know. And since this circumstance in its turn is closely connected with your question to me about *Poor Folk*— a question to which you demand a speedy reply, I will go straight to *Poor Folk*.

You want, my friend, to sell it to Kushelev. That would be fine, but I ask that you not do it, because I have a different idea. Here it is: I'm now finishing the novel for Katkov (it came out long: about 14 or 15 signatures). 3/4 of it is already sent off. I'll send off the rest in the first part of June. Listen, Misha! This novel, of course, has great shortcomings and the main one, perhaps, is longwindedness; but what I'm just as certain of as I am of an axiom is that at the same time it has great merits and that it is my *best work.* I spent two years writing it (with a break in the middle for *Uncle's Dream).* The beginning and middle have been polished, the end was written hastily. But I put my soul, my flesh and blood into it. I don't mean to say that I've said everything I have to say in it; that would be nonsense! There will still be a lot to say. Moreover, there's little tenderness in the novel (that is, little of the passionate element, as for example in *Nest of Gentlefolk)*—but there are two enormous typical characters that I *have been creating* and *writing down* for five years, polished beyond reproach

---

2. Ivan Goncharov's *Oblomov* was published in 1859. Turgenev's royalty for *Nest of Gentlefolk* is exaggerated by Dostoevsky— he received 200 rubles a signature. Dostoevsky retained his good opinion of Turgenev's novel, and in *Diary of a Writer* Dostoevsky singles out both *Oblomov* and *Nest of Gentlefolk* for their authors' understanding of the people *(narod).*

3. Souls: serfs.

(in my opinion)—characters that are completely Russian and which until now have been poorly pointed out by Russian literature. I don't know whether Katkov will appreciate it, but if the public receives my novel coldly, then, I confess, I may fall into despair. My best hopes are founded on it and, mainly, the consolidation of my literary name. Now consider: the novel will appear this year, perhaps, in September. I think that if it's talked about, if it's praised, then I'll be able to propose to Kushelev the 300 rubles a signature, etc. He will no longer be dealing with the writer who wrote only *Uncle's Dream*. Of course, I can be very wrong about my novel and its merit, but all of my hopes are on it.[4] Now: if the novel in *The Russian Messenger* is a success and, maybe a significant one, then instead of publishing *Poor Folk* separately, a new idea has occurred to me: after arriving in Tver and, it goes without saying, with your help, my dear friend, my constant helper—to publish by January or February of the coming year a 2-volume collection of my works, in the following order: 1st volume: *Poor Folk, Netochka Nezvanova*, the first 6 chapters, polished (which everyone liked, "White Nights," "A Children's Tale" and "The Christmas Tree and the Wedding"—in all about 18 printed signatures. The *2nd volume: The Village of Stepanchikovo* (the novel for Katkov) and *Uncle's Dream*. There are 24 printed signatures in the 2nd volume.[5] (NB. Later on it will be possible to publish the polished or more accurately, the completely rewritten *The Double*[6] and so forth. This will be the 3rd volume, but this is *later on*, but now there are only 2 volumes.) An edition of 2000 copies will cost 1500 rubles, not more. It can be sold for 3 rubles. And therefore if I'll be writing my long novel for 1 1/2 years, the gradual sale of copies can support me and I'll have money. It can be done this way, too: sell the edition to Kushelev for 3 thousand or even 2 1/2; but *it goes without saying, it's quite out of the question* to enter into negotiations now; we must wait for the success of the Katkov novel. That's my hope, and that success will facilitate all of the negotiations.

NB. I'll send Katkov 15 signatures in all at 100 rubles—1,1500 rubles, I took 500 from him, and also, when I sent the 3/4 of the novel asked him for 200 rubles for the journey, in sum I've taken 700. I'll arrive in Tver without a kopeck, but I'll be getting 700 or 800 rubles from Katkov in the near future. That's quite all right. I can get by.

I'm alarmed by rumors that if Pasha is taken out of the academy, I'll have to pay 200 rubles a year for his support, 400 rubles in all, and where

---

4. Dostoevsky's hopes for *The Village of Stepanchikovo* were not realized. Both *The Russian Messenger* and *The Contemporary* turned it down, and there was little critical response when it finally appeared.

5. An edition of Dostoevsky's collected works was published in 1860.

6. A revised version of *The Double* was not published until 1866. For a complete account of the revisions see Evelyn Harden's "Introduction," *The Double: Two Versions* (Ann Arbor, 1985).

will I get it? That will strike me like a thunderbolt. I have in all 600 rubles now, and with Katkov's it will be 800, but I have to buy a carriage and so forth and travel 4000 versts, in summer, when traveling is the most expensive (they'll be harnessing 4 horses and sometimes 5), and so I only have enough money for the journey. What will I pay for Pasha with?

Good-bye, my dear, my darling, my sweet Misha, be happy and *healthy* and may I embrace you soon. Regards to your wife and kiss the children. There may still be a lot that I didn't write in my letter, but I'm hurrying terribly. I have a matter to attend to. Good-bye, my dear! Regards to Pleshcheev; why doesn't he write me? Is he by chance angry because of the request for money? That can't be!—My wife sends you her regards. Regards to everyone who remembers me. *Until we meet*, my friend.

149. To Mikhail Dostoevsky
End of June 1859. Semipalatinsk

...and so on Tuesday I'm writing you a 2nd letter in any event, whether I receive one or not.[1] But, my dear, Misha, my benefactor, this isn't the whole request yet. There's another, huge one. Hear me out about it. I'm moving from here painfully and in need; I will leave on Wednesday 31 June,[2] I don't have enough money; the expenses have crushed me. Kushelev's 1000 rubles melted away like wax; a journey of 4000 versts is difficult, unprofitable. And we still have to get Pasha out of Omsk. And therefore I've calculated (correctly) that I will have enough money for only as far as Kazan. I have no hope whatsoever that *The Russian Messenger* will send money. And therefore I beg you, my friend and brother, save me once more: immediately upon receiving this letter, the next day if possible (without waiting for a second one on Tuesday)—send 200 rubles to Kazan for me. You will definitely have time to do this, as I will be in Kazan *by no means earlier* than the first part of August, perhaps a bit earlier. You will utterly save me. If you don't send it, imagine what I will do in Kazan completely without money, living on credit in an inn with the entire family. You yourself wrote me, my dear friend, that you'll have about 150 or 200 rubles for me when I arrive, and you expected me earlier, so you'll have it by that time. Don't refuse, Misha! Upon arriving in Tver I should receive

1. The opening of the letter has not survived.
2. Dostoevsky surely means *30* June. He finally left Semipalatinsk 2 July 1859.

from *The Russian Messenger,* by even the most modest reckoning, 800 rubles (but when will I receive it?—maybe in December). Then I'll pay you back. Help me now! All my hopes are on you. Here's how to do it: immediately upon receiving *this* letter send the money to *Kazan: For F. M. Dostoevsky, retired second lieutenant, who is travelling through Kazan, poste restante, sent by so-and-so.*[3] Upon arriving in Kazan, I'll go to the post office immediately and without delay will set off straight for Tver, it's 1300 versts from Kazan to Tver by my route, that is, bypassing Moscow Province.

I'm entrusting my fate and that of my family to you, I heartily embrace you and ask you once again to save me, as you have already saved me several times.

Now in a few words I'll finish writing the rest of what I wanted to write. (The rest until Tuesday.)

1st, I inform you that I will arrive in Tver around August 15th.

2nd, that I'm not entirely well now and am swamped with horrible worries in connection with the departure.

3rd, that with tears I dream of our seeing each other, and 10 times a day pray to God to protect you. If you die, I will die, and besides, I don't want to live after you.

4) Inform our sisters that I'm coming.

5) If it's necessary and if you're well, go to Moscow yourself to see about my novel or entrust somebody else with this. Or better leave it until my arrival. We'll decide everything in Tver. But forward the letter and manuscript to them immediately, and urgently demand an answer. I'll write them that I authorize you to take care of everything.[4]

6) Don't read the end of the novel and give me your word on this. 1st, you won't understand anything, everything will seem nonsense and strange, and 2nd, I would very much like you to read all of it, in order and to give me an answer, otherwise the impression will be completely ruined.

7) Pleshcheev hasn't written me for a long time.

8) I didn't receive *Le Nord,*[5] but perhaps I'll receive it on Monday.

9) I rely on God and on our Tsar, benefactor to us and all of Russia. He is merciful and will permit me to go to Moscow. I shall ask him. May God allow him to reign another 60 years!

10)Italia[m]! Italia[m]![6] I heartily embrace you! I thank you for everything. I pray to God that he protect you. I kiss you. And all of yours.

---

3. Mikhail sent the requested sum on 28 July.

4. Enclosed with Dostoevsky's letter were the ending of *The Village of Stepanchikovo* and a letter for *The Russian Messenger.*

5. The Brussels newspaper *Le Nord* published a short notice about Dostoevsky's *Uncle's Dream* on 29 April 1859.

6. A quotation from Virgil's *Aeneid* (Book III). The expression, according to the editors of the Academy edition, was used in the sense of "in conclusion," "finally."

My wife sends her regards.

Your Dostoevsky.

I received everything—the waistcoats, shirts, photographs—thank you very much.

150. To Mikhail Dostoevsky
1 July 1859. Semipalatinsk

Semipalatinsk, July 1st, 59.

My dear, darling Misha, here's the promised letter for you with an enclosure of letters for the proper persons. The mail didn't bring me anything.[1] Read all of these letters carefully. I pretend not to know the names of the present editors. I think, my priceless friend, that you will not censure me for this trick. But after all they've treated me in quite ungentlemanly fashion. What else can I do! One musn't forget oneself. I figure that you will have this letter at the end of July, and that they will already have it in their hands by August 1st. Send it by the post. I'll arrive in Tver toward the middle of August (perhaps a little earlier) and then there may already be an answer. If there isn't, if they act haughtily and seal themselves off in their Olympian calm, in stupid, ungentlemanly vulgar silence, then when you come to Tver it would be good, dear friend, if you made a trip to Moscow yourself to find out definitely what's the matter and, if possible, to call them swine. It goes without saying that all of the costs will be at my expense. Even with their rate per signature I can count on 700-800 rubles. But when I'll get it—nobody knows.

When you send the letter, novel and comments (all together) write them 6 lines or so that you are authorized to act, are expecting a speedy

1. Dostoevsky was waiting for Katkov's reply to his request for 200 rubles. The cause for the delay is partially explained by a letter written by D. Boputsky, who worked on the staff of *The Russian Messenger:* "Dear Fyodor Mikhailovich, On the instructions of the editorial board of *The Russian Messenger* I have the honor to inform you that 3/4 of your novel, *The Village of Stepanchikovo,* was received by the editorial board at the moment of Mikhail Nikiforovich's departure for abroad, where he has gone for his health. From abroad he sent orders about sending you the 200 rubles you had requested. But the editorial board will not take it upon itself until we receive from you the correct address of your present residence, since you will be in Semipalatinsk only until June 15th."

reply from them, etc., however, the most polite lines, I ask you, and give your address. If, dear friend, you for any important reason censure my action, if moreover, you have any news, then don't send the letter. It's all up to your discretion. But send only the conclusion of the novel with a letter in which you state all of my *comments,* after having softened them and discarding the unnecessary. However, I don't understand what the reason would be to stop you. I would very much like to end all dealings with them. I apologized so to those peasants in my 2 previous letters that now I'm annoyed! The ass! He thinks he's Jupiter.[2] It makes me sick to be a contributor for them. Can it really be that my proposals even now are highly dishonest and indelicate?

I foresee 3 situations. 1) That they, owing to their exorbitant pride, turn down the novel. Then I will have to get some money right away and repay them. My darling, my dear. If it were possible not to borrow from Nekrasov, but get 500 rubles for only just a few days, repay them, and then go and sell to Nekrasov. But if it's impossible to get the money, then go to Nekrasov yourself, talk with him in person, tell him the whole story frankly, give him my regards and offer the novel on the condition that for approximately half, that is, for 7 signatures, the money be paid in advance, at 125 rubles per signatures. As he already offered me through Pleshcheev. Give him a receipt signed in your name. Add that since I still owed him (Nekrasov) 165 rubles in '49, I'm prepared to pay this at the final accounting. It should be published this year and, if possible, in two installments. If you repay the 500 rubles to *The Russian Messenger,* then go yourself, of course at my expense. Don't refuse, my dear friend.

2nd situation.) Apologies, reservations, some circumstance I don't know about and agreement to all of my conditions. That could happen: the novel is good and if they've read it, perhaps they won't want to let it slip by. In such a case you could hint about an advance, one as large as possible. They have the manuscript, and the censor won't strike out even two words. I vouch for that.[3]

3rd situation.) They answer politely, coldly and *vaguely* that since this is a matter more for Mikhail Nikiforovich Katkov, they can't even decide it without him. Consequently, they have to either wait for him or send to him for an answer. But this will be only a dodge and petty revenge—to drag the business out. And after all, what kind of editorial board is it that doesn't know how to carry on business? In such a case there's nothing to be done, but they must be informed that I'm not relinquishing any of my conditions and that if they drag things out until next year I will reprint the novel separately. And if they give me 100, then I will complain to both the public

2. Mikhail Katkov, the editor of *The Russian Messenger.*

3. Ivan Goncharov was the censor for *The Village of Stepanchikovo* when it was published in *Notes of the Fatherland.* According to Mikhail's letter (dated 23 November 1859) to his brother, Goncharov struck only one word from the first part.

and the court simultaneously. I'm right and clean; they will be very embarrassed. However, in the last case, in case of difficulties, wait for my arrival. But send the letter, novel and comments just as soon as you can.

Forgive the trouble I'm giving you. But after all, you are my guardian angel! Save me now, too. I hope to find the money from you in *Kazan*. My brother, if it's not there, I'm ruined.

I leave tomorrow. Today my head is spinning and I have a stomach ache on top of it. Forgive the business-like nature of this letter. I heartily embrace you. Finally, perhaps, we will see each other, my dear.

Until we meet!

F. Dostoevsky.

I leave tomorrow at 5 in the afternoon.

151. To Mikhail Dostoevsky
24 August 1859. Tver

Tver. Monday. 24 August 59.

Here's yet another letter to you, Misha, my dear friend, and it's all about my affairs. 1st, did you receive, my dear, the letter that I sent you in answer to your first letter?[1] I received your second letter (on the octavo) the day before yesterday, and since yesterday was Sunday, I couldn't answer you the following day, but am answering today, on the third day. All that you advise me is very fine. I have proceeded almost precisely that way; but what it cost me to find an apartment, what trouble! I have all of 20 rubles cash and the unsold carriage in which I arrived. They offered 30 rubles for it, but it cost me 115. That hurts. I'm looking for buyers who will pay at least 40. But when will they turn up? You advise me not to buy even cups. Cups, fine; but I definitely have to buy a samovar. There's an expense. Moreover, my boots and shoes are in bad shape. In a word, we're lodged as though on the head of a pin. But it doesn't really matter. Everything will work out, God will provide. How's your health, my dear? The weather has changed now, rain, and it will be even harder for you to come see me. Don't risk your health at all, though God knows how I wish to embrace you. I

1. Dostoevsky arrived in Tver on August 18th or 19th and sent Mikhail a telegram on arrival. His first letter from Tver has not survived.

miss you. Tver is the most hateful city on earth. I hope, however, that this letter will still find you in Petersburg.[2]

Now here's how things stand: yesterday I received 2 letters. The first from Milyukov, with the article in *Le Nord*. It had been sent to Semipalatinsk, dated June 5th, and in accordance with the instructions I gave when leaving Semipalatinsk, it was forwarded to me in Tver. Thus I received it only yesterday. I ask you, my dear, to write me what Milyukov's name and patronymic are; I've forgotten. I very much want to answer him as soon as possible. *The second letter,* which I also received yesterday and also by way of Semipalatinsk, was a letter from the editorial board of *The Russian Messenger.* How do you like that! It was sent from Moscow on June 15th. The point of my letter to the *Messenger* which I sent through you, with its reproaches and conditions—thus disappears, but not entirely. Here's what they write. It's written by a factotum of theirs, an editorial assistant or something like that (I can't make out the signature to the letter at all), but it's not Kapustin or Leontiev (whom Katkov left in charge as editors). This gentleman writes me that he "is informing me (1st) on the instructions of the editorial board of *The Russian Messenger* that 3/4 of my novel has been received." Oh, a fine time to be informing me. I wrote clearly that I was leaving for Tver on the 15th. But they didn't mail this letter until the 15th. Next: that "my manuscript was received at the editorial office at the moment of Katkov's departure for abroad, so that he sent this order when he was already abroad" (but not an answer to the letter). All of this is untrue. From information from Pleshcheev it's clear that he received my letter and manuscript not at the moment of departure, but several days beforehand. *Next:* Katkov gave instructions that I be sent 200 rubles, but the editorial board, he says, is afraid to do so, because, since I myself wrote that I was leaving Semipalatinsk on June 15th, consequently the money wouldn't reach me in Semipalatinsk and therefore they ask me to send my correct address. 1st, they were written clearly that I was leaving for Tver and nowhere else;—and that's the address; 2nd, why the devil did they send me the letter when they knew definitely that it wouldn't reach me in Semipalatinsk? What sort of strange instructions are these? But the letter, by the way, is one I need.

Then they ask me to send the novel's conclusion—but that's all.

Now what can one conclude from this letter? 1st, Katkov doesn't answer himself (this is in response to my 2nd letter already). Well, let's assume that such public figures don't have time to answer such small fry as I. Away with politeness! But I, it seems, asked to be clearly informed as to how much he will give me per signature and whether he will give 100. Let's assume that I owe him money, but it doesn't follow from that that Katkov, as a creditor, receives as well the right to be the sole and unchecked appraiser. It's business after all, how can he not answer? It's both improper and discourteous! Now, after receiving the letter and manuscript from you they don't even want to inform you that they received the manuscript. The boors! Let's assume that I apologize for my letter and am the first to do so. In a word, I do everything that a decent person can; but what will they say? Finally, Muscovites are all so petty, ticklish and irritable. They may still say that my letter (with the reproaches) has to be sent to Katkov and that nothing can be decided otherwise. The devil only knows what's going on! I would like to answer them, but I don't know what; it's impossible now to ask them to send the 200 rubles to Tver. 1st, having become angered by that letter, they may say that now, after such a letter, without Katkov's permission—it's impossible. Consequently, an affront. 2nd, there's no answer: do they agree to the 100 rubles and the conditions? But they can't publish it without that. And therefore I'm venturing not to answer, but to write them today just the following: that I received their letter. That the answer will follow through my representative, Mikhail Mikhail[ovich] Dostoevsky, who will be in Moscow *in person* in a week or ten days *on business of his own.*

My friend! You wrote that *perhaps* you would go to Moscow for me. That's just what I was hoping for. If you go, talk things over with the editorial board *thoroughly.* But if you can't go (which is very likely), then I will just write them a letter, which you and I will compose here together. Is that all right, my dear? In general I am impatiently waiting for you. We'll decide *about everything.* But take note, my dear friend: if it will be difficult for you to go to Moscow, or impossible, then I don't at all insist on it and won't be angry. Would I do that, my dear!

Now another request and a big one. Here it is: my wife has no hat at all (we sold the hats on our departure. It didn't make sense to haul them 4000 versts!). Although my wife, seeing our poverty, doesn't even want a hat, judge for yourself: is she really to be locked in for a month, in a room? Become jaundiced and grow thin, not enjoy the fresh air? Exercise is essential for health and therefore I definitely wish to buy her a hat. There isn't anything in the local stores, there are summer hats, horrible things, but my wife wants a fall one, for everyday, and as inexpensive as possible. And so this is my most urgent request of you. Send someone or go yourself to Mme Vikhman's and if there's something ready-made, buy it, and if there isn't, order one. The hat should be gray or lilac, without any decorations or doodads, without flowers, in a word, as simple, inexpensive and elegant as possible (by no means a white one)—*an everyday one in the full sense of the word.* We'll have another good winter hat made later. But now just something to put on her head, she can't go around out bare headed, after all. If Mme Vikhman says that the hats are all summer ones, and the *fall fashions aren't in yet,* then order a fall one and let her do any fall fashion, even if it's last year's. Without decorations, inexpensive, but as elegant as possible. In Semipalatinsk there was an everyday hat for 9 rubles (i.e., 5 here), but so elegant that it was fit for a countess.

For God's sake brother, don't refuse. We'll sell the carriage—and pay back the money right away. Vikhman's has ribbons (we saw samples here from Vikhman's) with thin gray and white stripes going lengthwise. That's the sort of ribbons for the hat. It's a pity that I can't send a sample. If you can—bring the hat with you. If not—order it and when it's ready, have them send it by rail. Just so it doesn't detain you in Petersburg.

My dear! Don't be annoyed with me for my requests! My head is spinning. Good-bye! I embrace you and all of your family. My wife sends you her regards. To Kolya as well.[3] My best to Milyukov.

If my novel went to *The Contemporary,* then I'd have, after paying you 200 rubles, 1,000 silver rubles, but now at *The Messenger* there won't be more than 600 left.[4] What should I do? 600 is nothing for me. My needs are so great! We'll think together about how to get money.

And don't think that I'm playing up to you so as not to pay you the 200! I'll definitely pay! I want to so—and I'll pay!

152. To Mikhail Dostoevsky
25 August 1859. Tver

Tuesday 25 August 59. Tver.

I just received, my dear, your *couple of words* and hurry to answer you, also on the run, with a couple of words (the post is leaving; it's after 1). I wrote you yesterday and informed you about the letter from *The Russian Messenger.* The letter sent to you (and which I just had the pleasure of reading) is amazing![1] Not one clear word, they didn't accept the terms—which ones, precisely! They were all extraordinarily easy. 2) They contradict themselves on the same page: they are firmly convinced that the

---

3. Nikolay (Kolya) Dostoevsky was also planning to visit his brother in Tver, but according to a letter from Mikhail, Kolya was forced to give up the idea in order to keep his job.

4. *The Contemporary* was offering Dostoevsky 125 rubles per printed signature, while *The Russian Messenger* offered only 100.

1. In his letter of 23 August Mikhail informed his brother that he had received two letters from *The Russian Messenger.* In the first letter, addressed to Mikhail, *The Russian Messenger* stated that Dostoevsky's terms were not acceptable and that the manuscript would be returned after repayment of the 500-ruble advance. The second letter, addressed to Fyodor Dostoevsky, is not extant.

money could not reach me, then they are surprised that I did not mention anything about the letter they sent on August 13th! But how could I have received it if they are absolutely certain that there was no way I could have had time to receive the letter with the money. It's stupid! Finally: they answer and justify themselves not at all on those points about which I asked. I asked Katkov clearly, after laying out all of my circumstances (that is, moving, shortage of money and so forth)—to inform me how much he would give me for the novel, whether he would give 100 so *that I, a poor man and ruined by a journey of 4 thousand versts, could know what I could count on when I arrived in Tver.* Can it really be that this isn't an important question for me? Not a vital one, not the most essential one? Consequently, what angers me more than anything is that Katkov pointedly did not pay any attention to my request, not only did he delay his answer, ignore my most delicate requests, that is, requests made by a person in an extreme and unusual state—but even now, even from their letter (dated June 13th) that I received here, I don't know whether he agreed to 100 rubles; consequently, I don't know even now what I could have counted on. (Note that he hasn't answered two of my letters now.) His departure for abroad has in no way prevented him from saying to that same secretary just two words, just two words, that he agrees to the 100 rubles, giving instructions that I be written about this immediately.

Now they are pretending that I have become angry because they didn't send me the 200 rubles! God knows that's not true! If I had been annoyed that they didn't send anything, then not for anything would I have written such a reproachful letter, which you forwarded to them. I was simply offended by Katkov's extremely insulting behavior towards me.

Here's another new idea that I've had: either they were very angry over my letter, thought and finally decided to return the novel; or another thing: namely—they did not like the novel.

If they had liked the novel, then perhaps they would have agreed to swallow the pill, so as not to let a good thing get away. But who knows, perhaps vanity overcame all other considerations. Now here's what, my friend: I'm certain that there are lots of revolting and weak things in my novel. But I'm certain—I'd stake my life on it!—that there are wonderful things, too. They poured out of my soul. There are scenes of high comedy that Gogol would immediately have put his name to. The whole novel is extremely drawn out; I know that. The story is uninterrupted and therefore, perhaps is tiresome. And therefore, I implore you, dear Misha, don't read a single line of it when you get the novel, but when you get it— come to visit me and we'll read it here, together; and together we'll decide where to send it; I'll also correct a few things (what I wanted to correct— changing some verbs, etc.). Don't give it to Nekrasov now. However, you could gently forewarn them. Together you and I would agree on the terms as well, how much to ask them for.

True, I'm horrified that a payment of 500 has fallen upon you; but one thing comforts me: that this loan is not a long-term one. After all, the novel is worth something. I'll certainly repay it—all the money I have now is 12 rubles. Sasha's present was very timely. Kiss her for me and thank her. It's very kind on her part, all the more so as she doesn't know me at all.[2] The carriage isn't selling—there aren't any buyers. I wrote you yesterday about the hat, don't forget, my friend, for God's sake. The sample of ribbons is for decorating the hat. These ribbons are from Vikhman's in Petersburg (so a local lady store owner said). The color of the hat should be like the gray stripe on the ribbons.

Last night I worried a lot about your health and reproached myself for wanting to send you to Moscow on my business. But now, thank God, there's nothing to be done in Moscow. For God's sake, guard you health and if you feel even a bit unwell, then it's better to postpone your trip to see me. But if your health doesn't interfere, then, for God's sake, don't be hampered by either the novel, or the hat—or by anything, come as soon as you can.

I'll be at the train station late Thursday night and will meet you.

153. To Mikhail Dostoevsky
19 September 1859. Tver

Tver, 19 September 59.

I received your letter yesterday, my dear Misha, but late, and therefore I couldn't answer you right away. Your letter made me terribly happy, first, because I'm completely alone, and 2nd, because it arrived sooner than I had thought. I thought that it would come on Saturday. I'm happy for you that you are again at home and satisfied.[1] But when will we see each other? Even though I'm stuck in Tver, I'm still *continuing to wander;* someday fate will unite us again.

I went to Baranov with the letter for Dolgoruky. He promised me that he would do everything (that is, nothing more than forward the letter), but said that I was wasting my time submitting it now, that Prince Dolgoruky isn't in Petersburg now, and won't make reports when he's traveling, and therefore he advised me to postpone it until the middle of October, when the Prince returns to Petersburg. He asked me to come with the letter then.

2. Dostoevsky's sister Alexandra (Sasha), who had not yet turned 14 when Dostoevsky was arrested, gave Mikhail 100 rubles for their brother Fyodor.
1. Mikhail's letter was written upon his return from Tver and Moscow.

After thinking it over I imagine that that is right.

All the more so since if the Prince is in Petersburg in a month, he will take care of the matter quickly, especially in view of the petitions and recommendations, for example from Eduard Ivanovich.[2] So I'm even hoping to be with you by the 1st of December. And therefore we'll wait.

I read in your letter about Vrangel with extraordinary pleasure. I was so happy for him. Give him my regards, tell him that I badly want to see him and that if he comes to Tver, even for a day, he will be doing a wonderfully good thing. I'll write him in a few days.[3] I'll also write Eduard Iv[anovich] a little later.

Regards to Maykov and tell him that I don't love and remember him less, and if he comes, he will be doing a *fine* thing; even for a day; tell him that I'm waiting for him with extreme impatience.

I wrote our sisters.

You write that you didn't catch Nekrasov at home. But here's the problem, my friend: if you didn't catch him on the 16th either, then won't you be late with the manuscript? Time will run out—and they'll publish something else in the October issue. He still has to read it; but you don't write whether you left the manuscript with him. And whether you delivered the letter to him. You promise to write on the 17th, if you see Nekrasov. Of course, you'll see him and that's why I'm waiting for your letter today with extreme impatience. NB: Take note of all the details and all of his words in your dealings with Nekrasov and I implore you, for God's sake, describe all this in detail. This is all of great *interest* to me.

Kiss the fibber Kolka for me. And your kittens as well.[4] Warm regards to Emilia Fyodorovna. My wife also sends all of you her regards. There's really nothing more to add about me: I think about the future, I wonder how to begin work on the novel, I'm distressed that there are many letters to write and I tormented myself terribly over the letter to the Prince. I also ordered pants from the tailor (but you were there)—he ruined them. The weather is horrible in Tver, and the boredom is dreadful.

I think about you, my dear. Now you've left, but I know that we still haven't become acquainted with each other as we should, somehow we didn't say everything, didn't show ourselves in everything. No, brother: we must live together, not a hurried life, but an ordinary one, and then we'll get used to each other completely; you are all I have; even ten years didn't separate us. You don't write anything about your health, and mainly, what Rozenberg said to you. Please consult with him. Good-bye, my dear. I embrace you, write, for God's sake.

Your D.

<hr />

2. Dostoevsky planned to write Eduard Totleben to request assistance in receiving permission to live in Moscow.

3. Vrangel visited Tver in the fall of 1859.

4. Kolya: Nikolay Dostoevsky. Mikhail called his children "kittens."

NB. I remember you telling me to write as we said good-bye. I'm thinking over the novel that I recounted to you, and together with you feel bad about the long novel. I thought about writing it. Oh, if only there were money and security!

Don't neglect the clap. Go to see Rozenburg.

154. To Alexander Vrangel
22 September 1859. Tver

Tver 22 September 59.

My dear friend, Alexander Yegorovich, I almost didn't write you, but I couldn't restrain myself. Really, what can one write after 4 years of separation? We need, first of all, to see each other again, and I was so happy that you (according to my brother) are thinking of coming here and seeing me. Even for a day, my priceless one! What a talk we would have! And for such a gentleman, who traveled the whole planet over, to come by train from Petersburg to Tver is a trifle.[1]

My brother writes that you are planning to go on another expedition. That's bad—bad for me. I thought that now we wouldn't part, after we are united in Petersbrug. And so—you can imagine my impatience to see you—even for a couple of days, even for a few hours. After all, you and I have a lot to cover. There are a lot of wonderful memories. Although since I saw you off from your apartment, at 10 in the evening (remember?)—so much has been added to your life, surely it can't be that we won't understand each other now. We were very close back then. Come. We'll talk about the old times, when things were so good, about Siberia, which now has become dear to me after leaving it, about the Kazakov garden[2] (remember?), about *beans*[3] and other garden plants, about the most dear places—Zmeinogorsk and Barnaul, which I visited rather often after you left... well, about everything! And you'll tell me something of your subsequent life; we'll become close again and do an even better job of storing up memories. We'll have plenty of things to remember in our old age.

What are you planning now? What are you expecting and what are

---

1. Alexander Vrangel had just returned from an around-the-world voyage.

2. The dacha that Dostoevsky shared with Vrangel.

3. A nickname that both Dostoevsky and Vrangel used to refer to an unidentified Semipalatinsk acquaintance of theirs.

your hopes? How is your father and all of your family? Who has replaced X.?[4] It's a pity if X. is in Petersburg and has influence over you. But this is nonsense and I'm a fool for suspecting this:

It's not for flowers to bloom after autumn.[5]

I hope to hear all about you, in detail, from you yourself. I also hope that you'll drop me a line.

If you ask about me, then what can I tell you: I took on the worries of family life and am dragging them along. But I believe that my life hasn't ended yet and don't want to die. My illness is as before—so-so. I'd like to consult with doctors. But I won't be treated until I get to Petersburg. Why should I mess around with fools? Now I'm locked up in Tver, and that's worse than Semipalatinsk. Although recently Semipalatinsk had completely changed (not one likeable person, not one bright memory was left), Tver is a thousand times more vile. It's gloomy, cold, stone houses, no movement, no interests—not even a decent library. A veritable prison! I intend to get out of here as soon as possible. But my situation is most unusual: for a long time I've considered myself completely pardoned. Even my hereditary nobility was returned to me, by special order, two years ago already. But meanwhile, I know that without a special, formal request (to live in Petersburg) I can't enter either Petersburg or Moscow. I missed the right time; I should have asked a month ago. Now Prince Dolgoruky is absent. I have written Dolgoruky a letter. I went with it to Count Baranov (our governor) and asked him to forward it to the Prince. Baranov promised, but said—when the Prince returns, there's no point even in thinking of it earlier. The Prince will return in the middle of October; consequently until that time I have to sit tight and not undertake anything. I, of course, am almost certain that my request will be honored. There have already been examples: many of our people are in Petersburg. Moreover, the Sovereign is incomparably kind and merciful. And I have been continually well recommended. But here's what I'm afraid of: the business will be dragged out and I'll have to live in Tver. And therefore I wanted to write Eduard Ivanovich, and I shall write; I want to ask him to write or talk about me with Prince Dolgoruky; then the latter, having taken note of his intercession, will not dawdle and will curtail the formalities.[6] I also wanted to ask Eduard Ivanovich to write Baranov, so that they will not drag out the business here either. But, again, I'm in doubt: what terms is Eduard Ivanovich on with the Prince and does he know our Count? Perhaps it's difficult for him to ask something of them, and he's already done so much

4. Yekaterina Gerngross.

5. An inexact quotation from Alexey Koltsov's poem "Russian Song" (1838).

6. Eduard Ivanovich Totleben did facilitate Dostoevsky's return to Petersburg (see Letter 157).

for me as it is. I wanted to send the letter to Ed[uard] Iv[anovich] through you. (If only he were in Petersburg and you could talk with him in person! That would be better; but my brother has already written me that Ed[uard] Iv[anovich] is in Riga.) And therefore, my friend, advise me what to do. I'm relying on you and hope that you won't abandon me, particularly if Ed[uard] Iv[anovich] arrives soon. I don't know when to write. What do you think? Tell me something and I'll follow your advice completely.

Now about another matter: I have a lot of your books, which I brought from Siberia with me. 2 packets of your private correspondence and your rug. All of this has to be sent to you. I hope that you've already received several of the books, which I sent you more than two years ago (with Semyonov, a member of the Geographic Society)—namely, the works of Simashko.[7] Your books are rather good ones. Write me your arrangements concerning them.

Well, that's enough for now. It's your turn. Write me something, my dear friend, my priceless one. I was so happy when my brother wrote that you stopped by his place. I had just instructed my brother to move heaven and earth to find you in Petersburg. Marya Dmitrievna and I have thought of you so often and with such pleasure all these three years. She would very much like to see you. She is still ailing. Good-bye, I embrace you.

Your Dostoevsky.

The post office here is so rotten, careless and vile that I even wanted to insure this letter. But maybe it will get there this way. My letters are held up three days.

My brother wrote me on the 16th and suddenly stopped writing, and today's the 22nd. What's wrong with him? Is he by any chance ill? I'm waiting for a letter from him with impatience and am alarmed.

155. To Mikhail Dostoevsky
1 October 1859. Tver

Tver, 1 October 59.

My dear Misha, I received your letter yesterday after I'd sent you mine, with the reproaches. The trouble is, my friend, that I was on the verge

---

7. Yu. Simashko was the author of *The Russian Fauna* (1856-61) and *The Animal Kingdom* (1857).

of becoming completely despondent, because of not having received anything from you. And therefore I implore you—in the future even if there's nothing to write—simply write that there's nothing, and don't leave me in an anxiety that only increases the nastiness and hopelessness of my situation. I hope that you aren't angry with me for my letter. Don't be angry, dear, and write me more often.

I confess that your letter surprised me. What's with Nekrasov? They aren't boasting, are they? But perhaps he simply hasn't read it yet. I've heard that Nekrasov is gambling something dreadful. Panaev[1] doesn't care about the journal either, and if it weren't for Chernyshevsky and Dobrolyubov, everything would collapse. You say that we have to wait a bit and that this is even more tactful. But, my friend, we've already waited enough. And so, please go (I earnestly beg you) to Nekrasov yourself, try to catch him at home (that's the main thing) and speak to him in person about the fate they are preparing for my novel.[2] The main thing is to find out if they are making the novel into three or two books, what precisely are their comments about the novel, and having talked about this, towards the end you can mention money too. Do this, for Christ's sake, and drag the final word out of them. And if you don't go yourself—perhaps you'll never see him at your place, particularly if he's gambling. I'm relying on you.

Now, my dear, I want to write you about what I've decided on after mature consideration, I decided to begin writing a novel (a long one— that's already decided)—I'll write it in a year. I don't wish to hurry. It's shaped up so well that it's impossible to lay a hand on it, that is, to hurry to meet some deadline. I want to write freely. This novel has an idea and will give me a start. But I need to be provided for to write it. It's suicide to sell it in advance and live on that. That means taking 100 or 120, when I perhaps could try to get 150 or 200. I will be my own judge and if the novel succeeds—I'll set the price myself. And so I must not sell it in advance and must write while being provided for. But the question is: where to get the money to support myself for at least a year? After considering it seriously—I've firmly decided to publish my previous works and to publish them myself, and not to sell them—unless I'd be given a lot, but I won't be given a lot. Listen: let's assume that the works sell slowly. But that doesn't mean anything to me. I need 120 or 150 rubles a month. If they would just make that, consequently they will feed me. You will ask where I will get the money to publish them. Here is what I have thought up: 1st, not to publish them all at once, but book by book. Three books in all. In the 1st) *Poor Folk, Netochka Nezvanova* 2 parts, "White Nights," "A Children's Tale," "The Christmas Tree and the Wedding," "An Honest Thief" (revised),

---

1. Ivan Ivanovich Panaev (1812-62) was both an editor and contributor to *The Contemporary*.

2. *The Village of Stepanchikovo.*

"The Jealous Husband." In all—about 23 signatures of small type. 2nd part: *The Double* (completely revised[3])and *Uncle's Dream*. 3rd part: *The Village of Stepanchikovo*. I think the 1st part will sell out fairly quickly. But it needs to be revised some. *Poor Folk* will be without any changes from the 2nd edition, but the rest of the 1st part will need to be slightly revised. For this I'm going to ask you to help me, namely: get hold of all the other stories from the 1st part, some, like *Netochka Nezvanova* you may have, but search and search as soon as possible for the rest, at once, at Maykov's, Milyukov's, etc. Give them my regards and earnestly ask them whether they won't let these stories be torn out of the journals. If they will— send them to me as soon as possible, I'll correct the printed text and without delay will send them back to you. If by the end of October we polish all of that and you have all the stories, corrected, then on November 1st they could be submitted to the censor. Let's suppose that the censor keeps them until December 1st. Then beginning December 1st the 1st volume can be printed. Where to get the money from? Here's how: again a bow to you: get the necessary quantity of paper for the 1st part from a merchant and give him a promissory note from you for 6 months or even sooner. It's a matter of 300 rubles or a bit more. I swear, Misha, my dear, I will pay the note that you give now (for me). If the book doesn't sell and doesn't even pay for the paper, then I'll raise heaven and earth to get the money somehow and redeem the note by the deadline. Nothing will fall on you. As far as the printer goes, if it's impossible to use a promissory note, then I'll give half the money for the printing, and I'll borrow the other half from somebody (wouldn't it be possible from Sashenka?).

This way the printing can be finished in January, in the middle—and it can go on sale! I'm certain that the 1st volume will produce a certain effect. 1st, the best things are collected, second, I'll remind them of myself, 3rd, the *name* is interesting, 4th, if the novel in *The Contemporary* succeeds, then this will sell too. Meanwhile, by the middle of December I'll send you (or bring myself) the revised *The Double*. Believe me, brother, that this revision, provided with an introduction, will be the equivalent of a *new novel*. They will finally see what *The Double* is! I hope even to interest them too much. In a word, I'm challenging everybody to a battle (and finally, if I don't revise *The Double* now, then when will I revise it? Why should I lose a superb idea, a great type in its social importance, which I was the first to discover and of which I was the herald?).

In December—*The Double* and *Uncle's Dream* will go to the censor. We'll print it in January, and towards the end of February the 2nd volume will appear, and after it, almost at the same time, the 3rd could come too—*Stepanchikovo*. For the money—either a loan, or the 1st volume will pay

---

3. A revised version of *The Double* was not included in the 1860 edition of Dostoevsky's works.

for it. Finally, the last two volumes (depending on the success of the 1st) could even as a last resort be sold. I will pay for the edition, and until then live on the money from *The Contemporary,* and later, after the printing is paid for, even if it sells slowly, it doesn't matter to me: because even slow sales will suffice for my keep, and meanwhile, in December, I'll begin working *seriously* on my long novel (which, if it produces an effect in a year, might carry along the remaining copies of *The Collected Works* too). And therefore the 1st step: give me your opinion immediately, and as soon as possible, send me copies of the stories for the 1st volume for correction.

My friend, if you delay your answer, understand that my time will be wasted. I won't do anything (and can't do anything) until there's a definite settlement, that is, will you approve or not and will you help me? For God's sake, answer soon.

Maykov hasn't come, I received a letter from Vrangel. Golovinsky is here and acquainted me at one go with all of local society. I'm not planning to keep up too much with all of them, but it's impossible with friends. You can't hide anywhere in the provinces. This is in part a burden for me. There are two or three good people. I became well acquainted with Baranov and the Countess. She several times *most earnestly* invited me to visit them without formality in the evenings. It's impossible not to visit them. She turned out to be somewhat acquainted with me already. About 12 years ago Sollogub (she's his cousin) introduced me to her, when she was still a girl, Miss Vasilchikova.

Marya Dmitrievna sends her regards. I embrace you with all my heart and would like with all my might to get out of Tver. They'll interfere with my writing in Tver now.

For God's sake, my dear friend, answer. Good-bye, I kiss you affectionately. Regards to everybody. Guard your health like a treasure. Greetings to Emilia Fyodorovna, Kolya, Sasha. Write more often. We need Nekrasov's money. 1st, for you, and 2nd, for me.

156. To Mikhail Dostoevsky
2 October 1859. Tver

Tver, 2 October 59.

Dear brother, I'm writing you again and implore you: for God's sake, go to Nekrasov yourself, succeed in catching him at home and finish my business with him.[1] I need money, I need very much specifically the entire amount that I had counted on, that is, 500 silver rubles. After all, he promised to give 1,200 in advance for 10 printed signatures, of which 700 are immediately earmarked for you, and 500 for me. Right now I need this 500 badly. Don't refuse me, my dear friend, you who are the only one I can rely on. I'm begging you. The main thing, finally, is that you will solve my predicament.

I wrote you yesterday about the publication of my works. Attend to this idea and, for God's sake, help me. You alone can save me. A little effort on your part and everything could work out.

My situation here is difficult, awful and sad. My heart will dry up. Will my calamities ever end and will God finally grant me the possibility of embracing you all and being renewed in a new and better life!

I'm not going to write you any details of my life here. I'm writing these few words only to remind you once more about Nekrasov and to finish the business with him soon. For God's sake, do this and inform me immediately, as soon as possible. I'll be terribly anxious until then.

Good-bye, my dear friend, all my hopes are on you. Set me at ease soon.

Your F. Dostoevsky

P.S. I just received from you the letter you wrote yesterday.[2] Thank you for the news. But the trouble is that there's still no news from Nekrasov. For God's sake, don't dawdle. It's an important matter. Don't drag it out. And I need the 500 rubles very much. For God's sake, hurry. I'll write Vrangel tomorrow, Eduard Ivanovich too.[3]

You are thinking about me—thank you. You yourself know how dear you are to me. I'd love to tear myself away from everything and escape to you. Answer soon, for God's sake. You are all I have.

D.

---

1. Mikhail was Dostoevsky's intermediary with Nekrasov regarding the publication of *The Village of Stepanchikovo* in *The Contemporary*.
2. In his letter of 1 October 1859 Mikhail informed Dostoevsky that Pleshcheev had moved to Moscow.
3. See Letters 157 and 158.

157. To Eduard Totleben
4 October 1859. Tver

Dear Eduard Ivanovich,

I am once more appealing to all the indulgence and goodness of your heart. Forgive me for this new request. Ever since you did me so much good and by taking an interest in my fate gave me the opportunity to begin a new life—ever since then I have looked upon you as my deliverer in my difficult situation, which has still not come to an end. I finally have received my discharge, which, I don't know why, dragged on for a year-and-a-half. Suffering from falling sickness, I traveled with my wife and stepson 4000 versts and have settled for now in Tver. But my situation has almost not improved at all. Allow me, most noble Eduard Ivanovich, to explain to you this situation and forgive my new request, with the same kindness, with the same magnanimity as three years ago when you saved and resurrected me—which I will never forget.

When I was leaving Siberia I hoped that I would achieve the possibility, quickly and without difficulty, of living in Petersburg upon my arrival in Russia. Since I knew that I would have to ask permission for entry into Petersburg, I decided, for the time being, to stay in the city of Tver. And now I've already been here a month-and-a-half and I don't know how and when all these difficulties will end. Meanwhile, it's impossible for me not to live in Petersburg. I am ill with falling sickness; I need to be treated, seriously, radically. I have been given hope that the attacks I suffer can still be completely cured; if, however, I am not treated, I will perish. I know that such an illness as mine is a difficult illness, not only for an ordinary doctor, but even for a specialist in this area. Provincial doctors, as far as I have been able to size them up, are of two kinds: either young, just graduated from the university, or old men, people worthy of every sort of respect, but who have completely forgotten medicine. To be treated by them is to injure and torment oneself. I would like to consult with a learned medic, a specialist, in Petersburg. But apart from my illness, I have other reasons, no less important and, perhaps, even more important, which make it absolutely essential for me to live in Petersburg. I am married; I have a stepson; I must support my wife and raise my son. I do not have any fortune whatsoever. I live by my own work and hard work— literary work. I lose an extraordinary amount by dealing with the literary entrepreneurs by correspondence. I have already lost a lot of money this way. Even now I have some business, the publication of a selection of my works, which can in no way be arranged without my personal participation, and meanwhile, it could provide for me for two years or so, and with some success, for much longer, so that, perhaps, for the first time in my life I would have the opportunity, by having provided for myself, to not write to order, for money, for a deadline, but conscientiously, honestly, with care, without selling my pen for a piece of daily bread. I am not even mentioning all the other reasons—for example, my brothers from whom I have been separated for ten years. Two weeks ago I saw the local governor, Count Baranov. I set forth for him my case and asked him to give my letter to Prince Dolgoruky, the chief of the gendarmes; in my letter I ask the Prince to petition to the Sovereign on my behalf for permission to settle in Petersburg for the treatment of my illness and for all the reasons that I have just mentioned. Already many of those who were exiled in connection with our case have received permission to enter and reside in the capitals;[1] and therefore, I could hope. Count Baranov received me wonderfully and on his part promised everything; but he advised me to wait until the middle of October, because the Prince is away from Petersburg. I know that I can hope; but I also know that because of formalities the business can be dragged out for an extraordinarily long time. It will be good if they confine themselves to inquiries about my conduct in Tver, but perhaps they'll send to Siberia to ask about this. I have also heard that the Prince is exceedingly mistrustful in these matters, and therefore, perhaps, he will not venture to bring the matter before the Sovereign soon... Eduard Ivanovich! Save me once again! Use your influence, as you did three years ago. Perhaps, if you would speak about me to Prince Dolgoruky, you would persuade him to end the business quickly. All of my hopes are on you. I know that I am troubling you, and perhaps a great deal. But forgive a sick man, an unfortunate man; I am still an unfortunate man.

Accept the most sincere assurance of the most sincere respect, devotion and gratitude to you with which my heart is overflowing.

Fyodor Dostoevsky.[2]

Tver 4 October. 59.

---

1. In fact, only four of the Petrashevsky group had been allowed to reside in the capitals: Toll, Akhsharumov, Timovsky and Pleshcheev.

2. Dostoevsky received the following reply from Totleben (dated 29 October 1859):

"I, unfortunately, was deprived of the opportunity to fulfill your request immediately upon receiving your letter. Prince Dolgorukov was with the Sovereign in Warsaw.

Yesterday I had occasion to speak with Prince Dolgoruky and Count Timashev, both expressed their full consent to your permanent residence in St. Petersburg and asked that you apply to them in writing. Write, please, without fail to both the Prince and Count Timashev—your permission will follow soon after the receipt of your letters.

Cordial regards from one who greatly respects you and who is always at your service. E. Totleben."

158. To Alexander Vrangel
4 October 1859. Tver

Tver 4 October 59.

My priceless friend, Alexander Yegorovich, I received your kind letter three days ago, wanted to answer immediately, but a letter to Eduard Ivanovich[1] and some other matters delayed me. And therefore I hasten to write now. First, business. I enclose here the letter for Eduard Ivanovich. Read it, seal it, write the address and give it to Eduard Ivanovich, if possible, in person. I'm relying on you in everything. Support me and ask him for me. My situation in Tver is awful. I made the acquaintance here, by the way, of Count Baranov (the governor). The Countess is a wonderful woman (née Vasilchikova) whom I used to see when she was just a girl in Petersburg, at the home of her relative, Sollogub, of which she herself was the first to remind me. I liked her very much even then. But despite all of these acquaintanceships, it's unbearable for me here. Everything that I wrote Eduard Ivanovich is accurate to the last letter. I am suffering both mentally and physically, and my work is being neglected. And so, my priceless Alexander Yegorovich, I rely on you. Inform me, for God's sake, when you give him the letter, how he received it and what Eduard Ivanovich said.

I am very happy that you will spend the winter in Petersburg. There will really be time to talk and remember the past. And that time will finally arrive, surely I'm not to keep on languishing! The news that X. is ready *to begin again* worries me a bit.[2] For God's sake, be careful. Besides bad things, besides new *fetters*—there can be nothing. And what passed long ago will not return. This woman should know that. And, finally, her age. Of course, it's all to her advantage to entice you again, but not to yours.

You write me about another person and about hard circumstances.[3] What you say is really not joyous. I would like to know this in detail, only, it goes without saying, not in a letter. Nothing comes out in a letter. Much as I've thought about you, my dear friend, these last days, it still seems to me that you have stayed exactly the same as you were, that is, your heart. That's both good and, partly, bad. I was so happy for you two years ago when you set out to travel. I thought that it would help you, make a new man of you. I'm very happy that things are better between you and your

---

1. See Letter 157 to Eduard Totleben.
2. X: Yekaterina Gerngross.
3. Dostoevsky is responding to Vrangel's letter of 29 September, where he writes that he "has become intimate with a wonderful woman, an angel, but her husband is jealous, torments her and me, and we aren't even allowed to talk heart to heart at balls."

father. Do you know that this is almost the main thing and that it must be cherished very, very much?

You write that you need to get settled. But can it be that these things aren't yet resolved between you and your father? My God, what then is your situation? It's essential to resolve it, but as gently as possible. That's my opinion. However, we will talk a lot about that, and talk heart to heart. You are right when you speak about my friendship. Nobody ever wished you as much good as I do. How are your sisters?[4] I have two fat and unsealed packets of your private correspondence. It goes without saying that I haven't read anything. If I'm allowed to come to Petersburg, I will first come alone, without my wife, and will stay with my brother. I'll stay in Petersburg for about a week. I'll rent an apartment, arrange everything, and then leave to get my wife and Pasha, who has to be fixed up. Write me where my boy can be fixed up, but well, where it is easy, where it is possible and quick? Advise me. A propos: are you acquainted with Pyotr Petrovich Semyonov, who was with us in Siberia, after you my best friend? He is a wonderful person, and one must search for wonderful people. If you are acquainted, give him my regards and tell him about me.

Marya Dmitrievna sends her regards to you. I already wrote you that she remembers you very often. Your portrait is always on our table. Good-bye, my priceless one, visit my brother. I embrace you. Remember your friend—write.

F. Dostoevsky

---

159. To Mikhail Dostoevsky
9 October 1859. Tver

Tver, 9 October 59.

Yesterday I received, my priceless Misha, your letter dated the 6th, at that very moment when I was writing a letter to you. Your letter distressed me. I put aside the message I'd begun until today so I could think over everything rationally and coolly—and it's good that I did that. Now I've arranged everything in my mind and am letting you know my final decision. This whole letter will be most egoistic, only about my business.

---

4. Vrangel was waiting for the return of his sisters and father from Paris.

Prepare yourself to listen.

First, my dear, it's *impossible* to agree to Nekrasov's offer.[1] You speak the truth: it's all because they're *shysters.* It's also true that they didn't like the novel *a lot,* or, at least, they're still in doubt. It's not the first time for them to reach a deadlock and reject good things. It's true that the novel doesn't make an *external* impact. Nekrasov subtly hinted that he was in doubt with the news that he had given it to one of his closest contributors to *The Contemporary* to read. But that they don't find it thoroughly bad is proved by the fact that they are offering money for it. Nobody anywhere would give so much as a kopeck for a thoroughly bad thing.

It's true, finally, as well, that their doubts are not very strong and that perhaps they find it to be a good piece. But they've been seized by mercantilism. I see their mode of operation perfectly. *First,* I wager that Nekrasov asked around at *The Russian Messenger* and found out the whole story. And there has been enough time to check. The *R[ussian] M[essenger]* probably adhered to the line that "it's green; the berry isn't ripe."[2] Both journals have been exchanging caustic remarks for a long time. It's awkward to print something *The R[ussian] Messenger* rejected and to give 120 rubles for something for which *The R[ussian] Messenger* didn't give even 100. They had to strike a pose. To definitely buy it for *less* than 100 and put it in next year, in the *summer* months to show the writers and the public that they bought it for ballast. This way they've protected themselves in the event of failure. And if it's successful—so be it! They aren't losing anything. First, they paid appallingly little for a good piece— this means they know how to make a good deal. *And 2nd,* they were able to guess it was something good, when the *Messenger* couldn't make anything out... But in addition to that, in addition to all these intrigues with the *Messenger,* Nekrasov is a keen animal. Having learned the story with the *Messenger* and knowing that I, after arriving from Siberia, have spent everything, am in need—how can he not offer such a proletarian a reduced price? They're thinking "He'll certainly agree!" That's why he's purposely held out for such a long time, knowing for certain that I, expecting and certain of the money, will dig myself even deeper into need and will surely agree to everything that they will give me—as long as there is at least some money.

But here's my opinion: it would be possible to agree due to my extreme need. 1000 rubles is still money and for me a lot. But that entails intense psychological humiliation. Let's suppose that I could agree to the humiliation; to hell with them! But I'm injured afterwards. I will

---

1. In his letter of 6 October Mikhail enclosed a copy of Nekrasov's letter regarding the terms for publishing *The Village of Stepanchikovo.* Nekrasov offered to pay 1000 rubles for the work and to print an extra 300-500 copies for the author.

2. A quotation from Ivan Krylov's fable "The Fox and the Grapes." See Letters 150-153 about Dostoevsky's rift with *The Russian Messenger.*

completely forfeit all subsequent literary reputation. They will offer me 50 silver rubles. Even if *Stepanchikovo* is a success—there won't be anything. The Contemporaries deliberately won't support me, precisely so that I wouldn't take a lot in the future either. The scoundrels! My friend, Misha! It's impossible to accept. There's one thing: I owe you 700 and now, without a livelihood, for a time I will look to you for help, and you yourself are in straitened circumstances. That one thing may force me to change my mind. You write that I should not worry about my debt to you. Oh, Misha! You are all generosity and nothing else. Your affairs will not improve because of that. But, my friend, I've thought for a long time and foolproof, reliable projects have occurred to me. Let's wait a bit, we'll refuse Nekrasov and if we succed—then honor and glory to us and mainly, *independence!* I will make it up to you for that! But before I explain my reliable and foolproof project to you, let's finish with Nekrasov. Here's how we should proceed: if I won't ruin you with the seven hundred, and you can wait a bit longer—then Nekrasov shall be refused and refused without fail. But this should be done in the most gentle, sweet and delicate way. For God's sake, my friend, see him in person for this. If he writes me a letter (as he said)—I'll answer him in the sweetest way. It would be excellent if you were to say to him in passing, "But for now this novel will be in my possession, my brother doesn't want to offer it to the other journals now. My brother has some special plans for it." If you can, say it like that. However, I leave this to your discretion. Say that I am extremely sorry that I couldn't agree with them *in this instance.* It would be good, dear Misha, if you would try to find out something, at close hand, what happened there and what their opinion of the novel is. Of course, it's clear that it's impossible to find out everything, but something will filter through. Find out and write me immediately. Finally, in the event that Nekrasov says: "I'll think about it" and offers an increase, answer him that you will inform me immediately. In general I have a most urgent request of you: see him to get the novel, in person, and describe your entire conversation with him to me, your *impressions* and *observations*—in complete detail. Even if there's nothing, write even then. Also write me what you hear about this episode later (from Maykov, for example). Then take the novel and the matter is closed.

Having taken the novel, keep it in your possession. *Do not* offer it to *Notes of the Father*[land] or any other people, no matter who. The novel has been spat upon and,*for the time being,* has lost its reputation. (Minaev was here; I promised to contribute to *The Torch*, without, however, obligating myself in any way.[3]) If *Notes of the Father*[land] or even

---

3. Dmitry Minaev (1835-89), satirical poet and journalist, visited Dostoevsky as a representative of the journal *The Torch (Svetoch* 1860-62), which was then being organized. Both Dostoevsky brothers were close to the new journal, but Mikhail was the only one to contribute anything.

Minaev's journal should begin to look and offer—I don't think we should give them the novel. It's been spat upon and if it appears now anywhere other than in *The Contemporary,* it will be spat upon even more. Only perhaps if Kraevsky or the Minaevs will give 120. Then it can be given some more thought. You will inform me then and write me what you think. But all of this is only in the event that *Notes of the Father*[land] *themselves* or someone else makes an offer. Don't offer it to anyone *yourself* and don't even look as though you're thinking of making them an offer. Let the novel remain with you for now—and the matter is closed! I'll write you, at the end of the letter, what to do with it. But now, to my plan. Listen carefully:

NB. My priceless friend, I only just now received your letter from yesterday (the 7th). And here's what I will say: that you went to see Nekrasov is good. But, for God's sake, be more gentle and more tactful with him. Don't even give the appearance that we are grieving and frightened. Don't show them our disappointment. I'm certain that we will win *later on.* Now we just have to save ourselves from scandal. If Nekrasov starts to barter or just hints at it, then answer him courteously that you will inform me about it, but that you, however, know my thoughts and as my representative you are giving notice that I will not back down from the previous terms (120 rubles). As far as reading it to Dudyshkin[4]—that's fine; but just so that this remains between Maykov, you and Dudyshkin. (I can't write to Maykov now. I'm swamped with business, extremely important things, which I will write you about at the end of the letter. Press his hand and say that I am relying on him. He's a friend to me and sincerely wishes me well. But best of all, read this letter to him, confidentially.)

But here's what I don't like: if we *foist* ourselves on *Notes of the Fatherland.* The novel has been spat upon and they will bury it with a deathly silence. Besides it really is not spectacular. *In view of these intrigues* it's not the right time even to have it printed in *Notes of the Father*[land] now. I already told you that I would write you at the end of the letter how I intend to act as far as the novel is concerned. However, if *Notes of the Father*[*land*] will give 120 without trouble—I will agree. I'm in such need that I don't have the right not to agree. Don't call my ideas arrogance. It's simply a calculation, because I have *a lot* in mind. Let Maykov consider this too. But, I repeat, I will agree to 120 rubles and 1200 in advance. I will certainly agree to *The Torch,* however, if it's for 150. That's good money. In everything else I will proceed according to your advice (that is, if Nekrasov will write me a letter).

Now to my plan. Consider it carefully, inform Maykov in secret and consult with him too.

First, you write that I can't spend a year writing now, but that I should hurry to prepare the novel I told you about by the New Year (the one with

---

4. Stepan Dudyshkin (1820-66) headed the criticism section of *Notes of the Fatherland.*

the passionate element) and in this way attract attention to myself at a single stroke. I answer: I can't do that. I'd sooner die of hunger than ruin it and rush. And besides, the novel has already been destroyed. I have another idea: I don't know if you paid attention, my dear friend, to my last letter, in which I wrote you that I want to write *Notes from the House of the Dead* (about penal servitude)—and asked you then to hint about this to Nekrasov and Kraevsky.[5] (In general, you sometimes don't write that you received such-and-such letter; and I can think that it didn't reach you. Always inform me that you've received them.) These *Notes from the House of the Dead* have taken on a full and definite plan in my head now. It will be a book of 6 or 7 printed signatures. My person will disappar. These are the notes of an unknown person; but I vouch for their interest. The interest will be most capital. There will be serious and gloomy and humorous things, and popular speech with the special convict coloring (I read you some of the expressions I recorded *on the spot)* and the depiction of personalities *unheard of* in literature, and touching things, and finally, the main thing— my name. Remember that Pleshcheev attributed the success of his poems to his name (do you understand?).[6] I'm certain that the public will read it avidly. But we shouldn't publish it in the journals now! We will publish it in a separate edition. I figure that I will finish it by December 1st; have it go through the censorship in December (give it to an educated censor), print it in January and already have it on sale in January.[7] Print it in Milyukov's format (about *Russian Poetry*) and in the same typeface. If the book comes out as thick as Milyukov's,[8] then the price can be 1 ruble 50 kopecks, if it's smaller, then 1 ruble 25 kopecks. Definitely print it ourselves, and not through the booksellers. I'm as *certain* of it's interest as that I am alive. 2000 copies will sell out in a year (in half a year, *I'm certain*). Let's suppose 1 ruble 25 kopecks—that's 2000 rubles in a year. That, for a start, is money, and money that is certain.

But there might be a terrible misfortune: it could be forbidden. (I'm convinced that I'll write it in a way absolutely passable by the censor.) If it is forbidden, then everything can be broken up into articles and published as excerpts in journals. They'll give money and good money. But this is a misfortune! To be afraid of the wolf and not go into the forest. If it is forbidden, I could ask again. I'll be in Petersburg, through Ed[uard] Iv[anovich Totleben] I'll go to His Royal Highness Nikolay Nikolaevich,

5. This is the first mention in Dostoevsky's extant correspondence of *Notes from the House of the Dead.*

6. Pleschcev, who was now living in Moscow, had published in *The Russian Messenger, The Contemporary, The Moscow Messenger,* and *The Library for Reading.*

7. Dostoevsky did not manage to write *Notes from the House of the Dead* in two months. It was published serially from September 1860 to December 1862.

8. Dostoevsky is referring to Milyukov's book on Russian poetry that was sent to him as a gift (see Letter 141).

I'll go to Maria Nikolaevna.[9] I'll petition and the book will acquire even greater interest.

But if it is forbidden, there's another source, another project, that is essential to carry out in any event, whether it is forbidden or not. This is an edition of my works. They can be published in three forms (consult with Maykov, my dear).

1st form. Poor Folk, Netochka Nezvanova 6 chapters, "White Nights," "A Children's Tale," "The Christmas Tree and the Wedding," "An Honest Thief," "The Jealous Husband."—All of this in one book in the format of Pisemsky's 1858 *Sketches from Peasant Life.* 2 silver rubles for the book. Title of the book: *Old Stories.*

2nd form. 2 books in the same Pisemsky format and on the same thick (excellent) paper (each part will come out thicker than Pisemsky's).

1st part. *Poor Folk,* "White Nights," "A Chilren's Tale," "The Christmas Tree and the Wedding."

2nd part. *Uncle's Dream, Netochka Nezvanova* 6 chapters, "An Honest Thief" and "The Jealous Husband."—Both parts for 3 silver rubles.

NB. (*The Double* is excluded, I'll publish it later on, *in the case of a success,* separately, completely revised and with an introduction.)

So as not to delay, I beg you, my dear, to send me as soon as possible my works (except for *Poor Folk, The Double, Uncle's Dream* and all those which are not included in the above plan of the edition). I'll revise them quickly, on the printed text, lightly, without getting the least distracted from writing *The House of the Dead,* and send them to you immediately. They can be printed in two ways: either at our expense, or by selling them to a bookseller.

1) If at our expense: I'll send you everything corrected by the end of October. November—the censorship. December—printing and in the middle of January it will be on the market together with *The House of the Dead.*

It will cost 300 rubles to print *The House of the Dead* (maximum). The works in the 1st form: from 600 to 700, *in the 2nd form* 1000 silver rubles, 1300 silver rubles in all.

I will ask you all, my saviors, for money for the printing: you, Sasha, Varya, Verochka (I wrote them letters) and, if possible, uncle.[10] I won't take money from you; instead give a promissory note for 6 months for the paper; I'll redeem it by the deadline.

NB. But while I'm writing now, I have to live! That's what is terrible! And I have only 30 rubles left. I need to be provided for for 4 months or so. Where am I to get it? Don't abandon me, brother! Appeal to Sasha, rouse

---

9. Maria Nikolaevna, daughter of Nicholas I, was the president of the Academy of the Arts.

10. Dostoevsky's letters to his sisters and his uncle, Alexander Kumanin, are not extant.

all the relatives. After all, I need at least 300-400 rubles. Just to tide me over here, later on, there, it will be fine. The works will begin to sell fairly well, I'm certain, the more so as *Notes from the House of the Dead*, which will be sold separately, will get the public's interest and *will carry* the works as well, which will come out at the same time. Even if I sell up to 1000 copies in a year (print 2000), then I'll have 1200 rubles if it's published in the *1st form*. With the two thousand for *The House of the Dead* I'll have 3200.

The accounting: 700 to you for debts, 900 for printing, 400 for living expenses, 2000 in all: 1200 rubles is left to live on. That's good.

If it's published in the 2nd form then, after all expenses 2000 remains. That's something to live on. And it's quite possible to hope that both books will help each other.

If they're published through a bookseller (just the works), then they can be sold for 1000 rubles, in the 1st form, *in the second form* for 1500 and not any less. It goes without saying that we must first ask for more. The amount received this way, at one go, would fully enable me to pay all my debts, and the sales from *The House of the Dead* would give me good and certain means to live on. Here are instructions for you concerning the booksellers, and, I implore you, follow these instructions to the letter. First, *in any case*, start acting now. Ask Maykov for help. Speak to the booksellers about the 1st and 2nd forms immediately. Bargain. Mention that it's a *name* (do you understand?). After all, now is the *best* and most opportune moment to begin action. If the bookseller isn't an ass, he'll realize what a name means. If they agree—an advance immediately. After passing the censorship—a contract (I will send you power of attorney in good form, in accordance with the law). The contract is the following: 1)Manuscript in hand—money in hand. 2) To print 2000 copies— absolutely no more (2400 at most would be possible). 3) I have the right to publish 2 years after this edition. 4) During this time, if all copies are sold, the bookseller does not have the right to do a 2nd printing. 5) To begin the edition immediately.

If it's sold to a bookseller, it can be printed in a third form as well. I'll agree. It's this: 3 volumes. The 1st and 2nd volumes the same as in the 2nd form, and the 3rd *Stepanchikovo* (never published before), ask 3500 for everything, you could agree to 3300, that is, 1800 for *Stepanchikovo*, 1500 for the works. Offer it this way too; if they accept, I agree.

These are my means, my dear, and calculations for next year. But there's one other thing. In December I'll begin a novel (but not that one— the young man who was flogged and who ended up in Siberia).[11] No. Do you remember that I spoke to you about a certain *Confession*—a novel that I wanted to write after all the other ones, and said that I myself needed

---

11. The plan for this novel has not been mentioned before in Dostoevsky's correspondence and the plot does not figure in *Notes from the House of the Dead*.

to experience more. Recently I definitely decided to write it without delay. It has become combined with the novel (the passionate element) that I told you about. It will be, 1st, striking, passionate and, 2nd, all my heart and blood will go into the novel. I conceived it in prison, lying on my plank bed, in a difficult moment of sadness and demoralization. It will fall naturally into 3 novels (different periods of life), each novel about 12 printed signatures. I'll print the 1st novel in some journal in March or April. The effect will be greater than *Poor Folk* (much!) and *Netochka Nezvanova*. I swear. My friend, Misha! You are thinking that I have lost heart. I swear I have only been roused still more after your letter from yesterday, to work, to fight, to make a name for myself in literature—that's what I want now. But don't abandon me, you, my guardian angel. Support me. I will write our sisters to ask them to give me something to live on. *A Confession* will secure my name once and for all.[12] Then, perhaps, the Contemporaries themselves will come to me for *Stepanchikovo*, or I could publish it separately then. But I've already said that if *Notes of the Father*[land] will give 120—that's fine. I agree, but I would so like it if Ap[ollon] Nikol[aevich Maykov] were to read *Stepanchikovo* himself, *alone*, before Dudyshkin, and to give his frank opinion.

I'm very busy now: I'm not writing to Dolgoruky, but to the Sovereign directly.[13] Baranov will deliver it. The Sovereign is merciful. It is up to Him; but if says *yes*, then I'm in Petersburg right away, without any delay. For God's sake. This is a secret, don't tell anyone. I wrote our sisters. I'm running out of money. Brother! Don't think me an egoist! Realize that my entire career, perhaps, depends on this. Forgive my egoism and save me. I wrote our sisters, I'll write again. But, for God's sake, answer me soon, and in as much detail as possible.

NB. My life here is terrible, you will understand me. I don't understand how I have not completely lost heart yet. Good-bye, write as soon and in as much detail as possible. Yours.

12. Dostoevsky's journal *Time* announced a work under the title *A Confession* in 1862 and 1863, but nothing was ever published under that title. Dostoevsky's confession was published in considerably altered form as *Notes from Underground* (1864).

13. See Letter 7 in the section of Dostoevsky's official and business correspondence for the letter to Alexander II.

160. To Mikhail Dostoevsky
11 October 1859. Tver

Tver 11 October 59.

My dearest Misha, I received your letter dated October 9th and am answering it immediately. I'm very concerned: did you receive my letter (a big one, on 2 sheets)? You should have received it yesterday. I wrote it on the 9th. The postmark on your letter indicates that it was sent from Petersburg on the 10th. However, why lose hope; I hope that you received it and therefore know that I didn't get angry and that there wasn't even a shadow of such nonsense. Would I get angry with you, my dear friend? But to business:

You already know from the long letter all my hopes and instructions. Now the business with Kraevsky is beginning.[1] It's an important thing. You ask about the price, and here's the final word for you on that score: 120 rubles per signature of the usual large type that the journals use to print stories—and not a kopeck less. If it's *en bloc* [a lump sum]—that's a different matter. In that case I authorize you to sell it to Kraevsky for 1700 and not a kopeck less, and that only if he'll give at least 1000 rubles *right now,* that is, in a few days. (You should ask for and insist on the whole 1700 in advance, that is: when the manuscript is delivered, so is the money. As far as the censorship goes, there can't be even a shadow of doubt; they won't cross out a single comma.) If Kraevsky will *definitely* print it this year, then we could take just 1000 in advance, and 700 on publication. If it's the beginning of next year, however, then 1700 *immediately,* and *not a kopeck less.*

For God's sake, explain to Kraevsky that if it's 120 rubles per signature, then 15 signatures comes to 1800 rubles, consequently, I lose 100. And after all, I think that *surely* it will be more than fifteen signatures. Consequently, it's all the more to his advantage to buy it for 1700.

If *The Torch* gives 2500 rubles—(for *Stepanchikovo*), then it goes without saying—give it to them. What could be better? Even if they don't have a single subscriber, there's 2500 rubles and the other journals will be convinced of the value of my works, that is, they will be ashamed to give less than 2000 or 1800 for such a piece for which I immediately, without thinking, can get 2500. In addition next year I'll have two other pieces that may be published: *The House of the Dead* and *the first episode from the long novel.*[2] That will go to *The Contemporary.* I dare say they won't let it

---

1. Kraevsky, the publisher of *Notes of the Fatherland*, had offered Mikhail 1500 rubles for *The Village of Stepanchikovo*.

2. Dostoevsky's novel *A Confession* probably provided material for the works *The Insulted and the Injured* and *Notes from Underground.*

slip by and I'll deliver it with a recommendation. As far as *The House of the Dead* is concerned, they don't have sheep's heads after all. They realize what curiosity such a piece can arouse in the first (January) issues of a journal. If they'll give 200 rubles per signature, then I'll publish it in the journal. If not, then I don't need to. Don't think, dear Misha, that I have my nose in the air or am boasting about my *House of the Dead,* because I'm asking 200 rubles? Not at all; but I understand very well curiosity and the piece's *importance* and don't want to lose what's mine.

This piece and the future novel (if it's carefully spoken of beforehand, now, to the effect that it's being written) can shut up *Notes of the Father*[*land*] and *The Contemporary* so they won't criticize me in the journals for not letting them have *Stepanchikovo,* because I hoped to have a future collaborator. And it doesn't matter that *The Torch* has few readers. All the better for me. When I publish it separately the novel will be little known to the public and it will have the appearance of something new.

By the way, about *Stepanchikovo.* I wrote Pleshcheev to have him find out *for certain* why exactly *The Russian Messenger* returned the manuscript to me. And I received the answer that he made inquiries and knows *for certain* that they were frightened by the 100 rubles per signature, which Katkov would have given, but the whole journal is run by Leontiev and he has Katkov under his thumb and the world has never seen such skinflints. About the novel they say that they were simply delighted with the beginning, but that the ending, in their opinion, is weak and that in general the novel requires cuts.

Finally, I will conclude with a *most important observation,* which I forgot in the last (long) letter. Namely: if Nekrasov starts to bargain and is *more reasonable,* then, in any event, he is to be preferred. How sorry, how extremely sorry I am that he didn't find you at home! Then we would know his thoughts for certain. Couldn't you, my dear friend, *somehow* see him soon! You see: it's very important that the novel will be published in *The Contemporary.* That journal persecuted me before, and now is soliciting my piece. That's very important for my literary reputation. 2nd) Nekrasov, who returned the manuscript to you and who *came again for it* and (if it were like that) finally has seen reason, gives the novel an extraordinary significance through all these pranks. It means the novel isn't bad, if they are soliciting and bargaining so because of it. In passing tell Nekrasov frankly *The Russian Messenger's* opinion of the novel (and about Leontiev and call him a skinflint); and in addition, tell Nekrasov that I myself know very well my novel's faults, but that I think that there are several good pages in my novel as well. Tell him in those words, because that really is my opinion. And it wouldn't be bad to tell Kraevsky that, too. Tell them frankly. Frankness is power.

NB. I'm swamped with business. I'll start writing (*The House of the Dead*) after the 15th. My eyes hurt, I absolutely can't work by candlelight, everything is worse and worse. I received a letter from Sasha. Good-bye, my dear, I embrace you. Write me. Try to see Nekrasov. Send my old works for revision. Talk with the booksellers. I think that it's best to publish them in the 2nd form.[3] Good-bye, my dear friend. Thank you for all your efforts. Write.

161. To Pyotr Davydov[1]
14 October 1859. Tver

Tver, 14 October 1859

Dear Pyotr Andreevich,

I am certain that you are extremely surprised and are even indignant with me for my silence. I promised to write and *inform* you soon, and, meanwhile, not a word, as if we had vanished. But don't be very angry, my dear and most obliging Pyotr Andreevich: I'm blamelessly guilty before you. I never forget my good friends. And long ago I singled you out as a most honest and noble person. If I have been silent until now, despite the fact that I promised to write you as soon as possible about a certain matter, it's solely due to the enormous troubles that have befallen me here. The most varied troubles. It's the question of my moving to Petersburg. This matter has taken on such varied and difficult manifestations, has required so many different troubles, of which I had not even suspected, that my mind has become somewhat preoccupied until I settle and arrange all these things, which, however, are going better. It's not that my time is occupied; my mind is preoccupied. That's why I've been silent and have been waiting all the time for the main thing that worries me to be settled. Then, I repeated to myself, then I'll write all of my friends in Siberia. Will you believe that I still haven't written anyone in Semipalatinsk—neither Mikhail Alexandrovich,[2] nor the Geyboviches[3] (though I did receive a letter from him from Ayaguz). I'll definitely write Geybovich this week. I promised him a long and detailed letter; and besides, he didn't forget me. I'll also inform the good and noble Mikhail Alexandrovich. Every day my

3. See the preceding letter for the three proposals Dostoevsky made to his brother in regard to publishing a collection of his works.

1. Pyotr Andreevich Davydov was a Semipalatinsk acquaintance of Dostoevsky's.

2. Mikhail Alexandrovich Sytnikov, the assistant postmaster in Semipalatinsk.

3. Artemy Ivanovich Geybovich had moved from Semipalatinsk to Ayaguz (present-day Sergiopol). See Letter 164 for Dostoevsky's letter to Geybovich.

wife plans to write Elena Ivanovna[4] and has been putting everything aside until the necessary settlement of certain matters. It turns out that I am writing you first, since I am guilty before you (although blamelessly). I know that I should have informed you earlier. But, to business: my first word to my brother on the first day of our meeting was about you. He said that it would be a wonderful thing, but that he doesn't have exactly the kind of position you need. I explained to him in detail and conscientiously your requirements. A salary of 35 rubles a month won't do for your support. My brother would have gladly agreed to those terms. But I know that those terms are definitely no good for you. My brother told me reasonably that if you are summoned from Siberia, with your family, and suddenly, you see that your needs in Petersburg will outweigh your means, then—my brother said to me—"you will have to blame yourself for encouraging a person in vain and acting thoughtlessly." I understand all this very well. I asked my brother about other positions; he said that salaries everywhere are the same as he gives; but that in general positions are so varied and numerous that, it goes without saying, with time something suitable can be found. And so this is my conclusion: there's no point in looking for anything for next year. But next year, if you will allow me, I will work for you and your hopes may be realized next year. First, I myself will be in Petersburg, and 2nd, in Petersburg one can find anything, absolutely anything through people (and I have them). I repeat my promise that if I inform you of anything during the coming year, I will inform you of it *precisely* and *definitely,* and not thoughtlessly. However, you have nothing to lose. I would very much like you not to remain in Siberia, and therefore I have your interests at heart. If anything good is found, it will be all the better for you; the information which will be reported to you will be exact and definite, and the final decision will depend wholly on you. Write me something and inform me of your plans. I am certain, most noble Pyotr Andreevich, that you will not want to break off our friendship just because of my being too lazy to write. I will answer your letter in greater detail than now; for now I have in mind just to inform you about the main thing. My compliments to Nastasya Petrovna.[5] My wife also sends her regards. My compliments also to your household, *if you want to inform them of this letter.*

Good-bye, dearest Pyotr Andreevich. I wish you health and every success, write me something about Semipalatinsk. My address: city of Tver, Galyanov's house, by the post office. I'll write you about myself in greater detail too.

Yours truly Fyodor Dostoevsky

4. Elena Ivanovna was a Semipalatinsk aquaintance of Marya Dostoevskaya.
5. Nastasya Petrovna is probably Davydov's wife.

Mikhail Dostoevsky (1847)

Mikhail Dostoevsky (1860s)

162. To Mikhail Dostoevsky
18 October 1859. Tver

Tver, 18 October 1859

I received two letters from you, one with money (50 rubles), the other with the news that you had visited Kraevsky. Thank you very much for the money, my dear Misha. It came very opportunely. But, my dear friend, I need it all, that is, all that could be expected upon receipt of the advance for the novel minus the 750 silver rubles for you. I need it very much. Why?— it's better not to ask. But the business with my novel is dragging on and on, and, it seems, will never come to an end. I'm not reproaching you, my dear. But why are they giving themselves airs? It's really funny. Can it be that Maykov's recommendation isn't enough for Kraevsky, and for Dudyshkin as well? But, let's grant that Dudyshkin needs to read it. Why is he taking such a long time to read it? In a word, it seems to me that they are putting on a lot of airs and are pretending that they have accepted a flawed novel out of kindness. I think, my friend, that it would be possible to hurry them a bit.[1]

Because you were there on Thursday (evidently with the view to find out about the novel) and, apparently, didn't dare even to bring up the novel with them. I just mean to say that they probably realize that that's precisely the case. But, my friend, I have no grudge against you. You write that Kraevsky is very friendly and attentive and note that this is a good sign. But in my opinion that's a very bad sign. They'll definitely begin to bargain! But before this it would have been possible not to allow that. In a word: it would really be better, more impressive somehow, if you acted more persistently and independently. We ought to give the appearance that we don't need them very much. I think they must definitely be hurried a bit. I dare say, if they need the novel, they won't return it. And when do they want to publish it? I would very much like it to be published this year. Announcements about the publication of *Notes of the Fatherland* have appeared in the papers with a listing of the names of their future contributor's names; my name isn't listed. Listen, dear, we must strike while the iron is hot, while there's still time. We must make use of all the advantages of our position and all permissible wiles; and for this take my advice and think about it, and think it over carefully. Here it is:

1. In his letter dated 16 October, Mikhail writes his brother about the negotiations concerning *The Village of Stepanchikovo:* "I was at Kraevsky's today. And found Dudyshin there. He asked a lot about you. I learned that he is reading your novel, but hasn't finished it yet, and therefore it wasn't possible to get an answer from Kraevsky yet. I think that I'll learn something in a few days. Krae\[sky] is very attentive towards me— that's a good sign. I'm afraid that they'll haggle."

You see, while Kraevsky has the novel and *the final word has still not been said,* in a word—while there's still time—shouldn't we threaten him with some competition? They regard the novel (and during negotiations will definitely pretend) to be almost flawed. They must be definitely shown that the novel isn't flawed at all. Then not only will they not bargain, but they will even add something. The primary means to this end is Nekrasov. After all, he called on you, didn't find you in, said that he would stop by again, consequently, he had something to say. Why don't you visit him yourself (but not write a letter to which you have to wait for a reply; consequently, time will be lost), but simply drop by yourself. The business with *The Contemporary,* after all, is finished, there's hardly anything to be expected from them, consequently, there's nothing to lose either, so it's not only possible to go, but even imperative. You may stumble upon something unexpectedly. If you go to see Nekrasov and *find him at home,* you would say to him straightaway: "You, Nikolay Alexeevich, came to visit me that time. It's a pity that I wasn't in. I wrote my brother and he, too, regrets very much that I didn't see you. You probably came about the novel and perhaps wanted to propose something new. But you see: Kraevsky has the novel, and I'm now on the verge of concluding the final agreement with him, *however, I have not yet bound myself with anything to him* (that is, to Kraevsky). And so, if your have something to say to me, say it now. I am authorized by my brother to conclude the business whenever I please, and, moreover, have very detailed instructions. Moreover, I can tell you frankly that my brother will always give preference to *The Contemporary.* He himself stated that to me. And so, what did you wish to say to me?" Either Nekrasov will answer immediately, or he will request time for his answer. In that case give him only one day, declaring that after that *they will not wait.* Do you see what will happen: if Nekrasov starts to talk the least bit reasonably, then we can scare Kraevsky with Nekrasov right away. They will both start to fight over it. And then, whoever gives more gets the novel. In addition, remember, my dear, that I particularly asked you to see Nekrasov in order to find out from him all his *thoughts* and what he thinks about the novel, that is, what his opinion is. That is very important. This is the future voice of *The Contemporary,* their review, if they in fact discuss the novel in print. This is all of great interest to me. Listen to me, my dear friend, do this. You will not in any way humiliate either me or yourself before Nekrasov. Noble frankness is power. And you're not hiding anything from them. We are proceeding openly. And finally, *The Contemporary* on its part has nothing to lose, and may win, if only by our frightening Kraevsky. Realize also, Misha, that all of this must be done as soon as possible. Because when *Notes of the Father*[*land*] announces its terms—it will be too late. Then Nekrasov, too, will realize that, evidently, we're not having any luck with *Notes of the Father*[land] either. But now you will go to him without yet having begun serious negotiations with Kraevsky. That's a different matter altogether. You could also tell

Nekrasov that Maykov likes the novel. Maykov is Dudyshkin's friend. That would influence Nekrasov: he would think that *Notes of the Father*[*land*] will definitely accept the novel and will hold onto it as a good thing. It would be splendid if Maykov were to praise the novel, in person, to Nekrasov. In general, we must hurry.

Now, the *second means* is to frighten Kraevsky.

I wrote you that Minaev visited me and that I promised to contribute to *The Torch*. Go to see Kalinovsky, the *Torch's* main publisher and backer. For God's sake go and go immediately. Ask Milyukov for the address. Milyukov is one of the editors. When you go in to see Kalinovsky, you frankly, simply and openly say to him: "There is a novel. Nekrasov didn't offer the right terms. Kraevsky has asked for the novel and we are on the verge of concluding the final terms with him. But I have not yet bound myself in any way. Meanwhile Nekrasov stopped by to see me, promised to stop by another time; consequently, he wants to propose different terms. In a word, *The Contemporary* and *Notes of the Father*[*land*] are outbidding each other. Nekrasov is offering up to 100 rubles a signature, Kraevsky will probably give 120, but my brother needs money. He wrote me the other day that Mr. Minaev visited him and requested his participation in *The Torch*. My brother asked me to talk it over with you. You, as a new journal, have neither significance nor subscribers. Of course it's better for a known writer and one with an *interesting* name to contribute to journals that have both significance and a reputation. Consequently, if he doesn't refuse to contribute something to yours, then, it goes without saying, it is in the hope that you will give more. What would you give?" (In addition, definitely add that I am now writing the very interesting *Notes from the House of the Dead,* that this will appear in one of the well-known journals, it seems, in *The Contemporary,* and that this work may interest the public even more in the author. And, add as well that *Notes of the Father*[*land*] wants to publish my novel *this year*. Consequently, I could publish it in a separate edition next year. But having published it in *The Torch,* I will have to wait a year to reprint it, consequently, I lose.) If Kalinovsky asks for a postponement, tell him to decide soon. If he reachs a decision at once and names a price, we have an enormous advantage. When dealing with Kraevsky, you will tell him straight out that *The Torch* is giving more and money in advance. That your brother isn't concerned now with fame; he needs money. That, finally, your brother is seeking neither patronage, nor well-known journals, but is behaving honestly with the public. If the novel is good, then it will be good in Kalinovsky's journal and the public will notice it there, though not immediately, but it will be noticed. If it's bad, then it will be bad in *Notes of the Father*[*land*] too; consequently, it's not worth it to your brother to look at it that way and *he doesn't need to pay extra for the honor of seeing his name in Notes of the Father*[*land*]. But if Kalinovsky offers 150 rubles, give it to him with joy, with God's blessing, and give it to him immediately. You can't imagine anything better than this. 2000 and something; why, that's a hoard. I don't care that *The Torch* has no subscribers. If the novel is good, it won't fall by the wayside. And I'm not afraid of rage and contempt on the part of *The Contem*[*porary*] and *Notes of the Father*[land]. First, I'm simply not afraid, and 2nd, they'll already have discovered that I have *The House of the Dead.* I dare say they won't even think of criticizing *Stepanchikovo.* And so, there you have, my friend Misha, the terms for Kalinovsky: 150 rubles per signature. One half in advance immediately, the other half on publication. To be published in January or February. My dear! Do this for me, do it, for God's sake, be a friend, prove that you're a friend to me. Realize that this is my future support and that we must strike while the iron is hot. If you are my friend, then you'll do this. Forgive me for bothering you. I'll make it up to you. I'm really tired of this novel. In any case *answer* quickly.

My letter to the Sovereign will go to Petersburg tomorrow, via Adlerberg.[2] That was already decided before. But you, however, Misha don't talk a lot about that. At least now. What will happen—I don't know. The Sovereign is merciful. However, there may be delays, inquiries made of Dolgoruky, etc. In any case, I am not counting, my friend, on seeing you very soon. I foresee that. As for Zhdan-Pushkin's letter and the package for Marya Dmitrievna—send them immediately. Good-bye, my priceless one, I embrace you, don't be angry with me. It's difficult for me to live here, very, very difficult.

Your Dost.

Be very polite, obliging and concise with Nekrasov. Make it look like you just dropped in for a minute and are in a great hurry.

163. To Mikhail Dostoevsky
20 October 1859. Tver

This time I'm writing you just a few words, my priceless Misha. I received your letter dated the 17th, but still have not received your package, I haven't even received the notice from the post office. Our post office is extremely unreliable. However, I don't know for certain when the package was sent from Petersburg. Perhaps it's being delayed there.

I thank you, my friend, for your efforts and trouble in collecting my

2. See Offical Letter 7 for Dostoevsky's petition to the Tsar to be allowed residence in Petersburg. The letter was sent via General-Adjutant Alexander Vladimirovich Adlerberg (1819-88).

works. I realize how much you are doing for me and I sense it. I'll repay you someday.

Did you receive my letter (the last one) in which I ask you to go to see Nekrasov and Kalinovsky? In general, my friend, once again *I implore* you, inform me in each letter that "such-and-such a letter of yours was received by me," etc. That's important. Realize that. And I implore you as well, my priceless one, to act in accordance with my request in the last letter, that is to go to see both Nekrasov and Kalinovsky. Of course, I leave everything to your discretion. (Circumstances about which I know nothing may arise.) But agree that my advice is rather sound and that it would not be a bad thing to see these people.

Already on Thursday Kraevsky promised to let you know something in a few days. It's already Tuesday. You must admit that they're delaying.

I, of course, agree as far as Kushelev is concerned and thank you both (you and Maykov). 2000 isn't bad, but what 3 parts? Perhaps *Stepanchikovo* is to be in the 3rd?[1] But this is in the event that Kraevsky publishes it this year (insist, dear friend, that it be this year).

NB. And one other thing: remember Col. Rostanev's literary judgments on literature, journals, *Notes of the Father[land]*'s erudition, etc. An absolute condition: that Kraevsky not throw out even one line of this conversation. Col. Rostanev's opinion cannot humiliate or offend Kraevsky. Please, insist on this. Mention this in particular.[2]

I received your money and thanked you, as you already know.

My request has been dispatched to Petersburg.[3] I'm waiting. But I will not see you, perhaps, for a very long time still. There will be inquiries, etc. That's what I foresee. Perhaps only in two months of so.

Good-bye, my priceless one. I embrace and kiss you. Your devoted brother

Dost.

My regards to all of your family. Vrangel doesn't write, what's with him? I sent Totleben a letter through him. I haven't received an answer.[4] About two weeks have passed.

Y[ours]

1. Dostoevsky is referring to a proposed edition of his collected works.

2. See Colonel Rostanev's description of *Notes of the Fatherland* in Part II, Chapter 3 of *The Village of Stepanchikovo*.

3. Dostoevsky's petition to Alexander II to be allowed residence in Petersburg.

4. In his letter of 21 October 1859 Mikhail wrote his brother: "Vrangel visited me today. He received your letter on the day of his departure for the country, and therefore couldn't answer you. He'll write you the day after tomorrow. The letter for Eduard Ivan[ovich Totleben] was delivered at the same time."

164. To Artemy Geybovich
23 October 1859. Tver

Tver, 23 October 1859

Our most kind and never-to-be-forgotten friend, most noble Artemy Ivanovich, I am not about to justify myself to you for my long silence, but if I am guilty before you, I swear I am blameless! My wife and I not only have not forgotten you and all of your dear family, but it seems not a day has passed that we haven't reminisced about you and reminisced with ardent hearts. When I received your letter here, which began so unlike a friend, "Dear Sir," I was tormented by remorse and I reproached myself for my long silence. It's true, I could have written a letter earlier, but my affairs were so far from being settled that I would hardly get ready to write when some difficult matter would befall me: I would have to run, seek advice, petition and make a formal reply. However, that's no way to tell it; it's better if I describe for you our entire journey from July 2nd, and from my story you will see for yourself what kept me so unusually busy and what precisely alarmed me.—I will never forget our last day of parting, when (speaking in passing) I clinked glasses with everybody a fair amount. On the next day of our journey we talked about you all the time. We finally arrived in Omsk; the weather was superb and the road was wonderful. I was in Omsk three of four days. We took Pasha out of the academy; I visited old acquaintances and superiors, for example: de Grave[1] and others. Valikhanov announced to me that his presence was required in Petersburg and that he was going there in a month. Through him I became acquainted with a good family, the Kapustins (do you know them?), they're in Tomsk now; they are simple-hearted and noble people with a good heart. In case you happen to be in Tomsk (well, someday), be sure to make their acquaintance and remember me to them. We got along well; they are people without any pretensions. But in general I disliked Omsk a lot and it inspired sad thoughts and memories in me. When we left Omsk, I truly bade farewell to Siberia. The road was horrendous, but Tyumen is a splendid city—mercantile, industrial, populous, comfortable—everything you could want. We stayed there (I don't remember why) for about two days. During the first half of the journey I had two attacks on the road, and since then they've ceased. Our postmaster Nikolaev turned out to be a superb fellow, obliging, kind, though not entirely businesslike. As a character, as a type, he's a most remarkable fellow. The kindest and noblest heart, though a bit of a braggart. We became friends and got as used to each other on the road as is possible, and he remained content and

---

1. Major-General Alexey de Grave, commandant of the Omsk fortress.

cried like a child when we parted. If he's in Ayaguz with the mail, lure him to your place, he will tell you a lot.[2] I'm leaving out a great deal of my traveling observations and impressions. The weather was exemplary for almost the entire journey, the carriage didn't break down (not once!), there weren't any delays with the horses, but the expense, the prices at the stations—God preserve us! You ask for a piece of something, you ask the price—and then you look at him in the eyes with terror, even fearing that maybe he's mad! There aren't prices like that anywhere in the world! But the landscape made up for it. The magnificent Perm forests and later the Vyatka forests are perfection. But already in Perm you seldom see a deserted place alongside the road: everything is ploughed, everything is cultivated, everything is valued. So, at least, it seemed to me. We spent a day in Yekaterinburg and were seduced: we spent about 40 rubles on assorted wares—rosaries and 38 assorted minerals, studs, buttons and so on. We bought them for gifts and, there's no point in fibbing, we paid terribly little—here they cost almost twice as much. One fine evening, about five p.m., wandering in the spurs of the Urals, in the middle of a forest, we finally came upon the border between Europe and Asia. A marvelous column with inscriptions has been placed there, and beside it a disabled veteran lives in a hut. We got out of the carriage and I crossed my-self to thank God for having finally allowed me to see the Promised Land. Then your wicker flask, filled with bitter orange-blossom (Shtreiter's recipe) was brought out, and we drank with the veteran to our parting with Asia, and Nikolaev also drank, and the coachman, too (and how he drove later on). We talked a little and then went to walk in the forest to gather wild strawberries. We gathered a fair amount. However, if I tell the story this way we'll never get to business. We got stuck in Kazan. 120 silver rubles remained, which was obviously too little to get to Tver. When I was still in Semipalatinsk I had written my brother to send me 200 rubles in Kazan, to the post office, poste restante. We decided to wait for the money and took a good room in a hotel. The expense was unbearable. We waited 10 days, it cost almost 50 rubles. I had already subscribed to read books in the Kazan library, but meanwhile didn't know what to do. But my brother received the letter unpardonably late and finally sent the 200 rubles. We set off at once. We arrived in Nizhny at the height of the fair; we arrived at night and for two hours wandered around the city, stopping at all the hotels; everything was full. We finally found something in the way of a kennel and were glad for that. The next day we went to see Annenkov (a Tobolsk exile; he's now a counselor in Nizhny). But he was on leave and the whole family was in the country. I at once set out to look at the market. Well, Artemy Ivanovich, a strong impression! I wandered around for two-three hours

2. In his reply (dated 25 March 1860) to Dostoevsky's letter Geybovich informs his friend that Nikolaev died as the result of an accident in a snowstorm.

and saw only a small part. You need a month to survey all of this. But the effect is still significant. Even too impressive. Not for nothing is it famed. That very day we left Nizhny for Vladimir. In Vladimir I saw Khomentovsky; he's the supervisor of the provisions commission there. He's a splendid, most noble fellow—but he's going to be the ruination of himself. You know: the public house. He's surrounded by God knows what people who are unworthy of him. He visited us, told us about his adventures abroad and told them wonderfully. We got quite tipsy that evening. We finally left Vladimir. It would have been shorter to go to Moscow; but, first, it was formally forbidden for me to enter Moscow. And, second, to arrive in Moscow, see my sisters, and not spend a week would have been impossible. There could be trouble, so I decided not to go to Yaroslavl as I had planned the itinerary in Semipalatinsk, but to go to the St. Sergey Monastery[3] (60 versts from Moscow) and, cutting through Moscow Province, to enter the Tver Province. I had decided on that, but vowed not to do that again. There's no main road; the coachmen are freelance and made me pay for 150 versts three times as much as on the public post roads. But the St. Sergey Monastery completely made up for that. I hadn't been there in 23 years. What architecture, what monuments, Byzantine rooms, churches! The sacristy amazed us. In the sacristy the pearls (magnificent) are measured in bushels, emeralds an inch in diameter, diamonds worth a half-million each. Clothing from several centuries, handmade articles produced by the tsarinas and their daughters, Ivan the Terrible's at-home clothing, coins, old books, all kinds of rarities—I didn't want to leave there. Finally, after a long journey, we arrived in Tver, stayed at a hotel, the prices were exorbitant. We had to rent an apartment. There were a lot of apartments, but not a single furnished one, and it's inconvenient for me to buy furniture for a few months. Finally, after several days of searching I found not exactly an apartment, not exactly a hotel room, but three small, furnished rooms for 11 silver rubles a month. And thank God for even that. I started to wait for my brother. My brother had been so ill that he had been on the point of death. He finally recovered and came. That was happiness. The train arrives after two in the morning, and the station is three versts from Tver. I set off at night to meet him there. We talked about a lot of things; but what's the point. You can't describe such moments. He stayed with me 5 days or so, went to Moscow and then on the return trip stayed another two days or so. He and I decided everything about my affairs. We decided, first, to wait until September 8th (everybody was talking about a manifesto, everyone was expecting it), but there wasn't any manifesto,[4] though there

3. The Holy Trinity-St. Sergey Monastery, founded in the fourteenth century by Sergey of Radonezh, is located in Zagorsk, north of Moscow.

4. A manifesto was expected to be issued on 8 September 1859 in conjunction with the tsarevich's coming of age.

were many pardons. Then I went to the local colonel of the gendarmes, asked his advice, and he told me that the most direct way was to write Prince Dolgoruky (the chief of the gendarmes). And that's just what we decided on. I am writing letters, by the way, to Totleben as well, through Vrangel, who turned out to be in Petersburg. Meanwhile a former acquaintance of mine,[5] who is acquainted with everybody in Tver, is passing through Tver. Through him I have made the acquaintance here of two or three households and, most importantly, with the governor, Adjutant-General Baranov. Count Baranov turned out to be a most outstanding fellow, one in a million. Incidentally, I told him that I wanted to write Dolgoruky; he was very interested, but said that I should wait, because Our Imperial Sovereign is on a journey and Prince Dolgoruky is with him (NB.—five days ago the Sovereign returned to Petersburg). I began to wait, but meanwhile I composed a lot of letters; I wanted to write Dolgoruky, Totleben and Rostovtsev.[6] A wonderful idea occurred to me all of a sudden: to write to Our Imperial Sovereign directly. I went to see Baranov, sought his advice, and Baranov approved completely, and moreover volunteered to send my letter in his name, through his cousin Count Adlerberg. I wrote the letter; I requested in the letter at the same time that Pasha be admitted to a school or academy, and now it's already been five days since the letter was sent. I'm waiting for the answer, and can you imagine, most kind Artemy Ivanovich, how agitated I am? At this very moment my fate, perhaps, has already been decided. There can be two outcomes: either the Sovereign will write right on my letter: *I give my permission.* Then in a few days I will go to Petersburg and all of my worries are over; or the Sovereign will order that my case be turned over to Dolgoruky for inquiry as to whether there are *special obstacles* in my case. There cannot be any special obstacles, but the permission and the closing of the case will in this instance be much later; perhaps, only by Christmas. In a word, I'm almost beside myself now from the waiting. One hope is unshakable: the Sovereign's mercy. What a person, what a great person for Russia, Artemy Ivanovich! One can see everything and hear everything better here. I've heard a lot, a lot here. And what difficulties he is fighting![7] There are scoundrels who do not like his salutary measures, and they are all backward, incorrigible people. God help Him! Parallel with these worries I had worries about my finances. Finally these, too, have ended. I broke with *The Russian Messenger,* and *Notes of the Fatherland* gave me 120

5. Dostoevsky's "former acquaintance" is Vasily Golovinsky, a member of the Petrashevsky group. Golovinsky's rights were returned to him in 1857. He lived in Tver and occupied a post in the civil service.

6. Yakov Rostovtsev (1803-60) was a member of the committee of inquiry on the Petrashevsky affair.

7. One of the difficulties Alexander II faced was the question of peasant reforms. The Emancipation Edict was issued in February 1861.

rubles per signature, all in all I will have 1800 or 2000 silver rubles. Moreover, I want to sell a selection of my previous works; they will yield one-and-a-half or two thousand in silver. I will live for the time being on these two sales. All this has been horribly troublesome. And even now I'm writing at a moment when my main worries are not yet over. That's why, being in endless worry and agitation, I kept not writing you, our priceless friend, Artemy Ivanovich! But now it's already a different story. Soon all the troubles will end. Only the ordinary, everyday ones will remain, but write, too, our dear friend. And don't even think that I could ever forget you! There's no person in all the world perhaps, who is more devoted to you and respects you more than I! Well, now that I have told you about myself in detail, and only about myself, allow me to speak, my dear, about you and your unforgettable family too.

And, first, I remember life in Semipalatinsk so well, and how you received us, how cordially we met the last time. And kind Praskovya Mikhaylovna, and the sweet faces of your girls Zinaida Artemievna and Lizaveta Nikitishna—all this is memorable and unforgettable.[8] And so write and write in more detail. But about that at the end of the letter, but for the present *a certain little matter*. You surely remember, Artemy Ivanovich, how I always wished for you to move to Russia, to a better position for the education of your dear children, and being devoted to you with all my heart, with sadness told you that you now were not in the right place, were contenting yourself with a paltry salary and were losing your life, but meanwhile, you were working, fussing with things, putting up with job worries and troubles and so forth. You remember all this, and surely don't think that I have forgotten about it. In Vladimir, at a good moment, I talked with Khomentovsky (and, first, above all, rest assured, noble Artemy Ivanovich, that I will not speak lightly or breezily, no matter with whom, about your affairs; moreover, everyone who knows you, regards you with respect; so do I in my conversations with *people* act in such a way that, though it is in your absence, they must look upon you with respect. I in speaking about you finally by no means represent you as a suppliant, but speak simply for myself, and in such a tone as to suggest that you are capable of improving any place with your presence). Khomentovsky is a very noble person and I was able to speak to him; I won't even speak to others. After attentively listening to me, Khomentovsky said to me very sensibly that, of course, there are positions in Russia; that there are good, comfortable positions in his department; but the salaries are not as large and, if they are much larger than in the Siberian battalions, the prices for everything in Russia are much higher than in Siberia and that therefore you need a position with *at least* a salary of 600 or 700 rubles. Otherwise, there's no

8. Praskovya Mikhaylovna (Dostoevsky incorrectly gives her patronymic below as Maximovna) was Geybovich's wife; Zinaida Artemievna, Geybovich's daughter; Lizaveta Nikitishna, probably Geybovich's niece or adopted daughter.

point in even considering it, but that there are few positions with those salaries, and there are very many candidates for them. But that a person who is honest and wishes to do serious work, in his opinion, is always capable of getting a start; but that private positions are the best of all. So many private companies, institutions, societies have started up that *honest* and conscientious people are very badly needed, the salaries are stupendous. The only bad thing is that you are in Siberia. In Russia the matter would be accomplished quickly with a recommendation, and these private positions don't require either any particular technical knowledge or any particular difficulties and snags, but simply the major requirement is work and honesty. After I finished this, I got to talking with Khomentovsky about Vasilchikov.[9] I wanted to find out what terms he's on with him. Splendid ones, it turned out (and Khomentovsky wouldn't lie). Then I said to him that if, for instance, you by some necessity, that is through oppressions at work, transfers and so forth, in a word, if due to work you needed the help of such a person as Vasilchikov, then would it be possible to count on the assistance of Khomentovsky (who is connected with Vasilchikov by an earlier friendship)? Then Khomentovsky told me that if you need to ask for something or write something in connection with work, he gives his word of honor to forward your request to Vasilchikov and that in the majority of cases one can count on certain success. I am writing you this, noble Artemy Ivanovich, so that you will have this in mind, *just in case.* Well, just in case something is needed: then a powerful person, like Vasilchikov, is not superfluous. Furthermore, after I began to feel at home here in Tver, I, in the middle of a conversation, once said to Countess Baranova: "Does the Count need a thoroughly *honest man* for any position?" She answered: "If only you knew how much." Then I said a few words about you; I described you, your family and so forth. But I spoke *in general,* I didn't even name you or say where you are. (I wanted to talk later on with the Count himself.) But she herself told him about this the same day, and when we met again at certain acquaintances' place, she said to me: "I spoke to my husband about the officer you told me about; where is he and who is he?" I told her. She was surprised to hear that you were in Siberia: "How can he travel so far away to Russia?" I answered that let's assume that it's difficult, but let's imagine that this difficulty is removed, what then? She answered: "Anyone will take an honest man, my husband first of all from what you say; but you are speaking of a family, and do you know the local prices? It's impossible to give a position with *a large salary* at first, but one with a small salary is always possible. Perhaps, however, private employment." And that's how the matter ended for the present. I was very happy that I had spoken so lightly this time; I'm happy because I intend to talk with the

9. Lieutenant-General Viktor Illarionovich Vasilchikov (1820-78), governed the Ministry of War for the period 1858-60.

Count myself later on, and seriously this time. But I will not talk about a position in Tver or in the Tver Province; I have different plans and here's what they are—I have two options: the first course: I become acquainted through the Count with his relatives in Petersburg (I hope), incidentally, with Adlerberg too; through other people, with Rostovtsev, to whom I definitely will present myself and with whom Pyotr Petrovich Semyonov, the explorer who visited us in Semipalatinsk, is well acquainted. I very much hope to make the acquaintance of many people in Moscow through another acquaintance of mine. I will get acquainted with these gentleman because I will need them. They're all powerful people, and it's not possible that if anything can be done regarding a comfortable, government position for you, that it couldn't be done through these people. I repeat again, Artemy Ivanovich, I will speak neither idly, nor thoughtlessly; I won't even mention your name where I needn't, and in general I will keep my eyes open. If there isn't a position through these people, then there won't be one through anybody. Then there is the second course: to search for a private position with a large salary, because I hope to make the acquaintance of those gentlemen, the industrialists, too. At least I won't avoid it.

Now the conclusion. I know very well, Artemy Ivanovich, that you consider all of this to be almost impossible; I remember that in Semipalatinsk you looked at me with a smile. But hear me out: first, I am not at all representing myself as some dispenser of positions and will never take upon myself such an *unbearably* ridiculous role. I am a little person and know my place. But I have some idea of the reality around me and I know what I can use to my advantage and to the advantage of my friends. I am acting sincerely on your behalf as a friend of yours who wishes you good fortune with all his heart. You yourself, though you looked at me incredulously when I spoke to you about this in Semipalatinsk, did not forbid me to try, however. Finally, I am acting entirely for your benefit, that is I am acting in my name, not in yours, I am not representing you as a suppliant, I am observing respect for you, will not even mention your name when it's not necessary. In addition I'm scrutinizing the people and the matter in advance. I well know myself that this may all end in trifles and nothing, that is, it may not succeed. But if only God will help, then I will not begin to act before I have shown you clear proof of the matter's certainty and trustworthiness. Then you will make the final decision. You are the master of your fate, and no one else, and the moment something should seem vague or shaky to you, you can reject it absolutely. As far as your moving from Siberia is concerned—that's a purely external matter, a completely possible one and only depends on money. But financial matters are settled in various ways. Finally, I am telling you all of this without misgivings: I know with whom I am speaking; you are a rational, positive person and will not be lured by idle hopes, you will not chase after a crane when you have a tomtit in hand, you will not waste the certain on the uncertain. So *I advise you:* namely, look upon my dreams and hopes as fantasies, but meanwhile permit me to try and search. Well, if God grants success—all the better, why waste it? And you cannot laugh at my impetuosity. You are a most noble person and will realize that I am acting completly disinterestedly and solely out of friendship for you, because I sincerely love you and all of your family. If my dreams are ridiculous, then I myself will be the first to laugh; but my conscience will be clear, because I know that I cannot disturb or upset you; you are a rational person and will not give credence to anything until you have been shown something definite. And I cannot harm you in any other way. And, finally, this is still remote, not soon, even in the event of success. But enough about this. Later we will talk again; there's still a lot that we need to talk over. I will write you again soon, and without waiting for your reply; I am waiting only for my affairs to be settled; I'll definitely inform you as soon as they are settled. Perhaps I'll write even earlier than that. I ask in return that you, too, write as a friend, as a brother. And here's a friendly order for you: inform us in your very first letter, first *about Ayaguz,* about your acquaintances and in general about your life *in more detail:* what people, what faces. Second, how are things at work for you, speaking in general? Third, more details about your family, and in particular about Zinaida Artemievna and Lizaveta Nikitishna: what are they doing, what are they keeping themselves busy with, do they remember us? Tell them that I kiss their hands and ask that they not be angry that I still have not sent them letters and am not sending any now. I will send them letters specially very soon. I remember my promise, after all. Write about how Praskovya Maximovna's health is and whether she remembers us. Marya Dmitrievna sometimes even cries when she recalls you. Honest to God! She has, it seems, even prepared a letter for you. Write, finally, about all the people in Semipalatinsk and Ayaguz, if there's anyone there who knows us; inform us about Mikhail Ivanovich Protasov—the dear man. If he is already in Russia, then it can't be that we won't run into each other. What are you reading? Do you have any books? We're also living a rather boring life while we wait. We aren't buying even the most essential things until we move to Petersburg. I alone keep up acquaintances, Marya Dmitrievna doesn't want to because we have nowhere to receive. And besides, there are only three or four households of acquaintances. I'm acquainted with many people, but visit only a few, those whom it is pleasant to visit. As a city Tver is unbelievably boring. There are few comforts. The expense is horrible. It's built up very well, but boring. The theater is worthless. I still can't sell my carriage; people were offering 30 silver rubles, meanwhile people praise it and say that in another place I would be offered twice as much, but here it's unnecessary because of the railroad. Although the railroad station is three versts from town, you hear the whistle of different trains day and night. We have been at the station several times. It's fine there. But now the letter is already ended. Good-bye, dear Artemy Ivanovich. Good-bye, don't be lazy and not write and remember us. And we will not forget you. I embrace you. My sincere regards to Praskovya Maximovna, I kiss the girls' hands. I will write again soon. And in the meantime I remain, as always, yours truly

F. Dostoevsky.

P.S. Thank Vasily for his letter.[10] My regards to him. What has become of the Novoveyskys?[11] I'll write Mikhail Alexandrovich in a few days.[12]

165. To Mikhail Dostoevsky
29 October 1859. Tver

Tver, 29 October 59.

I hasten to write you just a few words, my dear. There's literally no time. S. D. Yanovsky is here and I'm going to see him now, at his hotel; and I still have to stop in at the post office to get the money. Thank you for the money.[1] But to business: don't bury me alive! It's impossible (I'm certain of this) to end the 1st part earlier, that is, not with the 12th chapter.[2] For Christ's sake, save me. Ask, beg. Show my leter to And[rey] Alexandrovich. Even Nekrasov decided right away that not to end with the 12th chapter means ruining the entire effect right away. If you end with another chapter, then, that means nothing other than concluding with the chapter "Your Excellency," so that the chapter "Mizinchikov" will begin the 2nd part. But remember, judge for yourself: is that possible? The 12th chapter is the only one with which it's possible to end. The effect is lost. Is it possible to work against yourself to such an extent, to be an enemy to *yourself*, to ruin something of yours that is being published in a journal?

10. Vasily: Dostoevsky's former orderly.

11. Zinaida Sytina (neé Geybovich) writes in her memoirs that Dostoevsky was fond of Novoveysky and helped him out financially.

12. Mikhail Alexandrovich Sytnikov, assistant postmaster in Semipalatinsk, died in November 1859.

1. Mikhail sent 125 of the 500 rubles received from Kraevsky for *The Village of Stepanchikovo*.

2. The subject under discussion for the rest of this paragraph is the publication of *The Village of Stepanchikovo* in *Notes of the Fatherland*. Dostoevsky wanted the first installment to end with Chapter 12. Andrey Alexandrovich Kraevsky wanted to shorten the first installment of *The Village of Stepanchikovo* so that the two installments would be more equal. Kraevsky ultimately agreed to Dostoevsky's wishes.

Ask, beg, insist, for God's sake! And answer quickly what was decided. I'll be in a fever until I receive your reply.

Oh, my dear friend, what a favor you would have rendered me if, when you were in Moscow, you had, with your own hand, struck out in the proofs half of what I added to the 1st chapter. That revision was a mistake. The chapter is unbearably boring and long, and it's the 1st.

Good-bye. I feel a bit unwell (don't worry, hemorrhoids). Yanovsky is leaving today. When you read this letter, he'll already be in Petersburg.

Your D.

P.S. Nothing has been heard about my request.³ No reply. I received a letter from Vrangel.

166. To Alexander Vrangel
31 October 1859. Tver

Tver 31 October 59.

I thank you with all my heart, my dear friend, for all your efforts on my behalf. Thank Eduard Ivanovich for me as well.¹ I would have written to him myself, but I keep thinking that perhaps I will soon be in Petersburg and then will see him in person. But meanwhile, despite my hopes, I don't know what to think. I'm definitely like a man suspended between heaven and earth. You know that I wrote the Sovereign directly and that my letter was sent by the local governor, Count Baranov, to Adlerberg, who will give it to the Sovereign Emperor in person. It's now 12 days since the letter was sent. I don't know and haven't heard anything about whether it was shown to the Emperor. If it was shown, then, perhaps, there would have been an answer immediately; at least Count Adlerberg would have written something to me through Count Baranov, our governor, about the result of presenting the letter; and Count Baranov would have informed me right away. But there's nothing so far. I'm lost in conjecture. I wonder (which, moreover, is very likely) whether His Imperial Highness didn't send my letter to Prince

---

3. Dostoevsky is referring to his petition for permission to take up residence in Petersburg.

1. In his letter of 25 October Vrangel wrote Dostoevsky that Eduard Ivanovich Totleben had already spoken with Prince Dolgoruky and had received the Prince's promise to do everything possible.

Dolgoruky to ask him whether there are any particular obstacles to my request. (That's the way it seems to me, the matter should proceed; this is a formal step.) But since there definitely cannot be any particular obstacles to my request (I know that for certain) and since the Prince already promised Ed[uard] Iv[anovich] to give my case his attention—then, it seems to me, he could not hold it up. Are they really about to start making inquiries of Count Baranov, as the governor of the city of Tver, that is, about my conduct? I don't think so. After all Count Adlerberg will transmit the letter in Count Baranov's name. What more could be wanted? (That means that Count Baranov finds me worthy if he himself is exerting himself on my behalf.) In addition, if there were official inquiries, Count Bar[anov], I think, would inform me about that and I would know. My friend, I know you love me and will not refuse me. I would ask you to do something, but I don't even know what to ask. Here's the problem: it would be good to inquire, but of whom? Trouble Ed[uard] Iv[anovich]? Ask Adlerberg through somebody (without making it too public)? Ask Dolgoruky?—I absolutely don't know what to think. If you hear anything, inform me, for God's sake, I beg you, most kind Alexander Yegorovich. I'm on tenterhooks. I'm practically living at the station. I'm spending time in vain and losing at my business dealings. And I have dealings concerning the sale of my works, that is, financial ones; consequently, important ones for me. After all, that is all I'm living on. However, I still am not losing hope. God and the Sovereign are merciful...

I was extremely concerned when I read your letter. What is this you are writing me, my dear one, about your heart, that it can no longer live as before? And when? At the age of 26.[2] But is this really possible? You simply don't know your strength. After having twice sustained heartbreak, you think that you have exhausted everything. However, it's natural to think that. When there's nothing *new*, then it really seems that you're already quite dead. Everyone thinks like that. But the human heart lives and demands life. Yours is also demanding life—and that is a sign of its freshness and strength. It is waiting and pining. But wait a bit. Life will have its way, I'm certain. There's still a lot ahead... How I would like to see and talk with you! I've heard a lot of good things about Polonsky.[3] I met your Dm[itry] Bolkhovsky here. But I don't know anything about Lvov.[4] What's

---

2. Vrangel had written Dostoevsky: "I can get carried away, passionately and ardently, for two days, no more. ...the greater the intensity, the sooner my strength is sapped. There's youth for you! 26 years old, no hopes or dreams."

3. Vrangel had written Dostoevsky that Yakov Polonsky (1819-98), poet and editor of *The Russian Word*, wanted to meet him.

4. This sentence is written in reply to Vrangel's letter: "To my pleasure I hear that Tver isn't so boring for you now; I'm told that my friend and comrade Fyodor Lvov works for Baranov, get acquainted with him—he's the officer for special commissions, as is Dmitry Bolkhovsky."

this Baden story?⁵ This is absolutely the first time I've heard of it. Oh, my God! How much time has passed since we saw each other! Both you and I have lived a bit and lived through a lot.

I'm utterly bored in Tver, though there are 2 or 3 people here. Some of your books have been saved, though they got a bit worn from the journey. But I had only the list (now mislaid) from your mineral collection and not more than 3 or four minerals. I left them in Semipalatinsk. I don't know what became of the whole collection. I considered your game bag and small dagger (as it was in the suitcase) to be my property, since you gave me everything, and, on leaving, I in turn, by the way, gave the little dagger to Valikhanov. Forgive me for this. Valikhanov is a most kind and remarkable fellow. He, it seems, is in Petersburg? Did I write you about him? He's a member of the Geographical Society. Inquire about Valikhanov there if there's time. I like him very much and am very interested in him. Good-bye, my friend. I embrace you. I planned to write more; but I'm in a hurry. Perhaps we will see each other. God grant it.

M[arya] Dmitrie[vna] sends you her regards.

Yours truly Dostoevsky

167. To Eduard Totleben
2 November 1859. Tver

Your Excellency,
Eduard Ivanovich,

I do not know how to thank you even for your letter and for everything that you are doing for me.¹ May God reward you. But I am guilty before you, though unintentionally. After my letter to you I, on the advice of some people who are concerned about me, wrote a letter to the Sovereign. In my letter I requested permission to live in Petersburg, and at the same time for the placement of my twelve-year-old stepson in one of the Petersburg schools; and if a school is not possible, then in one of the Petersburg cadet academies. That is the essence of my letter. The local Tver governor, Count

---

5. Vrangel wrote Dostoevsky: "I should tell you, as a friend, of my second adventure with Z. pendant X [i.e., Yekaterina Gerngross], a drama acted out publicly in Baden-Baden, which made a lot of noise in Petersburg and the spas, but it's long, and sad, and so I'm putting it aside until our first meeting."

1. Totleben had personally interceded with Prince Dolgoruky on behalf of Dostoevsky.

Baranov, who shows sincere concern for me, undertook to forward my letter in his name to his relative Adjutant-General Count Adlerberg, for delivery to His Imperial Highness. It's already been two weeks since the letter was sent, but there has still been no news from Count Adlerberg. I am guilty before you in that asking you to be my mediator with Prince Dolgoruky, I did not inform you until now about my letter to the Emperor. But forgive me, noble Eduard Ivanovich! My guilt is unintentional. I was waiting for Alexander Yegorovich Vrangel's reply. But he was in the country and informed me of giving you my letter almost a week after I had sent my letter to the Sovereign. In response to his letter I asked him to notify you of the new measures that I have taken. Most importantly: having sent my letter to the Emperor, I very much hoped that I would soon receive a reply from Count Baranov through Count Adlerberg. Then I, at that very moment, would have been in Petersburg and would have thanked you in person. If there is anyone who sincerely, with all the warmth of a noble heart has pitied me and helped me, it is you. I know that, I feel it, and my heart knows how to be grateful.

You have done more for me than anyone else and particularly now, having received Prince Dolgoruky's promise and his consent to my living in Petersburg. The Emperor, after reading my letter, will definitely ask the Prince for information about me, that is, whether there are any particular observations concerning me. I am certain that there are no such observations against me. But the matter could drag on because of inquiries. Now, at your request, the Prince will pay particular attention to my case. On your instructions I am sending a letter this very day to the Prince and also one to Adjutant-General Timashev.[2] I thank them both, explain my request in detail, ask for their assistance and inform each of them of my letter to the Emperor. Count Baranov, on his part, wants to write to Prince Dolgoruky immediately about me.

I rely on our magnanimous Tsar. God grant that He see the success of his great initiatives. How fortunate you are, Eduard Ivanovich, that you can serve Him so close to His person!

I repeat once more: I do not have words to express to you all my gratitude for your concern for me.

I know absolutely nothing of the fate of my letter to the Sovereign. I do not know whether Count Adlerberg passed it on. But I hope that if my letter is in the Sovereign's hands, He will pardon me. His mercy is boundless.

Accept, most noble Eduard Ivanovich, assurance of the feelings of my most profound respect and ardent devotion for you.

Tver   Yours truly Fyodor Dostoevsky.
November 2nd 1859.

---

2. Alexander Yegorovich Timashev (1818-93) was the director of the Third Department. See Official Letters 8 and 9 for Dostoevsky's petitions to Dolgoruky and Timashev.

168. To Alexander Vrangel
2 November 1859. Tver

Tver 2 November 59.

My priceless friend, Alexander Yegorovich, my letter this time is a *business* one and is all about my affairs. I have requests for you. I'm relying upon you completely. The point is this: Ed[uard] Iv[anovich] sent me a letter in which he notifies me that he spoke about me to Prince Dolgoruky and Adjutant-General Timashev; they have both given their consent to my living in Petersburg and ask that I write them letters about this.[1] With this same post I am informing Ed[uard] Iv[anovich] and sending the letters to Prince Dolgoruky and Timashev. I particularly and most earnestly ask you, my friend, to pass on my letter to Ed[uard] Iv[anovich] immediately, after making an envelope and addressing it. Read my letter carefully. I confess to you that I am in great trouble. After having chosen Ed[uard] Iv[anovich] to be my mediator with Prince Dolgoruky, I suddenly wrote a letter to the Sovereign and it was passed on to Adlerberg through Count Baranov for presentation to His Imperial Highness (which I informed you about in my last letter). I wonder whether Ed[uard] Ivanovich was not offended. Understand me: Ed[uard] Iv[anov]ich is a most noble person and will not be bothered by trifles, but he has not known me personally *for a long time.* I would so not want him to think badly of me! The bad thing is this: *it's as if I, not trusting his efforts and pains on my behalf, am appealing to other people, expecting more from them than from him.* At least *I should have* informed Ed[uard] Iv[anovi]ch of this right away, when I made up my mind to write the Sovereign. Even then I felt the necessity of that. But you *had left* for the country then, I did not have a letter from you and therefore could not know whether you had managed to pass on my letter to Ed[uard] Iv[anovi]ch. I did not venture another letter without notification from you. And besides, through whom would I have sent another letter to Ed[uard] Iv[anovi]ch, without even knowing his address? I am writing him about all of this.

That same circumstance, that I *apparently* trust the efforts on my behalf of others more than Ed[uard] Iv[anovich]'s, is absolutely unjust, and I am not at all to blame. Count Baranov is the governor. Prince Dolgoruky certainly would have made an inquiry about me to him *as the governor,* regarding whether I am trustworthy—if I had petitioned the Prince about residing in Petersburg. This would have resulted in a waste of time. Count Baranov forwarded my letter to the Sovereign *in his name* as the governor, and consequently, there is no need to make inquiries about me if the

---

1. See Letter 167.

governor himself is making an effort on my behalf; consequently, the case may have won a lot of time. In addition, in my letter to the Sovereign I ask for the placement of my stepson, Pasha, in a school. Marya Dmitrievna is terribly worried about her son's fate. She keeps thinking that I if I die, she will again be left with a growing son in the same misery as after her first widowhood. She is frightened, and although she does not tell me everything, I see her anxiety. And since I still do not know when life in Tver will come to an end, and Pasha is not settled and is losing valuable time, in a decisive moment I ventured on an extreme measure and, relying on His mercy, wrote the Sovereign. That's the story of my letter. I reasoned that if I am refused one thing, then, perhaps, I will not be refused the other, and if the Sovereign does not deign to permit me to live in Petersburg, then at least He will admit Pasha so as not to refuse completely.

My friend, I believe absolutely in Ed[uard] Iv[anovi]ch's nobility and clear sight; but if you notice that he is angry that I did not inform him right away about my letter to the Sovereign, defend me. It will be too painful for me if he reproaches me. I expect everything from your friendship. Inform me, for God's sake, about all of this in detail.

I already wrote you about the letter I sent through Adlerberg. Baranov has not had any news from Adlerberg yet—and I am at a loss as to what this means. Probably, Count Adlerberg is being slow with delivering it. I do not know what will happen! My only hope is on the Sovereign's mercy and on good people.

I do not know when I will embrace you, my dear. Forgive me for the endless requests and tasks. But soon, perhaps, everything will end, and end for the better.

I am not writing anything else this time. I have to prepare the letters to Prince Dolgoruky and Timashev by tomorrow. A horror of a job. Goodbye. I embrace you heartily and, I repeat, am relying on your friendship for me.

Your devoted Fyodor Dostoevsky.

169. To Mikhail Dostoevsky
12 November 1859. Tver

Tver 12 November 59.

Yesterday I received your letter (dated the 9th), my friend Misha, and I want to write you at least a couple of lines. You won't believe how nauseating it is for me now to stay in Tver and not have any idea about the present status of my case. If only there were some estimate, but I can't even estimate, since I have absolutely no idea what is happening about me in Petersburg. I've written everybody, asked everybody—and no news at all. I agree with you that I chose the most difficult route in this matter. I grumble at myself every day and—wait. If only somebody would remind Adlerberg about me! What if my letter hasn't even been presented? Would you, in a spare moment (if you'll have one), go to see Vrangel and drop a hint: wouldn't Totleben undertake to tell Adlerberg or Dolgoruky to tell Dolgoruky to speak to Adlerberg, or himself present on his part my request to His Imperial Highness?[1] Oh, if it were soon! The Sovereign is merciful; we all know that; but the formalities, the delay! [3 undecipherable words] The main thing is that I need to be in Petersburg to sell my works. I have, however, a plan in mind. Namely: not to sell them for money, but, if it's possible, to have them printed by Shchepkin and Soldatenkov in Moscow in an edition of 2000 copies.[2] They don't give money, but will print it and as the book is sold, they first deduct their investment along with a reasonable percentage. That seems to me to be best for a number of reasons that would take a long time to explain, and I would certainly do that, if on my arrival in Petersburg I got some money for living expenses right away (besides what I'll get from Kraevsky). You realize that this is all of great interest for me. It's my living and future. However, don't take my words à la letter [literally], and if the occasion should arise, sell them for money; look for this occasion, without waiting for me to come to Petersburg. Realize that time is passing. It's already time to publish them. Time is passing, and meanwhile financial opportunities are being lost...

But to hell with money! I'd like to embrace you—that's what I'd like! To settle near you soon, in your circle. It's hard for me to live here. I can't tackle anything because of various mental anxieties; time is passing... You will not believe, my dear Misha, what waiting means! A month! But will it be over in a month? Perhaps three or four months will pass.. You write about an idea for which you need 15 to 20 thousand to begin with. All of that worries me too, brother. It's as if we've turned out to be some sort of cursed beings. You look at others: neither talent, nor abilities—but the person goes out into the world, makes his capital. And we struggle on... I'm certain, for example, that you and I have a lot more smarts, abilities and business know-how (sic) than Kraevsky and Nekrasov. They're peasants in

1. In October 1859 Dostoevsky appealed to Alexander II for permission to reside in Petersburg (see Official and Business Letter 7). Count Adlerberg had promised his relative, Count Pavel Baranov, to deliver the letter to the Tsar personally. Eduard Totleben had written to Dostoevsky that both Dolgoruky and Timashev of the Third Section had given their verbal approval to Dostoevsky's request.

2. The booksellers Shchepkin and Soldatenkov had published books by Nekrasov, Ogaryov, Koltsov, Polezhaev and Belinsky in the period 1856-59.

literature, after all. Nevertheless, they're getting rich and we're sitting on the rocks. You, for example, started your own business. How much work, and what results? What did you gain? And thank God that you had something to live on and raise your children. Your business reached a certain point and stopped. That's sad for a man with abilities. No, brother, we have to think, and seriously; we have to take a risk and undertake some literary venture—a journal, for instance... However, we'll think and talk about that together. The matter isn't closed.

My novel really did come out short; 13-14 signatures.[3] Very small, and I'll get less than I had counted on. But what the heck! Send me, for God's sake, a separate copy even before the issue is out; realize how all of this is of great interest to me. I'll get 1050 rubles for 8 3/4 signatures, consequently, when the issue is published I'll have, after deducting the debt to you (375 rubles)—175, and not 125. I beg you: get the money as soon as possible and, just in case, send it to me immediately. Who knows, perhaps my fate will actually be decided. Then the money will be needed for my departure from here. And so send it as soon as possible.

Good-bye, I embrace you, write me something, and soon.

Your Dostoevsky

As soon as the novel appears—inform me right away in all particulars everything you hear. What the talk is, if there is any.

170. To Varvara Karepina
12 November 1859. Tver

Tver. 12 November 59.

It's already been four days since I've been back in Tver, and only now have I gotten around to informing you of my arrival, dear Varenka. There are various matters and little bothers all the time. I traveled without mishap, but was 5 minutes late for the first train and was forced to take the passenger train. I arrived home after 10 and told my wife about my adventures the whole evening. I praised you, darling Varenka, to the skies (Verochka, too)—and could I have done differently? I so much want to see you again. As I calculate now, I see that I need to stay in Moscow a bit

---

3. *The Village of Stepanchikovo.*

longer.[1] Apart from the pleasure of becoming closer to you, there may be business (literary), I sense that. And so, perhaps, I'll spend some time in Moscow before the holidays. I have so fired my wife's imagination that she wants to go too. I don't know if we'll manage be able to go together. If we both come, we'll stay in a hotel, and, without even stopping for tea, will come straight to see you, my darling sister. But when will this be! And will it be?

There's not yet a word from Petersburg about my affairs: I'll receive permission someday. And until that time I wait—and waiting is the most unbearable position. I received a letter from our brother Misha; part of my novel has already been printed and will soon be out, but it turned out to be fewer signatures in print than I had estimated, and, consequently, I'll get less money, some 250 or 300 rubles less.[2] Misfortune on all sides.

Misha writes that for a time they expected me any day. The rumor had spread that I had already been given permission to come. It's very sad that the rumor was not justified. He keeps inviting me, wants to see me, and I do too, no less than he. It's so nauseating in Tver. There's nothing more unbearable than an uncertain situation.

I kiss you, dear Varenka, with all my heart. You and Misha are dearer to me than anyone else. Give Verochka my regards and a kiss, regards from me to her husband, uncle, auntie and grandmother. My regards to your children. I kiss Mashenka's hand.[3] By my arrival she probably will have learned something cute. Kiss all of Verochka's children;[4] especially Katya and the diplomat-cook. Good-bye, my darling, until we meet.

Your brother F. Dostoevsky.

171. To Alexander Vrangel
19 November 1859. Tver

Tver 19 November 1859

My dear friend, Alexander Yegorovich, I hasten to write you. Various circumstances positively prevented me from answering you earlier. And

1. This is the only letter that mentions Dostoevsky's trip to Moscow in November 1859, most likely taken without official permission.

2. The first installment of *The Village of Stepanchikovo* was published in November 1859.

3. Mashenka is Varvara's daughter.

4. Vera Ivanovna had six children at this time: Sofia, Maria, Alexander, Yulia, Nina, Yekaterina.

even now I am taking up my pen to write about business again. Someday it will end and someday I will embrace all of you, my dear ones. Again I have a request of you, and God grant that it be the last one! I've worn you out with these requests. But you were always like a brother to me. Don't refuse me now.

Here is the matter: you write and ask me why I don't come to see you, since I have Dolgoruky's and Timashev's consent to my settling in Petersburg. That's the trouble, my friend, it's impossible; for the case now rests with the Sovereign. I wrote Him myself, and now He will decide. I had thought of coming for a time; because if Dolgoruky consents *even to my permanent move to Petersburg,* then he will not be angry if I, while waiting for the final decision, come to Petersburg for several days. I had decided to go and told Count Baranov about it. But he advised me against it, fearing that I would do harm to myself by willfully taking advantage of a right that I had so recently requested and about which I have still not received an answer. You have to agree, my friend, that I can't go if Baranov doesn't wish it. And I can't leave without telling him. He forwarded my letter to the Sovereign (through Adlerberg) and asked that it be delivered in *his name,* consequently, he vouched for me as the governor; and so if I went on the sly from him, it would be indiscreet on my part. And so here's what I've thought up and what the Count himself advised me. Namely: to write Prince Dolgoruky a letter in which I request a temporary stay in Petersburg, while waiting for the final decision regarding my first request, that is, my permanent residency in Petersburg. I've already written this letter to Dolgoruky and am sending it today. I cite my financial circumstances as the reason for my request to go to Petersburg; that is, that I plan to publish a selection of my earlier works, that I must find a publisher, that is, a buyer, and that it's imperative to do this in person. Because I may lose a lot, which has already happened to me more than once, if I proceed by way of correspondence; and any loss in my present extreme position is significant to me. (This is all correct and true; I want to consult with Kushelev. He's a publisher and might pay me decently for my works. In addition, he and I still have settling up to do in connection with the journal, and I need to speak about this in person.[1] That's why I've given that reason in the letter to Dolgoruky, it goes without saying, without mentioning Kushelev.) What do you think now, my dear? If Prince Dolgoruky had consented even to my settling in Petersburg, will he really refuse me permission to come for a short time while waiting for the final decision? I don't think so; but they may *delay the answer.* That's why I have the following request of you:

---

1. Mikhail Dostoevsky had begun negotiations with Kushelev, the editor of *The Russian Word,* about publishing Dostoevsky's collected works. The "settling up" refers to the final accounting for *Uncle's Dream,* which appeared in Kushelev's journal.

If possible, my dear, inform Eduard Ivanovich about the fact that I, today, on the 19th, sent a letter to Dolgoruky with this request, and inform him as soon as possible.[2] I would have written Eduard Ivanovich myself, but I'm afraid that I've already been bothering him too much. You—my brother and friend, I don't stand on ceremony with you; we are bound together by old, good memories. And Eduard Ivanovich is only troubling himself about me because of his extreme kindness and nobility. I am so afraid, so afraid of bothering him too much! He's so tactful with me that I too must be tactful with him. On the other hand, I understand his situation too. Who knows what his relationship is with all those people? Perhaps, it's difficult for him to ask them for something. And so, *the main point, spirit and sense* of my request to you: go (if only you can) to Eduard Ivanovich, having called to your aid all the tact of your heart, and observe carefully how Eduard Ivanovich would receive my request. If you see that it won't burden him, then tell him everything. Namely: tell him what the trouble is, that on November 19th I sent a letter to Dolgoruky with such-and-such a request and ask whether he could support this letter of mine to Dolgoruky with his own appeal to him on my behalf. If he says that he can, then tell him the whole truth. If you find, however, that I am troubling him too much—if you find this without even going to see him, then don't go at all. Everything is left to your discretion, my friend, and I am relying on your sympathy for me. The request, you see, is a fateful one! They may refuse, they may not answer, and finally, they may drag the business out; they may, finally, answer very quickly, but with a refusal. And therefore, it's important not to lose time! However, everything is left to your discretion.

My regards to Ed[uard] Iv[anovich] and thank him for me. For now, good-bye, my dear friend. I'm not writing you anything else. Soon, perhaps, we'll see each other. I'm not even answering my brother today—I'm in such a hurry.

Entirely yours, Dostoevsky.

19 November

2. See Official and Business Letter 10 for Dostoevsky's petition to Prince Dolgoruky. By writing to the Tsar directly, Dostoevsky had made things considerably more difficult for Eduard Totleben and others to help him, since it was now necessary to wait for the Tsar's decision. Dostoevsky finally did receive permission to reside in Petersburg, and arrived there with his family in December 1859.

Official Correspondence

1. To the Chief of the Officers' Departments
Of the Main Academy of Engineering
Captain Gartong[1]
8 June 1843. Petersburg

To the Chief of the Officers' Departments
Of the Main Academy of Engineering
Captain Gartong

2nd Lieutenant-Engineer Dostoevsky

Report

Suffering from a pain in the chest and continuous rheumatic pains, I have sought the advice of a doctor, State Counselor Valkenau, who has informed me that bathing in the sea would bring me undoubted benefit. But since the water at Kronstadt, where the practical training for the higher officer class is to be held, in the opinion of Doctor Valkenau, is quite weak, bathing in it cannot at all be considered a curative method. Therefore I request most humbly, Your Excellency, that you petition His Excellency the Director of the Academy to grant me a twenty-eight-day furlough to Revel for the use of the waters there, at a favorable time of the year, that is, in the middle of the summer, when the water has not yet turned cold.—I consider it my duty to add that if the Director sees fit to entrust me with training and work in Revel corresponding to that impending for us at Kronstadt, I will do everything in my power in order through diligence and industry to justify his indulgence.

2nd Lieutenant-Engineer Dostoevsky

1843
June 8

1. Vasily Andreevich Gartong.

2. To the Chief of the Officers' Departments
Of the Main Academy of Engineering
Captain Gartong
13 June 1843. Petersburg

To the Chief of the Officers' Departments
Of the Main Academy of Engineering
Captain Gartong

2nd Lieutenant-Engineer Dostoevsky

Report

I have the honor of presenting to Your Excellency a petition to His Imperial Majesty for a furlough to Revel for medical treatment.—At the same time I am presenting a certificate from the doctor of medicine Valkenau.

2nd Lieutenant-Engineer Dostoevsky

1843
June 13

3. To the Commander of the 7th Siberian Line Battalion Lieutenant-Colonel Belikhov 27 July 1857. Semipalatinsk

To the Commander of the 7th Siberian Line Battalion
Lieutenant-Colonel Belikhov

From Ensign Dostoevsky of the Same Battalion

Report

Yesterday, upon returning from a two-month furlough given me for the treatment of chronic epilepsy at the Ozyorny outpost,[1] I received a notice from the Semipalatinsk city police that my stepson, the nine-year-old Isaev, has been accepted at the Siberian Cadet Corps. The duty office of the corps headquarters informed the Semipalatinsk city police, on July 17, 1857, memo No. 5207, that His Excellency the Corps Commander was pleased to issue an order for the release from the Tobolsk District Treasury, to be signed for by Mrs. Isaeva (now my wife, Dostoevskaya), of travel funds and an order for relay horses for the delivery to the Siberian Cadet Corps by August 1 of this year of her son, Isaev. But since my wife, upon marrying me, moved from the city of Kuznetsk, Tomsk Province, to the city of Semipalatinsk, the Chief of the Corps Headquarters, notified of this circumstance, has already asked the Tobolsk Treasury Office for the issuance of travel funds and an order for relay horses for the delivery of Pavel Isaev to the city of Omsk, from the Semipalatinsk District Treasury, at the request of his mother, Mrs. Dostoevskaya, formerly Isaeva.

Having the honor to notify you most humbly of this circumstance, Your Excellency, I find myself compelled to add that the Semipalatinsk District Treasury, without a ukase from the Tobolsk Treasury Office, cannot issue Pavel Isaev the proper travel funds. And therefore I ask you most humbly to inform His Excellency the Semipalatinsk Military Governor of this circumstance. As Pavel Isaev's stepfather, I am obliged to arrange his delivery to the Siberian Cadet Corps, definitely by August 1 of this year, or at least the first few days of the month. Having a person entrusted with accompanying Pavel Isaev, namely, the mailman of the Semipalatinsk post office Lyapukhin,[2] I, if I cannot immediately receive travel funds, must definitely provide my stepson with an order for relay horses, so that there be no delays on the road.

Having the honor of explaining to Your Excellency all these

---

1. The Ozyorny outpost was located about 15 miles from Semipalatinsk.
2. See Letter 128.

circumstances, I make bold to ask Your Excellency most humbly to bring this to the attention of His Excellency the Semipalatinsk Military Governor and petition His Excellency for a government order for relay horses for delivering Pavel Isaev to the Siberian Cadet Corps. Without it I cannot arrange for his delivery to Omsk during the first few days of August, and if he fails to report on time, he may lose his right to enroll in the Corps.

Ensign of the 7th Siberian Line Battalion
Dostoevsky

Semipalatinsk
27 July 1857

4. Waiver
16 January 1858. Semipalatinsk

I, the undersigned, affirm that if, in accordance with my most humble petition, my resignation from service is granted, I will not ask for any further government funds anywhere. My place of residence following my retirement will be the capital city of Moscow.

16 January 1858. The regional city of Semipalatinsk.

From Ensign Dostoevsky of the 7th Siberian Line Battalion.[1]

---

1. The waiver was attached to the letter to Alexander II that follows.

5. To Alexander II
Beginning of March, 1858. Semipalatinsk

Most Serene, August, Grand Sire
Emperor Alexander Nikolaevich,
Autocrat of All the Russias, Most Merciful Sovereign!

Fyodor Mikhaylovich Dostoevsky,
Ensign of the 7th Siberian Line
Battalion, petitions for the
Following:

I, of the nobility of St. Petersburg Province, entered Your Imperial Majesty's service as a petty officer on January 16, 1838, in the Petty Officer Company of the Main Academy of Engineering, on the assent of His Imperial Majesty's Inspector-General of Engineering Matters, for good conduct and knowledge of drill service was promoted to the rank of noncommissioned officer on November 19, 1840, by Imperial decree renamed a porte-épée cadet in the same company on December 27, 1840. Promoted after an examination to the rank of field ensign engineer on the fifth day of August, 1841, at the age of nineteen, with retention in the Main Academy of Engineering for continuing the full course of studies in the higher officer class, entered active service in the Engineering Corps August 12, 1843, attached to the St. Petersburg Engineering Command for use in the drafting room of the engineering department on August 23, 1843, by Imperial order released from service by reason of health with the rank of lieutenant October 19, 1844, removed from the ranks of the St. Petersburg Engineering Command December 17, 1844, by Imperial order reduced to the ranks December 19, 1849 and sent to convict labor in fortresses. On finishing the term as a common soldier, March 2, 1854, assigned to this 7th Siberian Line Battalion, by Imperial order promoted to the rank of noncommissioned officer January 15, 1856, for distinction in service promoted by Imperial order to the rank of ensign October 1, 1856, in the same battalion, did not serve in the elections of the nobility. In the course of my service I have not been in campaigns and actions against the enemy. Have not had special assignments at Your Imperial Majesty's command or from my commanders. Was not awarded orders and medals of distinction, did not receive the Imperial favor of munificent rescripts and awards. I was under punishment by Imperial sentencing, which occurred December 19, 1849, following the report of the Auditor-General, for participation in criminal designs, the dissemination of the letter by the writer Belinsky, full of insolent expressions against the Orthodox Church and higher authority,[1] and an attempt along with others to disseminate works against the government by means of a private printing press. Stripped of the rank of lieutenant and all rights of station and sent to convict labor in fortresses for four years. But by decree of Your Imperial Majesty, transmitted by the Minister of War on April 18, 1857, in memo No. 2468, to the Commander of the Separate Siberian Corps, I and my legitimate children are granted our former rights of station, but without the right to former possessions. I was on furlough for 28 days beginning June 21, 1843, and reported on time. Studied at the Main Academy of Engineering. Married to Marya Dmitrievna Isaeva, widow of a district secretary, have no children. Of the Orthodox faith, she is with me. Neither I, my parents, nor my wife have hereditary or acquired property. I am 35 years old. *Attach to this petition.*[2]

Now, because of my health, which has been completely undermined in service, I feel a general weakness of energy in my organism, in view of my emaciated figure, and I often suffer from a nervous pain in the face, as a consequence of the organic suffering of my brain, I can no longer continue in Your Majesty's service, about which fact I am enclosing a certificate, No. 26, signed by Doctor Yermakov, who is assigned to the 7th Siberian Line Battalion, and made out in the presence of Junior Captain Bakhirev of the 7th Line Battalion.[3] And I petition most humbly for the following. *The 7th Siberian Line Battalion*

That the present petition be accepted and that I, mentioned in connection with the above-stated illnesses, listed in certificate No. 26, be released from military duty on the basis of article 469 of the 1st continuation of the 11th copy of Part II of the military code, with a promotion in rank, for which after my retirement I will not ask for any other government support, I attach my waiver of January 16, 1858, to be delivered to the Commander of the 7th Siberian Line Battalion. This petition was recopied by noncommisioned officer Andrey Andreevich Shilitsyn of the 7th Siberian Line Battalion but composed by the petitioner himself.

Signed by Ensign Fyodor Mikhaylovich Dostoevsky.
I will have my residence in the capital city of Moscow.[4]

---

1. A reference to Belinsky's famous "Letter to Gogol" (1847), written in outraged response to Gogol's *Selected Passages from a Correspondence with Friends.* A powerful indictment of serfdom and virtual credo of the left-leaning Westernizing intelligentsia, Belinsky's letter circulated for decades clandestinely, in manuscript form only. Dostoevsky read the letter aloud at meetings of both the Durov-Palm Circle and the Petrashevsky Circle.

2. In the present letter the use of italics indicates passages added in Dostoevsky's own hand.

3. The document refers specifically to Dostoevsky's epilepsy.

4 Dostoevsky's petition to be allowed to resign from service was granted 18 March 1859. He was allowed to live in Tver (now Kalinin), without the right to visit Moscow or St. Petersburg, and secret police surveillance over him was established.

6. To Alexander Pavlovsky,[1]
Director of the Siberian Cadet Corps
Second Half of May, 1858. Semipalatinsk

Your Excellency, Alexander Mikhaylovich,

At the end of 1857 my stepson, Pavel Isaev, the son of district secretary Alexander Isaev, who died in service, enrolled in the Siberian Cadet Corps as a government-supported pupil. I asked you at that time to accept him in the corps, in the first place, so that the boy would not become accustomed to idleness at home and lose his hard-won primary education, when such a significant amount of time had already been lost in idleness. And in the second place, I myself, being in service in the 7th Siberian Line Battalion and still considering myself an exile, did not foresee a return soon to Russia, and therefore was obliged to raise my stepson here, in Siberia.

Having now received permission to retire and along with it permission to go to Russia, I find it absolutely impossible to leave the young Isaev in Siberia. Besides the fact that it is difficult and disadvantageous to raise children far away from their family, I would not like to leave him here as a complete orphan, abandoned by his stepfather. Lastly, he is the only child of a mother who cannot part with him forever: such a separation would be almost eternal.

Forgive me, Your Excellency, for making bold to trouble you by setting forth such details. I just wanted to depict for you all of the necessity that forces me now to appeal to Your Excellency with a most humble request for the release of Isaev, completely, from the Corps, for his further education in Russia, near his family. In submitting my petition to you, I consider myself obliged to hope for your just and philanthropic decision on this matter.

With the most profound respect I remain Your Excellency's most humble servant.

Fyodor Dostoevsky

Semipalatinsk 58

---

1. Alexander Mikhaylovich Pavlovsky (1800-67), director of the Siberian Cadet Corps, where Pavel Isaev studied from 1857 to 1859.

7. To Alexander II
Between October 10 and October 18, 1859. Tver

Your Imperial Majesty,

I, a former state criminal, make bold to cast my humble petition before Your throne. I know that I am unworthy of Your Imperial Majesty's kindnesses and am the last person who could hope to earn Your Imperial mercy. But I am unfortunate, and You, our Emperor, are infinitely merciful. Forgive me for my letter and do not punish with Your ire an unfortunate person in need of Your mercy.

I was convicted of a state crime in 1849, in St. Petersburg, reduced to the ranks, stripped of the rights of station and exiled to Siberia, to convict labor of the second degree, in fortresses, for four years, with enrollment in the ranks of common soldiers at the end of the term of labor. In 1854, on leaving the Omsk fortress prison, I joined the 7th Siberian Line Battalion as a common soldier; in 1855 was promoted to the rank of non-commissioned officer, and the next year, 1856, was favored with Your Imperial Majesty's kindness and promoted to the rank of officer. In 1858 Your Imperial Majesty deigned to grant me the right to hereditary noble status. The same year I retired as a consequence of epilepsy, which manifested itself in me during the first year of my penal servitude,[1] and now, having received permission to retire, I have moved and taken up residence in the city of Tver. My illness is growing worse and worse. I seem to lose consciousness, imagination, spiritual and bodily strength from each attack. The outcome of my illness is debilitation, death or insanity. I have a wife and stepson about whom I must concern myself. I have no independent means of support and earn my livelihood exclusively through literary work, which is difficult and exhausting in my ill condition. But meanwhile my doctors offer me hope for treatment, based on the fact that my illness is acquired, not hereditary. But I can only receive serious and definitive medical help in Petersburg, where there are doctors who specialize in the study of nervous illnesses. Your Imperial Majesty! My entire fate, health, and life are in Your hands! Have the kindness to allow me to move to St. Petersburg in order to use the advice of the capital's doctors. Resurrect me and grant me the opportunity with the repair of my health to be useful to my family and perhaps even in some way to my

---

1. The statement that Dostoevsky's epilepsy first manifested itself while he was in prison is untrue. Dostoevsky had had epileptic seizures well before prison. For an exhaustive study of Dostoevsky's epilepsy, see James L. Rice, *Dostoevsky and the Healing Art* (1986).

fatherland! Two of my brothers, from whom I was separated for 10 years, live in Petersburg; their brotherly care of me could make my difficult situation easier. But in spite of all my hopes, a sad outcome of my disease or my death could leave my wife and stepson without any help. As long as I have even a drop of health and strength in me, I will work to support them. But the future is in the hands of God, and human hopes are unreliable. Most Merciful Emperor! Forgive me my second request as well, and please render the extraordinary kindness of having my stepson, the twelve-year-old Pavel Isaev, enrolled in one of the St. Petersburg gymnasiums[2] at public expense. He is a hereditary noble, the son of district secretary Alexander Isaev, who died in Siberia in Your Imperial Majesty's service, in the city of Kuznetsk in Tomsk Province, who died exclusively because of a lack of medical assistance, impossible in the remote area where he served, and who left his wife and son without any means of support. If, however, acceptance in a gymnasium for Pavel Isaev is impossible, then please, Sire, have him accepted at one of the St. Petersburg cadet corps. You will gladden his poor mother, who teaches her son daily to pray for Your Imperial Majesty's good fortune and that of Your entire august family. You, Sire, are like the sun which shines on the just and the unjust. You have already gladdened millions of Your people; now gladden one more poor orphan, his mother, and an unfortunate sick man from whom the status of outcast has not yet been removed and who is ready to give his whole life for the Tsar who has done much good for His people!

With feelings of reverence and passionate, infinite devotion I make bold to call myself the most loyal and grateful of Your Imperial Majesty's subjects.[3]

Fyodor Dostoevsky

2. "Gymnasium" here refers to a European secondary school, not a sports facility.

3. Alexander II received Dostoevsky's petition after permission to move to St. Petersburg had already been granted by V. A. Dolgorukov, the head of the Third Department. See official letter No. 8, which follows.

8. To Vasily Dolgorukov,[1]
Head of the Third Department
Of His Imperial Majesty's Chancellery
3 November 1859. Tver

Your Highness,

Forgive me for making bold to trouble you with my most humble request. I, a former political criminal, who was under investigation and on trial in St. Petersburg in 1849, and, by Imperial order, that same year was exiled to Siberia to penal servitude in fortresses for 4 years, with enrollment, at the conclusion of the term of labor, in the ranks of common soldiers. After completing the full term of labor, I joined the 7th Siberian Line Battalion as a common soldier in 1854. In 1856, by Imperial order, I was promoted to the rank of noncommissioned officer and on October 1st of the same year to ensign with retention in service in the same battalion. In 1858 I was favored with the Imperial kindness of returning me hereditary noble status. I applied for retirement the same year by reason of severe epilepsy, and in the present year, 1859, was released from service with the rank of second lieutenant and moved to the city of Tver, where I have been about three months.

His Excellency Eduard Ivanovich Totleben has informed me that he has appealed to you with a request: to petition the Emperor for permission for me to live in St. Petersburg. He added in his letter that Your Highness gave Your benevolent consent to that. Encouraged by Eduard Ivanovich's message, I have made up my mind to ask Your Highness most humbly myself, too, not to abandon me in my onerous position.[2] I am ill with epilepsy and meanwhile I must work, support my wife, arrange the fate of my young stepson. The hope for the treatment of my disease calls me to Petersburg, where, availing myself of the advice of very experienced doctors, I might still recover my health and be useful to my family. Moreover, two of my brothers live in Petersburg: I can rely firmly on their constant brotherly help, which is essential for me in my ill state. By giving me the opportunity to return to Petersburg, Your Highness will do me a kindness that will remain in my grateful heart forever.

I consider it my duty to inform Your Highness that two weeks ago I wrote a letter to His Imperial Majesty. The governor of the city of Tver,

---

1. Prince Vasily Andreevich Dolgorukov (1803-68), head of the gendarmerie and Third Department (secret police) from 1858 on.

2. Totleben had informed Dostoevsky that Dolgorukov had already given tentative consent to his, Dostoevsky's, request for permission to live in St. Petersburg, but Totleben added that Dostoevsky needed to write to Prince Dolgorukov himself.

His Excellency Count Baranov,[3] transmitted that letter to his Excellency Count Adlerberg[4] for presentation personally to the Emperor. In that letter, setting forth my whole grievous situation, I asked our monarch most humbly to show me charity and allow me to move to St. Petersburg for treatment of my illness. In the same letter I asked his Imperial Majesty to have my stepson, a hereditary noble, the twelve-year-old Pavel Isaev, accepted at public expense in one of St. Petersburg's gymnasiums. Count Baranov has not yet had any information about that letter from His Excellency Count Adlerberg.

I make bold to nurse the sweet hope that Your Highness will see fit to receive the letter favorably as well as my request and will advocate it to the most magnanimous of monarchs. Forgive me for my hope; but I am writing *to you,* I am asking *you;* how can I not expect compassion and charity!

Please deign, Your Highness, to accept the assurance of the feelings of most profound respect with which I make bold to have the honor of calling myself Your Highness's most humble servant.

Fyodor Dostoevsky

Tver.
3 November 1859.

3. Pavel Trofimovich Baranov (1815-64), Governor of Tver, helped Dostoevsky win permission to return to St. Petersburg. Some scholars have suggested that Baranov served as the prototype for the character von Lembke in the novel *The Devils.*

4. Alexander Vladimirovich Adlerberg (1819-88), adjutant-general, cousin of P. T. Baranov.

9. To Alexander Timashev,[1]
Director of the Third Department
Of His Imperial Majesty's Chancellery
3 November 1859. Tver

Your Excellency, Alexander Yegorovich,

Forgive me for making bold to trouble you with my most humble request. You are being appealed to by a former political criminal who was in penal servitude in fortresses for four years, who was then a common soldier in the 7th Siberian Line Battalion and then thanks to Imperial benevolence finally awarded with promotion to the rank of officer and the return again of hereditary noble status. As a consequence of epilepsy I am now in retirement. His Excellency Eduard Ivanovich Toleben has informed me that he has appealed to you with a request to petition his Imperial Majesty for permission for me to live in St. Petersburg and that Your Excellency has deigned to declare your consent to favorable action on your part. My gratitude to you is infinite. A move to Petersburg for me in my present situation is a great kindness. Only there can I hope to treat my severe illness by availing myself of the advice of experienced doctors. In addition, in any event I can find help for me and for my family in Petersburg from my relatives—help which is essential because of my illness.

I consider it my duty to inform Your Excellency that two weeks ago I wrote a letter to His Imperial Majesty. The governor of Tver Province, His Excellency Count Baranov, forwarded the letter to to His Excellency Count Adlerberg for delivery personally to the Emperor. In that letter I set forth all my grievous situation and asked our magnanimous monarch to have mercy on me and allow me to move to St. Petersburg for the treatment of my illness. In the same letter I asked His Imperial Majesty to have my stepson, a hereditary noble, twelve-year-old Pavel Isaev, accepted at government expense in one of St. Petersburg's gymnasiums. His Excellency Count Baranov has not yet received any information about that letter from His Excellency Count Adlerberg.

Making bold to hope for your favorable and compassionate interest in my fate, I most humbly beg Your Excellency to deign to accept the assurance of my feelings of most profound respect and complete devotion.

Tver   Fyodor Dostoevsky

3rd of November, 1859

---

1. Alexander Yegorovich Timashev (1818-93), director of the Third Department 1856-61. In the 1870s he served as Minister of Internal Affairs.

10. To Vasily Dolgorukov,
Head of the Third Department
Of His Imperial Majesty's Chancellery
19 November 1859. Tver

Your Highness,

Recently, having received from His Excellency Adjutant-General Totleben notification of your consent to my settling in St. Petersburg, I wrote you a letter in which, setting forth the reasons for my move, I asked Your Highness not to ignore my request and to receive it favorably.

I would not make bold to trouble you another time in such a short time; but the extreme nature of my situation forces me to appeal to you again with another request. I most humbly ask you to allow me, while waiting for the final decision on my first request, to go to Petersburg for a while, even if only for a very short time.

The reasons forcing me to ask for this are the necessity of my earning means of livelihood for myself and for my family. I am a writer, I write for the journals, and that is what I live on. At the present time, not having anything in view, I have decided to publish a collection of my earlier works and must find a publisher, that is, a buyer. I must do that in person. In acting without seeing the person directly, I may lose a lot, which has already happened to me more than once. And for me in my present situation any financial loss is quite significant, since all the means of my livelihood are in my labor.

In addition, two of my brothers and a sister[1] whom I have not seen in many years, after such a long separation, live in St. Petersburg.

Making bold to hope for your favorable attention to my request, I most humbly beg Your Highness to honor me with your notification.

Please deign to accept the assurance of my feelings of most profound respect.

Fyodor Dostoevsky

Tver. 19 November 1859

---

1. Alexandra Mikhaylovna Dostoevskaya.

Dostoevsky's Correspondents

The following is a listing of the letters in volume 1 by addressee. The numbers refer to letter number, not page number. Letters from Dostoevsky's official correspondence are designated by the abbreviation OC.

Alexander II. OC 5, 7.

Annenkova, A. P. 101.

Davydov, P. A. 161.

Dolgorukov, V. A. OC 8, 10.

Dostoevskaya, D. I. 94.

Dostoevskaya, M. F. 2-9.

Dostoevskaya, V. M. *see* Karepina.

Dostoevsky, A. M. 35-37, 51, 61, 66, 80, 84, 93.

Dostoevsky, M. A. 1, 10-15, 17-19, 21, 23, 25.

Dostoevsky, M. M. 20, 22, 26, 28, 32-34, 40-44, 48, 50, 52-60, 62-65, 67-69, 71-72, 76, 85-89, 91-92, 96, 99, 102-3, 106, 113, 116, 123, 131, 135, 137, 141-43, 145-53, 155-56, 159-60, 162-63, 165, 169.

Fonvizina, N. D. 90.

Gartong. OC 1, 2.

Geybovich, A. I. 164.

Isaeva, M. D. 97.

Karepin, P. A. 38, 45-47, 49.

Karepina, V. M. 39, 117, 121, 124, 130, 170.

Katkov, M. N. 134, 139.

Khotyaintsev, A. F. 24.

Konstant, D. S. 125, 129, 138.

Konstant, V. D. 128, 133.

Kraevsky, A. A. 79, 81-83.

Kumanin, A. A. and A. F. 27. 29.

Maykov, A. N. 104.

Maykova, E. P. 77.

Nechaeva, O. Ya. 31.

Nekrasov, N. A. 75.

Pavlovsky, A. M. OC 6.

Poretsky, A. U. 70.

Starchevsky, A. V. 73-74.

Timashev, A. Ye. OC 9.

Totleben, E. I. 107, 157, 167.

Valikhanov, Ch. Ch. 114.

Vrangel, A. Ye. 98, 100, 105, 108-12, 115, 120, 122, 154, 158, 166, 168, 171.

Yakushkin, Ye. I. 95, 126, 132, 136, 144.

Zhdan-Pushkin, I. V. 127, 140.

Index

The numbers following names in this index refer to letter numbers, not pages. Biographical information can usually be found in the notes to the first letter in which a person's name appears. Letters from Dostoevsky's official correspondence are designated by the abbreviation OC.